VIETNAM
THE WAR ZONE
DICTIONARY
In Their Own Words

SHARON O. LIGHTHOLDER

The opinions expressed in this manuscript are solely the opinions of the author and do not represent the opinions or thoughts of the publisher. The author has represented and warranted full ownership and/or legal right to publish all the materials in this book.

Vietnam: The War Zone Dictionary In Their Own Words
All Rights Reserved.
Copyright © 2016 Sharon O. Lightholder
v3.0

Cover Photo © 2016 thinkstockphotos.com. All rights reserved - used with permission.

This book may not be reproduced, transmitted, or stored in whole or in part by any means, including graphic, electronic, or mechanical without the express written consent of the publisher except in the case of brief quotations embodied in critical articles and reviews.

Albedo Press

Paperback ISBN: 978-0-578-17135-7
Hardback ISBN: 978-0-578-17136-4

Library of Congress Control Number: 2015917080

PRINTED IN THE UNITED STATES OF AMERICA

*To the women and men who served
and those who serve our nation today.*

Thank you.

Welcome home.

TABLE OF CONTENTS

Author's Note i
Explanatory Notes iii
A – ALFA (ALPHA) 1
B – BRAVO 63
C – CHARLIE 96
D – DELTA 161
E – ECHO 195
F – FOXTROT 214
G – GOLF 245
H – HOTEL 263
I – INDIA 280
J – JULIET 305
K – KILO 311
L – LIMA 316
M – MIKE 335
N – NOVEMBER 378
O – OSCAR 399
P – PAPA 415
Q – QUEBEC 451
R – ROMEO 453
S – SIERRA 486
T – TANGO 547
U – UNIFORM 584
V – VICTOR 592
W – WHISKEY 598
X – X–RAY 609
Y – YANKEE 612
Z – ZULU 613

ALSO BY THE AUTHOR

Historical Fiction

The English Rendition

The Baldwin Portolano

AUTHOR'S NOTE

More than a half a century after the start of the war in Vietnam, we are at the transition between the living memory of the American experience in Vietnam and its history being written and documents read by subsequent generations. This reference is a time capsule that preserves the words and definitions unique to that war zone in the words of the men and women of the Armed Forces of the United States and its allied nations, journalists, photographers, contractors, and the extraordinary women who volunteered for the Army Nurse Corps, Red Cross, and USO.

As a writer who grew up in a military family where words mattered, I soon learned that the languages of the military and civilian worlds are not the same. The Vietnam War gave us new words for new technology as well as new social and military challenges. This reference began as a personal glossary to help me understand the war stories of my friends. As it grew, I shared it with co-workers who also were working with vets just back from Nam. I continued to add new words as I verified them, and researched the official terms adopted by the military. It is at the urging of veterans and historians that this collection is now published as a reference for all.

This is an unauthorized, uncensored dictionary of the English language used during the Vietnam War in the war zone. There is much to offend today's reader. The slang is often racist, sexist, homophobic, and derogatory. Much of the official language is designed to mask the reality of death and war. The few entries with French, Chinese, Japanese or Vietnamese words are spelled and used as reported. Because this is a collection of their words, there will be inconsistencies in spelling and style in both the slang and the official terms. All words and phrases are reported as collected, not sanitized or edited into a uniform style. Details of the methodology are found in the Explanatory Notes that follows.

Publishing this reference is a thank you to those who served and to those who had the patience to share their words and stories with me. I hope it will serve as a resource for those who want to understand this time and place in fiction and non-fiction. Whether the reader is a linguist, historian, sociologist, genealogist, or a relative reading the diary of their grandmother who was an Army nurse or letters of an uncle who flew a dust-off chopper, I want their words from the war zone to carry the specific meaning they intended and pierce the fog of time.

What is not here is the ongoing and unchanging language of duty, compassion, honor, valor, comradeship, hope, fear, and loss. These values and words transcend time. I hope this collection will be a reference of interest and use to you.

Respectfully Submitted,
Sharon O. Lightholder
August 16, 2015

EXPLANATORY NOTES

Time, Place and Sources: The time frame for words in this collection coincides with the dates of the award of the Vietnam Service Medal, which was awarded to eligible members of the United States Armed Forces serving between 15 November 1961 and 30 April 1975. The place is in the war zone in Vietnam for both military and civilian sources. Military sources from the offshore fleet, aviation, and support operations were included. Civilian sources were limited to Vietnam.

Method: Spelling, abbreviation, hyphenation, capitalization, and definitions are true to their sources, whether officially adopted by the United States and her allied nations, or slang. Inconsistencies have been retained because imposing a uniformity of style would reduce accuracy. When there are official and slang definitions of the same word, the definitions are entered separately to preserve the accuracy of the official source. Names of places, people, battles, campaigns or unit references, which are readily available through other references, are generally omitted. Exceptions are made as a specific thank you to the men and women contributing to this reference over the past fifty years.

<u>The unofficial language</u> of the war grew organically from necessity and spread from the bottom up. It is essential, primal, often crude, and consistently clear. The average infantryman was under drinking age. The average age for all Armed Forces was just 26 years old. A quarter of them had been drafted, and others enlisted when they felt the hot breath of the draft on their neck, which increased the ranks of those not wanting to be there. Gallows humor, escapism, sex, alcohol and drugs are predictable topics of conversation that developed their own language. Slang, acronyms, abbreviations, radio code, nicknames, euphemisms, and commonly used foreign words and phases were shortcuts that arose from necessity not planning. The unofficial words are not noted as to source. This is a personal collection that began informally in 1965 on an index card. Only when the list grew to several hand-written pages did a system of verification start:

- Primary: Personal sources included informal discussions and formal interviews with men and women who were in the war zone, on military, news-gathering, nursing, civilian contracting, Red Cross, USO, or other war-related assignments.

- Secondary: Documentary research included legal transcripts, oral histories, written documents that were time and place specific such as newspapers, magazines, letters, diaries as well as fiction and non-fiction works by authors with direct knowledge.
- Verification: A verification process was adopted to avoid the addition of later used words, author invented words, or words that were unique to one unit and not of general interest. Primary sourced words required a second source, either primary or secondary. Secondary sourced words required a primary source validation so there could not be a self-validation by using other written material.

<u>The official language</u> of the war was crafted by military and political planners. This usage was mandated from the top down. It is verbose, unambiguous, and sanitary. Spelling often favors British English in deference to the allied partners or invents a "military conjunction" mashing words together into new meanings. Style too is variable such as the three variants of the word: takeoff, take off and take-off. These words are from unclassified government documents, not individuals. Variations in spelling and errors are retained as collected. The abbreviation reflecting the military or political organization(s) adopting each term precedes the definition.

- **DOD:** reflects adoption by the United States Department of Defense which includes the Army, Navy, Marine Corps, Air Force, Coast Guard, and U.S. Reserve units.
- **I:** reflects adoption by the United States for intergovernmental usage.
- **NATO:** reflects adoption by nations that are members of the North Atlantic Treaty Organization.
- **NESN:** reflects adoption by the English speaking nations of the NATO alliance (United States, Canada, and the United Kingdom).
- **NFSN:** reflects adoption by French speaking nations of the NATO alliance (France and Belgium).
- **SEATO:** reflects adoption by nations that are members of the Southeast Asia Treaty Organization.
- **CENTO:** reflects adoption by nations that are members of the Central Treaty Organization. Originally known as the Bagdad Pact, or the Middle East Treaty Organization (METO), which existed between 1955 and 1979 as an alliance between Iran, Iraq, Pakistan, Turkey, and the United Kingdom.
- **IADB**: reflects adoption by the Inter-American Defense Board. Note: This is an advisory body to the Organization of American States representing North, Central and South America.

Technical:
Several editorial decisions simplify this reference in both print and digital formats.
- The alphabetization system is computer-generated. It is letter-by-letter, not word-by-word and ignores dashes and spaces. Numbers are sorted by the first digit so 1, 2, 3, 33, 100 would appear as 1, 100, 2, 3, 33. This speeds digital searching.
- A pronunciation guide is provided only for oddities. This keeps it simple.
- Notes are provided only when necessary to explain a term, and as few cross-references as possible are used. This keeps it brief.
- A single column format with the defined word in bold type is used to facilitate both reading and searching for similar words in the printed format as it proved to be faster, easier and better with our test readers than the traditional double column dictionary format.
- Numbers are spelled out as pronounced and then followed by the numeric. This allows better manual searching on words and digital searching for both the alpha and numeric.

A – ALFA (ALPHA)

A - 1. Designated in the military phonetic alphabet, as Alfa, more commonly spelled Alpha. 2. The designation for aircraft used as an attack or attack bomber.

A Kit - See ACAV Kit.

A Shau Valley - The area of Vietnam where the "Hamburger Hill" battle took place in 1969.

A-1 - See Skyraider.

A-130 - See Hercules.

A-26 - See Invader.

A-3 - See Skywarrior.

A-37 - See Dragonfly.

A-4 - See Skyhawk.

A-5 - See Vigilante.

A-6 - See Intruder.

A-7 - See Corsair II.

A-gunner - Assistant gunner.

A-Shaped Ambush - A troop formation in an A shape allowing enemy to enter the open area and then be ambushed. Also called U-Shaped Ambush.

A-Team - Field operating units of the U.S. Special Forces of 10-12 soldiers, cross-trained in specialized weapons, medical aid, communications, counterinsurgency operations and tactics.

A-Team-B-Team - The Special Forces tactic in the field, to have two teams, in which the A-Team is in the lead and is supported by the B-Team.

A. J. Squaredaway - Slang for a sharp looking soldier.

A&D - Admission and Deposition, the entry point of a field hospital.

A1C - Airman First Class (Air Force).

AA - 1. Antiaircraft guns. 2. Air-to-air weapon. 3. Airman Apprentice (Coast Guard).

AA gun sites - Locations holding antiaircraft gun emplacements whether mobile or fixed.

AA-2 AAM - See Atoll missile.

AAA - Antiaircraft artillery. See triple A.

AADS - Army Authorization Documents System. Also TAADS.

AAM - Air-to-air missile.

AAR - After Action Report.

Aardvark - Also called Edsel. See F-111.

AB - Airman Basic (Air Force).

abatis - A perimeter defense of sharpened stakes or sticks, embedded in the ground pointing out at a 30-90 degree angle to prevent or slow ground assaults. See Porcupine Fence.

abeam - (DOD, NATO, CENTO, IADB) Bearing approximately 090 degrees or 270 degrees relative; at right angles to the longitudinal axis of a vehicle.

Able Dog - See A-1.

abn - Airborne.

aboard - 1. Marine and Navy slang for being on a ship or base. 2. In agreement.

abort - (DOD, NESN, NFSN, CENTO, IADB) Failure to accomplish a mission for any reason other than enemy action. It may occur at any point from initiation of operation to destination.

Above the Rest - Slang for the 101st Airborne Division.

abrasions - (NATO, CENTO) In photography, scratches or marks produced mechanically on emulsion surfaces or film base.

Absent Without Leave - A soldier absent without permission from his unit or post. Abbreviated AWOL.

absolute altitude - (DOD, NATO, CENTO, IADB) The height of an aircraft directly above the surface or terrain over which it is flying. See also altitude.

absolute dud - (DOD) A nuclear weapon, which when launched at or emplaced on a target, fails to explode.

absorbed dose - (DOD, NATO, CENTO) The amount of energy imparted by nuclear (or ionizing) radiation to unit mass of absorbing material. The unit is the rad.

AC or A/C - 1. Aircraft Commander. 2. Acting Commander. 3. Army Corps. 4. Air Corps.

AC-1 - See C-7.

AC-119 - The C-119 cargo aircraft modified to be a U.S. Air Force gunship. Nicknames: for AC-119G Shadow and Gunship III; for AC-119K Stinger.

AC-130 - The C-130 cargo aircraft modified to be a U.S. Air Force gunship. Nicknames: Specre or Gunship II.

AC-47 - The C-47 aircraft modified to be a U.S. Air Force gunship. Nicknames: Spooky, Dragonship, Gooney Bird, and Puff the Magic Dragon.

VIETNAM: THE WAR ZONE DICTIONARY IN THEIR OWN WORDS

ACAV - Armored cavalry assault vehicle. Pronounced A-cav.

ACB - See Amphibious Construction Battalion.

ACAV Kit - A retrofit kit to convert armored personnel carriers into armored cavalry assault vehicles.

acceptable loss level - The level of casualties deemed acceptable in combat.

acceptable product - (NATO, CENTO, IADB) One which may be used in place of another product for extended periods without technical advice. See also emergency substitute; NATO unified product; standardized product.

acceptance trials - (NATO, SEATO, CENTO, IADB) Trials carried out by nominated representatives of the eventual military users of the weapon or equipment to determine if the specified performance and characteristics have been met.

access to classified information - (DOD) The ability and opportunity to obtain knowledge of classified information. A person has access to classified information if he is permitted to gain knowledge of the information or if he is in a place where he would be expected to gain such knowledge. A person does not have access to classified information by being in a place where classified information is kept if security measures prevent him from gaining knowledge of the information.

accessory packet - The waterproof packet in each C-ration box containing matches, instant coffee, cream substitute, sugar, chewing gum, four cigarettes and folded toilet paper.

accidental attack - (DOD, IADB) An unintended attack which occurs without deliberate national design as a direct result of a random event, such as a mechanical failure, a simple human error, or an unauthorized action by a subordinate.

accidental war - (DOD) Not to be used. See accidental attack.

accommodation - (NATO, CENTO) The ability of the human eye to adjust itself to give sharp images of objects of different distances. In stereoscopy, the ability of the human eyes to bring two images into superimposition for stereoscopic viewing.

accommodations - See Live and Let Live.

accompanied tour - A tour of duty in which military personnel were allowed to bring dependents. Accompanied tours were allowed until 1964.

accompanying cargo - (NATO, CENTO) All classes of cargo carried by units into the objective area. See also accompanying supplies.

accompanying supplies - (DOD, NATO, SEATO, CENTO, IADB) All classes of supplies carried by units into the objective area. See also accompanying cargo.

accordion wire - See concertina wire.

accountability - (DOD, IADB) The obligation imposed by law or lawful order or regulation of an officer or other person for keeping accurate record of property, documents, or funds. The person having this obligation may or may not have actual possession of the property, documents, or funds. Accountability is concerned primarily with records, while responsibility is concerned primarily with custody, care, and safekeeping. See also responsibility.

accubuoy - A noise activated sensor, usually buried with antenna remaining above ground.

accuracy of fire - (DOD, NATO, SEATO, CENTO, IADB) The measure of the deviation of fire from the point of aim, expressed in terms of the distance between the point of aim and the mean point of bursts.

accuracy of information - See evaluation (intelligence).

ace - 1. Designation for a pilot who shot down five or more enemy aircraft. Extended to the Radar Intercept Officer in some aircraft such as the F-4 in which the shooting was not done exclusively by the pilot. 2. To kill someone. 3. Marine slang for being killed.

Ace of Spades - Taken as symbol of death by Vietnamese as American troops left that playing card on dead Viet Cong. Note playing card makers produced packs of cards containing only the Ace of Spades for troops to use.

acetylene gas - The gas used in welding which was also pumped into Viet Cong tunnels and lighted to remove oxygen, burn, or flush out the enemy.

Acey-Deucy Club - A NCO club, named from the card game frequently played.

acft - Aircraft.

acid - LSD.

acknowledgment - (NATO, SEATO, CENTO, IADB) A message from the addressee informing the originator that his communication has been received and is understood.

ACM - Air combat maneuver, a dogfight.

ACMR - Army Court of Military Review.

ACOU-SID - See Acoustic Sound Intrusion Device.

Acoustic Bullet Detector - A system designed as an early warning to helicopter pilots that ground fire had started based on the sound of the shot being fired. Practically, it provided little advance warning.

acoustic jamming - (DOD) The deliberate radiation or reradiation of mechanical or electro-acoustic signals with the objectives of obliterating or obscuring signals which the enemy is attempting to receive and of deterring enemy weapon systems. See also barrage jamming; electronic jamming; jamming; spot jamming.

acoustic sensors - A noise sensing device, most commonly dropped from aircraft to hang in the jungle canopy to detect enemy sound from movement or speech.

Acoustic Sound Intrusion Device - Devices which used sound to monitor and report enemy troop movement. Devices were about a yard long and 4 inches across and could be hand planted or dropped from aircraft using a drag chute.

acoustical intelligence - (DOD) The technical and intelligence information derived from foreign sources which generate acoustical waves.

acoustical surveillance - (DOD) Employment of electronic devices including sound recording, receiving, or transmitting equipment for the collection of information.

ACP - Automatic Colt pistol.

acquire - (DOD) 1. When applied to acquisition radars, the process of detecting the presence and location of a target in sufficient detail to permit identification. 2. When applied to tracking radars, the process of positioning a radar beam so that a target is in that beam to permit the effective employment of weapons. See also target acquisition.

acquire (radar) - See acquire.

ACR - Armored Cavalry Regiment.

across the fence - Slang for across the border of South Vietnam into North Vietnam, Laos, or Cambodia.

ACT - Air combat tactic.

acting jack - Slang for an acting noncommissioned officer, usually an E-4 Corporal acting as Sergeant but without the pay raise.

action agent - (DOD) In intelligence usage, one who has access to and performs action against the target.

action deferred - (DOD) Tactical action on a specific track is being withheld for better tactical advantage. Weapons are available and commitment is pending.

action information center - See combat information center.

ACTIV - Army Concept Team in Vietnam. The U.S. Army personnel in South Vietnam assigned to evaluate new weapons and techniques and offer solutions to problems with and improvements to new technology.

activate - (DOD, NATO, SEATO, CENTO, IADB) 1. To put into existence by official order a unit, post, camp, station, base, or shore activity which has previously been constituted and designated by name or number, or both, so that it can be organized to function in its assigned capacity. (DOD, IADB) 2. To prepare for active service a naval ship or craft which has been in an inactive or reserve status. See also commission; constitute.

activation detector - (DOD, NATO, CENTO) A material used to determine neutron flux or density by virtue of the radioactivity induced in it as a result of neutron capture.

active air defense - (DOD, NATO, SEATO, CENTO, IADB) Direct defensive action taken to destroy or reduce the effectiveness of an enemy air attack. It includes such measures as the use of aircraft, antiaircraft guns, electronic countermeasures, and surface-to-air guided missiles. See also air defense.

active aircraft - (DOD, IADB) Aircraft currently and actively engaged in supporting the flying missions either through direct assignment to operational units or in the preparation for such assignment or reassignment through any of the logistic processes of supply, maintenance, and modification. See also aircraft.

active communications satellite - See communications satellite.

active defense - (DOD, NATO, SEATO, CENTO, IADB) The employment of limited offensive action and counterattacks to deny a contested area or position to the enemy. See also passive defense.

active homing guidance - (DOD, NESN, IADB) A system of homing guidance wherein both the source for illuminating the target, and the receiver for detecting the energy reflected from the target as the result of illuminating the target, are carried within the missile. See also guidance.

active material - (DOD, NATO, CENTO, IADB) Material, such as plutonium and certain isotopes of uranium, which is capable of supporting a fission chain reaction.

activity - (DOD, IADB) 1. A unit, organization, or installation performing a function or mission, e.g., reception center, redistribution center, naval station, naval shipyard. 2. A function or mission, e.g., recruiting, schooling. See also establishment.

actual - Slang for the person who was the official commander of a military unit as opposed to the name of the unit. A request to put your actual on, means the commander, not just any personnel.

actual ground zero - (DOD, NATO, CENTO, IADB) The point on the surface of the earth at, or vertically below or above, the center of an actual nuclear detonation. Also called AGZ. See also desired ground zero; ground zero.

acute dose - (DOD, NATO, CENTO) Total dose received at one time over a period so short that biological recovery cannot occur.

acute situation reaction (ASR) - See combat fatigue.

AD - 1. Active Duty. 2. Air Division. 3. Accidental discharge.

add - (DOD) A correction used by an observer or a spotter to indicate that an increase in range along a spotting line is desired.

ADF - Automatic direction finder.

ADIZ - See air defense identification zone.

adjust - (DOD) An order to the observer or spotter to initiate an adjustment on a designated target.

adjust fire - (DOD) 1. An order or request to initiate an adjustment. 2. A method of control transmitted in the call for fire by the observer or spotter to indicate that he will control the adjustment.

adjustment - See adjustment of fire.

adjustment of fire - (DOD, NATO, CENTO) Process used in artillery and naval gunfire to obtain correct bearing, range and height of burst (if time fuzes are used) when engaging a target by observed fire. See also spot.

adjutant - An officer responsible for all correspondence except combat orders.

ADM - Admiral Chief of Naval Operations/Commandant of the Coast Guard (Navy, Coast Guard).

ADM-20 - See Quail.

admin - See administration.

admin-o - An administrative officer. Also spelled admino.

administration - (DOD, NATO, SEATO, CENTO, IADB) 1. The management and execution of all military matters not included in tactics and strategy; primarily in the fields of logistics and personnel management. 2. Internal management of units.

administrative airlift service - (DOD, IADB) The airlift service normally provided by specifically identifiable aircraft assigned to organizations or commands for internal administration.

administrative chain of command - (DOD, NATO, SEATO, CENTO, IADB) The normal chain of command as determined by the administrative organization. See also chain of command; operational chain of command.

administrative control - (DOD, NATO, SEATO, CENTO, IADB) Direction or exercise of authority over subordinate or other organizations in respect to administrative matters, such as personnel management, supply, services, and other matters not included in the operational missions of the subordinate or other organizations. See also control; operational command; operational control.

Administrative Discharge (AD) - All discharges from military service except those resulting from a court martial.

administrative landing - (DOD) An unopposed landing involving debarkation from vehicles which have been administratively loaded. See also administrative loading; administrative movement; logistics over the shore operations.

administrative lead time - (DOD, IADB) The time interval between initiation of procurement action and letting of contract or placing of order. See also procurement lead time.

administrative leave - Leave from duty that is authorized but not charged against annual leave allowances, usually to attend some civic event or religious service.

administrative loading - (DOD, NATO, CENTO, IADB) A loading system which gives primary consideration to achieving maximum utilization of troop and cargo space without regard to tactical considerations. Equipment and supplies must be unloaded and sorted before they can be used. See also commercial loading; loading.

administrative map - (DOD, IADB) A map on which is graphically recorded information pertaining to administrative matters, such as supply and evacuation installations, personnel installations, medical facilities, collecting points for stragglers and prisoners of war, train bivouacs, service and maintenance areas, main supply roads, traffic circulation, boundaries, and other details necessary to show the administrative situation in relation to the tactical situation. See also map.

administrative movement - (DOB, NATO, SEATO, CENTO, IADB) A movement in which troops and vehicles are arranged to expedite their movement and conserve time and energy when no enemy interference, except by air, is anticipated. (DOD, IADB) Also called administrative march.

administrative order - (DOD, NATO, SEATO, CENTO, IADB) An order covering traffic, supply, maintenance, evacuation, personnel, and other administrative details.

administrative shipping - (DOD) Support shipping that is capable of transporting troops and cargo from origin to destination, but which cannot be loaded or unloaded without non-organic personnel and/or equipment; e.g., stevedores, piers, barges, boats. See also administrative loading; administrative movement.

adrenalin junkie - Thrill seeker. A soldier actively seeking enemy engagement and danger.

ADSID - Air-delivered seismic intruder detection device, consisting of a microphone and transmitter.

advance - (DOD) A request from a spotter to indicate that he desires the illuminating projectile to burst earlier in relation to the subsequent bursts of high explosive projectiles.

advance force (amphibious) - (DOD, NATO, SEATO, CENTO, IADB) A temporary organization within the amphibious task force which precedes the main body to the objective area. Its function is to participate in preparing the objective for the main assault by conducting such operations as reconnaissance, seizure of supporting positions, minesweeping, preliminary bombardment, underwater demolitions, and air support.

advance guard - (DOD, IADB) Detachment sent ahead of the main force to insure its uninterrupted advance; to protect the main body against surprise; to facilitate the advance by removing obstacles, repairing roads, and bridges; and to cover the deployment of the main body if it is committed to action.

advance guard reserve - (DOD, IADB) Second of the two main parts of an advance guard, the other being the advance guard support. It protects the main force and is itself protected by the advance guard support. Small advance guards do not have reserves.

advance guard support - (DOD, IADB) First of the two main parts of an advance guard, the other being the advance guard reserve. It is made up of three smaller elements, in order from front to rear, the advance guard point, the advance party, and the support proper. The advance guard support protects the advance guard reserve.

advanced base - (DOD, NATO. SEATO, CENTO, IADB) A base located in or near a theater of operations whose primary mission is to support military operations.

advanced fleet anchorage - (DOD, NATO, CENTO, IADB) A secure anchorage for a large number of naval ships, mobile support units, and auxiliaries, located in or near a theater of operations. See also emergency anchorage. (Note: NATO and CENTO uses the words "naval vessels" instead of "naval ships".)

advanced fleet anchorage - (SEATO) A secure anchorage for a large number of naval vessels, mobile support units, and auxiliaries.

advanced guard - (NATO, CENTO) The leading element of an advancing force. The primary mission is to insure the uninterrupted advance of the main body. It has the following functions: a. to find and exploit gaps in the enemy's defensive system; b. to prevent the main body of the advancing force running blindly into enemy opposition; and c. to clear away minor opposition or, if major opposition is met, to cover the deployment of the main body.

Advanced Individual Training - Training beyond basic training for special such as mechanic, dog handler, medic. Not Advanced Infantry Training. See AIT.

advanced landing field - (DOD, NATO, SEATO, CENTO, IADB) An airfield, usually having minimum facilities, in or near an objective area. See also airfield.

advanced leave - Leave of 30 days per year was granted from combat duty usually to a designated R&R location and taken at one time. Occasionally leave was granted prior to the 12 month period particularly when expedited from training into combat.

Advanced Technological Training (ATT) - The training provided to those troops returning from Vietnam who could not be reassigned due to their remaining length of service, (usually 5-10 months) and who did not qualify for the Early Out Program.

adverse weather - (DOD) Weather in which military operations are generally restricted or impeded. See also marginal weather.

advisors - The personnel providing military instruction and assistance, usually from one nation to another, as opposed to engaging in combat, see MAAG, Military Assistance Advisory Group Note: this was the pre-war position of U.S. personnel in Vietnam.

advisory area (air traffic) - (DOD, NATO, CENTO, IADB) A designated area within a flight information region where air traffic advisory service is available.

aerial flares - Illuminating flares suspended from small parachutes.

aerial photograph - See air photograph.

aerial pickets - (SEATO, IADB) Aircraft disposed around a position, area, or formation, primarily to detect, report, and track approaching enemy aircraft.

aerial port - (DOD, IADB) A facility located on an air base, consisting of one or more air terminals, and constituting an authorized port of entry to and clearance from a country.

aerial port squadron - (DOD) An Air Force organization which operates and provides the functions assigned to aerial ports to include the processing of personnel and cargo, rigging for airdrop, packing parachutes and loading equipment, preparing air cargo and load plans, loading and securing aircraft, ejection of cargo for inflight delivery, and supervision of units engaged in aircraft loading and unloading operations.

aerial supply - (SEATO) The act or process by which aerial delivery of supplies is made to ground units.

aerodrome - See airfield.

aerodrome traffic - (SEATO) All traffic on the maneuvering area of an aerodrome and all aircraft flying in the vicinity of an aerodrome.

aerodynamic missile - (DOD, NATO, CENTO, IADB) A missile which uses aerodynamic forces to maintain its flight path, generally employing propulsion guidance. See also ballistic missile; guided missile.

aeromedical evacuation - (DOD, NATO, SEATO, CENTO, IADB) The movement of patients to and between medical treatment facilities by air transportation.

aeromedical evacuation control center - (DOD, IADB) The control facility established by the commander of an air transport division, air force, or air command. It operates in conjunction with the command transport movement control center and coordinates overall medical requirement with transport airlift capability. The center also assigns medical missions to appropriate aeromedical evacuation elements in the system, and monitors patient movement activities.

aeromedical evacuation control officer - (DOD, IADB) An officer of the air transport force or air command controlling the flow of patients by air.

aeromedical evacuation coordinating officer - (NATO, SEATO, CENTO) An officer of an originating, intransit, or destination medical facility/establishment who coordinates aeromedical evacuation activities of the facility/establishment.

aeromedical evacuation system - (DOD, NATO, SEATO, CENTO, IADB) A system which provides: a. control of patient movement by air transport; b. specialized medical attendants and equipment for in-flight medical care; c. facilities, on or in the vicinity of air strips and air bases, for the limited medical care of in-transit patients entering, en route via, or leaving the system; and d. communication with destination and en route medical facilities concerning patient airlift movements.

aeromedical evacuation unit - (DOD, IADB) An operational medical organization concerned primarily with the management and control of patients being transported via an aeromedical evacuation system or system echelon.

aeronautical chart - (DOD, IADB) A specialized representation of mapped features of the earth, or some part of it, produced to show selected terrain, cultural and hydrographic features, and supplemental information required for air navigation, pilotage, or for planning air operations.

aeronautical chart - (NATO, CENTO) A representation of a portion of the earth, its culture and relief, specifically designed to meet the requirements of air navigation.

aeronautical information overprint - (DOD, NATO, CENTO, IADB) Additional information which is printed or stamped on a map or chart for the specific purpose of air navigation.

aeronautical topographic chart - (NATO) A representation of features of the surface of the earth, designed primarily as an aid to visual or radar navigation, which shows selected terrain, cultural or hydrographic features and supplementary aeronautical information.

aeropause - (NATO, SEATO, CENTO, IADB) Region in which functional effects of the atmosphere on man and aircraft cease to exist.

aerospace - (DOD, NATO, CENTO, IADB) Of, or pertaining to, the earth's envelope of atmosphere and the space above it; two separate entities considered as a single realm for activity in launching, guidance, and control of vehicles which will travel in both entities.

aerospace control operations - (DOD) The employment of air forces, supported by ground and naval forces, as appropriate, to achieve military objectives in vital aerospace areas. Such operations include destruction of enemy aerospace and surface-to-air forces, interdiction of enemy aerospace operations, protection of vital air lines of communication, and the establishment of local military superiority in areas of air operations.

aerospace defense - (DOD, IADB) All measures designed to reduce or nullify the effectiveness of hostile acts by aircraft, missiles, and space vehicles after they leave the earth's surface; an inclusive term encompassing air defense and space defense.

Aerospace Rescue and Recovery Service - The U.S. Air Force search and rescue specialists.

AF - Air Force.

AFB - Air Force Base.

AFC - Airman First Class.

AFDL - Floating dry dock.

AFFE - Armed Forces Far East.

afloat support - The form of logistic support outside the harbor area in which the supply of troops and vessels, at anchor or underway, is accomplished.

AFM - Air Force Manual.

AFN - Armed Forces Network. See AFVN.

AFPAC - Armed Forces Pacific.

AFQT - The Armed Forces Qualification Test. The military entrance exam given to all draftees and volunteers that sorted out abilities and rejected those unfit for duty.

AFRS - Armed Forces Radio Saigon. The initial U.S. operated radio in Vietnam, Later changed to Armed Forces Vietnam Network. See AFVN.

AFRTS - Armed Forces Radio and Television Service.

After Action Report (AAR) - The report of any enemy engagement written after the event for intelligence analysis.

after-flight inspection - The general examination of an aircraft after landing for obvious defects, repair and replenishment of expendables such as fuel.

afterburner - The added thrust of a jet engine to assist in short runway, carrier or heavy load takeoffs or in combat for added speed by adjusting the fuel mixture or employing a specific afterburner mechanism.

afterburning - (DOD, NATO, CENTO, IADB) 1. The characteristic of some rocket motors to burn irregularly for some time after the main burning and thrust has ceased. 2. The process of fuel injection and combustion in the exhaust jet of a turbojet engine (aft or to the rear of the turbine).

afterwinds - (DOD) Wind currents set up in the vicinity of a nuclear explosion directed toward the burst center, resulting from the updraft accompanying the rise of the fireball.

AFU - All fucked up.

AFUS - Air Force of the United States.

AFVN - Armed Forces Vietnam Network, the U.S. operated radio station. Initially named Armed Forces Radio Saigon. See AFRS.

AGC - See amphibious command ship.

AGCT - Army General Classification Test.

age of moon - The elapsed time from the last new moon expressed in days.

Agency - Central Intelligence Agency. See CIA.

agent - (DOD, NATO, SEATO, CENTO, IADB) In intelligence usage, one who is authorized or instructed to obtain or to assist in obtaining information for intelligence or counterintelligence purposes.

agent - The chemical agents that were defoliants were named for the color band on the drums of the liquid as follows: Agent Blue, the defoliant chemical used in Vietnam between 1964 and 1971. Agent Orange, the defoliant applied by air to vegetation between 1964 and 1971. The herbicide contained a type of Dioxin. Agent Pink, the defoliant applied by air in Vietnam pre-1964. Agent Purple, the defoliant applied by air in Vietnam pre-1964. Agent White, the defoliant used in Vietnam between 1964 and 1971.

agent authentication - (DOD) The technical support task of providing an agent with personal documents, accoutrements, and equipment which have the appearance of authenticity as to claimed origin and which support and are consistent with the agent's cover story.

agent net - (DOD) An organization for clandestine purposes which operates under the direction of a principal agent.

Agent Orange - The defoliant applied by air to vegetation between 1964 and 1971. The herbicide contained a type of Dioxin that was linked to many medical issues for those exposed to it and birth defects in their children. See agent.

aggressor forces - (DOD, IADB) Forces engaged in aggressive military action. In the context of training exercises, the "enemy" created to add realism in training maneuvers and exercises. This method replaces the less realistic system of fictional "red" and "blue" armies.

agiprop - Agitation and propaganda. A Communist tactic for indoctrination. Also spelled AgiProp and agitprop.

AGL - Above Ground Level.

AGM - Air to Ground Missile

AGM-28 - See Hound Dog.

AGM-45 - See Shrike.

AGM-62 - See Walleye.

AGM-78A - See Standard.

AGM-l2 - See Bullpup.

AGO - Adjutant General's office.

agonic line - (DOD, NATO) A line drawn on a map or chart joining points of zero magnetic declination for a specified epoch.

agreed point - (DOD, NATO, SEATO, CENTO, IADB) A predetermined point on the ground, identifiable from the air, and used when aircraft assist in fire adjustment.

Agreement on Ending the War and Restoring the Peace in Vietnam - Signed 27 January 1973. Also called the Paris Peace Accords.

Agroville - A town developed under a South Vietnamese government program that relocated peasants from areas believed to be under or subject to Viet Cong control to government built and protected "Agrovilles" Later merged with the strategic hamlet program.

AGZ - Actual ground zero.

AH - See hospital ship.

AH-1G - See Cobra.

AHB - Assault Helicopter Battalion.

AHB-1J - The single rotor, two crew light attack helicopter. See Sea Cobra.

AID - Agency for International Development.

aim dot - The spot on aircraft radar indication lock-on to a target.

AIM-4, 26, 47 - See Falcon.

AIM-7 - See Sparrow.

AIM-9 - See Sidewinder.

aiming stakes - Stakes driven into the ground around a gun pit as reference points to allow rapid aiming

air - (DOD) A spotting, or an observation, by a spotter or an observer to indicate that a burst or group of bursts occurred before impact.

air - Slang for: 1. Atmosphere. 2. Aviation section of the military. 3. Airpower. 4. Pointless chatter.

air alert - (IADB) The alerting against possible enemy air attack. See also air defense warning conditions; alert; ground alert.

air alert - (SEATO) The operational status of aircraft in the air that are ready for the immediate accomplishment of a mission.

air alert mission - (SEATO, IADB) Aircraft airborne in the battle area to answer calls for immediate air support from the ground forces.

Air America - 1. The name of the airline used in covert operations by the CIA. 2. The aircraft operated to support the activities of the CIA personnel in South East Asia.

air and naval gunfire liaison company - (DOD, IADB) An organization composed of Marine and Navy personnel specially qualified for shore control of naval gunfire and close air support. Also known as ANGLICO.

air attack - (DOD) 1. (coordinated) - A combination of two or more types of air attack (dive, glide, low-level) in one strike, using one or more types of aircraft. 2. (deferred) - A procedure in which attack groups rendezvous as a single unit. It is used when attack groups are launched from more than one station with their departure on the mission being delayed pending further orders. 3. (divided) - A method of delivering a coordinated air attack which consists of holding the units in close tactical concentration up to a point, then splitting them to attack an objective from different directions.

air base (photogrammetry) - (DOD, NATO, CENTO, IADB) 1. The line joining two air stations or the length of that line. 2. The distance, at the scale of the stereoscopic model, between adjacent perspective centers as reconstructed in the plotting instrument. See also air station (photogrammetry).

air blowers - Gasoline powered blowers used to deploy gas or smoke into enemy tunnels. Also called tunnel flushers.

air boat - A flat bottomed shallow draft boat driven by a huge caged propeller on the rear. Used over marsh and swampy areas and able to carry 6-8 troops at speeds up to 40 knots.

Air Boss - Aviation term for the head of aviation on a carrier.

air burst - An explosive (bomb, artillery or grenade) set to explode before hitting the ground.

air cartographic camera - (NATO, CENTO, IADB) A camera having the accuracy and other characteristics essential for air survey or cartographic photography.

air cartographic photography - (NATO, CENTO) The taking and processing of air photography for mapping and charting purposes.

Air Cav - See Air Cavalry.

Air Cavalry - The army troops using helicopters and helicopter gunships to reconnoiter and shield infantry from the enemy.

air command - (DOD, IADB) A major subdivision of the Air Force; for operational purposes it normally consists of two or more air forces. See also command.

Air Command and Staff College - The Air Force's war college for senior officers.

air control - See air controller; air traffic control center; airway; area control center; control and reporting center; control area; control zone; controlled airspace; tactical air control center; terminal control area; transport control center (air transport).

air control and reporting center - (SEATO, IADB) A subordinate air control element of the Tactical Air Control Center from which control and warning operations within its area of responsibility are conducted.

air control team - (NATO, SEATO, CENTO, IADB) A team especially organized to direct close air support strikes in the vicinity of forward ground elements by visual or other means. See also tactical air control party.

air controller - (DOD, NATO, SEATO, CENTO, IADB) An individual especially trained for and assigned the duty of the control (by use of radio, radar, or other means) of such aircraft as may be allotted to him for operation within his area. See also air traffic controller; air weapons controller; tactical air controller.

air corridors - (DOD, NATO, SEATO, CENTO, IADB) Restricted air routes of travel specified for use by friendly aircraft and established for the purpose of preventing friendly aircraft from being fired on by friendly forces.

air cushion vehicles - 1. A vehicle capable of being operated so that its weight is supported all or in part by a cushion of air to elevate it above the ground. 2. Boats with a fan-like mechanism to lift it out of the water and provide propulsion, see hovercraft, PACV. Also called Ground Effect Machines by NATO staff.

air defense - (DOD, IADB) All measures designed to reduce or nullify the effectiveness of hostile acts by vehicles (including missiles) in the earth's envelope of atmosphere. See also active air defense; passive air defense.

air defense - (NATO, SEATO, CENTO) All measures designed to nullify or reduce the effectiveness of the attack of aircraft or guided missiles in flight. See also active air defense; passive air defense.

air defense action area - (DOD, NATO, SEATO, CENTO, IADB) An area and the airspace above it within which friendly aircraft or surface-to-air weapons are normally given precedence in operations except under specified conditions. See also air defense operations area.

air defense area - (DOD, IADB) 1. (overseas) A specifically defined airspace for which air defense must be planned and provided. 2. (United States) Airspace of defined dimensions designated by the appropriate agency within which the ready control of airborne vehicles is required in the interest of national security during an air defense emergency. (Note: IADB does not use "(overseas)" in Part 1 definition.)

air defense area - (NATO, CENTO) A specifically defined airspace for which air defense must be planned and provided.

air defense area - (SEATO) A specifically defined, established territory that includes objectives of possible enemy air attack, and for which air defense must be provided.

air defense artillery - (DOD) Weapons and equipment for actively combating air targets from the ground. Weapons are classed as: light-20-57-mm, medium-58-99-mm; heavy-100-mm or greater.

air defense battle zone - (DOD) A volume of airspace surrounding an air defense fire unit or defended area, extending to a specified altitude and range, in which the fire unit commander will engage and destroy targets not identified as friendly under criteria established by higher headquarters.

air defense control center - (DOD, NATO, CENTO, IADB) The principal information, communications, and operations center from which all aircraft, antiaircraft operations, air defense artillery, guided missiles, and air warning functions of a specific area of air defense responsibility are supervised and coordinated. See also combat information center.

air defense direction center - (DOD, IADB) An installation having the capability of performing air surveillance, interception control and direction of allocated air defense weapons within an assigned sector of responsibility. Also may have an identification capability.

air defense division - (DOD) A geographical subdivision of an air defense region. See also air defense sector.

air defense early warning - (NATO, SEATO, CENTO, IADB) Early notification of approach of enemy airborne weapons or weapons carriers obtained by electronic or visual means. See also early warning.

air defense element - (DOD) A section representing the force air defense commander that operates as a functional portion of the Army tactical operations center when air defense units are assigned or attached to the force. It coordinates Army air defense operations with other tactical support operations, use of airspace over the force area and air defense of the commander's area of responsibility.

air defense emergency - (DOD) An emergency condition, declared or confirmed by either the Commander in Chief, North American Air Defense Command or Commander in Chief, Continental Air Defense Command, or higher authority, which exists when attack upon the continental United States, Alaska, Canada, or United States installations in Greenland by hostile aircraft or missiles is considered probable, is imminent, or is taking place.

air defense identification zone - (DOD) Airspace of defined dimensions within which the ready identification, location, and control of airborne vehicles is required. Commonly referred to as ADIZ. See also air defense operations area.

air defense identification zone - (NATO, SEATO, CENTO, IADB) Airspace of defined dimensions within which the ready identification, location, and control of aircraft is required. See also air defense operations area.

air defense interrogation formation - Aviation term for an aerial formation of two fighter planes in proximity to an unknown aircraft. The lead plane is at the same level and with a visual of the cockpit of the unknown plane. The trail plane is directly behind the unknown plane and slightly lower.

air defense operations area - (DOD) An area and the airspace above it within which procedures are established to minimize mutual interference between air defense and other operations and which may include designation of one or more of the following: air defense action area, air defense identification zone, and/or fire power umbrella. See also air defense action area; air defense identification zone; fire power umbrella; positive identification and radar advisory zone.

air defense operations area - (NATO, SEATO, CENTO, IADB) A geographical area defining the boundaries within which procedures are established to minimize interference between air defense and other operations and which may include designation of one or more of the following: air defense area; air defense action area; air defense identification zone; fire power umbrella.

air defense readiness - (DOD, IADB) An operational status requiring air defense forces to maintain higher than ordinary preparedness for short periods of time.

air defense region - (DOD, IADB) A geographical subdivision or an air defense area.

air defense sector - (DOD, NATO, CENTO, IADB) A geographical subdivision of an air defense region. See also air defense division.

air defense ship - (NATO, SEATO, CENTO, IADB) The ship detailed to assume responsibility for air defense. (Note: SEATO and IADB term has qualifier "(naval term)".)

air defense warning conditions - (DOD) A degree of air raid probability according to the following code. The term air defense division/sector referred to herein may include forces and units afloat and/or deployed to forward areas, as applicable. Air defense warning yellow-attack by hostile aircraft and/or missiles is probable. This means that hostile aircraft and/or missiles are en route toward an air defense division/sector, or unknown aircraft and/or missiles suspected to be hostile are en route toward or are within an air defense division/sector. Air defense warning red-attack by hostile aircraft and/or missiles is imminent or is in progress. This means that hostile aircraft and/or missiles are within an air defense division/sector or are in the immediate vicinity of an air defense division/sector with high probability of entering the division/sector. Air defense warning white-attack by hostile aircraft and/or missiles is improbable. May be called either before or after air defense warning yellow or red. The initial declaration of air defense emergency will automatically establish a condition of air defense warning other than white for purposes of security control of air traffic.

air defense warning conditions - (IADB) A degree of air raid probability according to the following code. The term air defense sector referred to herein may include forces and units afloat and/or deployed to forward areas, as applicable. Air defense warning yellow: Attack by hostile aircraft is probable. (This means that hostile aircraft are en route toward an air defense sector, or unknown aircraft suspected to be hostile are en route toward or are within an air defense sector.) Air defense warning red: Attack by hostile aircraft is imminent or is taking place. (This means that hostile aircraft are within an air defense sector or are in the immediate vicinity of an air defense sector with high probability of entering the sector.) Air defense warning white: Attack by hostile aircraft is improbable. May be called either before or after air defense warning yellow or red.

Air Delivered Seismic Intrusion Devices - Seismic sensors two feet long and four inches wide that were dropped from aircraft and embedded into the ground intended to send a signal when disturbed by ground vibration.

air delivery - See airdrop; air landed; air movement; air supply.

air delivery container - (DOD) A sling, bag or roll, usually of canvas or webbing, designed to hold supplies and equipment for air delivery.

air delivery equipment - (DOD) Special items of equipment, such as parachutes, air delivery containers, platforms, tie downs, and related items used in air delivery of personnel supplies, and equipment.

air despatcher (cargo) - (NATO, SEATO, CENTO, IADB) A person trained in the ejection of cargo from aircraft in flight.

air division - (DOD) A unit or its headquarters, on a level of command above wing level, composed of two or more combat wings, but sometimes adapted to other organizational structures.

air evacuation - (NATO, SEATO, CENTO, IADB) Evacuation by aircraft of personnel and cargo.

air facility - (DOD, IADB) An installation from which air operations may be or are being conducted. See also facility.

air fire plan - (DOD) A plan for integrating and coordinating tactical air support of ground forces with other fire support.

Air Force - See Department of the Air Force, established in 1947.

Air Force base - (DOD, SEATO) An air base for support of Air Force units consisting of landing strips and all components or related facilities for which the Air Force has operating responsibility, together with interior lines of communications and the minimum surrounding area required for local security. (Normally, not greater than an area of 20 square miles.) See also base complex.

Air Force Component Headquarters - (DOD) The field headquarters facility of the Air Force commander charged with the overall conduct of Air Force operations. It is composed of the command section and appropriate staff elements.

Air Force Cross - The nation's second highest award for bravery, parallel to the Navy Cross and the Army's Distinguished Service Cross.

air freighting - (NATO, CENTO, IADB) The non-tactical movement of cargo by air.

air ground operations system - (DOD, NATO, SEATO, CENTO, IADB) An Army/Air Force system providing the ground commander with the means for receiving, processing, and forwarding the requests of subordinate ground commanders for air-support missions and for the rapid dissemination of information and intelligence.

air intercept control common - (DOD) A tactical air-to-ground radio frequency monitored by all air intercept control facilities within an area, which is used as a back-up for other discrete tactical control frequencies.

air intercept zone - (DOD) A subdivided part of the destruction area in which it is planned to destroy or defeat the enemy airborne threat with interceptor aircraft. See also destruction area.

air interception - (DOD) To effect visual or electronic contact by a friendly aircraft with another aircraft. Normally the air intercept is conducted in the following five phases: a. climb phase - Airborne to cruising altitude; b. maneuver phase - Receipt of initial vector to target until beginning transition to attack speed and altitude; c. transition phase - Increase or decrease of speed and altitude required for the attack; d. attack phase - Turn to attack heading, acquisition of target, completion of attack and turn to breakaway heading; and e. recovery phase - Breakaway to landing. See also broadcast controlled air interception; close controlled air interception.

air interception - (NATO, CENTO, IADB) To effect visual or radar contact by a friendly aircraft with another aircraft. See also broadcast controlled air interception; close controlled air interception.

air interception - (SEATO) To effect visual or radar contact by a friendly aircraft with an unidentified aircraft. See also broadcast controlled air interception; close controlled air interception.

air interdiction - (DOD, NESN) Air operations conducted to destroy, neutralize, or delay the enemy's military potential before it can be brought to bear effectively against friendly forces, at such distance from friendly forces that detailed integration of each air mission with the fire and movement of friendly forces is not required. See also interdict.

air landed - (DOD) Moved by air and disembarked, or unloaded, after the aircraft has landed or while a helicopter is hovering.

air landed - (SEATO, IADB) Moved by air and disembarked, or unloaded, after the aircraft has landed.

air landing - (NATO, CENTO) Moved by air and disembarked, or unloaded, after the aircraft has landed. See also air movement.

air liaison officer - (DOD) An officer (aviator/ pilot) attached to a ground unit who functions as the primary advisor to the ground commander on air operation matters.

air liaison officer - (NATO, CENTO, IADB) A tactical air force or naval aviation officer attached to a ground unit or formation as air adviser.

air liaison officer - (SEATO) A tactical air force or naval aviation officer attached to a ground formation.

air logistic support - (DOD, NATO, CENTO, IADB) Support by air landing or airdrop including air supply, movement of personnel, evacuation of casualties and prisoners of war, and recovery of equipment and vehicles.

Air Medal - The medal recognizing heroism in aerial flight but less than that required for the Distinguished Flying Cross.

air mission - See mission.

air mission intelligence report - (DOD, NATO, SEATO, CENTO, IADB) A detailed report of the results of an air mission, including a complete intelligence account of the mission.

air movement - (DOD, NATO, CENTO, IADB) Air transport of units, personnel, supplies, and equipment including airdrops and air landings. See also airdrop; free drop; free fall; high-velocity drop; low velocity drop.

air movement - (SEATO) Air transport of units, personnel, supplies, and equipment, including airdrops and air landings. See also airdrops; free dropping; high velocity drop; low velocity drop.

air movement column - (DOD, IADB) In airborne operations, the lead formation and the serials following, proceeding over the same flight path at the same altitude.

air movement officer - (NATO, CENTO) An officer trained for duties in air movement/ traffic sections.

air movement section - See air traffic section.

air movement table - (DOD, NATO, SEATO, CENTO, IADB) A table prepared by a ground force commander in coordination with an air force commander. This form, issued as an annex to the operation order: a. indicates the allocation of aircraft space to elements of the ground units to be airlifted; b. designates the number and type of aircraft in each serial; c. specifies the departure area, time of loading, and takeoff.

air movement/traffic section - (NATO, SEATO, CENTO, IADB) A section located on those airfields which serve transport aircraft. It is responsible for the loading and unloading of aircraft, and for the handling of passengers, mail, and material.

air observation - See air observer.

air observation post - See observation post.

air observer - (DOD, NATO, SEATO, CENTO, IADB) An individual whose primary mission is to observe or take photographs from an aircraft in order to adjust artillery fire or obtain military information.

air observer adjustment - (DOD) The correcting of gunfire from an aircraft. See also spot.

air offensive - (DOD) Sustained operations by strategic and/or tactical air weapon systems against hostile air forces or surface targets.

air operations center - See tactical air control center.

air photograph - (NATO, CENTO) Any photograph taken from the air.

air photographic reconnaissance - (DOD, NATO, CENTO, IADB) The obtaining of information by air photography-divided into three types: a. strategic photographic reconnaissance; b. tactical photographic reconnaissance; and c. survey/ cartographic photography-air photography taken for survey/ cartographic purposes and to survey/ cartographic standards of accuracy. It may be strategic or tactical.

air pickets - (DOD, NATO, CENTO, IADB) Airborne early warning aircraft disposed around a position, area, or formation primarily to detect, report, and track approaching enemy aircraft or missiles, and to control intercepts. See also airborne early warning and control.

air plot - (DOD, NATO, CENTO, IADB) 1. A continuous plot used in air navigation of a graphic representation of true headings steered and air distances flown. 2. A continuous plot of the position of an airborne object represented graphically to show true headings steered and air distances flown. 3. Within ships, a display which shows the positions and movements of an airborne object relative to the plotting ship.

air portable - (DOD, NATO, SEATO, CENTO, IADB) Denotes materiel which is suitable for transport by an aircraft loaded internally or externally, with no more than minor dismantling and reassembling within the capabilities of user units. This term must be qualified to show the extent of air portability.

air position - (DOD, NATO, SEATO, CENTO, IADB) The calculated position of an aircraft assuming no wind effect.

air priorities committee - (DOD, NATO, SEATO, CENTO, IADB) A committee set up to determine the priorities of passengers and cargo.

air raid reporting control ship - (DOD, NATO, SEATO, CENTO, IADB) A ship to which the air defense ship has delegated the duties of controlling air warning radar and air raid reporting.

air reconnaissance - (DOD) The acquisition of intelligence information employing visual observation and/or sensors in air vehicles.

air reconnaissance - (NATO, CENTO, IADB) The acquisition of intelligence information employing aerial vehicles in visual observation or the use of sensory devices.

air reconnaissance liaison officer - (DOD) An Army officer especially trained in air reconnaissance and imagery interpretation matters who is attached to a tactical air reconnaissance unit. He assists and advises the air commander and staff on matters concerning ground operations and informs the supported ground commander on the status of air reconnaissance requests.

air route - (DOD, NATO, CENTO, IADB) The navigable airspace between two points, identified to the extent necessary for the application of flight rules.

air route traffic control center - (DOD, IADB) The principal facility exercising en route control of Instrument Flight Rules flights within its area of jurisdiction. (DOD) Approximately 26 such centers cover the United States. Each has communication capability to adjacent centers.

air space warning area - See danger area.

air spot - (DOD, IADB) The correcting adjustment of gunfire based on air observation.

air staging unit - (DOD, NATO, CENTO, IADB) A unit situated at an airfield and concerned with the reception, handling, servicing, and preparation for departure of aircraft and control of personnel and cargo.

air stair - The ladder attached to an airplane for passengers to enter and exit, often folding.

air station (photogrammetry) - (DOD, NATO, CENTO, IADB) The point in space occupied by the camera lens at the moment of exposure. See also air base (photogrammetry).

air strike - (DOD, IADB) An attack on specific objectives by fighter, bomber, or attack aircraft on an offensive mission. May consist of several air organizations under a single command in the air.

air strike coordinator - (DOD) The air representative of the force commander in a target area. He is responsible for directing all aircraft in the target area and coordinating their efforts to achieve the most effective use of air striking power.

air strip - (DOD, NATO, SEATO, CENTO, IADB) An unimproved surface which has been adapted for takeoff or landing of aircraft, usually having minimum facilities. See also airfield.

air superiority - (DOD, NATO, SEATO, CENTO, IADB) That degree of dominance in the air battle of one force over another which permits the conduct of operations by the former and its related land, sea, and air forces at a given time and place without prohibitive interference by the opposing force.

air supply - (DOD, NATO, CENTO, IADB) The delivery of cargo by airdrop or air landing.

air support - (DOD, NATO, SEATO, CENTO, IADB) All forms of support given by air forces to forces on land or sea. See also air interdiction; call mission; close air support; immediate air support; indirect air support; preplanned air support; tactical air support.

air support radar team - (DOD) A subordinate operational component of a tactical air control system which provides ground controlled precision flight path guidance and weapons release.

air supremacy - (DOD, NATO, SEATO, CENTO, IADB) That degree of air superiority wherein the opposing air force is incapable of effective interference.

air surface zones - (DOD, NATO, SEATO, CENTO, IADB) Restricted areas established for the purpose of preventing friendly surface ships and aircraft from being fired upon by friendly forces and for permitting antisubmarine operations, unrestricted by the operations of friendly submarines. See also restricted area. (Note: NATO and CENTO definition uses the word "vessels" instead of the word "ships".)

air surveillance - (DOD, NATO, SEATO, CENTO, IADB) The systematic observation of airspace by electronic, visual, or other means primarily for the purpose of identifying and determining the movements of aircraft and missiles, friendly and enemy, in the airspace under observation. See also satellite and missile surveillance; surveillance.

air surveillance plotting board - (NATO, SEATO, CENTO, IADB) A gridded, small scale, air defense map of an appropriate area. It is maintained at the air control center. On it are posted current locations, number, and altitudes of all friendly or enemy aircraft within range of radar or ground observer facilities.

air survey camera - See air cartographic camera.

air survey photography - See air cartographic photography.

air target chart - (DOD) A display of pertinent air target intelligence on a specialized graphic base. It is designed primarily to support operations against designated air targets by various weapon systems.

air target materials program - (DOD) A Department of Defense program established for the production of medium and large-scale target materials and related items in support of long-range, worldwide requirements of the unified and specified commands, the military departments, and allied participants. It is under the management control of the Defense Intelligence Agency and encompasses the determination of production and coverage requirements, standardization of products, establishment of production priorities and schedules, and the production, distribution, storage, and release/exchange of the air target materials items and related products.

air target mosaic - (DOD) A large-scale mosaic providing photographic coverage of an area and permitting comprehensive portrayal of pertinent target detail. These mosaics are used for intelligence study and in planning and briefing for air operations.

air terminal - (DOD, IADB) An installation provided with the facilities for loading and unloading aircraft and the in-transit handling of traffic (passengers, cargo, and mail) which is moved by aircraft.

air to mud - Slang for air to ground bombing.

air traffic control center - (DOD, NATO, CENTO, IADB) A unit combining the functions of an area control center and a flight information center. See also area control center; flight information region.

air traffic control clearance - (DOD, NATO, SEATO, CENTO, IADB) Authorization by an air traffic control authority for an aircraft to proceed under specified conditions.

air traffic control service - (DOD, NATO, CENTO) A service provided for the purpose of: 1. Preventing collisions; a. between aircraft; and b. between aircraft and obstructions, and 2. Expediting and maintaining an orderly flow of air traffic.

air traffic controller - (DOD) An air controller especially trained for and assigned to the duty of airspace management and traffic control of airborne objects. See also air controller.

air traffic section - (DOD, IADB) The link between the staging post and the local air priority committee. It is the key to the efficient handling of passengers and cargo at a staging post. It must include load control (including Customs and Immigration facilities), freight, and mail sections.

air transport allocations board - (DOD, NATO, CENTO, IADB) The joint agency responsible within the theater for the establishment of airlift priorities and for space allocation of available aircraft capabilities allotted to the theater.

air transport liaison officer - (DOD, NATO, SEATO, CENTO, IADB) An officer attached for air transport liaison duties to a headquarters or unit.

air transport liaison section (army) - (NATO, CENTO, IADB) A subunit of the movement control organization deployed to airfields and responsible for the control of Service movement at the airfield in connection with air movement operations and exercises.

air transportable units - (DOD, NATO, CENTO, IADB) Those units, other than airborne, whose equipment is adapted for air movement. See also airborne; airborne operation.

air transportable units - (SEATO) Those ground units, other than airborne, which are trained and whose equipment is adapted for movement and delivery by transport aircraft. See also airborne; airborne operation.

air transported forces - (NATO, SEATO, CENTO, IADB) Forces which are moved by air. See also force(s).

air transported operations - (DOD, SEATO, IADB) The movement by aircraft of troops and their equipment for an operation.

air trooping - (NATO, CENTO, IADB) The non-tactical movement by air of personnel. See also air movement.

air weapons controller - (DOD) An air controller especially trained for and assigned to the duty of employing and controlling weapons against airborne objects. See also air controller.

Air Wing - Aviation term for all aircraft related to a carrier.

AIR-2A - See Genie.

AIR-2B - See Genie.

air-breathing missile - (DOD) A missile with an engine requiring the intake of air for combustion of its fuel, as in a ramjet or turbojet. To be contrasted with the rocket missile, which carries its own oxidizer and can operate beyond the atmosphere.

air-launched ballistic missile - (DOD) An air-launched ballistic missile launched from an airborne vehicle.

air-launched ballistic missile - (IADB) A ballistic missile launched from an airborne vehicle.

air-sea rescue - See search and rescue.

air-to-air missile - (DOD, IADB) A missile launched from an airborne carrier at a target above the surface.

air-to-surface missile - (DOD, IADB) A missile launched from an airborne carrier to impact on a surface target.

airborne - (DOD, NESN, NFSN, SEATO, CENTO, IADB) 1. Applied to personnel, equipment, etc., transported by air, e.g., airborne infantry. 2. Applied to materiel being or designed to be transported by aircraft, as distinguished from weapons and equipment installed in and remaining a part of the aircraft. 3. Applied to an aircraft from the instant it becomes entirely sustained by air until it ceases to be so sustained. A lighter-than-air aircraft is not considered to be airborne when it is attached to the ground, except that moored balloons are airborne whenever sent aloft. See also air transportable units.

airborne - 1. Parachute qualified soldier. 2. Anything dropped by parachute.

airborne alert - (DOD, NATO, CENTO, IADB) A state of aircraft readiness wherein combat-equipped aircraft are airborne and ready for immediate action. (DOD, IADB) It is designed to reduce reaction time and to increase the survivability factor. See also combat air patrol; fighter cover.

airborne assault - See assault.

airborne assault weapon - (DOD, IADB) An unarmored, mobile, full-tracked gun providing a mobile antitank capability for airborne troops. Can be airdropped.

airborne battlefield command and control center - (DOD) A United States Air Force aircraft equipped with communications, data link, and display equipment; it may be employed as an airborne command post or a communications and intelligence relay facility.

airborne command center - The U.S. Air Force aircraft serving as a command center for ground as well as aviation.

airborne command post - (DOD) A suitably equipped aircraft used by the commander for the control of his forces.

airborne copulation - Euphemism for "flying fuck" as in "I don't give a flying fuck."

airborne early warning - (DOD) The detection of enemy air or surface units by radar or other equipment carried in an airborne vehicle and the transmitting of a warning to friendly units.

airborne early warning - (IADB) An airborne aircraft that has the capability, through radar or other means, of detecting the approach of enemy air or surface units and of transmitting an alert to friendly units.

airborne early warning and control - (DOD, NATO, CENTO, IADB) Air surveillance and control provided by airborne early warning vehicles which are equipped with search and height-finding radar and communications equipment for controlling weapons. See also air pickets.

airborne early warning and control - (SEATO) An airborne radar station providing early warning and control facilities.

airborne force liaison officer - (NATO, SEATO, CENTO, IADB) An officer who is the representative of the airborne units and who works with the air force on airfields being used for airborne operations.

airborne forces - (DOD, NATO, SEATO, CENTO, IADB) Forces composed primarily of ground and air units organized, equipped, and trained for airborne operations. See also force(s).

airborne intercept equipment - (DOD) A fire control system, including radar equipment, installed in interceptor aircraft used to effect air interception.

airborne lift - (DOD IADB) The total capacities expressed in terms of personnel and cargo that are, or can be, carried by available aircraft in one trip.

airborne operation - (DOD, IADB) An operation involving the air movement into an objective area, of combat forces and their logistic support for execution of a tactical or a strategic mission. The means employed may be any combination of airborne units, air transportable units and types of transport aircraft, depending on the mission and the overall situation.

airborne operation - (NATO, SEATO, CENTO) An operation involving the movement of combat forces and their logistic support into an objective area by air.

airborne order - (DOD) A command and authorization for flight when a predetermined time greater than five minutes is established for aircraft to become airborne.

airborne platform - A support for the Howitzer with adjustable legs.

airborne radio relay - (DOD) Airborne equipment used to relay radio transmission from selected originating transmitters.

airborne radio relay - (NATO, CENTO) A technique, employing aircraft fitted with radio relay stations for the purpose of increasing the range, flexibility or physical security of communications systems.

airborne sensor operator - (DOD) An individual trained to operate sensor equipment aboard aircraft and to perform limited interpretations of imagery produced in flight.

airborne troops - (DOD, IADB) Those ground units whose primary mission is to make assault landings from the air. See also troops.

airburst - (DOD, NATO, SEATO, CENTO, IADB) An explosion of a bomb or projectile above the surface as distinguished from an explosion on contact with the surface or after penetration. See types of burst.

aircraft - See active aircraft; inactive aircraft; nonprogram aircraft; program aircraft; reserve aircraft; supporting aircraft; unit aircraft.

aircraft arresting barrier - (DOD, NATO, CENTO, IADB) The device, not dependent on an aircraft hook, used to engage and absorb the forward momentum of an emergency landing or aborted take-off. See also aircraft arresting system.

aircraft arresting gear - (DOD, NATO, CENTO, IADB) The device used to engage hook equipped aircraft to absorb the forward momentum of a routine or emergency landing, or aborted take-off. See also aircraft arresting system.

aircraft arresting hook - (NATO, CENTO, IADB) A device fitted to an aircraft to engage arresting gear. See also aircraft arresting system.

aircraft arresting hook wire - (NATO, CENTO) A wire engaged by an aircraft arresting hook used in certain types of aircraft arresting systems. See also aircraft arresting hook; aircraft arresting system.

aircraft arresting system - (DOD, NATO, CENTO, IADB) A series of components used to engage an aircraft and absorb the forward momentum of a routine or emergency landing (or aborted takeoff). See also aircraft arresting barrier; aircraft arresting gear; aircraft arresting hook.

aircraft block speed - (DOD) True air speed in knots under zero wind conditions adjusted in relation to length of sortie to compensate for take-off, climb-out, let-down, instrument approach and landing.

aircraft carrier - A large ship which served as a floating airport for military aircraft. Specifically, the U.S. Navy ships that carried 70-100 planes each from the two fighter and three attack squadrons that were used in Vietnam from 1964. Helicopters augmented the fixed wing aircraft capacity. Two to four aircraft carriers were on station at any one time. A total of 19 carriers served.

aircraft climb corridor - (NATO, CENTO, IADB) Positive controlled airspaces of defined vertical and horizontal dimensions extending from an airfield.

aircraft control and warning system - (DOD, IADB) A system established to control and report the movement of aircraft. It consists of observation facilities (radar, passive electronic, visual, or other means), control centers, and necessary communications.

aircraft dispersal area - (NATO, SEATO, CENTO, IADB) An area on a military installation designed primarily for the dispersal of parked aircraft, whereby such aircraft will be less vulnerable in the event of an enemy air raid.

aircraft flat pallet - (NATO, CENTO) A stressed pallet capable of supporting and restraining a specifically rated load. It is specifically designed for tiedown in an aircraft. See also palletized unit load.

aircraft guide - See aircraft marshaller.

aircraft handover - (NATO, SEATO, CENTO, IADB) The process of transferring control of aircraft from one controlling authority to another.

aircraft inspection - (NATO, CENTO, IADB) The process of systematically examining, checking and testing aircraft structural members, components and systems, to detect actual or potential unserviceable conditions.

aircraft loading table - (DOD, NATO, SEATO, CENTO, IADB) A data sheet used by the force unit commander containing information as to the load that actually goes into each aircraft.

aircraft marshaller - (NATO, CENTO) A person trained to direct by visual or other means the movement of aircraft on the ground, into and out of landing, parking or hovering points. Also known as aircraft guide.

aircraft marshalling area - (NATO, SEATO, CENTO, IADB) An area in which aircraft may form up before take-off or assemble after landing.

aircraft mission equipment - (DOD, NATO, CENTO, IADB) Equipment that must be fitted to an aircraft to enable it to fulfill a particular mission or task.

aircraft modification - (DOD, NATO, CENTO, IADB) A change in the physical characteristics of aircraft, accomplished either by a change in production specifications or by alteration of items already produced.

aircraft monitoring and control - (DOD) That equipment installed in aircraft to permit monitoring and control of safing, arming, and fuzing functions of nuclear weapons or nuclear weapon systems.

aircraft picketing - (NATO, CENTO) Securing aircraft when parked in the open to restrain movement due to the weather or condition of the parking area. See also aircraft tiedown.

aircraft repair - (DOD, NATO, CENTO) The process of restoring aircraft or aircraft material after damage or wear to a serviceable condition.

aircraft replenishing - (NATO, CENTO, IADB) The refilling of aircraft with consumables such as fuel, oil, and compressed gases to predetermined levels, pressures, quantities, or weights. Rearming is excluded.

aircraft role equipment - See aircraft mission equipment.

aircraft scrambling - (DOD, NATO, SEATO, CENTO, IADB) Directing the immediate takeoff of aircraft from a ground alert condition of readiness.

aircraft tiedown - (DOD, IADB) Securing aircraft when parked in the open to restrain movement due to the weather or condition of the parking area. See also aircraft picketing.

aircraft utilization - (DOD, IADB) Average number of hours during each 24-hour period that an aircraft is actually in flight.

aircraft vectoring - (DOD, NATO, CENTO, IADB) The directional control of in-flight aircraft through transmission of azimuth headings.

aircraft vectoring - (SEATO) The directional control of in-flight aircraft through transmission of azimuth headings. (Not used for homing headings.)

airdrop - (DOD, SEATO, IADB) The unloading of personnel or materiel from aircraft in flight. See also air movement; free drop; free fall; high velocity drop; low velocity drop; (Note: SEATO term is "airdrops".)

airdrop - (NATO, CENTO) Delivery of personnel or cargo from aircraft in flight. See also air movement; free drop; high velocity drop; low velocity drop.

airdrop platform - (DOD, NATO, CENTO, IADB) A base on which vehicles, cargo, or equipment is loaded for airdrop or low altitude extraction. See also airdrop.

airfield - (DOD, NATO, CENTO, IADB) An area prepared for the accommodation, (including any buildings, installations, and equipment), landing and take-off of aircraft. See also alternative airfield; departure airfield; landing area; landing point; landing site; landing zone; main airfield; redeployment airfield; regroup airfield. (Note: IADB definition does not have the parenthetical phrase beginning with the word "including".)

airfield traffic - (DOD, NATO, CENTO) All traffic on the maneuvering area of an airfield and all aircraft flying in the vicinity of an airfield.

airframe - (DOD, IADB) 1. The structural components of an airplane, including the framework and skin of such parts as the fuselage, empennage, wings, landing gear (minus tires), and engine mounts. 2. The framework, envelope, and cabin of an airship. 3. The assembled principal structural components, less propulsion system, control, electronic equipments, and payload of a missile.

airhead - (DOD, NATO, CENTO, IADB) 1. A designated area in a hostile or threatened territory which, when seized and held, insures the continuous air landing of troops and materiel and provides maneuver space necessary for projected operations. Normally, it is the area seized in the assault phase of an airborne operation. 2. A designated location in an area of operations used as a base for supply and evacuation by air.

airhead - (SEATO) 1. A designated area in a hostile or threatened territory which, when seized and held, ensures the continuous air landing of troops and materiel and provides the maneuver space necessary for projected operations. 2. A designated location in an area of operations and used as a base for supply and evacuation by air. See also beachhead; bridgehead.

airhead - Slang for a stupid, or disconnected person, usually drug related.

airlift - (DOD, NATO, SEATO, CENTO, IADB) 1. The total weight of personnel and/or cargo that is, or can be, carried by air, or that is offered for carriage by air. 2. To transport passengers and cargo by use of aircraft. (DOD, NATO, CENTO, IADB) 3. The carriage of personnel and/or cargo by air. See also payload.

airlift capability - (DOD, NATO, CENTO, IADB) The total capacity expressed in terms of number of passengers and/or weight/cubic displacement of cargo that can be carried at anyone time to a given destination by the available air transport service. See also airlift requirement; allowable cabin load (air); allowable cargo load (air); payload; planned load (aircraft).

airlift requirement - (DOD, NATO, CENTO, IADB) The total number of passengers and/or weight/cubic displacement of cargo required to be carried by air for a specific task. See also airlift capability.

airlift service - (DOD, IADB) The performance or procurement of air transportation and services incident thereto required for the movement of persons, cargo, mail, or other goods.

airmobile operations - (DOD, NATO, CENTO, IADB) Operations in which combat forces and their equipment move about the battlefield in air vehicles under the control of a ground force commander to engage in ground combat.

airport surface detection equipment - (DOD) Short range radar displaying the airport surface. Aircraft and vehicular traffic operating on runways, taxiways, and ramps, moving or stationary, may be observed with a high degree of resolution.

airport surveillance radar - (DOD) Radar displaying range and azimuth which is normally employed in a terminal area as an aid to approach and departure control.

airport traffic area - (DOD) Unless otherwise specifically designated, that airspace within a horizontal radius of five statute miles from the geographical center of any airport at which a control tower is operating, extending from the surface up to, but not including, 2000 feet above the surface.

airspace reservation - (DOD) The airspace located above an area on the surface of the land or water, designated and set apart by Executive Order of the President or by a state, commonwealth, or territory, over which the flight of aircraft is prohibited or restricted for the purpose of national defense or for other governmental purposes.

airspace reservation - (IADB) The airspace located above an area on the surface of the land or water, designated and set apart by competent authority, over which the flight of aircraft is prohibited or restricted for the purpose of national defense or for other governmental purposes.

airspeed - (DOD, IADB) The speed of an aircraft relative to its surrounding air mass. The unqualified term "airspeed" can mean anyone of the following: a. calibrated airspeed - Indicated airspeed corrected for instrument installation error, b. equivalent airspeed - Calibrated airspeed corrected for compressibility error, c. indicated airspeed - The airspeed shown by an airspeed indicator, d. true airspeed - Equivalent airspeed corrected for error due to air density (altitude and temperature).

airspeed - (NATO, SEATO, CENTO) The speed of an aircraft relative to its surrounding air mass.

airway - (DOD, NATO, CENTO, IADB) A control area or portion thereof established in the form of a corridor marked with radio navigation aids.

airways station - (DOD, IADB) A ground communication installation established, manned, and equipped to communicate with aircraft in flight, as well as with other designated airways installations, for the purpose of expeditious and safe movements of aircraft. These stations mayor may not be located on designated airways.

AIT - Abbreviation for advanced individual or infantry training.

AJ - See Acting Jack.

AK - See AK-47.

AK amp - Hospital slang for an at knee amputation. See BK amp.

AK-47 - Soviet made military assault rifle. It used a standard 7.62-mm bullet and could be fired on full automatic or as a single shot weapon. The name comes from the Russian Avtomat (for automatic) Kalashnikov (the name of the designer Milhail Kalashnikov) 47 (the year that the weapon was put into production 1947). The AK-47 is a derivative of the 1944 German assault rifle, and the source for the Chinese copy, the T-56 which was the standard issue for the North Vietnamese Army and the Viet Cong. Also called AK.

AKA - See attack cargo ship.

AKL - Light cargo ship used by Navy to transfer cargo in harbor or for resupply. Called lighter.

Alabama black snake - A black soldier's penis.

Alamo Apartments - The apartment complex in Da Nang occupied by civilian contractors.

Alamo Hilton - The heavily fortified bunker at Khe Sanh Combat Base built by Navy Sea-Bees.

Albatross - The HU-16 amphibious plane.

ALC - Radio call for all concerned to pay attention to the mesage.

Alcatraz - The high security prison near Hanoi.

Alcoholics Anonymous - Slang for 82nd Airborne Division (using double As on uniform patch).

alert - (DOD, NATO, SEATO, CENTO, IADB) 1. Readiness for action, defense, or protection. 2. A warning signal of a real or threatened danger, such as an air attack. 3. The period of time during which troops stand by in response to an alarm. 4. To forewarn; to prepare for action. See also air alert; airborne alert; air defense warning conditions; ground alert.

alert force - (DOD, IADB) Specified forces maintained in a special degree of readiness.

alert status - The color coded system for identification of the level of readiness needed. White is a low alert status allowing normal operations. Yellow is increased readiness placing 50% of troops in readiness on the line expecting an enemy attack. Red is high alert status with 75-100% of troops in combat readiness expecting that an enemy attack is imminent.

Alert-15 - Having an aircraft and crew able to launch within fifteen minutes.

Alert-30 - Having an aircraft and crew able to launch within thirty minutes.

Alert-5 - Having an aircraft and crew able to launch within five minutes.

Alert-60 - Having an aircraft and crew able to launch within sixty minutes.

alerting service - (DOD, NATO, SEATO, CENTO, IADB) A service provided to notify appropriate organizations regarding aircraft in need of search and rescue aid, and assist such organizations as required.

Alfa - The adopted military phonetic alphabet designation for the letter "A". More commonly spelled Alpha in practice.

ALICE - All Purpose Lightweight Individual Carrying Equipment. The soldier's field backpack for all personal gear. See ruck.

alighting area - (NATO) A specified surface, reserved to vehicles that depend upon water surfaces for their landing.

alignment - (NATO) 1. The bearing of two or more conspicuous objects (such as lights, beacons etc.) as seen by an observer. 2. Representation of a road, railway, etc., on a map or chart in relation to surrounding topographic detail.

All African - Derogatory reference to the 82nd Airborne division.

All American - Nickname for the 82nd Airborne division.

all available - (DOD) A command or request to obtain the fire of all artillery able to deliver effective fire on a given target.

all hands - Everyone.

all out war - (DOD) Not to be used. See general war.

all purpose capsule - See Army aspirin, APC.

all purpose hand-held weapon - (DOD, IADB) A light-weight, hand-held, small arms weapon capable of projecting munitions required to engage both area and point-type targets.

all the way - The goal of some officers for promotions to the top.

all weather fighter - (DOD, NATO, SEATO, CENTO, IADB) A fighter aircraft with radar devices and other special equipment which enable it to intercept its target in dark or daylight weather conditions which do not permit visual interception.

allied headquarters - See allied staff.

allied staff - (NATO, SEATO, CENTO, IADB) A staff or headquarters composed of two or more allied nations working together.

alligator clip - 1. A toggle that attached an IBS (rubber raft) to an aircraft. 2. The small clip used in electrical soldering that was also used to hold the small butt end of a marijuana cigarette.

allocation - (DOD) The designation of specific numbers and types of aircraft sorties for use during a specified time period or for carrying out an assigned task.

allocation (nuclear) - (DOD) The apportionment of specific numbers and types of nuclear weapons to a commander for a stated time period as a planning factor for use in the development of war plans. (Additional authority is required for the actual deployment of allocated weapons to locations desired by the commander to support his war plans. Expenditures of these weapons are not authorized until released by proper authority.)

allocation (nuclear) - (NATO, CENTO) The specific numbers and types of nuclear weapons allocated to a commander for a stated time period as a planning factor only.

allocation (transportation) - (DOD) Apportionment by designated authority of available transport capability to users.

allotment - The portion of a soldier's pay allocated to the living allowance of his dependent(s) and removed from his pay and paid to the dependent(s).

allowable cabin load (air) - (DOD, NATO, CENTO) The amount of cargo and passengers, determined by weight, cubic displacement and distance to be flown, which may be transported by specified aircraft.

allowable cargo load (air) - (DOD, NATO, SEATO, CENTO, IADB) The amount of cargo, determined by weight, cubic displacement, and distance to be flown, which may be transported by specified aircraft.

ALMAR 65 - The Order from Marine Corps Headquarters intended to reduce racial tension by permitting the Black Power salute and Afro haircuts.

Almost Airborne - The 82nd Airborne Division.

Almost American - Slang for 82nd Airborne Division (using double As on uniform patch).

Alpha - The common spelling of Alfa.

Alpha Alpha - Slang for automatic ambush.

Alpha Bravo - Slang for ambush.

Alpha Hotel - Slang for ass hole.

Alpha Mike/ Foxtrot Mike - AM/FM radio methods of communication.

Alpha Sierra - Slang for air support.

Alpha Strike - A major bombing mission.

Alpha-Sierra-Sierra-Romeo-Sierra (ASSRS) - The Marine radio code for unchanged calm status, specifically All Secure Situation Remains Same.

alphabet code - See phonetic alphabet.

alternate aerodrome - (NATO, SEATO, CENTO, IADB) An aerodrome specified in the flight plan to which a flight may proceed when a landing at the intended destination becomes inadvisable.

alternate command authority - (DOD) One or more predesignated officers empowered by the commander through pre-delegation of authority to act for him under stipulated emergency conditions in the accomplishment of previously defined functions.

alternate command post - (DOD, IADB) Any location designated by a commander to assume command post functions in the event the command post becomes inoperative. It may be partially or fully equipped and manned or it may be the command post of a subordinate unit.

alternate escort operating base - (NATO, SEATO, CENTO, IADB) A base providing the facilities and activities required for the support of escort units for short periods of time.

alternate water terminal - (DOD, NATO, CENTO, IADB) A water terminal with facilities for berthing from two to five ships simultaneously at wharves and/or working anchorages, located within sheltered coastal waters, adjacent to reliable highway and/or rail transportation nets. It covers a relatively small area and is located away from population centers. The scope of operation is such that it is not designated a probable nuclear target. See also water terminal.

alternative airfield - (DOD, NATO, SEATO, CENTO, IADB) An airfield with minimum essential facilities for use as an emergency landing ground, or when main or redeployment airfields are not of action, or as required for tactical flexibility. See also airfield.

alternative service - Humanitarian services performed at home or in Vietnam by conscientious objectors to the war.

altimeter - The instrument displaying altitude.

altitude - (DOD, NATO, CENTO, IADB) The vertical distance of a level, a point, or an object considered as a point, measured from mean sea level. See also absolute altitude; critical altitude; density altitude; drop altitude; elevation; height; minimum safe altitude; pressure altitude; transition altitude; true altitude.

altitude acclimatization - (DOD, NATO, CENTO, IADB) A slow physiological adaptation resulting from prolonged exposure to significantly reduced atmospheric pressure.

altitude acclimatization - (SEATO) A slow physiological adaptation to significantly reduced atmospheric pressure, resulting from prolonged exposure.

altitude datum - (DOD, NATO, CENTO) The arbitrary level from which vertical displacement is measured. The datum for height measurement is the terrain directly below the aircraft or some specified datum; for pressure altitude, the level at which the atmospheric pressure is 29.92 inches of mercury (1013.2 mbs); and for true altitude, mean sea level.

altitude height - See altitude datum.

altitude hole - (NATO, CENTO) The blank area at the origin of a radial display, on a radar tube presentation, the center of the periphery of which represents the point on the ground immediately below the aircraft. In side looking airborne radar, this is known as the altitude slot.

altitude sickness - (DOD, NATO, SEATO, CENTO, IADB) The syndrome of depression, anorexia, nausea, vomiting, and collapse, due to decreased atmospheric pressure, occurring in an individual exposed to an altitude beyond that to which acclimatization has occurred.

altitude slot - See altitude hole.

altitude tint - See hypsometric tinting.

ambulatory patient - See walking patient.

ambush academy - Slang for jungle fighting school.

Ambush Alley - Slang for the portion of highway 19 that was frequently ambushed.

AMEMB - American Embassy.

Amer-Asian - The term for children with an American father and Asian mother (and rarely the reverse).

Americal - The 23d Infantry Division. Involved in the Mai Lai massacre.

American Gold Star Mothers - The maternal organization of mothers who have lost sons in wars. Prior to the Korean War, the government awarded a gold star to such mothers in addition to medals earned by the soldier.

American Red Cross (ARC) - The charity providing non-combat services to troops, particularly refreshment and entertainment at bases and support to those hospitalized.

American Services Radio - The radio service that replaced Armed Forces Radio in 1973. Noted for its playing of "I'm Dreaming of a White Christmas" on April 29, 1975 as the alert code to evacuate the American Embassy in Saigon.

Amerikill - Derogatory term for the Americal Division.

AMF - Adios, motherfucker or Aloha, mother fucker. Slang for goodbye after an unpleasant encounter or battle.

ammo (plus, minus, zero) - (DOD) In air intercept, a code meaning I have amount of ammunition indicated left (type may be specified). For example: ammo plus-I have more than half my ammunition left; ammo minus-I have less than half my ammunition left; ammo zero - I have no ammunition left.

ammo dump - Storage location for ammunition.

ammo humper - Artilleryman.

ammunition - (DOD, NATO, SEATO, CENTO, IADB) A contrivance charged with explosives, propellants, pyrotechnics, initiating composition, or nuclear, biological, or chemical material for use in connection with defense or offense including demolitions. Certain ammunition can be used for training, ceremonial, or nonoperational purposes. See also chemical ammunition; fixed ammunition; semifixed ammunition; separate-loading ammunition.

ammunition and toxic material open space - (DOD, NATO, CENTO, IADB) Area especially prepared for storage of explosive ammunition and toxic material. For reporting purposes, it does not include the surrounding area restricted for storage because of safety distance factors. It includes barricades and improvised coverings. See also storage.

ammunition supply point - See distribution point.

Amn - Abbreviation for Airman (Air Force).

amnesty box - The receptacle for contraband disposed of by departing troops before being searched before leaving Vietnam.

amphibious assault landing - See amphibious operation, Part e.

amphibious assault ship - (DOD, IADB) A ship designed to transport and land troops, equipment, and supplies by means of embarked helicopters. (DOD) Designated as LPH. Some of these ships were formerly CVAs or CVSs.

amphibious command ship - (DOD, NATO, SEATO, CENTO, IADB) A naval ship from which a commander exercises control in amphibious operations.

Amphibious Construction Battalion - Large SEABEE construction units.

amphibious control group - (DOD, NATO, CENTO, IADB) Personnel, ships, and craft designated to control the waterborne ship-to-shore movement in an amphibious operation.

amphibious demonstration - (DOD, NATO, CENTO, IADB) A lesser included type of amphibious operation conducted for the purpose of deceiving the enemy by a show of force with the expectation of deluding the enemy into a course of action unfavorable to him.

amphibious force - (DOD, NATO, SEATO, CENTO, IADB) 1. A naval force and landing force, together with supporting forces that are trained, organized, and equipped for amphibious operations. 2. In naval usage, the administrative title of the amphibious-type command of a fleet.

amphibious group - (DOD, NATO, CENTO) A command within the amphibious force, consisting of the commander and his staff, designed to exercise operational command of assigned units in executing all phases of a division-size amphibious operation.

amphibious lift - (DOD, NATO, CENTO, IADB) The total capacity of assault shipping utilized in an amphibious operation, expressed in terms of personnel, vehicles, and measurement or weight tons of supplies.

amphibious objective study - (DOD) Studies designed to provide basic intelligence data of a permanent or semipermanent nature required for planning amphibious operations. Each study deals with a specific area the selection of which is based on strategic location, susceptibility to seizure by amphibious means, and other considerations.

amphibious operation - (DOD, IADB) An attack launched from the sea by naval and landing forces, embarked in ships or craft involving a landing on a hostile shore. As an entity, the amphibious operation includes the following phases: a. planning - The period extending from issuance of the initiating directive to embarkation. b. embarkation - The period during which the forces, with their equipment and supplies, are embarked in the assigned shipping. c. rehearsal - The period during which the prospective operation is rehearsed for the purpose of: (1) testing adequacy of plans, the timing of detailed operations, and the combat readiness of participating forces; (2) insuring that all echelons are familiar with plans; and (3) testing communications. d. movement - The period during which various components of the amphibious task force move from points of embarkation to the objective area. e. assault - The period between the arrival of the major assault forces of the amphibious task force in the objective area and the accomplishment of the amphibious task force mission.

amphibious operation - (NATO, CENTO) An attack launched from the sea by naval and landing forces, embarked in ships or craft involving a landing on a hostile shore.

amphibious raid - (DOD, IADB) A lesser included type of amphibious operation: a landing from the sea on a hostile shore involving swift incursion into, or a temporary occupancy of an objective, followed by a planned withdrawal.

amphibious raid - (NATO, CENTO) A limited type of amphibious operation; a landing from the sea on a hostile shore involving swift incursion into, or a temporary occupancy of an objective, followed by a planned withdrawal.

amphibious reconnaissance - (DOD) An amphibious landing conducted by minor elements, normally involving stealth rather than force of arms, for the purpose of securing information and usually followed by a planned withdrawal.

amphibious shipping - (DOD) Organic Navy ships specifically designed to transport, land, and support landing forces in amphibious assault operations and capable of being loaded or unloaded by naval personnel without external assistance in the amphibious objective area.

amphibious squadron - (DOD, NATO, CENTO, IADB) A tactical and administrative organization composed of amphibious assault shipping to transport troops and their equipment anchored for an amphibious assault operation.

amphibious striking forces - (DOD, IADB) Forces capable of projecting military power from the sea upon adjacent land areas for initiating and/or conducting operations there in the face of enemy opposition.

amphibious transport dock - (DOD, IADB) A ship designed to transport and land troops, equipment, and supplies by means of embarked landing craft, amphibious vehicles, and helicopters. (DOD) Designated as LPD.

amphibious vehicle - (DOD, NATO, CENTO, IADB) A wheeled or tracked vehicle capable of operating on both land and water. See also landing craft; vehicle.

amphibious vehicle availability table - (DOD, IADB) A tabulation of the type and number of amphibious vehicles available primarily for assault landings and for support of other elements of the operation.

amphibious vehicle employment plan - (DOD, IADB) A plan showing in tabular form the planned employment of amphibious vehicles in landing operations including their employment after the initial movement to the beach.

amphibious vehicle launching area - (DOD, NATO, CENTO, IADB) An area, in the vicinity of and to seaward of the line of departure, to which landing ships proceed and launch amphibious vehicles.

amplifying report - See contact report.

amtrack - The amphibious armored troop and supply transport vehicle armed with a .30-caliber machine gun, used by Marines (see APC).

AN - Airman (Coast Guard).

AN-109 - A long range radio used by Special Forces.

AN-2 - A type of aircraft used by North Vietnamese and/or Viet Cong Forces made by Antonov.

AN-24 - A type of aircraft used by North Vietnamese and/or Viet Cong Forces made by Antonov.

analysis - (DOD) A stage in the intelligence cycle in which information is subjected to review in order to identify significant facts and derive conclusions therefrom.

analysis staff - See central analysis team.

ANC - Army Nurse Corps.

anchor - Slang for mid-air refueling tracks.

anchor cable (air transport) - (DOD, NATO, CENTO, IADB) A cable in an aircraft to which the parachute static lines or strops are attached.

anchor line extension kits - (DOD, NATO, CENTO) A device fitted to an aircraft equipped with removable clamshell doors to enable paratroopers to exit from the rear.

anchor-clankers - Slang for navy personnel.

anchored - (DOD) In air intercept, a code meaning am orbiting a visible orbit point.

Androck - A name stamped on the P-38 can opener. See P-38.

angel - See angels.

angel track - Slang for the armored personnel carrier transporting the wounded to a medical aid station.

angels - 1. (DOD) In air intercept and close air support, a code meaning aircraft altitude (in thousands of feet).

angels - Slang for: 1. A rescue helicopter, in general, and those stationed near a carrier for planned rescues. 2. A false image in radar screen. 3. Women of the Army Nurse Corps and Red Cross in hospital service.

angle of convergence - (NATO, CENTO) The angle subtended by the eyebase of an observer at the point of focus. Also known as angular parallax; parallactic angle.

angle of depression - (DOD, NATO, CENTO) 1. The angle in a vertical plane between the horizontal and a descending line. 2. In air photography, the angle between the axis of an obliquely mounted air camera and the horizontal. See also tilt angle.

angle of safety - (DOD, NATO, SEATO, CENTO, IADB) The minimum permissible angular clearance at the gun, of the path of a projectile above the friendly troops. It is the angle of clearance corrected to insure the safety of the troops.

angle of view - (NATO, CENTO) 1. The angle between two rays passing through the perspective center (rear nodal point) of a camera lens to two opposite corners of the format. 2. In photogrammetry, twice the angle whose tangent is one half the length of the diagonal of the format divided by the calibrated focal length.

angle of view (photography) - (IADB) 1. When the format is square - the angle between two rays passing through the perspective center (rear nodal point) to two opposite sides of the format. 2. When the image format is rectangular - it is necessary to define the sides of the format to which the angle refers. 3. Photogrammetrically, it is twice the angle whose tangent is one-half the length of the diagonal of the format divided by the calibrated focal length.

angle T - (DOD) The angle formed at the target by the intersection of the gun-target line and the observer-target line.

Angry 109 - The AN-109 radio.

angular mil - Angular mil. Angular milliradian. A measurement used on artillery gunsights. A mil is an angular measure that is 1/6400 of a circle in NATO countries or 1/18 of a degree. See mil.

angular parallax - See angle of convergence.

animal - A series of claymore mines designed to explode as a unit.

Animals of the Army - Army Rangers.

ankle express - Slang for on foot.

Annam - The Chinese name for the area called Vietnam, the former French Indochina broadly defined as the Central Lowlands and Central Highlands between Tonkin and Cochin China.

annex - (DOD, IADB) A document appended to an operation order or other document to make it clearer or to give further details.

annotated print - (NATO, CENTO) A photograph on which interpretation details are indicated by words or symbols.

annotation - (DOD) A marking placed on imagery or drawings for explanatory purposes. Annotations are used to indicate items or areas of special importance.

annotation - (NATO, CENTO) A marking placed on imagery or drawings for explanatory purposes or to indicate items or areas of special importance.

antenna mine - In naval warfare, a mine with an antenna that creates a galvanic response when it contacts the metal of a ship and triggers the mine.

anti-G suit - (DOD, NATO, SEATO, CENTO, IADB) A device worn by aircrew to counteract the effects on the human body of positive acceleration.

anti-smash - Aviation term for any of the warning lights on a carrier, air field or in the cockpit to warn of a collision.

antiair warfare - (DOD) A United States Navy/United States Marine Corps term to indicate that action required to destroy or reduce to an acceptable level the enemy air and missile threat. It includes such measures as the use of interceptors, bombers, antiaircraft guns, surface-to-air and air-to-air missiles, electronic countermeasures, and destruction of the air or missile threat both before and after it is launched. Other measures which are taken to minimize the effects of hostile air action are: cover, concealment, dispersion, deception (including electronic), and mobility. See also counter air.

antiairborne minefield (land mine warfare) - (DOD, NATO, SEATO, CENTO, IADB) A minefield laid primarily for protection against airborne attack. See also minefield (land mine warfare).

antiaircraft guns - Weapons used to shoot down enemy aircraft from the ground. See AA.

antiaircraft operations center - (NATO, SEATO, CENTO, IADB) The tactical headquarters of an antiaircraft commander. The agency provided to collect and evaluate information, and disseminate intelligence for the antiaircraft defense, and through which operational control over subordinate units is exercised.

antiaircraft weapon - See Duster (antiaircraft weapon).

antiamphibious minefield (land mine warfare) - (DOD, NATO, SEATO, CENTO, IADB) A minefield laid primarily for protection against amphibious attack. See also mine-field (land mine warfare).

anticrop agent - (DOD, NATO, CENTO) A living organism or chemical used to cause disease or damage to selected food or industrial crops. See also antiplant agent; herbicide.

anticrop operations - (DOD, NATO, CENTO) The employment of anticrop agents in military operations to destroy the enemy's source of selected food or industrial crops.

antilift device (land mine warfare) - (DOD, NATO, SEATO, CENTO, IADB) A device arranged to detonate the mine to which it is attached, or to detonate another mine or charge nearby, if the mine is disturbed.

antimateriel agent - (DOD, NATO, CENTO) A living organism or chemical used to cause deterioration of or damage to selected materiel.

antimateriel operations - (DOD, NATO, CENTO) The employment of antimateriel weapons or agents in military operations.

antipersonnel mine (land mine warfare) - (DOD, NATO, SEATO, CENTO, IADB) A mine designed to cause casualties to personnel. See also mine; mine (land mine warfare).

antipersonnel minefield (land mine warfare) - (DOD, NATO, SEATO, CENTO, IADB) A minefield laid primarily for protection against infantry attack. See also minefield (land mine warfare).

antiplant agent - (DOD) A microorganism or chemical which will kill, disease or damage plants. See also anticrop agent; herbicide.

antiradiation missile - (DOD, NATO, CENTO) A missile which homes passively on a radiation source.

antisubmarine action - (DOD, IADB) An operation by one or more antisubmarine ships or aircraft, or a combination of the two, against a particular enemy submarine. It begins when contact has been gained by any ship or aircraft of the unit. Any number of antisubmarine attacks may be carried out as part of the action. The action ends when the submarine has been destroyed or when contact has been lost and cannot be regained.

antisubmarine action - (NATO, SEATO, CENTO) An operation by one or more antisubmarine ships or aircraft, or a combination of both, against a particular enemy submarine.

antisubmarine air area operations - (DOD) Carrier-based and shore-based aircraft operated singly and in coordination with other aircraft, ships, or both, to conduct offensive operations. While the purpose of such operations differs fundamentally from that of operations in distant support, the search localization and attack tactics are similar to those in the conduct of antisubmarine air distant support.

antisubmarine air close support - (DOD) Air operations for the antisubmarine warfare protection of a supported force. These operations are normally carried out within 80 nautical miles of the force, but this limit may be varied at the discretion of the controlling officer in tactical command.

antisubmarine air distant support - (DOD, NATO, SEATO, CENTO, IADB) Antisubmarine air support at a distance from, but directly related to, specific convoys or forces.

antisubmarine air escort and close support - (NATO, SEATO, CENTO, IADB) The provision of air protection to a particular convoy or force threatened by imminent submarine attack. Aircraft provide increased defense in depth and are under the tactical control of the officer in tactical command.

antisubmarine air offensive operations - (NATO, SEATO, CENTO, IADB) Carrier-based and shore-based aircraft operated singly and in coordination with other aircraft, ships, or both, to conduct offensive operations. While the purpose of such operations differs fundamentally from that of operations in distant support, the search localization and attack tactics are similar to those in the conduct of antisubmarine air distant support.

antisubmarine air search attack unit - (DOD) The designation given to one or more aircraft separately organized as a tactical unit to search for and destroy submarines.

antisubmarine barrier - (DOD, NATO, CENTO, IADB) The line formed by a series of static devices or mobile units arranged for the purpose of detecting, denying passage to, or destroying hostile submarines.

antisubmarine carrier group - (NATO, SEATO, CENTO) A formed group of ships consisting of one or more antisubmarine carriers and a number of escort vessels whose primary mission is to detect and destroy submarines. Such groups may be employed in convoy support or hunter-killer roles.

antisubmarine operation - (DOD, IADB) Operation contributing to the conduct of antisubmarine warfare.

antisubmarine patrol - (DOD, NATO, CENTO, IADB) The systematic and continuing investigation of an area or along a line to detect or hamper submarines, used when the direction of submarine movement can be established.

antisubmarine rocket - (DOD) A surface ship-launched, rocket-propelled, nuclear depth charge or homing torpedo. Designated as RUR-5. Popular name is Asroc.

antisubmarine screen - (DOD, NATO, CENTO, IADB) An arrangement of ships and/or aircraft for the protection of a screened unit against attack by a submarine.

antisubmarine search - (DOD, NATO, CENTO, IADB) Systematic investigation of a particular area for the purpose of locating a submarine known or suspected to be somewhere in the area. Some types of search are also used in locating the position of a distress incident.

antisubmarine support aircraft carrier - (DOD, IADB) A ship primarily designed to support and operate aircraft and for sustained antisubmarine warfare and escort convoys. It also may be used to provide close air support. (DOD) Designated as CVS. These are former CVAs which have been redesignated.

antisubmarine support operations - (DOD, NATO, CENTO, IADB) Operations conducted by an antisubmarine force in the area around a force or convoy, in areas through which the force or convoy is passing, or in defense of geographic areas. Support operations may be completely coordinated with those of the force or convoy, or they may be independent operations coordinated only to the extent of providing operational intelligence and information.

antisubmarine torpedo - (DOD, IADB) A submarine-launched, long-range, high-speed, wire-guided, deep-diving, wakeless torpedo capable of carrying a nuclear warhead for use in antisubmarine and antisurface ship operations. Also known as Astor.

antisubmarine warfare - (DOD, NATO, SEATO, CENTO, IADB) Operations conducted with the intention of denying the enemy the effective use of his submarines.

antisubmarine warfare forces - (DOD, IADB) Forces organized primarily for antisubmarine action. May be comprised of surface ships, aircraft, submarines, or any combination of these, and their supporting systems.

antitank mine (land mine warfare) - (DOD, NATO, SEATO, CENTO, IADB) A mine designed to immobilize or destroy a tank. See also mine; mine (land mine warfare).

antivigneting filter - (NATO, CENTO) A filter bearing a deposit which is graduated in density to correct for the uneven illumination given by certain lenses, particularly wideangle types.

Antonov - Soviet aircraft builder.

anvil and hammer - An infantry tactic in which an infantry unit (hammer) drives the enemy toward the coast which functions as the anvil. See hammer and anvil.

AO - 1. Area of operations. 2. Aerial Observer.

ao baba - The black pajama attire of the Vietnamese peasants.

ao dai - The traditional long dress-like Vietnamese attire with side slits from hem to waist and worn over loose fitting trousers. The hem was at ankle length for women and knee high when worn by men ceremonially.

AOA - Angle of Attack, the wind to airfoil relationship.

AOBC - Armored Officers Basic Course.

AOC - Air operations center.

AOD - Administrative Officer on Duty.

AP - 1. Air Police (Air Force MPs). 2. Armor piercing. 3. Ambush Patrol. 4. Antipersonnel.

APA - See attack transport.

APC - 1. Armored Personnel Carrier. 2. See Army Aspirin.

APD - Airborne Personnel Detector.

APE - Air Force Military Police.

aperture - (NATO, CENTO) The opening in a lens diaphragm through which light passes.

APH-5 - The helmet worn by helicopter pilots.

APL - A barracks ship.

APO - Army Post Office, located in San Francisco. The mailing address for soldiers in Vietnam.

apogee - (DOD, NATO, CENTO, IADB) The point at which a missile trajectory or a satellite orbit is farthest from the center of the gravitational field of the controlling body or bodies.

apparent horizon - (DOD, NATO, CENTO, IADB) The visible line of demarcation between land/sea and sky.

appendix - (DOD, IADB) A subsidiary addition to a main paper. Details essential to the main paper but too bulky or numerous to include therein are usually embodied in appendixes.

applesauce enema - Slang for a mild reprimand or criticism.

applicable materiel assets - (DOD) That portion of the total acceptable materiel assets which meets the military or other characteristics as defined by the responsible military service and which is in the right condition and location to satisfy a specific military requirement.

application - (DOD, IADB) The system or problem to which a computer is applied. Reference is often made to an application as being either of the computational type, wherein arithmetic computations predominate, or of the data processing type, wherein data handling operations predominate.

applied research - (DOD, IADB) Research concerned with the practical application of knowledge, material, and/or techniques directed toward a solution to an existent anticipated military requirement. See also basic research; research.

apportionment - (DOD) A commander's decision on division of the total tactical air capability among air strike tasks to be performed for a specified period.

appreciation of the situation - See estimate of the situation.

appreciations - The facts, estimates and assumptions about the enemy's intentions and ability which are used in military planning and decision making.

approach clearance - (DOD) Authorization for a pilot conducting flight in accordance with instrument flight rules to commence an approach to an airport.

approach end - The end of a runway nearest to the direction from which the final approach is made.

approach lanes - (DOD, NATO, CENTO, IADB) Extensions of the boat lanes from the line of departure toward the transport area. They may be terminated by marker ships, boats, or buoys.

approach schedule - (DOD, NATO, CENTO, IADB) The schedule which indicates for each scheduled wave the time of departure from the rendezvous area, from the line of departure, and from other control points, and the time of arrival at the beach.

approach sequence - (NATO, SEATO, CENTO, IADB) The order in which aircraft are to approach a given point.

approach time - (DOD, IADB) The time at which an aircraft is expected to commence approach procedure.

approach time - (NATO, SEATO, CENTO) The time at which an aircraft commences its final approach preparatory to landing.

apricot ears - The illegal practice of taking trophy ears from the dead enemy. When dried they resemble dried apricots.

apron (airfield) - (NATO, CENTO, IADB) A paved, surfaced, or prepared area where aircraft stand for purposes of loading or unloading passengers or cargo, refueling, parking, or servicing.

APU - Auxiliary Power Unit.

AR - Army Regulations.

ARA - 1. Aerial Rocket Artillery, for example, the helicopter had 4 XM-159C, 19 rocket pods for 2.75 inch rockets. 2. Australian Regular Army.

Arabic method - The interrogation method by which the subject is stripped, blindfolded and tied to a straight-backed chair before questioning.

ARC - American Red Cross.

arc light - 1. The light caused by the ordinance of a B-52 bomber strike. 2. Reference to the sound and earth shaking generated from a bombing.

arc light missions - Slang for the B-52 bombing missions, usually dropping thirty tons of bombs at night. Guidance in targeting was from the ground-controlled radar.

arcing around – Slang for aimless but rapid activity.

area - See advisory area (air traffic); aircraft dispersal area; aircraft marshalling area; air defense action area; alighting area; amphibious vehicle launching area; area control center; assembly area; closed area; concentration area; control area; danger area; defensive coastal area; embarkation area; fire support area; homogeneous area; impact area; initial approach area; key area; landing area; maneuvering area; maritime area; naval support area; objective area; prohibited area; runup area; signal area; staging area; submarine patrol areas; summary areas; terminal control area; transit area. See also zone.

area air defense commander - (DOD) Within an overseas unified command, subordinate unified command, or joint task force, the commander will assign overall responsibility for air defense to a single commander. Normally, this will be the Air Force component commander. Representation from the other Service components involved will be provided, as appropriate, to the area air defense commander's headquarters.

area bombing - (DOD, NATO, SEATO, CENTO, IADB) Bombing of a target which is in effect a general area rather than a small or pinpoint target.

area command - (DOD, NATO, SEATO, CENTO, IADB) A command which is composed of those organized elements of one or more of the armed Services, designated to operate in a specific geographical area, which are placed under a single commander, e.g., commander of a unified command, area commander. See also command.

area control center - (DOD, NATO, CENTO) A unit established to provide air traffic control service to controlled flights in control areas under its jurisdiction. See also air traffic control center; flight information region.

area control center - (IADB) A unit established to provide air traffic control service to Instrument Flight Rules flights. See also flight information region.

area coordination group - (DOD) A composite organization to include representatives of local military, paramilitary and other governmental agencies and their United States counterparts responsible for planning and coordinating internal defense and development operations.

area damage control - (DOD, NATO, CENTO, IADB) Measures taken before, during, or after hostile action or natural or man-made disasters, to reduce the probability of damage and minimize its effects. See also damage control; disaster control; rear area security.

area evacuation - (NATO, CENTO, IADB) The movement of merchant ships, under naval control, from a threatened general area to safer localities. See also movement of shipping (in the early days of war).

area of burst - The immediate impact area after an explosion.

area of influence - (NATO, CENTO, IADB) The portion of the assigned zone and the area of operations wherein a commander is directly capable of influencing the progress or outcome of operations by maneuvers of his ground-gaining elements or by delivery of firepower with the fire support systems normally under his control or command. It is a geographical area the size of which depends upon the mission, organization, and equipment of the force involved.

area of interest - (DOD, NATO, CENTO, IADB) That area of concern to the commander, including the area of influence, areas adjacent thereto, and extending into enemy territory to the objectives of current or planned operations. This area also includes areas occupied by enemy forces who could jeopardize the accomplishment of the mission.

area of militarily significant fallout - (DOD, NATO, CENTO, IADB) The area in which radioactive fallout affects the ability of military units to carry out their normal mission.

area of northern operations - (DOD) A region of variable width in the Northern Hemisphere that lies north of the 50 degrees isotherm - a line along which the average temperature of the warmest four month period of the year does not exceed 50 degrees Fahrenheit. Mountain regions located outside of this area are included in this category of operations provided these same temperature conditions exist.

area of operations - (DOD) That portion of an area of conflict necessary for military operations, either offensive or defensive, pursuant to an assigned mission, and for the administration incident to such military operations.

area of operations - (NATO, CENTO, IADB) That portion of an area of war necessary for military operations, either offensive or defensive, pursuant to an assigned mission, and for the administration incident to such military operations.

area of responsibility - (DOD, NATO, SEATO, CENTO, IADB) 1. A defined area of land in which responsibility is specifically assigned to the commander of the area for the development and maintenance of installations, control of movement and the conduct of tactical operations involving troops under his control along with parallel authority to exercise these functions. 2. In naval usage, a predefined area of enemy terrain for which supporting ships are responsible for covering by fire on known targets or targets of opportunity and by observation.

area of war - (DOD, IADB) That area of land, sea, and air which is, or may become, involved directly in the operations of war.

area radar prediction analysis - (DOD) Radar target intelligence study designed to provide radar significant data for use in the preparation of radar target predictions.

area search - (DOD) Visual reconnaissance of limited or defined areas.

area target - (DOD, NATO, SEATO, CENTO, IADB) A target consisting of an area rather than a single point.

area warfare - General warfare without a specific front battle line.

areodesy - (DOD) That branch of mathematics which determines by observation and measurement, the exact positions of points and the figures and areas of large portions of the surface of the planet Mars, or the shape and size of the planet Mars.

areodetic - (DOD) Of, or pertaining to, or determined by areodesy.

Arizona Territory - Slang for the area south of Da Nang known for ambush.

ARM - Anti-radiation Missile, an air to ground guided missile with radar equipment which when hitting the ground gave off a signal to guide pilots to targets.

armed forces - (DOD, NATO, CENTO, IADB) The military forces of a nation or a group of nations. See also force(s).

armed forces - (SEATO) All the naval, ground, and air forces of a nation or group of nations. See also force(s).

armed forces censorship - (DOD) The examination and control of personal communications to or from persons in the Armed Forces of the United States and persons accompanying or serving with the Armed Forces of the United States. See also censorship.

armed forces censorship - (IADB) The examination and control of personal communications to or from persons in the Armed Forces. See also censorship.

armed forces courier - (DOD) An officer or enlisted member in the grade of E-7 and above, of the United States Armed Forces, assigned to perform Armed Forces Courier Service duties and identified by having in his possession an Armed Forces Courier Service Identification Card (ARFCOS Form 9). See also courier.

Armed Forces Courier Service - (DOD) A joint service of the Departments of the Army, the Navy, and the Air Force, with the Chief of Staff, United States Army, as Executive Agent. The courier service provides one of the available methods for the secure and expeditious transmission of material requiring protected handling by military courier.

armed forces courier station - (DOD) An Army, Navy, or Air Force activity, approved by the respective military department and officially designated by Headquarters, Armed Forces Courier Service, for the acceptance, processing and dispatching of Armed Forces Courier Service material.

Armed Forces Expeditionary Medal - The Armed Forces Expeditionary Medal is the award by the U.S. for service in the United States military when there is no other medal available. The Vietnam Service Medal replaced it. See Expeditionary Medal.

Armed Forces of the United States - (DOD) A term used to denote collectively all components of the Army, Navy, Air Force, Marine Corps, and Coast Guard. See also United States Armed Forces.

Armed Forces Radio - The English Language radio station in Vietnam until 1973 when it was replaced by American Services Radio.

Armed Forces Staff College - The staff college that trained officers from all service branches in joint operations and procedures, located in Norfolk, Virginia.

armed mine - (DOD, NATO, SEATO, CENTO, IADB) A mine ready for actuation. See also mine.

armed reconnaissance - (DOD) A mission with the primary purpose of locating and attacking targets of opportunity, i.e., enemy materiel, personnel, and facilities, in assigned general areas or along assigned ground communications routes, and not for the purpose of attacking specific briefed targets.

armed reconnaissance - (NATO, CENTO, IADB) An air mission flown with the primary purpose of locating and attacking targets of opportunity, i.e., enemy materiel, personnel, and facilities, in assigned general areas or along assigned ground communications routes, and not for the purpose of attacking specific briefed targets.

arming - (DOD) As applied to weapons and ammunition, the changing from a safe condition to a state of readiness for initiation.

arming - (NATO, SEATO, CENTO, IADB) As applied to explosives, the changing from a safe condition to a state of readiness for initiation.

arming system - (DOD) That portion of a weapon which serves to ready (arm), safe, or re-safe (disarm) the firing system and fuzing system and which may actuate devices in the nuclear system.

armor - Slang for: 1. Tanks and armored personnel carriers. 2. Body armor as the flack jackets.

Armored Cavalry - The Army forces equipped with tanks and armored personnel carriers.

armored personnel carrier - A light armored, highly mobile, full tracked vehicle that is amphibious and air droppable. Equipped with a .50-caliber machine gun, used by Army named Green Dragons by Vietnamese for color and ability to spew fire. See amtrack and APC.

armored reconnaissance airborne assault vehicle - (DOD, IADB) A lightly-armored, mobile, full-tracked vehicle serving as the main reconnaissance vehicle in infantry and airborne operations and as the principal assault weapon of airborne troops.

armpit sauce - Slang for the Vietnamese fermented fish sauce (nuoc mam).

arms control - (DOD, IADB) A concept which connotes: a. any plan, arrangement, or process, resting upon explicit or implicit international agreement, governing any aspect of the following: the numbers, types, and performance characteristics of weapon systems (including the command and control, logistics support arrangements, and any related intelligence-gathering mechanisms); and the numerical strength, organization, equipment, deployment or employment of the armed forces retained by the parties. (It encompasses "disarmament".) and b. on some occasions, those measures taken for the purpose of reducing instability in the military environment.

arms control agreement - (DOD, IADB) The written or unwritten embodiment of the acceptance of one or more arms control measures by two or more nations.

arms control agreement verification - (DOD) A concept that entails the collection, processing, and reporting of data indicating testing or employment of proscribed weapons systems, including country of origin and location, weapon and payload identification, and event type.

arms control measure - (DOD, IADB) Any specific arms control course of action.

armstrong - (DOD) The term, peculiar to the Air Support Radar Team, indicating both the command and response for arming and fuzing circuit activation.

Army Air Defense Command Post - (DOD) The tactical headquarters of an Army air defense commander.

Army air ground system - (DOD) The Army system which provides for interface between Army and tactical air support agencies of other Services in the planning, evaluating, processing, and coordinating of air support requirements and operations. It is composed of appropriate staff members, including G-2 air and G-3 air personnel, and necessary communications equipment.

Army Aspirin - Standard military Aspirin compound containing Aspirin, Phenacetin and caffeine. See APC, all purpose capsule.

Army banjo - The entrenching tool.

Army base - (DOD, SEATO) A base or group of installations for which a local commander is responsible, consisting of facilities necessary for support of Army activities including security, internal lines of communications, utilities, plants and systems, and real property for which the Army has operating responsibility. See also base complex.

Army brat - The son or daughter from career Army family. See brat.

Army call signs - Radio communications call signs designated the function of the speaker. Examples: 2 was the intelligence officer, 3 was the operations officer, 4 was the command NCO or Sergeant, 5 was the executive officer or second in command, 6 was the unit commander. Added alpha-numeric designations were made for units and operations, and frequently changed.

Army corps - (DOD, IADB) A tactical unit larger than a division and smaller than a field army. A corps usually consists of two or more divisions together with auxiliary arms and services.

Army corps - (NATO, SEATO, CENTO) An organization larger than a division and smaller than a field army; usually consists of two or more divisions together with supporting arms and services.

Army forces - (NATO, CENTO) The armies of a nation.

Army forces - (SEATO, IADB) A term used to describe the armies of a nation. See also force(s).

Army green - The uniform approved for all ranks in Vietnam.

Army group - (DOD, NATO, CENTO) Several field armies under a designated commander.

Army group - (IADB) Several field armies under a designated commander. Primarily a tactical command.

Army group - (SEATO) Several field armies under a designated commander. Primarily a tactical command, but may be given logistic responsibilities.

Army service area - (DOD, NATO, SEATO, CENTO, IADB) The territory between the corps rear boundary and the combat zone rear boundary. Most of the Army administrative establishment and service troops are usually located in this area. See also rear area.

Army tan - The tropical worsted uniform.

ARPA - Advanced Research Projects Agency. A research and development agency of the Department of Defense.

arresting barrier - See aircraft arresting barrier.

arresting gear - See aircraft arresting gear.

Article 118 - The section of the Uniform Code of Military Justice that addresses the murder of a civilian.

Article 15 - The section of the Uniform Code of Military Justice that allows punishment imposed at the company level by a commander, less than a court martial. Usually having as a penalty a loss of pay or privileges.

artie/arty - See artillery.

artificial daylight - (NATO, CENTO, IADB) Illumination of an intensity greater than the light of a full moon on a clear night. (The optimum illumination is the equivalent of daylight.) See also battlefield illumination.

artificial horizon - (NATO, CENTO) A device that indicates attitude with respect to the true horizon. A substitute for a natural horizon, determined by a liquid level, bubble pendulum, or gyroscope.

artificial moonlight - (NATO, CENTO, IADB) Illumination of an intensity between that of starlight and that of a full moon on a clear night. See also battlefield illumination.

artillery - (DOD) Complete projectile-firing weapons consisting of cannon or missile launchers on suitable carriages or mounts. Field artillery cannons are classified according to caliber as: light - 120-mm and less; medium - 121-160-mm; heavy - 161-210-mm; very heavy - greater than 210-mm.

artillery - (SEATO, IADB) Complete projectile-firing weapons, consisting of cannon or missile launchers on suitable carriages or mounts.

artillery preparation - (DOD, NATO, SEATO, CENTO, IADB) Artillery fire delivered before an attack to disrupt communications and disorganize the enemy's defense.

Arvin - Nickname for ARVN soldier.

ARVIN - One of the three telephone systems in South Vietnam. Also PTT and tiger exchange.

ARVN - 1. The Army of the Republic of Vietnam (south). 2. A soldier in the Army of Republic of Vietnam.

ARVN attitude - Derogatory reference to cowardly behavior.

as loud - Slang for heroin smoked with tobacco.

as you were - Resume your prior activity.

ASAP - Abbreviation for as soon as possible. Pronounced either ASAP or A-sap.

ASEAN - Association of Southeast Asian Nations, included Philippines, Thailand, Singapore, Malaysia and Indonesia. Designed to foster growth and cooperation between member nations south.

ashtray - Slang for the scene of downed aircraft.

Asking for six and going airborne. - Going home. From the travel allowance of six cents a mile and flying home.

ASN - Army Serial Number. Replaced by Social Security Number in 1969.

aspect angle - (DOD) The angle between the longitudinal axis of the target (projected rearward) and the line-of-sight to the interceptor measured from the tail of the target.

aspect change - (NATO, CENTO) The different appearance of a reflecting object viewed by radar from varying directions. It is caused by the change in the effective reflecting area of the target.

ASR - See acute situation response.

Asroc - See antisubmarine rocket.

ass and trash mission - Slang for troop and cargo transport by aircraft. Also called ash and trash.

ass in the grass test - An audit of the number of troops in the field.

ass kicker - 1. Anything particularly difficult, a big problem, bad news. 2. An overly demanding superior.

assault - (DOD) 1. The climax of an attack; closing with the enemy in hand-to-hand fighting. 2. In an amphibious operation, the period of time between the arrival of the major assault forces of the amphibious task force in the objective area and the accomplishment of the amphibious task force mission. 3. To make a short, violent, but well-ordered attack against a local objective, such as a gun emplacement, a fort, or a machine gun nest. 4. A phase of an airborne operation beginning with delivery by air of the assault echelon of the force into the objective area and extending through attack of assault objectives and consolidation of the initial airhead. See also landing attack.

assault - (NATO, CENTO, IADB) 1. The climax of an attack; closing with the enemy in hand-to-hand fighting. 2. In an amphibious operation, the period of time from the crossing of the line of departure by the first scheduled wave, to the seizure of the initial objectives. 3. To make a short, violent, but well-ordered attack against a local objective, such as a gun emplacement, a fort, or a machine gun nest. 4. A phase of an airborne operation beginning with delivery by air of the assault echelon of the force into the objective area and extending through attack of assault objectives and consolidation of the initial airhead. See also landing attack.

assault - (SEATO) 1. The climax of an attack; closing with the enemy in hand-to-hand fighting. 2. In an amphibious operation, the landing of troops for attack on the enemy's beach defenses. 3. To make a short, violent, but well-ordered attack against a local objective, such as a gun emplacement, a fort, or a machine gun nest.

assault aircraft - (DOD, NATO, SEATO, CENTO, IADB) Powered aircraft, including helicopters, which move assault troops and cargo into an objective area and which provide for their resupply.

assault area diagram - (DOD, IADB) A graphic means of showing for amphibious operations the beach designations, boat lanes, organization of the line of departure, scheduled waves, landing ship area, transport areas, and the fire support areas in the immediate vicinity of the boat lanes.

assault craft - (DOD, IADB) A landing craft or amphibious vehicle employed for landing troops and equipment in the assault waves of an amphibious operation.

assault echelon (air transport) - (DOD, NATO, SEATO, CENTO, IADB) The element of a force which is scheduled for initial assault on the objective area.

assault schedule - See landing schedule.

assault shipping - (DOD, NATO, CENTO, IADB) Shipping assigned to the amphibious task force and utilized for transporting assault troops, vehicles, equipment, and supplies to the objective area.

assault waves - See wave.

assembly anchorage - (NATO, CENTO, IADB) An anchorage intended primarily for the assembly and onward routing of oceangoing shipping. See also emergency anchorages.

assembly area - (DOD, NATO, CENTO, IADB) 1. An area in which a command is assembled preparatory to further action. 2. In a supply installation, the gross area used for collection and combining components into complete units, kits, or assemblies.

assessment - (DOD) 1. Analysis of the security, effectiveness, and potential of an existing or planned intelligence activity. 2. Judgment of the motives, qualifications, and characteristics of present or prospective employees or "agents".

asset (intelligence) - (DOD) Any resource -person, group, relationship, instrument, installation, or supply- at the disposition of an intelligence organization for use in an operational or support role. Often used with a qualifying term such as agent asset, propaganda asset.

asshole of the world - Slang for Vietnam.

assholes and elbows - In a hurry.

assholes to bellybuttons - Close marching or standing in line.

assign - (DOD, NATO, SEATO, CENTO, IADB) 1. The placement of units or personnel in an organization where such placement is relatively permanent and/or where such organization controls and administers the units or personnel for the primary function, or greater portion of the functions of the unit or personnel. 2. The detailing of individuals to specific duties or functions where such duties or functions are primary and/or relatively permanent. See also attach.

assigned forces - (NATO, SEATO, CENTO, IADB) Forces in being which have been placed under the operational command or operational control of a commander. See also force(s).

assignment (nuclear) - (DOD) A specified number of complete nuclear rounds authorized for expenditure by a commander. An assignment may be made for a specific period of time, for a phase of an operation, or to accomplish a particular mission.

assumed azimuth - (DOD) The assumption of azimuth origins as a field expedient until the required data is available.

assumed grid - (DOD) A grid constructed using an arbitrary scale superimposed on a map, chart, or photograph for use in point designation without regard to actual geographic location. See also grid.

assumption - (DOD, IADB) A supposition on the current situation, or a presupposition on the future course of events, either or both assumed to be true in the absence of positive proof, necessary to enable the commander, in the process of planning, to complete his estimate of the situation and make a decision on his course of action.

Astor - See antisubmarine torpedo.

at my command - (DOD) The command used when it is desired to control the exact time of delivery of fire.

ATC - 1. Air Traffic Control. 2. Armored Troop Carrier.

Atlas - (DOD) A liquid-propellant, one-and-a half stage, rocket-powered intercontinental ballistic missile, equipped with a nuclear warhead; designated as CGM-16. The CGM-16D is equipped with radio-inertial guidance and dispersed by complexes. The CGM-16E and HGM-16F are equipped with all-inertial guidance and deployed in a hardened and dispersed configuration.

Atlas Heavy Lift Helicopter - CH-35 or H-35.

atmosphere - (DOD, NATO, CENTO) The air surrounding the earth. See also ionosphere; stratosphere; tropopause; troposphere.

atmospheric environment - (DOD) The envelope of air surrounding the earth, including its interfaces and interactions with the earth's solid or liquid surface.

Atoll missile - The Soviet made air to air missile used by North Vietnamese troops.

atomic air burst - See airburst.

atomic defense - See nuclear defense.

atomic demolition munition - (DOD) A nuclear device designed to be detonated on or below the ground surface, or under water as a demolition munition against material-type targets to block, deny and/or canalize the enemy.

atomic demolition munition - (NATO, CENTO, IADB) A nuclear device designed or adapted for use as a demolition munition.

atomic energy - (IADB) All forms of energy released in the course of nuclear fission or nuclear transformation. See nuclear energy.

atomic underground burst - See nuclear underground burst.

atomic underwater burst - See nuclear underwater burst.

atomic warfare - See nuclear warfare.

atomic weapon - See nuclear weapon.

attach - (DOD, NATO, SEATO, CENTO, IADB) 1. The placement of units or personnel in an organization where such placement is relatively temporary. Subject to limitations imposed by the attachment order, the commander of the formation, unit, or organization receiving the attachment will exercise the same degree of command and control thereover as he does over units and persons organic to his command. However, the responsibility for transfer and promotion of personnel will normally be retained by the parent formation, unit, or organization. 2. The detailing of individuals to specific functions where such functions are secondary or relatively temporary, i.e., attach for quarters and rations; attach for flying duty. See also assign.

attached airlift service - (DOD) The airlift service provided to an organization or command by an airlift unit attached to that organization.

attack aircraft carrier - (DOD, IADB) A warship designed to support and operate aircraft, engage in attacks on targets afloat or ashore, and engage in sustained operations in support of other forces. (DOD) Designated as CVA and CVAN. CVAN is nuclear powered.

attack altitude - (DOD) The altitude at which the interceptor will maneuver during the attack phase of an air intercept.

attack cargo ship - (DOD, IADB) A naval ship designed or converted to transport combat-loaded cargo in an assault landing. Capabilities as to carrying landing craft, speed of ship, armament, size of hatches and booms are greater than those of comparable cargo ship types. Designated as AKA.

attack carrier striking forces - (DOD, IADB) Naval forces, the primary offensive weapon of which is carrier-based aircraft. Ships, other than carriers, act primarily to support and screen against submarine and air threat, and secondarily against surface threat.

attack condition alpha - (DOD) Considers there is adequate warning of attack and the command and control facility supporting a decision authority becomes ineffective prior to the performance of essential functions.

attack condition bravo - (DOD) Considers there is inadequate warning of attack and the command post or headquarters of a decision authority becomes ineffective prior to the performance of essential functions.

attack group - (DOD, NATO, CENTO, IADB) A subordinate task organization of the Navy forces of an amphibious task force. It is composed of assault shipping and supporting naval units designated to transport, protect, land, and initially support a landing group.

attack heading - (DOD) 1. The interceptor heading during the attack phase which will achieve the desired track-crossing angle. 2. The assigned magnetic compass heading to be flown by aircraft during the delivery phase of an air strike.

attack origin - (DOD) 1. The location or source from which an attack was initiated. 2. The nation initiating an attack.

attack pattern - See target pattern.

attack position - (DOD, IADB) The last position occupied by the assault echelon before crossing the line of departure. See also forming up place.

attack speed - (DOD) The speed at which the interceptor will maneuver during the attack phase of an air intercept.

attack transport - (DOD, IADB) A naval ship designed for combat loading a battalion landing team with its equipment and supplies, and having the facilities, including landing craft, for landing them on a hostile beach. Designated as APA.

attacking - (DOD) In air intercept, a term meaning am commencing attacking run with weapon indicated (size may be given).

attenuation - (DOD, NATO, CENTO) Decrease in intensity of a signal, beam, or wave as a result of absorption of energy and of scattering out of the path of a detector, but not including the reduction due to geometric spreading, i.e., the inverse square of distance effect.

attenuation factor - (DOD, NATO, CENTO) The ratio of the incident radiation dose or dose rate to the radiation dose or dose rate transmitted through a shielding material. This is the reciprocal of the transmission factor.

attitude - (DOD, NATO, CENTO, IADB) 1. The position of a body as determined by the inclination of the axes to some frame of reference. If not otherwise specified, this frame of reference is fixed to the earth. (DOD) 2. Grid bearing relative to the long axis of the target.

attrition - (DOD, NATO, CENTO, IADB) The reduction of the effectiveness of a force caused by loss of personnel and materiel.

attrition - (SEATO) A loss in personnel or material suffered by a force, whereby its effectiveness is worn down or drained away.

attrition rate - (DOD, NATO, SEATO, CENTO, IADB) A factor, normally expressed as percentage, reflecting the degree of losses of personnel or materiel due to various causes within a specified period of time.

attrition reserve aircraft - (DOD) Aircraft procured for the specific purpose of replacing the anticipated losses of aircraft due to peacetime and/or wartime attrition.

auger in - Slang for crashing an aircraft, particularly jets, straight into the earth.

Aussie - Slang for Australian troops.

authentic document - (NATO, CENTO, IADB) A document bearing a signature or seal attesting that it is genuine and official. If it is an enemy document it may have been prepared for purposes of deception and the accuracy of such document, even though authenticated, must be confirmed by other information, e.g., conditions of capture.

authenticate - (DOD) A challenge given by voice or electrical means to attest to the authenticity of a message or transmission.

authentication - (DOD, IADB) 1. A security measure designed to protect a communications system against acceptance of a fraudulent transmission or simulation by establishing the validity of a transmission, message, or originator. 2. A means of identifying individuals and verifying their eligibility to receive specific categories of information. 3. Evidence by proper signature or seal that a document is genuine and official.

authentication - (NATO, SEATO, CENTO) 1. Evidence by proper signature or seal that a document is genuine and official. 2. A security measure designed to protect a communication system against fraudulent transmissions.

authenticator - (DOD) A symbol or group of symbols, or a series of bits, selected or derived in a prearranged manner and usually inserted at a predetermined point within a message or transmission for the purpose of attesting to the validity of the message or transmission.

authenticator - (NATO, SEATO, CENTO, IADB) A letter, numeral, or groups of letters or numerals, or both, attesting to the authenticity of a message or transmission.

auto-gettem - Firing on full automatic. Also auto-get-'em.

automated intelligence file - (DOD) A combination of manual and automatic data processing systems designed to store, retrieve, and display large volumes of intelligence data. Its data base is composed of individual records of specific installations.

automatic approach and landing - (DOD, NATO, CENTO, IADB) A control mode in which the aircraft's speed and flight path are automatically controlled for approach, flair-out, and landing.

automatic flight control system - (DOD, NATO, CENTO) A system which includes all equipment to automatically control the flight of an aircraft or missile to a path or attitude described by references internal or external to the aircraft or missile.

automatic pilot - A flight control system which provides attitude stabilization with respect to internal references.

automatic supply - (DOD, IADB) A system by which certain supply requirements are automatically shipped or issued for a predetermined period of time without requisition by the using unit. It is based upon estimated or experience-usage factors.

automatic throttle - A flight control system which provides throttle based on its own computation and feedback.

automatic voice network - (DOD) The Automatic Voice Network is the principal long-haul, unsecure voice communications network within the Defense Communications System. Also known as AUTOVON.

automation - (DOD, IADB) The technique of improving human productivity in the processing of materials, energy, and information, by utilizing in various degrees, elements of automatic control, and of automatically executed product programming.

autonomous operation - (DOD) In air defense, the mode of operation assumed by a unit after it has lost all communications with higher echelons. The unit commander assumes full responsibility for control of weapons and engagement of hostile targets.

autonomous operation - (NATO, CENTO) One mode of operation of a unit in which the unit commander assumes full responsibility for control of weapons and engagement of hostile targets. This mode may be either directed by higher authority or result from a loss of all means of communication.

autorotation - In helicopter flight, the term for a controlled landing when the power of the helicopter fails. The maneuver requires the rotors to be set to a minimum drag position while falling and shifted to a maximum drag position about a hundred feet before the ground to act as a type of parachute.

autovon - The telephone system connecting the U.S. military worldwide. Also spelled AUTOVON.

auxiliary contours - (NATO) Additional contours used to portray unique ground forms not adequately portrayed by the selected contour interval.

available payload - (DOD, IADB) The passenger and/or cargo capacity expressed in weight and/or space available to the user.

available supply rate (ammunition) - (DOD, NATO, SEATO, CENTO, IADB) The rate of consumption of ammunition that can be allocated, considering the supplies and facilities available, for a given period. For ammunition items fired from weapons, this rate is expressed in rounds per weapon per day. For other items, such as antitank mines, hand grenades, demolition explosives, etc., the rate is expressed in terms of units of measure for specified items, e.g., per day, per week (each unit of measure, kilos, pounds, or tons, metric, short, long, is to be specified).

average speed - (DOD, NATO, CENTO) The average distance traveled per hour, calculated over the whole journey, excluding specifically ordered halts.

average speed (transport vehicles) - (SEATO, IADB) The average number of miles traveled per hour, calculated over the whole journey, excluding specifically ordered halts.

aviation medicine - (DOD, NATO, SEATO, CENTO, IADB) The special field of medicine which is related to the biological and psychological problems of flight.

avionics - (DOD, IADB) The application of electronics to aviation and astronautics.

avn - Aviation.

AWAC - Airborne Warning and Control System. Radar and communications equipment installed in a transport aircraft to allow commanders to assess conditions for hundreds of miles. Often distinguished by large radar antenna on top. Used to guide aircraft to combat and assess enemy response.

AWL - Absent with leave.

AWLS - All weather landing system.

AWOL - Absent Without Leave.

AWOL bag - Any small carry-on luggage. Usually cheap and opened at the top like a doctor's bag.

axial mining (land mine warfare) - (DOD, NATO, SEATO, CENTO, IADB) Continuous or intermittent nuisance mining in great depth along the axes of enemy advance.

axial route - (DOD, NATO, CENTO) A route running through the rear area and into the forward area. See also route.

axis of advance - (DOD, NATO, SEATO, CENTO, IADB) A line of advance assigned for purposes of control; often a road or a group of roads, or a designated series of locations, extending in the direction of the enemy.

azimuth - (DOD) Quantities may be expressed in positive quantities increasing in a clockwise direction, or in X, Y coordinates where south and west are negative. They may be referenced to true north or magnetic north depending on the particular weapon system used. (a navigational bearing measured from the north).

azimuth angle - (NATO, CENTO) An angle measured clockwise in the horizontal plane between a reference direction and any other line.

azimuth resolution - (NATO, CENTO) The ability of the radar equipment to separate two reflectors at similar ranges but different bearings from a vehicle. Normally the minimum separation distance between the reflectors is quoted and expressed as the angle subtended by the reflectors at the vehicle.

VIETNAM: THE WAR ZONE DICTIONARY IN THEIR OWN WORDS

B – BRAVO

B - 1. Designated in the military phonetic alphabet, as "Bravo". 2. The aviation designation for bomber.

B and B, B&B - Booze and Broads. A parody of R&R.

B and S Ration - The daily beer or soda ration allowed, usually collected after duty in the field or at locations without a post or base exchange. Amounts varied but were usually in the range of two cans a day, some required one of each others allowed two of the same.

B-1 Unit (B-2, B-3) - The ancillary food pack (usually in a tin) that accompanies the main entree in a C-Rations meal, which usually contained biscuits and peanut butter, jam or cheese spread.

B-12 - The vitamin, often injected to cure a hangover.

B-26 - The World War II vintage bomber used by the South Vietnamese Air Force.

B-4 Bag - See Valpak.

B-40 - The Chinese rocket, shoulder fired model, refers either to projectile or to the launcher.

B-40 Magnet - The APC, thought to be an easy target.

B-47 - See Stratojet.

B-5 Front - A communist military command just south of the DMZ.

B-52 - See Stratofortress. Also, slang for a can opener, a piercer of the "church key" type.

B-57 - See Canberra.

B-58 - See Hustler.

B-66 - See Destroyer; Skywarrior.

B-Team - The support group for a Special Forces A-Team in the field.

B/N - Bombardier/Navigator.

BA - Base area.

Ba - Vietnamese for many things but became GI slang for "woman".

ba mui ba (33) - A Vietnamese brand of beer. Also spelled Ba Mu'o'i Ba and Ba Me Ba.

baby 007 - An agent of the Army's Criminal Investigation Division working undercover narcotics. From the fictional James Bond character.

baby hero - A brave person.

baby shit - Slang for mustard.

baby-san - Slang for: 1. Any youthful Vietnamese. 2. A new soldier, virgin.

bac bac - Slang for the order "to shoot", from the Vietnamese ban.

bac si - Vietnamese for medic or doctor.

bac si de - Homebrewed rice whiskey.

back - See guy in back.

back bird - The part of a resupply effort removing trash and unused equipment.

Back Porch - Code for the communication system linking U.S. soldiers in Vietnam and Thailand.

back tell - (DOD) The transfer of information from a higher to a lower echelon of command. See also track telling.

back time - Duty away from the combat area.

back-scratching - 1. Doing reciprocal favors. 2. Removing the enemy from a tank by small weapons fire.

back-up - (NATO) Sometimes used to indicate printing on the reverse of a sheet, e.g. to supplement marginal information.

background count - (DOD, NATO, CENTO, IADB) The evidence or effect on a detector of radiation, other than that which it is desired to detect, caused by any agency. In connection with health protection, the background count usually includes radiations produced by naturally occurring radioactivity and cosmic rays.

background radiation - (DOD, NATO, CENTO) Nuclear (or ionizing) radiations arising from within the body and from the surroundings to which individuals are always exposed.

backwards hat - Slang for the student pilots who had not yet soloed. Until a successful solo flight, those students in flight school had to wear their billed baseball caps backwards.

bad ass territory - Enemy territory.

Bad Conduct Discharge (BCD) - The discharge that is less than Honorable but better then Dishonorable, limiting or denying benefits.

bad news - The Patton tank.

bad paper - Slang for a less than honorable discharge.

bad scene - Negative event, awful enemy engagement, any dispute.

bad time - Time not counted against the enlistment period, such as that spent in the brig.

bad trip - Negative effect of an illegal drug usage.

badges - Uniform devices showing proficiency in some skill such as marksmanship.

Badlands - Enemy territory.

bag - Aviation term for: 1 A flight suit. 2. The acquisition of a target on radar of visually.

bag and tag - The removal of dead from a combat area, in which they were placed in body bags with identification tags.

bag drag - Get transferred, from dragging sea bag or duffle bag. Also drag bag.

bag it - Get some sleep

bagged - Drunk.

Bailey bridge - A bridge made of pre-fabricated steel panels.

balance - (DOD, IADB) A concept as applied to an arms control measure which connotes: a. adjustments of armed forces and armaments in such manner that one state does not obtain military advantage vis-a-vis other states agreeing to the measure; and b. internal adjustments by one state of its forces in such manner as to enable it to cope with all aspects of remaining threats to its security in post arms control agreement era.

balance station zero - See reference datum.

balanced collective forces - (NATO, SEATO, CENTO, IADB) The requirement for "balance" in any military force stems from the consideration that all elements of a force should be complementary to each other. A force should function as a combined arms team, and the term "balance" implies that the ratio of the various elements of this team is such that the force is best constituted to execute its assigned mission effectively and efficiently. Applied multinationally, the term "balanced collective force" may be defined as a force comprised of one or more Services furnished by more than one nation, the total strength and composition of which is such as best to fulfill the specific mission for which it is designed. See also force(s).

balanced stock(s) - (DOD, IADB) 1. That condition of supply when availability and requirements are in equilibrium for specific items. 2. An accumulation of supplies in quantities determined necessary to meet requirements for a fixed period.

bale cubic capacity - (DOD, NATO, CENTO, IADB) The space available for cargo measured in cubic feet to the inside of the cargo battens, on the frames, and to the underside of the beams. In a general cargo of mixed commodities, the bale cubic applies. The stowage of the mixed cargo comes in contact with the cargo battens and as a general rule does not extend to the skin of the ship.

balisage - (DOD, NATO, CENTO) The marking of a route by a system of dim beacon lights enabling vehicles to be driven at near day time speed, under blackout conditions.

ball - Slang for: 1. The number zero. 2. Testicle. 3. See meatball.

ball-bearing BAM - A male Marine assigned to an administrative function usually done by a female Marine.

ballgame - Slang for an operation, mission or enemy contact.

ballistic - 1. Unguided, as in missile. 2. Going crazy or angry.

ballistic missile - (DOD, NATO, SEATO, CENTO, IADB) Any missile which does not rely upon aerodynamic surfaces to produce lift and consequently follows a ballistic trajectory when thrust is terminated. See also aerodynamic missile; guided missile.

ballistic missile early warning system - (DOD, IADB) An electronic system for providing detection and early warning of attack by enemy's intercontinental ballistic missiles.

ballistic trajectory - (DOD, NATO, SEATO, CENTO, IADB) The trajectory traced after the propulsive force is terminated and the body is acted upon only by gravity and aerodynamic drag.

ballistic wind - (DOD, NATO, CENTO, IADB) That constant wind which would have the same effect upon the trajectory of a bomb or projectile as the wind encountered in flight.

ballistics - (DOD, IADB) The science or art that deals with the motion, behavior, appearance, or modification of missiles or other vehicles acted upon by propellants, wind, gravity, temperature, or any other modifying substance, condition, or force.

balloon barrage - See barrage, Part 2.

balloon reflector - In electronic warfare, the support of a reflector system by balloons to confuse the radio or radar of the enemy.

balls - Slang for: 1. The double zero. 2. Testicles. 3. Exclamation of disgust or anger.

BAM - Big Assed Marine or Broad Assed Marine. A female Marine.

bamboo litter - A stretcher improvised in the field of cut lengths of bamboo and shirts or ponchos to move the wounded.

bamboo mine - A piece of bamboo into which rocks or other projectiles and an explosive charge have been placed, similar to a pipe bomb.

bamboo telegraph - Word of mouth communications.

bamboo whip - A booby trap in which bamboo spikes on the end of a bent section of bamboo would release when tripped, whipping the spikes into whoever tripped it.

ban - Vietnamese for "shoot".

banana clip - Slang for curved ammo clip for an automatic weapon.

band pass - (DOD) The number of cycles per second expressing the difference between the limiting frequencies at which the desired fraction (usually half power) of the maximum output is obtained. Term applies to all types of amplifiers.

Band-Aid - Slang for a medic, from the adhesive bandage trademarked Band-Aid.

bandit - Aviation code for an enemy aircraft. Red bandit was MiG-17, White bandit was a MiG-19. Blue bandit was a MiG-21.

bandolier - The cotton sling made to hold ammunition across the chest or over the shoulder.

bang out - To eject from an aircraft.

Bang-clap - Slang for Bangkok, a R&R location with readily available sex.

Bangalore torpedoes - A torpedo used on land to penetrate a fire base fencing equipped with a delayed fuse, allowing it to explode inside the base. Named after those used in Bangalore.

bank shot - A ricochet shot with a delayed fuse shell.

BAR - 1. Air Force term for beyond visual range. 2. Browning automatic rifle.

BAR belt - An ammo belt.

bar scale - See graphic scale; scale.

BARCAP - Barrier Combat Air Patrol, this is an air cover mission usually to provide protection to naval craft, initiated from carrier based aircraft of bases near the sea such as Da Nang or Chu Lai.

bare ass - Slang for barracks.

bareback - Having sex without a condom. Also riding bareback.

barracks - Shared housing space.

barracks bag - A large cloth drawstring bag for indoor use as a laundry bag or containing miscellaneous barracks items. See ditty bag.

barracks cover - The garrison cap with an internal frame.

barrage - (DOD, IADB) 1. A prearranged barrier of fire, except that delivered by small arms, designed to protect friendly troops and installations by impeding enemy movements across defensive lines or areas. 2. A protective screen of balloons that are moored to the ground and kept at given heights to prevent or hinder operations by enemy aircraft. This meaning also called balloon barrage. 3. A type of electronic counter-measures intended for simultaneous jamming over a wide area of frequency spectrum. See also barrage jamming; electronic counter-measures; electronic jamming; fire.

barrage fire - (DOD, NATO, SEATO, CENTO, IADB) Fire which is designed to fill a volume of space or area rather than aimed specifically at a given target. See also fire.

barrage jamming - (DOD, NATO, CENTO) Simultaneous electronic jamming over a broad band of frequencies. See also jamming.

barrage jamming - (IADB) The simultaneous jamming of a number of adjacent channels or frequencies. See also jamming.

barrage rocket - (DOD, NATO, CENTO, IADB) A combined blast and fragmentation weapon designed for firing from ship to shore in amphibious attack.

barrel roll - 1. Aviation maneuver to climb, roll and level flight, to either trap an enemy who used a break (turning out of sights) or increase speed and gain a better angle of attack. 2. A class of air missions in northern Laos in support of the Royal Laotian forces against the forces of the Pathet Lao.

barrier - (DOD, NATO, SEATO, CENTO, IADB) A coordinated series of obstacles designed or employed to canalize, direct, restrict, delay, or stop the movement of an opposing force, and to impose additional losses in personnel, time, and equipment on the opposing force. See also aircraft arresting system.

barrier combat air patrol - (DOD) One or more divisions or elements of a fighter aircraft employed between a force and an objective area as a barrier across the probable direction of enemy attack. It is used as far from the force as control conditions permit, giving added protection against raids that use the most direct routes of approach. See also combat air patrol.

barrier forces - (DOD, IADB) Air, surface, and submarine units, and their supporting systems positioned across the likely courses of expected enemy transit for early detection and providing rapid warning, blocking, and destruction of the enemy.

barrier minefield (land mine warfare) - (DOD, NATO, SEATO, CENTO, IADB) A minefield laid to block enemy attack formations in selected areas, especially to the flanks, and to deflect his approach into selected battle areas. See also minefield (land mine warfare).

BAS - Battalion Aid Station

base - (DOD, NATO, SEATO, CENTO, IADB) 1. A locality from which operations are projected or supported. 2. An area or locality containing installations which provide logistic or other support. (DOD) 3. Home airfield, or home carrier. See also emergency fleet operating base; establishment; island bases.

base area - A general area of fortification or supplies.

base camp - 1. A brigade to division size headquarters. 2. The rear area.

base command - (DOD, NATO, SEATO, CENTO, IADB) An area containing a military base or a group of such bases organized under one commander. See also command.

base complex - See Air Force base; Army base; Marine base; naval base; naval or Marine (air) base. See also noncontiguous facility.

base defense - (DOD, IADB) The local military measures, both normal and emergency, required to nullify or reduce the effectiveness of enemy attacks on, or sabotage of, a base so as to insure that the maximum capacity of its facilities is available to our forces.

base development - (DOD, NATO, SEATO, CENTO, IADB) The improvement or expansion of the resources and facilities of an area or a location to support military operations.

base development plan - (DOD) A plan for the facilities, installations and bases required to support military operations.

base ejection shell - (NATO, CENTO, IADB) A type of shell which ejects its load from its base.

base fuze - (NATO, CENTO, IADB) Fuze located in the base of a projectile or bomb. See also fuze.

base line - (DOD, NATO, CENTO, IADB) 1. (surveying) A surveyed line established with more than usual care, to which surveys are referred for coordination and correlation. 2. (photogrammetry) The line between the principal points of two consecutive vertical air photographs. It is usually measured on one photograph after the principal point of the other has been transferred.

base map - (DOD, NATO) A map or chart showing certain fundamental information, used as a base on which additional data of specialized nature are compiled or overprinted. Also a map containing all information from which maps showing specialized information can be prepared. See also chart base; map.

base map symbol - (NATO) A symbol used on a base map chart as opposed toll.one used on an overprint to the base map or chart.

base of operations - (DOD, IADB) An area or facility from which a military force begins its offensive operations, to which it falls back in case of reverse, and in which supply facilities are organized.

base period - (DOD) That period of time for which factors were determined for use in current planning and programming.

base section - (DOD, IADB) An area within the communications zone in an area of operations organized to provide logistic support to forward areas.

base surge - (DOD, NATO, CENTO, IADB) A cloud which rolls out from the bottom of the column produced by a subsurface burst of a nuclear weapon. For underwater bursts the surge is, in effect, a cloud of liquid droplets which has the property of flowing almost as if it were a homogeneous fluid. For subsurface land bursts the surge is made up of small solid particles but still behaves like a fluid.

base symbol - See base map symbol.

base unit - (DOD, IADB) Unit or organization in a tactical operation around which a movement or maneuver is planned and performed; base element.

baseball - A baseball shaped grenade.

baseball team - Radio code for squad of 13 soldiers.

basement - The lower deck on an aircraft carrier where aircraft are housed.

basic - Slang for basic training, boot camp.

basic cover - (DOD) Coverage of any installation or area of a permanent nature with which later coverage can be compared to discover any changes that have taken place.

basic cover (photogrammetry) - (NATO, CENTO, IADB) Air coverage of any installation or area of a permanent nature with which later cover can be compared to discover any changes that have taken place.

basic encyclopedia - (DOD) A compilation of identified installations and physical areas of potential significance as objectives for attack.

basic intelligence - (DOD) General intelligence concerning the capabilities, vulnerabilities, and intentions of foreign nations; used as a base for a variety of intelligence products for the support of planning, policy making, and military operations. See also intelligence.

basic intelligence - (NATO, CENTO) General reference material for use in planning, concerning other countries, which pertains to capabilities, resources or potential theaters of operations. See also intelligence.

basic intelligence - (SEATO, IADB) General reference material for use in planning, concerning enemies or potential enemies, which pertains to capabilities, resources, or potential theaters of operations. See also intelligence.

basic load (ammunition) - (DOD) That quantity of nonnuclear ammunition which is authorized and required by each Service to be on hand within a unit or formation at all times. It is expressed in rounds, units, or units of weight as appropriate.

basic load (ammunition) - (NATO, CENTO) That quantity of nonnuclear ammunition which is authorized and required by each nation to be on hand within a unit or formation at all times. It is expressed in rounds, units, or units of weight as appropriate.

basic load (ammunition) - (SEATO, IADB) That quantity of ammunition which is authorized and required by each nation to be on hand within a unit of formation at all times. It is expressed in terms of rounds for ammunition items fired by weapons, and other units of measure for bulk allotment and other ammunition items.

basic psychological operations study - The document describing the characteristics of the country, a geographic area of the country or of a group of people in the area to assist in the planning of psychological operations.

basic research - (DOD, IADB) Research directed toward the increase of knowledge, the primary aim being a greater knowledge or understanding of the subject under study. See also applied research; research.

Basic School - The Marine Corps school in Quantico Virginia, abbreviated TBS.

basic tactical organization - (DOD, IADB) The conventional organization of landing force units for combat, involving combinations of infantry, supporting ground arms, and aviation for accomplishment of missions ashore. This organizational form is employed as soon as possible following the landing of the various assault components of the landing force.

basic undertakings - (DOD, NATO, SEATO, CENTO, IADB) The essential things, expressed in broad terms, that must be done in order to implement the commander's concept successfully. These may include military, diplomatic, economic, psychological, and other measures.

basket case - Crazy.

basket head - Slang for local farmers who wore a conical straw hat.

basket leave - An illegal method of giving a favor to a subordinate by which the subordinate filled out leave papers which sat in the in-basket during the leave. The request was destroyed if the leave was uneventful, and processed if the absent soldier was arrested, injured or otherwise discovered to be absent from duty.

basketball ship - A helicopter that provides illumination on an area by dropping flares.

basketball team - Radio code for fire team of Marines, usually five.

Bat-turn - Aviation slang for a high speed, high-G force turn of a jet, from the Batman TV series in the 1960s in which the Batmobile made instant 180 degree turns.

bathymetric contour - See depth contour; depth curve.

bats - Slang for the 106-mm recoilless rifle.

batsman - The term for the Landing Signal Officer used by pilots of the British commonwealth countries.

battalion landing team - (DOD, IADB) In an amphibious operation, an infantry battalion normally reinforced by necessary combat and service elements; the basic unit for planning an assault landing.

battery - (DOD, NATO, SEATO, CENTO, IADB) 1. Tactical and administrative artillery unit or subunit corresponding to a company or similar unit in other branches of the Army. 2. All guns, torpedo tubes, searchlights, or missile launchers of the same size or caliber or used for the same purpose, either installed in one ship or otherwise operating as an entity.

battery (troop) left (right) - (DOD) A method of fire in which weapons are discharged from the left (right), one after the other, at 5-second intervals.

battery center - (DOD) A point materialized on the ground at the approximate geometric center of the battery position; the chart location of the battery.

battle casualty - (DOD, IADB) Any person lost to his organization because of death, wound, missing, capture, or internment provided such loss is incurred in action. "In action" characterizes the casualty status as having been the direct result of hostile action; sustained in combat or relating thereto; or sustained going to or returning from a combat mission provided that the occurrence was directly related to hostile action, or, through misadventure, friendly action. However, injuries due to the elements or self-inflicted wounds are not to be considered as sustained in action and are thereby not to be interpreted as battle casualties. See also died of wounds received in action; nonbattle casualty; wounded.

battle fatigue - See combat fatigue.

battle group - (IADB) Army tactical and administrative infantry or airborne unit, on a command level below a division or brigade whose next lower echelons are companies, the entire organization of which is prescribed by a table of organization.

battle map - (DOD, IADB) A map showing ground features in sufficient detail for tactical use by all forces, usually at a scale of 1: 25,000. See also map.

Battle Phrog - See CH-46 helicopter.

battle pin - Marine slang for tie clip.

battle reserves - (DOD, IADB) Reserve supplies accumulated by an army, detached corps, or detached division in the vicinity of the battlefield, in addition to unit and individual reserves. See also reserve supplies.

battle star - A small metal star on a uniform's campaign ribbon denoting participation in a battle of significance.

battle-sight zeroing - The process of adjusting the sight and windage controls on a weapon to the individual firing technique of the soldier so that the soldier will hit the object that is aimed at when it is fired.

battlefield illumination - (NATO, CENTO, IADB) The lighting of the zone of action of ground combat and combat support troops by artificial means other than invisible rays. See also artificial daylight; artificial moonlight.

battlefield religion - The emergence of a moral objection to killing that arises after field combat, primarily a ruse to get lighter or safer duty.

battlefield surveillance - (NATO, CENTO, IADB) The continuous (all weather, day and night) systematic watch over the battle area to provide timely information for combat intelligence. See also surveillance.

bazooka - Nickname for the shoulder held rocket launcher.

BC - Body count.

BCD - Bad Conduct Discharge.

BCT - Basic Combat Training.

BDA - Bomb Damage Assessment, the report prepared at the end of a bombing mission. by the controller of the flight.

Bde - Abbreviation for brigade.

BDU - Battle Dress Uniform. Fatigues.

be nice - A phrase used to get the other person to back off.

beach - (DOD, IADB) 1. The area extending from the shoreline inland to a marked change in physiographic form or material, or to the line of permanent vegetation (coastline). 2. In amphibious operations, that portion of the shoreline designated for landing of a tactical organization.

beach capacity - (DOD, NATO, SEATO, CENTO, IADB) An estimate, expressed in terms of measurement tons, or weight tons, of cargo that may be unloaded over a designated strip of shore per day. See also clearance capacity; port capacity.

beach group - See shore party.

beach marker - (DOD, SEATO, IADB) A sign or device used to identify a beach or certain activities thereon, for incoming waterborne traffic. Markers may be panels, lights, buoys, or electronic devices.

beach organization - (DOD, IADB) In an amphibious operation, the planned arrangement of personnel and facilities to effect movement, supply, and evacuation across beaches and in the beach area for support of a landing force.

beach party - (DOD, IADB) The naval component of the shore party. See also beachmaster unit; shore party.

beach party commander - (DOD, IADB) The naval officer in command of the naval component of the shore party.

beach photography - (DOD) Vertical, oblique, ground, and periscope coverage at varying scales to provide information of offshore, shore, and inland areas. It covers terrain which provides observation of the beaches and is primarily with the geological and tactical aspects of the beach.

beach reserves - (DOD, NATO, SEATO, CENTO, IADB) In an amphibious operation, an accumulation of supplies of all classes established in dumps in beachhead areas. See also reserve supplies.

beach support area - (DOD, IADB) The area to the rear of a landing force or elements thereof, established and operated by shore party units, which contains the facilities for the unloading of troops and materiel and the support of the forces ashore; it includes facilities for the evacuation of wounded, prisoners of war, and captured materiel.

beach survey - (DOD) The collection of data describing the physical characteristics of a beach; that is, an area whose boundaries are a shoreline, a coastline, and two natural or arbitrary assigned flanks.

beach width - (DOD, NATO, CENTO, IADB) The horizontal dimensions of the beach measured at right angles to the shoreline from the line of extreme low water inland to the landward limit of the beach (the coastline per DOD). (Note: The words "(the coastline)" are DOD and IADB approved only.)

beachhead - (DOD, NATO, SEATO, CENTO, IADB) A designated area on a hostile shore which, when seized and held, insures the continuous landing of troops and materiel, and provides maneuver space requisite for subsequent projected operations ashore. It is the physical objective of an amphibious operation. See also airhead; bridgehead.

beachmaster - (DOD, IADB) The naval officer in command of the beachmaster unit of the naval beach group.

beachmaster unit - (DOD, IADB) A commissioned naval unit of the naval beach group designed to provide to the shore party a naval component known as a beach party which is capable of supporting the amphibious landing of one division (reinforced). See also beach party; shore party.

beacon - (DOD) A light or electronic source which emits a distinctive or characteristic signal used for the determination of bearings, courses, or location. See crash locator beacon; fan marker beacon; localizer; beaconing; personal locator beacon; radio beacon; Z marker beacon.

beacon double - (DOD) In air intercept, a code meaning pilot select double pulse mode on your tracking beacon.

beacon off - (DOD) In air intercept, a code meaning turn off your tracking beacon.

beacon on - (DOD) In air intercept, a code meaning turn on your tracking beacon.

beaded up - Aviation slang for sweaty, worried.

beam attack - (DOD) In air intercept, an attack by an interceptor aircraft which terminates with a heading crossing angle greater than 45 degrees but less than 135 degrees. See also heading crossing angle.

VIETNAM: THE WAR ZONE DICTIONARY IN THEIR OWN WORDS

beam rider - (DOD, IADB) A missile guided by an electronic beam.

beam rider - (NATO, SEATO, CENTO) A missile guided by a radar or radio beam.

beam width - (DOD, NATO, CENTO) The angle between the directions, on either side of the axis, at which the intensity of the radio frequency power drops to one-half the value it has on the axis. (Note: NATO and CENTO definition uses the word "emission" instead of the word "frequency").

beannies - Special Forces.

beannies and weenies - See beans and franks.

beans - Slang for any meal.

beans and dicks - See beans and franks.

beans and franks - The dinner of beans and frankfurters. Also beannies and weenies.

beans and motherfuckers - The dinner in the C-ration pack that consisted of lima beans and ham. Pronounced "mutherfuckers".

bear hunting with a stick - A phrase indicating being under powered or understaffed for a mission, or the entire war.

bear trap - The booby trap that uses two blocks of wood with wood or metal spikes that close on a leg when stepped on, like a spring loaded metal bear trap.

bearing - (DOD, NATO, SEATO, CENTO, IADB) The horizontal angle at a given point measured clockwise from a specific reference datum to a second point.

beast - A white person.

beaten zone - (DOD) The area on the ground upon which the cone of fire falls.

beaucoup - French for "many", used by locals and adopted by service personnel in Vietnam to indicate many or much or a great deal, often pronounced "boo coo", thought by many to be a Vietnamese word.

Beaver - The U-6 Canadian made single engine prop aircraft.

bed check - A night time check of personnel present against the roster to insure all are accounted for, and none are AWOL or living off base.

bed pan commando - A medic, usually of enlisted rank.

beef and rocks - The meal composed of sliced beef and potatoes.

beehive it - To depart rapidly due to danger.

beehive rounds or beehive ammunition - M-46 an artillery shell that had 7-8,000 steel darts that acted as projectiles on impact, used in artillery shells, rockets and recoilless rifles. Also canister round.

been there medal - Slang for the Vietnam Service Medal.

Beer 33 - A Vietnamese beer brand.

beer can grenade - An improvised grenade made by nesting two discarded soda cans with rocks or other shrapnel and explosive charge between two cans which explodes on contact.

beer can house - A house shingled with flattened beer cans.

beetle stompers - Infantry.

Beginning of Morning Nautical Twilight - Navy term for the early morning just barely light.

behind the eight ball - In a difficult position, from the hard to make pool shot.

behind the power curve - Aviation slang for: 1. A lagging aircraft that is operating at a less than the optimum lift-to-drag ratio. 2. A pilot or others not operating well, failing to meet expected performance.

being interviewed for the morning papers - Morning roll call.

belay - Navy and Marine term for stop it, quit, put something away.

believer - A dead enemy soldier, from "now he is a believer (in our power)".

Bell Telephone Hour - 1. The use of electric current from field radios to shock prisoners during questioning. 2. The name of a popular radio program of classical music sponsored by Bell Telephone in the 1940s and 1950s.

bells - The Navy shipboard time system. By ringing a bell, all on board know the time. Split into 4-hour sections, each matching a watch, one bell is struck at 8:30 (a.m. or p.m.), one bell is then added each half hour, at eight bells (8, 12, 4, and 8) a watch changes and the bell cycle begins again.

belly landing - A wheels-up landing, a controlled crash.

below - Navy and Marine slang for downstairs.

below the zone - An early promotion.

Bend over here it comes again. - A phrase denoting an undesirable assignment. See BOHICA

bends and motherfuckers - An exercise in which there is a squat and then a leg thrust.

bennies - 1. Benefits from home such as beer or mail. 2. Benzedrine.

Bennington School for Boys - The Army's Officer Candidate School at Fort Bennington.

Benny - See Jack Benny.

bent - (DOD) In air intercept and close air support, a code meaning equipment indicated is inoperative (temporarily or indefinitely). Cancelled by OKAY.

BENT - Getting dark, from Beginning of Nautical Twilight.

BEQ - Bachelor Enlisted Quarters.

berm - The line of fortification at the perimeter, usually a raised area.

Betty Crocker - Derogatory term for a soldier in safe Saigon desk duty. From the trademarked cake mixes featuring a homemaker.

BFA - Blank Firing Apparatus. A metal attachment to a rifle to prevent burns when shooting blanks.

BG - Brigadier General (Army).

BGen - Brigadier General (Marine Corps).

bi-margin format - (NATO) The format of a map or chart on which the cartographic detail is extended to two edges of the sheet, normally North and East, thus leaving two margins only.

bicycle mine - An explosive in which a frame of a bicycle is loaded with explosives and the timer in a headlamp is set to explode at a set time.

Big Belly - Nickname for B-52 aircraft that was modified to hold 60,000 pounds of bombs

Big Bird - See Freedom Bird.

big boy - A tank.

big boys - Slang for artillery.

big chicken dinner - A Bad Conduct Discharge.

big dad - Drill Instructor.

Big Dead One - Derogatory for the Big Red One, the First Infantry Division.

Big Eye - Air Force airborne early warning radar system. Renamed in 1967 to College Eye.

big orange pill - Antimalaria pill.

Big Os - Marijuana cigarettes.

big pond - Pacific Ocean.

big PX - The United States.

big PX in the sky - Killed. Going to the big PX in the sky.

big R - Rotation home.

Big Red One - The First Infantry Division from the unit patch with a red 1.

big shotgun - The 106-mm rifle when using canister ammunition.

big stuff - Artillery or ordinance dropped from planes.

big twenty - Slang for a twenty year career in the military. Also Big 20.

bilateral infrastructure - (DOD, NATO, SEATO, CENTO) Infrastructure which concerns only two (NATO) (SEATO) (CENTO) members and is financed by mutual agreement between them (e.g., facilities required for the use of forces of one (NATO) (SEATO, CENTO) member in the territory of another). See also infrastructure.

billet - (DOD, IADB) 1. Shelter for troops. 2. To quarter troops. 3. A personnel position or assignment which may be filled by one person.

binding - (DOD, NATO, CENTO) The fastening or securing of items to a moveable platform called a pallet. See also palletized unit load.

bingo - (DOD) 1. (when originated by controlling authority) - Proceed to alternate airfield or carrier as specified. 2. (when originated by pilot) - I have reached minimum fuel for safe return to base or to designated alternate.

bingo field - (DOD) Alternate airfield.

bingo field - Aviation slang of carrier pilots for a land based air strip for emergency landings.

bingo fuel - Slang for out of gas.

Binh Xuyen - A political racketeering organization that was strong after WWII.

Binoctal - A barbiturate sold as a headache powder.

biographical intelligence - (DOD, NATO, CENTO) That component of intelligence which deals with individual foreign personalities of actual or potential importance.

biological agent - (DOD, NATO, CENTO, IADB) A microorganism which causes disease in man, plants, or animals or causes the deterioration of materiel. See also chemical agent.

biological half-time - See half-life.

biological operations - (DOD, NATO, CENTO, IADB) Employment of biological agents to produce casualties in man or animals and damage to plants or materiel; or defense against such employment.

biological warfare - (SEATO, IADB) Employment of living organisms, toxic biological products, and plant growth regulators to produce death or casualties in man, animals, or plants; or defense against such action. See also biological operations.

biological weapon - (DOD, NATO, CENTO, IADB) An item of materiel which projects, disperses, or disseminates a biological agent including arthropod vectors.

bipod - Two stabilizing legs at the front of a weapon.

bird - Slang for 1. A helicopter. 2. Any aircraft. 3. The obscene gesture extending the middle finger in a "fuck you" salute, also "The Bird".

bird colonel - Slang for full colonel.

bird dog - To labor intensively at something.

bird farm - Slang for aircraft carrier.

bird watching - Girl watching.

bird-shit - Paratroopers.

birdbath - That area of a motor pool used to wash vehicles.

Birddog - 1. See O-1 an aircraft. 2. A FAC (Forward Air Controller) usually stationed in the air in a small fixed wing aircraft, a Nickname for the L-19 a light slow flying reconnaissance plane.

Birdland - Slang for officer's quarters.

Birthday Ball - The Marine Corps annual celebration of the founding of the Marine Corps on November 10, 1775. Traditions include formal dress attire and a cake cutting ceremony. The cake is cut with an officer's sword, the first slice presented to the guest of honor, the second to the oldest Marine present, and the third to the oldest Marine to present to the youngest Marine present.

biscuit - Slang for C-rations.

biscuit bitches - See Donut Dolly.

BIT, Built In Test - 1. The systems checks on the radar of the Phantom jet that permits the identification and correction of system problems. 2. Generally any self-identification and correction of a problem.

bitch box - 1. A radio amplification box in the field. 2. A speaker system on board Navy ships over which announcements are made.

BK amp - Hospital slang for a below the knee amputation. See AK amp.

black - (DOD) In intelligence handling, a term used in certain phrases (e.g., living black, black border crossing) to indicate reliance on illegal concealment rather than on cover.

black - 1. A Negro. Often capitalized as Black. 2. Clandestine.

black belt - A Senior Drill Instructor from color of his belt.

Black Beret - A member of the Army Rangers.

black box - Sensors dropped from helicopters to detect enemy movement.

black crow - A device for locating engine ignition, used to locate enemy vehicles.

black death - VC term for M-16 rifle.

black flights - Secret evacuation of CIA operatives.

black hats - Army teams serving to prepare advanced landing zones, named for black ball caps they wore. See Pathfinders.

Black Hawks - Slang for black painted Huey helicopters.

Black Horse - The call sign and nickname of the Army 11th Armored Cavalry Regiment that had a rearing black horse on its patch.

black horse - The name of the code for sending numbers over the radio.

black list - (DOD) An official counterintelligence listing of actual or potential enemy collaborators, sympathizers, intelligence suspects, and other persons whose presence menaces the security of friendly forces.

black magic - The M-16 rifle.

black operations - Clandestine activities, secret missions, may be unauthorized.

black ops - See black operations.

Black Power - The militant faction of the black civil rights movement.

Black Power salute - A raised fist held overhead as the symbol of the Black Power movement.

black propaganda - (DOD, I, NATO, SEATO, CENTO, IADB) Propaganda which purports to emanate from a source other than the true one. See also propaganda.

black propaganda; grey propaganda; white propaganda.

black radio - In psychological warfare broadcasts of one side disguised as broadcasts of the other.

black rifle - See M-16.

black shoe - A Navy officer who is not in aviation (as aviators wore brown shoes).

black widow - The M-16 rifle with a night scope.

blackbird - An unmarked aircraft.

Blackbird - See SR-71, an aircraft.

Blackwater fever - Malaria.

bladder - A collapsible drum made of rubberized fabric holding 2,000 to 5,000 gallons, usually holding a petroleum product. See blivet.

bladder boat - An inflatable boat that used oars or paddles.

blade time - 1. The allocated time that a unit could use helicopter support for logistics. 2. Slang for the pilot's flight time in a helicopter.

Blanket Division - The First Cavalry Division from the large patch.

blanket party - Unauthorized discipline of one soldier by his peers, by throwing a blanket over him at night and administering several blows by fist or soap in a sock.

blast - (DOD, NATO, CENTO, IADB) The brief and rapid movement of air vapor or fluid away from a center of outward pressure, as in an explosion or in the combustion of rocket fuel; the pressure accompanying this movement. This term is commonly used for "explosion", but the two terms may be distinguished.

blast - Slang for a parachute jump.

blast effect - (DOD, IADB) Destruction of or damage to structures and personnel by the force of an explosion on or above the surface of the ground. Blast effect may be contrasted with the cratering and ground-shock effects of a projectile or charge which goes off beneath the surface.

blast line - (DOD) A horizontal radial line on the surface of the earth originating at ground zero on which measurements of blast from an explosion are taken.

blast wave - (DOD, NATO, CENTO, IADB) A sharply defined wave of increased pressure rapidly propagated through a surrounding medium from a center of detonation or similar disturbance.

blasting cap - The device used to detonate explosives.

bleeding edge - (DOD, NATO, IADB) That edge of a map or chart on which cartographic detail is extended to the edge of the sheet.

blind blast - A parachute jump at night into an unsupported area.

blind bombing zone - (DOD, NATO, IADB) A restricted area (air, land, or sea) established for the purpose of permitting air operations, unrestricted by the operations or possible attack of friendly forces.

blind fire - Spraying an area with fire, usually by machine gun, without aiming.

blinker - A quadriplegic.

blip - (DOD, NATO, SEATO, CENTO, IADB) The display of a received pulse on a cathode ray tube.

blip - Slang for the aircraft visible on a radar screen.

blister agent - A chemical agent which blisters the skin and lungs and burns the eyes, also called vesicant agent.

blister bandit - A recruit who gets blisters and is excused from duties.

blivet - A collapsible drum made of a rubberized fabric holding 250 or 500 gallons. See bladder.

block shipment - (DOD, IADB) A method of shipment of supplies to overseas areas to provide balanced stocks for an arbitrary balanced force for a specific number of days, e.g., shipment of 30 days' supply for an average force of 10,000 individuals.

block stowage loading - (DOD, NATO, SEATO, CENTO, IADB) A method of loading whereby all cargo for a specific destination is stowed together. The purpose is to facilitate rapid off-loading at the destination, with the least possible disturbance of cargo intended for other points. See also loading.

block time - (NATO, CENTO) The period from the moment the chocks are withdrawn and brakes released, or moorings dropped, to the return to rest or take up of moorings after the flight.

blocking and chocking - (DOD, NATO, CENTO) The use of wedges or chocks to prevent the inadvertent shifting of cargo in transit.

blocking position - A defensive position sited so as to prevent the advance of the enemy or deny the enemy access to a set area.

blood - Slang for a black soldier in Vietnam used primarily by other black soldiers.

blood chit - (DOD) A small cloth chart depicting an American Flag and a statement in several languages to the effect that anyone assisting the bearer to safety will be rewarded.

blood stripe - 1. A promotion in rank achieved at the expense of others. 2. The red stripe on the outside seam of Marine Corps dress blues uniform honoring those who died in battle.

blooker - See blooper.

blooper - Slang for: 1. A bad round. 2. The M-79 grenade launcher.

blooper balls - Ammunition for the M-79 grenade launcher.

blouse - 1. Marine slang for the uniform jacket. 2. To tuck in or make secure.

bloused - Pant legs tucked into boot tops. See unbloused.

blousing bands - Rubber or elastic bands used to secure the cuff area of trouser legs.

blow - (DOD) To expose, often unintentionally, personnel, installations, or other elements of a clandestine organization or activity.

blow and go - 1. An underwater emergency move to empty lungs before a fast ascent when evacuating a submarine to prevent lung damage. 2. When using a breathing apparatus, to vent used air.

blow away - Slang for to kill.

blow bath - A steam or sauna followed by oral sex.

blow smoke - Slang for: 1. To obscure. 2. To lie. 3. To confuse the situation. 4. To pander to superiors.

blow the rag - To deploy the emergency parachute.

blow Zs - To sleep.

blowback - (DOD, NATO, SEATO, CENTO, IADB) 1. Escape, to the rear and under pressure, of gases formed during the firing of the weapon. Blowback may be caused by a defective breech mechanism, a ruptured cartridge case, or a faulty primer. 2. Type of weapon operation in which the force of expanding gases acting to the rear against the face of the bolt furnishes all the energy required to initiate the complete cycle of operation. A weapon which employs this method of operation is characterized by the absence of any breech-lock or bolt-lock mechanism.

blower - Aviation term for a jet's afterburner.

blown away - Killed.

BLT - Battalion Landing Team

blue - Slang for water.

Blue Dragon - A South Korean Marine unit.

blue feature - Slang for water, named from the designation on maps of water as blue areas.

blue forces - (NATO, SEATO, CENTO, IADB) Denotes those forces used in a friendly role during exercises. See also force(s).

blue key - (NATO) A blue image on any medium which is not reproduced when the superimposed work is reproduced, used as a guide for scribing or drawing.

blue line - River or stream, from how it is shown on a map.

blue line sweep - Searching a river area.

Blue Max - Medal of Honor.

blue ticket - Discharge from the military for mental issues.

blue water ops - Aviation slang for carrier based flight operations over water, without a bingo field, land based landing field.

blue water sailor - A ocean-going Navy personnel as opposed to the Coast Guard.

blue-eyed soul brother - A white soldier who related well with black soldiers.

blues - The Marine Corps formal dress uniform.

BMNT - Beginning of Morning Nautical Twilight.

bn - Abbreviation for Battalion.

boards out - Aviation slang for deploying speed brakes. Particularly important on short fields or carrier landings.

boat diagram - (DOD, IADB) In the assault phase of an amphibious operation, a diagram showing the positions of individuals and equipment in each boat.

boat group - (DOD, IADB) The basic organization of landing craft. One boat group is organized for each battalion landing team (or equivalent) to be landed in the first trip of landing craft or amphibious vehicles.

boat lanes - (DOD, NATO, SEATO, CENTO, IADB) Lanes, for amphibious assault landing craft, which extend seaward from the landing beaches to the line of departure. The width of the boat lanes is determined by the length of the corresponding beach.

boat people - Refugees escaping from Vietnam, mainly after the war ended.

boat space - (DOD, IADB) The space and weight factor used to determine the capacity of boats, landing craft, and amphibious vehicles. With respect to landing craft and amphibious vehicles, it is based on the requirements of one man with his individual equipment. He is assumed to weigh 224 pounds and to occupy 13.5 cubic feet of space. See also man space.

boat space - (SEATO) The space and weight factor used to determine the capacity of boats and landing craft. With respect to landing craft, it is based on the requirements of one man with his individual equipment. He is assumed to weigh 224 pounds and to occupy 13.5 cubic feet of space.

boat wave - See wave.

boattail - (DOD, NATO, CENTO, IADB) The conical section of a ballistic body that progressively decreases in diameter toward the tail to reduce overall aerodynamic drag.

Bobbie - 1. The American female weather reporter on American Services Radio's TV show, Miss Bobbie Keith, introduced as "Bobbie the bubbling bundle of barometric brilliance". 2. Any American female held in high regard. Note: Uniformly, sources have referenced Miss Keith as Miss, not the emerging Ms., and talked about her in a protective and sisterly manner in stark contrast to most references to females. Most commented on her dancing, wearing minidresses and giving the weather at home as well as in Vietnam.

body armor - Protective body armor, also chicken plate.

body bag - The heavy plastic bag used for encasing and transporting bodies from a battle zone.

body count - 1. The statistical report of deaths in a battle. 2. The main analytical tool of the Department of Defense in Vietnam 3. The often inflated official report of a battle.

body of a map or chart - (NATO) That area of a map or chart contained within the neatline.

bogey - (DOD) An air contact which is unidentified but assumed to be enemy. (Not to be confused with "unknown".) See also friendly; hostile.

bogus - Slang for 1. Any poorly planed event. 2. A bad or defective item.

BOHICA - See Bend over here it comes again.

Bolo badge - Purple Heart medal for injury in combat acquired by foolish action.

bolter - An aircraft on a carrier that is not stopped by the arresting cable even when the wheels touch down. Requires a go around and try again.

Bomarc - (DOD) A long-range, surface-to-air guided missile with nuclear warhead for area air defense, powered by twin ramjet engines with either liquid or solid rocket boosters, and terminal guidance. Designated as CIM-10.

bomb alarm system - (DOD) A fully automatic system of detectors ringing key target areas in North America for transmitting to display centers reports of nuclear bursts. See also nuclear detonation detection and reporting system.

bomb damage assessment - (DOD) The determination of the effect of all air attacks on targets (e.g., bombs, rockets, or strafe).

bomb disposal unit - See explosive ordnance disposal unit.

bomb impact plot - (DOD) A graphic representation of the target area, usually a pre-strike air photograph, on which prominent dots are plotted to mark the impact or detonation points of bombs dropped on a specific bombing attack.

bomb line - (SEATO, IADB) An imaginary line arranged, if possible, to follow well-defined geographical features, prescribed by the troop commander and coordinated with the air force commander, forward of which air forces are free to attack targets, without danger to or reference to the ground forces. Behind this line all attacks must be coordinated with the appropriate troop commander. See fire support coordination line.

bomb lines - (IADB) Lines (land) established to delimit attacks by friendly aircraft. See also forward bomb lines; tactical bomb lines.

bomb pocket - A target so attractive that it was bombed regardless of cost.

bomb release line - (DOD) An imaginary line around a defended area or objective over which an aircraft should release its bomb in order to obtain a hit or hits on an area or objective.

bomb release point - (DOD, NATO, SEATO, CENTO, IADB) The point in space at which bombs must be released to reach the desired point of detonation.

bomber - (DOD) 1. light: A bomber designed for a tactical operating radius of under 1,000 nautical miles at design gross weight and design bomb load. 2. medium: A bomber designed for a tactical operating radius of between 1,000 to 2,500 nautical miles at design gross weight and design bomb load. 3. heavy: A bomber designed for a tactical operating radius over 2,500 nautical miles at design gross weight and design bomb load.

bombing angle - The angle between the vertical and a line joining the aircraft to what would be the point of impact of a bomb released from it at that instant.

bombing errors - (NATO, SEATO, CENTO, IADB) 1. (50% circular error)- The radius of a circle, with the center at a desired mean point of impact, which contains half the missiles independently aimed to hit the desired mean point of impact. 2. (50% deflection error)- Half the distance between two lines, drawn parallel to the aircrafts track and equidistant from the desired mean point of impact, which contains half the missiles independently aimed to hit the desired mean point of impact. 3. (50% range error)- Half the distance between two lines, drawn perpendicular to the aircraft's track equidistant from the desired mean point of impact, which contains half the missiles independently aimed to hit the desired mean point of impact. (Note: Above errors should imply overall errors unless otherwise stipulated by inclusion of the word "random" or "systematic" as necessary.)

bombing height - (NATO, CENTO) Distance above target at the moment of bomb release, measured vertically from the target to the level of the bombing aircraft.

bombing run - In air bombing, that part of the flight that begins from an initial point with the approach to the target, includes target acquisition, and ends on release of the ordinance.

Bonanza - A small twin engine utility transport. See U-8.

bong - A device for smoking marijuana that collected a large quantity of smoke to be inhaled quickly. Made in the field of a section of bamboo or a shotgun barrel. From the Thai word baung - meaning a large wooden cylinder.

bong son bomber - A huge marijuana cigarette.

booby trap - (DOD, NATO, SEATO, CENTO, IADB) An explosive or nonexplosive device or other material, deliberately placed to cause casualties when an unsuspecting person disturbs an apparently harmless object or performs a normally safe act.

booby trap - Slang see widow-maker or Automatic Ambush.

boocoo or boo coo - The local pronunciation of the French word beaucoup meaning many.

book - Slang for: 1. The Book, rules and regulations. 2. Departure, usually fast. Note: Book and book it may have come from Navy and Marine Corps personnel signing out in a ship's "book" before leaving it.

boom boom - Slang for sex.

boom boom girl - Slang for prostitute.

boom boom house - Slang for whorehouse.

boom de boom - Ba Muoi Ba beer.

boomer - Slang for one who refuels aircraft in flight.

boondockers - Marine slang for the low-top work boots issued to reservists.

boondocks - Back country, rugged area.

boonie - Slang for infantry soldier.

boonie hat - The soft olive drab or camouflage hat with a floppy brim on all sides worn by infantrymen in the field.

boonie rat - Slang for an infantryman with significant time in the field.

boonies - Slang for in the jungle, far away from anything, isolated terrain.

booster - (DOD, NATO, SEATO, CENTO, IADB) 1. A high-explosive element sufficiently sensitive so as to be actuated by small explosive elements in a fuze or primer and powerful enough to cause detonation of the main explosive filling. 2. An auxiliary or initial propulsion system which travels with a missile or aircraft and which mayor may not separate from the parent craft when its impulse has been delivered. A booster system may contain or consist of one or more units.

boot - Slang for a soldier who has recently graduated from boot camp, untested, new to a field assignment.

boot camp - Slang for basic training for Navy and Marine personnel.

boot it - A long patrol on foot.

bootleg whiskey - A black market combination of beer and Coca Cola.

booze - Alcoholic beverage.

boozer - One who drinks excessively.

BOQ - Bachelor Officers' Quarters.

border - (NATO) In cartography, the area of a map or chart lying between the neatline and the surrounding framework.

border break - (DOD, NATO, IADB) A cartographic technique used when it is required to extend a portion of the cartographic detail of a map or chart beyond the sheetlines into the margin.

border crosser - (DOD, NATO, SEATO, CENTO, IADB) An individual living close to a frontier who normally has to cross the frontier frequently for legitimate purposes.

boresafe fuze - (NATO, CENTO, IADB) Type of fuze having an interrupter in the explosive train that prevents a projectile from exploding until after it has cleared the muzzle of a weapon. See also fuze.

boresight - 1. Aviation term for the aiming of a gun by lining up the axis of the gun with its sights. 2. Aviation slang for a guy who gets lost in the details and misses the big picture.

bottle baby - An alcoholic.

bottlecap colonel - Lieutenant Colonel, from ruffled edge of the silver insignia.

bottom mine - A mine with negative buoyancy that remains on the sea or river bed after placement.

bought it - Slang for to kill or die.

bought lunch - Slang for to kill or die.

bought the farm - Slang for to kill or die. The most popular background story is that student pilots often landed in farm fields, occasionally dying. Reimbursement of the farmer for damage was routine, but some farmers inflated the loss value so the government 'bought the farm' not just the area damaged.

Bouncing Betty - A cone shaped land mine that when triggered bounced up to groin-level and exploded causing severe injury.

bound - (DOD, NATO, SEATO, CENTO, IADB) 1. Single movement, usually from cover to cover, made by troops often under artillery fire or small arms fire. (DOD, IADB) 2. Distance covered in one movement by a unit which is advancing by bounds. (IADB) 3. Change of firing data to move the center of impact in direction or range.

boundary (de facto) - (NATO) An international or administrative boundary whose existence and legality is not recognized but which is a practical division between separate national and provincial administering authorities.

boundary (de jure) - (NATO) An international or administrative boundary whose existence and legality is recognized.

boundary disclaimer - (NATO) A statement on a map or chart that the status and/or alignment of international or administrative boundaries is not necessarily recognized by the Government of the publishing nation.

bounty - A price to be paid on the death of specified individuals, particularly U.S. troops.

bouquet mine - In naval mine warfare, a mine with a number buoyant mine cases attached to a sinker so that when a mine is cut another mine rises to the same depth.

bow - The front of a ship or aircraft.

bowl - Slang for a pipe used for smoking marijuana, or the amount of marijuana smoked.

box - Vagina.

box formation - Aviation term for an aerial formation of four planes forming a square.

boys in Saigon - Newspaper reporters.

bra chute - A parachute malfunction in which the lines cross the canopy forming two smaller shapes resembling a bra. This is fatal if the reserve chute is not deployed.

brace - An exaggerated form of coming to attention.

bracketing - (DOD, NATO, SEATO, CENTO, IADB) A method of adjusting fire in which a bracket is established by obtaining an over and a short along the spotting line, and then successively splitting the bracket in half until a target hit or desired bracket is obtained.

brain housing group - Aviation sarcastically technical term for the skull and brain.

branch - (DOD, IADB) 1. A subdivision of any organization. 2. A geographically separate unit of an activity which performs all or part of the primary functions of the parent activity on a smaller scale. Unlike an annex, a branch is not merely an overflow addition. (DOD) 3. An arm or service of the Army.

brass - 1. Officers. 2. Brass fittings.

brass band - A support unit into rescue another unit.

brass monkey - An interagency term asking for help.

Brasso - The name of a trademarked brass and copper cleaner.

brat - The son or daughter raised in a career military family.

brave - Infantryman, from MOS of 11-B.

Bravo - 1. The military phonetic alphabet designation for the letter "B". 2. Some infantry company slang for a medic.

Bravo Zulu - Well done.

breaching - (DOD, NATO, SEATO, CENTO, IADB) The employment of any available means to secure a passage through an enemy minefield or fortification. See also deliberate breaching (land mine warfare); hasty breaching (land mine warfare). (Note: SEATO and IADB term has qualifier "(Land mine warfare)".)

break - 1. A radio communication term indicating the end of communication with one receiver and that the next thing said by the sender is intended for a second receiver, as in "Tango One reduce speed, break - Tango Two, increase speed". 2. The termination of a flight pattern of aircraft either for landing or evasive action (also called a kiss off, from the visual of the flight leader blowing a kiss to other aircraft), 3. Aviation maneuver involving a hard turn that is employed when an enemy aircraft is in a position to fire at you from behind. 4. Luck, as in "to get a break".

break off - (DOD) In close air support, a command utilized to immediately terminate an attack.

break starch - Slang for putting on a new set of heavily starched fatigues.

break tape - To fire a weapon.

break-up - (NATO, CENTO) In detection, the separation of one solid return into a number of individual returns which correspond to the various objects or structure groupings. This separation is contingent upon a number of factors including range, beam width, gain setting, object size and distance between objects.

breakaway - (DOD, NATO, CENTO) 1. The onset of a condition in which the shock front moves away from the exterior of the expanding fireball produced by the explosion of a nuclear weapon. (DOD) 2. After completion of attack, turn to heading as directed.

Breakbone fever - Dengue fever.

breaking contact - Disengaging from enemy contact in flight.

breaking squelch - The interruption of the ongoing static and hum of a radio that is open for communication, used to signal on a radio when a verbal signal would disclose position or be too time consuming. This is done by depressing the microphone button or transmission bar on the radio without talking. Sounds like "click-hiss".

breakoff position - The position at which a leaver or leaver section leaves a convoy to proceed to a different destination.

Bren Gun - A submachine gun with a silencer used by Special Forces.

Brevie Line - The navigational and political demarcation between South Vietnam and Cambodia.

brevity code - (DOD, NATO, CENTO) A code which provides no security but which has as its sole purpose the shortening of messages rather than the concealment of their content.

brevity or condensation code - (SEATO, IADB) A code which has as its sole purpose the shortening of messages rather than the concealment of their content.

brew - 1. Coffee. 2. Beer.

bridge trap - A trap in which a small foot bridge is cut and the damage disguised so when passed over, the bridge collapses onto spikes.

bridgehead - (DOD, NATO, SEATO, CENTO, IADB) An area of ground held or to be gained on the enemy's side of an obstacle. See also airhead; beachhead.

bridgehead line - (DOD, NATO, CENTO) The limit of the objective area in the development of the bridgehead. See also objective area.

briefing - (NATO, SEATO, CENTO, IADB) The act of giving in advance specific instructions or information.

brig - Military jail.

brig chaser - The Military Police assigned to escort prisoners.

Brig Gen - Brigadier General (Air Force).

brig rat - Inmate in brig.

brigade - (DOD) A unit usually smaller than a division to which are attached groups and/or battalions and smaller units tailored to meet anticipated requirements.

brigadier general - A one star general, lowest of the general ranks.

brightlight team - A small team that rescues other teams in trouble, usually in special operations.

brightwork - Navy term for brass or other metal that is polished.

bring smoke - Send intense artillery fire onto an enemy position. Also Fire for effect.

bringing red leg - Calling for artillery fire.

bringing up the rear - The last man in a patrol.

bro - Short for brother, meaning soul brother or black brother, designation of black soldier by other black soldiers, a term of camaraderie later adopted within some units without the racial distinction.

broadcast controlled air interception - (DOD, NATO, SEATO, CENTO, IADB) An interception in which the interceptor is given a continuous broadcast of information concerning an enemy raid and effects interception without further control. See also air interception; close-controlled air interception.

broken arrow - Radio code for the position being overrun and a request for immediate assistance.

broken down - Taken apart.

Bronco - 1. A light twin turbo prop, twin seat observation and support aircraft which may be equipped with machine guns and light ordinance for close direct support missions. 2. See OV-10, an aircraft.

Bronze Star Medal - A medal for heroic or meritorious action against an armed enemy not involving flight.

brother - Slang for black soldier.

brown bar - A lieutenant, the bar is from the single insignia on the collar, the brown is from the brown or black colored camouflage insignia. (see butter bar).

brown bomber - A laxative pill.

brown derby - Slang for a hot meal in the field, from the famed Brown Derby restaurant in Los Angeles.

brown nosing - Kissing up to superiors.

brown shoe Army - 1. The Army prior to 1 September 1956 when the uniform was changed from brown to black shoes. 2. Old timer.

brown shoes - 1. Navy and Marine personnel in aviation as pilot or crew as all other Navy wore black or white shoes or jungle boots. 2. A old-timer Marine still wearing "brown" shoes after the shoe color was changed from cordovan to black in the early 1960s.

brown side out - 1. Marine slang for confusion. 2. The order to display the brown camouflage pattern on helmet covers and shelters (the other side being green).

brown water navy - Navy personnel on river and canal patrols.

BS - 1. Abbreviation for bullshit. 2. Border surveillance.

BT - Benocotol, a French made drug available without prescription in Vietnam. Taken as a pill or mixed with other drugs, it induced violence.

BTZ - Below the zone. Referring to one who gets an undeserved promotion.

bubble - The two man Ott-13 Sioux helicopter.

bubbler - A SCUBA diver.

bubbles - The MUST, portable hospital that was inflated and looked like a mass of bubbles. See MUST.

Buck Rogers decoder - A field encryption and decryption device named for the comic book character. See circle wheel.

buck sergeant - The lowest grade sergeant.

buckle - Marine slang for a fistfight.

buckle for your dust - Marine slang for a violent fistfight.

Buddah grass - Drugs mixed with tobacco and smoked.

Buddah zone - Death, heaven.

Buddhist Barbeques - The self-immolation by Buddhist monks to protest the discrimination of the Catholic Diem regime.

Buddhist priest - An expression of surprise, similar to Judas priest.

buddy system - The technique of placing a new soldier with one more experienced for training.

Budweiser - 1. Slang for the SEALS insignia whish resembles the Budweiser logo. 2. An American beer.

BUFE - Big Ugly Fucking Elephant, painted ceramic elephants sold as souvenirs.

BUFF - Big Ugly Fat Fellow/Fucker, the B-52 bomber.

Buffalo - See CV-7, a troop transport aircraft.

buffer distance (nuclear) - (DOD, NATO, CENTO, IADB) 1. The horizontal distance which, when added to the radius of safety will give the desired assurance that the specified degree of risk will not be exceeded. The buffer distance is normally expressed quantitatively in multiples of the delivery error. 2. The vertical distance which is added to the fallout safe height of burst in order to determine a desired height of burst which will provide the desired assurance that militarily significant fallout will not occur. It is normally expressed quantitatively in multiples of the vertical error.

bug - (DOD) 1. A concealed microphone or listening device or other audiosurveillance device. 2. To install means for audiosurveillance.

bug juice - 1. Insect repellant. While marginally effective, it killed leaches on contact and made a good fuel for heating rations when mixed with peanut butter. 2. Slang for Kool-Aid mixed with disinfected water in the field

bugged - (DOD) Room or object which contains a concealed listening device.

Bugsmasher - The Beech aircraft used by Navy and Marine aviation.

build-up - (DOD, NATO, SEATO, CENTO, IADB) The process of attaining prescribed strengths of units and prescribed levels of vehicles, equipment, stores, and supplies. Also may be applied to the means of accomplishing this process.

bulk cargo - (DOD) That which is generally shipped in volume where the transportation conveyance is the only external container; such as liquids, ore, or grain.

bulk petroleum - (IADB) Liquid petroleum products which are normally transported by pipeline, rail, tank car, tank truck, tank trailer, barge and/or ocean tanker, and stored in tank or container having a fill capacity greater than 55 gallons. See also petroleum.

bulk petroleum products - (DOD, NATO, CENTO) Liquid petroleum products which are normally transported by pipeline, rail tank car, road tank truck, road tank trailer, barge, harbor or coastal tanker and oceangoing tanker and stored in a tank or container having a fill capacity greater than 55 United States gallons (45 Imperial gallons).

bulk storage - (DOD, IADB) 1. Storage in a warehouse of supplies and equipment in large quantities, usually in original containers, as distinguished from bin storage. 2. Storage of liquids, such as petroleum products in tanks, as distinguished from drum or packaged storage. See also storage.

bulkhead - Navy and Marine slang for wall.

bull boat - A small round boat used by Vietnamese fishermen.

bullet catcher - The front seat of a helicopter, particularly the Cobra.

bullet stabber - The man loading shells in a tank.

Bullpup - (DOD) An air-to-surface guided missile, visually guided by launching aircraft command, for use by fighter, light attack aircraft, and possibly helicopters, in close support of ground troops and for interdiction, and small tactical targets ashore and afloat. Designated as AGM-12.

bullseye - A mission specific bombing target.

bullshit - Slang for lies, falsehoods.

bullshit bombers - Aircraft used for dropping propaganda materials.

bullshitting - Slang for telling tall tales, talking about nothing in particular, killing time.

bum's roll - Slang for light pack of C-rations, bedroll, dry socks, and jungle blanket.

bummer - A bad occurrence or drug trip.

bunji cord - The elastic cord used to stabilize a door mounted machine gun offering the gunner greater range than a fixed mount.

bunk - A bed, Navy term. See rack.

bunker - A defensive fighting postion dug into the ground with a top cover ranging from sandbags to concrete.

bunker buster - A satchel charge explosive with short fuze.

bunker mentality - Limiting fights to the area close to your bunker and failing to engage in broader efforts.

BuNo - Bureau Number. The number assigned an aircraft when built.

burial - See emergency burial; group burial; trench burial. See also graves registration.

burn - (DOD) 1. Deliberately expose the true status of a person under cover. 2. The legitimate destruction and burning of classified material, usually accomplished by the custodian as prescribed in regulations.

burn call - The order to clean up of an area after an engagement in which all trash was burned to deprive the enemy of access to anything of value or disclose injuries such as medical dressings, spent equipment or food.

burn notice - (DOD) An official statement by one intelligence agency to other agencies, domestic or foreign, that an individual or group is unreliable for any of a variety of reasons.

burn-through range - (DOD) The distance at which a specific radar can discern targets through the external interference being received.

burned - (DOD) Used to indicate that a clandestine operator has been exposed to the operation (especially in a surveillance) or that his reliability as a source of information has been compromised.

burner - See afterburner.

burning shitters - The sanitation duty to collect the drums of fecal material from latrines and add fuel and burn it off. As this required stirring, it was particularly objectionable task, often contracted to locals or used as discipline.

burnout - (DOD, NATO, SEATO, CENTO, IADB) The point in time or in the missile trajectory when combustion of fuels in the rocket engine is terminated by other than programmed cutoff.

burnout velocity - (DOD, NATO, SEATO, CENTO, IADB) The velocity attained by a missile at the point of burnout.

burp - Infantry slang for Marines.

Burp gun - The .45 cal. machine gun as it has a distinctive burping sound when fired.

burst - Explosion.

burst interval - The time between explosions.

bursting fart - Slang for a Marine gunner's insignia.

bus driver hat - Slang for billed cap with internal frame and flat top, often with embellishments on brim.

bush - 1. A location away from base, in the field. 2. An area in which enemy contact is a high probability, an infantry term. See boonies. 3. Short for ambush. 4. Pubic hair.

bush time - Time spent in the field or in combat.

bush towel - Military issue green bath towel, 24x48 inches used to pad backpack straps and drape around neck to wipe sweat. Also bush rag.

Bushmaster - 1. A unit specializing in jungle operations. 2. A deadly snake.

bust - To reduce in rank, demote.

bust your cherry - To initiate into the first combat or sexual experience.

busted - Reduced in rank.

buster - (DOD) In air intercept, a code meaning fly at maximum continuous speed (or power).

Buster! - Aviation term used by an air controller directing a pilot to go as fast as you can, to haul ass.

busting caps - Firing a weapon, possibly from toy cap guns or from the older historical percussion cap weapons of the civil war era, a Marine Corps term.

bustle rack - A storage unit of pipe on the rear of a tank turret.

butt fuck - 1. In tactics, to attack (or be attacked) from the rear. 2. Really bad news or assignment. 3. To sodomize.

butt pack - A small field pack attached to a pistol belt that carried about half the contents of a rucksack. See M-1956.

butt plates - Slang for infantry.

butter bar - A lieutenant denoting rank by the use of the usual gold bar.

butterfly - 1. A field tactical maneuver to flit from place to place. 2. To depart, walk out on someone.

button bombs - A small mine with button sized projectiles in it set to blow up an enemy's foot when stepped on.

buy it - Slang for to die or be killed.

buy the farm/ranch - To die.

buzz - Slang for to fly low over an area or airfield.

BX - Base Exchange. The general store on base, see PX.

by the numbers - 1. Perform an activity in sequence. 2. A person who is in strict adherence to the rules.

C – CHARLIE

C - 1. Designated in the military phonetic alphabet, as "Charlie". 2. The aviation designation for cargo aircraft.

C and C, C&C - Command and Control, the operations center for air missions by helicopters.

C and S, C&S - Cordon and search.

C-1 - See Tracker.

C-117 - See Hummer.

C-118 - See Liftmaster.

C-119 - See Flying Box Car.

C-121 - See Constellation.

C-123 - See Provider, Lightship and Candlestick.

C-124 - See Globemaster.

C-130 - See Hercules.

C-133 - See Cargomaster.

C-135 - See Stratolifter.

C-140 - See Jetstar.

C-141 - See Starlifter.

C-2A - See Greyhound.

C-3 - The plastic explosive that was replaced by C-4.

C-4 - Composition 4. A plastic explosive. A malleable explosive that could be cut with a knife or shaped by hand. It came in bars 1x3x12 inches and looked like white putty wrapped in olive drab cellophane. Ignition as an explosive was by blasting caps. It would burn with a white-hot flame as well. Also spelled "plastique".

C-40 - See claymore.

C-45 - See Expediter.

C-46 - See Curtis Commando.

C-47 - See Skytrain.

C-5 - See Galaxy.

C-54 - See Skymaster.

C-7 - See Caribou.

C-8A - See Buffalo.

C-biscuit/cookies/crackers - See John Wayne Crackers.

C-day - (DOD, IADB) The unnamed day on which a deployment operation commences or is to commence. The deployment may be movement of troops, cargo, weapon systems, or a combination of these elements utilizing any or all types of transport. The letter "C" will be the only one used to denote the above. The highest command or headquarters responsible for coordinating the planning will specify the exact meaning of C-day within the aforementioned definition. The command or headquarters ctly responsible for the execution of the operation, if other than the one coordinating the planning, will do so in light of the meaning specified by the highest command or headquarters coordinating the planning.

C-rat grenade - An improvised grenade using a used C-ration box or can to contain shrapnel and explosives.

C-rations - Combat rations which are metal tins and boxed with plastic utensils, heat tabs and tobacco.

C-rats - See C-rations.

C-rats stove - An improvised stove made of an empty can from the ration box, and C-4 explosive which burns very hot when ignited in an empty can to heat the item placed above it.

C.O. - Conscientious objector.

C's - See C-rations.

C&E - Clothing and equipment.

CA - 1. Heavy cruiser. 2. Combat Assault

CAB - Combat Aviation Battalion.

cabin - (NATO, CENTO) In an aircraft, all the compartments used for the carriage of passengers or cargo.

cable drag drop - (NATO, CENTO) Ultra low level airdrop technique using the drag of an arrester cable ground installation to extract and halt airdrop loads.

cables - Slang for threads hanging from a uniform.

CAC - Combined Acton Company.

Caca dau. - Vietnamese for I'll kill you.

cache - A hidden store of ammunition or food.

CACO - See Casualty Assistance Call Officer.

CADC - Central Air Data Computer the calibrated data to in flight aircraft instruments.

Cadre - The central leadership group of the North Vietnamese army or Viet Cong, which sent orders to field operatives.

CAG - 1. See guided missile heavy cruiser. 2. Combined Action Group. 3. Commander of Air Group.

cairn - Very subtle trail markings, such as a broken twig, used by North Vietnamese to mark a trail, booby traps or identify food or weapon caches.

cal - Abbreviation for caliber, expressed in a decimal fraction of an inch, so a .50 cal round is a half inch in diameter.

calibrated airspeed - See airspeed.

calibrated focal length - (NATO, CENTO) An adjusted value of the equivalent focal length, so computed as to equalize the positive and negative values of distortion over the entire field used in a camera.

call fire - (DOD, IADB) Fire delivered on a specific target in response to a request from the supported unit. See also fire.

call for fire - (DOD, NATO, SEATO, CENTO, IADB) A request for fire containing data necessary for obtaining the required fire on a target.

call mission - (DOD, NATO, SEATO, CENTO, IADB) A type of air support mission which is not requested sufficiently in advance of the desired time of execution to permit detailed planning and briefing of pilots prior to take-off. Aircraft scheduled for this type of mission are on air, ground, or carrier alert, and are armed with a prescribed load.

call sign - (DOD, NATO, SEATO, CENTO, IADB) Any combination of characters or pronounceable words which identifies a communication facility, a command, an authority, an activity, or a unit; used primarily for establishing and maintaining communications. See also collective call sign; indefinite call sign; international call sign; net call sign; tactical call sign; visual call sign; voice call sign.

calling cards - Some units had calling cards or playing cards printed identifying them as the force attacking a location or killing a enemy soldier. These were left near or on the dead.

calls - The verbal calls by a leader to marching troops to keep cadence. The simplest is "Hup, two, three, four". Other calls get very complex and move into the realm of folk story telling or call and response songs. See Jody call.

cam on - Vietnamese for thank you.

camera axis - (DOD, NATO, CENTO, IADB) An imaginary line through the optical center of the lens perpendicular to the negative photo plane.

camera axis direction - (NATO, CENTO) Direction on the horizontal plane of the optical axis of the camera at the time of exposure. This direction is defined by its azimuth expressed in degrees in relation to True Magnetic North.

camera calibration - (DOD, NATO, CENTO, IADB) The determination of the calibrated focal length, the location of the principal point with respect to the fiducial marks and the lens distortion effective in the focal plane of the camera referred to the particular calibrated focal length.

camera magazine - (NATO, CENTO) A removable part of a camera in which the unexposed and exposed portions of film are contained.

camera nadir - See photo nadir.

camera station (photogrammetry) - See air base (photogrammetry); air station (photogrammetry).

camera window - (NATO, CENTO) A window in the camera compartment through which photographs are taken.

cammies - Jungle camouflage uniforms.

camouflage - (DOD) The use of concealment and disguise to minimize the possibility of detection and/or identification of troops, materiel, equipment and installations. It includes taking advantage of the natural environment as well as the application of natural and artificial materials. See also concealment; cover.

camouflage - (NATO, CENTO) The use of concealment and disguise to minimize the possibility of detection and/or identification. See also concealment; cover.

camouflage detection photography - (DOD) Photography utilizing a special type of film (usually infrared) designed for the detection of camouflage.

camouflet - (NATO) The resulting cavity in a deep underground burst when there is no rupture of the surface. See also crater.

camp - (DOD, IADB) A group of tents, huts, or other shelter set up temporarily for troops, and more permanent than a bivouac. A military post, temporary or permanent, may be called a camp.

campaign hat - The distinctive hat worn by Drill Sergeants in the Army and Marine Corps called Smokey-the Bear hat.

Campaign Medal - See Republic of Vietnam Campaign Medal. See also Vietnam Service Medal for the medal issued by the U.S.

campaign plan - (DOD, NATO, SEATO, CENTO, IADB) A plan for a series of related military operations aimed to accomplish a common objective, normally within a given time and space.

Can Lao Party - The Personalist Revolutionary Labor Party known as Can Lao which was pro-government, based on French "personalist" philosophy.

can of worms - 1. A fouled up mission. 2. Canned spaghetti.

can opener - 1. The P38. 2. A tank with a bulldozer front.

Canberra - (DOD, IADB) A two-place, twin-engine turbojet, all-weather tactical bomber capable of delivering nuclear and nonnuclear weapons. Designated as B-57, RB-57 is the reconnaissance version. Made by Martin from the British design, noted for its accuracy; however its slowness and age required its replacement in 1969.

cancel check firing - (DOD) The order to rescind "check firing".

cancel converge - (DOD) The command used to rescind "converge".

Candlestick - The C-123 aircraft when using flares to illuminate a battlefield.

candy ass - A person who is emotionally or physically weak. Also wimp, flake, pussy.

canister round - An antipersonnel projectile containing flechettes to spray the enemy with multiple projectiles.

canker mechanic - A medic dealing with non-combat wounds.

Cannabis - Marijuana.

cannibalize - (DOD, NATO, SEATO, CENTO, IADB) To remove serviceable parts from one item of equipment in order to install them on another item of equipment.

cannon cocker - Slang for artilleryman.

cannot observe - (DOD) A type of fire control which indicates that the observer or spotter will be unable to adjust fire but believes a target exists at the given location and is of sufficient importance to justify firing upon it without adjustment or observation.

Canoe U - Nickname for the United States Naval Academy at Annapolis.

canopy - The thick overhead jungle foliage, concealing the jungle floor from the air.

cans and vans - Pilot slang for spotting and targeting a convoy.

Canton - A political subdivision similar to a county in the US.

Cao Dai - A politically active religious group that was formed from several sects and philosophical traditions.

CAP - 1. Combat Air Patrol. 2. Combined Action Platoon, a platoon composed of U.S. Marines and South Vietnamese to defend specific villages.

capability - (DOD, IADB) The ability to execute a specified course of action. (A capability may or may not be accompanied by an intention.)

capacity load (navy) - (DOD, NATO, CENTO) The maximum quality of all supplies (ammunition, petroleum, oils, and lubricants, rations, general stores, maintenance stores, etc.) which each vessel can carry in proportions prescribed by proper authority. See also combat load (air force).

capping - Slang for shooting at.

capsule - (DOD, NATO, SEATO, CENTO, IADB) 1. A sealed, pressurized cabin for extremely high altitude or orbital space flight which provides an acceptable environment for man, animal, or equipment. 2. An ejectable sealed cabin having automatic devices for safe return of the occupants to the surface.

Capt - Captain (Marine Corps, Air Force).

CAPT - Captain (Navy and Coast Guard).

Captain's Mast - Navy and Marine Corps usage indication action or activity by the commanding officer which may include informal investigation and low level discipline, hearing complaints, or calling an assembly to award medals or citations.

captive firing - (DOD, NATO, SEATO, CENTO) A firing test of short duration, conducted with the missile propulsion system operating while secured to a test stand.

CAR - Combined Action Ribbon. The Marine decoration for being under fire in a combat zone.

car wash - A business set up outside a base that did provide a wash for dirty vehicles and added services such as a barber shop and whorehouse.

CAR-15 - A carbine rifle.

cardinal point effect - (DOD, NATO, CENTO, IADB) The increased intensity of a line or group of returns on the radar scope occurring when the radar beam is perpendicular to the rectangular surface of a line or group of similarly aligned features in the ground pattern.

cardinal points - (NATO, SEATO, CENTO, IADB) The directions: north, south, east, and west.

CARE (Cooperative for American Relief Everywhere) - The non-profit relief organization.

care package - The package of items from home (socks, cookies etc.), named after the relief CARE agency.

caretaker status - (DOD, IADB) A nonoperating condition in which the installations, materiel, and facilities are in a care and limited preservation status. Only a minimum of personnel is required to safeguard against fire, theft, and damage from the elements.

cargo - See chemical ammunition cargo; flatted cargo; general cargo; heavy-lift cargo; high explosive cargo; inflammable cargo; perishable cargo; special cargo; troop space cargo; vehicle cargo. See also loading.

cargo classification (combat loading) - (DOD) The division of military cargo into categories for combat loading aboard ships. See also cargo.

cargo outturn message - (DOD, IADB) A brief message report transmitted within 48 hours of completion of ship discharge to advise both the Military Sealift Command and the terminal of loading of the condition of the cargo, including any discrepancies in the form of overages, shortages, or damages between cargo as manifested and cargo as checked at time of discharge.

cargo outturn report - (DOD, CENTO, IADB) A detailed report prepared by a discharging terminal to record discrepancies in the form of over, short, and damaged cargo as manifested, and cargo checked at a time and place of discharge from ship.

cargo sling - (NATO, CENTO, IADB) A strap, chain, or other material used to hold cargo items securely which are to be hoisted, lowered, or suspended.

cargo tie-down point - (DOD, IADB) A point on military materiel designed for attachment of various means for securing the item for transport.

cargo transporter - (DOD, IADB) A reusable, metal shipping container designed for worldwide surface and air movement of suitable military supplies and equipment through the cargo transporter service.

cargoes - See essential cargo; immediately vital cargo; nonvital cargo; valuable cargo.

Cargomaster - (DOD, IADB) A four-engine turboprop cargo transport capable of carrying outsize freight. Designated as C-133.

Caribou - A small cargo plane, twin prop made by de Havilland Corporation in Canada. This twin engine, 32 passenger transport built by de Havilland of Canada required a very short takeoff or landing area and allowed rapid loading and unloading of cargo through the rear door, see CV-2.

carpet bombing - (DOD, NATO, SEATO, CENTO, IADB) The progressive distribution of a mass bomb load upon an area defined by designated boundaries, in such a manner as to inflict damage to all portions thereof.

CarQual - Aviation term for carrier qualified. A certification that a pilot is qualified to land on a carrier. Also carqual.

carriage - See gun carriage.

carrier - An aircraft carrier.

carrier air group - (DOD, NATO, CENTO, IADB) Two or more aircraft squadrons formed under one command for administrative and tactical control of operations from a carrier.

carrier striking force - (DOD, NATO, SEATO, CENTO, IADB) A naval task force composed of aircraft carriers and supporting combatant ships capable of conducting strike operations.

carry on - An order to resume what you were doing.

cartesian coordinates - (NATO) A coordinate system in which locations of points in space are expressed by reference to three mutually perpendicular planes, called coordinate planes. The three planes intersect in three straight lines called coordinate axes. See also coordinates.

cartridge - Shell casing.

cartridge belt - Belt to hold ammo pouch, canteen, first aid kit and other items at waist.

cartridge mine - An empty shell casing used as a mine, so when stepped on it exploded. Also cartridge trap.

cartwheel - A two plane defensive maneuver in which both protect the rear of the other by circling.

CAS - 1. Close Air Support, aircraft fire or bombing intended to provide direct support to ground troops. 2. Calibrated Air Speed, the raw air speed reflecting the sensor error. 3. Controlled American Services, the Saigon office of the CIA, pronounced cass.

CAS-team - Controlled American Services team. South Vietnamese trained by CIA who performed clandestine sabotage and intelligence gathering in North Vietnam.

case - (DOD) 1. An intelligence operation in its entirety. 2. Record of the development of an intelligence operation, including personnel, modus operandi, and objectives.

casevac - Australian slang for medevac of battle casualties. Pronounced cas evac.

Casey - See Hercules, KC-130.

cash - See cache.

cash sales - 1. The military store, requiring cash, which sold uniforms. 2. The new soldier whose uniform still smelled newly purchased due to the chemically treated cotton.

cassette - (NATO, CENTO) In photography, a reloadable container for either unexposed or exposed sensitized materials which may be removed from the camera or darkroom equipment under lightened conditions.

cast iron mike - An egg shaped enemy mine.

casual - See transient.

casual company - A unit waiting for reassignment.

casuals - Soldiers in transit.

casualty - (DOD, IADB) Any person who is lost to his organization by reason of having been declared dead, wounded, injured, diseased, interned, captured, missing; or a person whose whereabouts or status has not been determined. See also battle casualty; non-battle casualty; wounded.

Casualty Assistance Call Officers - The Marine Corps officer assigned to notify the next of kin of a fellow Marine's death and assist in funeral arrangements. See also Survival Assistance Officer.

casualty prioritization - See triage.

cat - A Caterpillar tractor.

CAT - Civil Air Transport, airline based in Taiwan.

cat fever - Slang for Catarrhal Gastroenteritis, an inflammation of the stomach and intestines causing diarrhea.

cat hole - A individual latrine dug for excrement in the field and covered immediately.

cat shot - Catapult assisted takeoff of a plane from a carrier deck.

catalytic attack - (DOD, IADB) An attack designed to bring about a war between major powers through the disguised machinations of a third power.

catalytic war - (DOD) Not to be used. See catalytic attack.

catapult - (DOD, NATO, SEATO, CENTO, IADB) A structure which provides an auxiliary source of thrust to a missile or aircraft; must combine the functions of directing and accelerating the missile during its travel on the catapult; serves the same function for a missile as does a gun tube for a shell.

catch a hit - Marine slang for getting chewed out. A minor reprimand.

catch Zs - To sleep.

caterpillar - 1. A supply or other non-combat convoy on a safe road. 2. A road used for logistical convoys that is safe.

Caterpillar Club - Those who have parachuted from a disabled aircraft to safety are awarded a caterpillar pin and inducted into the Caterpillar Club, founded by The Irvin Air Chute Co. in 1922. Early parachutes were made of silk, spun by worms; thus the caterpillar represents a safe descent on silk.

cattle truck - Troop transport truck.

Caucasian - The white race. Slang during this time of racial unrest used by black troops included, honky, whitey, chuck, Mister Charlie, cracker, redneck, beast and the white beast.

caught his lunch - Killed.

caution area - See danger area.

Cav - American Cavalry units, specifically the 1st Air Cavalry Division of the U.S. Army, infantry that is delivered to and removed from a battle area by helicopter. The helicopter gunship assault teams.

cavu - (DOD) Ceiling and visibility unlimited.

Cayuse - A Hughes made helicopter.

CB - Construction Battalion.

CBR - Chemical, Biological, Radiological, referring to weapons using these means to kill.

CBU - Cluster or Canister Bomblet Unit, a generic term or any of a number of weapons that are delivered by air and which contain and deliver a number of smaller bomblets such as flechettes, ball bearing or shot-put size projectiles.

CBU-24 - A cluster bomb that is dropped from an aircraft and detonate at a pre-set height above the ground.

CBW - Chemical Biological Warfare.

CC - 1. Company Commander. 2. Corrective Custody, in jail. 3. See tactical command ship.

CCC - Command and Control Central. The field command for operations in the central area of South Vietnam.

CCE - Civil Engineering Corps.

CCI - National Committee for a Citizens' Commission of Inquiry of the American involvement in war crimes in Vietnam.

CCM - Command Chief Master Sergeant (Air Force).

CCM - Counter counter-measures.

CCN - Command and Control North. The field command for operations in the northern area of South Vietnam.

CCR-1000 - An underwater breathing device that reused air to prevent surface detection of bubbles.

CCS - Command and Control South. The field command for operations in the southern area of South Vietnam.

CCT - Command and Control Team.

CDR - Commander (Navy, Coast Guard).

CE - 1. Corps of Engineers. 2. Combat emergency.

cease engagement - (DOD) An order that weapons will disengage a particular target or targets and prepare to engage another target. Missiles in flight will continue to intercept. The order terminates engagement on a particular target.

cease fire - (DOD) A command normally given to air defense artillery units to refrain from firing on, but to continue to track, an airborne object. Missiles already in flight will be permitted to continue to intercept.

ceiling - (DOD) The height above the earth's surface of the lowest layer of clouds or obscuration phenomena that is reported as "broken," "overcast," or "obscured" and not classified as "thin" or "partial".

celestial guidance - (DOD, IADB) The guidance of a missile or other vehicle by reference to celestial bodies. See also guidance.

celestial sphere - (DOD, NATO, CENTO) An imaginary sphere of infinite radius concentric with the earth, on which all celestial bodies except the earth are imagined to be projected.

cell - (DOD) Small group of individuals who work together for clandestine or subversive purposes.

cell - Slang for a cluster of planes on a mission.

censorship - See armed forces censorship; civil censorship; field press censorship; military censorship; national censorship; primary censorship; prisoner of war censorship; secondary censorship.

center of burst - (SEATO, IADB) A point about which the burst of projectiles fired under like conditions are evenly distributed. See also mean point of impact.

center of gravity limits - (NATO, CENTO, IADB) The limits within which an aircraft's center of gravity must lie to ensure safe flight. The center of gravity of the loading aircraft must be within these limits at take-off, in the air, and on landing. In some cases take-off and landing limits may also be specified.

center of gravity limits - (SEATO) The range of movement which the center of gravity can have without making the aircraft unsafe to fly. The center of gravity of the loaded aircraft must be within these limits at take-off, in the air, and on landing. In some cases, take-off and landing limits may also be specified.

centerline tank - The fuel tank on a plane that is located along the plane's centerline.

CENTO - 1. An indication modifying a military definition that CENTO approval has been granted for a term to be used in military use by CENTO. 2. The abbreviation for the Central Treaty Organization, an alliance formed in 1955 by Iran, Iraq, Pakistan, Turkey, and the United Kingdom that ended in 1979. Also known initially as Middle East Treaty Organization or METO, later known as the Baghdad Pact.

central analysis team - (IADB) A team composed of representatives from two or more commanders, responsible jointly to their superiors for the detailed analysis and reporting of a large scale naval exercise. If an analysis is being done by one commander or his subordinate (s) it will be called an analysis staff.

central analysis team - (NATO, CENTO) A team composed of representatives from two or more major (NATO) (CENTO) commanders, responsible jointly to their superiors for the detailed analysis and reporting of a large-scale (NATO) (CENTO) exercise.

central analysis team - (SEATO) A team composed of representatives from two or more major SEATO commanders, responsible jointly to their superiors for the detailed analysis and reporting of a large scale SEATO naval exercise. If an analysis is being done by one major SEATO commander or his subordinate(s) it will be called an analysis staff.

Central Highlands - The area of Vietnam of about 5,000 square miles bounded by Ban Me Thuot in the North and Kontum Province in the South.

Central Intelligence Agency - The United States intelligence gathering agency.

central planning team - (IADB) A team composed of representatives of two or more commanders, responsible jointly to their superiors for the production of the general instructions for the exercise in accordance with the agreed concept. Regional planning groups may be set up prior to the formulation of the central planning team in order to provide the central planning team with information of certain phases of the exercise. If exercise planning is done by a joint command, or by one commander or his subordinate (s), it will be called a planning staff. The central planning team issues "instructions," whereas the planning staffs issue "general exercise orders".

central planning team - (NATO, SEATO, CENTO) A team composed of representatives of two or more major (NATO) (SEATO) (CENTO) commanders, responsible jointly to their superiors for the production of the general instructions for the exercise in accordance with the agreed concept. Regional planning groups may be set up prior to the formulation of the central planning team in order to provide the central planning team with information of certain phases of the exercise. (SEATO) If exercise planning is done by a joint command, or by one major SEATO commander or his subordinate (s), it will be called a planning staff. The central planning team issues "instructions", whereas the planning staffs issue "general exercise orders".

central war - (DOD) Not to be used. See general war.

centralized control - (DOD, NATO, CENTO) In air defense, the control mode whereby a higher echelon makes direct target assignments to fire units.

centralized items - (DOD, IADB) Those items of supply for which appropriate authority has prescribed central management and procurement within a Military Department or Service.

Centurion patch - Aviation award for a pilot making 100 landings on one carrier. The patch was carrier specific and worn on a flight jacket, not uniform.

Cercle Sportif - A private Saigon club, similar to an country club, featuring dining, dancing, tennis courts and a swimming pool. The French name translates as Sporting Club or Sports Club.

CES request - Emergency resupply request.

CFB - Slang for clear as a fucking bell.

CG - 1. Commanding General. 2. See guided missile cruiser.

CGM-l6 - See Atlas.

CGN - See guided missile cruiser.

CGT - Confederation General du Travail (General Confederation of Labor) a Communist-led French labor party.

Ch-21 - See Flying Banana.

CH-3 - See Jolly Green Giant.

CH-34 - See Choctaw.

CH-35 - See Atlas Heavy Lift Helicopter.

CH-37 - See Mojave.

CH-46 - See Sea Knight.

CH-47 - See Chinook.

CH-53 - See Sea Stallion.

CH-54 - See Skycrane or The Flying Crane

chaff - (DOD, NESN, CENTO, IADB) Radar confusion reflectors, which consist of thin, narrow metallic strips of various lengths and frequency responses, used to reflect echoes for confusion purposes. See also rope; rope-chaff; window.

chaff corridor - The area in which chaff is in the air protecting aircraft by disrupting ground-to-air missile radar.

Chaffee - 1. M-24 light tank. 2. The light tank used by the French.

chain - See net, chain, cell system.

chain of command - (DOD, NATO, SEATO, CENTO, IADB) The succession of commanding officers from a superior to a subordinate through which command is exercised. Also called command channel. See also administrative chain of command; operational chain of command.

chairborne - Slang for doing desk duty.

chairborne commando - Slang for personnel in the rear doing paperwork.

chalk commander - (NATO, CENTO, IADB) The commander of all troops embarked under one chalk number.

chalk number - (NATO, CENTO, IADB) The number given to a complete load and to the transporting carrier.

chalk number - Slang for: 1. The number put on a helmet by a jumpmaster in chalk for troops who will be parachuting to insure they are loaded in the correct order, accounted for, and jump in the correct order. 2. The position of a specific aircraft in a formation.

challenge - (DOD, NATO, SEATO, CENTO, IADB) Any process carried out by one unit or person with the object of ascertaining the friendly or hostile character or identity of another. See also countersign; password; reply.

Champagne formation - Aviation term for an aerial formation of three or four planes in which the two leading planes act as a decoy to lure enemy aircraft into a fight or away from a target, then the trailing plane(s) attack. This is only used in combat.

chancre mechanic - Slang for a medic.

Chandelle - Aviation term for a full-throttle climb and turn.

change of operational control - (DOD, NATO, SEATO, CENTO, IADB) The date and time (Greenwich mean time/Greenwich civil time) at which the responsibility for operational control of a force or unit passes from one operational control authority to another.

changing tune - A retreat.

Channel _____ - (DOD) Used in conjunction with a predetermined letter, number, or code word to reference a specific radio frequency.

channel airlift - (DOD) Common-user airlift service provided on a scheduled basis between two points.

Chaplin - An officer who is a clergyman.

chaptered out - Discharged in lieu of a court martial, per Chapter 10.

charge - (DOD) The propellant of semifixed or separate loading ammunition.

Charge of Quarters - A duty assignment, usually for an officer, to be in charge of headquarters, usually when minimally staffed, like a night supervisor.

charged demolition target - (DOD, NATO, SEATO, CENTO, IADB) A target on which all charges have been placed and which is in one of the states of readiness, i.e., safe or armed. See also demolition target.

charging point - (NATO, CENTO, IADB) A connection on an aircraft, or aircraft component, through which the aircraft or aircraft component can be replenished with a specific commodity, e.g., oxygen, air, or hydraulic fluid, etc.

Charles - Slang for Viet Cong.

Charlie - 1. The military phonetic alphabet designation for the letter "C". 2. The designation for the Viet Cong, a shortening of Victor Charlie for V.C. 3. Aviation term for a landing time on a carrier.

Charlie Mike - Continue the mission.

Charlie rats - C-rations.

Charlie Tango - Slang for control tower.

Charlie-Alpha - Combat Assault, by a helicopter delivery of soldiers.

Charlie-Bird - The Command and Control helicopter or fixed wing aircraft.

Charlie-Charlie - Slang for the Command and Control function.

Charlie-Cong - Marine slang for the Viet Cong.

Charlie-Four - Slang for a C-4 explosive.

Charlie-Foxtrot - Cluster fuck. A hopelessly fouled up mess.

chart base - (DOD, NATO) A chart used as a primary source for compilation or as a framework on which new detail is printed. Also known as topographic base. See also map.

chart index - See map index.

chart series - See map series.

chart sheet - See map sheet.

Chas - Abbreviation for Charles, the enemy.

chase ship - The second of two aircrafts, the function of the rear one is security both in the air and as a backup for evacuation for added security.

chatter - 1. Multiple conversations on the same shared radio frequency. 2. Meaningless talk.

cheap Charlie - A soldier who is tight with his money, especially in a bar.

cheap heart - A wound that is minor but adequate to get the Purple Heart award.

check firing - (DOD) A command to cause a temporary halt in firing.

check point - (DOD, NATO, CENTO, IADB) 1. A predetermined point on the earth's surface used as a means of controlling movement, a registration target for fire adjustment, or a reference for location. 2. Center of impact; a burst center. 3. Geographical location on land or water above which the position of an aircraft in flight may be determined by observation or by electronic means. 4. A place where military police check vehicular or pedestrian traffic in order to enforce circulation control measures and other laws, orders, and regulations.

check port/starboard - (DOD) In air intercept, a term meaning alter heading ____ degrees to port/starboard momentarily for airborne radar search and then resume heading.

Check Six. - Aviation slang phrase for: 1. A greeting, particularly between fighter pilots. 2. Watch your backside, politically rather than in combat.

Check your six. - A warning to look behind, usually in aviation. See clock code.

checkerboard - A tactic in which a map is gridded into squares, each of which is swept by a team.

Checking for light leaks. - Aviation slang for taking a nap, closing eyelids.

checking the dictionary - 1. Referring to the manual. 2. Getting clarification on orders that are vague or conflicting.

checkmate - A security roadblock or temporary checkpoint.

checkout - (DOD, NATO, SEATO, CENTO, IADB) A sequence of functional, operational, and calibrational tests to determine the condition and status of a weapon system or element thereof.

checkpoint - 1. A call-in point for field units on the move to verify their location. 2. The entrance to a base or location controlled by military police verifying identity before allowing entrance.

CHECO - Contemporary Historical Examination of Current Operations

cheese - Slang for sucking up to a superior, to brown nose.

cheeseburger - See daisy-cutter.

chemical agent - (DOD, IADB) A solid, liquid, or gas which through its chemical properties produces lethal or damaging effects on man, animals, plants, or material, or produces a screening or signaling smoke.

chemical agent - (NATO, CENTO) A chemical compound which, when suitably disseminated produces incapacitating, lethal, or damaging effects on man, animals, plants, or materials. See also biological agent.

chemical agent cumulative action - (DOD) The building up, within the human body, of small ineffective doses of certain chemical agents to a point where eventual effect is similar to one large dose.

chemical ammunition - (DOD, IADB) A type of ammunition, the filler of which is primarily a chemical agent (toxic chemical agent), a training and riot control agent, a smoke, or an incendiary. See also ammunition.

chemical ammunition - (NATO, CENTO) A type of ammunition the filler of which is primarily a chemical agent.

chemical ammunition cargo - (DOD, IADB) Cargo such as white phosphorous munitions (shell and grenades). See also cargo.

chemical defense - (DOD, NATO, CENTO) The methods, plans, and procedures involved in establishing and executing defensive measures against attack by chemical agents.

chemical mine - (DOD, NATO) A mine containing a chemical agent designed to kill or disable personnel or to contaminate materiel or terrain.

chemical operations - (DOD, NATO, CENTO) Employment of chemical agents (excluding riot agents) to: a. kill, or incapacitate for a significant period of time, man or animals; and b. deny or hinder the use of areas, facilities or materials.

chemical operations - (IADB) Employment of chemical agents to produce casualties in man or animals, damage to plants or materiel, to make hazardous the occupation of certain areas, to produce a screening or signaling smoke; or defense against such employment.

chemical, biological, and radiological operations - (DOD, IADB) A combining term used only when referring to the three areas of chemical operations, biological operations, and radiological operations in the collective sense.

chemical, biological, and radiological operations - (NATO, CENTO) A collective term used only when referring to combined chemical, biological, and radiological operations.

cherry - 1. A new soldier. 2. A sexual virgin.

cherry juice - Hydraulic fluid, from its color.

cherry unit - Slang for a unit that has not seen combat.

Cherrypicker - See M-578 VTR.

Cherubs - Aviation slang for an altitude under 1000 feet (angels), measured in 100 feet increments, so Cherubs three is 300 feet.

Chic - Slang for the Huey helicopter.

Chickasaw - Slang for the Sikorsky utility helicopter.

chicken - Any petty action or individual.

chicken coop - Interrogation room.

chicken plate - Chest armor worn by flight crews.

Chickenman - A humorous radio series on Armed Forces Radio 1969-70 of a crime fighting chicken, aired in short segments called the Fabulous Fowl or Wonderful Winged Weekend Warrior.

chickenshit - Any petty action or individual.

chicks - (DOD) Friendly fighter aircraft.

chicks - Slang for women.

chicomm or Chi-Comm - 1. Chinese communist. 2. Used as a description of the point of origin or supply for a good, such as a Chi-comm rocket, 3. Chi-comm used alone means a hand grenade of Chinese communist manufacture, which looked like a hand potato masher, thus one nickname.

chief interceptor controller - (SEATO, IADB) The senior interception controller who is responsible for supervising and coordinating the work of a number of interception controllers.

chief of staff - (DOD, IADB) The senior or principal member or head of a staff, or the principal assistant in a staff capacity to a person in a command capacity; the head or controlling member of a staff, for purposes of the coordination of its work; a position, which in itself is without inherent power to command by reason of assignment, except that which is invested in such a position by delegation to exercise command in another's name. (DOD) In the Army and Marine Corps, the title is applied only to the staff on a brigade or division level or higher. In lower units, the corresponding title is executive officer. In the Air Force, the title is applied normally in the staff on an Air Force level and above. In the Navy, the title is applied only on the staff of a commander with rank of rear admiral or above. The corresponding title on the staff of a commander of rank lower than rear admiral is chief staff officer, and in the organization of a single ship, executive officer.

Chief, Army, Navy, Air Force or Marine Corps Censor - (DOD) An officer appointed by the commander of the Army, Navy, Air Force, or Marine Corps component of a unified command to supervise all censorship activities of his Service.

Chieu Hoi (or Chieu boi) - 1. A Vietnamese term for "Open Arms". 2. The designation of an amnesty program to promote soldiers from the north (NVA or VC) joining the forces of the south, operated between 1963 and 1973.

chimpo - Slang for penis, from the Japanese.

China Beach - The Marine Corps R&R facility in Vietnam for short recreation, often only one day in duration.

Chinook - The CH-47 twin rotor cargo helicopter, used to transport up to 33 personnel or supplies in the interior and added cargo such as light artillery by the use of slings. Also called Shit-hook.

chit - 1. A receipt. 2. Approval in writing of a request.

chit book - A book of 20 or 40 chits to be used to pay for food or drinks at the Enlisted or NCO Clubs in place of money. See also MPC, Military Payment Certificates.

chloracne - The rash or boils from Dioxin exposure.

Chlorobenzamalononitrile - CS gas.

Chloroquine-primaquine - Antimalarial pill, Also horse pill or Monday pill.

chock - 1. A wedge put by a tire to secure a plane or vehicle from rolling. 2. See chalk number.

chocolate bunnies - Vietnamese prostitutes favoring black soldiers.

Choctaw - The Sikorsky transport helicopter.

chogi stick - A balancing pole, usually bamboo, 4-6 feet in length, with baskets or buckets on each end, carried over shoulders.

chogie - Army slang from move out quickly, brought from Korea era. Also chogie out.

Choi oi - My God! From the Vietnamese.

chop - See change of operational control.

chop-chop - 1. Hurry. 2. Oral sex. 3. Vietnamese slang word for food.

chopped rag - An altered parachute, usually by removing some panels.

chopper - Helicopter, army and civilian term.

chops - Chief of Operations.

chow - Slang for food.

chow down - Eat a meal.

chow hall - Mess hall.

chrome dome - 1. A bald person. 2 The fiber helmets with reflective aluminum paint for heat management in hot season.

chron - Chronology. The written record on a timeline.

chronic dose - (DOD, NATO, CENTO) Radiation dose absorbed in circumstances such that biological recovery may have been possible. It is arbitrarily accepted that a chronic dose can only mean absorption occurring after 24 hours following the burst.

Chu hoi - Vietnamese for "I surrender", literally "open arms", also spelled chieu hoi.

Chu Lai - A coastal city in Vietnam which was constructed as a military site during the war. It has no historical roots prior to the war. There is a story that the site was selected by Lt. Gen. Victor Krulak who named it with the mandarin Chinese characters that were his initials.

chuck - 1. Slang term for white soldier, may be used in friendly (he's a chuck-dude) or derogatory manner (acting like chuck). 2. Abbreviation for Charlie, the enemy.

chuck cookies - 1. The vanilla wafer sandwich cookies filled with white crème, also see spib cookies. 2. To vomit.

chuffing - (DOD, NATO, CENTO) The characteristic of some rockets to burn intermittently and with an irregular noise.

chumming - The aviation technique of having two planes work together, the first to draw fire, which exposes the enemy location and the second to fire on the enemy, from the fishing term.

Chunker - The M-5 grenade launcher.

church key - Slang for a bottle and can opener, a piercer (not lid remover).

churning butter - Having sex.

chute - Parachute.

CI - Counter Intelligence.

CIA - Central Intelligence Agency.

CIB - Combat Infantry Badge, insignia worn on dress and fatigue uniforms designating that the soldier was Army infantry and had been under fire in a combat zone.

CIC - 1. Commander in Chief. 2. Combat Information Center. 3. Counterintelligence Corps.

CID - Criminal Investigation Division.

CIDG - Civilian Irregular Defense Group, Local defense forces established by CIA and later run by Special Forces. Pronounced sid-gee.

cigarette roll - A parachute malfunction in which lines twist around the canopy forming a tube. This malfunction is fatal unless the reserve chute is deployed.

CIM-10 - See Bomarc.

CINCPAC - Commander In Chief for the American troops in the Pacific Region

Cinderella Liberty - A relief from duty ending at midnight, often restricted to confines of base, but off duty.

CIO - Chief Intelligence Operations, South Vietnam.

CIP - Counterinsurgency Plan.

cipher - (DOD, IADB) Any cryptographic system in which arbitrary symbols or groups of symbols represent units of plain text of regular length, usually single letters, or in which units of plain text are rearranged, or both, in accordance with certain predetermined rules. See also cryptosystem.

circle jerk - 1. Activity with no reason or function. 2. Multiple party masturbation.

circle wheel - A encrypting device using two or more rotating bands on a disk to form an exchange code. Also called Buck Rogers Decoder.

circuit - (DOD, IADB) 1. An electronic path between two or more points capable of providing a number of channels. 2. A number of conductors connected together for the purpose of carrying an electrical current.

circuitry - (DOD, IADB) A complex of circuits describing interconnection within or between systems.

circular error probable - (DOD, IADB) An indicator of the delivery accuracy of a weapon system, used as a factor in determining probable damage to a target. It is the radius of a circle within which half of the missiles/projectiles are expected to fall. Also called CEP. See also delivery error; deviation; dispersion error; horizontal error.

circular error probable - (NATO, CENTO) An indicator of the accuracy of a missile/projectile, used as a factor in determining probable damage to a target. It is the radius of a circle within which half of missiles-projectiles are expected to fall. See also delivery error; deviation; dispersion error; horizontal error.

cirvis - (DOD) Communications instructions for reporting vital intelligence sightings.

CIT - Counter Intelligence team.

citadel - A fortified defensive position in a battle.

civic action - See military civic action.

civil disturbance - (NATO, SEATO, CENTO, IADB) Group acts of violence and disorder prejudicial to public law and order.

civil affairs - (DOD, SEATO, IADB) Those phases of the activities of a commander which embrace the relationship between the military forces and civil authorities and people in a friendly country or area, or occupied country or area when military forces are present. Civil affairs include, inter alia: a. matters concerning the relationship between military forces located in a country or area and the civil authorities and people of that country or area usually involving performance by the military forces of certain functions or the exercise of certain authority normally the responsibility of the local government. This relationship may occur prior to, during, or subsequent to military action in time of hostilities or other emergency and is normally covered by a treaty or other agreement, expressed or implied; and b. military government: the form of administration by which an occupying power exercises executive, legislative, and judicial authority over occupied territory. See also phases of military government.

civil affairs - (NFSN, CENTO) Questions relating to relations in war time between the commander of an armed force and the civilian populations and governments in areas where the force is employed, and which are settled on the basis of a mutual agreement, official or otherwise.

civil affairs agreement - (DOD, IADB) An agreement which governs the relationship between allied armed forces located in a friendly country and the civil authorities and people of that country. See also civil affairs.

civil censorship - (DOD, IADB) Censorship of civilian communications, such as messages, printed matter, and films, entering, leaving, or circulating within areas or territories occupied or controlled by armed forces. See also censorship.

civil defense - (DOD, IADB) All those activities and measures designed or undertaken to: a. minimize the effects upon the civilian population caused or which would be caused by an enemy attack upon the United States; b. deal with the immediate emergency conditions which would be created by any such attack; and c. effectuate emergency repairs to, or the emergency restoration of, vital utilities and facilities destroyed or damaged by any such attack.

civil defense - (NATO, SEATO, CENTO) Mobilization, organization, and direction of the civil population, designed to minimize by passive measures the effects of enemy action against all aspects of civil life.

civil defense emergency - See domestic emergencies.

civil defense intelligence - (DOD) The product resulting from the collection and evaluation of information concerning all aspects of the situation in the United States and its territories that are potential or actual targets of any enemy attack to include, in the pre-attack phase, the emergency measures taken and estimates in the civil populations' preparedness. In the event of an actual attack, a description of conditions in the affected area with emphasis on the extent of damage, fallout levels, and casualty and resources estimates. The product is required by civil and military authorities for use in the formulation of decisions, the conduct of operations and the continuation of the planning processes.

civil disturbances - See domestic emergencies.

civil military cooperation - (NATO, CENTO) All actions or measures undertaken between (NATO) (CENTO) commanders and national authorities, military or civil, in peace or war, which concern the relationship between allied armed forces and the government, civil population, or agencies in the areas where such armed forces are stationed, supported, or employed.

civil nuclear power - (DOD, NATO, CENTO) A nation which has potential to employ nuclear technology for development of nuclear weapons, but has deliberately decided against doing so. See also nuclear power.

civil requirements - (DOD, IADB) The computed production and distribution of all types of services, supplies, and equipment during periods of armed conflict or occupation to insure the productive efficiency of the civilian economy and to provide civilians the treatment and protection to which they are entitled under customary and conventional international law.

civil reserve air fleet - (DOD) A group of commercial aircraft with crews which is allocated in time of emergency for exclusive military use in both international and domestic service.

civil transportation - (DOD) The movement of persons, property, or mail by civil facilities, and the resources (including storage, except that for agricultural and petroleum products) necessary to accomplish the movement. (Excludes transportation operated or controlled by the military, and petroleum and gas pipelines.)

civil-military relations (in non-(NATO)(CENTO) countries) - (NATO, CENTO) All activities undertaken by (NATO) (CENTO) commanders in war directly concerned with the relationship between allied armed forces and the government, civil population, or agencies of non-(NATO) (CENTO) countries where such armed forces are stationed, supported or employed.

civilian construction workers - See tiger ladies.

Civilian Irregular Defense Group - The mountain people of South Vietnam who were trained by U.S. Army Special Forces to defend their rural and remote villages from the Northern Vietnamese Forces.

civilian preparedness for war - (NATO, CENTO) All measures and means taken in peacetime, by national and allied agencies to enable a nation to survive an enemy attack and to contribute more effectively to the common war effort.

civilization - The U.S.A.

CL - See light cruiser.

clacker - The small hand-held firing device that launched claymore mines. See M-57 hand detonator.

CLAK - Clandestine kill.

clandestine kill - A silent killing, usually by a two-man ambush.

clandestine operation - (DOD, I, IADB) Activities to accomplish intelligence, counterintelligence, and other similar activities sponsored or conducted by governmental departments or agencies, in such a way as to assure secrecy or concealment. (DOD, I) (It differs from covert operations in that emphasis is placed on concealment of the operation rather than on concealment of identity of sponsor.)

clap - Venereal disease.

clap checker - A lower rank medical corps personnel.

clara - (DOD) In air intercept, a code meaning radar scope is clear of contacts other than those known to be friendly.

Class A, Class As - Army green lightweight uniform that replaced Army Tan in 1964.

Class Six Store - Military store authorized to sell liquor to Officers and NCOs.

classification - (DOD, IADB) The determination that official information requires, in the interests of national defense, a specific degree of protection against unauthorized disclosure, coupled with a designation signifying that such a determination has been made. See also defense classification.

classification of bridges and vehicles - (DOD, NATO, CENTO) Standard procedure for the parallel classification of bridges (or rafts, including their landing stages) and vehicles based on a range of vehicle types. The classification is applied by the allocation of class numbers to be marked on each vehicle and each bridge (or raft). See also military load classification; route classification.

classified contract - (DOD) Any contract that requires or will require access to classified information by the contractor or his employees in the performance of the contract. (A contract may be classified even though the contract document itself is not classified.)

classified information - (DOD, IADB) Official information which has been determined to require, in the interests of national defense, protection against unauthorized disclosure and which has been so designated.

classified matter - (DOD, NATO, CENTO, IADB) Official information or matter in any form or of any nature which requires protection in the interests of national security.

classified matter - (SEATO) Official information or material which requires protection in the national interest. See also unclassified matter.

claymore - The claymore mine.

claymore mine - An American made fan shaped antipersonnel mine carried by the infantry The mine is composed of a pound of C-4 explosive and 600 steel balls that explode in a fan shaped pattern of 50 yards and six feet in height. The mine can be detonated by a remote electrical command. Named for the Scottish broadsword by inventor Norman MacLeod. Designated M-18.

clean aircraft - (DOD, IADB) 1. An aircraft in flight configuration, versus landing configuration, i.e., landing gear and flaps retracted, etc. 2. An aircraft that does not have external stores.

clean sheets - Sleeping in a bed, not in the field.

clean weapon - (DOD, NATO, CENTO) A nuclear weapon in which measures have been taken to reduce the amount of residual radioactivity relative to a "normal" weapon of the same energy yield. See also salted weapon.

cleansing station - See decontamination station.

clear - (DOD, IADB) 1. To approve or authorize, or to obtain approval or authorization for: a. a person or persons with regard to their actions, movements, duties, etc.; b. an object or group of objects, as equipment or supplies, with regard to quality, quantity, purpose, movement, disposition, etc.; and c. a request, with regard to correctness of form, validity, etc. 2. Specifically, to give one or more aircraft a clearance. 3. To give a person a security clearance. 4. To fly over an obstacle without touching it. 5. To pass a designated point, line, or object. The end of a column must pass the designated feature before the latter is cleared. 6. a. To operate a gun so as to unload it or make certain no ammunition remains; and b. to free a gun of stoppages. 7. To clear an engine; to open the throttle of an idling engine to free it from carbon. 8. To clear the air to gain either temporary or permanent air superiority or control in a given sector.

clear a weapon - 1. Fire several rounds to confirm functioning. 2. Empty a weapon particularly a door mounted machine gun, before returning to base.

clear and hold - A military tactic used in Vietnam in which a unit would drive the Northern troops out of an area and other troops would keep the area clear of enemy as a maintenance effort. Also known as clear and secure.

clear and secure - See clear and hold.

clearance - 1. Requesting or granting permission to engage in combat. This can involve both the military and political approval. 2. The act of removal of the enemy from a specific area.

clearance capacity - (DOD, IADB) An estimate expressed in terms of measurement or weight tons per day of the cargo that may be transported inland from a beach or port over the available means of inland communication, including roads, railroads, and inland waterways. The estimate is based on an evaluation of the physical characteristics of the transportation facilities in the area. See also beach capacity; port capacity.

cleats - A tie down, usually of metal on a dock, allowing a line to be wrapped and tied down on it.

clenched fist salute - See Black Power salute.

clerks and jerks - Slang for rear echelon support staff. Also clerks-n-jerks.

CLG - See guided missile light cruiser.

click - One stop on a gun sight. See klick for slang for a kilometer.

clock code position - (DOD) The position of a target in relation to an aircraft or ship with dead-ahead position considered as twelve o'clock.

close - Aviation order to get closer, have less distance between planes. Pronounced kloz.

close air support - (DOD, NATO, SEATO, CENTO, IADB) Air attacks against hostile targets which are in close proximity to friendly forces and which require detailed integration of each air mission with the fire and movement of those forces. See also air interdiction; air support; immediate mission request; preplanned mission request. Note: NATO, SEATO, CENTO and IADB definition uses the words "air action" instead of the words "air attacks".

close support - (DOD, NATO, SEATO, CENTO, IADB) That action of the supporting force against targets or objectives which are sufficiently near the supported force as to require detailed integration or coordination of the supporting action with the fire, movement, or other actions of the supported force. See also support.

close supporting fire - (DOD, NATO, SEATO, CENTO, IADB) Fire placed on enemy troops, weapons, or positions which, because of their proximity, present the most immediate and serious threat to the supported unit. See also supporting fire.

close-controlled air interception - (DOD, NATO, SEATO, CENTO, IADB) An interception in which the interceptor is continuously controlled into a position from which the target is within visual range or radar contact. See also air interception; broadcast-controlled air interception.

closed area - (DOD, NATO, SEATO, CENTO, IADB) A designated area in or over which passage of any kind is prohibited.

closing the back door - 1. Army slang for the last man in a patrol formation who provides rear security and monitors for stragglers. 2. Air Force slang for the last aircraft in formation providing security from rear attack.

cloud chamber effect - See condensation cloud.

cloud nine - Elation, feeling good, happy.

cloud top height - (DOD) The maximum altitude to which a nuclear mushroom cloud rises.

cloverleaf - An infantry tactic used on patrol to send two small groups a forward of a main group. The advance groups would loop one far to the left and the other far to the right and then return to the main unit. If seen from above, the pattern left would resemble a cloverleaf.

cluster - (DOD, NATO, CENTO, IADB) l. Fireworks signal in which a group of stars burns at the same time. 2. Groups of bombs released together. A cluster usually consists of fragmentation or incendiary bombs. 3. (land mine warfare) Component of a pattern-laid minefield. It may be anti-tank, anti-personnel or mixed. It consists of one to five mines and no more than one anti-tank mine. 4. Two or more engines coupled together so as to function as one power unit. 5. Two or more parachutes for dropping light or heavy loads.

cluster (land mine warfare) - (SEATO) The unit of minelaying. It may be antitank, antipersonnel, or mixed. It normally consists of several mines but may contain only one mine.

cluster belt - Marine slang for cartridge belt.

cluster fuck - Slang for totally botched operation or screwed up personnel. Also rat fuck, boondoggle, Chinese fire drill.

clutch belt - Marine slang for cartridge belt.

clutter - (DOD) Permanent echoes, cloud, or other atmospheric echo on radar scope, or contact has entered scope clutter.

Clyde - Nickname for the enemy.

CM - Court martial.

CMH - 1. Casket with metal handles. 2. Center of Military History.

CMR - Court martial reports.

CMSAF - Chief Master Sergeant of the Air Force (Special- during wartime only.) (Air Force).

CMSgt - Chief Master Sergeant (Air Force).

CN - A type of tear gas. See CS.

CO - Commanding Officer.

co - Vietnamese for girl.

Co. - Abbreviation for company.

Coast Guard - The United States group attached to the Department of Transportation that saw service in Vietnam from 1965 securing the coastal waterways, providing security in port cities and supervising the transportation of munitions. In the United States, the Coast Guard provides aids to navigation and secures the coastal waterways.

coast-in point - (DOD) The point of coastal penetration heading inbound to a target or objective.

coastal convoy - (NATO, CENTO, IADB) A convoy whose voyage lies in general in coastal waters and whose ports/water terminals of departure and arrival lie in the same country. See also convoy.

coastal frontier - (DOD, IADB) A geographical division of a coastal area, established for organization and command purposes in order to insure the effective coordination of military forces employed in military operations within the coastal frontier area.

coastal frontier defense - (DOD) The organization of the forces and materiel of the armed forces assigned to provide security for the coastal frontiers of the continental United States and its overseas possessions.

coastal frontier defense - (IADB) The organization of the forces and materiel of the armed forces assigned to provide security for coastal frontiers.

coastal refraction - (NATO, CENTO) The change of the direction of travel of a radio ground wave as it passes from land to sea or from sea to land. Also called land effect and shore line effect.

Coasties - Slang for Coast Guardsmen.

coastwise traffic - (DOD) Sea traffic between continental United States ports on the Atlantic coast, Gulf coast, and Great Lakes, or between continental United States ports on the Pacific coast.

COBOL - A computer programming language. See common business oriented language.

Cobra - The assault helicopter, the AH-1G, with mini-guns, rockets and grenade launchers to provide close air support to ground troops. Service began in 1968 in significant numbers.

COC - 1. Combat Operations Center. 2. Combined Operations Center, an operational headquarters in the field.

cock bang - Slang for Bangkok.

cock rot - Venereal disease.

cockroach races - For entertainment troops would capture and race huge cockroaches for money.

cocksuckers - Leeches in the swampy water.

cocoanut mine - An improvised mine using a cocoanut to hold the shrapnel and explosive.

cocooning - (NATO, CENTO, IADB) The spraying or coating of an aircraft or equipment with a substance, e.g., a plastic, to form a cocoon-like seal against the effects of the atmosphere.

COD - 1. Carrier Onboard Delivery, an aircraft which moves personnel or supplies from shore to a carrier. 2. Close Order Drill.

code - (DOD, IADB) 1. Any system of communication in which arbitrary groups of symbols represent units of plain text of varying length. Codes may be used for brevity or for security. (DOD) 2. A cryptosystem in which the cryptographic equivalents (usually called "code groups") typically consisting of letters or digits (or both) in otherwise meaningless combinations are substituted for plain text elements which are primarily words, phrases, or sentences. See also cryptosystem.

Code of Conduct - The rules for U.S. military personnel if taken prisoner.

code word - (DOD) 1. A word which has been assigned a classification and a classified meaning to safeguard intentions and information regarding a classified plan or operation. 2. A cryptonym used to identify sensitive intelligence data.

code word - (NATO, CENTO, IADB) A word which conveys a meaning other than its conventional one, prearranged by the correspondents. Its aim is to increase security.

Codel - A Congressional delegation, visiting VIPs.

codeword - (SEATO) A classified word which conveys a classified meaning other than its conventional one, prearranged by using agencies. See also exercise codeword; inactive codeword; using agency.

COFRAM - Controlled fragmentation munitions, which contained bomblets.

COIN - Counterinsurgency.

COL - Colonel (Army).

Col - Colonel (Marine Corps, Air Force).

cold - No active fighting, as in a cold area. See hot.

cold LZ - A safe landing zone.

cold war - (DOD, SEATO, IADB) A state of international tension, wherein political, economic, technological, sociological, psychological, paramilitary and military measures short of overt armed conflict involving regular military forces are employed to achieve national objectives.

COLD/SOP - Standard Operating Procedures for clothing, and procedures for weather between 15 October and 15 April, which reduced the need for the heat related protections. See HOT/SOP.

collaborative purchase - (DOD, IADB) A method of purchase whereby, in buying similar commodities, buyers for two or more departments exchange information concerning planned purchases in order to minimize competition between them for commodities in the same market. See also purchase.

collapsible canteen - A 2-quart canteen with soft plastic sides which eliminated air in the canteen and sloshing that could disclose a soldier's presence.

collate - (DOD, NESN, CENTO) 1. The grouping together of related items to provide a record of events and facilitate further processing. (DOD) 2. To compare critically two or more items or documents concerning the same general subject; normally accomplished in the processing phase in the intelligence cycle.

collateral civilian damage - Damage to the property of or injury to civilians resulting from military action.

collecting point - (DOD, IADB) A point designated for the assembly of personnel casualties, prisoners of war, stragglers, disabled materiel, salvage, etc., for further movement to collecting stations or rear installations.

collection - (DOD) The exploitation of sources of information by collection agencies and the delivery of this information to the proper intelligence processing unit for use in the production of intelligence. The collection phase is divided into four main functions: a. guidance is the direction of the collection effort to insure meeting information needs in accordance with an established intelligence plan; b. coverage is the complete fulfillment of their missions by the collection agencies through full exploitation of all available sources of information and the use of initiative to discover new sources; c. reporting is the timely transmittal of information from the collection agency to the intelligence-producing unit; and d. selection is the process by which incoming information is made available to the appropriate researcher, insuring that each receives all the reports pertinent to his subject and a minimum of those in which he has no interest. Additionally, all material processed in the past is kept accessible to all researchers. See also intelligence cycle.

collection agency - (DOD, NATO, CENTO, IADB) Any individual, organization, or unit that has access to sources of information and the capability of collecting information from them.

collective call sign - (DOD, NATO, SEATO, CENTO, IADB) Any call sign which represents two or more facilities, commands, authorities, or units. The collective call sign for any of these includes the commander thereof and all subordinate commanders therein. See also call sign.

College Eye - Air Force airborne early warning radar system. Known as Big Eye from 1963 to 1967.

collimating marks - (NATO, CENTO) Index marks, rigidly connected with the camera body, which form images on the negative. These images are used to determine the position of the optical center or principal point of the imagery. Also known as fiducial marks.

collision course interception - (NATO, SEATO, CENTO, IADB) Any course whereby the interception is accomplished by the constant heading of both aircraft.

colors - 1. The flag. 2. The ceremony for raising or lowering the flag. 3. LSD.

Colt - A gun maker.

Colt commando - The 5.56-mm machine gun.

column cover - (DOD) Cover of a column by aircraft in contact therewith, providing for its protection by reconnaissance and/or attack of air or ground targets which threaten the column.

column cover - (NATO, SEATO, CENTO, IADB) Cover of a column by aircraft in radio contact therewith, providing for its protection by reconnaissance and/or attack of air or ground targets which threaten the column.

column formation - (DOD, NATO, CENTO, IADB) A formation in which elements are placed one behind the other.

column gap - (DOD, NATO, CENTO) The space between two consecutive elements proceeding in the same direction on the same route. It can be calculated in units of length or in units of time measured from the rear of one element to the front of the following element.

com rats - See commuted rations.

combat air patrol - (DOD, NATO, SEATO, CENTO, IADB) An aircraft patrol provided over an objective area, over the force protected, over the critical area of a combat zone, or over an air defense area, for the purpose of intercepting and destroying hostile aircraft before they reach their target. See also airborne alert; barrier combat air patrol; force combat air patrol; patrol; rescue combat air patrol; target combat air patrol.

combat area - (DOD, IADB) A restricted area (air, land, or sea) which is established to prevent or minimize mutual interference between friendly forces engaged in combat operations. See also combat zone.

combat cargo officer - (DOD, SEATO, IADB) An embarkation officer assigned to major amphibious ships or naval staffs, functioning primarily as an adviser to and representative of the naval commander in matters pertaining to embarkation and debarkation of troops and their supplies and equipment. See also embarkation officer.

combat control team - (DOD) A team of Air Force personnel organized, trained, and equipped to establish and operate navigational or terminal guidance aids, communications, and aircraft control facilities within the objective area of an airborne operation.

combat control team - (NATO, CENTO) A team of specially trained air force personnel who can airdrop into forward areas, to advise on all aspects of landing area requirements and to provide local air control.

combat crazy - See combat fatigue and flip out.

combat dump - Aviation slang for a having a bowel movement before taking off in a plane.

combat engineers - The group that prepared landing fields, roads, bridges and other infrastructure needed by troops prior to their arrival.

combat fatigue - Mental health diagnosis for a wide spectrum of issues arising from combat exposure.

combat film - (NATO, SEATO, CENTO , IADB) A film exposed to record combat.

combat forces - (DOD, IADB) Those forces whose primary missions are to participate in combat. See also operating forces.

Combat Infantry Badge - The Army award for infantrymen under fire in a combat zone.

combat information center - (DOD, NATO, SEATO, CENTO, IADB) The agency in a ship or aircraft manned and equipped to collect, display, evaluate, and disseminate tactical information for the use of the embarked flag officer, commanding officer, and certain control agencies. Certain control, assistance, and coordination functions may be delegated by command to the combat information center. See also air defense control center.

combat information ship - (DOD, IADB) A designated ship charged with the coordination of the intership combat information center functions of the various ships in a task force so that the overall combat information available to commands will be increased. This ship normally is the flagship of the task force commander. See also fighter direction aircraft; fighter direction ship.

combat intelligence - (DOD) That knowledge of the enemy, weather, and geographical features required by a commander in the planning and conduct of combat operations. See also intelligence.

combat intelligence - (NATO, SEATO, CENTO, IADB) That knowledge of the enemy, weather, and geographical features required by a commander in the planning and conduct of tactical operations. See also intelligence.

combat load (air force) - (NATO, CENTO) The total warlike stores carried by an aircraft.

combat loading - (DOD, NATO, SEATO, CENTO, IADB) The arrangement of personnel and the stowage of equipment and supplies in a manner designed to conform to the anticipated tactical operation of the organization embarked. Each individual item is stowed so that it can be unloaded at the required time. See also loading.

Combat Medic Badge - The Army award for medical personnel under fire in a combat zone available to Marine, Navy and Air Force medical personnel as well.

combat patrol - (NATO, CENTO) Tactical unit sent out from the main body to engage in independent fighting; detachment assigned to protect the front, flank, or rear of the main body, by fighting if necessary. See also airborne alert; combat air patrol; patrol; reconnaissance patrol (ground).

combat pay - An addition to base pay of $65 a month in Vietnam. See hazardous duty pay.

combat professor - Military advisors.

combat readiness - (DOD) Synonymous with "operational readiness," with respect to missions or functions performed in combat.

combat readiness - (IADB) The capability of a unit/ship to perform its assigned missions as derived from approved plans. The status of personnel, equipment, supplies, maintenance, facilities, and training is considered in determining this capability.

combat ready - (DOD) Synonymous with "operationally ready," with respect to missions or functions performed in combat.

combat ready/readiness - (NATO, SEATO, CENTO) 1. Applied to organizations or equipment, means availability for combat operations. 2. Applied to personnel, means qualified to carry out combat operations in the unit to which they are assigned.

combat refusal - Euphemism for "mutiny" to avoid legal charges.

combat service support - (DOD) The assistance provided operating forces primarily in the fields of administrative services, chaplain service, civil affairs, finance, legal service, maintenance, medical service, military police, supply, transportation, and other logistical services.

combat service support elements - (DOD, IADB) Those elements whose primary missions are to provide service support to combat forces and which are a part, or prepared to become a part, of a theater, command, or task force formed for combat operations. See also operating forces; service troops; troops.

combat sky strike - A bombing run controlled by radar from the ground.

combat spread - In aviation, a formation with significant space between planes to allow maximum visibility

combat support elements - (DOD, IADB) Those elements whose primary missions are to provide combat support to the combat forces and which are a part, or prepared to become a part, of a theater, command, or task force formed for combat operations. See also operating forces.

combat support troops - (DOD, IADB) Those units or organizations whose primary mission is to furnish operational assistance for the combat elements. See also troops.

combat surveillance - (DOD, IADB) A continuous, all-weather, day-and-night, systematic watch over the battle area to provide timely information for tactical combat operations.

combat surveillance radar - (DOD) Radar with the normal function of maintaining continuous watch over a combat area.

combat survival - (DOD, NATO, SEATO, CENTO, IADB) Those measures to be taken by service personnel when involuntarily separated from friendly forces in combat, including procedures relating to individual survival, evasion, escape, and conduct after capture.

combat tracker team - A team of five men and a tracker dog searching for the enemy.

combat trail - (DOD) Interceptors in trail formation. Each interceptor behind the leader maintains position visually or with airborne radar.

combat tree - In aviation, the code name of a secret system allowing enemy MiG aircraft to be identified from their electronic IFF (Identification Friend or Foe) signals well before the plane could be seen visually.

combat troops - (DOD, IADB) Those units or organizations whose primary mission is destruction of enemy forces and/or installations. See also troops.

combat vehicle (fighting) - (DOD, IADB) A vehicle, with or without armor, designed for a specific fighting function. Armor protection or armament mounted as supplemental equipment on noncombat vehicles will not change the classification of such vehicles to combat vehicles. See also vehicle.

combat zone - (DOD, NATO, SEATO, CENTO, IADB) 1. That area required by combat forces for the conduct of operations. 2. The territory forward of the Army rear area boundary. See also combat area; communications zone.

combat/fighting patrol (ground) - (SEATO, IADB) Tactical unit sent out from the main body to engage in independent fighting; detachment assigned to protect the front, flank, or rear of the main body, by fighting, if necessary. See also combat air patrol; patrol; reconnaissance patrol (ground).

combination mission/level of effort-oriented items - (DOD) Items for which requirements computations are based upon the criteria used for both level of effort-oriented and mission-oriented items.

combined - (DOD, NATO, SEATO, CENTO) Between two or more forces or agencies of two or more allies. (When all allies or Services are not involved, the participating nations and Services shall be identified, e.g., combined Navies.) See also joint.

combined - (IADB) Between two or more forces or agencies of two or more allies. See also joint.

Combined Action Group - A small group of Marines and local militia to protect villages.

Combined Action Platoon - Marine Corps pacification program in rural areas in which Marines were stationed in hamlets and provided security, road building and medical support.

combined common user items - (NATO, SEATO, CENTO, IADB) Items of an interchangeable nature which are in common use by two or more nations.

combined force - (DOD, NATO, SEATO, CENTO, IADB) A military force composed of elements of two or more allied nations. See also force(s).

combined operation - (DOD, NATO, SEATO, CENTO, IADB) An operation conducted by forces of two or more allied nations acting together for the accomplishment of a single mission.

combined staff - (DOD, NATO, SEATO, CENTO, IADB) A staff composed of personnel of two or more allied nations. See also integrated staff; joint staff; parallel staff; staff.

combustor - (DOD, NATO, SEATO, CENTO, IADB) A name generally assigned to the combination of flame holder or stabilizer, igniter, combustion chamber, and injection system of a ramjet or gas turbine.

comics - Slang for the topographical maps, used sarcastically due to the unreliability of the old French maps used at the start of the war.

command - (DOD, IADB) 1. The authority which a commander in the military Service lawfully exercises over his subordinates by virtue of rank or assignment. Command includes the authority and responsibility for effectively using available resources and for planning the employment of, organizing, directing, coordinating, and controlling military forces for the accomplishment of assigned missions. It also includes responsibility for health, welfare, morale, and discipline of assigned personnel. 2. An order given by a commander; that is, the will of the commander expressed for the purpose of bringing about a particular action. 3. A unit or units, an organization, or an area under the command of one individual. 4. To dominate by a field of weapon fire or by observation from a superior position. See also air command; area command; base command.

command - (NATO, SEATO, CENTO) 1. The authority vested in an individual of the armed forces for the direction, coordination, and control of military forces. 2. An order given by a commander; that is, the will of the commander expressed for the purpose of bringing about a particular action. 3. A unit or units, an organization, or an area under the command of one individual. 4. To dominate by a field of weapon fire or by observation from a superior position. See also area command; base command; full command; national command; operational command.

command altitude - (DOD) Altitude which must be assumed and/or maintained by the interceptor.

command and control - (DOD) The exercise of authority and direction by a properly designated commander over assigned forces in the accomplishment of his mission. Command and control functions are performed through an arrangement of personnel, equipment, communications, facilities, and procedures which are employed by a commander in planning, directing, coordinating, and controlling forces and operations in the accomplishment of his mission.

command and control - (IADB) An arrangement of personnel, facilities, and the means for information acquisition, processing, and dissemination employed by a commander in planning, directing, and controlling operations.

command and control system - (DOD) The facilities, equipment, communications, procedures, and personnel essential to a commander for planning, directing, and controlling operations of assigned forces pursuant to the missions assigned.

command axis - (DOD, NATO, SEATO, CENTO, IADB) A line along which a headquarters will move.

command bird - The plane with the unit commander on board, issuing orders while looking at the area of combat from above.

command center - (DOD) A facility from which a commander and his representatives direct operations and control forces. It is organized to gather, process, analyze, display and disseminate planning and operational data and perform other related tasks.

command channel - See chain of command.

command destruct signal - (DOD, NATO, CENTO) A signal used to operate intentionally the destruction system in a missile.

command guidance - (DOD, NESN, IADB) A guidance system wherein intelligence transmitted to the missile from an outside source causes the missile to traverse a directed flight path. See also guidance.

command heading - (DOD) Heading that the controlled aircraft is directed to assume by the control station.

command net - (DOD, NATO, SEATO, CENTO, IADB) A communications network which connects an echelon of command with some or all of its subordinate echelons for the purpose of command control.

command post - (DOD, NATO, SEATO, CENTO, IADB) A unit's or subunit's headquarters where the commander and the staff perform their activities. In combat, a unit's or subunit's headquarters is often divided into echelons; the echelon in which the unit or subunit commander is located or from which he operates is called a command post.

command post exercise - (DOD, NATO, SEATO, CENTO, IADB) An exercise involving the commander, his staff, and communications within and between headquarters. See also exercise; maneuver.

command speed - (DOD) The speed at which the controlled aircraft is directed to fly.

command sponsored dependent - (DOD) A dependent entitled to travel to oversea commands at Government expense and indorsed by the appropriate military commander to be present in a dependent's status.

commander's concept of operations - See concept of operations.

commander's estimate of the situation - (DOD, IADB) A logical process of reasoning by which a commander considers all the circumstances affecting the military situation and arrives at a decision as to a course of action to be taken to accomplish his mission. A commander's estimate which considers a military situation so far in the future as to require major assumptions is called a commander's estimate of the situation. See also estimate of situation.

commander(s) - See executing commander (nuclear weapons); exercise commander; major NATO commanders; national commander; national force commanders; national territorial commander; releasing commander (nuclear weapons).

commercial items - (DOD) Articles of supply readily available from established commercial distribution sources, which the Department of Defense or inventory managers in the military Services have designated to be obtained directly or indirectly from such source.

commercial loading - (SEATO, IADB) The loading of personnel and/or equipment and supplies for maximum use of space. Sometimes called "administrative loading". See also administrative loading; loading.

commercial-type vehicle - (DOD, IADB) A vehicle designed to meet civilian requirements and used, without major modifications, for routine purposes in connection with the transportation of supplies, personnel, or equipment. See also vehicle.

commfu - Slang for military situation that is hopelessly fucked up.

COMMIKE - A microphone that could be activated or closed remotely.

commission - (DOD, IADB) 1. To put in or make ready for service or use, as to commission an aircraft or a ship. 2. A written order giving a person rank and authority as an officer in the armed forces. 3. The rank and the authority given by such an order. See also activate; constitute.

commit - (DOD) The process of committing one or more air interceptors or surface-to-air missiles for interception against a target track.

commo - Slang for communications.

commo bunker - The communications center and/or equipment located in a protected bunker.

commo check - Checking communications equipment and operation.

commo track - See M-577 ACC.

commo wire - All purpose electrical wire used in communication and electrical applications, WD-1.

commodity loading - (DOD, NATO, SEATO, CENTO, IADB) A method of loading in which various types of cargo are loaded together, such as ammunition, rations, or boxed vehicles, in order that each commodity can be discharged without disturbing the others. See also loading.

commodity manager - (DOD) An individual within the organization of an inventory control point or other such organization assigned management responsibility for homogeneous grouping of materiel items.

Commodore - A title, not a rank, for most of the Vietnam War. Retained in some areas as a holdover from the use in WWII. Commodore titles were converted into one of the two Rear Admiral ranks after the war ended. See Rear Admiral.

common business oriented language - (DOD, IADB) A specific language by which business data processing procedures may be precisely described in a standard form. The language is intended not only as a means for directly presenting any business program to any suitable computer, for which a compiler exists, but also as a means of communicating such procedures among individuals.

common control - (DOD, NATO, CENTO) Horizontal and vertical map or chart location of points in the target area and position area, tied in with the horizontal and vertical control in use by two or more units. May be established by firing, survey or combination of both, or by assumption. See also control point; field control; ground control. (Note: NATO and CENTO term has qualifier "artillery".)

common infrastructure - (DOD, NATO) Infrastructure essential to the training of NATO forces or to the implementation of NATO operational plans which, owing to its degree of common use or interest and its compliance with criteria laid down from time to time by the North Atlantic Council, is commonly financed by NATO members. See also infrastructure.

common infrastructure - (SEATO) Infrastructure essential to the training of SEATO forces or to the implementation of SEATO operational plans which is commonly financed by SEATO members.

common item - (DOD) 1. Any item of materiel which is required for use by more than one activity. 2. Sometimes loosely used to denote any consumable item except repair parts or other technical items. 3. Any item of materiel which is procured for, owned by (service stock), or used by any military department of the Department of Defense and which is also required to be furnished to a recipient country under the grant-aid Military Assistance Program. 4. Readily available commercial items. 5. Items used by two or more military Services of similar manufacture or fabrication which may vary between the Services as to color or shape (as vehicles or clothing). 6. Any part or component which is required in the assembly of two or more complete end items.

common servicing - (DOD) That function performed by one military Service in support of another military Service for which reimbursement is not required from the Service receiving support. See also servicing.

common supplies - (DOD, IADB) Those supplies common to two or more Services.

common use - (DOD) Services materials or facilities provided by a Department of Defense agency or a military department on a common basis for two or more Department of Defense agencies.

common user airlift service - (DOD) In military transport service usage, the airlift service provided on a common basis for all Department of Defense agencies and, as authorized, for other agencies of the United States Government.

common user network - (DOD) A system of circuits or channels allocated to furnish communication paths between switching centers to provide communication service on a common basis to all connected stations or subscribers. It is sometimes described as a General Purpose Network.

common-user military land transportation - (DOD) Point-to-point land transportation service operated by a single Service for common use by two or more Services.

common-user ocean terminals - (DOD) A military installation, part of a military installation, or a commercial facility operated under contract or arrangement by the Military Traffic Management and Terminal Service which regularly provides for two or more Services, terminal functions of receipt, transit storage or staging, processing loading and unloading of passengers or cargo aboard ships.

commubird - A communication system based on an airborne linkage.

communication deception - (DOD) Use of devices, operations, and techniques with the intent of confusing or misleading the user of a communications link or a navigation system.

communication operation instructions - See signal operation instructions.

communication tunnel - The connecting tunnel between two chambers in the Viet Cong tunnels.

communications - (DOD, IADB) A method or means of conveying information of any kind from one person or place to another, except by direct unassisted conversation or correspondence through nonmilitary postal agencies.

communications center - (DOD) A facility responsible for the reception, transmission and delivery of messages. Its normal elements are a message center section, a cryptographic section and a sending and receiving section, using electronic communications devices.

communications center - (NATO, CENTO) An agency charged with the responsibility for receipt, transmission, and delivery of messages.

communications intelligence - (DOD, IADB) Technical and intelligence information derived from foreign communications by other than the intended recipients. Also called COMINT.

communications intelligence database - (DOD) The aggregate of technical and intelligence information derived from the intercept and analysis of foreign communications (excluding press, propaganda, and public broadcast), which is used in the direction and redirection of Communications Intelligence Intercept, analysis and reporting activities.

communications mark - (DOD) An electronic indicator used for directing attention to a particular object or position of mutual interest within or between command and control systems.

communications network - (DOD, IADB) An organization of stations capable of intercommunications but not necessarily on the same channel.

communications satellite - (DOD, NATO, CENTO, IADB) An orbiting vehicle, which relays signals between communications stations. They are of two types: a. active communications satellite-A satellite which receives, regenerates, and retransmits signals between stations; and b. passive communications satellite-A satellite which reflects communications signals between stations.

communications security - (DOD, IADB) The protection resulting from all measures designed to deny unauthorized persons information of value which might be derived from the possession and study of telecommunications, or to mislead unauthorized persons in their interpretation of the results of such possession and study.

COMSEC includes: (1) cryptosecurity; (2) transmission security; (3) emission security; and (4) physical security of communications security materials and information. a. (cryptosecurity) - The component of communications security which results from the provision of technically sound cryptosystems and their proper use. b. (transmission security) - The component of communications security which results from all measures designed to protect transmissions from interception and exploitation by means other than cryptanalysis. c. (emission security) - The component of communications security which results from all measures taken to deny unauthorized persons information of value which might be derived from intercept and analysis of compromising emanations from cryptoequipment and telecommunications systems. d. (physical security) - The component of communications security which results from all physical measures necessary to safeguard classified equipment, material, and documents from access thereto or observation thereof by unauthorized persons.

communications security equipment - (DOD, IADB) Equipment designed to provide security to telecommunications by converting information to a form unintelligible to an unauthorized interceptor and by reconverting such information to its original form for authorized recipients as well as equipment designed specifically to aid in, or as an essential element of, the conversion process. COMSEC equipment is cryptoequipment, cryptoancillary equipment, cryptoproduction equipment, and authentication equipment.

communications security material - (DOD, IADB) All documents devices, equipment, or apparatus, including cryptomaterial, used in establishing or maintaining secure communications.

communications security monitoring - (DOD) The act of listening to, copying, or recording transmissions of one's own circuits (or when specially agreed, e.g., in Allied exercises, those of friendly forces) to provide material for COMSEC analysis in order to determine the degree of security being provided to those transmissions. In particular, the purposes include providing a basis for (1) advising commanders on the security risks resulting from their transmissions, (2) improving the security of communications, and (3) planning and conducting manipulative communications deception operations.

communications zone - (DOD, NATO, SEATO, CENTO, IADB) Rear part of theater of operations (behind but contiguous to the combat zone) which contains the lines of communications, establishments for supply and evacuation, and other agencies required for the immediate support and maintenance of the field forces. See also combat zone; rear area.

communications/signal center - (SEATO, IADB) An agency charged with the responsibility for receipt, transmission, and delivery of messages. See also message center.

community relations - (DOD, IADB) The relationship between military and civilian communities.

community relations program - (DOD) That command function which evaluates public attitudes, identifies the mission of a military organization with the public interest, and executes a program of action to earn public understanding and acceptance. Community relations programs are conducted at all levels of command, both in the United States and overseas, by military organizations having a community relations area of responsibility. Community relations programs include, but are not limited to, such activities as liaison and cooperation with associations and organizations and their local affiliates at all levels; armed forces participation in international, national, regional, state, and local public events; installation open houses and tours, embarkations in naval ships, orientation tours for distinguished civilians; people-to-people and humanitarian acts; cooperation with government officials and community leaders; and encouragement of armed forces personnel and their dependents to participate in activities of local schools, churches, fraternal, social, and civic organizations, sports and recreation programs, and other aspects of community life to the extent feasible and appropriate, regardless of where they are located.

community relations program - (IADB) That command function which evaluates public attitudes, identifies the mission of a military organization with the public interest, and executes a program of action to earn public understanding and acceptance. Community relations programs include, but are not limited to, such activities as liaison and cooperation with associations and organizations and their local affiliates at all levels; armed forces participation in international, national, regional, state, and local public events; installation open houses and tours, embarkations in naval ships, orientation tours for distinguished civilians; people-to-people and humanitarian acts; cooperation with government officials and community leaders; and encouragement of armed forces personnel and their dependents to participate in activities of civic organizations, sports and recreation programs, and other aspects of community life to the extent feasible and appropriate, regardless of where they are located.

commuted rations - Pay in lieu of eating meals on base, compensation for meals eaten off base. See com rats.

COMNAVFORV - Commander of United States Naval Forces, Vietnam company, the military unit commanded by a Captain and the basic element of a military operation. It is composed of two or more platoons. The cavalry company is called a troop and the artillery company is called a battalion.

company - A group of two or more platoons and a headquarters.

company lift - The number of helicopters in a flight.

company uniform - 1. Radio code for the radio frequency assigned to a specific company. These were changed frequently. 2. Changing the radio frequency and announcing it to keep all in the company on the same frequency.

comparative cover - (DOD, NATO, CENTO, IADB) Coverage of the same area or object taken at different times, to show any changes in details. See also cover.

compartment marking - (NATO, CENTO) In an aircraft, a system of marking a cabin into compartments for the positioning of loads in accordance with the weight and balance requirements.

compartmentalization- (DOD) 1. Establishment and management of an intelligence organization so that information about the personnel, organization, or activities of one component is made available to any other component only to the extent required for the performance of assigned duties. 2. Effects of relief and drainage upon avenues of approach so as to produce areas bounded on at least two sides by terrain features such as woods, ridges, or ravines that limit observation or observed fire into the area from points outside the area.

compass - See deviation; grid magnetic angle; magnetic compass; magnetic variation.

compass north - (DOD, NATO, IADB) The uncorrected direction by the north-seeking end of a compass needle. See also magnetic north.

compass rose - (DOD, NATO, CENTO, IADB) A graduated circle, usually marked in degrees, indicating directions and printed or inscribed on an appropriate medium.

compassionate leave - Emergency leave to go stateside to attend to serious family emergency such as illness or death.

compassionate loan - The temporary reassignment of a soldier, not for military reasons. For example to be to be closer to relative who is also a soldier recovering in a hospital.

compatibility - (NATO, CENTO) Capability of two or more items or components of equipment or material to exist or function in the same system or environment without mutual interference. See also interchangeability.

compilation - (NATO) Selection, assembly and graphic presentation of all relevant information required for the preparation of a map or chart. Such information may be derived from other maps or charts or from other sources.

compilation diagram - (NATO) A diagram giving details of the source material from which the map or chart has been compiled, this does not necessarily include reliability information. See also reliability diagram.

complaint-type investigation - (DOD) A counterintelligence investigation in which sabotage, espionage, treason, sedition, subversive activity, or disaffection is suspected.

complete round - (DOD, IADB) A term applied to an assemblage of explosive and nonexplosive components designed to perform a specific function at the time and under the conditions desired. Examples of complete rounds of ammunition are: a.

(separate loading) - consisting of a primer, propelling charge and except for blank ammunition, a projectile and a fuze; b. (fixed or semifixed) - consisting of a primer, propelling charge, cartridge case, a projectile and a fuze except when solid projectiles are used; c. (bomb) - consisting of all component parts required to drop and function the bomb once; d. (missile) - consisting of a complete warhead section and a missile body with its associated components and propellants; and e. (rocket) - consisting of all components necessary for it to function.

complete round - (NATO, CENTO) A basic munition, such as a shell, when all the components, explosive and non-explosive, necessary for it to function, are included.

component life - (NATO, CENTO, IADB) The period of acceptable usage after which the likelihood of failure sharply increases and before which the components are removed in the interests of reliability of operation.

component search and rescue controller - (DOD, IADB) The designated search and rescue representative of a component commander of a unified command, who is responsible in the name of his component commander for the control of component search and rescue forces committed to joint search and rescue operations. See also search and rescue.

composite air photography - (DOD) Air photographs made with a camera having one principal lens and two or more surrounding and oblique lenses. The several resulting photographs are corrected or transformed in printing to permit assembly as verticals with the same scale.

Composite Air Strike Force - (DOD) A group of selected United States Air Force units composed of appropriate elements of tactical air power (tactical fighters, tactical reconnaissance, tankers, airlift, and command and control elements) capable of employing a spectrum of nuclear and nonnuclear weapons. Composite Air Strike Force forces are held in readiness for immediate deployment from the continental United States to all areas of the world to meet national emergency contingency plans.

Composite Marine Aircraft Group - A group of both fixed wing airplanes and helicopters.

compromise - (DOD) The known or suspected exposure of clandestine personnel, installations or other assets, or of classified information or material, to an unauthorized person.

compromised - (DOD, NATO, SEATO, CEN· TO, IADB) A term applied to classified matter, knowledge of which has, in whole or in part, passed to an unauthorized person or persons, or which has been subject to risk of such passing. See also classified matter.

computed air release point - (NATO, CENTO, IADB) A computer air position where the first paratroop or cargo item is released to land on a specified impact point.

COMSEC - Communications security. This includes the following equipment: cryptoequipment, cryptoancillary equipment, cryptoproduction equipment, and authentication equipment. See communications security.

COMUSMACV - Commander of United States Military Assistance Command, Vietnam

Con biet? - Vietnamese for do you understand?

concealment - (DOD, NATO, SEATO, CENTO, IADB) The protection from observation only. See also camouflage; cover.

concentrated fire - (NATO, SEATO, CENTO, IADB) 1. The fire of the batteries of two or more ships directed against a single target. 2. Fire from a number of weapons, directed at a single point or small area. See also fire; massed fire.

concentration area - (DOD, IADB) 1. An area, usually in the area of operations, where troops are assembled before beginning active operations. 2. A limited area on which a volume of gunfire is placed within a limited time.

concentration area - (NATO, SEATO, CENTO) 1. An area, usually in the theater of operations, where troops are assembled before beginning active operations. 2. A limited area on which a volume of gunfire is placed within a limited time.

concept of operations - (DOD, IADB) A verbal or written statement, in broad outline, of a commander's assumptions or intent in regard to an operation or series of operations. The concept of operations frequently is embodied in campaign plans and operation plans, in the latter case particularly when the plan covers a series of connected operations to be carried out simultaneously or in succession. The concept is designed to give an overall picture of the operation. It is included primarily for additional clarity of purpose, and is frequently referred to as commander's concept.

concept of operations - (NATO, SEATO, CENTO) A verbal or graphic statement, in broad outline, of a commander's assumptions or intent in regard to an operation or series of operations. The concept of operations frequently is embodied in campaign plans and operation plans; in the latter case particularly when the plan covers a series of connected operations to be carried out simultaneously or in succession. The concept is designed to give an overall picture of the operation. It is included primarily for additional clarity of purpose. Frequently referred to as commander's concept.

concertina or concertina wire - A type of barbed wire that is strung in loose circles reminiscent of the concertina musical instrument. It can be added to the top of chain link fences or laid on the ground without posts. Also accordion wire.

condensation cloud - (DOD) A mist or fog of minute water droplets which temporarily surrounds the fireball following a nuclear (or atomic) detonation in a comparatively humid atmosphere. The expansion of the air in the negative phase of the blast wave from the explosion results in a lowering of the temperature, so that condensation of water vapor present in the air occurs and a cloud forms. The cloud is soon dispelled when the pressure returns to normal and the air warms up again. The phenomenon is similar to that used by physicists in the Wilson cloud chamber and is sometimes called the cloud chamber effect.

condensation trail - (DOD, IADB) A visible cloud streak, usually brilliantly white in color, which trails behind a missile or other vehicle in flight under certain conditions. Also called vapor trail or contrail.

condensation trail - (NATO, CENTO) A visible cloud streak, usually brilliantly white in color, which trails behind a missile or other vehicle in flight under certain conditions. Also called vapor trail.

condition CAP - A warning to standby for a sudden helicopter liftoff.

conducting staff - See directing staff.

cone of silence - (NATO, SEATO, CENTO, IADB) An inverted cone-shaped space directly over the aerial towers of some forms of radio beacons in which signals are unheard or greatly reduced in volume. See also Z marker beacon. "

conex - A corrugated metal packing crate that was six feet long, often left at a base and used for shelter above ground at a fire base. From: Container, express. Also spelled connex.

Coney Island - Slang for Khe Sanh base for the intense nighttime illumination.

confidential - See defense classification.

confirmation of information (intelligence) - (DOD, NATO, CENTO, IADB) An information item is said to be confirmed when it is reported for the second time, preferably by another independent source whose reliability is considered when confirming information.

confirms - Number of confirmed kills.

confused - (DOD) In air intercept, a term meaning individual contacts not identifiable.

confusion agent - (DOD) An individual who is dispatched by his sponsor for the primary purpose of confounding the intelligence or counterintelligence apparatus of another country rather than for the purpose of collecting and transmitting information.

Cong - Slang for Viet Cong.

Congressional Medal of Honor - Although authorized by Congress and presented by the President of the United States, it is properly referred to as the Medal of Honor. The highest military honor for bravery and intrepidity in fighting an enemy. There were 246 Medals of Honor awarded during the Vietnam War.

Congressionals - Correspondence from a member of Congress on behalf of a constituent with a complaint or their own inquiry.

conning - Aviation term for making a contrail.

Conscientious Objector - A person objecting to the war or killing on moral grounds. The Selective Service allowed 170,000 requests for CO status, many of whom did non-military or non-combat duty.

consol - (DOD, NATO, SEATO, CENTO, IADB) A long-range radio aid to navigation, the emissions of which, by means of their radio frequency modulation characteristics, enable bearings to be determined.

console - (DOD, NATO, CENTO, IADB) A grouping of controls, indicators, and similar electronic or mechanical equipment, used to monitor readiness of and/or control specific functions of a system, such as missile check-out, countdown, or launch operations.

consolidated vehicle table - (DOD, IADB) A summary of all vehicles loaded on a ship, listed by types, and showing the units to which they belong.

consolidation of position - (DOD, NATO, SEATO, CENTO, IADB) Organizing and strengthening a newly captured position so that it can be used against the enemy.

constant of the cone - (NATO) 1. For Lambert Conical Orthomorphic projection, see grid convergence factor. 2. See also convergence factor.

Constellation - See EC-121, an aircraft.

constitute - (DOD, IADB) To provide the legal authority for the existence of a new unit of the armed Services. The new unit is designated and listed but it has no specific existence until it is activated. See also activate; commission.

consumable supplies and material - See expendable supplies and material.

consumer - (DOD) Person or agency that uses information or intelligence produced by either its own staff or other agencies.

consumer logistics - (IADB) Those basic elements of logistics, normally of concern to operational chain of command, involving: a. requirement determination; and b. asset distribution after delivery to control of a commander below departmental level.

consumption rate - (DOD, NATO, CENTO) The average quantity of an item consumed or expended during a given time interval, expressed in quantities by the most appropriate unit of measurement per applicable stated basis.

contact - (DOD) In air intercept, a term meaning unit has an unevaluated target.

contact - Slang radio term for contact with enemy and firing or being fired upon.

contact burst preclusion - (DOD) A fuzing arrangement which prevents an unwanted surface burst in the event of failure of the air burst fuze.

contact lost - (DOD, NATO, CENTO) A target tracking term used to signify that a target believed to be still within the area of visual, sonar, or radar coverage is temporarily lost but the termination of track plotting is not warranted.

contact point - (DOD) 1. In land warfare, a point on the terrain, easily identifiable, where two or more units are required to make contact. 2. In air operations, the position at which a flight leader makes radio contact with an air control agency. See also forward air controller; pull-up point; turn-in point.

contact point - (NATO, CENTO, IADB) 1. In land warfare, a point on the terrain, easily identifiable, where two or more units are required to make contact. 2. In close air support, a position at which the strike leader makes initial radio telephone contact with the forward air controller. See also air control team; pull-up point (close air support); turn-in point (close air support).

contact print - (DOD, NATO, CENTO) A print made from a negative or a diapositive in direct contact with sensitized material.

contact reconnaissance - (DOD) Locating isolated units out of contact with the main force.

contact report - (DOD, NATO, SEATO, CENTO, IADB) A report of visual, radio, sonar, or radar contact with the enemy. The first report, giving the information immediately available when the contact is first made, is known as an initial contact report. Subsequent reports containing additional information are referred to as amplifying reports. See also sighting.

contain - (DOD, NATO, SEATO, CENTO, IADB) To stop, hold, or surround the forces of the enemy or to cause the enemy to center his activity on a given front and to prevent his withdrawing any part of his forces for use elsewhere.

contamination - (DOD, NATO, SEATO, CENTO, IADB) The deposit and/or absorption of radioactive material, biological, or chemical agents on and by structures, areas, personnel, or objects. See also induced radiation; residual radiation.

contamination control line - (NATO, CENTO) A line established by competent authority identifying the area contaminated to a specific level of the contaminant of interest. See also contamination.

contamination control point - (NATO, CENTO) That portion of the contamination control line used by personnel to control entry to and exit from the contaminated area. See also contamination.

continental United States (CONUS) - (DOD, IADB) United States territory, including the adjacent territorial waters, located within the North American continent between Canada and Mexico.

contingency plan - (DOD, IADB) A plan for major contingencies which can reasonably be anticipated in the principal geographic subareas of the command.

contingency plan - (NATO, CENTO) A plan for contingencies which can reasonably be anticipated in an area of responsibility.

contingency planning facilities list program - (DOD) A joint Defense Intelligence Agency/unified and specified command program for the production and maintenance of current target documentation of all countries of contingency planning interest to United States military planners.

contingency retention stock - (DOD) That portion of the quantity of an item excess to the approved force retention level for which there is no predictable demand or quantifiable requirement, and which normally would be allocated as potential Department of Defense excess stock, except for a determination that the quantity will be retained for possible contingencies for United States forces. (Category C ships, aircraft, and other items being retained as contingency reserve are included in this stratum.)

contingency retention stock - (IADB) That portion of the quantity of an item in long supply for which no programmed requirement exists and which normally would be considered as excess stock, but which it has been determined will be retained for possible military or defense contingencies; however, no portion of any item to be retained as contingency retention stock may be retained as economic retention stock. See also reserve supplies.

contingent effects - (DOD) The effects, both desirable and undesirable, which are in addition to the primary effects associated with a nuclear detonation.

contingent zone of fire - (DOD) An area within which a designated ground unit or fire support ship may be called upon to deliver fire. See also zone of fire.

contingent zone of fire - (IADB) An area within the zone of fire, other than the normal zone, within which an artillery unit may be called upon to fire under certain contingencies. See also zone of fire.

continue port/starboard - (DOD) In air intercept, a term meaning continue turning port/ starboard at present rate of turn to magnetic heading indicated (3 figures) or continue turning port/starboard for number of degrees indicated.

continuity of command - (DOD) The degree or state of being continuous in the exercise of the authority vested in an individual of the armed forces for the direction, coordination and control of military forces.

continuity of operations - (DOD) The degree or state of being continuous in the conduct of functions, tasks or duties necessary to accomplish a military action or mission in carrying out the national military strategy. It includes the functions and duties of the commander, as well as the supporting functions and duties performed by his staff and other acting under the authority and direction of the commander.

continuous fire - (DOD) 1. Fire conducted at a normal rate without interruption for application of adjustment corrections or for other causes. 2. In artillery and naval gunfire support, loading and firing as rapidly as possible, consistent with accuracy, within the prescribed rate of fire for the weapon. Firing will continue until the command "check firing" or "end of mission" is given.

continuous illumination - (DOD) A type of fire in which illuminating projectiles are fired at specified time intervals to provide uninterrupted lighting on the target or specified area.

continuous processor - (NATO, CENTO) Equipment which processes film or paper in continuous strips.

continuous strip camera - (DOD, IADB) A camera in which the film moves continuously past a slit in the focal plane, producing a photograph in one unbroken length by virtue of the continuous forward motion of the aircraft.

continuous strip camera - (NATO, CENTO) A camera in which the film moves continuously past a slit in the focal plane, producing a photograph in one unbroken length by virtue of the continuous motion of the aircraft.

continuous strip photography - (DOD, NATO, CENTO, IADB) Photography of a strip of terrain in which the image remains unbroken throughout its length, along the line of flight.

contour interval - (NATO, CENTO, IADB) Difference in elevation between two adjacent contour lines.

contour line - (DOD, NATO, CENTO, IADB) A line on a map or chart connecting points of equal elevation.

contract - Aviation term for the specific operating rules agreed to by two fighter pilots, lead and wingman.

contract termination - (DOD) As used in Defense procurement, refers to the cessation or cancellation in whole or in part, or work under a prime contract, or a subcontract thereunder, for the convenience of, or at the option of, the government, or due to failure of the contractor to perform in accordance with the terms of the contract (default).

contrail - Aviation term for the visible water vapor trail left by high speed jets.

control - (DOD, NATO, CENTO, IADB) 1. Authority which may be less than full command exercised by a commander over part of the activities of subordinate or other organizations. (DOD, NATO, CENTO) 2. In mapping, charting and photogrammetry, a collective term for a system of marks or objects on the earth or on a map or a photograph, whose positions or elevations, or both, have been or will be determined. (DOD) 3. Physical or psychological pressures exerted with the intent to assure that an agent or group will respond as directed. 4. An indicator governing the distribution and use of documents, information, or material. Such indicators are the subject of intelligence community agreement and are specifically defined in appropriate regulations. See also administrative control; operational command.

control (intelligence) - See control, Parts 3 and 4.

control and reporting center - (DOD) An element of the United States Air Force tactical air control system, subordinate to the Tactical Air Control Center, from which radar control and warning operations are conducted within its area of responsibility.

control and reporting center - (NATO, CENTO) A subordinate air control element of the tactical air control center from which radar control and warning operations are conducted within its area of responsibility. See air control and reporting center.

control and reporting post - (DOD) An element of the United States Air Force tactical air control system, subordinate to the control and reporting center, which provides radar control and surveillance within its area of responsibility.

control and reporting system - (NATO, SEATO, CENTO, IADB) An organization set up for: a. early warning, tracking, and recognition of aircraft and tracking of surface craft; and b. control of all active air defenses. It consists primarily of a chain of radar reporting stations and control centers and an observer organization, together with the necessary communications network.

control area - (DOD, NATO, CENTO, IADB) A controlled airspace extending upwards from a specified height above the surface of the earth without an upper limit unless one is specified. See also airway; control zone; controlled airspace; terminal control area.

control area - (SEATO) An airspace of defined dimensions within which air traffic control is exercised.

control of electromagnetic radiation - (DOD) A national operational plan to minimize the use of electromagnetic radiation in the United States, its possessions and the Panama Canal Zone in the event of attack or imminent threat thereof, as an aid to the navigation of hostile aircraft, guided missiles, or other devices. See also emission control orders.

control of electromagnetic radiation - (IADB) An operational plan to minimize the use of electromagnetic radiation in the event of attack or imminent threat thereof, as an aid to the navigation of hostile aircraft, guided missiles, or other devices. See also emission control orders.

control point - (DOD, NATO, SEATO, CENTO, IADB) 1. A position along a route of march at which men are stationed to give information and instructions for the regulation of supply or traffic. 2. A position marked by a buoy, boat, aircraft, electronic device, conspicuous terrain feature, or other identifiable object which is given a name or number and used as an aid to navigation or control of ships, boats, or aircraft. 3. A point located by ground survey with which a corresponding point on a photograph is matched, as a check, in making mosaics. Note: SEATO definition Part 2. begins: "in amphibious operations, a position marked * * *".

control questions - A series of questions, the answers to which are known, to test the knowledge and truthfulness of the prisoner.

control system (missile) - (DOD, NATO, CENTO, IADB) A system that serves to maintain attitude stability and to correct deflections. See also guidance system (missile).

control zone - (DOD, NATO, CENTO, IADB) A controlled airspace extending upwards from the surface of the earth. See also airway; control area; controlled airspace; terminal control area.

control zone - (SEATO) An airspace of defined dimensions, designated by the appropriate authority, extending upwards from the ground or water, to include one or more airdromes and within which rules, additional to those governing flight in control areas, apply for the protection of air traffic.

controlled airspace - (DOD, NATO, CENTO, IADB) An airspace of defined dimensions within which air traffic control service is provided.

controlled effects nuclear weapons - (DOD) Nuclear weapons designed to achieve variation in the intensity of specific effects other than normal blast effect.

controlled firing area - (DOD, IADB) An area in which ordnance firing is conducted under controlled conditions so as to eliminate hazard to aircraft in flight. See also restricted area.

controlled forces - (DOD, IADB) Military or paramilitary forces under effective and sustained political and military direction.

controlled interception - (NATO, SEATO, CENTO, IADB) An aircraft intercept action wherein the friendly aircraft are controlled from a ground, ship, or airborne station. See also air interception.

controlled item - See regulated item.

controlled map - (DOD, IADB) A map with precise horizontal and vertical ground control as a basis. Scale, azimuth, and elevation are accurate. See also map.

controlled mosaic - (DOD, NATO, CENTO) A mosaic corrected for scale, rectified, and laid to ground control to provide an accurate representation of distances and direction. See also mosaic; rectification; uncontrolled mosaic.

controlled passing - (DOD, NATO, CENTO) A traffic movement procedure whereby two lines of traffic travelling in opposite directions are enabled to traverse alternately a point or section of route which can take only one line of traffic at a time.

controlled port - (DOD, NATO, CENTO, IADB) A harbor or anchorage at which entry and departure, assignment of berths, and traffic within the harbor or anchorage are controlled by military authorities.

controlled reprisal - (DOD) Not to be used. See controlled response.

controlled response - (DOD, IADB) The selection from a wide variety of feasible options of the one which will provide the specific military response most advantageous in the circumstances.

controlled route - (DOD, NATO, CENTO) A route, the use of which is subject to traffic or movement restrictions. See also route.

controlled war - (DOD) Not to be used. See limited war.

CONUS - The continental United States. Also stateside.

conventional forces - (DOD, IADB) Those forces capable of conducting operations using nonnuclear weapons.

conventional weapons - (DOD, IADB) Nonnuclear weapons. Excludes all biological weapons, and generally excludes chemical weapons except for existing smoke and incendiary agents, and agents of the riot-control type.

converge - (DOD) A command or request used in a call for fire to indicate that the observer or spotter desires a sheaf in which the planes of fire intersect at a point.

converged sheaf - (DOD) The lateral distribution of fire of two or more pieces so that the planes of fire intersect at a given point.

convergence - See convergence factor; grid convergence; grid convergence factor; map convergence; true convergence.

convergence factor - (DOD, NATO) The ratio of the angle between any two meridians on the chart to their actual change of longitude. See also convergence.

convergence zone (antisubmarine warfare) - (DOD) That region in the deep ocean where sound rays from sources near the surface, refracted from the depths, return to the surface.

conversion scale - (DOD, NATO) A scale indicating the relationship between two different units of measurement. See also scale.

convoy - (DOD, NATO, SEATO, CENTO, IADB) 1. A number of merchant ships or naval auxiliaries, or both, usually escorted by warships and/or aircraft, or a single merchant ship or naval auxiliary under surface escort, assembled and organized for the purpose of passage together. 2. A group of vehicles organized for the purpose of control and orderly movement with or without escort protection. See also coastal convoy; evacuation convoy; short-haul convoy; ocean convoy.

convoy assembly port - (NATO, SEATO, CENTO, IADB) A port from which convoys, whether oceangoing or coastal, sail.

convoy commodore - (DOD) A naval officer, or master of one of the ships in a convoy designated to command the convoy, subject to the orders of the Officer in Tactical Command. If no surface escort is present, he takes entire command.

convoy commodore - (NATO, CENTO, IADB) A naval officer, or master of one of the ships in a convoy designated to command the convoy, subject to the orders of the escort force commander. If no surface escort is present, he takes entire command.

convoy escort - (DOD, NATO, SEATO, CENTO, IADB) 1. Naval ships or aircraft in company with a convoy and responsible for its protection. 2. An escort to protect a convoy of vehicles from being scattered, destroyed, or captured.

convoy joiner - (DOD, NATO, SEATO, CENTO, IADB) A ship or group of ships sailing independently from, and subsequently joining, the main convoy. See also convoy leaver.

convoy leaver - (DOD, NATO, SEATO, CENTO, IADB) A section of the main convoy or an independent ship (independent leaver) which breaks off from the main convoy to proceed separately to its own prearranged terminal port. When detached, a leaver section becomes a leaver convoy. See also convoy joiner.

convoy loading - (DOD, NATO, SEATO, CENTO, IADB) The loading of troop units with their equipment and supplies in ships of the same movement group, but not necessarily in the same ship. See also loading.

convoy route - (NATO, SEATO, CENTO, IADB) The specific route assigned to each convoy by the appropriate routing authority.

convoy speed - (DOD, NATO, CENTO, IADB) For ships the speed which the convoy commodore orders the guide of the convoy to make good through the water.

convoy through escort - (NATO, SEATO, CENTO, IADB) Those ships of the close escort which normally remain with the convoy from its port of assembly to its port of arrival.

cooking off - Ammunition exploding due to a fire.

cool - Preparation of a heat seeking air-to-air missile with a cooling gas before launching from an airplane.

cooperative logistics - (DOD, IADB) The logistic support provided a foreign government/ agency through its participation in the United States Department of Defense logistic system with reimbursement to the United States for support provided.

cooperative logistics support arrangements - (DOD) The combining term for procedural arrangements (cooperative logistics arrangements) and implementing procedures (supplementary procedures) which together support, define, or implement cooperative logistic understandings between the United States and a friendly foreign government under peacetime conditions.

coordinated attack - (NATO, SEATO, CENTO, IADB) A carefully planned and executed offensive action in which the various elements of a command are employed in such a manner as to utilize their powers to the greatest advantage to the command as a whole.

coordinated exercise - See JCS-coordinated exercise.

coordinated illumination - (DOD) A type of fire in which the firing of illuminating and high explosive projectiles is coordinated to provide illumination of the target and surrounding area only at the time required for spotting and adjusting the high explosive fire. See also continuous illumination.

coordinated procurement assignee - (DOD) The agency or military Service assigned purchase responsibility for all Department of Defense requirements of a particular Federal Supply Group/Class, commodity, or item.

coordinates - (DOD, NATO) Linear or angular quantities which designate the position that a point occupies in a given reference frame or system. Also used as a general term to designate the particular kind of reference frame or system such as a plane rectangular coordinates or spherical coordinates. See also cartesian coordinates; geographic coordinates; grid coordinates; georef.

coordinating authority - (DOD) A commander or individual assigned responsibility for coordinating specific functions or activities involving forces of two or more Services, or two or more forces of the same Service. He has the authority to require consultation between the agencies involved, but does not have the authority to compel agreement. In the event he is unable to obtain essential agreement, he shall refer the matter to the appointing authority.

coordinating authority - (NATO, CENTO, IADB) The authority granted to a commander or individual assigned responsibility for coordinating specific functions or activities involving forces of two or more countries, or two or more Services, or two or more forces of the same Service. He has the authority to require consultation between the agencies involved or their representatives but does not have the authority to compel agreement. In case of disagreement between the agencies involved, he should attempt to obtain essential agreement by discussion. In the event he is unable to obtain essential agreement, he shall refer the matter to the appointing authority.

coordinating authority - (SEATO) A commander or individual assigned responsibility for coordinating operations of several forces who has the authority to require consultation between the commanders of the forces involved, but does not have the authority to compel agreement unless time does not permit otherwise. Except in the latter case, he shall refer the point of disagreement to higher authority.

coordinating point - (DOD, NATO, CENTO, IADB) Designated point at which, in all types of combat, adjacent units/formations must make contact for purposes of control and coordination.

Coors - Radio code for killed in action.

COR - Committee of Responsibility to Save War Burned and War Injured Vietnamese Children.

cordon and search - An order to cordon (surround, from French for "rope off") and search. Usually a village was surrounded and a hut-by-hut search conducted.

CORDS - Civil Operations and Revolutionary (Rural) Development Support, the group that coordinates American pacification efforts and involving civilian, MACV, and CIA. Formerly the OCO.

cork - 1. Slang for anti-diarrhea medicine. 2. Burnt cork applied to the face as camouflage.

Corporal - (DOD) A mobile, surface-to-surface, liquid-propellant guided missile, with nuclear warhead capability, designed to attack targets up to a range of 75 nautical miles. Designated as MGM-5.

Corps - 1. A group sharing a similar function as the Marine Corps or the Medical Corps. 2. The organizational unit composed of two or more divisions and commanded by a Lt. General, 3. The division of Vietnam into four Corps. See I Corps, II Corps, III Corps and IV Corps.

corps troops - (DOD, NATO, SEATO, CENTO, IADB) Troops assigned or attached to a corps, but not a part of one of the divisions that make up the corps.

corpseman - Slang for corpsman.

corpsman - Navy or Marine Corps medic. Slang "corpseman".

corpsman up - A Marine call for help from a corpsman.

correction - (DOD) 1. Any change in firing data to bring the mean point of impact or burst closer to the target. 2. A communication pro-word to indicate that an error in data has been announced and that corrected data will follow.

correlation - (DOD, NATO, CENTO) In air defense, the determination that an aircraft appearing on a radar scope, on a plotting board, or visually is the same vehicle as that on which information is being received from another source.

correlation factor - (DOD, NATO) The ratio of a ground dose rate reading to a reading taken at approximately the same time at survey height over the same point on the ground.

Corsair II - The single-seat, single turbo-fan jet engine, all weather light attack aircraft made by Ling-Temco-Vought, for Navy carrier use (replacing the A-6), also used by the Air Force. Ordinance included cannon and capacity for a variety of nuclear or non-nuclear conventional ordinance, as well as advanced air to air or air to ground missiles. Designated A-7. Also called SLUF, Short Little Ugly Fella.

Cosmoline - 1. A heavy grease put on weapons at the factory to prevent rust, most of which is removed before use. 2. The trademarked product.

cost contract - (DOD) 1. A contract which provides for payment to the contractor of allowable costs, to the extent prescribed in the contract, incurred in performance of the contract. 2. A cost reimbursement type contract under which the contractor receives no fee.

cost plus a fixed-fee contract - (DOD) A cost reimbursement type contract which provides for the payment of a fixed fee to the contractor. The fixed fee, once negotiated, does not vary with actual cost, but may be adjusted as a result of any subsequent changes in the scope of work or services to be performed under the contract.

cost sharing contract - (DOD) A cost reimbursement type contract under which the contractor receives no fee but is reimbursed only for an agreed portion of its allowable costs.

COSVN - Communist (Central) Office of South Vietnam, the logistics headquarters for the communists that orchestrated civil and political action in the South. It was thought to be in Cambodia, but was never located.

cotton balls - Flak burst.

Cougar - F-9 fighter jet.

countdown - (DOD, NATO, SEATO, CENTO, IADB) The step-by step process leading to initiation of missile testing, launching, and firing. It is performed in accordance with a predesignated time schedule.

counter - An air mission over North Vietnam.

counter air - (DOD) A United States Air Force term for air operations conducted to attain and maintain a desired degree of air superiority by the destruction or neutralization of enemy forces. Both air offensive and air defensive actions are involved. The former range throughout enemy territory and are generally conducted at the initiative of the friendly forces. The latter are conducted near to or over friendly territory and are generally reactive to the initiative of the enemy air forces. See also antiair warfare.

counterattack - (DOD, NATO, SEATO, CENTO, IADB) Attack by a part or all of a defending force against an enemy attacking force, for such specific purposes as regaining ground lost or cutting off or destroying enemy advance units, and with the general objective of denying to the enemy the attainment of his purpose in attacking.

In sustained defensive operations, it is undertaken to restore the battle position and is directed at limited objectives.

counterespionage - (DOD) That aspect of counterintelligence designed to detect, destroy, neutralize, exploit or prevent espionage activities through identification, penetration, manipulation, deception and repression of individuals, groups or organizations conducting or suspected of conducting espionage activities.

counterespionage - (NATO, CENTO, IADB) A category of counterintelligence, the objective of which is the detection and neutralization of foreign espionage. See counterintelligence.

counterfire - (DOD, NATO, CENTO, IADB) Fire intended to destroy or neutralize enemy weapons. (DOD, IADB) Includes counterbattery, counterbombardment, and countermortar fire. See also fire.

counterforce - (DOD, IADB) The employment of strategic air and missile forces in an effort to destroy, or render impotent, selected military capabilities of an enemy force under any of the circumstances by which hostilities may be initiated.

counterguerrilla warfare - (DOD, I, IADB) Operations and activities conducted by armed forces, paramilitary forces, or nonmilitary agencies of a government against guerrillas.

counterinsurgency - (DOD, I, IADB) Those military, paramilitary, political, economic, psychological, and civic actions taken by a government to defeat subversive insurgency.

counterinsurgency - A tactic of the Vietnam war by which the alliance of the people was to have repelled the advances of the Northern Vietnamese armies.

counterintelligence - (DOD, I, IADB) That aspect of intelligence activity which is devoted to destroying the effectiveness of inimical foreign intelligence activities and to the protection of information against espionage, individuals against subversion, and installations or material against sabotage. See also counterespionage; countersabotage; countersubversion.

counterintelligence - (NATO, SEATO, CENTO) That phase of intelligence covering all activity devoted to destroying the effectiveness of inimical foreign intelligence activities and to the protection of information against espionage, personnel against subversion, and installations or material against sabotage. See also counterespionage; countersabotage; countersubversion.

countermeasures - (DOD, IADB) That form of military science which by the employment of devices and/or techniques has as its objective the impairment of the operational effectiveness of enemy activity. See also electronic countermeasures.

countermilitary - See counterforce.

countermining - (DOD, IADB) The detonation of mines by nearby explosions, either accidental or deliberate.

counteroffensive - (DOD) A large scale offensive undertaken by a defending force to seize the initiative from the attacking force. See also counterattack.

counterpreparation fire - (DOD, NATO, SEATO, CENTO, IADB) Intensive prearranged fire delivered when the imminence of the enemy attack is discovered. (DOD, SEATO, IADB) It is designed to break up enemy formations; disorganize the enemy's systems of command, communications, and observation; decrease the effectiveness of his artillery preparation; and impair his offensive spirit. See also fire.

counterreconnaissance - (DOD, IADB) All measures taken to prevent hostile observation of a force, area, or place.

countersabotage - (DOD) That aspect of counterintelligence designed to detect, destroy, neutralize or prevent sabotage activities through identification, penetration, manipulation, deception and repression of individuals, groups or organizations conducting or suspected of conducting sabotage activities.

countersabotage - (NATO, SEATO, CENTO, IADB) Action designed to destroy the effectiveness of sabotage activities through the process of identifying, penetrating, and manipulating, neutralizing, or repressing individuals, groups, or organizations conducting or capable of conducting such activities.

countersign - (DOD, NATO, SEATO, CENTO, IADB) A secret challenge and its reply. See also challenge; password; reply.

countersubversion - (DOD) That aspect of counterintelligence designed to detect, destroy, neutralize or prevent subversive activities through the identification, exploitation, penetration, manipulation, deception and repression of individuals, groups or organizations conducting or suspected of conducting subversive activities.

countersubversion - (NATO, SEATO, CENTO, IADB) That part of counterintelligence which is devoted to destroying the effectiveness of inimical subversive activities through the detection, identification, exploitation, penetration, manipulation, deception, and repression of individuals, groups, or organizations conducting or capable of conducting such activities. See also counterintelligence. (Note: NATO and CENTO definition does not use the word "inimical".)

country cover diagrams - (NATO, CENTO) A small scale index, by country, depicting the existence of air photography for planning purposes only.

country fair - A Marine term for a program in which a village was surrounded by troops while South Vietnamese police searched it for weapons while the villagers were isolated and provided medial care and entertainment during the search.

country team - The Embassy team assigned to any country.

courier - (DOD, IADB) A messenger (usually a commissioned or warrant officer) responsible for the secure physical transmission and delivery of documents and material. Generally referred to as a command or local courier. See also armed forces courier.

Courier - (DOD) A delayed repeater communication satellite which had the capability of storing and relaying communications using microwave frequencies. This satellite gave a limited demonstration of instantaneous microwave communications.

course (air traffic control) - (DOD) The intended direction of flight in the horizontal plane.

course of action - (DOD, NATO, SEATO, CENTO, IADB) 1. Any sequence of acts which an individual or a unit may follow. 2. A possible plan open to an individual or commander which would accomplish or is related to the accomplishment of his mission. 3. The scheme adopted to accomplish a job or mission. 4. A line of conduct in an engagement. (Note: NATO, SEATO and CENTO definition uses the words "sequence of activities" instead of "sequence of acts".)

court martial - 1. The military court system. 2. A trial in the military court for violation of a military law.

cover - (DOD, NATO, SEATO, CENTO, IADB) 1. The action by land, air, or sea forces to protect by offense, defense, or threat of either or both. 2. Shelter or protection, either natural or artificial. 3. To maintain a continuous receiver watch with transmitter calibrated and available, but not necessarily available for immediate use. (DOD, NATO, CENTO, IADB) 4. Photographs or other recorded images which show a particular area of ground. (DOD) 5. Keep fighters between force/base and contact designated at distance stated from force/base (e.g., "cover bogey" twenty-seven to thirty miles.) 6. Protective guise used by a person, organization, or installation to prevent identification with clandestine activities. See also comparative cover; concealment.

cover - Slang for hat or headgear, usually a soft hat or the cloth cover on a helmet.

cover (intelligence) - See cover, Part 6.

cover down - Order to form up and straighten a formation in a military manner.

cover search - (DOD, NATO, CENTO) In air photographic reconnaissance, the process of selection of the most suitable existing cover for a specific requirement.

cover trace (reconnaissance) - (NATO, CENTO) One of a series of overlays showing all air reconnaissance sorties covering the map sheet to which the overlays refer.

coverage - (DOD, NATO, IADB) 1. The ground area represented on imagery, photomaps, mosaics, maps, and other geographical presentation systems. (DOD, IADB) 2. Cover or protection, as the coverage of troops by supporting fire. 3. The extent to which intelligence information is available in respect to any specified area of interest.

(DOD) 4. The summation of the geographical areas and volumes of aerospace under surveillance.

coverage index - (DOD) One or a series of overlays showing all photographic reconnaissance missions covering the map sheet to which the overlays refer.

covering fire - (DOD, NATO, SEATO, CENTO, IADB) 1. Fire used to protect troops when they are within range of enemy small arms. 2. In amphibious usage, fire delivered prior to the landing to cover preparatory operations such as underwater demolitions or mine-sweeping. See also fire.

covering force - (DOD, NATO, SEATO, CENTO, IADB) 1. A force operating apart from the main force for the purpose of intercepting, engaging, delaying, disorganizing, and deceiving the enemy before he can attack the force covered. 2. Any body or detachment of troops which provides security for a larger force by observation, reconnaissance, attack or defense, or by any combination of these methods. See also force(s).

covert operations - (DOD, I, SEATO, IADB) Operations which are so planned and executed as to conceal the identity of or permit plausible denial by the sponsor. They differ from clandestine operations in that emphasis is placed on concealment of identity of sponsor rather than on concealment of the operation.

cowboy - Slang for: 1. Reckless pilot. 2. Vietnamese youth adopting western attire and dealing in black market or prostitution.

COWIN - Conduct of the War In Vietnam. A report by the U.S. Army Deputy Chief of Staff for Military Operations in 1971.

coxswain flat - The location from which the coxswain steers a ship.

CP - 1. Command Post, often in field no physical structure but the location of team leader and radio. 2. Combat photographer.

CP pill - An antimalaria pill.

CPDC - Central Pacification and Development Council (GNV).

CPL - Corporal (Army)

Cpl - Corporal (Marine Corps).

CPO - Chief Petty Officer (Navy, Coast Guard).

CPT - Captain (Army).

CQ - 1. Charge of Quarters. 2. Carrier qualified pilot.

Crab - The American made amphibious cargo carrier, M-29C.

crab angle - (NATO, CENTO) The angle between the aircraft track or flight line and the fore and aft axis of a vertical camera, which is in line with the aircraft heading.

crabs - Pubic lice.

crachin - Constant drizzle, a French word.

cracker box - A field ambulance.

cramper - The small cage in which American prisoners of war were held that did not allow one to sit or lie down. See tiger cage.

crank time - Starting a helicopter.

crapper - Latrine.

crash locator beacon - (DOD, NATO, CENTO, IADB) An automatic radio beacon which will help searching forces to locate a crashed aircraft. See also personal locator beacon.

crash position indicator - See crash locator beacon.

crater - (DOD) The pit, depression, or cavity formed in the surface of the earth by an explosion. It may range from saucer shaped to conical, depending largely on the depth of burst. In the case of a deep underground burst, no rupture of the surface may occur. The resulting cavity is termed a camouflet.

crater depth - (DOD) The maximum depth of the crater measured from the deepest point of the pit to the original ground level.

crater radius - (DOD) The average radius of the crater measured at the level corresponding to the original surface of the ground.

crease - A small wound.

creeping barrage - (NATO, CENTO, IADB) A barrage in which the fire of all units participating remains in the same relative position throughout and which advances in steps of one line at a time.

crest - (DOD) A terrain feature of such altitude that it restricts fire or observation in the area beyond, resulting in dead space, or limiting the minimum elevation, or both.

crested - (DOD) A report which indicates that engagement of a target or observation of an area is not possible because of an obstacle or intervening crest.

crib - To tie gear to the deck of a submarine.

crispy critter - 1. War dead from napalm burns. 2. Burn victims in the hospital or in recovery.

critic report - See critical intelligence.

critical altitude - (DOD, NATO, CENTO, IADB) The altitude beyond which an aircraft or air-breathing guided missile ceases to perform satisfactorily. See also altitude.

critical intelligence - (DOD) Intelligence which is crucial and requires the immediate attention of the commander. It is required to enable the commander to make decisions which will provide a timely and appropriate response to actions by the potential/actual enemy. It includes but is not limited to the following: a. strong indications of the imminent outbreak of hostilities of any type (warning of attack); b. aggression of any nature against a friendly country; c. indications or use of nuclear-biological-chemical weapons (targets); and d. significant events within potential enemy countries that may lead to modification of nuclear strike plans.

critical item - (DOD, IADB) An essential item which is in short supply or expected to be in short supply for an extended period. See also critical supplies and materials; regulated item.

critical mass - (DOD) The minimum amount of fissionable material capable of supporting a chain reaction under precisely specified conditions.

critical point - (DOD, IADB) 1. A key geographical point or position important to the success of an operation. 2. In point of time, a crisis of a turning point in an operation. 3. A selected point along a line of march used for reference in giving instructions. 4. A point where there is a change of direction or change in slope in a ridge or stream. 5. Any point along a route of march where interference with a troop movement may occur.

critical supplies and materials - (DOD, NATO, SEATO, CENTO, IADB) Those supplies vital to the support of operations, which, owing to various causes, are in short supply or are expected to be in short supply. See also critical item; regulated item.

critical zone - (DOD, IADB) The area over which a bombing plane engaged in horizontal or glide bombing must maintain straight flight so that the bomb sight can be operated properly and bombs dropped accurately.

critically wounded - (DOD, IADB) A non-evacuable patient. See also wounded.

cross check - Everyone in a patrol checks everyone else for readiness, loose gear, any lights, or reflective material that may disclose their location.

cross over point - (DOD) That range in the air warfare area at which a target ceases to be an air intercept target and becomes a surface-to-air missile target.

cross tell - (DOD) The transfer of information between facilities at the same operational level. See also track telling.

cross-loading (personnel) - (DOD, IADB) A system of loading troops so that they may be disembarked or dropped at two or more landing or drop zones, thereby achieving unit integrity upon delivery. See also loading.

cross-servicing - (DOD) That function performed by one military Service in support of another military Service for which reimbursement is required from the Service receiving support. See also servicing.

cross-servicing - (NATO, CENTO) That servicing performed by one Service or national element for other Services or national elements and for which the other Services or national elements may be charged.

crossing _____ - (DOD) In air intercept, a term meaning passing from _____ to _____.

crotch, the - Slang for Marine Corps.

crow's foot - A booby trap that has four sticks or prongs protruding from it.

cruise - 1. Navy term for deployment of a ship. 2. Marine slang for term of enlistment. 3. Air Force term for parade formation with close maneuvers.

cruise formation - Aviation term for an aerial formation of multiple planes in which each plane is at 45 degrees off the leader's wing forming a V. Similar to parade formation but with more distance between planes.

cruise missile - (DOD) Guided missile, the major portion of whose flight path to its target is conducted at approximately constant velocity; depends on the dynamic reaction of air for lift and upon propulsion forces to balance drag.

cruising altitude - (DOD, NATO, CENTO) A level determined by vertical measurement from mean sea level, maintained during a flight or portion thereof.

cruising level - (NATO) A level maintained during a significant portion of a flight. See also altitude.

crunch cap - The boonie hat, as it could be crunched up and shoved in a pocket.

crunchies - Slang for infantrymen.

Crusader - (DOD, IADB) A single-engine, single-seat, limited all weather supersonic jet fighter aircraft designed for operating from aircraft carriers for the interception and destruction of enemy aircraft, and for troop support. Armament includes Sidewinder missiles, rockets, and cannons. This aircraft possesses air-to-air refueling capability. Other versions have an all-weather capability or reconnaissance capability. Designated as F-8.

cryogenic liquid - (DOD) Liquefied gas at very low temperature, such as liquid oxygen, nitrogen, argon.

cryptanalysis - (NATO, CENTO) The study of encrypted texts. The steps or processes involved in converting encrypted text into plain text without initial knowledge of the key employed in the encryption.

cryptochannel - (DOD, IADB) A complete system of crypto-communications between two or more holders. The basic unit for naval cryptographic communication. It includes: a. the cryptographic aids prescribed; b. the holders thereof; c. the indicators or other means of identification; d. the area or areas in which effective; e. the special purpose, if any, for which provided; and f. pertinent notes as to distribution, usage, etc. A cryptochannel is analogous to a radio circuit.

cryptologic - (DOD, IADB) Of or pertaining to cryptology.

cryptology - (DOD) The science which treats of hidden, disguised, or encrypted communications. It embraces communications security and communications intelligence.

cryptomaterial - (DOD, NATO, CENTO) All material including documents, devices, equipments and apparatus essential to the encryption, decryption or authentication of telecommunications. When classified, it is designated CRYPTO and subject to special safeguards.

cryptoparts - (DOD, NATO, CENTO) The divisions of a message as prescribed for security reasons. The operating instructions for certain cryptosystems prescribe the number of groups which may be encrypted in the systems, using a single message indicator. Cryptoparts are identified in plain language. They are not to be confused with message parts.

cryptosecurity - See communications security.

cryptosystem - (DOD, IADB) The associated items of cryptomaterial that are used as a unit and provide a single means of encryption and decryption. See also cipher; code; decrypt; encipher; encrypt.

crystal ball - (DOD) Radar scope.

crytanalysis - (DOD, IADB) The steps and operations performed in converting encrypted messages into plain text without initial knowledge of the key employed in the encryption.

CS - A type of tear gas, non-lethal (see CN).

CSM - Command Sergeant Major (Army).

CTZ - Corps Tactical Zone.

Cu Chi - An area north of Saigon noted for tunnels used to conceal Viet Cong.

cultivation - (DOD) A deliberate and calculated association with a person for the purpose of recruitment, obtaining information, or gaining control for these or other purposes.

culture - (NATO) Features of the terrain that have been constructed by man. Included are such items as roads, buildings and canals; boundary lines, and, in a broad sense, all names and legends on a map.

culture (cartographic) - (IADB) Man-made or artificial features of the terrain.

cumshaw - A bribe, from the Chinese into Pidgin English in WWII.

cumulo granite - Slang for a mountaintop obscured by clouds.

cunt cap - Derogatory term for the folding fabric cap shaped like an envelope. Navy and Marine slang for this cap a piss cutter.

curb weight - (DOD) Weight of a ground vehicle including fuel, lubricants, coolant and on vehicle materiel, excluding cargo and operating personnel.

currency - (NATO) The up-to-dateness of a map or chart as determined by comparison with the best available information at a given time.

current intelligence - (DOD, NATO, CENTO) Intelligence of all types and forms of immediate interest which is usually disseminated without the delays necessary to complete evaluation or interpretation.

Curtis Commando - A WWII era cargo aircraft.

curve of pursuit - (DOD, NATO, SEATO, CENTO, IADB) The curved path described by a fighter plane making an attack on a moving target while holding the proper aiming allowance.

custody - (DOD) The responsibility for the control of transfer and movement of, and access to, weapons and components. Custody also includes the maintenance of accountability for weapons and components.

cut a huss - Do a favor.

cut and slash - A day of walking through bamboo and elephant grass, as this is what it does to a person and their uniform.

cut some slack - To relax the rules, give a break.

cutoff - (DOD, NATO, SEATO, CENTO) The deliberate shutting off of a reaction engine.

cutoff - Slang for an air interception by another plane using the shortest route.

cutoff attack - (DOD) An attack that provides a direct vector from the interceptor position to an intercept point with the target track.

cutoff velocity - (DOD, NATO, SEATO, CENTO) The velocity attained by a missile at the point of cutoff.

cutout - (DOD) An intermediary or device used to obviate direct contact between members of a clandestine organization.

cutting trail - Making a train, often through dense jungle by cutting away plants.

CV-2 - Caribou, a light transport aircraft with an exceptionally short runway needed for takeoff and landings, e.g. about 250 feet and the ability to use an unprepared field as a runway.

CV-7 - Buffalo - A larger version of the CV-2 light transport able to move up to 41 troops who were fully combat equipped.

CVA - See attack aircraft carrier.

CVAN - See attack aircraft carrier.

CVS - See antisubmarine support aircraft carrier.

CW2 - Chief Warrant Officer 2 (Army).

CW3 - Chief Warrant Officer 3 (Army).

CW4 - Chief Warrant Officer 4 (Army).

CW5 - Chief Warrant Officer 5 (Army).

CWC - Civilian War Casualty.

CWO 2 - Chief Warrant Officer 2 (Marine Corp, Navy, Coast Guard).

CWO 3 - Chief Warrant Officer 3 (Marine Corp, Navy, Coast Guard).

CWO 4 - Chief Warrant Officer 4 (Marine Corp, Navy, Coast Guard).

CWO 5 - Chief Warrant Officer 5 (Marine Corp, Navy).

CY - Calendar Year

CYA - Slang, cover your ass, develop an alibi.

cyclo - A motorized pedicab used in Saigon (pronounced sick-low).

D – DELTA

D - Designated in the military phonetic alphabet, as "Delta".

D to P assets required on D-day - (DOD) As applied to the D to P concept, this asset requirement represents those stocks that must be physically available on D-day to meet initial allowance requirements, to fill the wartime pipeline between the producers and users (even if P-day and D-day occur simultaneously), and to provide any required D to P consumption/production differential stockage. The D to P assets required on D-day is also represented as the difference between the D to P Materiel Readiness Gross Requirement and the cumulative sum of all production deliveries during the D to P period. See also D to P concept.

D to P concept - (DOD) A logistic planning concept by which the gross materiel readiness requirement in support of approved forces at planned wartime rates for conflicts of indefinite duration will be satisfied by a balanced mix of assets on hand on D-day and assets to be gained from production through P-day when the planned rate of production deliveries to the users equals the planned wartime rate of expenditure (consumption). See also D to P materiel readiness gross requirement; D to P materiel readiness gross capability; D to P assets required on D-day; D-day pipeline assets, D-day consumption/ production differential assets.

D to P materiel readiness gross requirement - (DOD) As applied to the D to P concept, the gross requirement for all supplies/materiel needed to meet all initial pipeline and anticipated expenditure (consumption) requirements between D-day and P-day. Includes initial allowances, CONUS and overseas operating and safety levels, intransit levels of supply, and the cumulative sum of all items expended (consumed) during the D to P period. See also D to P concept.

D-day - (DOD, IADB) 1. The unnamed day on which a particular operation commences or is to commence. An operation may be the commencement of hostilities; the date of a major military effort; the execution date of an operation (as distinguished from the date the order to execute is issued); the date the operations phase is implemented, either by land assault, air strike, naval bombardment, parachute assault, or amphibious assault. The highest command or headquarters responsible for coordinating the planning will specify the exact meaning of D-day within the aforementioned definition. If more than one such event is mentioned in a single plan, the secondary events will be keyed to the primary event by adding or subtracting days as necessary. The letter "D" will be the only one used to denote the above. The command or headquarters directly responsible for the execution of the operation, if other than the one coordinating the planning, will do so in light of the meanings specified by the highest planning headquarters. 2. Time in plans will be indicated by a letter which shows the unit of time employed, and figures, with a minus or plus sign to indicate the amount of time before or after the reference event, e.g., "D" is for a particular day, "H" for an hour. Similarly, D+7 means 7 days after D-day, H+2 means 2 hours after H-hour. If the figure becomes unduly large, for example, D-day plus 90, the designation of D+3 months may be employed, i.e., if the figure following a letter plus a time unit (D-day, H-hour, etc.) is intended to refer to units of time other than that which follows the letter, then the unit of time employed with the figure must be spelled out. See also H-hour; K-day; M-day.

D-day - (NATO, SEATO, CENTO) The day on which an operation commences or is due to commence. This may be the commencement of hostilities or any other operation. See also K-day; M-day.

D-day consumption/production differential assets - (DOD) As applied to the D to P concept, these assets are required to compensate for the inability of the production base to meet expenditure (consumption) requirements during the D to P period. See also D to P concept.

D-day materiel readiness gross capability - (DOD) As applied to the D to P concept, this capability represents the sum of all assets on hand on D-day and the gross production capability (funded and unfunded) between D-day and P-day. When this capability equals the D to P Materiel Readiness Gross Requirement, requirements and capabilities are in balance. See also D to P concept.

D-day pipeline assets - (DOD) As applied to the D to P concept, these assets represent the sum of CONUS and overseas operating and safety levels and intransit levels of supply. See also D to P concept.

D-ring - See STABO rig.

D5E - Bulldozer.

D7E - Caterpillar Tractor.

DA - Department of the Army.

DA 483/2635 - See dream sheet.

dadcap - (DOD) Dawn and dusk combat air patrol.

daily movement summary (shipping) - (DOD, NATO, CENTO, IADB) A tabulation of departures and arrivals of all merchant shipping (including neutrals) arriving or departing ports during a 24-hour period. (IADB) These summaries are prepared by area commanders (or operational control authorities if designated by area commanders) and are classified confidential.

daily-daily - Dapsone, the anti-malaria pill administered daily.

daisy chain - A series of several claymore mines.

daisy cutter - 1. A bomb used to open a landing area in a dense jungle area by cutting the trees down and blowing the area clean, See instant LZ. 2. A GI improvised field explosive made of C-4, ammunition, grenades flares or other material to create a jungle clearing explosion.

damage - See nuclear damage (land warfare).

damage assessment - (DOD, NATO, CENTO, IADB) 1. The determination of the effect of attacks on targets. (DOD) 2. A determination of the effect of a compromise of classified information on the national security.

damage assessment - (SEATO) The appraisal of the effect of attacks on targets.

damage control - (DOD, NATO, SEATO, CENTO, IADB) In naval usage, measures necessary aboard ship to preserve and reestablish watertight integrity, stability, maneuverability, and offensive power; to control list and trim; to effect rapid repairs of materiel; to limit the spread of, and provide adequate protection from fire; to limit the spread of, remove the contamination by, and provide adequate protection from toxic agents; and to provide for care of wounded personnel. See also area damage control; disaster control; rear area security.

damage criteria - (DOD) The critical levels of various effects, such as blast pressure and thermal radiation, required to achieve specified levels of damage.

danger - (DOD) Information in a call for fire to indicate that friendly forces are within 600 to 1500 meters of the target.

danger area - (DOD, NATO, CENTO, IADB) A specified area above, below, or within which there may exist potential danger. See also prohibited area; restricted area.

danger close - (DOD) Information in a call for fire to indicate that friendly forces are within 600 meters of the target.

danger space - (DOD) That space between the weapon and the target where the trajectory does not rise 1.8 meters (the average height of a standing man). This includes the area encompassed by the beaten zone. See also beaten zone.

dangerous cargo - (NATO, CENTO) Cargo, which because of its dangerous properties, is subject to special regulations for its transport.

DAO - Defense Attaché Office, a division of the U.S. Embassy that assumed responsibility for the military assistance between the 1973 cease fire and 1975 end of war.

dap - The ritualistic handshake, hand slap routine that was used first by blacks as a greeting and later by some units without racial distinction.

Dapsone - The antimalarial pill taken daily.

dark green Marine - Marine slang for a black Marine.

dart - (DOD) Aircraft rocket.

Darvon - A painkiller of Aspirin and propoxyphene, often abused.

Dash - See Drone Antisubmarine Helicopter.

dash-thirteen - A helicopter maintenance record.

dash-twelve, Page 12 - The helicopter log book page used to record flight time and track performance.

dash-two - Aviation term for the second plane in a formation, the wingman.

data code - (DOD) A number, letter, character, or any combination thereof used to represent a data element or data item. For example, the data codes "E8," "03," and "06" might be used to represent the data items of sergeant, captain, and colonel under the data element "military personnel grade".

data element - (DOD) A basic unit of information having a unique meaning and which has subcategories (data items) of distinct units of values. Examples of data elements are military personnel grade, sex, race, geographic location, and military unit.

data item - (DOD) A subunit of descriptive information or value classified under a data element. For example, the data element "military personnel grade," contains data items such as sergeant, captain, and colonel.

data link - (DOD, NATO, CENTO) A communications link suitable for transmission of data.

data mile - (DOD) A standard unit of distance - 6000 feet.

date eligible to return from overseas - GI's term for last day of service in Vietnam. See DEROS.

date line - See international date line.

date of expected to return from overseas - Military's term for last day of service in Vietnam. See DEROS.

date-time group - (DOD, NATO, SEATO, CENTO, IADB) The date and time, expressed in digits and zone suffix, at which the message was prepared for transmission. (Expressed as six digits followed by the zone suffix; first pair of digits denoting the date, second pair the hours, third pair the minutes.)

datum - (DOD, NATO) Any numerical or geometrical quantity or set of such quantities which may serve as a reference or base for other quantities. Where the concept is geometric, the plural form is 'datums' in contrast to the normal plural 'data'.

datum (antisubmarine warfare) - (DOD) A datum is the last known position of a submarine, or suspected submarine, after contact has been lost.

datum (geodetic) - (DOD, IADB) A reference surface consisting of five quantities: the latitude and longitude of an initial point, the azimuth of a line from this point, and the parameters of the reference ellipsoid.

datum error (antisubmarine warfare) - (DOD) An estimate of the degree of accuracy in the reported position of datum.

datum level - (DOD, NATO) A surface to which elevations, heights or depths on a map or chart are related. See also altitude.

datum point - (DOD, NATO, SEATO, CENTO, IADB) Any reference point of known or assumed coordinates from which calculations or measurements may be taken.

datum time (antisubmarine warfare) - (DOD) The datum time is the time when contact with the submarine, or suspected submarine, was lost.

day of supply - See supply amount adequate for one day of operation.

day the eagle shits - Payday.

dazzle - (DOD, IADB) Temporary loss of vision, or a temporary reduction in visual acuity. See also flash blindness.

dazzle - (NATO, CENTO) Temporary loss of vision, or a temporary reduction in visual acuity by excess light or moving light.

DC - Radio codeword for east, as Washington D.C. is on the east coast of the United States.

DC-3 - A commercial prop aircraft, when armed and modified it became the AC-47 gunship.

DCIA - Director of the CIA.

DCPG - Defense Communication Planning Group, formerly The Jason Group, a think-tank for the development and design of electronic warfare methods.

DD - 1. Dishonorable discharge. 2. See dee-dee.

DD - See destroyer.

DD Four, DD 4 - Department of Defense Form 4, the enlistment contract.

DD Two Fourteen, DD 214 - The Department of Defense discharge form.

DDG - See guided missile destroyer.

DE - See escort ship.

deactivate - To demobilize or disband.

Dead Marine Zone - The DMZ.

dead space - (DOD, NATO, SEATO, CENTO, IADB) 1. An area within the maximum range of a weapon, radar, or observer, which cannot be covered by fire or observation from a particular position because of intervening obstacles, the nature of the ground, or the characteristics of the trajectory, or the limitations of the pointing capabilities of the weapon. 2. An area or zone which is within the range of a radio transmitter, but in which a signal is not received. 3. The volume of space about and around a gun or guided missile system into which it cannot fire because of mechanical or electronic limitations.

dead space - Slang for an area within range of a gun/weapon, but not visually available to gunner, such as target being in a ravine.

dead stick - 1. An aviation training exercise in which the power is cut and flight managed without power. 2 A landing without power is a dead stick landing.

dead time - Time not counted against the term of service, such as time in the brig.

dead zone - See dead space.

deadline - (DOD, IADB) To remove a vehicle or piece of equipment from operation or use for one of the following reasons: a. is inoperative due to damage, malfunctioning, or necessary repairs. The term does not include items temporarily removed from use by reason of routine maintenance, and repairs which do not affect the combat capability of the item; b. is unsafe; and c. would be damaged by further use.

Dear John/ Dear John letter - Letter ending relationship from a girlfriend back in the United States.

Dear Johned - To be dumped by your girlfriend in a letter. A romance break-up.

debarkation - (DOD, IADB) The unloading of troops, equipment, or supplies from a ship or aircraft.

debarkation - (NATO, SEATO, CENTO) The unloading of troops with their supplies and equipment from a ship.

debarkation net - (DOD, IADB) A specially prepared type of cargo net employed for the debarkation of troops over the side of a ship.

debarkation schedule - (DOD, NATO, CENTO, IADB) A schedule which provides for the timely and orderly debarkation of troops and equipment and emergency supplies for the waterborne ship-to-shore movement.

decay (radioactive) - (DOD, NATO, CENTO, IADB) The decrease in the radiation intensity of any radioactive material with respect to time.

decay curves (radioactive) - (DOD, NATO, CENTO, IADB) Graph lines representing the decrease of radioactivity with the passage of time.

decay rate (radioactive) - (DOD, IADB) The time rate of the disintegration of radioactive material generally accompanied by the emission of particles and/or gamma radiation.

decay rate (radioactive) - (NATO, CENTO) The rate of disintegration of radioactive material with respect to time.

decentralized control - (DOD, NATO, CENTO) In air defense, the normal mode whereby a higher echelon monitors unit actions, making direct target assignments to units only when necessary to insure proper fire distribution or to prevent engagement of friendly aircraft.

decentralized items - (DOD, IADB) Those items of supply for which appropriate authority has prescribed local management and procurement.

deception - (DOD, NATO, CENTO) Those measures designated to mislead the enemy by manipulation, distortion, or falsification of evidence to induce him to react in a manner prejudicial to his interests.

decision - (DOD, NATO, SEATO, CENTO, IADB) In an estimate of the situation, a clear and concise statement of the line of action intended to be followed by the commander as the one most favorable to the successful accomplishment of his mission.

deck - 1. Navy and Marine slang for floor. 2. Aviation term for the altitude just above the ground, or a specific altitude set per mission.

deck alert - See ground alert.

Deck Spotter - Aviation term for a pilot who takes his eye off the ball in a carrier landing and looks at the deck, which is bad form and dangerous.

declared speed - (DOD, NATO, CENTO, IADB) The continuous speed which a master declares his ship can maintain on a forthcoming voyage under moderate weather conditions (that is, moderate sea, wind force 4 on the Beaufort scale) having due regard to her present condition (trim, draft, state of bottom, state of machinery, and quality of bunkers). The declared speed is used by the naval control of shipping officer to determine whether a ship is qualified for inclusion in an x-knot convoy.

declassification - (DOD, IADB) The determination that classified information no longer requires, in the interests of national defense, any degree of protection against unauthorized disclosure, coupled with a removal or cancellation of the classification designation.

declassify - (NATO, SEATO, CENTO, IADB) To cancel the security classification of an item of classified matter. See also downgrade.

declination - (DOD, NATO, CENTO, IADB) The angular distance to a body on the celestial sphere measured north or south through 90 degrees from the celestial equator along the hour circle of the body. Comparable to latitude on the terrestrial sphere.

decompression - Medical term for a recommended period of transition between combat and return to stateside, but rarely offered.

decompression sickness - (DOD, NATO, SEATO, CENTO, IADB) A syndrome including bends, chokes, neurological disturbances, and collapse, resulting from exposure to reduced ambient pressure and caused by gas bubbles in the tissues, fluids, and blood vessels.

decontamination - (DOD, NATO, SEATO, CENTO, IADB) The process of making any person, object, or area safe by absorbing, destroying, neutralizing, making harmless, or removing, chemical or biological agents, or by removing radioactive material clinging to or around it.

decontamination station - (DOD, NATO, SEATO, CENTO, IADB) A building or location suitably equipped and staffed where personnel and their clothing are decontaminated from the effects of toxic attack.

decoy - (NATO) A model, electromagnetic reflector or other device which is used to deceive sensors. See also chaff.

decoy ships (Q-ships) - (DOD, NATO, CENTO, IADB) Warships or other ships camouflaged as merchantmen or converted commerce raiders with their armament and other fighting equipment hidden and with special provisions for unmasking their weapons quickly.

decrypt - (DOD, IADB) To convert encrypted text into its equivalent plain text by means of a cryptosystem. (This does not include solution by cryptanalysis.) Note: The term decrypt covers the meanings of decipher and decode. See also cryptosystem.

dee-dee - Slang from Vietnamese dee dee maow, to go away or hurry. Also di-di.

deep fording - (DOD, NATO, CENTO) The ability of a self-propelled gun or ground vehicle equipped with built-in waterproofing and/or a special waterproofing kit, to negotiate a water obstacle with its wheels or tracks in contact with the ground. See also flotation; shallow fording.

deep fording - (SEATO, IADB) The ability of a gun or vehicle equipped with built-in waterproofing with its suspension in contact with the ground to negotiate a water obstacle by application of a special waterproofing kit. See also flotation; shallow fording.

deep kimchi - In serious trouble, from the fermented Korean cabbage dish.

deep serious - Real trouble.

deep shit - A horrible situation.

deep six - 1. To kill. 2. To bury at sea.

deep supporting fire - (DOD, NATO, SEATO, CENTO, IADB) Fire directed on objectives not in the immediate vicinity of our forces, for neutralizing and destroying enemy reserves and weapons, and interfering with enemy command, supply, communications, and observations. See also close supporting fire; direct supporting fire; supporting fire.

defcon - Defensive contact artillery fire.

defector - (DOD) National of a country who has escaped from the control of such country or who, being outside such jurisdiction and control, is unwilling to return thereto and who is of special value to another country.

defector - (IADB) Nonmilitary person of enemy nationality who, for political or other nonmilitary reasons, has repudiated his country, and is in possession of information of sufficient interest to justify special treatment.

defector - (NATO, CENTO) A person who for political or other reasons has repudiated his country and may be in possession of information of sufficient interest to justify special treatment.

defense classification - (DOD) A category or grade assigned to defense information or material which denotes the degree of danger to national security that would result from its unauthorized disclosure and for which standards in handling, storage, and dissemination have been established. These categories are defined as follows: a. confidential - Defense information or material, the unauthorized disclosure of which could be prejudicial to the defense interests of the Nation. b. secret - Defense information or material, the unauthorized disclosure of which could result in serious damage to the Nation, such as jeopardizing the international relations of the United States, endangering the effectiveness of a program or policy of vital importance to the national defense, or compromising important military or defense plans, scientific or technological developments important to national defense, or information revealing important intelligence operations. c. top secret - Defense information or material which requires the highest degree of protection. The top secret classification shall be applied only to that information or material, the defense aspect of which is paramount, and the unauthorized disclosure of which could result in exceptionally grave damage to the Nation, such as leading to a definite break in diplomatic relations affecting the defense of the United States an armed attack against the United States or its allies, a war, or the compromise of military or defense plans, or intelligence operations, or scientific or technological developments vital to the national defense.

defense emergency - (DOD) An emergency condition which exists when: a. a major attack is made upon United States forces overseas, or on allied forces in any theater and is confirmed either by the commander of a command established by the Secretary of Defense, or higher authority; or b. an overt attack of any type is made upon the United States and is confirmed either by the commander of a command established by the Secretary of Defense, or higher authority.

defense in depth - (DOD, NATO, SEATO, CENTO, IADB) The siting of mutually supporting defense positions designed to absorb and progressively weaken attack, prevent initial observations of the whole position by the enemy, and to allow the commander to maneuver his reserve.

defense readiness condition - (NATO, CENTO) A number or code word indicating the readiness posture of a unit for actual operations or exercises.

defense readiness conditions - (DOD) A uniform system of progressive alert postures for use between the Joint Chiefs of Staff and the commanders of unified and specified commands, and for use by the Services. Defense Readiness Conditions are graduated to match situations of varying military severity (status of alert). Defense Readiness Conditions are identified by the short title DEFCON (5), (4), (3), (2), and (1), as appropriate.

defense suppression - An action that destroys the enemy's defensive procedures.

defensive coastal area - (DOD, NATO, SEATO, CENTO, IADB) A part of a coastal area and of the air, land, and water area adjacent to the coast line within which defense operations may involve land, sea, and air forces.

defensive minefield (land mine warfare) - (DOD, SEATO, IADB) A minefield which is laid in accordance with the divisional plan and with the purpose of defeating penetration between positions and also to strengthen the defense of the positions themselves. See also minefield (land mine warfare).

defensive minefield (land mine warfare) - (NATO, CENTO) Minefield laid in accordance with an established plan to prevent a penetration between positions and to strengthen the defense of the positions themselves. See also minefield (land mine warfare).

defensive sea area - (DOD, IADB) A sea area, usually including the approaches to and the waters of important ports, harbors, bays, or sounds, for the control and protection of shipping; for the safeguarding of defense installations bordering on waters of the areas; and for provision of other security measures required within the specified areas. It does not extend seaward beyond the United States territorial waters. See also maritime control area.

defensive spiral - Aviation maneuver of a high speed dive while rolling.

defensive split - Aviation maneuver for a two-plane element when attacked. Both planes turn away from each other and fly apart so the attacker can fire on only one while the other circles to defend.

deferment - A conditional exemption from being inducted into active duty, such as college attendance

defilade - (DOD, NATO, SEATO, CENTO, IADB) 1. Protection from hostile observation and fire provided by an obstacle such as a hill, ridge, or bank. 2. A vertical distance by which a position is concealed from enemy observation. 3. To shield from enemy fire or observation by using natural or artificial obstacles.

definition - (NATO, CENTO) In imagery interpretation, the degree of clarity and sharpness of an image.

defoliant operations - (DOD, NATO, CENTO) The employment of defoliating agents on vegetated areas in support of military operations.

defoliating agent - (DOD, NATO, CENTO) A chemical which causes trees, shrubs, and other plants to shed their leaves prematurely.

defoliation - The chemical removal of foliage. See Agent.

degree of risk (nuclear) - (DOD) As specified by the commander, the risk to which friendly forces may be subjected from the effects of the detonation of a nuclear weapon used in the attack of a close in enemy target; acceptable degrees of risk under differing tactical conditions are emergency, moderate, and negligible. See also emergency risk (nuclear); moderate risk (nuclear); negligible risk (nuclear).

delay (radar) - (NATO, CENTO) 1. The ground distance from a point directly beneath the aircraft to the beginning of the area of the radar scan. 2. The electronic delay of the start of the time base used to select a particular segment of the total.

delay - (DOD) A report from the firing ship to the observer or the spotter to inform him that the ship will be unable to provide the requested fire immediately. It will normally be followed by the estimated duration of the delay.

Delayed Stress Syndrome - An early term for Post Traumatic Stress. See Post Traumatic Stress Syndrome.

delaying action - An infantry tactic in which the main body retreats, leaving an ambush group behind to attack the enemy as it advances into the vacated area.

deliberate breaching (land mine warfare) - (DOD, NATO, CENTO, IADB) A major minefield operation requiring extensive planning, especially trained personnel and positive methods of locating and removing each mine to create demined lanes through minefields. See also breaching.

deliberate crossing - (DOD, NATO, SEATO, CENTO, IADB) A crossing of a river or stream that requires extensive planning and detailed preparations. See also hasty crossing.

deliberate defense - (DOD, NATO, CENTO, IADB) A defense normally organized when out of contact with the enemy or when contact with the enemy is not imminent and time for organization is available. It normally includes an extensive fortified zone incorporating pillboxes, forts, and communications systems. See also hasty defense.

delinquency report - A citation issued by Military Police to a soldier for some infraction such as improper uniform, traffic violation or other violations. The DR was sent to the soldier's headquarters for further disposition. Also DR.

delivery error - (DOD, NATO, CENTO, IADB) The inaccuracy associated with a given weapon system resulting in a dispersion of shots about the aiming point. See also circular error probable; deviation; dispersion error; horizontal error.

delivery forecasts - (DOD) 1. Periodic estimates of contract production deliveries, used as a measure of the effectiveness of production and supply availability scheduling and as a guide to corrective actions to resolve procurement or production bottlenecks. 2. Estimates of deliveries under obligation against procurement from appropriated or other funds.

delivery requirements - (DOD, IADB) The stipulation which requires that an item of material must be delivered in the total quantity required by the date required, and when appropriate, overpacked as required.

Delta - 1. The military phonetic alphabet designation for the letter "D". 2. The Mekong Delta region of Vietnam. See Mekong Delta. 3. Aviation term used by air controller on a carrier to tell the pilot to remain in the air and conserve gas that they are not ready for him to land.

Delta Dagger - (DOD, IADB) A single-engine turbojet interceptor employed in air defense. Its speed is supersonic and its armament is the AIM-4 series and AIM-26A (Falcon). It has an all-weather intercept capability. Designated as F-102.

Delta Dart - (DOD, IADB) A supersonic, single-engine turbojet interceptor aircraft. Its armament consists of Falcon (AIM-4 series) missiles with nonnuclear warheads and Genie (AIR-2A) rockets with nuclear warheads. The Delta Dart is similar to the earlier F-102 in appearance. It has an all-weather intercept capability. Designated as F-106.

Delta Delta - Donut Dolly.

Delta dust - A type of marijuana.

Delta Sierra - Dumb Shit!

delta sox - Nylon socks designed for a wet climate which replaced wool socks in 1970. Aviators continued to wear wool socks as the nylon was not flame resistant.

Delta Tango - Defensive Target.

demarcation line - The line dividing North from South Vietnam.

demilitarized zone - (DOD, NATO, CENTO, IADB) A defined area in which the stationing or concentrating of military forces, or the retention or establishment of military installations of any description, is prohibited.

Demilitarized Zone - Note the Demilitarized Zone in Vietnam was established by the 1954 Geneva Convention which created a five mile wide buffer zone in Vietnam between the North and South in which there was not to be military action. The area ran West along the Song Ben Hai River from the South China Sea to the city of Bo Ho Su, and followed the 17th parallel to the West from that point to the border of Laos. See DMZ.

demobilize - To deactivate or disband.

demolition - (DOD, NATO, SEATO, CENTO, IADB) The destruction of structures, facilities, or material by use of fire, water, explosives, mechanical, or other means. Note: SEATO term is "demolition (destruction)".

demolition belt - (DOD, NATO, CENTO, IADB) A selected land area sown with explosive charges, mines, and other available obstacles to deny use of the land to enemy operations, and as a protection to friendly troops. See also primary demolition belt; subsidiary demolition belt.

demolition firing party - (DOD, NATO, SEATO, CENTO, IADB) The party at the site which is technically responsible for the demolition. See also demolition guard.

demolition guard - (DOD, NATO, SEATO, CENTO, IADB) A local force positioned to insure that a target is not captured by an enemy before orders are given for its demolition and before the demolition has been successfully fired. The commander of the demolition guard is responsible for the operational command of all troops at the demolition site, including the demolition firing party. He is responsible for transmitting the order to fire to the demolition firing party.

demolition target - See charged demolition target; reserved demolition target; uncharged demolition target.

Demon - (DOD, IADB) A single-engine, single-pilot, supersonic, all-weather jet fighter designed for operating from aircraft carriers for interception and destruction of enemy aircraft, and troop support. This aircraft possesses a nuclear delivery capability, and armament includes Sparrow missiles. It has air-to-air refueling capability. Designated as F-3.

demonstration - (DOD, NATO, CENTO, IADB) An attack or a show of force on a front where a decision is not sought, made with the aim of deceiving the enemy. See also amphibious demonstration; diversion; diversionary attack.

demonstration - (SEATO) 1. An attack or a show of force on a front where a decision is not sought, made with the aim of deceiving the enemy. 2. In an amphibious operation, an exhibition of force which may be a feint or minor attack. See diversion.

Dengue fever - A viral fever accompanied by painful swelling of joints. Also Breakbone fever.

denial measures - (DOD, NATO, SEATO, CENTO, IADB) Action to hinder or deny the enemy the use of space, personnel, or facilities. It may include destruction, removal, contamination, or erection of obstructions.

density (land mine warfare) - (DOD, NATO, SEATO, CENTO, IADB) The average number of mines per meter of minefield front.

density altitude - (DOD, NATO) An atmospheric density expressed in terms of the altitude which corresponds with that density in the Standard Atmosphere.

DENTCAP - The Dental Civic Action Program that provided dental services to the Vietnamese.

dep - Pretty, from Vietnamese. Often modified with a slang of the French beaucoup, thus boo-coo dep means very pretty.

Department of the Air Force - (DOD) The executive part of the Department of the Air Force at the seat of government, and all field headquarters, forces, reserve components, installations, activities, and functions under the control or supervision of the Secretary of the Air Force. See also Military Department.

Department of the Army - (DOD) The executive part of the Department of the Army at the seat of government, and all field headquarters, forces, reserve components, installations, activities, and functions under the control or supervision of the Secretary of the Army. See also Military Department.

Department of the Navy - (DOD) The executive part of the Department of the Navy at the seat of government; the headquarters, United States Marine Corps; the entire operating forces of the United States Navy, including naval aviation, and of the United States Marine Corps, including the reserve components of such forces; all field activities, headquarters, forces, bases, installations, activities, and functions under the control or supervision of the Secretary of the Navy; and the United States Coast Guard when operating as a part of the Navy pursuant to law. See also Military Department.

departmental intelligence - (DOD) Intelligence which any department or agency of the Federal Government requires to execute its own mission.

departure - Aviation term for the awful moment that an aircraft departs from controlled flight, e.g. the pilot's control. It may be a stall, or a hydraulic failure. Some are recoverable. Others are fatal.

departure airfield - (DOD, SEATO, IADB) An airfield on which troops and/or materiel are emplaned for flight. See also airfield.

departure airfield - (NATO, CENTO) 1. An airfield from which aircraft depart. 2. An airfield on which passengers or cargo are emplaned for flights.

departure point - (DOD, NATO, SEATO, CENTO, IADB) A navigational check point used by aircraft as a marker for setting course.

deploy - (IADB) 1. In a strategic sense, to relocate forces to desired areas of operations. 2. To extend or widen the front of a military unit, extending from a close order to a battle formation. 3. To change from a cruising approach, or contact disposition to a disposition for naval battle.

deployed nuclear weapons - (DOD) 1. When used in connection with the transfer of weapons between the Atomic Energy Commission and the Department of Defense, this term describes those weapons transferred to and in the custody of the Department of Defense. 2. Those nuclear weapons specifically authorized by the Joint Chiefs of Staff to be transferred to the custody of the storage facilities, carrying or delivery units of the armed forces.

deployment - (DOD) 1. Act of extending battalions and smaller units in width, in depth or in both width and depth to increase its readiness for contemplated action. 2. In naval usage, the change from a cruising approach or contact disposition to a disposition for battle. 3. In a strategic sense, the relocation of forces to desired areas of operation. 4. Designated location of troops and troop units as indicated in a troop schedule. 5. The series of functions which transpire from the time a packed parachute is placed in operation until it is fully opened and is supporting its load.

deployment - (NATO, SEATO, CENTO, IADB) 1. The extension or widening of the front of a military unit, extending from a close order to a battle formation. 2. In naval usage, the change from a cruising approach, or contact disposition to a disposition for battle. 3. In a strategic sense, the relocation of forces to desired areas of operation.

deployment diagram - (DOD, IADB) In the assault phase of an amphibious operation, a diagram showing the formation in which the boat group proceeds from the rendezvous area to the line of departure and the method of deployment into the landing formation.

depot - (DOD, IADB) 1. (supply) - An activity for the receipt, classification, storage, accounting, issue, maintenance, procurement, manufacture, assembly, research, salvage or disposal of materiel. 2. (personnel) - An activity for the reception, processing, training, assignment, and forwarding of personnel replacements.

depot maintenance - (DOD, IADB) That maintenance performed on materiel requiring major overhaul or a complete rebuild of parts, assemblies, subassemblies, and end items, including the manufacture of parts, modifications, testing, and reclamation as required. Depot maintenance serves to support lower categories of maintenance by providing technical assistance and performing that maintenance beyond their responsibility. Depot maintenance provides stocks of serviceable equipment by using more extensive facilities for repair than are available in lower level maintenance activities.

DepTel - Department of State telegram.

depth - (NATO) The vertical distance from the plane of the hydrographic datum to the bed of the sea, lake or river.

depth contour - (NATO, CENTO, IADB) A line connecting points of equal depth below the hydrographic datum. See also depth curve.

depth curve - (DOD, IADB) A line connecting points of equal depth below the hydrographic datum. See also depth contour.

DePuy foxhole - A defensive tactic of having foxholes positioned close enough together to insure interlocking fire toward the enemy. Named for General DuPuy.

DER - See radar picket escort ship.

DEROS - 1. The day the soldier was scheduled to leave Vietnam permanently. 2. The act of leaving Vietnam. Pronounced dee ros.

description of target - (DOD) An element in the call for fire in which the observer or spotter describes the installation, personnel, equipment, or activity to be taken under fire.

descriptive name - (NATO, CENTO, IADB) Written indication on maps and charts, used to specify the nature of a feature (natural or artificial) shown by a general symbol. (Note: IADB definition does not use the parenthetical phrase "(natural or artificial)".)

deserter - A soldier who leaves his assignment with the intent of not returning.

desertion - Being absent from one's assigned duty station with the intent of remaining away permanently. Note: about 500,000 desertions were reported and the distinction between AWOL and desertion often was shaded.

desired effects - (DOD) The damage or casualties to enemy men or material which a commander desires to achieve from a nuclear weapon detonation. Damage effects on material are classified as light, moderate or severe. Casualty effects on personnel may be immediate, prompt, or delayed.

desired ground zero - (DOD, NATO, CENTO, IADB) The point on the surface of the earth at, or vertically below or above, the center of a planned nuclear detonation. Also called DGZ. See also actual ground zero; ground zero.

desk jockey - One assigned to office work, usually in the rear echelon.

DeSoto - Code name for the U.S. Navy surveillance and intelligence patrols along the North Vietnamese coast.

despatch route - (DOD, NATO, CENTO) A roadway over which full control, both as to priorities of use and the regulation of movement of traffic in time and space is exercised. See also route.

Dessert - Code for a bombing area in Cambodia. See Menu.

destination port - (NATO, SEATO, CENTO, IADB) A destination is the delivery port of discharge of an individual ship, as determined by the ship's destination authority. See also port.

destinations (merchant shipping) - See final destination; immediate destination; intermediate destination; original destination; terminal destination.

destroy (beam) - (DOD) The interceptor will be vectored to a standard beam attack for interception and destruction of the target.

destroy (cut off) - (DOD) Intercept and destroy. Command vectors will produce a cut-off attack.

destroy (frontal) - (DOD) The interceptor will be vectored to a standard frontal attack for interception and destruction of the target.

destroy (stern) - (DOD) The interceptor will be vectored to a standard stern attack for interception and destruction of the target.

destroyed - (DOD) A condition of a target so damaged that it cannot function as intended nor be restored to a usable condition. In the case of a building, all vertical supports and spanning members are damaged to such an extent that nothing is salvageable. In the case of bridges, all spans must be dropped and all piers must require replacement.

destroyer - (DOD, IADB) A high-speed warship designed to operate offensively with strike forces, with hunter-killer groups and in support of amphibious assault operations. Destroyers also operate defensively to screen support forces and convoys against submarine, air, and surface threats. (Normal armament consists of 3" and 5" dual-purpose guns and various antisubmarine warfare weapons.) Designated as DD.

Destroyer - (DOD, IADB) A twin-engine turbo-jet, tactical, all-weather, light-bombardment aircraft capable of delivering nuclear and nonnuclear weapons. Its range can be extended by in-flight refueling. The RB-66 is a two-place tactical reconnaissance version of the B-66 capable of day or night reconnaissance and can also be in-flight refueled. Designated as B-66. Navy version is the A-3.

destroyer minelayer - (DOD, IADB) Converted destroyers designed to conduct high-speed mine laying operations. Average load is 80 mines laid from two stern racks. Designated as DM.

destruct (missile) - (DOD, NATO, CENTO, IADB) Intentional destruction of a missile or similar vehicle for safety or other reasons.

destruct system (missile) - (DOD, NATO, CENTO, IADB) A system which, when operated by external command or preset internal means, destroys the missile or similar vehicle.

destruction - (DOD) A type of adjustment for destroying a given target.

destruction area - (DOD) An area in which it is planned to destroy or defeat the enemy airborne threat. The area may be further subdivided into air intercept, missile (long, medium, and short-range) or antiaircraft gun zones.

destruction fire - (DOD, NATO, SEATO, CENTO, IADB) Fire delivered for the sole purpose of destroying material objects. See also fire.

det cord - Detonating cord, used to set off explosives.

detachment - (DOD, NATO, SEATO, CENTO, IADB) 1. A part of a unit separated from its main organization for duty elsewhere. 2. A temporary military or naval unit formed from other units or parts of units.

detail - (NATO) The basic graphic representation of features.

detail - Slang for: 1. A work assignment. 2. A small group working on a specific task.

detailed report (photographic interpretation) - (DOD, NATO, CENTO) A comprehensive analytical intelligence report written as a result of the interpretation of photography usually covering a single subject, target, or target complex, and of a detailed nature.

detection - (DOD, IADB) In arms control, the first step in the process of ascertaining the occurrence of a violation of an arms control agreement.

détente - French for reduction of tension, specifically referring to the political tension between the Soviet and American governments.

deterrence - (DOD, IADB) The prevention from action by fear of the consequences. Deterrence is a state of mind brought about by the existence of a credible threat of unacceptable counter action.

detour - (DOD, NATO, CENTO) Deviation from those parts of a route where movement has become difficult or impossible, to ensure continuity of movement right to the destination. The modified part of the route is known as a detour.

detox - Detoxification from drug abuse.

deuce - 1. Slang for two. 2. The CH-37. 3. In aviation, the formation of two planes, with the lead plane in front and the wingman back and to the right (or less commonly left).

deuce and a half - Two and a half ton cargo truck.

deuce gear - The Marine slang for the basic gear needed in the field including the ALICE pack and web belt.

deuce point - The second man on a patrol.

deviation - (NATO, SEATO, CENTO, IADB) 1. The distance by which a point of impact or burst misses the target. 2. The angular difference between magnetic and compass headings. See also circular error probable; delivery error; dispersion error; horizontal error.

Devil Dog - A Marine. From being called that in WWI by Germans for their tenacity.

dew - Marijuana, from doobie.

Dexamphetamine - Amphetamines used to overcome exhaustion and remain alert. Often abused. Also uppers, greenies, green bomb, Special Forces popcorn.

DF - 1. Disposition form, a memo recounting the outcome of an action or mission. 2. Direction Finding. 3. Defense Support.

DFC - The Distinguished Flying Cross.

Dharma - Ideal truth, as taught by Buddha.

DI - Drill Instructor. The trainer of new recruits in boot camp. See boot and boot camp.

DI shack - The room of the on duty Drill Instructor with a desk and bunk.

di-di - See dee-dee.

DIA - Defense Intelligence Agency.

diamond formation - Aviation term for an aerial formation of four planes forming a diamond with the lead plane trailed by two which are trailed by one plane. Rarely used in combat.

DIANE - Digital Inertial Airborne Navigation System.

diaphragm - (NATO, CENTO) The physical element of an optical system which regulates the quantity of light traversing the system. The quantity of light determines the brightness of the image without affecting the size of the image.

diapositive - (DOD, NATO, CENTO) A positive photograph on a transparent medium. See transparency.

dich - Vietnamese term for dead, applied to enemy. Pronounced dick.

dick - Penis.

dicks - Derogatory description of the enemy.

diddy bag - See ditty bag.

diddy-bopping - Walking carelessly, non-combat walking, from the slang used by black soldiers for a free and easy walking style.

DIE - Draft induced enlistment. One who enlists to get a better deal than waiting for a draft call-up.

died of wounds received in action - (DOD, SEATO) The term used to describe all battle casualties who die of wounds or other injuries received in action, after having reached any medical treatment facility. It is essential to differentiate these cases from battle casualties found dead or who died before reaching a medical treatment facility (the "killed in action" group). It should be noted that reaching a medical treatment facility while still alive is the criterion. See also battle casualty; killed in action.

died of wounds received in action - (NATO, CENTO, IADB) A battle casualty who dies of wounds or other injuries received in action, after having reached any medical treatment facility. It is essential to differentiate these cases from battle casualties found dead or who died before reaching a medical treatment facility (the "killed in action" group). It should be noted that reaching a medical treatment facility while still alive is the criterion. See also killed in action.

Diem-ocracy - A slang for the political style of President Diem who blended dictatorship, monarchy and democracy.

Dien Bien Phu - The battle in which ended the French Indochina War in which the French were defeated and Vietnamese victorious.

diffraction loading - (DOD, NATO, CENTO) The force (or loading) on the structure during the envelopment process.

diffusion (light) - (NATO, CENTO) The scattering of light rays either when reflected from a rough surface or during the transmission of light through a translucent medium.

digger - Australian term for Australian infantryman.

digger hat - Wide soft brimmed hat worn by Australian infantryman.

dime - The number ten.

dime-nickel - Slang for the 105-mm howitzer.

dimes - GI slang for an illegal mixture of drugs, usually Speed and Quaaludes.

ding - 1. To hit a target, but not perfectly. 2. To do damage to something, as in to ding a fender while parking badly.

dinger - Marksman, sniper.

dink, dinks - GI's derogatory term for the enemy or Asians in general, from the Vietnamese term for U.S. soldiers.

dinky dau - To be crazy.

DIOCC - District Intelligence and Operation coordinating Center.

dip - Short form of dipshit.

diplomatic authorization (air) - (DOD, NATO, CENTO, IADB) Authority for overflight or landing obtained at government-to-government level through diplomatic channels.

dipstick - 1. The long thin metal blade with marks to show fluid levels in a container, such as testing engine oil level. 2. Euphemism for dipshit. 3. Medical slang for the chemically sensitive paper strips dipped into urine to test for some chemical such as glucose.

direct action fuze - See impact action fuze; proximity fuze; self-destroying fuze; time fuze; variable time fuze.

direct air support center - (DOD) A subordinate operational component of a tactical air control system designed for control and direction of close air support and other tactical air support operations and is normally collocated with fire support coordination elements. See also direct air support center (airborne).

direct air support center - (IADB) A subordinate operational component of the tactical air control system designed for control and direction of close air support and other direct air support operations. It is under the operational control of a tactical air control or tactical air direction center and is normally located near the command post of the supported ground unit.

direct air support center (airborne) - (DOD) An airborne aircraft equipped with the necessary staff personnel, communications, and operations facilities to function as a direct air support center. See also direct air support center.

direct damage assessment - (NATO, CENTO, IADB) A direct examination of an actual strike area by air observation, air photography, or by direct observation.

direct exchange - Exchange of military goods for other military goods. See DX.

direct fire - (DOD) Gunfire delivered on a target, using the target itself as a point of aim for either the gun or the director.

direct fire - (NATO, CENTO, IADB) Fire directed at a target which is visible to the aimer. See also fire. (Note: IADB term is "direct or visual fire".)

direct laying - (DOD, IADB) Laying in which the sights of the weapons are aligned directly on the target.

direct support - (DOD, IADB) A mission requiring a force to support another specific force and authorizing it to answer directly the supported force's request for assistance.

direct support - (NATO, CENTO) The support provided by a unit or formation, not attached or under command of the supported unit or formation, but required to give priority to the support required by that unit or formation. See also support.

direct support artillery - (DOD, NATO, CENTO, IADB) Artillery whose primary task is to provide fire requested by the supported unit.

direct supporting fire - (DOD, NATO, SEATO, CENTO, IADB) Fire delivered in support of part of a force, as opposed to general supporting fire which is delivered in support of the force as a whole. See also supporting fire; close supporting fire; deep supporting fire.

directed exercise - See JCS-directed exercise.

directing staff - (NATO, SEATO, CENTO) A group of officers who by virtue of experience, qualifications, and a thorough knowledge of the exercise instructions, are selected to direct, conduct, or control an exercise. Their knowledge of both BLUE and ORANGE roles will usually preclude them from specific BLUE or ORANGE duties.

direction - (DOD) A term used by a spotter or observer in a call for fire to indicate the bearing of the spotting line.

direction finding - (DOD) A procedure for obtaining bearings of radio frequency emitters with the use of a highly directional antenna and a display unit on an intercept receiver of ancillary equipment.

direction of attack - (DOD, NATO, CENTO, IADB) A specific direction or route which the main attack or center of mass of the unit will follow. The unit is restricted and required to attack as indicated and is not normally allowed to bypass the enemy. The direction of attack is used primarily in counter-attacks or to ensure that supporting attacks make maximum contribution to the main attack. (Note: NATO and CENTO term has qualifier "(ground forces)".)

directional radar prediction - (NATO, CENTO) A prediction made for a particular heading.

directive - (DOD, NATO, SEATO, CENTO, IADB) 1. A military communication in which policy is established or a specific action is ordered. 2. A plan issued with a view to placing it in effect when so directed, or in the event that a stated contingency arises. 3. Broadly speaking, any communication which initiates or governs action, conduct, or procedure.

dirty - Aviation term for a plane in position for a landing in which the landing gear and flaps are down.

dirty officer - Duty Officer.

disaffected person - (DOD) A person who is alienated or estranged from those in authority or has a lack of loyalty for his government; a state of mind.

disarmament - (DOD, IADB) The reduction of a military establishment to some level set by international agreement. See also arms control; arms control agreement; arms control measure.

disarmed mine - (NATO, SEATO, CENTO, IADB) A mine which has been rendered inoperative by breaking a link in the firing sequence. See also mine.

disaster control - (DOD, IADB) Measures taken before, during, or after hostile action, natural or man-made disasters, to reduce the probability of damage, minimize its effects, and initiate recovery. See also area damage control; damage control.

disembarkation schedule - See debarkation schedule.

disengagement - (DOD, IADB) In arms control, a general term for proposals which would result in the geographic separation of opposing nonindigenous forces without directly affecting indigenous military forces.

Disneyland East - Slang for the Pentagon.

Disneyland Far East - Slang for Vietnam.

dispensary - (DOD, IADB) A medical treatment facility primarily intended and appropriately staffed and equipped to provide out-patient medical service for non-hospital type patients. Examination and treatment for emergency cases are types of services rendered. (DOD) A dispensary is also intended to perform certain non-therapeutic activities related to the health of the personnel served, such as physical examinations, immunizations, medical administration, and other preventive medical and sanitary measures necessary to support a primary military mission. A dispensary will be equipped with the necessary supporting services to perform the assigned mission. A dispensary may be equipped with beds (normally less than 25) for observation of patients awaiting transfer to a hospital, and for care of cases which cannot be cared for on an outpatient status, but which do not require hospitalization. Patients whose expected duration of illness exceeds 72 hours will not occupy dispensary beds for periods longer than are necessary to arrange transfer to a hospital.

dispersal airfield - (DOD, IADB) An airfield, military or civil, to which aircraft might move before H-hour on either a temporary duty or permanent change of station basis and be able to conduct operations. See also airfield.

dispersed movement pattern - (DOD, NATO, CENTO, IADB) A pattern for ship-to-shore movement which provides additional separation of landing craft both laterally and in depth. This pattern is used when nuclear weapon threat is a factor.

dispersion - (DOD, NATO, SEATO, CENTO, IADB) 1. A scattered pattern of hits, by bombs dropped under identical conditions or by projectiles fired from the same weapon or group of weapons with the same firing data. 2. In antiaircraft gunnery, the scattering of shots in range and deflection about the mean point of impact. As used in flak analysis, the term includes scattering due to all causes, and the mean point of impact is assumed to be the target. 3. The spreading or separating of troops, materiel, establishments, or activities which are usually concentrated in limited areas, to reduce vulnerability to enemy action. 4. In chemical operations, the dissemination of agents in liquid or aerosol form from bombs and spray tanks. See also circular error probable; delivery error; deviation; dispersion error; horizontal error.

dispersion error - (DOD, NATO, SEATO, CENTO, IADB) The distance from the point of impact or burst of a round to mean point of impact or burst.

dispersion pattern - (DOD, NATO, SEATO, CENTO, IADB) The distribution of a series of rounds fired from one weapon or group of weapons under conditions as nearly identical as possible, the points of bursts or impacts being dispersed about a point called the mean point of impact.

displaced person - (DOD, NATO, SEATO, CENTO, IADB) A civilian who is involuntarily outside the national boundaries of his country. See also evacuees; refugee.

displacement - (DOD) In air intercept, separation between target and interceptor tracks established to position the interceptor in such a manner as to provide sufficient maneuvering and acquisition space.

disposition - (DOD, NATO, SEATO, CENTO, IADB) 1. Distribution of the elements of a command within an area, usually the exact location of each unit headquarters and the deployment of the forces subordinate to it. 2. A prescribed arrangement of the stations to be occupied by the several formations and single ships of a fleet, or major subdivisions of a fleet, for any purpose, such as cruising, approach, maintaining contact, or battle. 3. A prescribed arrangement of all the tactical units composing a flight or group of aircraft. (DOD) 4. The removal of a patient from a medical treatment facility by reason of return to duty, transfer to another treatment facility, death or other termination of medical care.

dissemination - See intelligence cycle.

distance - (DOD, IADB) 1. The space between adjacent individual ships or boats measured in any direction between foremasts. 2. The space between adjacent men, animals, vehicles, or units in a formation measured from front to rear. (DOD) 3. The space between a known reference point or a ground observer and a target, measured in meters (artillery), in yards (naval gunfire), or in units specified by the observer. See also interval.

Distinguished Flying Cross - The highest aviation decoration for heroism or extraordinary achievement in flight and voluntary action above and beyond the call of duty. See DFC.

Distinguished Service Cross - The second highest decoration for bravery.

distributed fire - (DOD, NATO, SEATO, CENTO, IADB) Fire so dispersed as to engage most effectively an area target. See also fire.

distribution - (DOD, IADB) 1. The arrangement of troops for any purpose, such as a battle, march, or maneuver. 2. A planned pattern of projectiles about a point. 3. A planned spread of fire to cover a desired frontage or depth. 4. An official delivery of anything, such as orders or supplies. 5. That functional phase of military logistics which embraces the act of dispensing materiel, facilities, and services. 6. The process of assigning military personnel to activities, units or billets.

distribution point - (DOD, NATO, SEATO, CENTO, IADB) A point at which supplies and/or ammunition, obtained from supporting supply points by a division or other unit, are broken down for distribution to subordinate units. Distribution points usually carry no stocks; items drawn are issued completely as soon as possible.

distribution system - (DOD, IADB) That complex of facilities, installations, methods, and procedures, designed to receive, store, maintain, distribute, and control the flow of military materiel between the point of receipt into the military system and the point of issue to using activities and units.

ditching - (DOD, IADB) Controlled landing of a distressed aircraft on water.

ditty bag - A small cloth drawstring bag for indoor use containing small miscellaneous barracks items. See barracks bag.

dive toss - A computerized bomb guidance system on the F-4 jet.

diversion - (DOD, IADB) 1. The act of drawing the attention and forces of an enemy from the point of the principal operation; an attack, alarm, or feint which diverts attention. 2. A change made in a prescribed route for operational or tactical reasons. A diversion order will not constitute a change of destination. (DOD) 3. The rerouting of cargo or passengers to a new transshipment point or destination or on a different mode of transportation prior to arrival at ultimate destination. See also demonstration.

diversion - (NATO, SEATO, CENTO) 1. The act of drawing the attention and forces of an enemy from the point of the principal operation; an attack, alarm, or feint which diverts attention. 2. A change made in a prescribed route for operational or tactical reasons. (NATO, CENTO) Except in the case of aircraft, a diversion order will not constitute a change of destination. See also demonstration.

diversionary attack - (DOD, NATO, SEATO, CENTO, IADB) An attack wherein a force attacks, or threatens to attack, a target other than the main target for the purpose of drawing enemy defenses away from the main effort. See also demonstration.

diversionary landing - (DOD, IADB) An operation in which troops are actually landed for the purpose of diverting enemy reaction away from the main landing.

divert - (DOD) 1. Proceed to divert field or carrier as specified. 2. To change the target, mission, or destination of an airborne flight.

division - (DOD, NATO, SEATO, CENTO, IADB) 1. A tactical unit/formation as follows: a. a major administrative and tactical unit/formation which combines in itself the necessary arms and services required for sustained combat, larger than a regiment/brigade and smaller than a corps; b. a number of naval ships of similar type grouped together for operational and administrative command, or a tactical unit of a naval aircraft squadron, consisting of two or more sections; and c. an air division is an air combat organization normally consisting of two or more wings with appropriate service units. The combat wings of an air division will normally contain similar type units. 2. An organizational part of a headquarters that handles military matters of a particular nature, such as personnel, intelligence, plans and training, or supply and evacuation. 3. A number of personnel of a ship's complement grouped together for operational and administrative command.

division artillery - (DOD, IADB) Artillery that is permanently an integral part of a division. For tactical purposes, all artillery placed under the command of a division commander is considered division artillery.

division direct support missile - See Missile A.

division formation - Aviation term for the air flight pattern in which a flight of two or more sections fly for mutual support and protection as a tactical air formation. See section.

division slice - See slice.

division support missile - See Missile B.

Dixie cup - Slang for the white all-brim cap worn by sailors, or winged white cap worn by nurses.

Dixie Station - The military designation of a location in the South China Sea, southwest of Cam Rahn Bay which was used as a staging area and a reference point for air operations by the U.S. Navy.

DKZ-57 - A Soviet made 57-mm recoilless rifle.

DKZ-75 - A Soviet made 75-mm recoilless rifle.

DKZ-B - Soviet-made rocket launcher.

DL - See frigate.

DLG - See guided missile frigate.

DLGN - See guided missile frigate.

DM - See destroyer minelayer.

DME - Distance Measuring Equipment, the aviation system used by the Navy that supplied the pilot with distance to a known point information. The plane sends a pulse to a ground station which sends back a response pulse. The time for the pulse to travel to the ground station and back is measured and provides distance data.

DMS - Jungle boot with a direct molded sole.

DMZ - Demilitarized Zone.

DO - 1. Duty Officer. 2. Defensive order.

Doc - Marine corps slang for the Navy medic.

doctrine - (DOD) Fundamental principles by which the military forces or elements thereof guide their actions in support of national objectives. It is authoritative but requires judgment in application.

DOD - The United States Department of Defense which includes the Army, Navy, Marine Corps, Air Force and Coast Guard.

dog and pony show - Slang for putting on some administrative presentation for visiting personnel, usually high ranking or dignitaries, that is more fluff than substance.

dog collar - The clerical collar worn by priests.

dog him out - Deride.

dog robbers - 1. Aids to general staff officers who would do anything, including rob dogs, to curry favor. 2. Rear area personnel.

dog shift - The work shift 1800 to 0600 (6 p.m. to 6 a.m.).

dog tags - The metal identification disk worn by military personnel that provided name, rank, service, identification number, blood type, religion and other data.

dogbone - The shape and the nickname of the panel in the F-4 fighter airplane's cockpit that is used to select weapons for deployment.

dogfight - Close range battle between two or more fighter planes.

doggie straps - Wider pack straps on Army backpacks than on Marine Corps issued packs.

doghouse - 1. Helicopter pilot slang for the box shaped area above the fuselage. 2. Trouble, as "he is in the doghouse".

Dogpatch - The shanty town erected outside a base that provided barbershop, truck wash, restaurant, and often a bordello. From the comic strip Li'l Abner.

dogs - 1. The service dogs which were used in Vietnam as scouts, for the detection of explosives or drugs, flushing the enemy out of tunnels and for sentry duty. 2. Slang for feet.

dolly - (DOD) Airborne data link equipment.

dome - See spray dome.

domestic air traffic - (DOD) Air traffic within continental United States.

domestic emergencies - (DOD) Emergencies affecting the public welfare and occurring in the United States, its territories and possessions, as a result of enemy attack, insurrection, civil disturbances, earthquakes, fire, flood, or other public disasters or equivalent emergencies which endanger life and property or disrupt the usual processes of government. The term domestic emergency includes any or all of the emergency conditions defined below: a. civil defense emergency - A domestic emergency disaster situation resulting from devastation created by an enemy attack and requiring emergency operations during and following attack. It may also be proclaimed by appropriate authority in anticipation of an attack. b. civil disturbances - Group acts of violence or disorder prejudicial to public law and order. c. major disaster - Any flood, fire, hurricane, or other catastrophe which, in the determination of the President, is or threatens to be of sufficient severity and magnitude to warrant disaster assistance by the Federal Government to supplement the efforts and available resources of state and local governments in alleviating the damage, hardship, or suffering caused thereby. d. natural disaster - All domestic emergencies except those created as a result of enemy attack or civil disturbance.

domestic intelligence - (DOD) Intelligence relating to activities or conditions within the United States which threaten internal security and which might require the employment of troops, and intelligence relating to activities of individuals or agencies potentially or actually dangerous to the security of the Department of Defense.

dominant user concept - (DOD) The concept that the Service which is the principal consumer will have the responsibility for performance of a support workload for all using Services.

Domino Theory - The political theory that suggests that if one country falls to communism then others will also fall after it, as in the image of a line of dominos on end and tipping over.

Don't mean nothing. - Phrase used to devalue or negate bad news, bad event. In the vein of Fuck it. Don't give a shit.

dong - 1. Vietnamese currency. 2. Penis.

donkey dick - The flexible metal tin spout attached to jerry cans to allow fuel or water to poured more accurately.

donkey sight - Gun sight on tank. Also, iron idiot.

Donut Dollies - The women of the American Red Cross, named for the custom of serving coffee and donuts. More important was the provision of comfort, stability, and a glimpse of normalcy in a foreign environment for military personnel. For those hospitalized, the visits and letters written by DDs to their families when a soldier could not write formed a link to the world. All were volunteers.

Donut Six - The commander of the American Red Cross in Vietnam, given the "six" associated with military commanders.

doo-mommie - Mother fucker, from the Vietnamese "du ma".

doobie - Marijuana cigarette.

doodad - Name for any piece of gear or component in lieu of knowing or using the technical term (such as hoo-ha, gizmo, thingamabob).

door bundle - (NATO, CENTO, IADB) A bundle for manual ejection in flight normally followed by parachutists.

door gunner - The soldier operating the machine gun from the open door of a helicopter.

doorstop - Useless soldier.

dope - 1. Slang for information. 2. Slang for a variety of narcotics. 3. An adjustment to a gun sight.

doper - One who used illegal drugs.

doppler effect - (DOD, NATO, CENTO, IADB) The phenomenon evidenced by the change in the observed frequency of a sound or radio wave caused by a time rate of change in the effective length of the path of travel between the source and the point of observation.

doppler radar - (DOD) A radar system which differentiates between fixed and moving targets by detecting the apparent change in frequency of the reflected wave due to motion of target or the observer.

dork - 1. Penis. 2. Idiot.

DOS - Department of State.

dose rate contour line - (DOD, NATO, CENTO, IADB) A line on a map, diagram, or overlay joining all points at which the radiation dose rate at a given time is the same.

dosimetry - (DOD, NATO, CENTO, IADB) The measurement of radiation doses. It applies to both the devices used (dosimeters) and to the techniques.

dot - 1. The spot on radar in a plane that appeared when the target was locked on. 2. Aviation slang for getting gone fast, as I am a dot on the horizon.

double agent - (DOD) Agent in contact with two opposing intelligence services only one of which is aware of the double contact or quasi-intelligence services.

double canopy - Thick jungle foliage in two layers. See triple canopy.

double hatted - Having two jobs.

double nuts - Aviation term for carrier Air Group commander's aircraft number ending in 00 or 100.

double point - An infantry tactic in which two point observers are used rather than the usual one.

double tap - To shoot twice.

double time - 1. Increasing the pace of a 36 inch stride to 180 per minute. 2. To go fast, at a run.

double veteran - A rapist-killer.

double-digit fidget - Nerves being a short timer. See short timer.

double-digit midget - Having under 90 days left in Vietnam. See short timer.

doubtful - (DOD) A term used by the observer or spotter to indicate that he was unable to determine the difference in range between the target and a round or rounds.

doubtfuls - Slang for Vietnamese who were not clearly friend or foe.

Doughnut Dollies - See Donut Dollies.

Doves - See Hawks and Doves.

DOW - Died of wounds.

down - (DOD) 1. A term used in a call for fire to indicate that the target is at a lower altitude than the reference point used in identifying the target. 2. A correction used by an observer or a spotter in time fire to indicate that a decrease in height of burst is desired.

down - 1. Aviation for a pilot too ill to fly. 2. Slang for generally depressed or sad.

downgrade - (DOD) To determine that classified information requires, in the interests of national defense, a lower degree of protection against unauthorized disclosure than currently provided, coupled with a changing of the classification designation to reflect such lower degree.

downgrade - (NATO, SEATO, CENTO, IADB) To reduce the security classification of a classified document or an item of classified matter or material. See also declassify.

downrange - The space between the artillery and its target.

Downtown - Aviation reference to Hanoi. Flight missions were Going Downtown if it involved Hanoi. From the 1964 song by Petula Clark, *Downtown*.

dozens, the dozens - An oral contest between black soldiers in which one insults the other's family, girlfriend, or other topic until the other has no witty reply, usually in good nature. The winner is usually decided by the audience with victory to the one who was the lowest or coldest.

DR - See Delinquency Report.

Dr Pepper - 1. The targeted area of a ground to air missile, aiming to hit the enemy aircraft at 10 o'clock, 2 o'clock and 4 o'clock locations. The slogan of the Dr Pepper soda company encouraged consumption at 10, 2 and 4 o'clock. 2. Nurse slang for pregnant as there is no period in the soda name.

draft - The involuntary conscription of males into military service, the draft began during the Civil War and was suspended in 1973.

draft classification - The classification for draft readiness determined by the Selective Service System. Classifications were given in an numeric-alpha system using Roman numerals, such as I-A or IV-F but usually written outside the military as 1-A, 4-F etc. See I-A, I-B, I-C, I-D, I-O, I-S, I-W, I-Y, II-A, II-B, II-C, II-D, II-S, II-A, III-A, IV-A, IV-B, IV-C, IV-D, IV-F, and V-A.

draft dodger - A male who was eligible for conscription who evaded the draft by technical evasion or fleeing the country.

draftees - See transient.

drafter - (DOD, IADB) A person who actually composes the message for release by the originator or the releasing officer. See also originator.

drag - (DOD) 1. Force of aerodynamic resistance caused by the violent currents behind the shock front.

drag - Slang for: 1. Having political or social influence or pull. 2. The last man in a patrol formation, often "the drag". 3. Not having fun.

drag bag - To depart, often due to a transfer.

drag bombs - Bombs dropped at a low altitude.

drag loading - (DOD) The force on an object or structure due to the transient winds accompanying the passage of a blast wave. The drag pressure is the product of the dynamic pressure and the drag coefficient which is dependent upon the shape (or geometry) of the structure or object.

drag squad - The squad left behind a main group to maintain security on a road. Or behind the advancing group.

Dragon's Jaw - Bridge 130 K south of Hanoi that was a critical supply link for the North.

Dragonfly - Light attack jet built by Cessna, with wing-tip fuel tanks. Called Super Tweet. Designated A-37.

drainage system - (NATO) Rivers, streams and other inland water features.

drawbar pull - (NATO, CENTO) The pulling force exerted at the drawbar of a ground vehicle.

drawing key - (NATO) An image or preliminary drawing used as a guide for scribing or drawing. See also blue key.

dream sheet - The official form on which to request your next duty assignment. DA 483 for officers, DA 2635 for enlisted men.

drift - To slide off course.

drift factor - 1. Aviation slang for someone who can't stay on target. A high drift factor made someone unreliable. 2. The distance off course.

drifting mine - (DOD, IADB) A mine which is designed with no provision for maintaining a fixed position after laying. It is free to move with the waves, current, and wind. Drifting mines may watch at the surface or may be kept at a set depth by depth control devices.

drifting mine - (NATO, SEATO, CENTO) A buoyant or neutrally buoyant mine, free to move under the influence of waves, wind, current or tide.

Drill Instructor - See DI.

drippy dick - Venereal disease.

driver - Aviation term for the pilot.

DRO - Dining Room Orderly.

drogue chute - A parachute used in low level cargo drops through a rear door of an aircraft.

drone - (DOD, IADB) A land, sea or air vehicle which is remotely or automatically controlled.

Drone Antisubmarine Helicopter - (DOD) Small, lightweight, remotely controlled helicopter capable of operating from a destroyer and delivering an antisubmarine warfare weapon to an enemy submarine. It provides destroyers with a stand-off weapon. Popular name is Dash. Designated as QH-50, the QH-50A can carry a 265-pound weapon within a combat radius of 29 miles, the QH-50B, a 500-pound weapon within a com - bat radius of 30 miles, and the QH-50C, a 750-pound weapon within a combat radius of 30 miles.

drop - (DOD) A correction used by an observer or a spotter to indicate that a decrease in range along a spotting line is desired.

drop altitude - (DOD, NATO, CENTO) The altitude above mean sea level at which airdrop is executed. See also altitude; drop height.

drop altitude - (SEATO, IADB) Actual altitude of an aircraft above the ground at the time of a parachute drop or the initiation of an aerial drop.

drop height - (DOD, NATO, CENTO, IADB) The vertical distance between the drop zone and the aircraft. See also altitude.

drop message - (DOD, NATO, SEATO, CENTO, IADB) A message dropped from an aircraft to a ground or surface unit.

drop track - (DOD) In air intercept, the unit having reporting responsibility for a particular track is dropping that track and will no longer report it. Other units holding an interest in that track may continue to report it.

drop zone - (DOD, NATO, SEATO, CENTO, IADB) A specified area upon which airborne troops, equipment, or supplies are airdropped.

dropmaster - (DOD, IADB) 1. An individual qualified to prepare, perform acceptance inspection, load, lash, and eject material for airdrop. 2. An air crew member who, during parachute operations, will relay any required information between pilot and jumpmaster.

drops - The reduction of the length of the tour of duty in Vietnam caused by the reduction in the level of American troops in Vietnam.

DRV - Democratic Republic of Vietnam (North) the name given to the north by Ho Chi Minh in 1950. The name was changed in 1975 to reflect the inclusion of the Southern part of the country to the Socialist Republic of Vietnam.

dry feet - 1. An infantryman's dream. 2. Going home alive and away from the wet jungle.

dry fire - 1. Training or practice without live ammunition. 2. Generally any practice session.

dry gap bridge - (NATO, CENTO) A bridge, fixed or portable, which is used to span a gap that does not normally contain water, e.g., anti-tank ditches, road craters, etc.

dry hole - An attack on an enemy target resulting in no explosion, from a well drilling enterprise that failed.

dry run - Practice, rehearsal.

dry shave - Shaving with a double edge razor without water or lather.

DSC - See Distinguished Service Cross.

DShKM .51 caliber machine gun - Degtyraoy and Shpagin (the developers) K is the abbreviation for caliber and M is model. North Vietnamese weapon used as antiaircraft against helicopters. See fifty-one.

DTG - Days to go. The short-timer's countdown for going home.

Du dit. - Fuck you, from the Vietnamese.

dual (multi)-capable weapons - (DOD, IADB) 1. Weapons, weapon systems, or vehicles capable of selective equipage with different types or mixes of armament or firepower. 2. Sometimes restricted to weapons capable of handling either nuclear or nonnuclear munitions.

dual (multi)-purpose weapons - (DOD, IADB) Weapons which possess the capability for effective application in two or more basically different military functions and/or levels of conflict.

dual agent - (DOD) One who is simultaneously and independently employed by two or more intelligence agencies covering targets for both.

dual carriage way - See dual lane highway.

dual lane highway - (NATO) Any highway in which opposing streams of traffic are physically separated by a divider.

dual purpose weapon - (DOD) A weapon designed for delivering effective fire against air or surface targets.

dual-capable forces - (DOD, IADB) Forces capable of employing dual-capable weapons.

duce - Slang for two.

duce and a half - The M-35 2.5 ton truck.

duck - (DOD) In air intercept, a code meaning trouble headed your way (usually followed by "bogey, salvos," etc.).

duck suit - A brown and tan camouflage suit.

duckbill - A 12 gauge shotgun.

dud - (DOD, NATO, SEATO, CENTO) Explosive munition which has not been armed as intended or which has failed to explode after being armed. See also absolute dud; nuclear dud; dwarf dud; flare dud.

dud probability - (DOD) The expected percentage of failures in a given number of firings.

duffel bag - A cylindrical canvas bag issued to soldiers to hold their belongings.

dumb bomb - A bomb that has to be dropped over a target without any guidance system. See smart bomb.

dummy message - (DOD, NATO, CENTO, IADB) A message sent for some purpose other than its content, which may consist of dummy groups or may have a meaningless text.

dummy run - (DOD) Any simulated firing practice, particularly a dive bombing approach made without release of a bomb. Same as dry run.

dump - (DOD, NATO, SEATO, CENTO, IADB) A temporary storage area, usually in the open, for bombs, ammunition, equipment, or supplies.

dump - Slang for the mortuary.

dumpster diving - Locals scavenging for food in GI dumpsters.

Dung lai. - Vietnamese for halt.

duplicate negative - (DOD, NATO, CENTO) A negative reproduced from an original negative or dispositive.

DuPont lure - Fishing by detonating plastic explosive, made by DuPont, in water and retrieving the dead fish.

dust - 1. Kill. 2. Leave.

dust eater - 1. The last man in a patrol formation. 2. The last vehicle in a convoy.

dust off line number - On arrival, every soldier was entered into a roster, all names occupying one numbered line. If wounded or killed, that line number, not the soldier's name, was used on the radio.

dust off, dust-off, dustoff - 1. Medical evacuation by helicopter 2. The helicopter used in the medical evacuation.

Duster (antiaircraft weapon) - (DOD, IADB) A self-propelled, twin 40-mm antiaircraft weapon for use against low-flying aircraft. Designated as M42.

Duster (tank) - The army tank of WWII used in Vietnam, had twin 40-mm Bofors air defense guns. Deployed in conjunction with quad .50 caliber machine guns that were mounted on trucks or set directly on the ground.

dwarf dud - (DOD) A nuclear weapon, which when launched at or emplaced on a target, fails to provide a yield within a reasonable range of that which could be anticipated with normal operation of the weapon. This constitutes a dud only in the relative sense.

DX - 1. Direct exchange. 2. Discard or dispose of. 3. Kill or dispose of a person.

dynamic. pressure - (DOD, NATO, CENTO, IADB) Pressure resulting from some medium in motion, such as the air following the shock front of a blast wave.

DZ - Drop zone.

E – ECHO

E - 1. Designated in the military phonetic alphabet, as "Echo". 2. The designations, by pay grade, for Enlisted personnel.

E and E, E&E - Escape and evasion. 1. The tactics used if captured or separated from your unit to get back to safety. 2. Slang for anyone who evades added duty assignments, a slacker.

E-1 - Private (Army and Marine Corps), Seaman Recruit (Navy, Coast Guard), Airman Basic (Air Force).

E-2 - Private 2 (Army), Private First Class (Marine Corps), Seaman Apprentice (Navy and Coast Guard), Fireman Apprentice and Airman Apprentice (Coast Guard), Airman (Air Force).

E-3 - Private First Class (Army), Lance Corporal (Marine Corps), Seaman (Navy and Coast Guard), Fireman and Airman (Coast Guard), Airman First Class (Air Force).

E-4 - Specialist and Corporal (Army), Corporal (Marine Corps), Petty Officer 3rd Class (Navy and Coast Guard), Senior Airman (Air Force).

E-5 - Sergeant (Army and Marine Corps), Petty Officer 2nd Class (Navy and Coast Guard), Staff Sergeant (Air Force).

E-6 - Staff Sergeant (Army and Marine Corps), Petty Officer 1st Class (Navy and Coast Guard), Technical Sergeant (Air Force).

E-7 - Sergeant First Class (Army), Gunnery Sergeant (Marine Corps), Chief Petty Officer (Navy and Coast Guard), Master Sergeant (Air Force).

E-8 - A tear gas launcher.

E-8 - Master Sergeant and First Sergeant (Army and Marine Corps), Senior Chief Petty Officer (Navy and Coast Guard), Senior Master Sergeant (Air Force).

E-9 - Sergeant Major, Command Sergeant Major, Sergeant Major of the Army (Special- during wartime only.) (Army), Master Gunnery Sergeant, Sergeant Major, Sergeant Major of the Marine Corps (Marine Corps), Master Chief Petty Officer (Navy and Coast Guard), Master Chief Petty Officer of the Navy (Special- senior person.) (Navy) Master Chief Petty Officer of the Coast Guard (Special- senior person.) (Coast Guard), Chief Master Sergeant, Command Chief Master Sergeant, Chief Master Sergeant of the Air Force (Special- during wartime only.) (Air Force).

E-nothing - Lower than starting pay grade, a recruit, worthless.

e-tool - Entrenching tool, a folding shovel with a two-foot handle used for digging (shallow fox holes or latrines) clearing brush, and occasionally as a weapon. Also spelled as E-tool.

Eagle Eye - The search for Viet Cong hiding in villages.

Eagle Flight - The name of a tactical operation that used helicopters to deploy a platoon or squad sized assault force or to reconnoiter enemy positions.

Eagle Pull Operation - The designation of the military operation that evacuated the U.S. Embassy and military personnel from Phnom Penh, Cambodia in 1975.

early resupply - (NATO, CENTO, IADB) The shipping of supplies during the period between D-day and the beginning of planned resupply. See also elements of resupply.

early outs - 1. A soldier with less than 90 days (or 150 days if enrolled in college) to serve in Vietnam. 2. A reduction of the time set to serve in Vietnam (See DROS, Drops, ETS).

Early Spring - (DOD) An anti-reconnaissance satellite weapon system.

early time - See span of detonation (atomic demolition munition employment).

early warning - (DOD) Early notification of the launch, or approach, of unknown weapons or weapons carriers. See also tactical warning.

earmarked for assignment - (NATO, CENTO) Forces which nations have agreed to assign to the operational command or operational control of a (NATO) (CENTO) commander at some future date. In designating such forces, nations should specify when these forces will be available in terms agreed to in the echelon or category systems.

earmarked for assignment - (SEATO) Forces which nations have agreed to assign to the operational command or operational control of a SEATO commander at some future date in peace or in the event of war. See also SEATO forces.

earmarked for assignment on mobilization - (NATO, SEATO, CENTO) Forces specifically designated by nations for assignment to a (NATO) (SEATO) (CENTO) commander in the event of mobilization or war. In designating such forces, nations should specify, in the terms agreed to in the echelon system, when these forces will be available. See also NATO forces; SEATO forces.

earthquake bomb - The CBU-55 bomb which contained other bombs within it.

ease turn - (DOD) Ease rate of turn.

easting - (NATO, CENTO, IADB) Eastward (that is left to right) reading of grid values.

eat the apple, fuck the Corps - a Marine expression of frustration or anger.

EB-66 - See B-66 a bomber.

EC - Engineering Corps.

EC-121 - The Lockheed made airliner. The Constellation.

EC-121 - The Lockheed piston driven airliner that was equipped with a radar sail and became a airborne command post for air missions. See Warning Star.

echelon - (DOD, NATO, SEATO, CENTO, IADB) 1. A subdivision of a headquarters, i.e., forward echelon, rear echelon. 2. Separate level of command. As compared to a regiment, a division is a higher echelon; a battalion is a lower echelon. 3. A fraction of a command in the direction of depth, to which a principal combat mission is assigned, i.e., attack echelon, support echelon, reserve echelon. 4. A formation in which the subdivisions are placed one behind another, extending beyond and unmasking one another wholly or in part.

echelon formation - Aviation term for an aerial formation of multiple planes in which each subordinate aircraft is to one specified side and progressively to the rear of the lead plane. "Echelon right" has all subordinate aircraft off to the right of the lead plane and slightly back. "Echelon left" has all subordinate aircraft off to the left of the lead plane and slightly back. In either case, each subsequent plane is off to the side and behind the one ahead of it.

echelon left - See echelon formation.

echelon right - See echelon formation.

echeloned displacement - (DOD, NATO, CENTO, IADB) Movement of a unit from one position to another without discontinuing performance of its primary function. Normally, the unit divides into two (base and advance) functional elements; and while the base continues to operate, the advance element displaces to a new site where, after it becomes operational, it is joined by the base element.

Echo - 1. The military phonetic alphabet designation for the letter "E". 2. Listening to an enemy radio transmission without detection.

ECM - Electronic counter-measures generic term for a wide variety of measures used to interfere with the electronic equipment of the enemy, especially the radar equipment.

economic action - (DOD, IADB) The planned use of economic measures designed to influence the policies or actions of another state, e.g., to impair the war-making potential of a hostile power, or to generate economic stability within a friendly power.

economic mobilization - (DOD, NATO, SEATO, CENTO, IADB) The process of preparing for and carrying out such changes in the organization and functioning of the national economy as are necessary to provide for the most effective use of resources in a national emergency.

economic potential - (DOD, NATO, SEATO, CENTO, IADB) The total capacity of a nation to produce goods and services.

economic potential for war - (DOD, IADB) That share of the total economic capacity of a nation which can be used for the purposes of war.

economic retention stock - (DOD) That portion of the quantity of an item excess to the approved force retention level which it has been determined will be more economical to retain for future peacetime issue in lieu of replacement of future issues by procurement. To warrant economic retention, items must have a reasonably predictable demand rate.

economic retention stock - (IADB) That portion of the quantity of an item in long supply which has been determined will be retained for future peacetime issue or consumption as being more economical than replenishment by procurement; however, no portion of any item to be retained as economic retention stock may be retained as contingency retention stock. See also reserve supplies.

economic warfare - (DOD, NATO, CENTO, IADB) Aggressive use of economic means to achieve national objectives.

economic warfare - (SEATO) The defensive use in peacetime, as well as during a war, of any means by military and civilian agencies to maintain or expand the economic potential for war of a nation and its (probable) allies, and, conversely, the offensive use of any measure in peace or war to diminish or neutralize the economic potential for war of the (likely) enemy and his accomplices.

edition - (NATO) In cartography, a particular issue of a map or chart which is different from other issues.

edition designation - (NATO) The number, letter, date or symbol distinguishing one edition from another.

Edsel - F-111.

EE-8 - A field radiophone.

EEI - Essential elements of intelligence. The specific items that a pilot would look for in a surveillance flight.

EENT - End of Evening Nautical Twilight.

EF-10 - See Willie the Whale.

effective damage - (DOD) That damage necessary to render a target element inoperative, unserviceable, nonproductive, or uninhabitable

effective range - (SEATO, IADB) The maximum distance at which a weapon may be expected to fire accurately to inflict casualties or damage.

effective strength of enemy forces - (IADB) That part, including logistic component, of the initial strength which is currently capable of combat employment. See also initial strength of enemy forces; strength of enemy forces.

efficiency report - The personnel evaluation report completed periodically for officers and at the end of a tour of duty for enlisted personnel.

egg sucker - A kiss-ass or suck up soldier.

Eggbeater - The Huey helicopter.

egress - Outbound aircraft leaving a target, going out. See ingress.

EGT - Exhaust gas temperature. A measure of effectiveness of jet engines.

Eidal laundry - A portable laundry unit on a trailer.

Eiffel bridge - A left-over bridge built by the French during their occupancy of Vietnam.

Eight - Master Sergeant, E-8 pay grade.

eight AA, 8-mm AA - Soviet made antiaircraft artillery.

eight ball - 1. A problem person who is an impediment to your work. 2. In a hard spot, a difficult position, from the pool shot behind the eight ball.

eight-inch Howie, 8-inch Howie - The 8-inch Howitzer. See M-110 8-inch SPA, M-55 SPA.

Eighth and I - The address of the United States Marine Corps Headquarters in Washington DC. Pronounced Eighth and Eye.

eighty-five, 85-mm AAA - A North Vietnamese antiaircraft artillery piece.

eighty-one - An American mortar, M-29.

eighty-one mortar, 81-mm mortar - See M-29 81-mm mortar.

eighty-one tubes, 81-mm tubes - See M-29 81-mm mortar.

eighty-one, 81 Mike Mike - See M-29 81-mm mortar.

eighty-two - Russian designed mortar used by North Vietnamese.

eighty-two, 82 Mike Mike - See Type 53 mortar.

ejection - (DOD, NATO, SEATO, CENTO, IADB) Escape from an aircraft by means of explosively propelled seats. (Note: NATO, SEATO, CENTO and IADB term has qualifier "aircrew".)

El Cid - 1. Slang for an operative of the Criminal Investigation Division. 2. Any spy.

El Tee - Lieutenant, from the abbreviation Lt.

electro-optics - (DOD) The interaction between optics and electronics leading to the transformation of electrical energy into light, or vice versa, with the use of an optical device.

electromagnetic radiation - (DOD) Radiation made up of oscillating electric and magnetic fields and propagated with the speed of light. Includes gamma radiation, X-rays, ultraviolet, visible and infrared radiation, and radar and radio waves.

electromagnetic spectrum - (DOD) The frequencies (or wave lengths) present in a given electromagnetic radiation. A particular spectrum could include a single frequency or a wide range of frequencies.

electronic counter-countermeasures - (DOD) That division of electronic warfare involving actions taken to insure friendly effective use of the electromagnetic spectrum despite the enemy's use of electronic warfare.

electronic counter-countermeasures - (NATO, CENTO) That major subdivision of electronic warfare involving actions taken to insure our own effective use of electromagnetic radiations despite the enemy's use of countermeasures.

electronic countermeasures - (DOD) That division of electronic warfare involving actions taken to prevent or reduce an enemy's effective use of the electromagnetic spectrum. See also electronic counter-countermeasures; barrage (Part 3); electronic deception; electronic jamming; jamming; electronic warfare support measures.

electronic countermeasures - (NATO, CENTO, IADB) That major subdivision of electronic warfare involving actions taken to prevent or reduce the effectiveness of enemy equipment and tactics employing or affected by electromagnetic radiations and to exploit the enemy's use of such radiations. See also active electronic countermeasures; barrage (Part 3); electronic deception; electronic jamming; jamming; passive electronic countermeasures.

electronic deception - (DOD) The deliberate radiation, reradiation, alteration, absorption, or reflection of electromagnetic energy in a manner intended to mislead an enemy in the interpretation or use of information received by his electronic systems. See also electronic countermeasures; radio deception.

electronic deception - (NATO, CENTO, IADB) The deliberate radiation, reradiation, alteration, absorption, or reflection of electromagnetic radiations in a manner intended to mislead an enemy in the interpretation of data received by his electronic equipment or to present false indications to electronic systems. See also electronic countermeasures; radio deception.

electronic intelligence - (DOD, IADB) The intelligence information product of activities engaged in the collection and processing, for subsequent intelligence purposes, of foreign, noncommunications, electromagnetic radiations emanating from other than nuclear detonations and radioactive sources. Also called ELINT.

electronic jamming - (DOD) The deliberate radiation, reradiation, or reflection of electromagnetic energy with the object of impairing the use of electronic devices, equipment or systems being used by an enemy. See also jamming.

electronic jamming - (NATO, CENTO, IADB) The deliberate radiation, reradiation, or reflection of electromagnetic signals with the object of impairing the use of electronic devices by the enemy. See also electronic countermeasures; jamming.

electronic line of sight - (DOD) The path traversed by electromagnetic waves which is not subject to reflection or refraction by the atmosphere.

electronic reconnaissance - (DOD) The detection, identification, evaluation, and location of foreign, electromagnetic radiations emanating from other than nuclear detonations or radioactive sources.

electronic warfare - (DOD) Military action involving the use of electromagnetic energy to determine, exploit, reduce or prevent hostile use of the electromagnetic spectrum and action which retains friendly use of the electromagnetic spectrum.

electronic warfare - (NATO, CENTO, IADB) That division of the military use of electronics involving actions taken to prevent or reduce an enemy's effective use of radiated electromagnetic energy and actions taken to insure our own effective use of radiated electromagnetic energy.

electronic warfare support measures - (DOD) That division of electronic warfare involving actions taken to search for, intercept, locate, record, and analyze radiated electromagnetic energy for the purpose of exploiting such radiations in support of military operations. Thus, electronic warfare support measures provide a source of electronic warfare information required to conduct electronic countermeasures, electronic counter-countermeasures, threat detection, warning, avoidance, target acquisition and homing.

electronics security - (DOD, IADB) The protection resulting from all measures designed to deny unauthorized persons information of value which might be derived from their interception and study of noncommunications electromagnetic radiations, e.g., radar.

element - The aviation term for a two-plane unit.

elements of national power - (DOD, IADB) All the means which are available for employment in the pursuit of national objectives.

elements of resupply - See early resupply; improvised (early) resupply; initial (early) resupply; planned resupply; resupply of Europe.

elephant - Slang for combat. See "seen the elephant".

elephant grass - Tall bamboo-like vegetation, over 6 feet tall with sharp blades.

elephant gun - The M-79 grenade launcher.

elephant intestines - Slang for the cotton tubes containing rice carried like bandoliers by Vietnamese soldiers. Note this technique was adopted by GIs for carrying added rations in tube socks tied to a pack.

elephant turd - Slang for the 500-gallon fuel bladder.

elevation - (DOD, NATO, CENTO, IADB) The vertical distance of a point or a level, on or affixed to the surface of the earth, measured from mean sea level. See also altitude.

elevation of security - (NFSN, CENTO) Minimum elevation permissible for firing above friendly troops without endangering their safety. This concept can only be applied to certain equipments having a flat trajectory.

elevation tint - See hypsometric tinting.

elevator - (DOD) In air intercept, a code meaning take altitude indicated (in thousands of feet) calling off each five thousand feet increment passed through.

eleven bang bang - An infantryman.

eleven bravo - The phonetic military term for 11-B, the job code for infantry.

eleven-b - The designation of the job title for the infantry assignment.

elicitation (intelligence) - (DOD) Acquisition of information from a person or group in a manner which does not disclose the intent of the interview or conversation. A technique of human source intelligence collection, generally overt, unless the collector is other than he purports to be.

eligible traffic - (DOD) Traffic for which movement requirements are submitted and space is assigned or allocated. Such traffic must meet eligibility requirements specified in joint travel regulations for the uniformed services and publications of the Department of Defense and military departments governing eligibility for land, sea, and air transportation and be in accordance with the guidance of the Joint Chiefs of Staff.

ELINT - Electronic intelligence. This usually related to the active efforts to get the radar data from the enemy on the electronic systems used to deploy the SAM or AA batteries.

elope - Hospital slang for patient self-discharging before treatment is completed.

ELS - Entry level separation. A recruit who is discharged from service.

EM - Abbreviation for enlisted man.

em - Slang for pal, servant, girlfriend from the Vietnamese word for good friend.

EM Club - Enlisted Men's Club.

embarkation - (DOD, IADB) The loading of troops with their supplies and equipment into ships and/or aircraft.

embarkation - (NATO, SEATO, CENTO) The loading of troops with their supplies and equipment into a ship.

embarkation and tonnage table - (DOD, IADB) A consolidated table showing personnel and cargo, by troop or naval units, loaded aboard a combat-loaded ship.

embarkation area - (DOD, NATO, SEATO, CENTO, IADB) An area ashore, including a group of embarkation points, in which final preparations for embarkation are completed and through which assigned personnel and loads for craft and ships are called forward to embark. See also mounting area.

embarkation element (unit) (group) - (DOD, IADB) A temporary administrative formation of personnel with supplies and equipment embarking or to be embarked (combat loaded) aboard the ships of one transport element (unit) (group). It is dissolved upon completion of the embarkation. An embarkation element normally consists of two or more embarkation teams; a unit, of two or more elements; and a group, of two or more units. See also embarkation organization; embarkation team.

embarkation officer - (DOD, IADB) An officer on the staff of units of the landing force who advises the commander thereof on matters pertaining to embarkation planning, loading, and embarkation of the command aboard ships. See also combat cargo officer.

embarkation order - (DOD, IADB) An order specifying dates, times, routes, and methods of movement to shipside and/or aircraft for both personnel and impedimenta.

embarkation order - (NATO, SEATO, CENTO) An order specifying dates, times, routes, and methods of movement to shipside for troops with their supplies and equipment.

embarkation organization - (DOD, IADB) A temporary administrative formation of personnel with supplies and equipment embarking or to be embarked (combat loaded) aboard amphibious shipping. See also embarkation element (unit) (group); embarkation team.

embarkation team - (DOD, IADB) A temporary administrative formation of all personnel with supplies and equipment embarking or to be embarked (combat loaded) aboard one ship. See also embarkation element (unit) (group); embarkation organization.

embassy ceiling price - The failed attempt of the Embassy to set the maximum value for goods to reduce the black market and its negative consequences.

emergency anchorage - (NATO, SEATO, CENTO, IADB) An anchorage, which may have a limited defense organization, for naval vessels, mobile support units, auxiliaries, or merchant ships. See also assembly anchorage; holding anchorage; working anchorage.

emergency burial - (DOD, NATO, CENTO, IADB) A burial, usually on the battlefield, when conditions do not permit evacuation for interment in a cemetery. See also burial.

emergency fleet operating base - (NATO, SEATO, CENTO, IADB) A base providing logistic support for fleet units operating in an area for limited periods of time. See also base.

emergency in war - (NATO, CENTO) An operational contingency in a limited area caused by a critical aggravation of combat operations and requiring special and immediate action by National and Allied commanders. The existence of such an emergency shall be determined by the Allied commander responsible for the limited area involved, in consultation with the National commander concerned.

emergency priority - (DOD) A category of immediate mission request which takes precedence over all other priorities, e.g., an enemy breakthrough. See also immediate mission request; priority of immediate mission requests.

emergency relocation site - (DOD) A prepared location to which all or portions of a civilian or military headquarters may be moved. It is manned only to provide the maintenance of the facility, communications, and data base. It should be capable of rapid activation, or supporting the initial requirements of the relocated headquarters for a predetermined period, and of expansion to meet the full wartime requirements of the relocated headquarters.

emergency resupply - The helicopter resupply of water and ammo to a pinned unit. Food was not included.

emergency risk (nuclear) - (DOD, NATO, CENTO, IADB) A degree of risk where anticipated effects may cause some temporary shock, casualties, and may significantly reduce the unit's combat efficiency. See also moderate risk (nuclear).

emergency scramble - (DOD) In air intercept, carrier(s) addressed immediately launch all available fighter aircraft as combat air patrol. If all available are not required, numerals and/or type may be added.

emergency substitute - (NATO, CENTO, IADB) A product which may be used, in an emergency only, in place of another product, but only on the advice of technically qualified personnel of the nation using the product, who will specify the limitations. See also acceptable product; (NATO) unified product; standardized product.

emission control orders - (DOD) Orders, referred to as EMCON orders, used to authorize, control, or prohibit the use of electronic emission equipment. See also control of electromagnetic radiation.

emission control orders - (IADB) Orders used to authorize, control, or prohibit the use of electronic emission equipment. See also control of electromagnetic radiation.

emplacement - (DOD, NATO, SEATO, CENTO, IADB) 1. A prepared position for one or more weapons or pieces of equipment, for protection against hostile fire or bombardment, and from which they can execute their tasks. 2. The act of fixing a gun in a prepared position from which it may be fired.

emulation - Communist theory by which one tries to imitate a leader holding the correct values.

encipher - (DOD, IADB) To convert plain text into unintelligible form by means of a cipher system.

encipher - (NATO, CENTO) To convert a plain-text message into unintelligible language by means of a cipher system. See also crypto-system.

enclave policy - A U.S. military strategy to protect specific "enclaves" or areas not engage in a full territorial battle, not implemented.

encounter - An aviation term for a multiple contact action with enemy aircraft.

encrypt - (DOD, IADB) To convert plain text into unintelligible form by means of a cipher system.

encrypt - In common usage, the term encrypt covers the meanings of encipher and encode. See also cryptosystem.

end item - (DOD, IADB) A final combination of end products, component parts, and/or materials which is ready for its intended use, e.g., ship, tank, mobile machine shop, aircraft.

End of Evening Nautical Twilight - When dark has fallen, Navy term.

end of mission - (DOD) An order given to terminate firing on a specific target.

endurance - (DOD, NATO, CENTO, IADB) The time an aircraft can continue flying or a ground vehicle or ship can continue operating under specified conditions, e.g. without refueling. See also endurance distance.

endurance - (SEATO) The time an aircraft can continue flying under given conditions without refueling.

endurance distance - (DOD, NATO, CENTO, IADB) Total distance that a ground vehicle or ship can be self propelled at any specified endurance speed.

endurance loading - (DOD, IADB) The stocking aboard ship for a period of time normally covering the number of months between overhauls of items with all of the following characteristics: a. low price; b. low weight and cube; c. a predictable usage rate; and d. non-deteriorative. See also loading.

endurance speed - (NATO, CENTO) The nautical miles per hour a ship will travel through the water under average conditions of hull, sea in temperate weather, and wartime readiness. Endurance speeds in each case will correspond with specific engine speeds.

endurance time - (NATO, CENTO) The total time for which any specified endurance speed of a ship can be maintained. If this value is dependent on factors other than fuel, it shall be so indicated.

enemy - The North Vietnamese, Viet Cong, and their allies.

enemy capabilities - (DOD, NATO, SEATO, CENTO, IADB) Those courses of action of which the enemy is physically capable, and which, if adopted, will affect the accomplishment of our mission. The term "capabilities" includes not only the general courses of action open to the enemy, such as attack, defense, or withdrawal, but also all the particular courses of action possible under each general course of action. "Enemy capabilities" are considered in the light of all known factors affecting military operations including time, space, weather, terrain, and the strength and disposition of enemy forces. In strategic thinking, the capabilities of a nation represent the courses of action within the power of the nation for accomplishing its national objectives in peace or war.

ENFF - Enemy initiated fire fight.

engage - (DOD) In air intercept, a code meaning attack designated contact.

engagement control - (DOD, NATO, CENTO) In air defense, that degree of control exercised over the operational functions of an air defense fire unit that are related to detection, identification, engagement, and destruction of hostile targets. Note: NATO and CENTO definition uses "air defense unit" instead of "air defense fire unit".

Engr - engineer.

ENI - An enemy initiated incident.

enlargement - (NATO, CENTO) A negative, diapositive or paper print made at a larger scale than the original.

ENS - Ensign (Navy, Coast Guard).

ENSURE - Expedited Non-standard Urgent Requirement for Equipment. A requisition form asking for unusual gear or materials, justifying the use, and suggesting a source.

Entac - (DOD) A French-designed, antitank, wire-guided missile using a solid fuel propellant. Can be dropped by parachute from planes, launched from the ground, a vehicle, or helicopter, and is man-transportable. Designated as MGM-32.

entrenching tool - A small folding shovel. See E-tool.

envelope - 1. Aviation term for the area needed for a weapon to deploy effectively. 2. The range of operational capacity for an aircraft. Flying at the edge of the envelope is dangerous and thrilling.

environmental services - (DOD) The various combinations of scientific, technical and advisory activities (including modification processes, i.e., the influence of man-made and natural factors) required to acquire, produce, and supply information on the past, present, and future states of space, atmospheric, oceanographic, and terrestrial surroundings for use in military planning and decision-making processes, or to modify those surroundings to enhance military operations.

EOD - See explosive ordinance detail.

EOD team - The bomb squad.

ephemeris - (DOD, IADB) A publication giving the computed places of the celestial bodies for each day of the year, or for other regular intervals.

equal area projection - (NATO, CENTO) One in which equal areas on the ground are represented by equal areas on the map.

equipment - (DOD, IADB) All articles needed to outfit an individual or organization. The term refers to clothing, tools, utensils, vehicles, weapons, and other similar items. As to type of authorization, equipment may be divided into special (or project) equipment, equipment prescribed by tables of allowances, and equipment prescribed by tables of organization and equipment. See also individual equipment; material; organizational equipment; special (or project) equipment.

equivalent airspeed - See airspeed.

equivalent focal length - (NATO, CENTO) The distance measured along the optical axis of the lens from the rear nodal point to the plane of best average definition over the entire field used in a camera. See also focal length.

ER - Efficiency report. a soldier's personnel report on performance, progress, fitness and advancement.

ERDL - A camouflage pattern of four woodland colors on a green background.

errand boy - The daily courier flights.

escalation - (DOD, IADB) An increase in scope or violence of a conflict, deliberate or unpremeditated.

escape and evasion -1. The tactics used if captured or separated from your unit to get back to safety. 2. Slang for anyone who evades added duty assignments, a slacker.

escape line - (DOD) A planned route to allow personnel engaged in clandestine activity to depart from a site or area when possibility of compromise or apprehension exists.

escape route - See evasion and escape route.

escapee - (DOD, IADB) Any person who has been physically captured by the enemy and succeeds in freeing himself. See also evasion and escape.

escort - (DOD, NATO, SEATO, CENTO, IADB) 1. To convoy. 2. A combatant unit or units assigned to accompany and protect another force. 3. Aircraft assigned to protect other aircraft during a mission. 4. An armed guard that accompanies a convoy, a train, prisoners, etc. 5. An armed guard accompanying persons as a mark of honor. (DOD) 6. A member of the Armed Forces assigned to accompany, assist, or guide an individual or group, e.g., an escort officer. (Note: SEATO definition Part 2 uses "a weaker force" instead of "another force".)

escort forces - (DOD, IADB) Combat forces of various types provided to protect other forces against enemy attack.

escort ship - (DOD, IADB) A warship designed to screen support forces and convoys, and to operate against submarines. (Normal armament consists of 5" or 3" dual-purpose guns and various antisubmarine warfare weapons). Designated as DE.

esker - (NATO) A narrow ridge or mound of sand and gravel deposited by a subglacial stream.

espionage - (DOD, NATO, CENTO) Actions directed toward the acquisition of information through clandestine operations.

essential cargo - See essential supply.

essential elements of information - (DOD) The critical items of information regarding the enemy and his environment needed by the commander by a particular time, to relate with other available information and intelligence in order to assist him in reaching a logical decision.

essential elements of information (intelligence) - (NATO, CENTO, IADB) The critical items of information regarding the enemy and his environment required in order to make timely decisions.

essential industry - (DOD, IADB) Any industry necessary to the needs of a civilian or war economy. The term includes the basic industries as well as the necessary portions of those other industries which transform the crude basic raw materials into useful intermediate or end products, e.g., the iron and steel industry, the food industry, and the chemical industry.

essential supply - (NATO, CENTO, IADB) A commodity which is essential for the prosecution of the war in the survival period, or for national survival in that period, and which should be discharged as soon as circumstances permit. This will comprise such things as food, refined petroleum, oils, and lubricants, and medical stores. See also cargoes.

EST - Essential Subjects Test. An annual academic test for all ranks under sergeant.

establishment - (DOD, NATO, SEATO, CENTO, IADB) 1. An installation, together with its personnel and equipment, organized as an operating entity. (NATO, SEATO, CENTO) 2. The table setting out the authorized numbers of men and major equipments in a unit/formation; sometimes called "table of organization" or "table of organization and equipment". See also activity; base.

estimate - (DOD) 1. An analysis of a foreign situation, development, or trend which identifies its major elements, interprets the significance, and appraises the future possibilities and the prospective results of the various actions that might be taken 2. An appraisal of the capabilities, vulnerabilities, and potential courses of action of a foreign nation or combination of nations in consequence of a specific national plan, policy, decision, or contemplated course of action. 3. An analysis of an actual or contemplated clandestine operation in relation to the situation in which it is or would be conducted, in order to identify and appraise such factors as available and needed assets and potential obstacles, accomplishments, and consequences. See also intelligence estimate. 4. In air intercept operations, means- Provide a quick estimate of the height/depth/range/size of designated contact or I estimate height/depth/range/ size of designated contact is _____.

estimate of the situation - (NATO, SEATO, CENTO, IADB) A logical process of reasoning by which a commander considers all the circumstances affecting the military situation and arrives at a decision as to the course of action to be taken in order to accomplish his mission. See also commander's estimate of the situation; intelligence estimate of the situation; logistic estimate of the situation.

ET - Entrenching tool.

ETA - Estimated time of arrival.

ETD - Estimated time of departure.

ETS - The "get out" date variously defined by different services as: expiration of term of service, estimated time of service, estimated time of separation, end of tour of service, or estimated termination of services.

EV - Escort vehicle.

evac - Medical slang for evacuation hospital.

evacuation - (DOD) 1. The process of moving any person who is wounded, injured, or ill to and/or between medical treatment facilities. 2. The clearance of personnel, animals, or materiel from a given locality. 3. The controlled process of collecting, classifying, and shipping unserviceable or abandoned materiel, United States and foreign, to appropriate reclamation, maintenance, technical intelligence, or disposal facilities.

evacuation - (IADB) 1. The process of moving casualties from a battlefield, and subsequently of moving them along the chain of evacuation, as necessary. 2. The clearance of personnel, animals, or materiel from a given locality.

evacuation control ship - (DOD, NATO, SEATO, CENTO, IADB) In an amphibious operation, a ship designated as a control point for landing craft, amphibious vehicles, and helicopters evacuating casualties from the beaches. Medical personnel embarked in the evacuation control ship effect distribution of casualties throughout the attack force in accordance with ships' casualty capacities and specialized medical facilities available, and also perform emergency surgery.

evacuation convoy - (NATO, CENTO, IADB) An ocean convoy which is used for area evacuation in the early days of war. See also convoy.

evacuation hospital - Semi-mobile medical facility for stabilization of wounded or ill before transport to a more permanent facility.

evacuation policy - (DOD) 1. Command decision, indicating the length in days of the maximum period of noneffectiveness that patients may be held within the command for treatment. Patients who, in the opinion of responsible medical officers, cannot be returned to duty status within the period prescribed are evacuated by the first available means, provided the travel involved will not aggravate their disabilities. 2. A command decision concerning the movement of civilians from the proximity of military operations for security and safety reasons, and involving the need to arrange for movement, reception, care, and control of such individuals. 3. Command policy concerning the evacuation of unserviceable or abandoned materiel, and including designation of channels and destinations for evacuated materiel, the establishment of controls and procedures, and the dissemination of condition standards and disposition instructions.

evacuee - (DOD, IADB) A civilian removed from his place of residence by military direction for reasons of his own security or the requirements of the military situation. See also displaced person; expellee; refugee.

evacuees - (NATO, CENTO) Civilians, either residents or transients, who have been ordered to move by competent authority, and whose movement and accommodation are planned and controlled. See also displaced person; refugee.

evader - (DOD) Any person who has become isolated in hostile or unfriendly territory who eludes capture.

evaluation - See operational evaluation; technical evaluation.

evaluation (intelligence) - (DOD, NESN, CENTO, IADB) Appraisal of an item of information in terms of credibility, reliability, pertinency, and accuracy. Appraisal is accomplished at several stages within the intelligence process with progressively different contexts. Initial evaluations, made by case officers and report officers, are focused upon the reliability of the source and the accuracy of the information as judged by data available at or close to their operational levels. Later evaluations, by intelligence analysts, are primarily concerned with verifying accuracy of information and may, in effect, convert information into intelligence. Appraisal or evaluation of items of information or intelligence is indicated by a standard letter-number system. The evaluation of the reliability of sources is designated by a letter from A through F, and the accuracy of the information is designated by numeral 1 through 6. These are two entirely independent appraisals, and these separate appraisals are indicated in accordance with the system indicated below. Thus, information adjudged to be "probably true" received from a "usually reliable source" is designated "B-2" or "B2" while information of which the "truth cannot be judged" received from a "usually reliable source" is designated "B-6" or "B6". Rating of Reliability of Source: A-Completely reliable, B-Usually reliable, C-Fairly reliable, D-Not usually reliable, E -Unreliable, F-Reliability cannot be judged. Rating of Accuracy of Information: 1-Confirmed by other sources, 2-Probably true, 3-Possibly true, 4-Doubtful, 5-Improbable, 6-Truth cannot be judged.

evaluation of information (intelligence) - See evaluation (intelligence).

evaluation rating (intelligence) - See evaluation (intelligence).

evasion and escape - (DOD, I, NATO, SEATO, CENTO, IADB) The procedures and operations whereby military personnel and other selected individuals are enabled to emerge from an enemy-held or hostile area to areas under friendly control.

evasion and escape intelligence - (DOD) Processed information prepared to assist personnel to escape if captured by the enemy or to evade capture if lost in enemy-dominated territory.

evasion and escape net - (DOD) The organization within enemy held or hostile areas that operates to receive, move, and exfiltrate military personnel or selected individuals to friendly control. See also unconventional warfare.

evasion and escape route - (DOD) A course of travel, preplanned or not, which an escapee or evader uses in his attempt to depart enemy territory in order to return to friendly lines.

event - Slang for a nuclear explosion (of which there were none).

every swinging dick - Everyone.

EW - Electronic warfare.

EWO - Electronic warfare officer.

ex-Marine - A fictional concept. None such. Also former Marine.

exaggerated stereoscopy - See hyperstereoscopy.

excess property - (DOD) The quantity of property in possession of any component of the Department of Defense which exceeds the quantity required or authorized for retention by that component.

excess property - (IADB) The quantity of property in possession of any component of the Armed Forces which exceeds the quantity required or authorized for retention by that component.

exec - See Executive Officer.

executing commander (nuclear weapons) - (DOD, NATO, SEATO, CENTO) A commander to whom nuclear weapons are released for delivery against specific targets or in accordance with approved plans. See also commander(s); releasing commander (nuclear weapons).

Executive Agent for the Joint Chiefs of Staff - (DOD) A member of the Joint Chiefs of Staff to whom they have assigned responsibility and delegated authority, which would otherwise be exercised by them collectively, to carry out for them certain of their duties.

Executive Officer - Second in command, aid to Commanding Officer, usually separated in combat so XO could assume command if the CO were disabled. Abbreviated as XO.

exercise - (DOD, NATO, CENTO, IADB) A military maneuver or simulated wartime operation involving planning, preparation, and execution. It is carried out for the purpose of training and evaluation. It may be a combined, unified, joint, or single Service exercise, depending on participating organizations. See also command post exercise; field exercise; maneuver.

exercise codeword - (SEATO) An exercise codeword is a codeword whose use is confined to a specific exercise. See also codeword; inactive codeword; using agency.

exercise commander - (NATO, SEATO, CENTO, IADB) A commander taking part in the exercise who will issue appropriate operation orders to forces placed under his control. He may be allocated responsibilities regarding controlling, conducting and/or directing the exercise in addition to that of command. See also commander(s).

exfiltration - (DOD) The removal of personnel or units from areas under enemy control.

existence load - (DOD) Consists of items other than those in the fighting load which are required to sustain or protect the combat soldier, which may be necessary for increased personal and environmental protection, and which are not normally carried by the individual. See also fighting load.

exoatmosphere - See nuclear exoatmospheric burst.

Expediter - Beechcraft twin engine aircraft.

expeditionary force - (DOD, IADB) An armed force organized to accomplish a specific objective in a foreign country.

Expeditionary Medal - The Armed Forces Expeditionary Medal is the award by the U.S. for service in the United States military when there is no other medal available. The Vietnam Service Medal replaced it. See Armed Forces Expeditionary Medal.

expellee - (DOD, IADB) A civilian outside the boundaries of the country of his nationality or ethnic origin, who is being forcibly repatriated to that country, or to a third country, for political or other purposes. See also displaced person; evacuee; refugee.

expendable property - (DOD, IADB) Property that may be consumed in use or loses its identity in use and may be dropped from stock record accounts when it is issued or used.

expendable supplies and material - (DOD, IADB) Supplies which are consumed in use, such as ammunition, paint, fuel, cleaning and preserving materials, surgical dressings, drugs, medicines, etc., or which lose their identity, such as spare parts, etc. Sometimes referred to as consumable supplies and material.

expendable supplies and material - (NATO, SEATO, CENTO) Items which are consumed in use, such as ammunition, or which lose their identity, such as certain repair parts, or which are of low intrinsic value, unworthy of full accounting procedures.

expiration of term of service - Date when term of service ends, See ETS.

exploitation - (DOD, NATO, SEATO, CENTO, IADB) 1. Taking full advantage of success in battle and following up initial gains. 2. Taking full advantage of any information that has come to hand for tactical or strategic purposes.(DOD). 3. In intelligence usage, the process of getting information from any source.

explosive ordinance detail - A military assignment in each of the services to disarm booby traps. See EOD.

explosive ordnance disposal unit - (DOD, IADB) Personnel with special training and equipment who render explosive ordnance safe (such as bombs, mines, projectiles, and booby traps), make intelligence reports on such ordnance, and supervise the safe removal thereof.

exposure dose - (DOD, NATO, CENTO) The exposure dose at a given point is a measurement of radiation in relation to its ability to produce ionization. The unit of measurement of the exposure dose is the roentgen.

exposure station - See air station (photogrammetry); camera station (photogrammetry).

extend - Voluntary extension of the term of service in Vietnam.

extent of damage - (DOD) The visible plan area of damage to a target element, usually expressed in units of 1,000 square feet in detailed damage analysis and in approximate percentages in immediate-type damage assessment reports (e.g., 50 percent structural damage).

extract - To remove, usually from combat by helicopter.

extraction parachute - (DOD, NATO, CENTO, IADB) An auxiliary parachute designed to release and extract cargo from aircraft in flight and deploy cargo parachutes. See also gravity extraction.

eye fuck - To inspect carefully.

eyes in the sky - Slang for heat sensors in aircraft that detected enemy activity.

F – FOXTROT

F - 1. Designated in the military phonetic alphabet, as "Foxtrot". 2. The aviation designation for fighter aircraft.

F and M - See Fire and maneuver.

F-1 - See Fury.

F-1 - Soviet made fragmentation grenade.

F-10 - See Skyknight and Whale, initially designated F-3D.

F-100 - See Super Sabre.

F-101 - See Voodoo.

F-102 - See Delta Dagger.

F-104 - See Starfighter.

F-105 - See Thunderchief.

F-106 - See Delta Dart.

F-11 - See Tiger.

F-111 - (DOD, IADB) A twin-engine turbofan-powered tactical fighter for delivering nuclear and non-nuclear weapons and for operating from very short, relatively unprepared air strips with a minimum of ground support. The aircraft will have an all-weather attack capability. Other versions are: an all-weather interceptor version having a long-range pulse doppler fire control system and nuclear air-to-air missiles; a reconnaissance version having all-weather reconnaissance and bombing capabilities with both nuclear and nonnuclear weapons.

F-111 - Slang also called Aardvark and Edsel. Pronounced One-Eleven.

F-227 - A light transport aircraft for troops and supplies.

F-3 - See Demon.

F-3D - See F-10.

F-4 - See Phantom II.

F-5 - See Freedom Fighter and Scoshie Tiger.

F-6 - See Skyray.

F-8 - See Crusader.

F-80 - Shooting star.

F-89 - See Scorpion.

F-9 - See Cougar.

FA - 1. Field artillery. 2. Fireman Apprentice (Coast Guard).

fabricator - (DOD) Individuals or groups who, without genuine resources, invent information or inflate or embroider overt news for personal gain or for political purposes.

FAC - Forward Air Controller, pronounced "fack".

FAC-man - Nickname of the person who was the FAC.

face-shot - Air to air missile shot.

Faceplate - A NATO term for early MiG 21 jets.

facility - (DOD, IADB) 1. A physical plant, such as real estate and improvements thereto, including buildings and equipment, which provides the means for assisting or making easier the performance of a function, e.g., base arsenal, factory. 2. Any part or adjunct of a physical plant, or any item of equipment which is an operating entity and which contributes or can contribute to the execution of a function by providing some specific type of physical assistance.

facility - (NATO, SEATO, CENTO) An activity which provides a specific kind of operating assistance to naval, ground, or air forces, thereby facilitating any action or operation. See also base.

facsimile - (DOD, NATO, SEATO, CENTO, IADB) A system of telecommunication for the transmission of fixed images with a view to their reception in a permanent form.

faded - (DOD) In air intercept, a code meaning contact has disappeared from reporting station's scope, and any position information given is estimated.

FADM - Fleet Admiral (Navy- reserved for wartime).

FAE - Fuel-Air-Explosive. A massive bomb in which the fuel contained within it burned on detonation and either burned or suffocated all life and the explosion cleared sufficient space to create a helicopter landing zone.

FAG - Forward Air Guide. A soldier who guided air strikes from a forward position on the ground. Often a South Vietnamese soldier.

fair drawing - (NATO) A drawing complete in all respects in the style and form specified for reproduction.

faker - (DOD) A known strike aircraft engaged in an air defense exercise.

falciparum - One of the two types of malaria. See vivax.

Falcon - (DOD) An air-to-air guided missile. The Falcon family (AIM-4 series, AIM-26A, and AIM-47A) can be carried either internally or externally on interceptor aircraft. The Falcon can be used on the F-89, F-101B, F-104, and F-106. Some of the Falcon family of missiles are equipped with nuclear warheads.

fall in - The order to assemble in formation.

fallout - (DOD, NATO, SEATO, CENTO, IADB) The precipitation to earth of radioactive particulate matter from a nuclear cloud; also applied to the particulate matter itself.

fallout contours - (DOD, NATO, CENTO, IADB) Lines joining points which have the same radiation intensity that define a fallout pattern, represented in terms of roentgens per hour.

fallout pattern - (DOD, NATO), CENTO, IADB) The distribution of fallout as portrayed by fallout contours.

fallout prediction - (DOD) An estimate, made before and immediately after a nuclear detonation, of the location and intensity of militarily significant quantities of radioactive fallout.

fallout safe height of burst - (DOD) The height of burst at or above which no militarily significant fallout will be reproduced as a result of a nuclear weapon detonation. See types of burst.

fallout wind vector plot - (DOD, IADB) A wind vector diagram based on the wind structure from the earth's surface to the highest altitude affecting fallout pattern.

fallout wind vector plot - (NATO, CENTO) A wind vector diagram based on the wind structure from the earth's surface to the highest altitude of interest.

false origin - (DOD, NATO, SEATO, CENTO, IADB) A fixed point to the south and west of a grid zone from which grid distances are measured eastward and northward.

false parallax - (NATO, CENTO) The apparent vertical displacement of an object from its true position when viewed stereoscopically, due to movement of the object itself as well as to change in the point of observation.

false stereo - (NATO, CENTO) An imaginary impression of stereoscopic relief.

FAME - Floating Aircraft Maintenance Facility.

family syndrome - The practice of the South Vietnamese soldier to relocate their families near them, thus slowing relocations or reducing troop effectiveness.

famished - (DOD) In air intercept, a code meaning have you any instructions for me?

fan camera photography - (DOD, NATO, CENTO) Photography taken simultaneously by an assembly of three or more cameras, systematically installed at fixed angles relative to each other so as to provide wide lateral coverage with overlapping images.

fan cameras - (DOD, NATO, CENTO, IADB) An assembly of three or more cameras systematically disposed at fixed angles relative to each other so as to provide wide lateral coverage with overlapping images. See also split cameras.

fan marker beacon - (NATO, SEATO, CENTO, IADB) A type of radio beacon, the emissions which radiate in a vertical, fan-shaped pattern. (NATO, SEATO, CENTO) The signal can be keyed for identification purposes. See also beacon; Z marker beacon.

fan song radar - NATO slang for the Soviet made ground radar detection device.

fangs out - Aviation term for a pilot that is combat ready, looking for a dogfight.

Fantastic Feathered Fowl - See Chickenman.

farangs - Slang for foreigners.

Farm Gate - The code name for early United States Air Force assistance to the ARVN troops.

farm gate type operations - (DOD, I) Operational assistance and specialized tactical training provided a friendly foreign air force by the United States Armed Forces to include, under certain specified conditions, the flying of operational missions in combat by combined United States/foreign aircrews as a part of the training being given when such missions are beyond the capability of the foreign air force.

Farmer - The NATO slang for the MiG 19 jet.

fart sack - Sleeping bag.

fast bird - Jet attack planes.

fast mover - Slang for the F-4 jet or fast land vehicles, such as M-1 Abrams tanks and M2 Bradley fighting vehicles.

fat - Over authorized unit strength.

fat bombs - Ordinance that is nonnuclear, from WWII or Korean War era.

Fat City - MACV headquarters.

fat rats - Slang for the 5-gallon collapsible water bladder. Note often inflated and used to float equipment over water.

fat rats jobs - See Skatin'.

fat unit - A unit staffed with more than the allotted personnel.

fatigues - Military work uniform. Also called fats, combat fatigues, utilities.

fatty-gews - Fatigues.

favorable kill ratio - More of the enemy was killed than your troops.

FAX - See facsimile. Note: The technology of facsimile telegraphy was in transition from thermal paper on a drum to a flat page printer toward the end of the war. The usage of FAX as a noun during this era was limited to those with this access. Usage as a verb emerges in 1979, after the period covered by this reference.

FAY - See FAE.

FB - See fire base.

FBIS - Foreign Broadcast Information Service.

FC - 1. Forward controller. 2. Fire control.

FCT - Fire control tower. An elevated structure like a lifeguard stand, protected by sandbags or plating in a base camp used to direct artillery, mortar or machine gun fire when the base was attacked.

FDC - Fire Direction Control. The guidance for artillery.

FDO - Fire Direction Officer.

feasibility test - (DOD, IADB) A test to determine whether or not a plan is within the capacity of the resources which can be made available. See also logistic implications test.

feather - To adjust a propeller into a neutral position.

feature - (NATO) In cartography, any object or configuration of ground or water represented on the face of the map or chart.

feature line overlap - (NATO, CENTO) A series of overlapping air photographs which follow the line of a ground feature, e.g., river, road, railway, etc.

FEBA - Forward edge of battle area. As close a definition of the 'front' as possible in the fluid dynamic of unconventional warfare.

FEC - Far East Command.

feet dry - (DOD) In air intercept and close air support and air interdiction, a code meaning I am, or contact designated is, over land.

feet wet - (DOD) In air intercept and close air support and air interdiction, a code meaning I am, or contact designated is, over water.

fence, the fence - The Mekong River which was the approximate location of most of the border between North and South Vietnam.

fenugie - Slang for fuckin' new guy, pronounced fa-nuggie. See FNG.

ferret - (DOD, IADB) An aircraft, ship, or vehicle especially equipped for the detection, location, recording, and analyzing of electromagnetic radiation.

few (raid size) - (DOD) In air intercept usage, 7 or less aircraft. See also many (raid size).

FF - 1. Fire Fighter. A fire truck. 2. Firefly, a night helicopter mission.

FFE - Fire for effect.

FFZ - Free fire zone. No specific permission was needed to engage the enemy.

fib - A diversionary tactic to make one group seem larger than it was to drive enemy into another area for ambush.

FID - Foreign internal defense. The training of locals by Special Forces to fight.

FIDO - Fuck it, drive on. Used when a decoy, ambush, or trouble is spotted.

fiducial marks - See collimating marks.

field - 1. The area in which enemy contact is possible and probable. 2. Any area away from the base or base camp.

field army - (DOD, IADB) Administrative and tactical organization composed of a headquarters, certain organic Army troops, service support troops, a variable number of corps, and a variable number of divisions.

field artillery direct support weapons - (DOD, IADB) Artillery assigned the task of executing the fire requested by the supported unit.

field artillery general support weapons - (DOD, IADB) Artillery which fires in support of the operation as a whole rather than a specific unit.

field artillery observer - (DOD, IADB) A person who watches the effects of artillery fire, adjusts the center of impact of that fire onto a target, reporting results to the firing agency. See also naval gunfire spotting team; spotter.

field control - (DOD, NATO, CENTO) A series of points whose relative positions and elevations are known. These positions are used in basic data in mapping and charting.

Normally, these positions are established by survey methods, and, are sometimes referred to as "trig control". See also common control; control point; ground control.

field cross - A memorial arrangement of a rifle, boots and helmet of a fallen soldier.

field day - Marine slang for general housecleaning. See GI.

field exercise - (DOD, NATO, SEATO, CENTO, IADB) An exercise conducted in the field under simulated war conditions in which troops and armament of one side are actually present, while those of the other side may be imaginary or in outline. See also command post exercise; maneuver.

field fire - Marksman training in simulated field conditions.

field first - The sergeant who runs the unit in actuality in the field while the official commander in the rear.

field fortifications - (DOD, NATO, CENTO) Emplacements and shelters of a temporary nature which can be constructed with reasonable facility by units requiring no more than minor engineer supervisory and equipment participation.

field grade officers - Officers of the ranks of Major, Lieutenant Colonel and Colonel.

field headquarters - See command post.

field jacket - A waterproof jacket with a zipper closure worn in cold weather.

field load - The basic issue of weapon and ammunition for a soldier's specific assignment. Also basic load.

field maintenance - (DOD) That maintenance authorized and performed by designated Army, Air Force, and Marine Corps maintenance activities in direct support of using organizations. It is normally limited to replacement of unserviceable parts, subassemblies, or assemblies.

field maintenance - (IADB) That maintenance authorized and performed by designated maintenance activities in direct support of using organizations. It is normally limited to replacement of unserviceable parts, subassemblies, or assemblies.

field manual - The books of Army policies and procedures.

field of fire - (DOD, NATO, SEATO, CENTO, IADB) The area which a weapon or a group of weapons may cover effectively with fire from a given position.

field of view - (NATO, CENTO) The angle between two rays passing through the perspective center (rear nodal point) of a camera lens to the two opposite sides of the format. Not to be confused with "angle of view". See also angle of view.

field phone - The hand cranked telephones used in bunkers.

field press censorship - (DOD, IADB) The security review of news material subject to the jurisdiction of the Armed Forces of the United States, including all information or material intended for dissemination to the public. See also censorship.

field radio - The battery operated portable radio the size of a backpack.

field scarf - Marine slang for a necktie.

field strip - To take apart, usually to clean.

field transport pack - A Marine system of packing gear carried in the field.

field utility - Non-military issues items either bought locally or made by troops.

field-grade night - A night in which it is bright enough to allow pilots to observe features on the ground.

fifteen and two - A common discipline sentence of fifteen days restriction and two hours a day of extra duty.

fifteen fifties, 1550s - The lightweight Class A Air Force uniform.

fifty cal, 50 cal - The .50 cal machine gun.

fifty caliber HMG, .50 cal HMG - See M-2 HMG.

fifty five, 55 - The number POWs scuffed into the dirt to alert pilots not to attack the location.

fifty-caliber (.50 cal) - Fifty-caliber American made machine gun.

fifty-foot roll of flight line - The imaginary supply that rookies were sent to supply to request as a prank. See flight line for the proper use.

fifty-one cal, 51 cal - The heavy machine gun used by the North Vietnamese.

fifty-seven AA, 57-mm AA - The S-60 North Vietnamese antiaircraft gun.

fifty-seven recoilless, 57-mm recoilless - See M-18A1 RCL.

fighter - A fixed wing aircraft designed for air-to-air combat.

fighter controller - See air controller.

fighter cover - (DOD, NATO, SEATO, CENTO, IADB) The maintenance of a number of fighter aircraft over a specified area or force for the purpose of repelling hostile air activities. See also airborne alert.

fighter direction aircraft - (DOD, NATO, SEATO, CENTO, IADB) An aircraft equipped and manned for directing fighter aircraft operations. See also combat information ship.

fighter direction ship - (DOD, NATO, SEATO, CENTO, IADB) A ship equipped and manned for directing fighter aircraft operations. See also combat information ship.

fighter director - See air controller.

fighter interceptor - (SEATO, IADB) A fighter aircraft designed to intercept its target. It mayor may not carry devices to assist in interception and in aiming its weapons. See also interceptor.

fighter jock - Pilot.

fighter sweep - (DOD, NATO, SEATO, CENTO, IADB) An offensive mission by fighter aircraft to seek out and destroy enemy aircraft or targets of opportunity in an allotted area of operations.

fighters - Fighter aircraft.

Fighting for peace is like fucking for virginity. - A common saying on the futility of war.

fighting hole - A small dug out position like a foxhole.

fighting load - (DOD) Consists of items of individual clothing, equipment, weapons, and ammunition which are carried by, and are essential to, the effectiveness of the combat soldier and the accomplishment of the immediate mission of his unit when he is on foot. See also existence load.

fighting patrol - See combat patrol.

fighting wing - The wingman in the fighting wing formation.

fighting wing formation - Aviation term for a two plane formation in which the wingman is to the side and slightly behind the lead plane. The wingman's plane is usually to the right. See wingman.

figmo - Fuck it I got my orders. Pronounced fig-mo.

filler - (DOD, IADB) 1. A substance carried in an ammunition container such as a projectile, mine, bomb, or grenade. A filler may be an explosive, chemical, or inert substance. 2. One of a number of individuals, officer or enlisted, required initially to bring a unit, organization, or approved allotment to authorized strength.

filler point - See charging point.

film badge - (DOD, NATO, CENTO, IADB) A photographic film packet to be carried by personnel, in the form of a badge, for measuring and permanently recording (usually) gamma ray dosage.

film rating system - GI's system of rating films shown on base on the Skin/Fuzz system, Skin was flesh shown on a 1-2-3 rating scale. Fuzz was pubic hair shown on the same scale. Both were rated on 1 (little) 2 (some) 3 (lots) scale. Such as a "Skin 3 Fuzz 2" rating.

filter center - (DOD, IADB) The location in an aircraft control and warning system at which information from observation posts is filtered for further dissemination to air defense control centers and air defense direction centers.

filtering - (NATO, SEATO, CENTO, IADB) The process of interpreting reported information on movements of aircraft, ships, and submarines in order to determine their probable true tracks and, where applicable, heights or depths.

fin - Navy term for one not qualified in SCUBA.

final destination (merchant shipping) - (NATO, CENTO, IADB) The final destination of a convoy or of an individual ship (whether in convoy or independent) irrespective of whether or not routing instructions have been issued. See also destinations.

final protective fire - (DOD) An immediately available prearranged barrier of fire designed to impede enemy movement across defensive lines or areas.

financial property accounting - (DOD, IADB) The establishment and maintenance of property accounts in monetary terms; the rendition of property reports in monetary terms.

find, fix, finish (FFF) - Strategy to locate, pin down and kill the enemy.

finger - 1. The obscene gesture of a middle finger extended representing "fuck you". 2. A unit of hashish based on the form of purchase which was by the amount that was under a fingernail when pulled across a block of hashish.

finger charge - An explosive used for setting booby traps, the size is that of a man's finger.

finger four formation - Aviation term for an aerial formation of four planes in a modified wedge. The lead plane had two planes trailing off one wing and one off the other,

fingertip formation - Aviation slang for the finger four formation.

fini flight - Air Force slang for a pilot's last mission.

fini-hut - Over. Blurring both the French *fini* and Vietnamese *hut* into an emphatic declaration that something has ended.

fire - (DOD) The command given to discharge a weapon(s). See also barrage fire; call fire; close supporting fire; concentrated fire; counterfire; counterpreparation fire; covering fire; deep supporting fire; destruction fire; direct fire; direct supporting fire; distributed fire; grazing fire; harassing fire; indirect fire; interdiction fire; neutralization fire; observed fire; prearranged or scheduled fire; preparation fire; radar fire; registration fire; searching fire; supporting fire; unobserved fire; visual fire; zone fire.

fire - Shoot. Also bust caps, light up, bring heat.

fire and maneuver - An infantry strategy to use two units to lure an enemy closer. The first unit advances, draws fire and retreats. The enemy follows to bring them closer to unit two, thereupon both units attack. See F and M.

fire arrow - A huge arrow of wood with gas cans on it that was lighted and pointed to the enemy to direct air support at night.

fire barrage (specify) - (DOD) An order to deliver a prearranged barrier of fire. Specification of the particular barrage may be by code name, numbering system, unit assignment, or other designated means.

fire base - The site from which artillery fire was initiated, usually this was a remote hill top location. It had supply by helicopter and support from infantry. It could be a temporary location or one of long duration as was tactically needed. Also fire support base.

fire base psychosis - Slang for the GI's fear of going too far from the protection of the base.

fire brigade - A mobile operation that was relocated quickly as needed.

fire capabilities chart - (DOD) A chart, usually in the form of an overlay, showing the areas which can be reached by the fire of the bulk of the weapons of a unit.

fire control radar - (DOD, NATO, SEATO, CENTO, IADB) Radar used to provide target information inputs to a weapon fire control system.

fire coordination - See fire support coordination.

fire coordination area - (DOD) An area with specified restraints into which fires in excess of those restraints· will not be delivered without approval of the authority establishing the restraints.

fire coordination line - (DOD) A line established to coordinate fires between helicopterborne or airborne forces and linkup forces or between any converging friendly forces.

fire direction center - (DOD, IADB) That element of a command post, consisting of gunnery and communication personnel and equipment, by means of which the commander exercises fire direction and/or fire control. The fire direction center receives target intelligence and requests for fire, and translates them into appropriate fire direction.

fire discipline - The discipline to fire rounds in short bursts to conserve ammunition and prevent overheating a machine gun barrel which can result in premature ignition of cartridges.

fire for effect - (DOD, NATO, SEATO, CENTO, IADB) 1. Fire which is delivered after the mean point of impact or burst is within the desired distance of the target or adjusting/ranging point. 2. Term in a fire message to indicate the adjustment/ranging is satisfactory and fire for effect is desired.

fire for record - The official test of small arms proficiency as marksman, sharpshooter or expert.

fire guard - A night watch of an hour to alert others of any fire in barracks, usually limited to a training location.

fire in the hole - A warning that explosives were about to be set off.

fire message - See call for fire.

fire mission - (DOD, NATO, SEATO, CENTO, IADB) 1. Specific assignment given to a fire unit as part of a definite plan. (DOD, NATO, CENTO, IADB) 2. Order used to alert the weapon/battery area and indicate that the message following is a call for fire.

fire plan - (NATO, SEATO, CENTO, IADB) A tactical plan for using the weapons of a unit or formation so that their fire will be coordinated.

fire registration - (SEATO, IADB) Fire delivered to obtain accurate data for subsequent effective engagement of targets.

fire storm - (DOD, NATO, CENTO) Stationary mass fire, generally in built-up urban areas, generating strong, inrushing winds from all sides; the winds keep the fires from spreading while adding fresh oxygen to increase their intensity.

fire support area - (DOD, NATO, SEATO, CENTO, IADB) An appropriate maneuver area assigned to fire support ships from which to deliver gunfire support of an amphibious operation. See also naval support area.

fire support coordination - (DOD, NATO, SEATO, CENTO, IADB) The planning and executing of fire so that targets are adequately covered by a suitable weapon or group of weapons.

fire support coordination center - (DOD, NATO, SEATO, CENTO, IADB) A single location in which are centralized communications facilities and personnel incident to the coordination of all forms of fire support. See also supporting arms coordination center.

fire support coordination line - (DOD) An imaginary line arranged, if possible, to follow well defined geographical features, prescribed by the troop commander and coordinated with appropriate supporting commanders, forward of which supporting forces may attack targets, without danger or reference to the ground forces. Behind this line the attack of targets by forces not under the control of the troop commander must be coordinated with the appropriate troop commander.

fire support coordination line - (NATO, CENTO, IADB) A line established by the appropriate ground commander to insure coordination of fire not under his control but which may affect current tactical operations. The fire support coordination line should follow well defined terrain features. The establishment of the fire support coordination line is normally coordinated with the appropriate tactical air commander and other supporting elements.

fire support group - (DOD, NATO, CENTO, IADB) A temporary grouping of ships under a single commander charged with supporting troop operations ashore by naval gunfire. A fire support group may be further subdivided into fire support units and fire support elements.

fire support station - (DOD) An exact location at sea within a fire support area, from which a fire support ship delivers fire.

fire task - See fire mission.

fire team - 1. The Marine four-man unit. 2. The smallest unit of a rifle company of four or fewer soldiers.

fire time - See span of detonation (atomic demolition munition employment).

fire track - A flamethrowing tank.

fireball - (DOD, NATO, CENTO, IADB) The luminous sphere of gases which forms a few millionths of a second after detonation of a nuclear weapon and immediately starts expanding and cooling.

fireballing - Bringing a massive amount of artillery fire on one location.

firebee - An aircraft without a pilot. See RPV.

Firecan - NATO slang for the North Vietnamese radar unit used to direct antiaircraft fire.

firefight - Exchange of small arms fire with the enemy.

firefly - A night helicopter mission. See FF, Foxtrot Foxtrot.

firepower - (DOD, NATO, SEATO, CENTO, IADB) 1. The amount of fire which may be delivered by a position, unit, or weapon system. (DOD, NATO, CENTO, IADB) 2. Ability to deliver fire. (Note: SEATO definition consists of Part 1 only and ends with "weapon".)

firepower umbrella - (DOD, NATO, SEATO, CENTO, IADB) An area of specified dimensions defining the boundaries of the airspace over a naval force at sea within which the fire of ships' antiaircraft weapons can endanger aircraft, and within which special procedures have been established for the identification and operation of friendly aircraft. See also air defense operations area.

firing chart - (DOD, IADB) Map, photo map, or grid sheet showing the relative horizontal and vertical positions of batteries, base points, base point lines, check points, targets and other details needed in preparing firing data.

First John - A First Lieutenant.

First Lieutenant - Abbreviated as: 1LT (Army), 1stLt (Marine Corps), 1st Lt (Air Force).

first light - (DOD, IADB) The beginning of morning nautical twilight, i.e., when the center of the morning sun is 12 degrees below the horizon.

first log - The First Logistics Command, responsible for all supplies.

first pig - First Sergeant.

first salvo at _____ - (DOD) In naval gunfire support, a portion of a ship's message to an observer or spotter to indicate that because of proximity to troops, the ship will not fire at the target but offset the first salvo a specific distance from the target.

First Sergeant - Abbreviated as: 1SG (Army), 1stSgt (Marine Corps).

first shirt - Marine slang for the First Sergeant.

first strike - (DOD, IADB) The first offensive move of a war. (Generally associated with nuclear operations.)

first up - The lead helicopter or aircraft in a formation.

fish - Torpedo.

Fishbed - NATO nickname for single engine Soviet MiG-21 jet fighter which reached Mach 2.

fishhook - The code name for the area in Cambodia near the border of South Vietnam.

fission - (DOD) The process whereby the nucleus of a particular heavy element splits into (generally) two nuclei of lighter elements, with the release of substantial amounts of energy.

fission products - (DOD, NATO, CENTO) A general term for the complex mixture of substances produced as a result of nuclear fission.

fission to yield ratio - (DOD, NATO, CENTO, IADB) The ratio of the yield derived from nuclear fission to the total yield; it is frequently expressed in percent.

five - 1. Expressed in radio code or slang as nickel. 2. In radio code, the second in command, the executive officer.

five by five - 1. A radio operator's report that radio signal strength and clarity from the sending radio were excellent. Signal strength (Loud) and clarity (Clear) were rated on a 1-5 scale with 5 being the best, so Loud and Clear was Five by Five, degraded status required numeric clarification, so a reduced volume but clear signal was a three by five, etc. 2. Anything else being excellent. Also Lima Charlie.

five fingers - A large amount of hashish. The form of purchase was by the amount that was under a fingernail when pulled across a block.

five o'clock follies - Military briefings at the Saigon Joint united States Public Affairs Office. Derisive, stemming from lack of candor.

five squared - See five by five.

five-inch rocket, 5-inch rockets - See Zuni.

five-star general - The special rank is awarded only during wartime, see O-11.

five-ton truck, 5-ton truck - See M54 truck.

fiver - Radio slang for the number five.

fix - (DOD, NATO, SEATO, CENTO, IADB) A position determined from terrestrial, electronic, or astronomical data.

fixed ammunition - (DOD, NATO, SEATO, CENTO, IADB) Ammunition in which the cartridge case is permanently attached to the projectile. See also ammunition.

fixed capital property - (DOD) 1. Assets of a permanent character having continuing value. 2. As used in military establishments, includes real estate and equipment installed or in use, either in productive plants or in field operations. Synonymous with fixed assets.

fixed medical treatment facility - (DOD, NATO, SEATO, CENTO, IADB) A medical treatment facility which is designed to operate for an extended period of time at a specific site.

fixed price incentive contract - (DOD) A fixed price type of contract with provision for the adjustment of profit and price by a formula based on the relationship which final negotiated total cost bears to negotiated target cost as adjusted by approved changes.

fixed price type contract - (DOD) A type of contract which generally provides for a firm price, or under appropriate circumstances may provide for an adjustable price, for the supplies or services which are being procured. Fixed price contracts are of several types so designed as to facilitate proper pricing under varying circumstances.

fixed station patrol - (DOD, NATO, CENTO, IADB) One in which each scout maintains station relative to an assigned point on a barrier line while searching the surrounding area. Scouts are not stationary but remain underway and patrol near the center of their assigned stations. A scout is a surface ship, submarine, or aircraft.

fixer network - (NATO, SEATO, CENTO, IADB) A combination of radio or radar direction-finding installations which, operating in conjunction, are capable of plotting the position relative to the ground of an aircraft in flight.

fixer system - See fixer network.

flack - A public relations spokesman, a bullshitter. See flak.

flag - A limitation placed on a soldier's personnel file that limits duty stations, awards or promotions. The file is flagged.

flag days (red or green) - (DOD) Red flag days are those during which movement requirements cannot be met; green flag days are those during which the requisite amount or a surplus of transportation capability exists.

flag officer - Navy equivalent of General officers.

flak - The fire from antiaircraft guns. From WWI term (German: Flieger Abwher Kanon, an antiaircraft gun).

flak apron - A protective apron, too restricting for everyday use but used by bomb disposal teams.

flak birds - Aircraft tasked with flak suppression.

flak bursts - See Cotton balls.

flak envelope - The area in which flak is effective.

flak girdle - Body armor like pants used by helicopter pilots.

flak jacket - Torso body armor for the infantry.

flak suppression fire - (DOD) Fire used to suppress antiaircraft fire immediately prior to and during an air attack on enemy positions.

flak trap - An enemy tactic to delay deploying flack, as a rescue helicopter approached a downed pilot, until well within range.

flaky - A person or operation that is unorganized.

flame bath - A tactic by which drums of gas are dropped from helicopters and ignited by trip flares.

flameout - Jet engine failure. Also flame out.

flamethrower - (DOD, NATO, CENTO, IADB) A weapon that projects incendiary fuel and has provision for ignition of this fuel.

Flaming Dart - Code name for air strikes in retaliation for attacks on U.S. installations.

flaming horse turd - Slang for the insignia of the Ordinance Corps.

flaming onion - Slang for the insignia of the Ordinance Corps.

flaming piss pot - Slang for the insignia of the Ordinance Corps.

flammable cargo - See inflammable cargo.

flank - Sides of a troop formation.

flank guards - (DOD, NATO, CENTO) A security element operating to the flank of a moving or stationary force to protect it.

flank speed - Navy slang for full speed. The maximum speed that is attainable from that specific ship.

flare - 1. A signaling device either shot from a gun or a hand held launcher by ground troops. Location and rescue flares used smoke and illumination flares used colors for specific functions: white for illumination, red to signal enemy troop contact or green to signal friendly troop contact. Illumination flares were also launched or dropped from helicopters or planes. 2. Aviation term for a nose up landing that is used for most land airstrips. Not used on carriers which use a hard contact with the deck and arresting gear. 3. In the helicopter autorotation maneuver when power is lost, just before hitting ground the rotors are changed to slow the drop and divert energy to forward motion, reducing the impact of the crash.

flare dud - (DOD) A nuclear weapon, which when launched at a target, detonates with anticipated yield but at an altitude appreciably greater than intended. This is not a dud insofar as yield is concerned but it is a dud with respect to the effects on the target and the normal operation of the weapon.

flare kicker - The crew on a helicopter assigned to launch flares.

flare ship - An aircraft used for battlefield illumination.

flash - Radio proword for an emergency message to follow, pay attention.

flash blindness - (DOD, NATO, CENTO, IADB) Temporary impairment of vision resulting from an intense flash of light. It includes loss of night adaptation and dazzle, and may be associated with retinal burns. See also dazzle.

flash burn - (DOD, NATO, CENTO) A burn caused by excessive exposures (of bare skin) to thermal radiation.

flash message - (DOD, IADB) A category of precedence reserved for initial enemy contact messages or operational combat messages of extreme urgency. Brevity is mandatory. See also message precedence; precedence.

flash ranging - (DOD, IADB) Finding the position of the burst of a projectile or of an enemy gun by observing its flash.

flash report - (DOD) Not to be used. See in-flight report.

flash suppressor - (DOD, NATO, CENTO) Device attached to the muzzle of the weapon which reduces the amount of visible light or flash created by burning propellant gases.

flat hatting - Aviation slang for flying very close to the ground in an unauthorized manner, often stunting as well. Results can range from discipline to death.

flatted cargo - (DOD, IADB) Cargo placed in the bottom of the holds, covered with planks and dunnage, and held for future use. Flatted cargo usually has room left above it for the loading of vehicles which may be moved without interfering with the flatted cargo. Frequently, flatted cargo serves in lieu of ballast. Sometimes called understowed cargo. See also cargo.

flattop - An aircraft carrier.

FLD - Final line of departure. The imaginary line when crossed signals engagement in battle, behind which troops wait for the signal to advance.

flechette - French for dart. Bombs or other antipersonnel ordinance containing darts.

fleet - (DOD, IADB) An organization of ships, aircraft, marine forces and shore-based fleet activities, all under the command of a commander or commander in chief who may exercise operational as well as administrative control. See also major fleet; numbered fleet.

fleet ballistic missile submarine - (DOD, IADB) A nuclear-powered submarine designed to deliver ballistic missile attacks against assigned targets from either a submerged or surfaced condition. Designated as SSNB.

fleet in being - (DOD, IADB) A fleet (force) which avoids decisive action but which, because of its strength and location, causes or necessitates counter-concentrations and so reduces the number of opposing units available for operations elsewhere.

Fleet Marine Force - (DOD) A balanced force of combined arms comprising land, air, and service elements of the United States Marine Corps. A Fleet Marine Force is an integral part of a United States Fleet and has the status of a type command.

flex gun - The M-60 machine gun. Also Flexgun.

flexible response - (DOD, IADB) The capability of military forces for effective reaction to any enemy threat or attack with actions appropriate and adaptable to the circumstances existing.

flight line - (NATO, CENTO) In air graphic reconnaissance, the prescribed ground path over which an air vehicle moves during the execution of its photo mission.

flight readiness firing - (DOD, SEATO) A missile system test of short duration conducted with the propulsion system operating while the missile is secured to the launcher. Such a test is performed to determine the readiness of the missile system and launch facilities prior to flight test.

flight - (DOD) 1. In Navy and Marine Corps usage, a specified group of aircraft usually engaged in a common mission. 2. The basic tactical unit in the Air Force, consisting of four or more aircraft in two or more elements. 3. A single aircraft airborne on a nonoperational mission.

flight - (IADB) 1. A specified group of aircraft usually engaged in a common mission. 2. A single aircraft airborne on a nonoperational mission.

flight advisory - (DOD, IADB) A message dispatched to aircraft in flight, or to interested stations to advise of any deviation or irregularity.

flight deck - (DOD, IADB) 1. In certain airplanes, an elevated compartment occupied by the crew for operating the airplane in flight. 2. The upper deck of an aircraft carrier that serves as a runway.

flight deck casualty crane - The large crane attached to the flight deck of a carrier which removes any crashed or disabled aircraft from the flight deck allowing operations to continue. See Tilly.

flight information center - (DOD, NATO, CENTO, IADB) A unit established to provide flight information service and alerting service.

flight information region - (DOD, NATO, SEATO, CENTO, IADB) An airspace of defined dimensions within which flight information service and alerting service are provided. See also air traffic control area; air traffic control center; area control center.

flight integrity - The aviation term for the positioning and operation of all craft in support of the mission.

flight level - (IADB) An altitude of constant atmospheric pressure which is related to a pressure datum of 1013.25 mb or 29.92 hg.

flight levels - (DOD, NATO, CENTO) Surfaces of constant atmospheric pressure which are related to a specific pressure datum, 1013.2 mb (29.92 in), and are separated by specific pressure intervals. Flight levels are expressed in three digits that represent hundreds of feet; e.g. flight level 250 represents a barometric altimeter indication of 25,000 feet and flight level 255 is an indication of 25,500 feet.

flight line - The airfield parking area for flight ready craft.

flight operations center - (DOD) The element of the tactical Army air traffic regulation system which provides for aircraft flight following, separation of aircraft under instrument conditions, and identification of friendly aircraft to friendly air defense agencies.

flight pay - The added pay for pilots who maintain flight hours and proficiency.

flight plan - (DOD, NATO, SEATO, CENTO, IADB) Specified information provided to air traffic services units, relative to the intended flight of an aircraft.

flight plan correlation - (DOD) A means of identifying aircraft by association with known flight plans.

flight readiness firing - (NATO, CENTO) Short duration tests relating to a rocket system, carried out with the propulsion device in operation, the rocket being fixed on the launcher. Such tests are carried out in order to define the state of preparation of the rocket system and of the launching facilities before the flight test.

flight surgeon - (DOD, NATO, SEATO, CENTO, IADB) A physician specially trained in aviation medical practice whose primary duty is the medical examination and medical care of aircrew.

flight test - (DOD, NATO, SEATO, CENTO, IADB) Test of an aircraft, rocket, missile, or other vehicle by actual flight or launching. Flight tests are planned to achieve specific test objectives and gain operational information.

flight visibility - (DOD) The average forward horizontal distance from the cockpit of an aircraft in flight at which prominent unlighted objects may be seen and identified by day and prominent lighted objects may be seen and identified by night.

fling wing - Slang for helicopter.

flip flops - Rubber thong sandals.

flip out - Mental instability. Also crazy, crack up, flack happy.

flip-flop - A tactic to remove and replace troops by the same helicopter so the enemy thought all were removed and the area was clear.

FLIR - Forward looking infrared device. A heat detection system on aircraft to locate the enemy.

float - Sea duty.

float phase - 1. Marine slang for a seaborne deployment of a Marine unit. 2. Transportation on a Naval ship.

floating base support - (DOD, NATO, CENTO) A form of logistic support in which supplies, repairs, maintenance and other facilities and services are provided for operating forces from ships and craft within a harbor or anchorage.

floating lines - (NATO, CENTO) In photogrammetry, lines connecting the same two points of detail on each print of a stereo pair, used to determine whether or not the points are intervisible. The lines may be drawn directly into the prints or superimposed by means of strips of transparent material.

floating mark or dot - (NATO, CENTO) A mark seen as occupying a position in the three dimensional space formed by the stereoscopic fusion of a pair of photographs, used as a reference mark in examining or measuring a stereoscopic model.

floating reserve - (DOD, NATO, SEATO, CENTO, IADB) In an amphibious operation, reserve troops which remain embarked until needed. See also general reserve.

flotation - (DOD, NATO, CENTO) The capability of a vehicle to float in water.

flotation - (SEATO, IADB) 1. The capacity of a vehicle, gun, or trailer to negotiate water obstacles without being in contact with the bottom. (IADB) 2. The capacity of a vehicle to negotiate soft, unfavorable terrain such as mud, sand, or snow.

flotilla - (DOD, IADB) An administrative or tactical organization consisting of two or more squadrons of destroyers or smaller types, together with such additional ships as may be assigned as flagships and tenders.

flower seeker - A soldier looking for a prostitute.

fluff and buff - 1. Uniform preparation by having uniform done at a wash-and-wear laundry and boots buffed not shined. 2. Marginal but acceptable performance.

flume - (NATO) An inclined channel for conveying water.

fly by - 1. An authorized flight over an airfield or reviewing parade area, ceremonial in nature. 2. A pilot's unauthorized buzzing of a tower or low level flight over a landing strip in personal celebration.

fly(ing) at speed - (DOD) In air intercept, a term meaning fly at (Mach____/____) indicated air speed, or, my indicated air speed is (____ knots/Mach____).

flyboys - Pilots.

flying bananas - The H-21 helicopter.

flying battle cruiser - The B-25.

flying box car - A twin engine cargo plane fitted with miniguns and flares for support of ground troops and supply, designated C-119. Also flying boxcar.

flying bubble - The OH-13 helicopter.

flying cow - The C-123 and C-130 when fitted with bladder and pump.

flying crane - The CH-54 helicopter.

flying gas station - The KC-135 Air Force Stratotanker.

flying Oscar - The Chinook helicopter for the resemblance to the Oscar Mayer Wienermobile.

flying telephone poles - The SA-2 missiles

FM - 1. General term for Field Manual. 2. Radio term for Frequency Modulation, the static free radio, usually with an added number designating the specific band that is to be used. 3. Fucking Magic. Aviation slang to explain any complex system that is beyond explanation, as it is FM.

FMF - Fleet Marine Force.

FMFM - Fleet Marine Force Manual.

FMFPAC - Fleet Marine Force Pacific.

FN - Fireman (Coast Guard).

FNG - Fucking new guy, a boot or soldier new to the unit or operation who is unseasoned.

FO - 1. Forward Observer. 2. Field Officer.

FOB - Forward operating base.

focal length - See calibrated focal length; equivalent focal length; nominal focal length.

focal plane - (NATO, CENTO) The plane, perpendicular to the optical axis of the lens, in which images of points in the object field of the lens are focused.

FOD - Foreign Object Damage.

fodding - Sabotage by use of a foreign object to inflict damage.

FOF - Field of fire.

follow-up (amphibious) - (DOD, NATO, CENTO, IADB) The landing of reinforcements and stores after the assault and assault follow-on echelons have been landed.

follow-up echelon (air transport) - (DOD, NATO, SEATO, CENTO, IADB) Elements moved into the objective area after the assault echelon.

foo gas - See fougasse.

food tube - The thin long sack on which South Vietnamese carried rice and other food. See elephant's intestines.

foot pounder - Infantryman.

FORCAP - Force Combat Air Force. The aviation group providing security for road convoys.

force - (DOD, IADB) 1. A body of troops, ships, or aircraft, or combination thereof. 2. A major subdivision of a fleet.

force combat air patrol - (DOD) A patrol of fighters maintained over the task force to destroy enemy aircraft which threaten the force. See also combat air patrol.

force recon - Marines with exceptional physical and tactical skills doing reconnaissance.

force rendezvous - (DOD, NATO, CENTO) A navigational checkpoint at which formations of aircraft or ships join and become part of the main force.

force rendezvous (air) - (SEATO, IADB) A navigational checkpoint over which formations of aircraft join and become part of the main force.

force tabs - (DOD, IADB) With reference to war plans, the statement of time-phased deployments of major combat units by major commands and geographical areas.

force(s) - See airborne force; air transported forces; armed forces; army forces; assigned forces; balanced collective forces; blue forces; combined force; covering force; garrison force; NATO forces; orange forces; SEATO forces; task force; underway replenishment forces.

forces allocated to (NATO) (SEATO) - (NATO, SEATO) Those forces made available to (NATO) (SEATO) by a nation under the categories of: a. assigned; b. earmarked for assignment; or c. earmarked for assignment on mobilization. See also force(s); NATO forces; SEATO forces.

Ford - Radio code for Killed in Action, followed by a number, so Ford three would indicate three dead of your troops.

fordability - See deep fording; shallow fording.

foreign intelligence - (DOD) Intelligence concerning areas not under control of the power sponsoring the collection effort.

foreign military sales - (DOD) That portion of United States military assistance authorized by the Foreign Assistance Act of 1961, as amended. This assistance is for both defense articles and services (including training). This assistance differs from Military Assistance Program Grant Aid in that it is purchased by the recipient country.

foreign military sales trainees - (DOD) Foreign nationals receiving training conducted by the Department of Defense on a reimbursable basis, at the country's request.

foreign object damage - Damage to an aircraft usually from foreign objects, such as birds hit in flight or debris on runways, but not enemy fire.

foreshore flats - (NATO) An area of sand, gravel, mud, etc., which is bare or awash at low tide but covered at high tide.

forest penetrator - Gear on a helicopter that allows a folded chair to be lowered through trees and jungle growth to a soldier on the ground, at ground level, it is opened into a chair that protects the soldier from branches and retracts to the airborne helicopter.

form line - (NATO) A line joining all points of approximately equal elevation. Form lines are not normally annotated with elevation figures.

format - (NATO, CENTO) 1. In photography, the size and/or shape of a negative or of the print therefrom. 2. In cartography, the shape and size of a map or chart.

formation - (NATO, CENTO) 1. An ordered arrangement of troops and/or vehicles for a specific purpose. 2. An ordered arrangement of two or more ships, units, or aircraft proceeding together.

formation - Aviation term for the design of aerial flight alignment for two or more aircraft. See: air defense interrogation formation, box formation, champagne formation, cruise formation, diamond formation, division formation, echelon formation, fighting wing formation, finger four formation, fingertip formation, ladder formation, lead trail formation, line abreast formation, missing man formation, parade formation, recce formation, section, trail formation, spread formation, two ship element, and V formation.

former Marine - A Marine who is no longer in the service, never an ex-Marine.

formerly restricted data - (DOD) Information removed from the Restricted Data category upon determination jointly by the Atomic Energy Commission and Department of Defense that such information relates primarily to the military utilization of atomic weapons and that such information can be adequately safeguarded as classified defense information. (Section 142d, Atomic Energy Act of 1954, as amended.) See also restricted data.

forming up place - (NATO, CENTO, IADB) The last position occupied by the assault echelon before crossing the start line/line of departure.

Fort Fucker - Fort Rucker.

Fort Lost in the Woods - Fort Leonard Wood.

Fort Knox East - The U.S. Army Central Finance and Accounting Office that had huge amounts of cash and controlled pay and other disbursements.

Fort Piss - Fort Bliss.

Fort Pricks - Fort Dix.

Fort Puke - Fort Polk.

Fort Rucker - The Army helicopter training and aviation safety center.

Fort Screw Us - Fort Lewis.

Fort Smell - Fort Still.

Fort Turd - Fort Ord.

Fort Useless - Fort Eustis.

forty-five whiskey - Rice whiskey.

forty-five, 45, .45 cal - The standard issue American made Colt .45 caliber semiautomatic pistol. See M-1911A1, .45 cal pistol.

forty-four mag, .44 Mag. - A .44 cal Magnum pistol, see tunnel pistol.

forward aeromedical evacuation - (DOD, NATO, SEATO, CENTO, IADB) That phase of evacuation which provides airlift for patients between points within the battlefield, from the battlefield to the initial point of treatment, and to subsequent points of treatment within the combat zone.

forward air control post - (DOD) A highly mobile United States Air Force tactical air control system radar facility subordinate to the control and reporting center and/or post used to extend radar coverage and control in the forward combat area.

forward air controller - (DOD) An officer (aviator/pilot) member of the tactical air control party who, from a forward ground or airborne position, controls aircraft engaged in close air support of ground troops.

forward air controller - (IADB) An officer (aviator) member of the tactical air control party/air control team who, from a forward position, controls aircraft engaged in close air support of ground troops.

forward area - (DOD, IADB) An area in proximity to combat.

forward bomb lines - (IADB) Lines (land) prescribed by a troop commander beyond which he considers that bombing need not be coordinated with his own forces. See also bomb lines.

forward edge of the battle area - (DOD, NATO, CENTO, IADB) The foremost limits of a series of areas in which ground combat units are deployed, excluding the areas in which the covering or screening forces are operating, designated to coordinate fire support, the positioning of forces, or the maneuver of units.

forward lap - See overlap.

forward motion compensation - See image motion compensation.

forward oblique air photograph - (DOD) Oblique photography of the terrain ahead of the aircraft.

forward observer - (DOD) An observer operating with front line troops and trained to adjust ground or naval gunfire and pass back battlefield information. In the absence of a forward air controller he may control close air support strikes. See also spotter.

forward observer - (NATO, CENTO, IADB) An observer operating with front line troops and trained to adjust ground or naval gunfire and air bombardment, and pass back battlefield information.

forward observer - (SEATO) An observer operating with front line troops and trained to adjust ground or naval gunfire and air bombardment.

forward operating base - A base close to the combat area. See FOB.

forward roll - A parachute landing technique.

forward slope - (NATO, CENTO, IADB) Any slope which descends toward the enemy.

forward support area - A fixed location for support services.

forward tell - (DOD) The transfer of information to a higher level of command. See also track telling.

fou gas - See fougasse. Also spelled foo gas.

fougasse - Jellied gasoline, often made on site by GIs as a substitute for Napalm and for use on land rather than from air. It is a direct flame weapon like a massive flamethrower. It may be improvised from 55-gallon drums of fuel. Misspelled as foo-gas.

found shipment - (NATO, CENTO) Freight received but not listed or manifested.

Four - 1. F-4 Phantom jet. 2. The Selective Service draft classifications for deferrals. See IV-A through IV-F. 3. Radio call sign for NCO or Sergeant.

four - Expressed in radio code and slang as quad.

four by - A light truck.

four deuce - The M-106 or 4.2 inch mortar.

Four F - See IV-F.

four finger formation - See finger four formation.

Four or The Four - The officer in charge of supply.

Four Party Joint Military Commission - 1. Established February 27, 1973 by the Paris Accords to oversee the creation of a cease fire and the orderly withdrawal of the 23,516 U.S. troops then in Vietnam. 2. The member nations of the Commission e.g the United States, the Republic of Vietnam (South), the Democratic Republic of Vietnam (North) and the Provisional Revolutionary Government of South Vietnam (Viet Cong). It was disbanded March 29, 1973.

Four Party Joint Military Team - 1. Established March 29, 1973 the successor to the Four Party Joint Military Commission 2. Responsible for determining the status of the American troops listed as Missing in Action (MIA).

four-holer - A latrine with four seats/holes.

four-star general - General.

fourteen and two - A common discipline sentence of fourteen days restriction and two hours a day of extra duty.

fourteen-five HMG, 14.5-mm HMG - See KPV HMG.

fox - To fire missile.

fox away - (DOD) In air intercept, a code meaning missile has fired or been released from aircraft.

Fox Four - Phantom jet.

Fox One - A radio call indicating the launch of a Sparrow missile.

Fox Two - A radio call indicating the launch of a Sidewinder missile.

foxhole - A hole, man made or a natural depression, sufficient to protect a soldier from enemy observation and or fire. Also fox hole.

foxhole convert - One who becomes devoutly religious after combat.

foxtail - A short handled whisk broom.

Foxtrot - 1. The military phonetic alphabet designation for the letter "F". 2. Slang for Vietnamese female.

Foxtrot Foxtrot - A night helicopter mission. See firefly.

Foxtrot Whiskey - Fixed wing aircraft.

Foxtrot Yankee - Fuck You.

FPL - 1. Final protective line. 2. Call for aid as the FPL is being breeched and the patrol/unit is being overrun.

FPO - 1. Fleet Post Office for Navy and Marines. 2. Field Post Office for Army.

frag - 1. A fragmentation grenade. 2. The shrapnel from a mine, grenade or bomb. 3. To deploy a fragmentation grenade. See fragging.

frag order - An addendum to a prior order

fragging - The anonymous killing of a military leader by his subordinates usually by use of a fragmentation hand grenade at night.

fragmentary order - (DOD) An abbreviated form of an operation order, usually issued on a day-to-day basis which eliminates the need for restating information contained in a basic operation order. It may be issued in sections.

frame - (DOD, NATO, CENTO) In photography, any single exposure contained within a continuous sequence of photographs.

Frankenstein - Slang for an improvised explosive using a spool of barbed wire and C-4 explosive in the center.

freak - (DOD) In air intercept usage, a word meaning frequency in megacycles.

freak - Slang for a dope using individual.

Fred - Girlfriend in Aussie slang.

freddie - (DOD) In air intercept usage, a controlling unit.

free - Postage was not required for mail from troops to the States, but writing 'free" where postage would have been placed was required.

free air anomaly - (DOD, IADB) The difference between observed gravity and theoretical gravity which has been computed for latitude and corrected for elevation of the station above or below the geoid, by application of the normal rate of change of gravity for change of elevation, as in free air.

free air overpressure - (DOD. NATO, CENTO) The unreflected pressure, in excess of the ambient atmospheric pressure, created in the air by the blast wave from an explosion. See also overpressure.

free drop - (DOD, NATO, CENTO, IADB) The dropping of equipment or supplies from an aircraft without the use of parachutes. See also airdrop; air movement; free fall; high velocity drop; low velocity drop.

free drop zone - An area of terrain designated as open at all times for any bombing, opposed to specific targets that may be authorized for a time.

free dropping - (SEATO) The dropping of equipment or supplies from an aircraft without the use of parachutes. See also air drops; air movement; high velocity drop; low velocity drop.

free fall - (DOD, NATO, CENTO, IADB) A parachute maneuver in which the parachute is manually activated at the discretion of the jumper or automatically at a pre-set altitude. See also airdrop; air movement; free drop; high velocity drop; low velocity drop.

free field overpressure - See free air overpressure.

free fire zone - An area of Vietnam in which advance permission had been given to fire, not permission for indiscriminate action, but a set zone without restrictions common to other areas, in 1965 the designation was changed to specified strike zones. See SSZ.

free lance - (DOD) In air intercept, a code meaning self-control of aircraft is being employed.

free rocket - (DOD, NATO, CENTO, IADB) A rocket not subject to guidance or control in in flight.

free time - Nonexistent leisure time. See ghost time.

freedom bird - The slang for the airplane taking military personnel from Vietnam to the United States.

Freedom Fighter - See F-5, a fighter aircraft.

Freeze - The policy of the Marine Corps to restrict a unit to quarters, do a roll call after a fragging incident, and continue the restriction until a suspect was identified. See Operation Freeze.

freight - (NATO, CENTO) Cargo transported, including mail and unaccompanied baggage.

freight consolidating activity - (DOD) A transportation activity which receives less than carload/truckload shipments of materiel for the purpose of assembling them into carload/ truckload lots for onward movement to the ultimate consignee or to a freight distributing activity or other break bulk point. See also freight distributing activity.

freight distributing activity - (DOD) A transportation activity which receives and unloads consolidated carloads/truckloads of less than carload/truckload shipments of materiel and forwards the individual shipments to the ultimate consignee. See also freight consolidating activity.

French leave - Desertion.

FRENG - Friendly initiated engagement.

freq - Radio frequency, usually followed by a band designation (UHF for ultra high frequency or VHF for very high frequency) and the number of the frequency. See freak.

Frequent Wind Operation - The designation of the military operation in April 29-30, 1975 to evacuate the U.S. Embassy in Saigon. The primary evacuation craft was the Marine CH-53 Sea Stallion helicopter.

Fresco - NATO slang for the MiG 17.

fresh meat - A new guy.

fresh target - (DOD) A request or command sent by the observer or spotter to the firing ship to indicate that fire will be shifted from the original target to a new target by spots (corrections) applied to the computer solution being generated.

Freshwater Navy - Coast Guard when operating in rivers.

FRI - Friendly initiated event, pronounced fry.

friend or foe - 1. Slang for deciding if you like a fellow soldier, agree with his politics etc. 2. The challenge made by a sentry, often with as a question requiring a reply known only to friendlies, such as what team won the last World Series. 3. The electronic IFF system.

friendlies - Allied soldiers and civilians.

friendly - (DOD) A contact positively identified as friendly. See also bogey; hostile.

friendly fire - Weapon or artillery fire directed into own troops. See Incontinent Ordinance Delivery.

friendship kits - Gifts for the Vietnamese.

frigate - (DOD, IADB) A warship designed to operate independently, or with strike, antisubmarine warfare, or amphibious forces against submarine, air, and surface threats. (Normal armaments consists of 3" and 5" dual-purpose guns and advanced antisubmarine warfare weapons.) Designated as DL. See also guided missile frigate.

frigging, friggin' - The polite substitute for the word fucking.

FRITA - Friend of soldier with anti-war beliefs.

frog hair - Mythical unit of measure for very small/little, as in "just a frog hair to the left" similar to gnat's gonads.

frogman - Underwater reconnaissance or demolition teams.

front - (DOD, NATO, SEATO, CENTO, IADB) 1. The lateral space occupied by an element, measured from the extremity of one flank to the extremity of the other flank. 2. The direction of enemy. 3. The line of contact of two opposing forces. 4. When a combat situation does not exist or is not assumed, the direction toward which the command is faced.

front leaning position - In pushup position. See position.

front seat guy - Pilot of a fighter aircraft. See GIB, guy in back.

front time - Time in combat.

frontal attack - (DOD) In air intercept, an attack by an interceptor aircraft which terminates with a heading crossing angle greater than 135 degrees.

FRTS - Short for Armed Forces Radio and Television Service. Pronounced Fritz.

fruit salad - Two or more rows of campaign ribbons on uniform.

frustrated cargo - (DOD) Any shipment of supplies and/or equipment which while en route to destination is stopped prior to receipt and for which further disposition instructions must be obtained.

FSA - Fire Support Area.

FSB - Fire Support Base.

FT - Flamethrower.

FTA - Fuck the Army.

FTE - 1. Front toward enemy, the instructions on a Claymore mine. 2. Something important to remember. 3. Telling someone to go by the instructions, behave.

FTR - Failure to return.

FTX - Field training exercise.

FUBAR - Fucked up beyond belief.

fuck a duck - Loafing, lounging around, or sleeping.

fuck stick - Penis.

fuck up - 1. To make a mistake. 2. The person who makes mistakes.

fuck-you lizard - The gecko that had a night time call sounding like "fuck-you".

fuck, fucked, fucking, - Slang for sexual intercourse. Used as a verb, an adjective or adverb to modify almost anything, e.g. pass the fuckin' butter, or this fucked airstrike.

fucked up - 1. Loaded on drugs. 2. Stupid. 3. A bad situation.

fucker - Bad guy, misfit, untrustworthy person or thing.

fucking A - Absolutely. An expression of great truth.

Fucking Magic - Aviation slang to explain any complex system that is beyond explanation, as it is FM.

fucking new guy - Abbreviated as FNG, greenhorn, boot, new person.

fucking off - Goldbricking, messing around, not working when it was required.

FUFA - Fed up with the fucking Army, a type of deserter.

fugazi - Slang from fucked up meaning a fouled up or confused situation or person.

full bird - Colonel.

full charge - (DOD) The larger of the two propelling charges available for naval guns.

full command - (NATO, SEATO, CENTO, IADB) The military authority and responsibility of a superior officer to issue orders to subordinates. It covers every aspect of military operations and administration and exists only within national Services. The term command, as used internationally, implies a lesser degree of authority than when it is used in a purely national sense. (NATO, SEATO, CENTO) It follows that no (NATO) (SEATO) (CENTO) commander has full command over the forces that are assigned to him. This is because nations, in assigning forces to (NATO) (SEATO) (CENTO), assign only operational command or operational control. See also command.

Fulton Recovery - A method of recovering downed pilots from remote areas by having the pilot in a harness attached to a lift line pulled up by balloons. An aircraft hooks onto the lift line and reels the pilot into the aircraft. Also called Fulton surface-to-air recovery system.

functions - (DOD, IADB) The appropriate or assigned duties, responsibilities, missions, or tasks of an individual, office, or organization. (DOD) As defined in the National Security Act of 1947, as amended, the term "function" includes functions, powers, and duties, (5 United States Code 171n (a).)

funeral detail - An Army personnel assignment to notify the next of kin and assist in making funeral arrangements.

funnies - See funny papers.

funny money - Military payment in script which looked like play money.

funny papers - From the comic strips, used to describe the topographical maps. See comics.

FUO - Fever of unknown origin. Hospital abbreviation for any unknown cause of a fever.

furball - Aerial combat with many participants and extreme confusion. Also fur ball.

Fury - (DOD, IADB) A single-engine, single-seat, jet fighter/bomber designed for operating from aircraft carriers. Armament consists of cannons, nuclear or non-nuclear bombs, Sidewinders, rockets and Bullpups for troop support. The aircraft possesses air-to-air refueling capability, and can carry a tanker package. Designated as F-l.

fuse - 1. Cord filled with pyrotechnics that burned at a set rate to ignite explosives. 2. The electrical safety device. See fuze for the munitions term.

fuse lighter - Infantryman in demolitions. See fuze lighter.

fusion - (DOD) The process accompanied by the release of tremendous amounts of energy, whereby the nuclei of light elements combine to form the nucleus of a heavier element.

fuze - See boresafe fuze; impact action fuze; proximity fuze; self-destroying fuze; time fuze; variable time fuze. Note "fuse" is the electrical impedance safety device.

fuze (specify) - (DOD) In artillery and naval gunfire support, a command or request to indicate the type of fuze action desired, i.e., delay, quick, time, variable time.

fuze lighter - Artilleryman. See fuse lighter.

FWMAF - Free World Military Assistance Forces, the allies of the United States

FY - Fiscal year.

G – GOLF

G - 1. Designated in the military phonetic alphabet, as "Golf". 2. Designation of divisional level duties. 3. Abbreviation for gravity.

G force - The force of gravity.

G-1 - Designation for divisional administration.

G-2 - Designation for divisional intelligence.

G-3 - 1. Designation for divisional operations. 2. Staff officer assignment at the divisional level as a tactical advisor.

G-4 - Designation for divisional supply.

G-5 - Designation for civilian affairs/community liaison.

G-load - The gravity pull on a pilot and aircraft in specific directional shifts or rapid acceleration.

G-suit - A pilot's apparel that has a pneumatically inflatable sections around the torso and lower body to keep blood in the upper parts of the body and head to prevent black outs during times of high gravity as in pulling out of a steep dive. See anti-G suit. Also speedjeans.

GA - General of the Army.

ga mug - Vietnamese for thank you.

Gabby Hayes hat - A field hat with a low crown and narrow brim like the ratty cowboy hat worn by the actor Gabby Hayes, sidekick to Roy Rogers, in Western films.

gadget - (DOD) Radar equipment. (Type of equipment may be indicated by a letter as listed in operation orders.) May be followed by a color to indicate state of jamming. Colors will be used as follows: a. green-Clear of jamming. b. amber-Sector partially jammed. c. red-Sector completely jammed. d. blue-Completely jammed.

GAF - General of the Air Force.

GAFer - A guy who could not care less, or give a fuck.

gaff off - Ignore.

gaggle - Slang for a multi-service air strike, not necessarily in formation. Perhaps from a gaggle of geese.

Gainesburgers - A hamburger patty in gravy, named after a popular dog food.

Gainful - NATO slang for a surface-to-air missile.

Galaxy - (DOD) A large cargo transport aircraft powered by four turbofan engines, capable of very large payload and cargo volume, intercontinental range, forward area airfield operations and air dropping of troops and equipment. Designated as C-5A.

galley - Navy and Marine slang for kitchen.

gamma rays - (DOD) High energy electromagnetic radiation emitted from atomic nuclei during a nuclear reaction. Gamma rays and very high energy X-rays differ only in origin. X-rays do. not originate from atomic nuclei but are produced in other ways.

gang way - Marine slang for move away, stand back.

gangplank policy - A policy permitting the extension of a tour of duty until the soldier was about to depart.

gangway - A raised walkway, usually between a ship and dock.

GAO - General Accounting Office. (Predecessor to the current Government Accountability Office.)

gap (imagery) - (DOD) Any space where imagery fails to meet minimum coverage requirements. This might be a space not covered by imagery or a space where the minimum specified overlap was not obtained. See also holiday.

gap marker (land mine warfare) - (DOD, NATO, SEATO, CENTO, IADB) Used to mark a minefield gap. Gap markers at the entrance to and exit from the gap will be referenced to a landmark or intermediate marker. See also marker (land mine warfare); minefield gap (land mine warfare).

GARAND - The M-1 rifle used by the South Vietnamese.

garble - (DOD, IADB) An error in transmission, reception, encryption, or decryption which changes the text of a message or any portion thereof in such a manner that it is incorrect or undecryptable.

Garden of Honor - A veteran's cemetery.

garrison force - (DOD, NATO, SEATO, CENTO, IADB) All units assigned to a base or area for defense, development, operation, and maintenance of facilities. See also force(s).

garritrooper - A term invented term in WWII by cartoonist Bill Mauldin for assignments too far forward to wear a tie and too far back to get shot.

GAS - Ground air speed.

gas cumulative action - (IADB) The building up within the human body of small, ineffective doses of certain war gases to a point where the eventual effect is similar to one large dose.

gas station in the sky - The Stratotanker.

gate - (DOD) In air intercept, a code meaning fly at maximum possible speed (or power). (To be maintained for a limited time only, depending on type of aircraft.) Use of afterburners, rockets, etc., in accordance with local doctrine.

gate ghetto - Bars, small shops, and brothels that cluster near a base entrance.

Gatling - A machine gun, named for the inventor Richard Gatling in the American Civil War, although the original used multiple barrels. Often misspelled as Gattling.

GBU - Short for God bless you, a message said or sent by tap code between POWs.

GCA - Ground Controlled Approach. 1. The all-weather landing systems and protocol used primarily by the Navy and Marine flyers. 2. An instrument landing (See ILS, Instrument Landing System for Air Force and commercial use).

GCI - Ground Controlled Intercept. A ground based radar operation that directs friendly aircraft to the location of enemy aircraft.

GCR - Ground controlled radar.

GCT - General Classification Test.

gear - Equipment.

GED - General Equivalency Diploma. The award is equivalent of a High School diploma after passing tests.

gedunk - Marine slang for a snack bar on a ship, or generally a candy or snack food store.

geeters - Money in Vietnamese.

Gelignite - A nitroglycerine based explosive for demolition mainly.

GEM - Ground Effect Machines (NATO) See Air Cushion Vehicle.

Gen - 1. General (Marine Corps). 2. General Air Force Chief of Staff (Air Force).

GEN - General (Army).

general and complete disarmament - (DOD, IADB) Reductions of armed forces and armaments by all states to levels required for internal security and for an international peace force. Connotation is "total disarmament" by all states.

general cargo - (DOD, IADB) Cargo which is susceptible for loading in general, non-specialized stowage areas, e.g., boxes, barrels, bales, crates, packages, bundles, and pallets.

General Classification Test - The test given to recruits to determine assignments and training.

general map - (DOD, IADB) A map of small scale used for general planning purposes. See also map.

general mobilization reserve materiel objective - (DOD) The mobilization reserve materiel objective less the sum of the prepositioned war reserve requirement. See also mobilization reserves.

general mobilization reserve stock - (DOD) The quantity of an item acquired and placed in stock against a general mobilization reserve materiel objective. See also mobilization reserves.

general orders - (DOD, IADB) 1. Permanent instructions, issued in order form, that apply to all members of a command, as compared with special orders, which affect only individuals or small groups. General orders are usually concerned with matters of policy or administration. 2. A series of permanent guard orders that govern the duties of a sentry on post.

general purchasing agents - (DOD) Agents who have been appointed in the principal overseas areas of operations to supervise, control, coordinate, negotiate, and develop the local procurement of supplies, services, and facilities by United States Armed Forces, in order that the most effective utilization may be made of local resources and production.

general purchasing agents - (IADB) Agents who have been appointed to supervise, control, coordinate, negotiate, and develop the local procurement of supplies, services, and facilities in order that the most effective utilization maybe made of local resources and production.

general quarters - (DOD, IADB) A condition of readiness when naval action is imminent. All battle stations are fully manned and alert; ammunition is ready for instant loading; guns and guided missile launchers may be loaded.

general reserve - (DOD, NATO, SEATO, CENTO, IADB) Reserve of troops retained under the control of the overall commander. See also floating reserve. (Note: NATO, SEATO and CENTO definition does not use the word "retained".)

general staff - (DOD) A group of officers in the headquarters of Army or Marine divisions, Marine brigades and aircraft wings, or similar or larger units which assist their commanders in planning, coordinating, and supervising operations. A general staff may consist of four or more principal functional sections: personnel (G-1), military intelligence (G-2), operations and training (G-3), logistics (G-4), and (in Army organizations) civil affairs/military government (G-5). (A particular section may be added or eliminated by the commander, dependent upon the need which has been demonstrated.) The comparable Air Force staff is found in the wing and larger units, with sections designated Personnel, Operations, etc. G-2 Air and G-3 Air are Army officers assigned to G-2 or G-3 at division, corps, and Army headquarters level, who assist in planning and coordinating joint operations of ground and air units. Naval staffs ordinarily are not organized on these lines, but when they are, they are designated N-1, N-2, etc. Similarly, a joint staff may be designated J-1, J-2, etc. In Army brigades and smaller units and in Marine Corps units smaller than a brigade or aircraft wing, staff sections are designated S-l, S-2, etc., with corresponding duties; referred to as a unit staff in the Army and as an executive staff in the Marine Corps. See also staff.

general staff - (IADB) A group of officers in the headquarters of divisions, or similar larger units which assist their commanders in planning, coordinating, and supervising operations. A general staff may consist of four or more principal functional sections: personnel (G-1), military intelligence (G-2), operations and training (G-3), logistics (G-4), and civil affairs/military government (G-5). (A particular section may be added or eliminated by the commander, dependent upon the need which has been demonstrated.) In brigades and smaller units, staff sections are designated S-l, S-2, etc., with corresponding duties. See also staff.

general support - (DOD, IADB) That support which is given the supported force as a whole and not to any particular subdivision thereof.

general support artillery - (DOD, IADB) Artillery which executes the fire directed by the commander of the unit to which it organically belongs or is attached. It fires in support of the operation as a whole rather than in support of a specific subordinate unit.

general support-reinforcing - (DOD) A tactical artillery mission. General support-reinforcing artillery has the mission of supporting the force as a whole and of providing reinforcing fires for another artillery unit.

general war - (DOD, IADB) Armed conflict between major powers in which the total resources of the belligerents are employed, and the national survival of a major belligerent is in jeopardy.

General's mess - The private dining room of a General to which officers may be invited.

Geneva Conference, Geneva Accords - The 1954 peace conference held in Geneva Switzerland ending the French Indochinese War and dividing the country of Vietnam at the 17th parallel into the North and South Vietnam.

Genie - (DOD) An air to air, unguided rocket equipped with nuclear warhead. Designed to be carried by the F-89, F-I01, and F-I06. Designated as AIR-2.

geodetic datum - See datum (geodetic).

geographic bachelor - Nurse slang for married doctors and other married male medical personnel who acted socially like bachelors in Vietnam.

geographic coordinates - (DOD, NATO) The quantities of latitude and longitude which determine the position of a point on the surface of the earth with respect to the reference spheroid. See also coordinates.

geographic reference points - (DOD, IADB) A means of indicating position, usually expressed either as double letters or as code words which are established in operation orders or by other means.

georef - (DOD, IADB) A worldwide position reference system that may be applied to any map or chart graduated in latitude and longitude regardless of projection. It is a method of expressing latitude and longitude in a form suitable for rapid reporting and plotting. (This term is derived from the words "The World Geographic Reference System".)

georef - (NATO) A grid system used in reporting positions, using the earth's graticule of latitude and longitude as the grid. See also coordinates.

German wire - Similar to concertina barbed wire but having 1-inch razor blades in place of barbs.

get button - Throttle on aircraft, as in to hit the get button, get going fast.

get it on - To fight.

get some - 1. Revenge killing of enemy. 2. Sex.

get wet - To kill with a knife.

getting high - Intoxicated on drugs.

getting short - Approaching end of tour of duty.

getting smoked - Being shot down.

getting tight - Making friends.

getting your rocks off - Masturbating.

GFU - A person who is a general fuck up.

GG shot - Gamma globulin injection to prevent hepatitis, particularly painful.

GGM - Ground-to-ground missile.

ghost time - Free time.

ghosting - The act of goofing off, being invisible when there is work to be done, goldbricking.

GHQ - General headquarters.

GI - 1. Government issue 2. Slang for U.S. soldier.

GI Bill - Federal legislation providing benefits to eligible discharged or retired members of the Armed Forces.

GI can - A large garbage can.

GI gin - Cough syrup.

GI Says - One of the underground newspapers.

GI shower - A peer imposed discipline on those failing to maintain hygiene as a group administered very rough shower.

GIB - 1. Guy in back: 2. The weapons officer. 3. Co-pilot in aircraft in which the co-pilot sits aft of the pilot such as the A-4 jet.

gig - 1. A notation of a minor offense by a superior. 2. Minor discipline or a warning.

VIETNAM: THE WAR ZONE DICTIONARY IN THEIR OWN WORDS

Gimlet - (DOD, IADB) Two-inch, folding fin, unguided, air-to-surface rocket.

Gimlets - Slang for the 21st Infantry due to cocktail glass shape of insignia.

gimme go - Vietnamese slang for asking for a ride.

gimp - Slang for disabled vet, usually amputee or wheelchair bound, commonly a term of self-description rather then being used by others.

give a shit - Care about, usually in the negative.

give a shit lobe - The frontal lobe of the brain.

gizmo - Name for any piece of gear or component in lieu of knowing or using the technical term (such as hoo-ha, doodad, thingamabob).

GL - Grenade launcher.

Glad bag - 1. Slang for a body bag. 2. The trademarked plastic sandwich or food storage bag.

glide bomb - (DOD, IADB) A bomb fitted with airfoils to provide lift, carried and released in the direction of a target by an airplane.

glide path - (DOD, NATO, SEATO, CENTO, IADB) 1. The flight path of an aircraft or winged missile as it glides downward, the line of which forms an angle with the longitudinal axis of the aircraft or missile. 2. The line to be followed by an aircraft as it descends from horizontal flight to land upon the surface. Also called glide slope.

glide ratio - The distance a plane can fly after power fails.

glide slope - See glide path.

Globemaster - (DOD, IADB) A heavy cargo, four engine transport which has clamshell nose doors, a built-in cargo ramp, and can carry bulky, outsize cargo as well as personnel. Designated as C-124.

glory hole - Aviation slang for a hole in the clouds allowing a pilot to get to his target.

GM - 1. Gunner's Mate. 2. Guided missile.

GMO - General Medical Officer.

GMT - See Greenwich Mean Time.

gnat's gonads - Mythical unit of measure for very small/little, as in "just a gnat's gonads to the left" similar to "frog hair".

go go bird - The CH-47 helicopter with Vulcan guns.

go juice - 1. Aviation fuel. 2. Coffee.

go minh money - Damages payments made to civilians. From Go minh - to extract oneself from a predicament.

go no-go - The request for status and permission to initiate a flight or a convoy.

go to hell rag - The bandana of an infantryman.

go-aheads - Plastic shower shoes, thonged sandals.

go-fer - 1. A helper who "goes for" things. 2. Aid to an officer or administrator who does minor assignments. Pronounced gopher.

goat rope - A confusing situation, as in trying to rope goats.

GOCO - Government owned, contractor operated.

GOER - M-553 cargo carrier.

goes away - Something hit with a missile.

going downtown - Air Force slang for a mission against Hanoi. See Downtown.

going low level - Flying as low as possible, see nap of the earth.

going south - 1. A flight from Okinawa to Vietnam. 2. Things getting strange, going bad.

goldbrick - Worthless. Slacker. Historically from a swindle of selling gold painted bricks as ingots of gold.

golden BB - Aviation slang for a small arms bullet aimed at an aircraft that can potentially hit some area of vulnerability and bring down the plane.

golden flow - Urine testing for drugs.

Golden Triangle - The opium poppy growing area where Burma, Thailand, Laos and China meet.

Goldfish bowl - OH-13 helicopter.

goldie - (DOD) The term, peculiar to air support radar team operations, indicating aircraft automatic flight control system and ground control bombing system are engaged and awaiting electronic ground control commands.

goldie - Navy and Marine slang for the Advanced Parachutist's insignia

goldie lock - (DOD) The term, peculiar to air support radar team operations, indicating ground controller has electronic control of the aircraft.

Golf - The military phonetic alphabet designation for the letter "G".

golf time - The time zone set for convenience at 12 hours between Washington D.C. and the Tonkin Gulf, as the real time difference was 13 hours. Also called gulf time.

gomer - 1. Medical slang for an uncommunicative patient or a repeat visitor to the hospital, possibly from the phrase, get out of my emergency room. 2. Infantry slang for a Marine or a hick, unsophisticated guy from the sticks.

gone on a walk - A 30-day field patrol.

goo - Bad weather, clouds that make it hard to see.

good chute - Aviation report of a positive airplane ejection, also suggesting the flyer is still alive.

good guy card - Identification card for civilians.

Good morning, Vietnam. - The greeting of the DJ on the Armed Forces Vietnam Network radio show, made popular by Adrian Cronauer.

good time - Time counted toward the period of enlistment. See bad time.

good to go - Fit for duty, flight, etc.

goodie - An ambush set for the enemy.

gooey louies - A second lieutenant.

gook - Derogatory term for Vietnamese persons, or other Asians.

gook bands - Asian entertainers in Enlisted Men's clubs.

gook sore - Any general skin infection.

gooner - Slang for North Vietnamese soldier.

Gooney Bird - The C-47 transport.

gopher - See go-fer.

gork - Army medical slang for patients (and status) in the intensive care unit, particularly those with a severe head wound or potentially brain dead, from the phrase "God Only Really Knows".

gotcha vine - A thick thorn covered vine that inflicts cuts prone to infection and generally slows progress.

gourd - Medical slang for head.

GP - General purpose.

GR - See Graves Registration.

grab a hat - To leave or depart.

Grab them by the balls... - Part of the phrase ...and their hearts and minds will follow... This emerged after the "winning their hearts and minds" failed.

grabass - Marine slang for frivolous activity, unorganized sports as in a pick up game.

Graduated Response - The Johnson administration strategy to force withdrawal from the south and peace negotiations as the gradual increase of bombing in the north was a prelude to even greater destruction.

GRAIL - NATO term for the SA-7 shoulder fired surface-to-air missile.

grand slam - (DOD) All enemy aircraft originally sighted are shot down.

graphic - (NATO) Any and all products of the cartographic and photogrammetric art. A graphic may be either a map, chart or mosaic or even a film strip that was produced using cartographic techniques.

graphic scale - (DOD, NATO, SEATO, CENTO) A graduated line by means of which distances on the map, chart, or photograph may be measured in terms of ground distance. See also scale.

graticule - (NATO, CENTO) In cartography, a network of lines representing the earth's parallels of latitude and meridians of longitude.

graticule (maps and charts) - (SEATO, IADB) A network of lines representing the earth's parallels of latitude and meridians of longitude.

graticule ticks - (NATO) In cartography, short lines indicating where selected meridians and parallels intersect.

gravel - 1. A small antipersonnel mine, XM-27, laid by low flying aircraft. 2. The projectile of choice in most improvised mines used by the enemy.

graves registration - (DOD, IADB) Supervision and execution of matters pertaining to the identification, removal, and burial of the dead, and collection and processing of their effects. See also burial.

graves registration point - The location where dead soldiers are identified, embalmed and processed.

gravity extraction - (DOD, NATO, CENTO, IADB) The extraction of cargoes from the aircraft by influence of their own weight. See also parachute extraction.

graze - (DOD) A spotting, or an observation, by a spotter or an observer to indicate that all bursts occurred on impact.

grazing fire - (DOD, NATO, SEATO, CENTO, IADB) Fire approximately parallel to the ground where the center of the cone of fire does not rise above one meter from the ground. See also fire.

grease - To kill.

Grease Gun - The .45 cal machine gun as it resembles a automotive grease gun.

great circle - (NATO, CENTO, IADB) A circle on the surface of the earth, the plane of which passes through the center of the earth.

great circle route - (NATO, CENTO, IADB) The route which follows the shortest arc of a great circle between two points.

green - 1. Safe, as in a green landing zone. 2. New, untested.

green bait - Reenlistment bonus.

green beanies - Green Berets of Army Special Forces.

green belt - Marine term for Drill Instructor.

VIETNAM: THE WAR ZONE DICTIONARY IN THEIR OWN WORDS

Green Berets - U.S. Army Special Forces.

green bomb - Amphetamines.

green cord uniform - The standard uniform for Woman Army Corps (WAC) consisting of short sleeved blouse or jacket and light green skirt.

green door - A secure location.

Green Dragon - The M-113 APC.

green eye - The night vision Starlight scope.

green line - A windbreak of a row of trees at the edge of a rice field providing excellent cover.

green machine - 1. Career U.S. Army and Marine Corps enlistees. 2. The Veterans Administration (renamed and elevated to the Department of Veterans Affairs in 1989). 3. The Marine Corps.

green pounders - Infantry.

green side up - The reverse of brown side up in order about how to wear reversible helmet covers and shelters. See brown side out.

green tape - A general purpose tape for patching things in the field and taping dogtags together so they are silent.

green up - The aircraft cockpit indicator that bombs or other ordinance was armed and ready to fire. From the indicator light going from red to green.

green weenie - The Army Commendation Medal.

greenbacking - Hiring mercenaries.

greenbacks - American money.

greenies - Green Berets of Army Special Forces.

greens - The Class A Army uniform.

Greenwich mean time - (DOD) Mean solar time at the meridian of Greenwich. England, used as a basis for standard time throughout the world. Normally expressed in four numerals 0001 through 2400. See ZULU.

Greenwich mean time - (NATO, SEATO, CENTO, IADB) Mean solar time at the meridian of Greenwich.

grenade - A hand held bomb with a short timer or fuse that is thrown or launched.

grenade launcher - The M-79 shoulder held weapon.

grenadier - The operator of the grenade launcher.

grey propaganda - (DOD, I, NATO, SEATO, CENTO, IADB) Propaganda which does not specifically identify any source. See also propaganda.

Greyhound - 1. A light armored car M-8. 2. Twin engine Navy prop plane for carrier transport.

grid - (DOD) 1. Two sets of parallel lines intersecting at right angles and forming squares; the grid is superimposed on maps, charts, and other similar representations of the earth's surface in an accurate and consistent manner to permit identification of ground locations with respect to other locations and the computation of direction and distance to other points. 2. A term used in giving the location of a geographic point by grid coordinates. See also military grid; military grid reference system.

grid bearing - (DOD) Bearing measured from grid north.

grid convergence - (DOD, NATO, CENTO, IADB) The horizontal angle at a place between true North and grid North. It is proportional to the longitude difference between the place and the central meridian. See also convergence.

grid convergence factor - (DOD, NATO) The ratio of the grid convergence angle to the longitude difference (see grid convergence). In the Lambert Conical Orthomorphic projection this is constant and is sometimes called the constant of the cone. See also convergence.

grid coordinates - (NATO) Plane-rectangular coordinates based on and mathematically adjusted to a map projection in order that geographic positions (latitudes and longitudes) may be readily transformed into plane coordinates and the computations relating to them made by the ordinary methods of plane surveying. See also coordinates.

grid interval - (NATO) The distance represented between the lines of a grid.

grid magnetic angle - (DOD, NATO, CENTO, IADB) Angular difference in direction between grid north and magnetic north. It is measured east or west from grid north. Grid magnetic angle is sometimes called grivation and/or grid variation.

grid north - (DOD, NATO, SEATO, CENTO, IADB) The northerly or zero direction indicated by the grid datum of directional reference.

grid square - A specific enclosed square on a gridded map.

grid ticks - (NATO) Small marks on the neat-line of a map or chart indicating additional grid reference systems included on that sheet. Grid ticks are sometimes shown on the interior grid lines of some maps for ease of referencing.

grid variation - See grid magnetic angle.

grievance payment - A payment made to civilians for injury or property damage. See Go minh money.

grinder - Marine slang for the parade ground.

grins and shakes - Marine term for a VIP or civilian tour.

gripe - Aviation slang for a problem with a plane. A plane with an up gripe is flyable. A plane with a down gripe is not flyable.

grivation - See grid magnetic angle.

gross error - (DOD) A nuclear weapon detonation at such a distance from the desired ground zero as to cause no nuclear damage to the target.

gross weight - (DOD, NATO, CENTO) Weight of a ground vehicle including fuel, lubricants, coolant, vehicle tools and spares, cargo and operating personnel. See also net weight.

ground alert - (DOD, IADB) That status in which aircraft on the ground/deck are fully serviced and armed, with combat crews in readiness to take off within a specified short period of time (usually 15 minutes) after receipt of a mission order. See also air alert; alert.

ground control - (DOD, NATO, CENTO) A system of accurate measurements used to determine the distances and directions or differences in elevation between points on the earth. See also common control; control point; field control; traverse.

ground control (geodetic) - See ground control.

ground controlled intercept - An interception of enemy aircraft directed from the ground to the pilot.

ground effect - Also ground wash, the aerodynamic oddity that reduces drag on an aircraft when its altitude is within two thirds of the distance of the wingspan, this allows significantly increased acceleration.

ground effect machine - (NATO, CENTO) A machine which normally flies within the zone of the ground effect or ground cushion. See Air Cushion Vehicle, GEM.

ground fire - (DOD) Small arms ground-to-air fire directed against aircraft.

ground liaison officer - (DOD) An officer trained in offensive air support activities. Ground liaison officers are normally organized into parties under the control of the appropriate army commander to provide liaison to air force and naval units engaged in training and combat operations.

ground liaison officer - (NATO, CENTO, IADB) An officer especially trained in air reconnaissance and/or offensive air support activities. These officers are normally organized into teams under the control of the appropriate ground force commander to provide liaison to air force and navy units engaged in training and combat operations.

ground liaison officer - (SEATO) An officer especially trained in either air reconnaissance or offensive air support activities. These officers are normally organized into teams under the control of the appropriate army commander to provide liaison to air force and navy units engaged in training and combat operations.

ground liaison party - (DOD) An Army unit consisting of a variable number of personnel responsible for liaison with a tactical air support agency.

ground liaison section - (DOD, NATO, SEATO, CENTO) An army unit consisting of a variable number of army officers, other ranks, and vehicles responsible for army/air liaison, under control of army headquarters.

ground nadir - (NATO, CENTO) The point on the ground vertically beneath the perspective center of the camera lens. On a true vertical photograph this coincides with the principal point.

ground observer center - (DOD, IADB) A center to which ground observer teams report and which in turn will pass information to the appropriate control and/or reporting agency.

ground observer organization - (NATO, SEATO, CENTO, IADB) A corps of ground watchers deployed at suitable points throughout an air defense system to provide visual and aural information of aircraft movements.

ground observer team - (DOD, IADB) Small units or detachments deployed to provide information of aircraft movements over a defended area, obtained either by aural or visual means.

ground position - (DOD, NATO, SEATO, CENTO, IADB) The position on the earth vertically below an aircraft.

ground pounder - Infantry.

ground readiness - (DOD, IADB) That status wherein aircraft can be armed and serviced and personnel alerted to take off within a specified length of time after receiving orders.

ground return - (NATO, CENTO) The reflection from the terrain as displayed and/or recorded as an image.

ground speed - The motion of the aircraft in relation to the ground.

ground visibility - (DOD) Prevailing horizontal visibility near the earth's surface as reported by an accredited observer.

ground week - The first week or paratrooper school.

ground zero - (DOD, NATO, SEATO, CENTO, IADB) The point on the surface of the earth at, or vertically below or above, the center of a planned or actual nuclear detonation. Also called GZ. See also actual ground zero; desired ground zero.

ground-controlled approach - (DOD, NATO, SEATO, CENTO, IADB) The technique or procedures for talking down, through the use of both surveillance and precision approach radar, an aircraft during its approach so as to place it in a position for landing.

ground-controlled intercept - See air interception.

grounded - See NORS-G.

group - (DOD, IADB) 1. A flexible administrative and tactical unit composed of either two or more battalions or two or more squadrons. The term also applies to combat support and service support units. 2. A number of ships and/or aircraft, normally a subdivision of a force, assigned for a specific purpose.

group burial - (DOD, NATO, CENTO, IADB) A burial in a common grave of two or more individually unidentified remains. See also burial.

group rendezvous - (DOD, CENTO, IADB) A check point at which formations of the same type will join before proceeding. See also force rendezvous.

grow your own - A system of promoting from within ranks.

groyne - (NATO) A low wall built out into the sea to resist the travel of sand and gravel along the beach.

GRP - Graves Registration Point.

grunt - Slang for foot soldier. Note only about 15% of troops served in field combat, the remainder were in rear or support positions. See Mud Marine and Zoomie.

Grunt Free Press - One of the underground magazines.

GS - 1. General Support. 2. Ground speed.

Gs - Slang for gravity as used a measure of the force of the acceleration when flying, so, pulling 2Gs is twice the force of gravity.

GSW - Hospital notation for gunshot wound.

GT - General Technical. One of the classification test categories.

guard - The emergency radio communication system that is monitored for rescue and other emergency uses.

guarding the radio - The assignment to monitor the radio for incoming messages.

guardship - (NATO, SEATO, CENTO, IADB) A ship detailed for a specific duty for the purpose of enabling other ships in company to assume a lower degree of readiness. Note: SEATO term has qualifier "(naval term)".

guava - A bomb with half a million bomblets in it.

guerrilla - (DOD, IADB) A combat participant in guerrilla warfare. See also unconventional warfare.

guerrilla warfare - (DOD, I, NATO, CENTO, IADB) Military and paramilitary operations conducted in enemy-held or hostile territory by irregular, predominantly indigenous forces. See also unconventional warfare.

guidance - (DOD, IADB) 1. Policy, direction, decision, or instruction, having the effect of an order when promulgated by a higher echelon. 2. The entire process by which target intelligence information received by the guided missile is used to effect proper flight control to cause timely direction changes for effective target interception. See also active homing guidance; celestial guidance; command guidance; homing guidance; inertial guidance; midcourse guidance; passive homing guidance; preset guidance; semiactive homing guidance; stellar guidance; terminal guidance; terrestrial reference guidance.

guidance station equipment - (DOD, NATO, CENTO, IADB) The ground-based portion of the missile guidance system necessary to provide guidance during missile flight. (IADB) It specifically includes the tracking radar, the rate-measuring equipment, the data link equipment, and the computer, test, and maintenance equipment integral to these items.

guidance system (missile) - (DOD, NATO, SEATO, CENTO) A system which evaluates flight information, correlates it with target data, determines the desired flight path of the missile and communicates the necessary commands to the missile flight control system. See also control system (missile).

guide signs - (NATO, SEATO, CENTO) Signs used to indicate locations, distances, directions, routes, and similar information. Note: SEATO and IADB term is "guide signs (road transport)".

guided missile - (DOD, NATO, SEATO, CENTO, IADB) An unmanned vehicle moving above the surface of the earth, whose trajectory or flight path is capable of being altered by an external or internal mechanism. See also aerodynamic missile; ballistic missile.

guided missile (air-to-air) - (NATO, SEATO, CENTO, IADB) An air-launched guided missile for use against air targets.

guided missile (surface-to-air) - (NATO, SEATO, CENTO, IADB) A surface-launched guided missile for use against air targets.

guided missile cruiser - (DOD, IADB) For designed mission, see heavy cruiser. With exception of CGNs, these ships are full conversion of heavy cruisers. All guns are removed and replaced with Talos/Tartar missile launchers. The CGN is a nuclear-powered, long-range ship equipped with Talos/Terrier missile and Asroc launchers. Designated as CG and CGN.

guided missile destroyer - (DOD) For designed mission, see destroyer. This destroyer type is equipped with Terrier/Tartar guided missile launchers, improved naval gun battery, long-range sonar, and antisubmarine warfare weapons, including Asroc. Designated as DDG.

guided missile frigate - (DOD, IADB) For designed mission, see frigate. Equipped with Terrier or Tartar missile launchers and 5-inch/54-gun battery; also Asroc. Designated as DLG and DLGN. The DLGN is nuclear powered.

guided missile heavy cruiser - (DOD, IADB) For designed mission, see heavy cruiser. These ships are converted heavy cruisers, with one triple 8-inch/55 turret removed and replaced with a twin Terrier missile launcher. Designated as CAG.

guided missile light cruiser - (DOD, IADB) For designed mission, see light cruiser. Converted light cruisers. In addition to 6-inch/47 guns, either Terrier or Talos missile launchers have been added to main armament. Designated as CLG.

guided missile submarine - (DOD, IADB) A submarine designed to have an additional capability to launch guided missile attacks from surfaced condition. Designated as SSG and SSGN. The SSGN is nuclear powered.

Guideline - NATO slang for the SA-3 Surface-to-air missile.

guidon - The pennant or flag of a military unit.

gulf time - See golf time.

GUMP - The standard pre-flight check of gas, undercarriage, mixture, and prop.

gun - (DOD) 1. A cannon with relatively long barrel, operating with relatively low angle of fire, and having a high muzzle velocity. 2. A cannon with tube length .30 to .50 calibers or more. See also howitzer; mortar.

gun - Not a rifle. A hazing ritual for recruits who stupidly refer to their rifle as a gun is to have them march with a rifle in one hand and their penis in the other chanting, "This is my rifle, this is my gun. One is for fighting and the other for fun."

gun ape - Artilleryman.

gun bunnie - Artilleryman.

gun carriage - (DOD, NATO, SEATO, CENTO, IADB) A mobile or fixed support for a gun. It sometimes includes the elevating and traversing mechanisms. Sometimes called carriage.

gun direction - (NATO, SEATO, CENTO, IADB) The distribution and direction of gunfire from a ship.

Gun Jeep - The standard U.S. quarter ton Jeep equipped with a pedestal mounted machine gun See M-151 Jeep.

gun-target line - (DOD) An imaginary straight line from the gun(s) to the target. See also spotting line.

gun-type weapon - (DOD, NATO, CENTO) A device in which two or more pieces of fissionable material, each less than a critical mass, are brought together very rapidly so as to form a supercritical mass which can explode as the result of a rapidly expanding fission chain.

gun, 280-mm (very heavy artillery) - (DOD, IADB) A mobile cannon designed specifically to fire a nuclear projectile. Mobility for this weapon is provided by a "double-ender" transporter.

gun, heavy, 175-mm - (DOD) A full-tracked, self-propelled gun with a maximum range of 32,000 meters.

Gunbird - The Cobra helicopter.

gunboat - Small surface craft with machine guns.

Gung Ho - 1. From China Marines meaning working together, unity. 2. One who is enthusiastic.

gunge - Tropical skin disease. See crotch rot.

Gunjy, gungey - Zealous, from Gung Ho.

gunny - Short for Gunnery Sergeant.

Guns - See M-55.

guns up - An order to bring machine guns or other guns to the bow of a ship or otherwise prepare for combat.

guns/weapons free - (DOD) In air intercept, means fire may be opened on all aircraft not recognized as friendly.

guns/weapons tight - (DOD) In air intercept, means do not open fire, or cease firing on any aircraft (or on bogey specified, or in section indicated) unless target(s) known to be hostile.

gunship - 1. A generic term for armed helicopters. Early in the war it meant the helicopter with heavy guns and fire power that offered support to the infantry. Later in the war the term was used to mean a specific reference to the AH-1H Cobra helicopter and its specific arms that included mini-guns, rocket launchers and 40-mm cannons. The craft that permitted the development of the major tactical innovation of close air support.

guppy - Sarcastic term for Navy personnel not SCUBA qualified.

gurney - Hospital term for a wheeled stretcher for use in a hospital, not field.

guy in back - 1. The weapons officer. 2. Co-pilot. See GIB.

GVN - Government of Vietnam (South).

GWink - Gin and Wink (a grapefruit soda).

Gypsy operations - Small very mobile bases.

gyrene - U.S. Marine.

GySgt - Gunnery Sergeant (Marine Corps).

H – HOTEL

H - Designated in the military phonetic alphabet as "Hotel".

H-13 - See OH 13.

H-19 - See Chickasaw.

H-21 - See OH-21.

H-34 - See CH 34.

H-34 - See CH.

H-35 - See CH 35.

H-37 - See CH 37.

H-43 - Huskie helicopter.

H-43 - See Husky.

H-46 - See CH 46.

H-48 - See CH 48.

H-hour - (DOD) The specific hour on D-day at which a particular operation commences. The operation may be the commencement of hostilities; the hour at which an operation plan is executed or to be executed (as distinguished from the hour the order to execute is issued); the hour that the operations phase is implemented, either by land assault, parachute assault, amphibious assault, air or naval bombardment. The highest command or headquarters coordinating the planning will specify the exact meaning of H-hour within the aforementioned definition. Normally, the letter "H" will be the only one used to denote the above. However, when several operations or phases of an operation are being conducted in the same area on D-day, and confusion may arise through the use of the same hour designation for two or more of them, any letter of the alphabet may be used except A, C, D, E, J, M, or others which may be reserved for exclusive use. See also D-day.

H-hour - (IADB) The specific hour on D-day at which a particular operation commences. The operation may be the commencement of hostilities; the hour at which an operations plan is executed or to be executed (as distinguished from the hour the order to execute is issued) ; the hour that the operations phase is implemented, either by land assault, parachute assault, amphibious assault, air or naval bombardment. The letter "H" will be the only one used to denote the above. The highest command or headquarters coordinating the planning will specify the exact meaning of H-hour within the aforementioned definition. See also D-day.

H-hour - (NATO, SEATO, CENTO) 1. The specific hour on D-day on which hostilities commence. 2. When used in connection with planned operations, it is the specific hour on which the operation commences.

H&I - Harassment and interdiction fire.

H&MS - Marine Headquarters and Maintenance Squadron.

H&S - Headquarters and Supply.

Habu - See SR-71 - an aircraft.

hachuring - (NATO) A method of representing relief upon a map or chart by shading in short disconnected lines drawn in the direction of the slopes.

hack it - To manage something, to accomplish it, to get it done, to survive.

hacker - A good soldier. One who can manage everything.

hail-and-farewell - A party that greets incoming and says goodbye to outgoing personnel, usually officers.

hairy - Dangerous, challenging.

half thickness - (DOD, NATO, CENTO) Thickness of absorbing material necessary to reduce by one-half the intensity of radiation which passes through it.

half-life - (DOD, NATO, CENTO) The time required for the activity of a given radioactive species to decrease to half of its initial value due to radioactive decay. The half-life is a characteristic property of each radioactive species and is independent of its amount or condition. The effective half-life of a given isotope is the time in which the quantity in the body will decrease to half as a result of both radioactive decay and biological elimination.

half-residence time - (DOD, NATO, CENTO) As applied to delayed fallout, it is the time required for the amount of weapon debris deposited in a particular part of the atmosphere, to decrease to half of its initial value.

half-track - The M-16 light armored vehicle equipped with a .50 cal machine gun.

HALO - High Altitude Low Opening. A parachute strategy to avoid detection as the delivery aircraft is above sight, sound, and radar. Jumps often began at 15,000 feet and required a long free fall time.

Halozone tablets - Water purification tablets.

HAM - Hairy assed Marine, a male Marine. See BAM.

ham - Someone in a full dress uniform.

ham and motherfuckers - Ham and beans.

ham radio operator - Amateur radio operator licensed by the FCC to operate over the air radio transmissions. Ham radio operators in the U.S. served a vital communication link between friends and family in the U.S. and service members in Vietnam. See MARS.

Hamburger Hill - The battle in the A Shau Valley in May 1969.

hamlet - A cluster of several buildings. Multiple hamlets composed a village.

hammer and anvil - An infantry tactic using two teams. One is set in place (anvil) while the other (hammer) drives the enemy toward it. See anvil and hammer.

hammerhead - 1. A hard driver, go-getter. 2. A stupid person.

hammerhead stall - A stall in an aircraft engine from going up at too steep an angle.

hammerhead turn - Aviation maneuver that replaces the motionless moment at the top of an Immelmann maneuver with a powered turn.

hand flare - A flare launched from a hand-held cardboard tube. Once launched, it illuminated an area by dropping slowly on a parachute.

handover - (DOD) The passing of control authority of an aircraft from one flight control agency to another. Handover action may be accomplished between control agencies of separate Services when conducting joint operations or between control agencies within a single command and control system. Handover action is complete when the receiving controller acknowledges assumption of control authority.

hang fire - Failure of a round to clear the barrel. A stuck round.

hanger - Covered storage for aircraft.

hanger flyer - One who exaggerates, usually a pilot.

hanger flying - Bragging, exaggerating.

hanger queen - A plane that has a lot of time in the hanger getting fixed. Often a plane used for parts needed on other planes.

Hanoi Hilton - The Hoa Loa Prison in Hanoi noted for its cruelty to American POWs.

harassing (air) - (DOD, NATO, SEATO, CENTO, IADB) The attack of any target within the area or land battle not connected with interdiction of close air support. It is designed to reduce the enemy's combat effectiveness.

harassing fire - (DOD, NATO, SEATO, CENTO, IADB) Fire designed to disturb the rest of the enemy troops to curtail movement and, by threat of losses, to lower morale. See also fire.

harassment - (DOD) An incident in which the primary objective is to disrupt the activities of a unit, installation, or ship, rather than to inflict serious casualties or damage.

Harassment and Interdiction - The type of artillery fire intended to impede the movement and effectiveness of the enemy, usually this was used to target specific limited ground that if secured by the enemy would provide a tactical advantage.

harbor - (DOD, IADB) A restricted body of water, an anchorage, or other limited coastal water area and its mineable water approaches from which shipping operations are projected or supported. Generally, a harbor is a part of a base, in which case the harbor defense force forms a component element of the base defense force established for the local defense of the base and its included harbor.

harbor defense - (DOD, NATO, CENTO, IADB) The defense of a harbor or anchorage and its water approaches against: a. submarine, submarine-borne, or small surface craft attack; b. enemy minelaying operations; and c. sabotage. The defense of a harbor from guided or dropped missiles while such missiles are airborne is considered to be a part of air defense.

harbor site - Marine term for a safe overnight position.

hard base - (DOD, SEATO) A launching base that is protected against a nuclear explosion.

hard beach - (DOD, IADB) A portion of a beach especially prepared with a hard surface extending into the water, employed for the purpose of loading or unloading directly into or from landing ships or landing craft.

hard bomb - A conventional bomb without incendiary or fragmentation elements.

hard charger - Marine slang for a motivated Marine, a go-getter.

hard core - 1. The regular North Vietnamese soldiers. 2 A by the book old school officer.

hard deck - Aviation term for the minimum altitude in a flight, particularly training flights. Flying below the hard deck is equal to hitting ground in scoring. Topgun School uses a 10,000 foot hard deck in training, unless otherwise specified for a training event.

hard hats - Slang for the well trained North Vietnamese special units which were issued metal or fiberglass helmets.

hard missile base - (NATO, CENTO) A launching base that is protected against a nuclear explosion.

hard port - (DOD) Alter heading to magnetic heading indicated, turning to the port in a tight turn (three digit group), or alter heading indicated number of degrees to the port in a tight turn (one or two digit group with word "degrees").

hard rice - Ammunition provided to south Vietnamese tribesman.

hard spot - 1. Infantry overnight stopping place. 2. Ambush set by armored vehicles. Also spelled hardspot.

hard starboard - (DOD) Alter heading to magnetic heading indicated, turning to the starboard in a tight turn (three digit group), or alter heading indicated number of degrees to the starboard in a tight turn (one or two digit group with word "degrees").

hard striped - A sergeant, with a rank of E-5 or E-6, having some greater authority than those of the same rank without striped, a term acknowledging authority.

hard target - A military target that requires more than small arms fire to destroy such as aircraft, buildings and other hard assets. See soft target.

hardened site - (DOD, NATO, CENTO) A site constructed to withstand the blast and associated effects of a nuclear attack and likely to be protected against a chemical, biological, or radiological attack.

hardly working - Doing a tough assignment well and not complaining.

hardstand - (DOD, NATO, CENTO, IADB) 1. A paved or stabilized area where vehicles are parked. 2. Open ground area having a prepared surface and used for storage of materiel.

hardstand - Slang for the sheet of pierced steel plate laid over sand or marsh to give a solid foundation for artillery, other emplacements, or an airstrip. See PSP.

hash mark - See service stripe.

hasty breaching (land mine warfare) - (DOD, NATO, CENTO) The creation of lanes through enemy minefields by expedient methods such as blasting with demolitions, pushing rollers or disabled vehicles through the minefields when the time factor does not permit detailed reconnaissance, deliberate breaching, or bypassing the obstacle. See also breaching.

hasty crossing - (DOD, NATO, SEATO, CENTO, IADB) A crossing of a river or stream using crossing means at hand or readily available without pausing to make elaborate preparations. See also deliberate crossing.

hasty defense - (DOD, NATO, CENTO, IADB) A defense normally organized while in contact with the enemy or when contact is imminent and time available for the organization is limited. It is characterized by improvement of the natural defense strength of the terrain by utilization of foxholes, emplacements, and obstacles. See also deliberate defense.

hat - Marine slang for Drill Instructor.

hatch - Navy and Marine slang for a door.

hatch list - (DOD, IADB) A list showing, for each hold section of a cargo ship, a description of the items stowed, their volume and weight, the consignee of each, and the total volume and weight of materiel in the hold.

hatchet team - A Special Operations team deployed to take out any targets discovered on reconnaissance.

havens (moving) - See moving havens.

haversack - Marine slang for the main backpack.

HAW - Heavy Attack Weapon.

Hawk - (DOD, IADB) A mobile, surface-to-air guided missile system designed to defend against enemy aircraft flying at low altitudes, and short-range rocket/missiles. Designated as MIM-23.

Hawkeye - Radar search aircraft for early warning of troop movement.

Hawks and Doves - The two diverse political and strategic views of pursuing the war in Vietnam; Hawks wanted all out warfare while Doves pressed for peaceful resolution.

hawsers - Heavy lines used for mooring a ship, often 6 inches in diameter.

hazard signs (road transport) - (NATO, SEATO, CENTO, IADB) Signs used to indicate traffic hazards. Military hazard signs should be used in a communications zone area only in accord with existing agreement with national authorities.

hazardous duty pay - The added pay for duty in a combat zone. This was $65 a month for part of the war. See combat pay.

HE - See high explosive. Also Hotel Echo.

head - 1. Navy and Marine slang for the toilet. 2. A dope smoker.

head call - Marine slang for a trip to the bathroom.

head detail - Bathroom cleanup assignment.

head doctor - Psychiatrist.

head on a swivel - Aviation term for continual observation in all directions.

head shed - Headquarters.

head shrinker - Psychiatrist.

headache bar - The safety roll bar over the operator's head in the Rome Plow bulldozer.

heading - (DOD) In air intercept, means my, or "bogey's" magnetic course is ____.

heading crossing angle - (DOD) In air intercept, the angular difference between interceptor heading and target heading at the time of intercept.

headquarters - Abbreviated as HQ.

heads - Marijuana smoking soldiers.

heads up - (DOD) In air intercept, a code meaning enemy got through (part or all) or I am not in position to engage target.

heart - Purple Heart decoration for an injury during combat.

Hearts and Minds - The term used to describe the tactic of counterinsurgency, as in "win their hearts and minds".

HEAT - High explosive antitank. Description of specific round of ammunition or rocket.

heat - High explosive, anti-tank or artillery projectile.

heat tabs - Short for heat tablets, a heat tablet was include in the C-ration box to heat food or water for coffee, it was a small block of flammable material that was easy to light and produced a rapid and high heat in a confined space.

heavies - High ranking officers or political officials.

Heavy - The M-109 (self-propelled) or M-114 (towed) 155-mm Howitzer.

heavy artillery - See howitzer, 8-inch (heavy artillery); gun, heavy, 175-mm.

heavy assault weapon - (DOD, IADB) A weapon capable of operating from ground or vehicle, used to defeat armor and other material targets.

heavy cruiser - (DOD, IADB) A warship designed to operate with strike, antisubmarine warfare, or amphibious forces against air and surface threats. Main battery consists of 8" guns; some CAs have Regulus capability. Full load displacement is approximately 21,000 tons. Designated as CA.

heavy duty - Slang for a bad break or something serious.

heavy stuff - 1. Large artillery pieces. 2. A large artillery barrage.

heavy-lift cargo - (DOD, IADB) 1. Any single cargo lift weighing over 5 long tons and to be handled aboard ship. (DOD) 2. In Marine Corps usage, individual units of cargo which exceed 800 pounds in weight or 100 cubic feet in volume. See also cargo.

heavy-lift ship - (DOD, NATO, CENTO, IADB) A ship specially designed and capable of loading and unloading heavy and bulky items. It has booms of sufficient capacity to accommodate a single lift of 100 tons.

Hedgehog - (DOD, IADB) 7.2" antisubmarine warfare, ahead-thrown, short-range weapon.

Hedgehogs - Slang for the isolated French outposts.

hedgerow - A thick line of shrubs or trees, often planted as a windbreak, used for cover.

height - (DOD) The vertical distance of an object, point, or level above the ground or other established reference plane. Height may be indicated as follows: very low - Below 500 feet (above ground level); low - 500 to 2,000 feet (above ground level); medium - 2,000 to 25,000 feet; high - 25,000 to 50,000 feet; very high - Above 50,000 feet.

height - (NATO, CENTO) 1. The vertical distance of a level, a point or an object, considered as a point, measured from a specified datum. 2. The vertical dimension of an object.

height datum - See altitude datum.

height of burst - (DOD) The vertical distance from the earth's surface or target to the point of burst. See also types of burst.

height of burst - (NATO, CENTO) 1. The vertical distance from the earth's surface or target to the point of burst. 2. For nuclear weapons, the optimum height of burst for a particular target (or area) is that at which it is estimated a weapon of a specified energy yield will produce a certain desired effect over the maximum possible area.

Heinemann's Hot Rod - See A-4.

heliborne - Slang for being airborne in a helicopter.

helicopter - An aircraft propelled by one or more fixed rotors allowing motion in all directions. A key aviation component in the Vietnam war, including the Utility Helicopter (designated as UH) Cargo Helicopter (designated as CH), and Observation Helicopter (designated as OH) and Assault Helicopter (designated as AH).

helicopter assault force - (DOD, NATO, CENTO, IADB) A task organization combining helicopters, supporting units, and helicopter-borne troop units for use in helicopter-borne assault operations.

helicopter break-up point - (DOD, IADB) A control point at which helicopters returning from a landing zone break formation and are released to return to base or are dispatched for other employment.

helicopter departure point - See departure point.

helicopter drop point - (DOD, IADB) A designated point within a landing zone where helicopters are unable to land because of the terrain, but in which they can discharge cargo or troops while hovering.

helicopter landing site - (DOD, IADB) A designated subdivision of a helicopter landing zone in which a single flight or wave of assault helicopters land to embark or disembark troops and/or cargo.

helicopter landing zone - (DOD, IADB) A specified ground area for landing assault helicopters to embark or disembark troops and/or cargo. A landing zone may contain one or more landing sites.

helicopter lane - (DOD, NATO, CENTO, IADB) A safety air corridor in which helicopters fly to or from their destination during helicopter operations.

helicopter team - (DOD, IADB) The combat-equipped troops lifted in one helicopter at one time.

helicopter transport area - (DOD, IADB) Areas to the seaward and on the flanks of the outer transport and landing ship areas, but preferably inside the area screen, to which helicopter transports proceed for launching or recovering helicopters. See also transport area.

helicopter wave - See wave.

helipad - (DOD, NATO, CENTO) A prepared area designated and used for the takeoff and landing of helicopters. (Includes touchdown or hover point).

heliport - (DOD, NATO, CENTO) A facility designated for operating, basing, servicing, and maintaining helicopters.

helo - Navy and Marine Corps slang for a helicopter. See chopper.

helo cast - A helicopter delivery of troops into water via an exiting platform while hovering just above the surface.

HEP - High explosive-plastic. C-4.

herbicide - (DOD, NATO, CENTO) A chemical compound which will kill or damage plants. See also anticrop agent; antiplant agent.

Hercules - (DOD, IADB) A medium-range troop and cargo transport designed for air-drop or air-land delivery into a combat zone as well as conventional airlift. This aircraft is equipped with four turbo-prop engines, and integral ramp and cargo door. The D model is ski-equipped. The E model has additional fuel capacity for extended range. Designated as C-130. The inflight tanker configuration is designated KC-130. Also called Herky Bird.

Herd - The nickname for the 173d Airborne Brigade.

Herky Bird - See Hercules.

herringbone formation - The defensive maneuver by a truck convoy when attacked in which trucks steer to the shoulder, alternating left and right. This creates a herringbone pattern which reduces the potential of friendly fire and increases flank coverage.

Hershey Tropical Bar - The chocolate bar in C-rations that did not melt in the tropical heat.

HES - Hamlet Evaluation System.

hex tent - A hexagonal tent, the smaller one holding 5 men and the larger size 10 men.

HG - Hand grenade.

HGM-25 - See Titan.

HH-3 - See Jolly Green Giant.

HHC - Headquarters and Headquarters Company.

hidey hole - Shallow foxhole for cover.

high - (DOD) A height between twenty-five thousand and fifty thousand feet.

high - Slang for drunk or under the influence of drugs.

high airburst - (DOD) The fallout safe height of burst for a nuclear weapon which increases damage to or casualties on soft targets, or reduces induced radiation contamination at actual ground zero. See also types of burst.

high altitude - (DOD, NATO, SEATO, CENTO, IADB) Conventionally, an altitude above 10,000 meters (33,000 feet). See also altitude.

high altitude bombing - (DOD, IADB) Horizontal bombing with the height of release over 15,000 feet.

high altitude burst - (DOD, NATO, CENTO) The explosion of a nuclear weapon which takes place at a height in excess of 100,000 feet. See also types of burst.

high and tight - Marine slang for the standard Marine haircut that is short on top with shaved sides.

high angle - (DOD) An order to request to obtain high-angle fire.

high angle fire - (DOD) Fire delivered at elevations greater than the elevation of maximum range; fire the range of which decreases as the angle of elevation is increased.

high angle hell - Mortar fire.

high explosive - The designation and description of one of the several types of bombs that was used. See HE.

high explosive cargo - (DOD, IADB) Cargo such as artillery ammunition, bombs, depth charges, demolition material, rockets, and missiles. See also cargo.

high oblique - See oblique air photograph.

high points - CIA and MACV terms for a several day event of intense fighting.

high school on the Hudson - West Point.

high side gun pass - Aviation maneuver in which the attack plane is well above the enemy, drops into a power dive, and fires at the rear quarter of the opponent's aircraft.

high speed submarine - (DOD, IADB) A submarine capable of submerged speeds of 20 knots or more.

high velocity drop - (DOD, NATO, CENTO) A drop procedure in which the drop velocity is greater than 30 feet per second (low velocity drop) and lower than free drop velocity. See also airdrop.

high velocity drop - (IADB) The act or process of delivering supplies or equipment from aircraft in flight wherein the rate of descent is greater than that obtained utilizing conventional cargo parachute methods (low velocity drop), but less than terminal velocity (free drop). The high velocity drop system consists of retarding means to limit the rate of descent, stabilizing means (usually combined with the retarding means) to orient the load to strike on a predetermined surface, and sufficient cushioning material to absorb the shock upon impact and preserve the load from damage. See also airdrop; air movement; free drop; free fall; low velocity drop.

high velocity drop - (SEATO) The delivery of supplies or equipment from aircraft in flight wherein the rate of descent is greater than that obtained utilizing conventional cargo parachute methods (low velocity drop), but less than terminal velocity (free drop). See also airdrop.

high Yo-Yo - Aviation maneuver in which the plane either climbs to slow while turning, either to defend against an attacker or find a better position for attack. See low Yo-Yo. See Yo-Yo for history.

high-speed low-drag - Something or someone exceptionally good at something, fast, reliable, no hassle.

Higher-Higher - Slang for the leaders, the upper officers.

highspeed motorway - (NATO) A highway designed for high speed vehicular traffic, often although not necessarily a dual lane highway.

hightop - See M577 ACC.

highway - (NATO) A main road or thoroughfare.

highway clover leaf - (NATO) An intersection of two or more highways the plan pattern of which resembles the shape of a clover leaf.

hill numbers - The map markings of hills in the number of meters of the hill's height.

hill shading - (DOD, NATO) A method of representing relief on a map by depicting the shadows that would be cast by high ground if light were shining from a certain direction.

Hilo Hattie - Code for the C-54 when outfitted with infrared gear. Named for the Hawaiian singer and actress.

Hilton - Hotel chain name used ironically to apply to crummy housing in general and POW locations in the extreme as in Hanoi Hilton.

HIMS - Historical Information Management System.

his-ass - Slang for HSAS, Headquarters Support Activity, Saigon.

Hit Parade - The record of strike damage (hits) by air strikes, taken from the show that ranked and played the top selling records of the week.

hitch - Term of enlistment.

hitting - To try to talk someone into something. Hitting on a girl was to convince her to go out with you. Hitting you up for a smoke.

Ho Chi Minh sandals - Sandals made from used tires, the tread used for the sole and inner tube used for strapping.

Ho Chi Minh Trail - The supply route for the Northern troops to supply the south.

HOBOS - Homing and Bombing Systems. A smart bomb guidance system.

Hobson's Choice - The choice low level criminals had to either enlist or face jail time. Not technically correct as Hobson's Choice is a free will choice in which only one option is given, a "take it or leave it" situation.

hog - 1. The M-60 machine gun. 2. The UH-1B Huey helicopter.

hog board - Marine slang for the bulletin board with family letters, kid's drawings and photos.

Hognose - See M-75 grenade launcher turret.

Hoi Chanh - The name given to a person defecting from the north to the south under the Chieu Hoi amnesty program, (See Chieu Hoi).

hold - (DOD, NATO, SEATO, CENTO, IADB) 1. A cargo stowage compartment aboard ship. 2. To maintain or retain possession of by force, as a position or an area. 3. In an attack, to exert sufficient pressure to prevent movement or redistribution of enemy forces. (NATO, SEATO, CENTO, IADB) 4. As applied to air traffic, to keep an aircraft within a specified space or location which is identified by visual or other means in accordance with air traffic control instructions.

hold fire - (DOD) Do not open fire, or cease firing on raid/track designated. Missiles in flight must not be permitted to continue to intercept raid/track designated. (Note: This is an emergency order that temporarily terminates the active status of antiair warfare weapons on raid/track designated.)

hold(ing) - (DOD) In air intercept, means remain, or am, in position indicated and await(ing) further instructions.

holdees - See transient.

holding anchorage - (DOD, NATO, CENTO, IADB) An alternative anchorage where ships may lie if; a. the assembly or working anchorage or port/water terminal to which they have been consigned is occupied: or b. when delayed by enemy threats or other factors from immediately proceeding on their next voyage; or c. when dispersed from a major port/major water terminal to avoid the effects of a nuclear attack. See also emergency anchorage.

holding and reconsignment point - (DOD, NATO, SEATO, CENTO, IADB) A rail or motor center with considerable capacity, to which cars or trucks may be sent and at which they may be held until their destination becomes known or until the proper time arrives for them to be moved farther toward their destination. Also, a place where railroad cars or trucks may be unloaded and the cargo held for future transshipment.

holding attack - (DOD, NATO, SEATO, CENTO, IADB) An attack designed to hold the enemy in position, to deceive him as to where the main attack is being made, to prevent him from reinforcing the elements opposing the main attack, and/or to cause him to commit his reserves prematurely at an indecisive location.

holiday - (DOD) An unintentional omission in imagery coverage of an area. See also gap (imagery).

VIETNAM: THE WAR ZONE DICTIONARY IN THEIR OWN WORDS

Hollywood Marine - A Marine completing training at San Diego, California (near Hollywood) not Parris Island, South Carolina.

home - The target to which a missile is locked and guiding itself to.

home plate - 1. Aviation slang for the carrier to which the aircraft is assigned. 2. A soldier's last base prior to deployment to Vietnam.

Homecoming - The operation resulting in the release and return of POWs after the Peace Accords were signed.

homerun - Artillery slang for a on-target hit.

homesteader - 1. Soldier able to retain in a choice assignment for longer than others. 2. Anyone staying in Vietnam over a year.

homing guidance - (DOD, NESN, IADB) A system by which a missile steers itself towards a target by means of self-contained mechanism which is activated by some distinguishing characteristics of the target. See also active homing guidance; guidance; passive homing guidance; semiactive homing guidance.

homing phase - (DOD, IADB) The period of flight of a missile between the end of midcourse guidance and arrival in the vicinity of the target. See also terminal guidance.

homogeneous area - (NATO, CENTO) An area which has uniform radar reflecting power at all points.

honcho - Boss, from the Japanese word used in WWII era.

Honda - 1. The auto and motorcycle maker. 2. The general term for all motorcycles, regardless of maker.

Honest John - (DOD, IADB) A surface-to-surface, free-flight, solid-propellant rocket with nuclear and nonnuclear warhead capability. It is designed to attack targets in support of ground forces up to a range of 40,000 meters, depending on the model. Designated as MGR-1.

honey - 1. Any bar girl. 2. The use of honey as a field antiseptic.

honey bucket - The 55-gallon drums used in latrines where the conditions did not allow slit earthen trenching.

honey dippers - Those responsible for burning off the human excrement from latrines.

Hong Kong - 1. The city. 2. Anything cheap or false. 3. Padded bras.

hoo-ha - The substitute name for any piece of gear or component in lieu of knowing or using the technical term, similar to gizmo, doodad, or thingamabob.

hooch - From the Vietnamese term for the small rural huts that the peasants lived in, used to mean a residence, or small quarters.

hooch girl - A Vietnamese woman hired by the military personnel to do laundry or maid work in their quarters or hooch.

hook - (DOD) A procedure used by an air controller to electronically direct the data processing equipment of a semi-automatic command and control system to take a specified action on a specific radar blip or symbol.

hook - 1. The radio pack element of field radio. 2. The arresting hook on an aircraft to assist in a carrier landing by hooking onto a cable on the carrier.

hook slap - Aviation term related to carrier landing, when the hook on the landing plane hits the roundown (tail of the flight deck).

hop - Aviation term for a flight, usually short, sometimes a mission.

horizon - (DOD) In general, the apparent or visible junction of the earth and sky, as seen from any specific position. Also called the apparent, visible, or local horizon. A horizontal plane passing through a point of vision or perspective center. The apparent or visible horizon approximates the true horizon only when the point of vision is very close to sea level.

horizontal action mine - (DOD, NATO) A mine designed to produce a destructive effect in a plane approximately parallel to the ground.

horizontal error - (DOD, NATO, CENTO, IADB) The error in range, deflection, or in radius, which a weapon may be expected to exceed as often as not. Horizontal error of weapons making a nearly vertical approach to the target is described in terms of circular error probable. Horizontal error of weapons producing elliptical dispersion pattern is expressed in terms of probable error. See also circular error probable; delivery error; deviation; dispersion error.

horizontal loading - (DOD) NATO, CENTO, IADB) Loading of items of like character in horizontal layers throughout the holds of a ship. See also loading.

horizontal loading - (SEATO) A type of loading whereby items of like character are loaded in horizontal layers throughout the holds of a ship. See also loading.

horn - Slang for the handset of a field radio.

horse - Heroin.

horse collar - The rescue gear on a helicopter lowered by cable to rescue individuals from the water. The individual hooks his arms and upper body into the horse collar and is winched up into the helicopter.

hose - To kill.

hose down - To spray with automatic fire.

hospital - (DOD, IADB) A medical treatment facility primarily intended to provide inpatient care. It is appropriately staffed and equipped to provide diagnostic and therapeutic services, as well as the necessary supporting services required to perform its assigned mission. A hospital may, in addition, discharge the functions of a dispensary.

hospital ship - (DOD, IADB) An unarmed ship, marked in accordance with the Geneva Convention, staffed and equipped to provide hospitalization for the armed forces and also used to evacuate casualties. Designated as AH. See also hospital transport.

hospital transport - (DOD, IADB) A transport provided with additional medical personnel and increased facilities for evacuation of casualties. See also hospital ship.

host country - (DOD) A nation in which representatives or organizations of another state are present because of government invitation and/or international agreement.

hostage - (DOD, NATO, CENTO, IADB) A person held as a pledge that certain terms or agreements will be kept. (The taking of hostages is forbidden under the Geneva Conventions, 1949.)

hostile - (DOD) A contact positively identified as enemy. See also bogey; friendly.

hostile acts - (DOD) Basic rules established by higher authority for defining and recognizing hostile acts by aircraft, submarines, surface units, and ground forces will be promulgated by the commanders of unified or specified commands, and by other appropriate commanders when so authorized.

hostile track - (DOD, NATO, CENTO) The classification assigned to a track which, based upon established criteria, is determined to be an enemy airborne, ballistic and/or orbiting threat. Note: NATO and CENTO term is "hostile track (air defense)".

hot - An area under enemy fire or control.

hot bunk - A bunk on a ship that is used by several sailors in shifts.

hot dog - A show-off.

hot hoist - The extraction of troops by helicopter while under fire.

hot hole - A tunnel with Viet Cong in it.

hot LZ - An unsafe landing zone.

hot pad alert - See ramp alert.

hot photo interpretation report - Not to be used. See Joint Tactical Air Reconnaissance/Surveillance Mission Report.

hot pursuit - The policy allowing an army under attack to peruse the attacker into otherwise prohibited areas. President Nixon allowed it, but President Johnson did not.

hot report - Not to be used. See Joint Tactical Air Reconnaissance/Surveillance Mission Report.

hot sheets - 1. Steel matting laid as sidewalks. 2. Hot bunking. 3. Latest orders.

hot skinny - News.

hot spot - (DOD, NATO, CENTO) Region in a contaminated area in which the level of radioactive contamination is considerably greater than in neighboring regions in the area.

HOT/SOP - Standard Operating Procedures for clothing, and procedures for weather between 15 April and 15 October, particularly to combat heat related illnesses. Pronounced hot S-O-P. See COLD/SOP.

Hotel - The military phonetic alphabet designation for the letter "H".

Hotel Alpha - Haul ass, leave quickly, evacuate.

Hotel Echo - High explosives.

hots - Hot food served in the mess and occasionally in the field.

Hound Dog - (DOD, IADB) A turbojet-propelled, air-to-surface missile designed to be carried externally on the B-52. It is equipped with a nuclear warhead and can be launched for either high or low altitude attacks against enemy targets, supplementing the internally-carried firepower of the B-52. Designated as AGM-28.

house mouse - 1. Marine slang for a Drill Instructor's go-fer. See go-fer. 2. Army slang for maid or mistress.

house of dark shadows - A home of a Viet Cong soldier.

housewife - Marine slang for a sewing kit.

hovercraft - The air supported low-draft boats which were used experimentally in Vietnam. The Navy used these until 1968. The Army Special Forces used them to deploy troops until 1970. Officially designated as Patrol Air Cushion Vehicles (PACV). See ground effect machine.

hovering - (DOD, NATO, CENTO, IADB) A self-sustaining maneuver whereby a fixed, or nearly fixed position is maintained relative to a spot on the earth's surface or underwater.

hovering ceiling - (DOD, NATO, CENTO, IADB) The highest altitude at which the helicopter is capable of hovering in standard atmosphere. It is usually stated in two figures: hovering in ground effect and hovering out of ground effect.

Howard Johnson - Firebase built with intention of ongoing occupancy, named after the motel chain.

Howie - Howitzer.

howitzer - (DOD) 1. A cannon which combines certain characteristics of guns and mortars. The howitzer delivers projectiles with medium velocities, either by low or high trajectories. 2. A cannon with tube length 20 to 30 calibers. See also gun; mortar.

Howtar - See mortar, 107-mm (4.2").

HQ - Headquarters.

HSAS - Headquarters Support Activity, Saigon. Nicknamed his-ass.

Huey - Slang for any of the UH-1A or UH-1B helicopter which was the primary transport of the infantry to and from combat missions (See dust off bird, C&C birds, slicks).

Huey slick - A Huey helicopter without weapons.

hug - Radio code for: 1. Close to the enemy 2. Pinned down close to the enemy.

Hummer - The stretched C-47 aircraft used by Marines for transportation and flare missions. Designated as C-117.

hump - 1. Walking on patrol carrying full pack and gear. 2. Being on patrol. 3. Doing any hard work. 4. Sexual intercourse.

humping - Walking patrol.

Hundred and Worst - The 101st Airborne.

hundred miles an hour tape - Duct tape, often mispronounced as duck tape. Officially called reinforcing tape. Tape was used to patch bullet holes or other small holes in the aircraft hull to preserve the aerodynamic skin of the craft. Also hundred mile an hour tape.

hundred mission crunch - 1. A pilot's view of the strain that the Air Force requirement to fly one hundred missions put on operations. 2. The goal of flying the required missions and getting transferred from combat.

hundreds - Marijuana cigarettes.

hunter-killer force - (DOD, IADB) A naval force consisting of an antisubmarine warfare carrier, associated aircraft and escorts combining specialized searching, tracking, and attacking capabilities of air and surface antisubmarine warfare units operated as a coordinated group for the conduct of offensive antisubmarine operations in an area of submarine probability.

hunter-killer group - See antisubmarine carrier group.

hunter-killer operations - (DOD, NATO, SEATO, CENTO, IADB) Offensive antisubmarine operations in a submarine probability area, combining the best searching, tracking, and attacking capabilities of air, surface, and subsurface units, and forces in coordinated action to locate and destroy submarines at sea.

hurting - Wounded or severely injured.

hush puppy - The S&W 9-mm pistol.

Huskie - A search and rescue helicopter. The HH-43.

huss - 1. A favor granted by a superior. 2. A lucky break. Also spelled hus.

Hustler - (DOD, IADB) A strategic all-weather medium bomber with nuclear delivery capability. It is powered by four turbojet engines and has a supersonic dash capability. The Hustler has an intercontinental range through in-flight refueling. Designated as B-58.

HUT - Hamlet Upgrading Team. An Army training program for local soldiers.

hydrographic chart - (DOD, NATO, SEATO, CENTO, IADB) A nautical chart showing depths of water, nature of bottom, contours of bottom and coastline, and tides and currents in a given sea or sea and land area.

hydrographic reconnaissance - (DOD) Reconnaissance of an area of water to determine depths, beach gradients, the nature of the bottom, and the location of coral reefs, rocks, shoals, and man-made obstacles.

hydrographic section (beach party) - (DOD, SEATO, IADB) A section of a beach party whose duties are to clear the beach of damaged boats, conduct hydrographic reconnaissance, assist in removing underwater obstructions, act as stretcher bearers and furnish relief boat crews.

hydrography - (DOD, NATO, CENTO) The science which deals with the measurements and description of the physical features of the oceans, seas, lakes, rivers, and their adjoining coastal areas, with particular reference to their use for navigational purposes.

hyperfocal distance - (NATO, CENTO) The distance from the lens to the nearest object in focus when the lens is focused at infinity.

hypergolic fuel - (DOD, NATO, CENTO, IADB) Fuel which will spontaneously ignite with an oxidizer, such as aniline with fuming nitric acid. It is used as the propulsion agent in certain missile systems.

hypersonic - (DOD, NATO, CENTO, IADB) Of, or pertaining to, speeds equal to or in excess of five times the speed of sound. See also speed of sound.

hyperstereoscopy - (NATO, CENTO) Stereoscopic viewing in which the relief effect is noticeably exaggerated, caused by the extension of the camera base. Also known as exaggerated stereoscopy.

hypsometric tinting - (DOD, NATO, CENTO, IADB) A method of showing relief on maps and charts by coloring in different shades those parts which lie between selected levels. Sometimes referred to as elevation tint, altitude tint, and layer tint.

I – INDIA

I - 1. Designated in the military phonetic alphabet as "India". 2. An indication modifying a military definition that U.S. Government interdepartmental approval has been granted for a term to be used in national military use.

I Corps - The northern sector of Vietnam. Pronounced "eye core". See Corps.

I do not understand. - Toi com biet. Frequently used Vietnamese expression.

I go - (DOD) I am leaving my patrol/mission in _____ minutes. See also I stay.

I shit you not. - An emphatic exclamation of truth.

I stay - (DOD) Am remaining with you on patrol/mission _____ hours. See also I go.

I-A - The Selective Service System draft classification for males eligible for the draft as mentally and physically ready for service. Pronounced One-A.

I-AO-CO - The Selective Service System draft classification for males eligible for the draft as fit for non-combat duty (such as medic). Pronounced One-A Oh-Cee Oh.

I-C - The Selective Service System draft classification males in the U.S. Armed Forces, Coast Guard. Public Health Service, or Geodetic Survey. Pronounced One-C.

I-D - The Selective Service System draft classification for males in a reserve component or a student in military training. Pronounced One-D.

I-O - The Selective Service System draft classification for males eligible for the draft as Conscientious Objector fit to perform alternative civilian service. Pronounced One-Oh.

I-S - The Selective Service System draft classification for males eligible for the draft but a student deferred by statute, usually in high school. Pronounced One-S.

I-W - The Selective Service System draft classification for males eligible for the draft performing work contributing to the national health, safety or interest as a conscientious objector. Pronounced One-W.

I-Y - The Selective Service System draft classification for males eligible for the draft as unfit for service except in a declared war or national emergency. Pronounced One-Y.

I&I - Intercourse and Intoxication, a play on the term R&R.

IADB - An indication modifying a military definition that approval has been granted for the term to be used in military use between member countries of the Inter-American System, the Inter-American Defense Board. Note: This is an advisory body to the Organization of American States representing North, Central and South America.

IAS - Indicated Air Speed.

IBRD - International Bank for Reconstruction and Development, a United Nations agency.

IBS - Inflatable boat, small.

IBS donut - Donut shaped 7-man inflatable boat.

IC - Innocent civilian.

ICAO - International Civil Aviation Organization, a United Nations agency.

ICC - International Control Commission, A commission appointed under the 1954 Geneva Accords to monitor the observation of its terms by warring sides.

ice cream cone with wings - The parachutist badge.

ice cream soldiers - Marine's slang for Army due to the relatively luxurious accommodations at Army base camps, such as ice cream.

ice it - Reconnaissance slang for mission over, leaving the area.

ICEX - Intelligence Coordination and Exploitation.

ICRC - International Committee of the Red Cross.

ICS - Inter-Communications System. The communications system over internal radio in a plane allowing all on the craft to communicate with each other.

ICU - Intensive Care Unit in hospitals.

ID - 1. Identification card. 2. Infantry Division.

IDA - International Development Association, a United Nations agency.

identification - (DOD, IADB) 1. In air defense and antisubmarine warfare, the process of determining the friendly or hostile character of a detected contact. 2. In arms control, the process of determining which nation is responsible for the detected violations of an arms control measure.

identification - (NATO, SEATO, CENTO) The indication by any act or means of your own friendly character or individually.

Identification Friend or Foe - (DOD) A system using electronic transmissions to which equipment carried by friendly forces automatically responds, for example, by emitting pulses, thereby distinguishing themselves from enemy forces. It is a method of determining the friendly or unfriendly character of aircraft and ships by other aircraft or ships and by ground forces using electronic detection equipment and associated Identification Friend or Foe units. See also selective identification feature.

Identification Friend or Foe - (NATO, SEATO, CENTO, IADB) A system using radar transmissions to which equipment carried by friendly forces automatically responds, for example, by emitting pulses, thereby distinguishing themselves from enemy forces. It is the primary method of determining the friendly or unfriendly character of aircraft and ships by other aircraft or ships and by ground forces employing radar detection equipment and associated Identification, Friend or Foe units.

Identification Friend or Foe personal identifier - (DOD) The discreet Identification Friend or Foe code assigned to a particular aircraft, ship, or other vehicle for identification by electronic means.

identification maneuver - (DOD) A maneuver performed for identification purposes.

identification tags - Metal identification tags. Dogtags.

identify - (DOD) A code meaning identify the contact designated by any means at your disposal.

IDS - In da shit, in trouble of any sort.

IDT box - A book sized secure communication device with a display screen.

IFF - Identification Friend or Foe system.

IFR - Instrument flight rules. The flight protocol when visibility is restricted. See VFR.

IG - Inspector General.

igloo space - (DOD, IADB) Area in an earth-covered structure of concrete and/or steel designed for the storage of ammunition and explosives. See also storage.

igloo white - Code for the data from all sources on enemy locations.

IHTFP - I hate this fucking place. Written on walls and gear everywhere.

II Corps - The central highlands region of Vietnam. See Corps.

II-A - The Selective Service System draft classification for males eligible for the draft who were occupationally deferred as performing vital work, in full-time study in a trade school, community college or junior college or apprenticeship program. Pronounced Two-A.

II-B - The Selective Service System draft classification for males eligible for the draft who were occupationally deferred as performing vital work in a defense industry. Pronounced Two-B.

II-C - The Selective Service System draft classification for males eligible for the draft who got an agricultural deferment. Pronounced Two-C.

II-D - The Selective Service System draft classification for males eligible for the draft who were in military reserve units or ROTC. Pronounced Two-D.

II-S- The Selective Service System draft classification for males eligible for the draft who were deferred as full time college students. Pronounced Two-S.

III Corps - The central area between Saigon and the highlands, a dense population area. See Corps.

III MAF - Third Marine Amphibious Force.

III-A - The Selective Service System draft classification for males eligible for the draft who were deferred due to dependency of children in his family relationship or other hardship on dependents. Pronounced Three-A.

illum - An illumination flare.

illumination flare - A flare shot from the ground by hand or artillery or dropped from aircraft to illuminate a battlefield.

Illuminator - The aircraft fitted with a laser that targeted enemy troop locations, held laser on it while smart bombs were deployed to hit the laser spot.

ILO - International Labor Organization, a United Nations agency.

image displacement - (NATO, CENTO) In a photograph, any dimensional or positional error.

image format - (DOD) Actual size of negative, scope, or other medium on which image is produced.

image intensifier - See Starlight Scope.

image motion compensation - (NATO, CENTO) The process of synchronizing the relative movement of the ground image, caused by all vehicle motion, with a recording sensor during exposure.

imagery - (DOD, NATO, CENTO) Collectively, the representations of objects reproduced electronically or by optical means on film, electronic display devices or other media.

imagery interpretation - (DOD, NATO) The process of location, recognition, identification, and description of objects, activities and terrain represented on imagery.

imagery interpretation key - (NATO, CENTO) Any diagrams, charts, tables, lists or sets of examples, etc., which are used to aid imagery interpreters in the rapid identification of objects visible on imagery.

imagery sortie - (DOD, NATO, CENTO) One flight by one aircraft for the purpose of recording air imagery.

IMF - International Monetary Fund, a United Nations agency.

imitative deception - (DOD) The introduction of radiations into enemy channels which imitate his own emissions.

immediate air support - (DOD, NATO, SEATO, CENTO, IADB) Air support to meet specific requests which arise during the course of a battle and which by their nature cannot be planned in advance. See also air support.

immediate destination (merchant shipping) - (NATO, CENTO, IADB) The next destination of a ship or convoy, irrespective of whether or not onward routing instructions have been issued to it. See also destinations.

immediate message - (DOD, IADB) A category of precedence reserved for messages relating to situations which gravely affect the security of national allied forces or populace, and which require immediate delivery to the addressee(s). See also precedence.

immediate mission request - (DOD) A request for an air strike on a target which by its nature could not be identified sufficiently in advance to permit detailed mission coordination and planning. See also preplanned mission request.

immediate mission request (reconnaissance) - (DOD) A request for a mission on a target which, by its nature, could not be identified sufficiently in advance to permit detailed mission coordination and planning.

immediate nuclear support - (DOD) Nuclear support to meet specific requests which arise during the course of a battle and which by their nature cannot be planned in advance. See also preplanned nuclear support; nuclear support.

immediate operational readiness - (DOD) Those operations directly related to the assumption of an alert or quick-reaction posture. Typical operations include strip alert, airborne alert/indoctrination, no-notice launch of an alert force, and the maintenance of missiles in an alert configuration. See also nuclear weapon exercise; nuclear weapon maneuver.

immediate operational readiness - (NATO, CENTO, IADB) The state in which any arm or Service is ready in all respects for instant combat.

immediately vital cargo - (NATO, CENTO, IADB) A cargo already loaded, which the consignee country regards as immediately vital for the prosecution of the war or for national survival and delivery of which may be authorized by the national authorities of the flag or ship carrying the cargo, notwithstanding the risk to the ship. (NATO, CENTO) (This definition is limited to the period of implementation of the shipping movement policy.) See also cargoes.

Immelmann - Aviation maneuver in which the plane does a steep dive to gain speed, then climbs into a half a loop, is almost motionless at the top of the arc, and rolls to upright. Named for German pilot Max Immelmann in WWI. Replaced by the hammerhead turn with more power of jet engines and to avoid the motionless moment at the top.

immersion foot - Trench foot, swelling, numbing and infection of feet in continual cold and wet conditions. Tropical impetigo.

impact action fuze - (DOD, NATO, SEATO, CENTO, IADB) A fuze that is set in action by the striking of a projectile or bomb against an object, e.g., percussion fuze, contact fuze. Synonymous with direct action fuze. See also fuze.

impact area - (DOD) An area having designated boundaries within the limits of which all ordnance will detonate or impact.

impact area - (NATO, SEA TO, CENTO, IADB) An area having designated boundaries within the limits of which all ordnance is to make contact with the ground.

impact award - An award for valor made soon after the event.

impact point - (DOD, NATO, CENTO, IADB) The point on the drop zone where the first parachutist or air-dropped cargo item should land.

implosion weapon - (DOD) A weapon in which a quality of fissionable material, less than a critical mass at ordinary pressure, has its volume suddenly reduced by compression (a step accomplished by using chemical explosives) so that it becomes supercritical, producing a nuclear explosion.

implosion weapon - (NATO, CENTO) A device in which a quantity of fissionable material, less than a critical mass, has its volume suddenly decreased by compression, so that it becomes supercritical and an explosion can take place. The compression is achieved by means of a spherical arrangement of specially fabricated shapes of ordinary high explosive which produce an inwardly-directed implosion wave, the fissionable material being at the center of the sphere.

imprest fund - (DOD) A cash fund of a fixed amount established through an advance of funds, without appropriation change, to an authorized imprest fund cashier to effect mediate cash payments of relatively small amounts for authorized purchases of supplies and nonpersonal services.

imprint - (NATO) Brief note in the margin of a map giving all or some of the following: date of publication, printing, name of publisher, printer, place of publication, number of copies printed, and related information.

improvised (early) resupply - (NATO, CENTO, IADB) The onward movement of commodities which are available on land and which can be readily loaded into ships. See also elements of resupply.

in country - In Vietnam. In the war zone.

in support of - (DOD, NATO, SEATO, CENTO, IADB) Assisting or protecting another formation, unit, or organization while remaining under original control.

in the dark - (DOD) In air intercept, a code meaning not visible on my scope.

in the field - Away from camp or base.

in the saddle - 1. Aviation term for the status of a pilot in position to lock on a target and fire. 2. In charge.

in the spaghetti - Aviation term for being in the arresting wires on a carrier deck during a landing.

in-flight engagement - Aviation term for a carrier landing in which the arresting hook under a plane is engaged before the wheels touch down. This slams the plane into the deck and can cause damage.

in-processing - The formal medical review for troops returning to the United States.

inactive aircraft - (DOD) Aircraft placed in storage, bailment, on loan outside the Defense establishment, or otherwise not available to the military Services.

inactive aircraft - (IADB) The total of the reserve and nonprogram aircraft. See also aircraft.

inbound traffic - (DOD) Traffic originating in an area outside continental United States destined for or moving in the general direction of continental United States.

incapacitating agent - (DOD) An agent that produces temporary physiological or mental effects, or both, which will render individuals incapable of concerted effort in the performance of their assigned duties.

incendiaries - Thermite grenades. Fire bombs.

incentive type contract - (DOD) A contract which may be of either a fixed price or cost reimbursement nature, with a special provision for adjustment of the fixed price or fee. It provides for a tentative target price and a maximum price or maximum fee, with price or fee adjustment after completion of the contract for the purpose of establishing a final price or fee based on the contractor's actual costs plus a sliding scale of profit or fee which varies inversely with the cost but which in no event shall permit the final price or fee to exceed the maximum price or fee stated in the contract.

incident (exercise) - (NATO, SEATO, CENTO, IADB) An occurrence injected by directing staffs into the exercise which will have an effect on the forces being exercised or their facilities and which will require action by the appropriate commander and/or staff being exercised.

incidents - (DOD, IADB) Brief clashes or other military disturbances generally of a transitory nature and not involving protracted hostilities.

incoming - Hostile artillery arriving.

incoming mail - Hostile artillery arriving.

Incontinent Ordinance Delivery - Accidental discharge of a weapon or ordinance. See friendly fire.

incursion - A raid into enemy territory.

indefinite call sign - (DOD, NATO, SEATO, CENTO, IADB) A call sign which does not represent a specific facility, command, authority, activity, or unit, but which may represent anyone or any group of these. See also call sign.

indefinite delivery type contract - (DOD) A type of contract used for procurements where the exact time of delivery is not known at time of contracting.

index contour line - (NATO) A contour line accentuated by a heavier line weight to distinguish it from intermediate contour lines. Index contours are usually shown as every fifth contour with their assigned values, to facilitate reading elevations.

index to adjoining sheets - See map index.

India - The military phonetic alphabet designation for the letter "I".

Indian country - Unsecured territory. Enemy territory.

Indian Heads - Nickname for the Second Infantry Division.

indicated airspeed - Air speed without sensor correction added. See airspeed.

indicated Mach number - The relationship between the aircraft speed and the speed of sound, without sensor correction.

indicating - (DOD) In air intercept, a code meaning contact speed, by plot, is _____.

indications (intelligence) - (DOD, NATO, SEATO, CENTO, IADB) Information in various degrees of evaluation, all of which bears on the intention of a potential enemy to adopt or reject a course of action.

indirect air support - (DOD) All forms of air support provided to land or naval forces which do not immediately assist those forces in the tactical battle.

indirect air support - (NATO, SEATO, CENTO, IADB) Support given to land or sea forces by air action against objectives other than enemy forces engaged in the tactical battle. It includes the gaining and maintaining of air superiority, interdiction, and harassing. See also air support.

indirect damage assessment - (NATO, CENTO, IADB) A revised target analysis based on new data such as actual weapon yield, burst height, and ground zero obtained by means other than direct assessment.

indirect fire - (DOD) Fire delivered on a target which is not itself used as a point of aim for the weapons or the director.

indirect fire - (NATO, SEA TO, CENTO, IADB) Fire delivered at a target which cannot be seen by the aimer. See also fire.

indirect laying - (DOD) Aiming a gun either by sighting at a fixed object, called the aiming point, instead of the target or by using a means of pointing other than a sight, such as a gun director, when the target cannot be seen from the gun position.

individual equipment - (DOD, IADB) Referring to method of use, signifies personal clothing and equipment, for the personal use of the individual. See also equipment.

individual reserves - (DOD, IADB) The supplies carried on a soldier, animal, or vehicle for his or its individual use in an emergency. See also reserve supplies.

individual sponsored dependent - (DOD) A dependent not entitled to travel to the oversea command at Government expense or who enters the command without indorsement of the appropriate oversea commander.

Indochina, French Indochina - Vietnam, Laos and Cambodia while under French colonial rule.

induced environment - (DOD, IADB) Any man-made or equipment-made environment which directly or indirectly affects the performance of man or materiel.

induced radiation - (DOD, NATO, SEATO, CENTO, IADB) Radiation produced as a result of exposure to radioactive materials, particularly the capture of neutrons, See also contamination; initial radiation; residual radiation.

industrial mobilization - (DOD, IADB) The transformation of industry from its peacetime activity to the industrial program necessary to support the national military objectives. It includes the mobilization of materials, labor, capital, production facilities, and contributory items and services essential to the industrial program.

industrial property - (DOD) As distinguished from military property, means any contractor-acquired or Government-furnished property, including materials, special tooling and industrial facilities furnished or acquired in the performance of a contract or subcontract.

industrial readiness - (DOD) The state of preparedness of industry to produce essential materiel to support the national military objectives.

inert mine (land mine warfare) - (DOD, NATO, SEATO, CENTO, IADB) An inert replica of a standard mine. It is used for instructional purposes. See also mine.

inertial guidance - (DOD, IADB) A guidance system designed to project a missile over a predetermined path, wherein the path of the missile is adjusted after launching by devices wholly within the missile and independent of outside information. The system measures and converts accelerations experienced to distance traveled in a certain direction. See also guidance.

inf - Infantry.

INFANT - Iroquois Night Fighter and Night Tracker. A low light intelligence and fighting system in the Iroquois helicopter.

infantry - 1. The ground troops. 2. The tactical group to engage the enemy on the ground and through firepower and maneuvering destroy him.

infantry search pattern - Any of several patterns used by the infantry in the field, including checkerboard, starburst, cloverleaf and others.

infantryman's prayer - The variant of the Lord's Prayer often written on helmet covers as one of the following: Yea, though I walk through the Valley of the Shadow of Death, I shall fear no evil for I am the baddest (or meanest) mother fucker (or son of a bitch) in the Valley. See Twenty-third Psalm.

infill - (NATO) In cartography, the filling of an area or feature with color e.g. roads, town shapes, lakes, etc.

infiltration - (DOD, NATO, CENTO, IADB) 1. The movement through or into an area or territory occupied by either friendly or enemy troops or organizations. The movement is made, either by small groups or by individuals, at extended or irregular intervals. When used in connection with the enemy, it infers that contact is avoided.

(DOD) 2. In intelligence usage, placing an agent or other person in a target area in hostile territory. Usually involves crossing a frontier or other guarded line. Methods of infiltration are: black (clandestine); grey (through legal crossing point but under false documentation); white (legal).

infiltration (intelligence) - See Part 2. infiltration.

infinity sight - The forward facing sight in a helicopter gunship.

inflammable cargo - (DOD, IADB) Cargo such as drummed gasoline and oils. See also cargo.

Inflatoplane - An experimental inflatable one-person airplane made by Goodyear that was dropped in a metal 55-gallon drum. Powered by a 60 hp McCulloch engine, it was a rescue vehicle for a downed pilot.

inflight report - (DOD) The transmission from the airborne system of information obtained both at the target and en route.

inflight report - (NATO, CENTO) A standard form of message whereby aircrews report mission results while in flight. It is also used for reporting any other tactical information sighted of such importance and urgency that the delay, if reported by normal debriefing, would negate the usefulness of the information.

informant - (DOD) 1. Person who, wittingly or unwittingly, provides information to an agent, a clandestine service, or the police. 2. In reporting, a person who has provided specific information and is cited as a source.

information (intelligence) - (DOD, NATO, CENTO, IADB) Unevaluated material of every description, including that derived from observations, reports, rumors, imagery, and other sources which, when processed, may produce intelligence.

information (intelligence) - (SEATO) Unprocessed material of every description including that derived from observations, reports, rumors, photographs, etc., which when analyzed, produces intelligence.

information box - (NATO, CENTO) A space on an annotated overlay, mosaic, etc., which is used for identification, reference and scale information.

information processing - See intelligence cycle.

information report - (DOD) Report used to forward raw information collected to fulfill intelligence requirements.

informer - (DOD) Person who intentionally discloses to police or to a security service information about persons or activities he considers suspect, usually for a financial reward.

infrared film - (DOD) Film carrying an emulsion especially sensitive to "near-infrared". Used to photograph through haze, because of the penetrating power of infrared light, and in camouflage detection to distinguish between living vegetation and dead vegetation or artificial green pigment.

infrared imagery - (DOD) That imagery produced as a result of sensing electromagnetic radiations emitted or reflected from a given target surface in the infrared portion of the electromagnetic spectrum (approximately 0.72 to 1,000 microns).

infrared photography - (DOD) Photography employing an optical system and direct image recording on film sensitive to near-infrared wave length (infrared film). Note: Not to be confused with infrared imagery.

infrastructure - (DOD, NATO, SEATO, CENTO) A term generally applicable for all fixed and permanent installations, fabrications, or facilities for the support and control of military forces. See also bilateral infrastructure; common infrastructure; national infrastructure.

infusion - A program of rotating personnel to have less time spent in the field.

ingress - Incoming aircraft approach to target, going in. See Egress.

initial (early) resupply - (NATO, CENTO, IADB) The onward movement of ships which are already loaded with cargoes which will serve the requirements after D-day. This includes such shipping evacuation from major ports/major water terminals and subsequently dispersed to secondary ports/alternate water terminals and anchorages. See also elements of resupply.

initial approach - (DOD, NATO, CENTO) That part of the instrument approach procedure consisting of the first approach to the first navigational facility associated with the procedure, or to a predetermined fix. When not associated with an instrument approach procedure, that portion of the flight of an aircraft immediately prior to arrival over the airfield of destination or over the reporting point from which the final approach to the airfield is commenced.

initial approach - (SEATO, IADB) That portion of the flight of an aircraft immediately prior to arrival over the aerodrome of destination or over the reporting point from which the final approach to the aerodrome is commenced.

initial approach area - (NATO) An area of defined width lying between the last preceding navigational fix or dead reckoning position and either the facility to be used for making an instrument approach or a point associated with such a facility that is used for demarcating the termination of initial approach.

initial contact report - See contact report.

initial entry into military service - (DOD) Entry for the first time in military status (active duty or reserve) by induction, enlistment, or appointment in any Service of the Armed Forces of the United States. Appointment may be as a commissioned or warrant officer; as a cadet or midshipman at the Service academy of one of the armed forces;

or as a midshipman, United States Naval Reserve, for United States Naval Reserve Officers Training Corps training at a civilian institution.

initial issue - (NFSN, CENTO, IADB) First combat supply; placed at the disposal of units of all arms of all Services in peacetime. In principle it enables these units to fulfill their first missions without further supply. It can be transported by the organic transport of the unit. The data is expressed in number of rounds (or in lots in the case of explosives).

initial operational capability - (DOD, IADB) The first attainment of the capability to employ effectively a weapon, item of equipment, or system of approved specific characteristics, and which is manned or operated by an adequately trained, equipped, and supported military unit or force.

Initial Photo Interpretation Report - (DOD) A first-phase interpretation report, subsequent to the Joint Tactical Air Reconnaissance/ Surveillance Mission Report, presenting the results of the initial readout of new imagery to answer the specific requirements for which the mission was requested.

initial point - (DOD, IADB) 1. The first point at which a moving target is located on a plotting board. 2. A well defined point, easily distinguishable visually and/or electronically used as a starting point for the bomb run to the target. 3. (airborne) - A point close to the landing area where serials (troop carrier air formations) make final alterations in course to pass over individual drop or landing zones. 4. (helicopter) - An air control point in the vicinity of the landing zone from which individual flights of helicopters are directed to their prescribed landing sites. 5. Any designated place at which a column or element thereof is formed by the successive arrival of its various subdivisions, and comes under the control of the commander ordering the move. See also target approach point.

initial point - (NATO, CENTO) 1. (air operations) A well defined point, easily distinguishable visually and/or electronically, used as a starting point for the bomb run to the target or to the pull-up point. 2. (air transport) A point close to the landing area where air transport serials make final alterations in course to pass over individual prescribed drop or landing zones. 3. (helicopters) An air control point in the vicinity of the landing zone from which individual flights of helicopters are directed to their prescribed landing sites. 4. (air traffic control) A point in the air from which individual aircraft proceed from stacking to landing approach. NFSN usage only. 5. (ground movement) See start point. 6. The first position at which a moving target is located on a plotting board.

initial provisioning - (DOD, IADB) The process of determining the range and quantity of items (i.e., spares and repair parts, special tools, test equipment, and support equipment) required to support and maintain an item for an initial period of service.

Its phases include the identification of items of supply, the establishment of data for catalog, technical manual, and allowance list preparation of instructions to assure delivery of necessary support items with related end articles.

initial radiation - (DOD, NATO, CENTO) The radiation, essentially neutrons and gamma rays, resulting from a nuclear burst and emitted from the fireball within one minute after burst. See also induced radiation; residual radiation.

initial radiation - (IADB) The nuclear radiation accompanying a nuclear explosion and emitted from the resultant fireball; immediate radiation. It includes the neutrons and gamma rays given off at the instant of the explosion, and the alpha, beta, and gamma rays emitted in the rising fireball and column of smoke. In contrast to residual radiation, its delivery to persons and objects on the earth's surface is terminated by the removal of the source (products in the nuclear cloud) from within effective radiation range of the earth by the rising cloud.

initial reserves - (DOD, IADB) In an amphibious operation, those supplies which normally are unloaded immediately following the assault waves; usually the supplies for the use of the beach organization, battalion landing teams, and other elements of regimental combat teams for the purpose of initiating and sustaining combat until higher supply installations are established. See also reserve supplies.

initial strength of enemy forces - (IADB) The number of men, weapons, and equipment laid down in the accepted War Establishment and War Equipment Tables. See also effective strength of enemy forces; strength of enemy forces.

initial vector - (DOD) The initial command heading to be assumed by an interceptor after it has been committed to intercept an airborne object.

initial velocity - See muzzle velocity.

initiation (nuclear) - (DOD, NATO, CENTO) Action which sets off a chain reaction in a fissile mass which has reached the critical state generally by the emission of a "spurt" of neutrons.

initiation of procurement action - (DOD, IADB) That point in time when the approved document requesting procurement and citing funds is forwarded to the procuring activity. See also procurement lead time.

injury - (DOD, IADB) A term comprising such conditions as fractures, wounds, sprains, strains, dislocations, concussions, and compressions. In addition, it includes conditions resulting from extremes of temperature or prolonged exposure. Acute poisonings, except those due to contaminated food, resulting from exposure to a toxic or poisonous substance are also classed as injuries. See also battle casualty; casualty; nonbattle casualty; wounded.

inland search and rescue region - (DOD) The inland areas of continental United

States, except waters under the jurisdiction of the United States. See also search and rescue region.

inner transport area - (DOD, IADB) The area where most of the unloading is accomplished, located as near the beach as conditions permit. Normally, the transport group moves into the inner transport area after the probability of enemy interference is reduced. See also transport area.

insect bar - Mosquito netting.

insect repellant - See bug juice.

insert - The act of deploying infantry by helicopter to a tactical area.

inserted grouping (radar) - (NATO, CENTO) The inclusion of one area of homogeneous surface material in an area of different material.

inset - (NATO) In cartography, a separate map positioned within the neatline of a larger map. Three forms are recognized: a. an area geographically outside a sheet but included therein for convenience of publication, usually at the same scale; b. a portion of the map or chart at an enlarged scale; c. a smaller scale map or chart of surrounding areas, included for location purposes.

inshore patrol - (DOD, NATO, CENTO, IADB) A naval defense patrol operating generally within a defensive coastal area and comprising all elements of harbor defenses, the coastal lookout system, patrol craft, supporting bases, aircraft, and Coast Guard stations. (Note: IADB definition ends with the word "aircraft".)

inspection - (DOD, IADB) In arms control, physical process of determining compliance with arms control measures.

Inspector General - The audit function of the military.

installation - (DOD) A grouping of facilities, located in the same vicinity, which support particular functions. Installations may be elements of a base. See also base.

installation - (IADB) A military facility in a fixed or relatively fixed location, together with its buildings, building equipment, and subsidiary facilities such as piers, spurs, access roads, and beacons. See also base; base complex.

Instant LZ - Result of the explosion of the tree-clearing daisy cutter bomb.

instrument flight - (DOD, NATO, SEATO, CENTO, IADB) Flight in which the path and attitude of the aircraft are controlled solely by reference to instruments.

instrument landing system - (NATO, SEATO, CENTO, IADB) A system of radio navigation intended to assist aircraft in landing which provides lateral and vertical guidance, including indications of distance from the optimum point of landing.

instrument recording photography - (NATO, CENTO) Photography of the presentation of instrument data.

insurgency - (DOD, I, IADB) A condition resulting from a revolt or insurrection against a constituted government which falls short of civil war. In the current context, subversive insurgency is primarily communist inspired, supported, or exploited.

integrated fire control system - (DOD) A system which performs the functions of target acquisition, tracking, data computation, and engagement control, primarily using electronic means assisted by electromechanical devices.

integrated logistic support - (NATO, CENTO, IADB) The pooling of specified resources by nations for use by the same nations as decided by coordinating agency or authority to which the subscribing nations have agreed. See also logistic assistance; mutual aid; reallocation of resources.

integrated material management - (DOD) The exercise of total Department of Defense management responsibility for a Federal Supply Group/Class, commodity or item by a single agency. It normally includes computation of requirements, funding, budgeting, storing, issuing, cataloging, standardizing, and procuring functions.

integrated staff - (DOD, NATO, SEATO, CENTO, IADB) A staff in which one officer only is appointed to each post on the establishment of the headquarters, irrespective of nationality and Service. See also combined staff; joint staff; parallel staff; staff.

integration - (DOD) The process of forming an intelligence pattern through selection and combination of evaluated information.

integration - (NATO, CENTO) In photography, a process by which the average radar picture seen on several scans of the time base may be obtained on a print, or, the process by which several photographic images are combined into a single image.

intel - Intelligence.

intel-rep - Intelligence report.

intelligence - (DOD) The product resulting from the collection, evaluation, analysis, integration, and interpretation of all information concerning one or more aspects of foreign countries or areas, which is immediately or potentially significant to the development and execution of plans, policies, and operations.

intelligence - (NATO, SEATO, CENTO, IADB) The product resulting from the collection, evaluation, analysis, integration, and interpretation of all available information which concerns one or more aspects of foreign nations or of areas of operations and which is immediately or potentially significant to military planning and operations. See also basic intelligence; combat intelligence; counterintelligence; military intelligence; strategic intelligence; target intelligence; technical intelligence.

intelligence annex - (DOD) A supporting document of an operation plan or order which provides detailed information on the enemy situation, assignment of intelligence tasks, and intelligence administrative procedures.

intelligence collection plan - (DOD, NATO, SEATO, CENTO, IADB) A plan for gathering information from all available sources to meet an intelligence requirement. Specifically, a logical plan for transforming the essential elements of information into orders or requests to sources within a required time limit. See also intelligence cycle.

intelligence contingency funds - (DOD) Appropriated funds to be used for intelligence activities when the use of other funds is not applicable or would either jeopardize or impede the mission of the intelligence unit.

intelligence cycle - (DOD, NATO, IADB) The steps by which information is assembled, converted into intelligence, and made available to users. These steps are in four phases: a. direction - Determination of intelligence requirements, preparation of a collection plan, issuance of orders and requests to information collection agencies, and a continuous check on the productivity of collection agencies. b. collection - The exploitation of sources of information by collection agencies and the delivery of this information to the proper intelligence processing unit for use in the production of intelligence. c. processing - The step whereby information becomes intelligence through evaluation, analysis, integration, and interpretation. d. dissemination - The conveyance of intelligence in suitable form (oral, graphic, or written) to agencies needing it. See also intelligence collection plan.

intelligence data base - (DOD) The sum of holdings of intelligence data and finished intelligence products at a given organization.

intelligence data handling systems - (DOD) Information systems which process and manipulate raw information and intelligence data as required. They are characterized by the application of general purpose computers, peripheral equipment, and automated storage and retrieval equipment for documents and photographs. While automation is a distinguishing characteristic of intelligence data handling systems, individual system components may be either automated or manually operated.

intelligence estimate - (DOD, NESN, SEATO, CENTO, IADB) An appraisal of the elements of intelligence relating to a specific situation or condition with a view to determining the courses of action open to the enemy or potential enemy and the probable order of their adoption. See also estimate; estimate of the situation. (Note: IADB term is "intelligence estimate of the situation".)

intelligence journal - (DOD) A chronological log of intelligence activities covering a stated period, usually 24 hours. It is an index of reports and messages that have been received and transmitted and of important events that have occurred and actions taken. The journal is a permanent and official record.

intelligence process - (NESN, SEATO, CENTO) The steps by which information is collected, converted into intelligence, and disseminated.

intelligence report - (DOD) A specific report of information, usually on a single item, made at any level of command in tactical operations and disseminated as rapidly as possible in keeping with the timeliness of the information. Also called INTREP.

intelligence reporting - (DOD, NATO, CENTO, IADB) The preparation and conveyance of information by any means. More commonly, the term is restricted to reports as they are prepared by the collector and as they are transmitted by him to his headquarters and by this component of the intelligence structure to one or more intelligence-producing components. Thus, even in this limited sense, reporting embraces both collection and dissemination. The term is applied to normal and specialist intelligence reports. See also normal intelligence reports; specialist intelligence reports.

intelligence requirement - (DOD, NATO, CENTO, IADB) Any subject, general or specific, upon which there is a need for the collection of information, or the production of intelligence. See also essential elements of information.

intelligence subject code - (DOD) A system of subject and area references to index the information contained in intelligence reports as required by general intelligence document reference service.

intelligence summary - (DOD) A specific report providing a summary of items of intelligence information normally produced at battalion/squadron or higher level in tactical operations, usually at six-hour intervals. Also called INTSUM.

Intensive Care Unit - ICU.

intention - (DOD, IADB) An aim or design (as distinct from capability) to execute a specified course of action.

inter-chart relationship - See map index.

inter-service education - (DOD, IADB) Military education which is provided by one Service to members of another Service. See also military education; military training.

inter-service support - (DOD) Action by one military Service or element thereof, to provide logistic and/or administrative support to another military Service or element thereof. Such action can be recurring or non-recurring in character, on an installation, area, or worldwide basis. See also interdepartmental/agency support; international logistic support; support.

inter-service training - (DOD, IADB) Military training which is provided by one Service to members of another Service. See also military education; military training.

intercept point - (DOD) A computed point in space toward which an interceptor is vectored to complete an interception.

intercepting search - (DOD, NATO, SEATO, CENTO, IADB) A type of search designed to intercept an enemy whose previous position is known and the limits of whose subsequent course and speed can be assumed.

interceptor - (DOD, NATO, CENTO) A manned aircraft utilized for identification and/or engagement of airborne objects.

interceptor controller - (NATO, SEATO, CENTO, IADB) An officer who controls fighter aircraft allotted to him for interception purposes.

interceptor/fighter - See fighter interceptor.

interchangeability - (DOD, NATO, CENTO) A condition which exists when two or more items possess such functional and physical characteristics as to be equivalent in performance and durability, and are capable of being exchanged one for the other without alteration of the items themselves or of adjoining items, except for adjustment, and without selection for fit and performance. See also compatibility.

intercoastal traffic - (DOD) Sea traffic between Atlantic, Gulf, and Great Lakes continental United States ports and Pacific continental United States ports.

intercom - (DOD, NATO, SEATO, CENTO) A telephone apparatus by means of which personnel can talk to each other within an aircraft, tank, ship, or activity.

intercontinental ballistic missile - (DOD, IADB) A ballistic missile with a range capability from about 3,000 to 8,000 nautical miles.

interdepartmental intelligence - (DOD) Integrated departmental intelligence which is required by departments and agencies of the United States Government for the execution of their missions but which transcends the exclusive competence of a single department or agency to produce.

interdepartmental/agency support - (DOD) Provision of logistic and/or administrative support in services or materiel by one or more military Services to one or more departments or agencies of the United States Government (other than military) with or without reimbursement. See also international logistic support; inter-Service support; support.

interdict - (DOD, IADB) To prevent or hinder, by any means, enemy use of an area or route.

interdict - (NATO, SEATO, CENTO) To isolate, or seal off an area by any means; to deny the use of a route or approach.

interdiction fire - (DOD, NATO, SEATO, CENTO, IADB) Fire placed on an area or point to prevent the enemy from using the area or point. See also fire.

interface - (DOD) A boundary or point common to two or more similar or dissimilar command and control systems, subsystems, or other entities against which or at which necessary information flow takes place.

interim financing - (DOD, IADB) Advance payments, partial payments, loans, discounts, advances, and commitments in connection therewith; and guarantees of loans, discounts, advances, and commitments in connection therewith; and any other type of financing necessary for both performance and termination of contracts.

interim overhaul - (DOD, IADB) An availability for the accomplishment of necessary repairs and urgent alterations at a naval shipyard or other shore-based repair activity, normally scheduled halfway through the established regular overhaul cycle.

interior lines - Lines of communication in a specified zone, usually a closed or small area.

interlock switch - The aircraft panel safety switch preventing accidental missile firing.

interlocking fire - Mutual support in defensive weapon placement.

intermediate area illumination - (NATO, CENTO) Illumination in the area, extending in depth from the far boundary of the close-in about 2,000 meters) to the maximum effective range of the bulk of artillery weapons (about 10,000 meters).

intermediate contour line - (NATO) A contour line drawn between index contours. Depending on the contour interval there are three or four intermediate contours between the index contours. See also index contour line.

intermediate destination (merchant shipping) - (NATO, CENTO, IADB) The port/water terminal, or anchorage between the port/water terminal or anchorage of departure and the terminal destination of an independent or convoy to which routing instructions have been issued. In certain circumstances the intermediate destination may be synonymous with the immediate destinations. See also destinations.

intermediate maintenance (field) - (DOD, IADB) That maintenance which is the responsibility of and performed by designated maintenance activities for direct support of using organizations. Its phases normally consist of calibration, repair, or replacement of damaged or unserviceable parts, components, or assemblies; the emergency manufacture of nonavailable parts; and providing technical assistance to using organizations.

intermediate marker (land mine warfare) - (DOD, NATO, SEATO, CENTO, IADB) A marker, natural, artificial, or specially installed, which is used as a point of reference between the landmark and the minefield. See also marker (land mine warfare).

intermediate scale map - (IADB) A map, normally of a scale from 1:200,000 to 1:500,000, intended for planning strategic operations, including the movement, concentration, and supply of troops. See also map.

intermediate-range ballistic missile - (DOD, IADB) A ballistic missile with a range capability from about 1,500 to 3,000 nautical miles.

intermittent illumination - (DOD) A type of illuminating fire in which illuminating projectiles are fired at irregular intervals.

internal defense - (DOD, I, IADB) The full range of measures taken by a government and its allies to free and protect its society from subversion, lawlessness, and insurgency.

internal net - Company level radio network.

internal radiation - (DOD, NATO, CENTO, IADB) Nuclear radiation (alpha and beta particles and gamma radiation) resulting from radioactive substances in the body.

internal security - (DOD, I, IADB) The state of law and order prevailing within a nation.

international arms control organization - (DOD, I, IADB) An appropriately constituted organization established to supervise, and verify the implementation of arms control measures.

international call sign - (DOD, NATO, SEATO, CENTO, IADB) A call sign assigned in accordance with the provisions of the International Telecommunications Union to identify a radio station. The nationality of the radio station is identified by the first or the first two characters. (When used in visual signaling, international call signs are referred to as signal letters.) See also call sign.

international date line - (DOD, NATO) The line coinciding approximately with the antimeridian of Greenwich, modified to avoid certain habitable land. In crossing this line there is a date change of one day.

international logistic support - (DOD, IADB) The provision of military logistic support by one participating nation to one or more participating nations, either with or without reimbursement. See also interdepartmental agency support; inter-Service support; support.

international logistics - (DOD, IADB) The negotiating, planning, and implementation of supporting logistics arrangements between nations, their forces and agencies. It includes furnishing logistic support (major end items, materiel, and/or services) to, or receiving logistic support from, one or more friendly foreign governments, international organizations, or military forces, with or without reimbursement. (DOD) It also includes planning and actions related to the intermeshing of a significant element, activity, or component of the military logistics systems or procedures of the United States with those of one or more foreign governments, international organizations, or military forces on a temporary or permanent basis. It includes planning and actions related to the utilization of United States logistics, policies, systems, and/or procedures to meet requirements of one or more foreign governments, international organizations, or forces.

international map of the world - (NATO) A map series at 1:1,000,000 scale published by a number of countries to a common internationally agreed specification.

International Peace Force - (DOD) An appropriately constituted organization established for the purpose of preserving world peace.

interocular distance - (NATO, CENTO) The distance between the centers of rotation of the eyeballs of an individual or between the oculars of optical instruments.

interphone - See intercom.

interpretability - (DOD) Suitability of the imagery for interpretation with respect to answering questions of a given type of target in terms of quality and scale. The three levels of interpretability are: a. poor interpretability - Unsuitable for interpretation to adequately answer requirements on a given type of target. b. fair interpretability - Suitable for interpretation to answer requirements on a given type of target but with only average detail. c. good interpretability - Suitable for interpretation to answer requirements on a given type of target in considerable detail.

interpretation of information - (DOD) The act of determining the significance of information in relation to the current body of knowledge pertaining to the subject; it involves the application of critical judgments in the analysis and integration of information.

interrogation (intelligence) - (DOD) Systematic effort to procure information by direct questioning of a person under the control of the questioner.

interrogation by altitude - An illegal interrogation technique by which two prisoners were taken up in the open door of a helicopter and interrogated at about 2,000 feet. One being pushed out to his death induced disclosures by the remaining prisoner.

interrogation of prisoner of war - See IPW.

interrogation room - Also quiz room.

interrupted line - (NATO) A broken, dashed or pecked line usually used to indicate the indefinite alignment or area of a feature on the chart.

intertheater traffic - (DOD) Traffic between theaters exclusive of that between the continental United States and theaters.

interval - (DOD, NATO, SEATO, CENTO, IADB) 1. The space between adjacent groups of ships or boats measured in any direction between the corresponding ships or boats in each group. 2. The space between adjacent individuals, ground vehicles, or units in a formation that are placed side by side, measured abreast. (DOD, NATO, CENTO) 3. The space between adjacent aircraft measured from front to rear in units of time or distance. 4. The time lapse between photographic exposures.

intervalometer - The cockpit control for the rate of fire of ordinance.

interview (intelligence) - (DOD) To gather information from a person who is aware that he is giving information although he may be ignorant of the true connection and purposes of the interviewer. Generally overt unless the collector is other than he purports to be.

intracoastal sealift - (DOD) Shipping used primarily for the carriage of personnel and/or cargo along a coast or into river ports to support operations within a given area.

intransit aeromedical evacuation facility - (DOD, IADB) A medical facility, on or in the vicinity of an air base, that provides limited medical care for intransit patients awaiting air transportation. This type of medical facility is provided to obtain effective utilization of transport airlift within operating schedules. It includes "remain overnight" facilities, intransit facilities at aerial ports of embarkation and debarkation, and casualty staging facilities in an overseas combat area. See also aeromedical evaluation unit.

intransit inventory - (DOD, IADB) That materiel in the military distribution system which is in the process of movement from point of receipt from procurement and production (either contractor's plant or first destination, depending upon point of delivery) and between points of storage and distribution.

intransit stock - See intransit inventory.

intratheater traffic - (DOD) Traffic within a theater.

Intruder - (DOD, IADB) A twin-engine, turbo-jet, two place, long-range, all-weather, aircraft carrier based, low-altitude attack aircraft, possessing an integrated attack-navigation and central digital computer system to locate, track, and destroy small moving targets, and large fixed targets. The armament system consists of an assortment of nuclear and/or nonnuclear weapons, Sidewinder, Bullpup, napalm, and all standard Navy rockets. This aircraft can be air refueled. Designated as A-6A.

Intruder - Note: Made by Grumman Aircraft, able to carry up to thirty 500 lb. bombs making it second only to the B-52 in ordinance it can carry. It had a crew of two, the pilot and a B/N (bombardier/navigator). The on board, integrated attack navigation system could go from base to target and back without assistance. This is the DIANE (Digital Inertial Airborne Navigation System). Additionally, it was equipped with a central digital computer to destroy small moving or large fixed targets.

intruder operations - (DOD, NATO, SEATO, CENTO, IADB) Offensive operations by day or night over enemy territory with the primary object of destroying enemy aircraft in the vicinity of their bases.

Invader - The single-seat, twin-engine light bomber, built by Douglas Aircraft during World War II and used in Vietnam until the late 60s. It was renamed the B-26 during the war (not to be confused with Martin B-26 Marauder bomber that was not used in Vietnam.) Range 1400 miles. Speed 350 mph. Designated A-26.

invasion currency - See military currency.

inventory control - (DOD, NATO, CENTO, IADB) That phase of military logistics which includes managing, cataloging, requirements determination, procurement, distribution, overhaul, and disposal of materiel. Synonymous with materiel control, materiel management, inventory management, and supply management.

inventory control point - (DOD) An organizational unit or activity within a Department of Defense supply system which is assigned the primary responsibility for the materiel management of a group of items either for a particular Service or for the Defense Department as a whole. Materiel inventory management includes cataloging direction, requirements computation, procurement direction, distribution management, disposal direction, and generally, rebuild direction.

inventory management - See inventory control.

inventory managers - See inventory control point.

Invert - The Air Force computer identifying enemy air traffic.

iodine spiller - Slang for enlisted personnel in the Medical Corps.

ionization - (DOD, NATO, CENTO) The process of producing ions by the removal or addition of electrons to atoms or molecules.

ionosphere - (DOD, NATO, CENTO) The region of the atmosphere, extending from roughly 40 to 250 miles altitude, in which there is appreciable ionization. The presence of charged particles in this region profoundly affects the propagation of electromagnetic radiations of long wavelengths (radio and radar waves). See also atmosphere.

IP - 1. Initial point. The set point to start a bombing run. 2. Instructor Pilot.

IR - 1. Infrared. 2. Intelligence report.

Irish banjo - Entrenching tool.

Irish pennant - Marine slang for loose threads on a uniform.

iron bomb - Conventional bomb from WWII or Korea era, nonnuclear.

Iron Brigade - The Third Brigade, First Infantry.

iron idiot - Sight on front of a tank. See donkey sight.

Iron Triangle - The name of the Viet Cong guerrilla base area in a densely forested area about 20 miles northwest of Saigon.

ironing - To flatten a village by bombing and bulldozing.

Iroquois - See UH-1, a helicopter.

irregular forces - (DOD) Armed individuals or groups who are not members of the regular armed forces, police, or other internal security forces.

irregular forces - (IADB) Armed individuals or groups who are not members of regular armed forces.

irregular outer edge (land mine warfare) - (DOD, NATO, SEATO, CENTO, IADB) Short mine strips laid in an irregular manner in front of a minefield facing the enemy, to deceive the enemy as to the type or extent of the minefield. Generally, the irregular outer edge will only be used in minefields with buried mines.

ISA - Internal Security Affairs, a section of the Department of Defense.

island bases - (NATO, SEATO, CENTO, IADB) Those islands, or groups of islands, belonging to individual nations and serving mainly as naval and air bases for the naval and air combat forces in the ocean areas. See also base.

isobar - (NATO) A line along which the atmospheric pressure is, or is assumed to be, the same or constant.

isocentre - (NATO, CENTO) In photography, the intersection of the interior bisector of the tilt angle with the film plane.

isoclinal - (NATO) A line drawn on a map or chart joining points of equal magnetic dip.

isodose rate line - See dose rate contour line.

isogonal - (NATO, CENTO, IADB) A line drawn on a map or chart joining points of equal magnetic declination for a given time.

isogonic line - See isogonal.

isogriv - (NATO, CENTO, IADB) A line drawn on a map or chart joining points of equal grivation.

isotopes - (DOD) Forms of the same element having identical chemical properties but differing in their atomic masses, due to different numbers of neutrons in their respective nuclei, and in their nuclear properties.

item manager - (DOD) An individual within the organization of an inventory control point or other such organization assigned management responsibility for one or more specific items of material.

ITR - Infantry Training Unit.

IV Corps - The southern region of Vietnam around the Mekong Delta. See Corps.

IV-A - The Selective Service System draft classification for males eligible for the draft but who were exempted as veterans (who had completed their military obligation) or the sole surviving son in a family in which the father, son(s) or daughter(s) died while in the Armed Forces or later as a result of injury or illness that occurred while in the service. Pronounced Four-A.

IV-B - The Selective Service System draft classification for males eligible for the draft but deferred as officials or elected officials. Pronounced Four-B.

IV-C- The Selective Service System draft classification for males eligible for the draft but as aliens meeting set criteria are exempted from duty. Pronounced Four-C.

IV-D - The Selective Service System draft classification for males eligible for the draft but who were exempted as ministers or divinity students. Pronounced Four-D.

IV-F - The Selective Service System draft classification for males eligible for the draft but who were unfit for duty. Pronounced Four-F.

Ivory Tower - The Pentagon.

Ivy - Nickname for the Fourth Army Division from the Roman Numeral IV.

J – JULIET

J - 1. Designated in the military phonetic alphabet as "Juliet". 2. Marijuana.

Jack - A shark alert for men in the water. Also Smiling Jack.

Jack Benny - The number 39, from the comedian's joke that his age was 39, when he was clearly older. Used in radio code as a base number for setting a radio frequency to be used on a mission. Jack Benny (or Benny) plus twenty would be the coded announcement to use frequency 59.

jack off flare - Foot-long hand-held flare held against the thigh to launch.

Jack, Jack in the Black - Jack Daniels whiskey.

jacket - Folder of personnel materials.

jacking - Aviation slang for an evasive maneuver.

Jacob's ladder - The rope ladder from the ground to a helicopter.

JAG - Judge Advocate General. The legal office of the military.

jail chokers - Shoelaces.

jamming - See acoustic jamming;· barrage jamming; electronic countermeasures; electronic jamming; spot jamming.

janking - Aviation slang for an evasive maneuver.

Jarhead - Marine.

JATO - See jet assisted takeoff.

jaws tight - Pissed off, angry.

JCS - See Joint Chiefs of Staff.

JCS-coordinated exercise - (DOD) A minor exercise, the scheduling of which requires coordination by the Joint Chiefs of Staff because it involves the units or forces of more than one commander in chief or agency. See also exercise.

JCS-directed exercise - (DOD) A strategic mobility or major commander in chief directed exercise of considerable interest to the Joint Chiefs of Staff. See also exercise.

Jeep - The Ford M-151 personnel vehicle.

jelly donut - A Red Cross woman who was overweight.

Jerry can, jerrican - Military 5-gallon metal can.

Jesus nut - 1. Slang for the lock nut that attached the rotor blades to the body of the helicopter. 2. A person with an evangelical penchant.

jet advisory service - (DOD) The service provided certain civil aircraft while operating within radar and nonradar jet advisory areas. Within radar jet advisory areas, civil aircraft receiving this service are provided radar flight following, radar traffic information, and vectors around observed traffic. In nonradar jet advisory areas, civil aircraft receiving this service are afforded standard instrument flight rules separation from all other aircraft known to Air Traffic Control to be operating within these areas.

jet assisted takeoff - 1. The extra thrust added to a plane taking off in a short runway or to gain elevation to clear an obstacle. 2. Any assistance to getting going. 3. The bottles holding the fuel for the lift.

jet conventional low altitude bombing system - (DOB) A maneuver used by jet aircraft to loft conventional ordnance by means of low altitude bombing system.

jet fuel - The fuel came in several grades and designations. The most common were J-4 and J-5. The J-4 was lighter and had a lower flash point, so it was easier to restart the engine in the air if there were a flameout. The J-5, which was developed for carrier usage had a higher flashpoint, was less inclined to catch fire on board ship, and weighed more per gallon. The heavier fuels expanded the range of the aircraft as the engine thrust in the jets is gained from the weight rather than the volume of the fuel burned.

jet jock - Jet pilot with attitude.

jet propulsion - (DOD, IADB) Reaction propulsion in which the propulsion unit obtains oxygen from the air as distinguished from rocket propulsion in which the unit carries its own oxygen-producing material. In connection with aircraft propulsion, the term refers to a gasoline or other fuel turbine jet unit which discharges hot gas through a tail pipe and a nozzle, affording a thrust which propels the aircraft. See also rocket propulsion.

Jet Ranger - The OH-58 helicopter.

Jet Star - (DOD, IADB) A small, fast, support-type transport aircraft powered by four turbojet engines which are podded two on either side of the fuselage. Designated as C-140.

jet stream - (DOD, NATO, CENTO, IADB) A narrow band of high velocity wind in the upper troposphere or in the stratosphere.

jettison - (DOD) The selective release of stores from an aircraft other than normal attack.

JGS - See Joint General Staff (of RVNAF).

jibs - Marine slang for teeth, incisors.

Jimmy Olsen - A photographer of still or motion picture photography, from the comic book character in the Superman comics.

jing - Marine slang from the Japanese for change, small amount of money.

jinking - Aviation slang for a fast evasive maneuver.

jitterbug - The tactic of inserting a small troop into an area and extracting them if no enemy is contacted and reinserting until contact is made at which time added troops are inserted.

JM - Jump Master.

JO - Junior Officer.

Jody - The guy in the states who takes your girl while you are in Vietnam.

Jody calls - Marching cadence calls that feature rhymes about Jody.

Joe Shit - Marine slang for a sloppy Marine.

John - 1. Lieutenant, "first John" is a First Lieutenant. 2. Latrine (john).

John Wayne - 1. Heroic soldier. 2. A soldier who acts up and exaggerates for media attention. 3. The thumb size can opener, officially the P-38 can opener.

John Wayne biscuits - The hard biscuits or crackers that were used with cheese or peanut butter and jelly in C-rations.

John Wayne cookies - The chocolate coated cookies in C-rations.

John Wayne High School - Army Special Warfare School at Fort Bragg.

John Wayneing it - Acting macho, bragging.

joint amphibious task force - (NATO, CENTO) A temporary grouping of units of two or more Services under a single commander, organized for the purpose of engaging in an amphibious operation.

joint - (DOD, IADB) 1. Connotes activities, operations, organizations, etc., in which elements of more than one Service of the same nation participate. See also combined. (DOD) 2. When prefixed to any of the materiel terms applicable to joint usage, connotes that the definition of the designated term is enlarged to embrace the sum of the Army, Navy, Air Force, and Marine Corps quantities.

joint - (NATO, CENTO) Connotes activities, operations, etc., in which elements of more than one Service of the same nation participate. (When all Services are not involved the participating Services shall be identified, e.g., joint Army-Navy.) See also combined.

joint - (SEATO) Between two or more Services of the same nation. (When all Services are not involved the participating Services shall be identified, e.g., joint Army-Navy.)

joint - Slang for marijuana in rolled in paper as a cigarette.

joint airborne training - (DOD, IADB) Training operations or exercises involving airborne and appropriate troop carrier units. This training includes; a. air delivery of personnel and equipment; b. assault operations by airborne troops and/or air transportable units; c. loading exercises and local orientation flights of short duration; and d. maneuvers/exercises as agreed upon by the Services concerned and/or as authorized by the Joint Chiefs of Staff. Note: IADB definition does not use the words "and/or as authorized by the Joint Chiefs of Staff".

joint amphibious operation - (DOD, NATO, CENTO, IADB) amphibious operation conducted by significant elements of two or more Services.

joint amphibious task force - (DOD, IADB) A temporary grouping of units of two or more Services under a single commander, organized for the purpose of engaging in an amphibious landing for assault on hostile shores.

joint Army-Navy-Air Force publications - (DOD) A series of publications produced by supporting agencies of the Joint Chiefs of Staff and intended for distribution through the approved offices of distribution within the Army, Navy, and Air Force.

Joint Chiefs of Staff - The military body representing the four services acting as an advisory body to the Secretary of Defense.

joint common user items - (NATO, SEATO, CENTO, IADB) Items of an interchangeable nature which are in common use by two or more Services of a nation.

joint force - (DOD, IADB) A general term applied to a force which is composed of significant elements of the Army, the Navy or the Marine Corps, and the Air Force, or two or more of these Services, operating under a single commander authorized to exercise unified command or operational control over such joint forces.

joint grave - A grave containing more than one person. Usually when all are known but identification of individuals is not ascertainable (such as in a helicopter crash). See mass grave.

joint intelligence - (DOD) Intelligence produced by elements of more than one Service of the same nation.

joint intelligence estimate for planning - (DOD) A worldwide series of strategic estimates prepared annually by Defense Intelligence Agency for the Joint Chiefs of Staff to be used as a base for development of intelligence annexes for Joint Chiefs of Staff plans. Also called JIEP.

joint mobilization reserves - See joint, Part 2.

joint nuclear accident coordinating center - (DOD) A combined Defense Nuclear Agency and Atomic Energy Commission centralized agency for exchanging and maintaining information concerned with radiological assistance capabilities and coordinating assistance activities, when called upon, in connection with accidents involving radioactive materials.

joint operational intelligence agency - (DOD, IADB) An intelligence agency in which the efforts of two or more Services are integrated to furnish that operational intelligence essential to the commander of a joint force and to supplement that available to subordinate forces of his command. The agency may or may not be part of such joint force commander's staff.

joint operations center - (DOD) A jointly manned facility of a joint force commander's headquarters established for planning, monitoring, and guiding the execution of the commander's decisions.

joint purchase - (DOD, IADB) A method of purchase whereby purchases of a particular commodity for two or more departments are made by an activity established, staffed, and financed by them jointly for that purpose. See also purchase.

joint rescue coordination center - (DOD, IADB) An installation staffed by supervisory personnel from all participating Services, and possessing sufficient facilities to direct and coordinate all available search and rescue facilities within a specified area. See also search and rescue.

joint servicing - (DOD) That function performed by a jointly staffed and financed activity in support of two or more military Services. See also servicing.

joint staff - (DOD) 1. The staff of a commander of a unified or specified command, or of a joint task force, which includes members from the several Services comprising the force. These members should be assigned in such a manner as to insure that the commander understands the tactics, techniques, capabilities, needs, and limitations of the component parts of the force. Positions on the staff should be divided so that Service representation and influence generally reflect the Service composition of the force. 2. The staff of the Joint Chiefs of Staff as provided for under the National Security Act of 1947, as amended. See also staff.

joint staff - (NATO, SEATO, CENTO, IADB) A staff of two or more of the Services of the same country. See also combined staff; integrated staff; parallel staff.

joint strategic capabilities plan - (DOD) A short-range, current capabilities plan which translates United States national objectives and policies for the next fiscal year into terms of military objectives and strategic concepts and defines military tasks for cold, limited, and general war which are in consonance with actual United States military capabilities.

joint strategic objectives plan - (DOD) A mid-range objectives plan which translates United States national objectives and policies for the time frame 5 to 8 years in the future into terms of military objectives and strategic concepts and defines basic undertakings for cold, limited, and general war which may be accomplished with the objective force levels.

Joint Tactical Air Reconnaissance/Surveillance Mission Report - (DOD) A preliminary report of information from tactical reconnaissance aircrews rendered by designated debriefing personnel immediately after landing and dispatched prior to compilation of the Initial Photo Interpretation Report. It provides a summary of the route conditions, observations, and aircrew actions and identifies sensor products. If available, items of significant interest obtained from initial readout of the sensor record are also included. Also called MISREP.

joint task force - (DOD) A force composed of assigned or attached elements of the Army, the Navy or the Marine Corps, and the Air Force, or two or more of these Services, which is constituted and so designated by the Secretary of Defense or by the commander of a unified command, a specified command, or an existing joint task force.

joint task force - (IADB) A force composed of assigned or attached elements of the Army, the Navy or the Marine Corps, and the Air Force, or two or more of these Services.

joint zone (air, land, or sea) - (DOD, IADB) An area established for the purpose of permitting friendly surface, air, and subsurface forces to operate simultaneously.

joker - Fuel planning information.

Jolly Green Giant - The largest helicopters, HH-53, HH-3E, CH-55 CH-3.

Jolly Green SAR - 1. The search and rescue unit which rescued downed pilots. 2. A member of the search and rescue team, possibly from the advertising figure the Jolly Green Giant for Green Giant vegetables who would reach out of the sky and save the little village character in an ad of the time. (See SAR, Search and Rescue).

JP-4 - The designation for a common jet fuel, like kerosene (See jet fuel).

JP-5 - The designation for the jet fuel, heavier than kerosene (See jet fuel).

ju ju - 1. A black militant group that included some soldiers. See mau mau. 2. Voodoo word for luck or amulets worn to bring good luck. 3. An assessment of a situation as having good or bad ju ju.

judy - (DOD) In air intercept, a code meaning I have contact and am taking over the intercept.

juicer - 1. A person who drinks excessively. 2. Boozer.

Juliet - The military phonetic alphabet designation for the letter "J".

jump CP - A temporary command post.

jump pay - Added pay for troops qualified to parachute.

jump week - The last week in parachute school.

jumpmaster - (DOD, NATO, CENTO, IADB) The assigned airborne qualified individual who controls parachutists from the time they enter the aircraft until they exit. See also stick commander (air transport).

jungle boots - A canvas and leather combination footwear that allowed rapid drying in the humid climate where a solid leather boot would rot.

jungle busting - Clearing jungle growth using a tank to make a trail.

Jungle Jim - Aerial commando operations.

jungle juice - Slang for: 1. The GI bug repellent. 2. Booze, locally made or combined with fruit juices and fermented.

jungle ladder - A ladder from a helicopter to the jungle floor. See Jacob's ladder.

jungle rot - A fungal infection of the groin and inner thigh or extremities caused by moist/wet conditions and poor sanitation in the field.

jungle utilities - The lightweight tropical fatigue uniform.

Junk Force - The Vietnamese navy used for coastal patrol in junks under power or sail.

Junk Marines - U.S. Marines assigned to the Junk Force.

junk on the bunk - Inspection with all gear on the bed.

junks - The low draft, high sided Asian sailing craft, either motor or sail powered.

JUSPAO - Joint U.S. Public Affairs Office.

Just doin' my time. - Often heard phrase to negate bad stuff, like "Don't mean nothin'."

K – KILO

K - 1. Designated in the phonetic military alphabet as "Kilo". 2. Abbreviation for kilometer pronounced kay.

K-135 - A tanker aircraft used by the Air Force for mid-air refueling, made by Boeing, the craft looked a lot like the Boeing 707 airliner. See Stratotanker.

K-20 - See UH-2.

K-44 Rifle - A Mosin-Nagant rifle.

K-50 SMG - See Type 50 SMG.

K-9 - Dog.

K-bar - See KA BAR.

K-day - (DOD, NATO, SEATO, CENTO, IADB) The basic date for the introduction of a convoy system on any particular convoy lane. See also D-day; M-day.

KA BAR - The trademarked name of an American-made combat knife with a very sturdy 7 inch blade.

KA-3 - See B-66.

KA-6 - See A6A.

KA-60 - A gun camera that takes still photographs, activated by the trigger mechanism in an aircraft.

KA-71 - A gun camera that takes motion pictures, activated by the trigger mechanism in an aircraft.

KAK wheel - A numeric exchange calculator used by Radio Telephone Operators to encrypt map coordinates. Usually worn around the neck on a thong or string for fast access.

Kalashnikov - The Russian inventor of the AK-47 assault rifle used by the north Vietnamese.

Kampuchea - The name given to Cambodia by the Khmer Rouge Communist government in 1975. Now obsolete.

kanat - (NATO) An underground aqueduct with breather tubes which project upward through the surface of the earth.

katha - A leather pouch containing a protective talisman worn by Montagnard mountain tribesmen.

KATY - Kill Team from initials KT.

KB-50 - See Superfortress. KC-97-See Stratofreighter. KC-130-See Hercules. KC-135-See Stratotanker.

KBA - 1. Killed by air. 2. Killed by artillery. 3. Killed by action (when cause is unknown but combat related).

KBH - Killed by helicopter.

KC - See Khmer Rouge.

KC-130 - See Hercules.

KC-135 - See Stratotanker.

KC-97 - See Stratofighter.

KCS - See Kit Carson Scout.

KD - Known distance, on a rifle range.

keep book - Slang for something to be remembered, often written down in a book.

Keep on steppin'. - See Don't mean nothin'.

KEKN - The Korean Express Stevedoring Company, a contractor providing unloading services to U.S. transport vessels.

KEKN Crew - Personnel of KEKN.

Kentucky windage - Adjusting rifle aim by intuition and experience.

key - (NATO) In cartography, term sometimes loosely used as a synonym for "legend". See also blue key; drawing key; legend.

key area - (NATO, SEATO, CENTO, IADB) An area which is of paramount importance.

key facility list - (DOD) A list composed of selected critical industrial facilities, utilities, and Government-owned installations, located within the continental United States as designated by the Assistant Secretary of Defense (Installations and Logistics) and J-4, Joint Staff, Joint Chiefs of Staff.

key point - (DOD, NATO, SEATO, CENTO, IADB) A concentrated site or installation, the destruction or capture of which would seriously affect the war effort or the success of operations.

key terrain - (DOD, NATO, SEATO, CENTO, IADB) Any locality, or area, the seizure or retention of which affords a marked advantage to either combatant.

key(s) - Slang for kilogram(s) or kilo(s). Standard unit of measure for illegal drugs in commerce.

KHA - Killed in Hostile Action.

Kha tribes - A mountain tribe in Laos.

khaki tit - Military as provider, career soldier is said to suck the khaki tit.

khakis - The standard Army summer uniform.

Khe Sanh - The location of the 77 day siege involving 6,000 Marines and ASVN Rangers in in 1968. See Coney Island.

Khe Sanh quick step - Darting from one protected location to another while under fire.

Khmer Rouge - 1. The communist party in Cambodia. 2. French for red Cambodian.

KIA - 1. Killed in Action. 2. Radio code used for KIA included Kilo India Alpha. Kool Aid Cadillac, Kilos, Routines, Peanut, Ford, and Whiskey.

kick - Dishonorable discharge.

kick ass and take names - The imposition of discipline on an unruly group.

kick the tires and light the fires - An abbreviated pre-flight inspection, usually of a jet before combat.

kickers - Civilians making air drops of supplies where military was barred. From "kicking" cargo out of plane to parachute to the ground.

kicking pots - Assigned to kitchen patrol, KP.

kicks - Shoes.

kill - Slang for killing the enemy includes: waste, off, dust, zap, DX, grease, nail, and hose.

kill probability - (DOD, NATO, CENTO, IADB) A measure of the probability of destroying a target.

kill ratio - The ratio of enemy to US/ASVN dead.

kill team - A two-man reconnaissance team.

kill zone - 1. The deadliest area of an ambush. 2. Within artillery range.

killed - Slang for "to be killed" includes: deep sixed, bought it, bought lunch, bought the farm.

killed in action - (DOD, NATO, SEATO, CENTO, IADB) A battle casualty who is killed outright or who dies as a result of wounds or other injuries before reaching any medical treatment facility. See also died of wounds received in action.

killer dolphins - The dolphins trained by the U.S. Navy to guard ships from enemy frogmen.

killer junior - Artillery rounds designed to detonate above the ground as crawling soldiers could not avoid the beehive darts in it using the 105-mm and 155-mm guns.

Killer Kiwis - Soldiers from New Zealand.

Killer MOS - Any of the military assignments related to combat.

killer patrol - An ambush team of 4-6 soldiers.

killer senior - Artillery rounds designed to detonate above the ground as crawling soldiers could not avoid the beehive darts in it using the 8 inch Howitzer.

killer team - Marine term for killer patrol.

killer weed - Strong marijuana.

Kilo - 1. The military phonetic alphabet designation for the letter "K". 2. Slang for a kilo of drugs, 3. The measure of about 2.2 pounds, especially for the sale of marijuana.

Kilo India Alpha - See KIA.

kilometers - The unit of distance equal to 1,000 meters. 2. Slang klick (not click).

kilos - Radio code for Killed in Action.

kiloton weapon - (DOD, NATO, CENTO, IADB) A nuclear weapon, the yield of which is measured in terms of thousands of tons of trinitrotoluene explosive equivalents, producing yields from 1 to 999 kilotons. See also nominal weapon; subkiloton weapon.

kim chee - 1. Fermented spiced cabbage. 2. Something stinky or disgusting as in being in deep kim chee.

kin - Vietnamese for "confidential" as stamped on documents.

king of battle - The artillery, after the chess piece that is powerful but relatively stationary.

Kiowa - The OH-58 helicopter.

kiss ass - A subordinate trying to curry favor. A suck up.

kiss off - The termination of a flight pattern of aircraft either for landing or evasive action (from the visual of the flight leader blowing a kiss to other aircraft).

Kit Carson Scout - 1. A Vietnamese working with American troops, usually an infantry platoon, as a scout and interpreter. 2. A Viet Cong defector working as a scout for the south for pay.

kitchen police - Military assigned to kitchen duty. See KP.

kite tails - Staff of General Officers.

kiwi - 1. Troops from New Zealand. 2. Marine slang for a goof off.

klick - Slang for a kilometer. See click.

KM-60s - See Quad 60s. Machine guns.

knapsack - An pack added to the usual haversack for added storage.

knee cards - See kneeboard cards.

kneeboard - A small clipboard with a strap allowing it to be attached to the thigh of a pilot allowing immediate access to flight critical data.

kneeboard cards - A summary of classified information on a card in a kneeboard holder. Usually a card would include the fuel capacity, flight path, ordinance, radio frequencies, and other data needed for immediate access by a pilot.

knife fight - See knife fight in a phone booth.

knife fight in a phone booth - Aviation slang for a dogfight in which both airplanes are close and at slower speed which requires fast nibble maneuvering. Also knife fight.

Kool Aid Cadillac - Radio code for Killed in Action.

Kool-Aid - 1. The trademarked powdered drink mix. 2. Water purification tablets. 3. Radio code for reporting a killed in action.

KP - Kitchen police or kitchen patrol, performance of menial kitchen duties, often for punishment in non-combat zones.

KSCB - Khe Sanh Combat Base.

KT - Kill Team. See KATY.

KYPIYP - Keep Your Pecker in Your Pants. The anti-venereal disease slogan.

L – LIMA

L - Designated in the military phonetic alphabet, as "Lima", note pronounced as lee-ma, often spelled lema.

L and M - Slang for the South Vietnam from "legal and magnanimous".

L-14 RCL - Swedish made rifle.

L-19 - See O-1E, Birddog.

L-20 - See U-6.

L-28 - See U-10.

L-hour - The specific time of a planned helicopter(s) landing in an operation.

L.A. - 1. Slang for the west, as in going L.A. Not the direction from Vietnam but the west" of the USA. 2. Light Armored.

L1A1 - Army ambush rifle.

L9A1 - Browning 9-mm pistol.

La mal jeune - French for the "yellow illness", meaning the longing for the Orient/Asian, not the disease of Yellow Fever.

LAAM - The Hawk missile.

LAAW - Light assault weapon, this is a shoulder held rocket launcher.

lace in zippers - Zippered boots.

Lacrosse - (DOD, IADB) A mobile, accurate, surface-to-surface guided missile, with a nuclear and nonnuclear warhead capability, designed to engage hardened point targets or area targets up to a range of 30,000 meters. Designated as MGM-18.

ladder - Navy and Marine slang for stairs.

ladder formation - Aviation term for two or more planes following the lead plane at the same altitude directly behind the lead plane. Also called trail formation.

laden weight (transport vehicles) - (SEATO, IADB) The unladen weight of the vehicle plus the payload. See also net weight (transport vehicles); unladen weight (transport vehicles).

lagger - A defensive circle formed by placing motorized unit elements pointing out. From the Dutch, a Boer War term.

lagging - Goldbricking.

Lai day. - Vietnamese for "Come here.".

Lai mau. - Vietnamese for "Come quickly.".

Lam on - Please from the Vietnamese.

Lambretta - 1. The motor driven pedicab. 2. The Lambretta brand motor scooter.

lame duck ambush - The ambush technique using a soldier to appear wounded to draw enemy into open and then attack.

Lancer - A scout dog.

land control operations - (DOD) The employment of ground forces, supported by naval and air forces, as appropriate, to achieve military objectives in vital land areas. Such operations include destruction of opposing ground forces, securing key terrain, protection of vital land lines of communication, and establishment of local military superiority in areas of land operations.

land mine warfare - See mine warfare.

land of the 24-hour generator - Vietnam due to frequent power failures.

land reform - A major tactic of the communist party in South Vietnam where about three quarters of the population was in agriculture.

land tail - An aviation term for those in air-transport joining a unit from a base assignment.

land, sea, or aerospace projection operations - (DOD) The employment of land, sea, or air forces, or appropriate combinations thereof, to project United States military power into areas controlled or threatened by enemy forces. Operations may include penetration of such areas by amphibious, airborne, or land transported means, as well as air combat operations by land-based and/or carrier air.

landing aids - (DOD, NATO, SEATO, CENTO, IADB) Any illuminating light, radio beacon, radar device, communicating device, or any system of such devices, for aiding aircraft in an approach and landing.

landing area - (DOD, NATO, SEATO, CENTO, IADB) 1. That part of the objective area within which are conducted the landing operations of an amphibious force.

It includes the beach, the approaches to the beach, the transport areas, the fire support areas, the air occupied by close supporting aircraft, and the land included in the advance inland to the initial objective. 2. (airborne) - The general area used for landing troops and materiel either by airdrop or air landing. This area includes one or more drop zones or landing strips. 3. Any specially prepared or selected surface of land, water, or deck designated or used for take off and landing of aircraft. See also airfield. (Note: SEATO and IADB, Part 2 definition uses "air delivery" instead of "airdrop".)

landing attack - (DOD, IADB) An attack against enemy defenses by troops landed from ships, aircraft, boats, or amphibious vehicles. See also assault.

landing beach - (DOD, NATO, CENTO, IADB) That portion of a shoreline usually required for the landing of a battalion landing team. However, it may also be that portion of a shoreline constituting a tactical locality (such as the shore of a bay) over which a force larger or smaller than a battalion landing team may be landed.

landing craft - (DOD, NATO, SEATO, CENTO, IADB) A craft employed in amphibious operations, specifically designed for carrying troops and equipment, and for beaching, unloading, and retracting. (DOD, NATO, CENTO, IADB) Also used for logistic cargo resupply operations.

landing craft and amphibious vehicle assignment table - (DOD, IADB) A table showing the assignment of personnel and materiel to each landing craft and amphibious vehicle and the assignment of the landing craft and amphibious vehicles to waves for the ship-to-shore movement.

landing craft availability table - (DOD, IADB) A tabulation of the type and number of landing craft which will be available from each ship of the transport group. The table is the basis for the assignment of landing craft to the boat groups for the ship-to-shore movement.

landing diagram - (DOD, NATO, SEATO, CENTO, IADB) A graphic means of illustrating the plan for the ship-to-shore movement.

landing force - (DOD, NATO, CENTO, IADB) A task organization of troop units, aviation and ground, assigned to an amphibious assault. It is the highest troop echelon in the amphibious operation. See also amphibious force.

landing mat - (DOD, NATO, CENTO, IADB) A prefabricated, portable mat so designed that any number of planks (sections) may be rapidly fastened together to form surfacing for emergency runways, landing beaches, etc.

landing platform - Used by the infantry to get to the beach in an amphibious landing situation.

landing point - (DOD, NATO, CENTO, IADB) A point within a landing site where one helicopter can land. See also airfield.

landing schedule - (DOD, IADB) In an amphibious operation, a schedule which shows the beach, hour, and priorities of landing of assault units, and which coordinates the movements of landing craft from the transports to the beach in order to execute the scheme of maneuver ashore.

landing ship - (DOD, NATO, SEATO, CENTO, IADB) An assault ship which is designed for long sea voyages and for rapid unloading over and onto a beach.

landing ship dock - (DOD, NATO, CENTO, IADB) A ship designed to transport and launch loaded amphibious craft and/or amphibian vehicles with their crews and embarked personnel and/or equipment and to render limited docking and repair services to small ship and craft.

landing site - (DOD, NATO, CENTO, IADB) A site within a landing zone containing one or more landing points. See also airfield.

landing threshold - (DOD) The beginning of that portion of a runway usable for landing.

landing vehicle, tracked, engineer, model 1 - (DOD, IADB) A lightly armored amphibious vehicle designed for minefield and obstacle clearance in amphibious assaults and operations inland. Equipped with line charges for projection in advance of the vehicle and bull-dozer-type blade with scarifier teeth. Designated as LVTE-1.

landing vehicle, tracked, howitzer, model 6 - (DOD, IADB) A lightly armored, self-propelled, amphibious 105-mm howitzer. Designed to provide close fire support during a landing operation by initially delivering direct fire on the landing beaches, and after landing, providing field artillery fire in support of operations ashore. Designated as LVTH-6.

landing zone - (DOD, NATO, SEATO, CENTO, IADB) A specified zone within an objective area used for the landing of aircraft. See also airfield.

landing zone control - See pathfinder drop zone control.

landing zone control party - (DOD, NATO, CENTO, IADB) A group of personnel specially trained and equipped to establish and operate communication and signal devices from the ground for traffic control of aircraft/helicopters for a specific landing zone. See also pathfinder aircraft; pathfinders.

landline - A telephone system over wires, above or below ground.

landmark (land mine warfare) - (DOD, NATO, SEATO, CENTO, IADB) A feature, either natural or artificial, that can be accurately determined on the ground from a grid reference.

lane grader - Slang for an Army instructor.

lane marker (land mine warfare) - (DOD, NATO, SEATO, CENTO, IADB) Used to mark a minefield lane. Lane markers at the entrance to and exit from the lane will be referenced to a landmark or intermediate marker. See also marker (land mine warfare); minefield lane (land mine warfare).

lanyard puller - Artilleryman.

Lao Dong Party - The Communist Workers Party of North Vietnam (See VWP).

Lao grass - Marijuana.

Lao green - Marijuana.

Lao red - Marijuana.

LAPES - Low Altitude Parachute Extradition System. A supply delivery technique by which fixed wing transport flies low (under 10 feet), opens rear ramp, lets parachute attached to specialized cargo pallet open and drag pallet out. Allows for resupply to area unsuitable for normal landings.

large spread - (DOD) A report by an observer or a spotter to the ship to indicate that the distance between the bursts of a salvo is excessive.

large-lot storage - (DOD, IADB) A quantity of material which will require four or more pallet columns stored to maximum height. Usually accepted as stock stored in carload or greater quantities. See also storage.

large-scale map - (DOD, IADB) A map having a scale of 1:75,000 or larger. See also map.

laser - Slang for shooting off all your ammunition at once. A salvo.

laser guided bomb - A self-guiding bomb that used a laser point on the ground which has been projected from a leading aircraft as its target. See Smart bomb.

lashing - (DOD, NATO, CENTO) The fastening or securing of a load to its carrier to prevent shifting during transit.

late time - See span of detonation (atomic demolition munition employment).

lateral gain - (NATO, CENTO) The amount of new ground covered laterally by successive photographic runs over an area.

lateral route - (DOD, NATO, CENTO) A route generally parallel to the forward edge of the battle area which crosses or feeds into axial routes. See also route.

lateral spread - (DOD) A technique used to place the mean point of impact of two or more units 100 meters apart on a line perpendicular to the gun-target line.

lateral tell - See cross tell.

latitude band - (NATO) Any latitudinal strip, designated by accepted units of linear or angular measurement, which circumscribes the earth. Sometimes called latitudinal band.

latrine - Outdoor field toilet.

lattice - (NATO, CENTO, IADB) A network of intersecting positional lines printed on a map or chart from which a fix may be obtained.

LAU - A class of rocket launcher.

launch - (DOD, SEATO, IADB) The transition from static repose to dynamic flight of a missile.

launch pad - (DOD, NATO, SEATO, CENTO, IADB) A concrete or other hard surface area on which a missile launcher is positioned.

launch time - (DOD) A specified time for flight to be airborne, normally preplanned. See also airborne order.

launcher - (DOD, NATO, SEATO, CENTO, IADB) A structural device designed to support and hold a missile in position for firing.

launching site - (NATO, CENTO, IADB) Any site of installation with the capability of launching missiles from surface to air or surface to surface.

laundry bag - 1. A cloth drawstring bag for laundry. 2. Slang for barracks bag.

LAW - See Light Anti-tank Weapon.

lay - (DOD, IADB) 1. Direct or adjust the aim of a weapon. 2. Setting of a weapon for a given range, or for a given direction, or both. 3. To drop one or more aerial bombs or aerial mines onto the surface from an aircraft. 4. To spread a smoke screen on the ground from an aircraft. 5. To calculate or project a course. 6. To lay on: a. to execute a bomber strike; and b. to set up a mission.

lay chilly - To lie still, motionless.

lay dead - Goofing off.

laydown bombing - (DOD, NATO, CENTO) A very low level bombing technique wherein delay fuzes and/or devices are used to allow the attacker to escape the effects of his bomb.

layer depth - (DOD) The depth from the surface of the sea to the point above the first major negative thermocline at which sound velocity is maximum.

layer tint - See hypsometric tinting.

laying-up position (fast coastal forces) - (NATO, CENTO, IADB) Any suitable position where light naval units during daylight hours can berth, camouflage, and replenish in preparation for coming operations.

lazy - (DOD) In air intercept, a rode meaning equipment indicated at standby.

lazy dog - 1. An Air Force rocket. 2. Nickname for a bomb that explodes just above ground with darts in it.

LB - 1. Light bomber. 2. Landing Barge.

LBE - Load Bearing Equipment. Suspender straps and a belt to help carry gear in the field.

LBFM - Derogatory term for the enemy. Little Brown Fucking Machine.

LC - Landing craft.

LC-1 combat outfit - A lightweight load carrying system of a belt, pack frame, suspenders to which a pack, canteen and other essentials were attached.

LC-PL - Landing craft, personnel, large.

LC-VP - Landing craft, vehicle, personnel.

LCA - Landing craft, armored.

LCB - See smart bomb.

LCDR - Lieutenant Commander (Navy and Coast Guard).

LCM-6 - Landing craft.

LCM-8 - Landing craft, medium. Also Mike Boat.

LCpl - Lance Corporal (Marine Corps).

LCU - Landing craft utility.

lead - 1. Aircraft in lead position of a formation. 2. Pilot in lead ship. 3. Shooting in front of the target to anticipate its future position in relation to the time it will take for your bullet to get there. All pronounced leed.

lead aircraft - (DOD) 1. The airborne aircraft designated to exercise command of other aircraft within the flight. 2. An aircraft in the van of two or more aircraft.

lead aircraft - (NATO, SEA TO, CENTO, IADB) 1. An airborne aircraft designated to provide certain command and air control functions. 2. An aircraft in the van of two or more aircraft.

lead angle - The angle between the current position of a moving target and its anticipated position to allow an aiming adjustment.

Lead Sled - See F-100, a fighter aircraft. Pronounced Led Sled.

lead trail formation - Aviation term for two planes with the second plane following the lead plane at the same altitude directly behind the lead plane. See ladder formation and trail formation for multiple planes.

leaflet drop - Spending money like there is no tomorrow usually on women. Derived from the practice of dropping information leaflets to villagers by helicopter.

leaning rest - The up position in a push up. Often used to hold a soldier in place while lecturing about some misdeed.

leapfrog - (DOD, NATO, CENTO, IADB) Form of movement in which like supporting elements are moved successively through or by one another along the axis of movement of supported forces.

Leatherneck - U.S. Marine, from leather collars of 19th century uniform intended to deflect sword attack.

leave - 1. Time off duty. 2. Authorized absence of more than 24 hours. Note: Leave of 30 days per year was granted after 12 months of military service. Distinguished from liberty.

leeches - Blood sucking slug like animals living in water.

left (or right) - (DOD, NATO, SEATO, CENTO, IADB) 1. A term used to establish the relative position of a body of troops. The person using the terms "left" or "right" is assumed to be facing in the direction of the enemy regardless of whether the troops are advancing toward or withdrawing from the enemy. 2. A directional deviation used by an observer or a spotter in adjusting ground or naval gunfire. (DOD, NATO, CENTO) 3. Fire correction used by an observer to indicate that a lateral shift perpendicular to the spotting line is desired. (Note: NATO and CENTO Part 2 definition does not use the words "or a spotter".)

left (right) bank - (DOD, IADB) That bank of a stream or river on the left (right) of the observer when he is facing in the direction of flow, or downstream.

left foot - right foot - Slang for getting marching orders, a new assignment, or a transfer.

Legal and Magnanimous - Slang for South Vietnam. See L and M.

legborne - Infantry soldier.

legend - (NATO, CENTO) An explanation of symbols used on a map, chart, sketch, etc., commonly printed in tabular form at the side of the map, etc.

lego - A soldier who is not airborne, a legborne soldier.

legs - Infantry.

lema - The pronunciation of Lima, the designation in the phonetic military alphabet for the letter "L", not like the bean. Often misspelled as leema.

lens coating - (NATO, CENTO) A thin transparent coating applied to a surface of a lens element.

lens distortion - (NATO, CENTO) Image displacement caused by lens irregularities and aberrations.

lensatic - A type of compass with a lid that has a slit with a wire in it and a lens, The lens and sighting slit fold up to open the compass. It was used to find your location on a map by taking an azimuth reading of a distant objects by looking through the lens, lining up the object with a wire in the cover and taking a reading off the compass face. By doing this to two distant objects, you could locate your position on a map. The other use was to keep a consistent direction of travel in rough terrain or night travel.

Leroy - 1. A white GI's nickname for black GI. 2. A guy with a lot of field experience.

Let's do it. - General go ahead order in the field.

Let's get it done. - General go ahead order in the field.

lethal envelope - Aviation term for the space in which a specific weapon is accurate.

lethal radius - The area in which half of known enemy is dead.

levee - (NATO) A natural or manmade embankment bordering a river.

level - (DOD) In air intercept, a word meaning contact designated is at your "angels".

level of effort-oriented items - (DOD) Items for which requirements computations are based on such factors as equipment and personnel density and time and rate of use. See also combination mission/level of effort-oriented items; mission-oriented items.

level of supply - (DOD, NATO, SEATO, CENTO, IADB) The quantity of supplies or materials authorized or directed to be held in anticipation of future demands. See also operating level of supply; order and shipping time; procurement lead time; requisitioning objective; safety level of supply; stockage objective; strategic reserve.

levies - Personnel on a levy list.

levy list - A roster of personnel in a mass troop call-up.

LGB - Laser Guided Bomb. 1. Smart bomb. 2. A bomb that followed a laser light aimed at the target for guidance.

LGH - Large green helicopter.

LGM-30 - See Minuteman.

LI - Light Infantry.

liaison - (DOD, NATO, CENTO) That contact or intercommunication maintained between elements of military forces to insure mutual understanding and unity of purpose and action.

liaison - (SEATO, IADB) That contact or intercommunication maintained between parts of the armed forces to insure mutual understanding and unity of purpose and action. It is often aided by exchange of personnel in order to facilitate an exchange of information.

liberated territory - (DOD, NATO, SEATO, CENTO, IADB) Any area, domestic, neutral, or friendly, which, having been occupied by an enemy, is retaken by friendly forces.

liberation radio - Slang for the radio station of the Viet Cong.

liberty - An authorized absence of less than 24 hours.

liberty call - Navy and Marine slang for authorized leave from duty and permission to leave the base.

lick - Slang for something going wrong.

lid - 1. Hat. 2. A measure of marijuana either one ounce or enough to fill a sandwich baggie.

lifeguard submarine - (DOD, NATO, SEATO, CENTO, IADB) A submarine employed for rescue in an area which cannot be adequately covered by air or surface rescue facilities because of enemy opposition, distance from friendly bases, or other reasons. It is stationed near the objective and sometimes along the route to be flown by the strike aircraft.

lifeline - The safety strap holding a door gunner in a helicopter.

lifer - Derogatory term for the career military personnel.

lifer's dream - A SKS rifle captured and brought stateside as a trophy.

lift - 1. One helicopter trip with cargo from a loading area to a landing zone. 2. A flight of several helicopters.

liftbird - Any fixed wing aircraft or helicopter transporting troops.

Liftmaster - Military version of the DC-6 passenger airliner.

liftoff - (DOD, NATO, SEA TO, CENTO, IADB) The initial motion of a space vehicle or missile as it rises from the launcher.

Light Anti-tank Weapon - The M-72 handheld, 66-mm rocket housed in a one-shot tube. See HEAT.

light artillery - See howitzer, 105-mm (light artillery).

light at the end of the tunnel - Optimistic statement of impending victory, not always correct, often sarcastic.

light cruiser - (DOD, IADB) A warship with 6" naval guns as main battery. It is designed to operate with strike, antisubmarine, or amphibious forces against air and surface threats. Full load displacement is approximately 18,000 tons. Designated as CL. See also guided missile light cruiser.

light damage - See nuclear damage (land warfare).

light fire team - Helicopters with rockets, machine guns and a 40-mm cannon, usually a UH-1 or Cobra.

light green - Marine slang for a Caucasian.

light infantry - Infantry with light weight gear and weapons.

light line - (DOD, NATO, SEATO, CENTO, IADB) A designated line forward of which vehicles are required to use black-out lights at night.

Light Machine Gun - The Soviet made machine gun called the RPD, like the American M-60, with a bi-pod stand and a belt fed ammo supply. The Soviet machine gun had ammunition that was interchangeable between the RPD, AK-47 and SKS carbine.

light off - To fire artillery, light, or turn on.

lighter - A small boat used to transfer cargo between a ship and shore.

lightning - Artillery.

lightning bug - A helicopter with searchlights.

lights - Infantrymen without full gear.

lights out - Aviation slang for turning radar off.

Lightship - C123 aircraft when equipped with belly lights to illuminate a battlefield. lightweight disposable tube.

Lima - The military phonetic alphabet designation for the letter "L". Pronounced Leema.

Lima Charlie - Radio slang indicating that the transmission is both Loud and Clear.

Lima Charlie Hotel Mike? - Radio slang indicating that the transmission is both Loud and Clear and asking How Me? By asking how me, the radio operator is requesting a radio status report from the other radio operator.

Lima Lima - Abbreviation for land line, letters "LL".

Lima Lima line - A wire telephone line.

Lima site - Code for clandestine landing strips in Laos.

Lima Zed - See landing zone.

limit of fire - (DOD, IADB) 1. The boundary marking off the area on which gunfire can be delivered. 2. Safe angular limits for firing at aerial targets.

limited (conventional) warfare - War that is non-nuclear.

limited denied war - (DOD) Not to be used. No substitute recommended.

limited production type item - (DOD) An item under development, commercially available or available from other Government agencies for which an urgent operational requirement exists and for which no other existing item is substitutable; which appears to fulfill an approved materiel requirement or other Military Department approved requirements, and to be promising enough operationally to warrant initiating procurement and/or production for service issue prior to completion of development and/or test or adoption as a standard item.

limited standard item - (DOD) An item of supply determined by standardization action as authorized for procurement only to support in-Service military materiel requirements.

limited war - (DOD, IADB) Armed conflict short of general war, exclusive of incidents, involving the overt engagement of the military forces of two or more nations.

Lindane powder - A potent insecticide.

line - (DOD) A spotting, or an observation, used by a spotter or an observer to indicate that a burst (s) occurred on the spotting line.

line - Slang for duty with an infantry unit in the field, as in on the line.

line abreast formation - Aviation term for an aerial formation of planes flying at the same altitude side by side, usually in elements of two planes.

line haul - A truck convoy.

line number - On arrival, every soldier was entered into a roster, all names occupied one numbered line. If wounded or killed, that line number, not the soldier's name, was used on the radio and on the identification tag (as well as his name).

line of arrival - 1. The grid line on a map indicating the end point or destination of a mission. 2. See line of impact.

line of departure - (DOD, NATO, SEATO, CENTO, IADB) 1. A line designated to coordinate the departure of attack or scouting elements; a jump-off line. 2. A suitably marked offshore coordinating line to assist assault craft to land on designated beaches at scheduled times.

line of departure - Slang for point of no return.

line of impact - (NATO, SEATO, CENTO, IADB) A line tangent to the trajectory at the point of impact or burst.

line of position - (DOD) In air intercept, a reference line which originates at a target and extends outward at a predetermined angle.

line-route map - (DOD, IADB) A map or overlay for signal communication operations that shows the actual routes and types of construction of wire circuits in the field. It also gives the locations of switchboards and telegraph stations. See also map.

linear building frontage - (NATO, CENTO) In air photographic interpretation, the side elevation of structures of homogeneous area.

linear scale - See scale; graphic scale.

liner - (DOD) In air intercept, a code meaning fly at speed giving maximum cruising range.

lines - Navy and Marine term for ropes.

lines of communication - (DOD, IADB) All the routes, land, water, and air, which connect an operating military force with a base of operations and along which supplies and military forces move. (Note: IADB term is: lines of communication (logistics).)

lines of communication (logistics) - (NATO, SEATO, CENTO) All the routes, land, water, and air, which connect an operating military force with one or more bases of operations, and along which supplies and reinforcements move.

link (communications) - (NATO, SEATO, CENTO, IADB) A general term used to indicate the existence of communications facilities between two points.

link encryption - (DOD, IADB) The application of on-line crypto-operation to a link of a communications system so that all information passing over the link is encrypted in its entirety.

link-lift vehicle - (DOD) The conveyance, together with its operating personnel, used to satisfy a movement requirement between nodes.

link-route segments - (DOD) Route segments that connect nodes wherein link-lift vehicles perform the movement function.

links - The metal connectors of an ammunition belt.

liquid cork - Anti-diarrhea medicine.

liquid propellant - (DOD, NATO, SEATO, CENTO, IADB) Any liquid combustible fed to the combustion chamber of a rocket engine.

Liser bag - A large canvas water bag used when water trailers or tanks are not practical to provide sanitary water. Usual size was 36 gallons and was suspended from a wood tripod. Named for Dr. Lyster, of the U.S. Army Medical Corps whose introduction in 1917 of a rubber lined canvas bag with tight cover and water purification using chlorine became essential equipment for providing safe drinking water to troops. Also spelled Lyster bag.

list of targets - (DOD) A tabulation of confirmed or suspect targets maintained by any echelon for informational and fire support planning purposes. See also target list.

listen up - An order to pay attention.

listening post - A forward position composed of two or three men in a forward observer role at night, well ahead of combat troops in unprotected area to detect enemy movement and signal the troops.

listening watch - (DOD, IADB) A continuous receiver watch established for the reception of traffic addressed to, or of interest to, the unit maintaining the watch, with complete log optional.

lit - The targeting of an area by laser from a lead aircraft allowing smart bombs to follow the lit point.

lit-up - Fired upon.

litter - (DOD, NATO, SEATO, CENTO, IADB) A basket or frame utilized for the transport of injured persons.

Litter Bug - Code for a psychological warfare mission that dropped leaflets in North Vietnam using a Remotely Piloted Vehicle.

litter patient - (DOD, NATO, SEATO, CENTO, IADB) A patient requiring litter accommodations while in transit.

Little Brother - Slang for the O-2 with side guns.

Little Bulldog - The M41 tank.

little people - Derogatory term for the enemy.

little R - R&R. See big R.

live and let live - Slang for the "accommodations" between North and South Vietnamese troops to avoid conflict.

LLLTV - Limited Low Light Television used for night monitoring.

LMG - See Light Machine Gun.

LN - Liaison.

LOACH - See LOCH.

load (air) - See payload (Part 1); also airlift; airlift capability; airlift requirement; combat load (air force); load manifest (air); maximum load; type load; planned load (aircraft).

load bearing equipment - The pack, suspenders and belt on which gear was loaded on an infantryman. See LBE.

load manifest (air) (DOD, NATO, SEATO, CENTO, IADB) A document specifying in detail the payload expressed in terms of passengers and/or freight carried in one aircraft for a specific destination. See also load (air).

load spreader - (DOD, NATO, CENTO, IADB) Material used to distribute the weight of a load over a given floor area to avoid exceeding designed stress.

loading - (DOD, NATO, CENTO, IADB) The process of putting troops, equipment, and supplies into ships, aircraft, trains, road transport, or other means of conveyance. See also administrative loading; block stowage loading; cargo; combat loading; commercial loading; commodity loading; convoy loading; cross-loading (personnel); endurance loading; horizontal loading; preload loading; selective loading; unit loading; vertical loading.

loading chart (aircraft) - (DOD, IADB) Any one of a series of charts carried in an aircraft which shows the proper location for loads to be transported and which pertains to check lists, balance records, and clearances for weight and balance.

loading plan - (DOD, NATO, CENTO) All of the individually prepared documents which, taken together, present in detail all instructions for the arrangement of personnel, and the loading of equipment for one or more units or other special grouping of personnel or materiel moving by highway, water, rail, or air transportation. See also load manifest (air); ocean manifest; stowage diagram.

loading point - (DOD, NATO, CENTO, IADB) A point where one aircraft can be loaded.

loading site - (DOD, NATO, CENTO, IADB) An area containing a number of loading points.

loading/unloading - Aviation term for the increase or decrease in the angle of attack and the G force related to each maneuver in combat.

LOC - Abbreviation of line of communication.

local procurement - (DOD) The process of obtaining personnel, services, supplies, and equipment from local or indigenous sources.

local purchase - (DOD) The function of acquiring a decentralized item of supply from sources outside the Department of Defense.

local purchase - (IADB) The function of acquiring a decentralized item of supply from sources outside the military establishment.

local war - (DOD) Not to be used. See limited war.

localizer - (NATO, SEATO, CENTO, IADB) A directional radio beacon which provides to an aircraft an indication of its lateral position relative to a specific runway. See also beacon; instrument landing system.

locap - (DOD) Low combat air patrol.

location diagram - See map or chart index.

LOCH - See OH-6, an aircraft. Pronounced loach.

lock and load - 1. Readying a weapon for use as weapons were carried without a round in the chamber in base to avoid accidental shooting. 2. A general "get yourself ready" call.

lock on - (DOD, NATO, CENTO, IADB) Signifies that a tracking or target seeking system is continuously and automatically tracking a target in one or more coordinates (e.g., range, bearing, elevation).

locked - Slang for locked on in aviation or artillery. See padlocked.

Loco Coco - Slang for Loud and Clear verifying radio communication status.

LOCSTAT - Requesting location statement on the radio. Where are you?

lodgement area - See airhead; beachhead.

loft bombing - (DOD, IADB) A method of bombing in which the delivery plane approaches the target at a very low altitude, makes a definite pull-up at a given point, releases bomb at predetermined point during the pull-up and tosses the bomb onto the target. See also over-the-shoulder bombing; toss bombing.

log run - A logistical resupply mission or flight.

logair - (DOD) Long term contract airlift service within continental United States for the movement of cargo in support of the logistics systems of the military Services (primarily the Army and Air Force) and Department of Defense agencies. See also quicktrans.

logbird - Logistical supply or resupply helicopter.

logging - A flight with supplies.

logistic assessment - (DOD, NATO, CENTO) An evaluation of: a. The logistic support required to support particular military operations in a theater of operations, country or area. b. The actual and/or potential logistics support available for the conduct of military operations either within the theater, country or area, or located elsewhere.

logistic assistance - (NATO, CENTO, IADB) A generic term used to denote types of assistance between and within military commands both in peace and war. See also integrated logistic support; mutual aid; reallocation of resources.

logistic estimate of the situation - (DOD, IADB) An appraisal resulting from an orderly examination of the logistic factors influencing contemplated courses of action to provide conclusions concerning the degree and manner of that influence. See also estimate of the situation.

logistic implications test - (DOD) An analysis of the major logistic aspects of a joint strategic war plan and the consideration of the logistic implications resultant therefrom as they may limit the acceptability of the plan. The logistic analysis and consideration are conducted concurrently with the development of the strategic plan. The objective is to establish whether the logistic requirements generated by the plan are in balance with availabilities, and to set forth those logistic implications which should be weighed by the Joint Chiefs of Staff in their consideration of the plan. See also feasibility test.

logistic routes - See lines of communication (logistics).

logistic support (medical) - (DOD, NATO, SEATO, CENTO, IADB) Medical care, treatment, hospitalization, evacuation, furnishing of medical services, supplies, materiel, and adjuncts thereto.

logistics - (DOD, NATO, SEATO, CENTO, IADB) The science of planning and carrying out the movement and maintenance of forces. In its most comprehensive sense, those aspects of military operations which deal with: a. design and development, acquisition, storage, movement, distribution, maintenance, evacuation, and disposition of materiel; b. movement, evacuation, and hospitalization of personnel; c. acquisition or construction, maintenance, operation, and disposition of facilities; and d. acquisition or furnishing of services.

logistics over the shore operations - (DOD, IADB) The loading and unloading of ships without the benefit of fixed port facilities, in friendly or nondefended territory, and, in time of war, during phases of theater development in which there is no opposition by the enemy.

LOH - Light Observation Helicopter.

Lomotil - Trademarked antidiarrheal medication.

long - Overshooting a target. See short.

long green line - Slang for infantry troops in a line in the field.

long haul - Long distance military truck convoy.

Long John - The 175-mm gun.

Long Range Reconnaissance Patrols - Because jungle warfare does not have a fixed classical front, a tactic developed to use patrols to: a. gather intelligence on enemy location, status and movement, b. direct air strikes, and c. evaluate the effectiveness of bombing.

longtime - Slang for having a hooker all night.

Looking for golf balls. - The humorous reply of American females in Vietnam to why they were in the brush in remote areas where few bathrooms existed.

loop - Aviation maneuver in which a plane climbs up and then completes a full circle vertically.

loose deuce - A deuce is a two-plane formation. It is "loose" when expanded to a four-plane formation offering mutual support.

loran - (DOD, NATO, CENTO, IADB) A long range radio navigation position fixing system using the time difference of reception of pulse type transmissions from two or more fixed stations. (This term is derived from the words "long-range electronic navigation".)

lost - (DOD) A spotting, or an observation, used by a spotter or an observer to indicate that rounds fired by a gun or mortar were not observed.

lost the bubble - Aviation slang for someone who got confused, lost, forgot what was happening, from the bubble in the level indicator in the cockpit used for orientation.

lot - (DOD, IADB) Specifically, a quantity of material all of which was manufactured under identical conditions, and assigned an identifying lot number.

lottery number - The assigned draft number based on a combination of birth date and another number. The higher the number the later reporting for service was.

loud and clear - A report on how a radio signal was received. Signal strength (Loud) and clarity (Clear) were rated on a 1-5 scale with 5 being the best, so Loud and Clear was Five by Five, degraded status required numeric clarification, so a reduced volume but clear signal was a three by five, etc.

loud handle - Aviation term for the handle on the ejection seat, which, when pulled, fired an explosive charge under the seat, shooting the pilot and seat into the air.

Louie - 1. Slang for lieutenant 2. Spit green phlegm, also lugie.

low - (DOD) A height between five hundred and two thousand feet.

low airburst - (DOD) The fallout safe height of burst for a nuclear weapon which maximizes damage to or casualties on surface targets. See also types of burst.

low altitude bombing - (DOD, IADB) Horizontal bombing with the height of release between 900 and 8,000 feet.

low angle - (DOD) An order or request to obtain low-angle fire.

low angle fire - (DOD) Gunfire delivered at angles of elevation below the elevation that corresponds to the maximum range of the gun and ammunition concerned.

low angle loft bombing - (DOD, NATO, CENTO, IADB) Type of loft bombing of free fall bombs wherein weapon release occurs at an angle less than 35 degrees above the horizontal. See also loft bombing.

low oblique - See oblique air photograph.

low pass - Aviation term for a carrier landing that was missed as the plane was too high to catch the arresting gear and wheels failed to hit the flight deck. It is a kind term for a major error.

low velocity drop - (DOD, NATO, CENTO) A drop procedure in which the drop velocity does not exceed 30 feet per second.

low velocity drop - (SEATO, IADB) The delivery of personnel, supplies, or equipment from aircraft in flight, utilizing sufficient parachute retardation to prevent injury or damage upon ground impact. See also air-drop; air movement; free drop; high velocity drop.

Low Yo-Yo - Aviation maneuver in which the plane dives to accelerate while turning, either to defend against an attacker or find a better position for attack. See High yo-yo. See also Yo-Yo for history.

lower than whale shit - 1. Despicable actions. 2. One who is despicable, 3. Lowest in rank.

LP - 1. Listening post. 2. Landing platform used in amphibious landings.

LPD - See amphibious transport dock.

LPH - 1. Assault Hospital Ship. 2. Amphibious assault ship.

LRP - See long range patrol, the later name of the LRRP.

LRRP - See long range reconnaissance patrol. Pronounced lurp.

LRRP Rations - Very light weight rations, often freeze dried foods.

LSA - Lubricant, small arms. Gun oil.

LSD - Lysergic acid diethylamide, the psychedelic drug.

LSO - Landing Signal Officer. The specially trained Naval Aviator on the deck of a carrier that provides visual landing instruction to a pilot to expedite the safe recovery of naval aircraft. See Paddles.

LST - A ship used for landing troops.

LT - Lieutenant (Navy, Coast Guard).

Lt Col - Lieutenant Colonel (Air Force).

Lt Gen - Major General (Air Force).

Lt. - Abbreviation for the rank of Lieutenant.

LTC - Lieutenant Colonel (Army).

LtCdr - Lieutenant Commander. See LCDR.

LtCol - Lieutenant Colonel (Marine Corps)

LTG - Lieutenant General (Army).

LtGen - Major General (Marine Corps).

LTJG - Lieutenant Junior Grade (Navy and Coast Guard).

Ltr - Letter.

Lucifer match - A wooden stick match that self-ignites on any friction. Not a safety match which required use of a special striking surface. Used to trigger booby traps.

Lufberry Circle - Aviation defensive maneuver involving multiple planes flying in a horizontal circular so at any time, ordinance is pointed out to provide mutual defense. An ineffective offensive maneuver of just chasing the plane in front of you in a circle that worked in WWI for underpowered aircraft. Also spelled Luffberry Circle.

lugie - Green phlegm.

Lunch - Code for a bombing area in Cambodia. See Menu.

Lurp - Special food ration for long range patrol members.

Lurps - Members of a long range reconnaissance patrol.

LVTE-1 - See landing vehicle, tracked, engineer, model 1.

LVTH-6 - See landing vehicle, tracked, howitzer, model 6.

Lyster bag - See Lister bag.

LZ - Landing zone, the area into which helicopters land to deliver or retrieve troops, often this is in a rural area that has been cleared by bombing or is a natural opening in the jungle area.

LZ prep - Aviation term for the clearing of a future landing zone by airstrikes.

M – MIKE

M - 1. Designated in the phonetic military alphabet as "Mike". 2. Abbreviation for Mach. 3. Abbreviation for model. 4. Abbreviation for mechanized.

M and M's, M&M's - 1. The trademarked hard-shell button-shaped chocolate candy. 2. The candy in the C-ration pack. See SP Pack

M Force - Mobile Strike Force.

M-1 Helmet - The GI helmet.

M-1 Mortar - The 81-mm mortar.

M-1 pencil - Cheating (from the puncture of paper targets by a pencil to simulate a round passing through the target to increase range score).

M-1-Carbine - Light weight semiautomatic rifle of WWII era.

M-1-Rifle - The .30 caliber American rifles from WWII.

M-101 - A 105-mm howitzer which was the standard light artillery piece. Called dime-nickel.

M-106 - A 4.2 inch mortar carrier mounted in the troop compartment of an APC. Also four-duce.

M-107 - The 175-mm self-propelled cannon-like gun used by Americans.

M-108 SPA - A self-propelled 105-mm howitzer with the tube enclosed in the armored turret.

M-109 SPA - A self-propelled 155-mm howitzer with a machine gun as well.

M-110 SPA - A self-propelled 8-inch howitzer weighing 29 tons.

M-113 APC - The most used armored personnel carrier with a crew of two, capable of carrying ten fully equipped troops who used a rear ramp for entry and exit. Speeds of 40 mph on land and 4mph in water were possible. Nicknamed The Green Dragon for its color and ability to spit fire from the top mounted machine gun.

M-114 - The 155-mm howitzer weighing 6-tons used by Americans. Unlike the self-propelled M109, the M-114 required towing by truck or helicopter transport. Nicknamed Heavy, 155s or Penny-nickel-nickel.

M-114 CRV - The light armored amphibious tracked carrier used as a command and reconnaissance vehicle. A smaller less able version of the M-113 APC.

M-116 cargo carrier - The fully tracked amphibious cargo carrier used by Marines.

M-123 tractor - The standard U.S. military 10-ton tractor that pulled a variety of trailers. The larger version of the 5-ton M-52.

M-125 mortar - The 81-mm mortar carrier.

M-127 flare - A hand flare.

M-127 trailer - The flatbed trailer used with the M-123 tractor.

M-131 tanker trailer - The fuel tanker holding 3,000 gallons.

M-132 flamethrower APC - The armored personnel carrier with a flamethrower. Nicknamed Zippo Track.

M-14 - The American infantry rifle at the start of the Vietnam war. It had a wood stock, weighed 9.3 pounds and used a 7.62-mm cartridge in a 20 round magazine. Although accurate to 460 meters, the weapon proved too heavy for the jungle conditions in Vietnam and was soon replaced by the M-16.

M-14 antipersonnel mine - A three-ounce mine similar to the M-16 antipersonnel mine. Called Toe Popper.

M-15 land mine - A land mine used in perimeter defense.

M-151 Jeep - See gun Jeep.

M-151 TOW - A tube launched, optically tracked, wire guided antitank missile

M-15A1 semitractor lowboy - A tank transported. See M-123 Tractor.

M-16 antipersonnel mine - The eight-pound cylindrical mine that when triggered bounced up from the ground. Called the Bouncing Betty.

M-16 Rifle - The American infantry rifle for most of the Vietnam war. It had a plastic stock and used 5.56-mm ammunition in a 20 round magazine. It is a gas operated, air cooled weapon that can operate on a fully automatic or semi automatic mode. It weighs about seven and a half pounds, making it about 2 pounds lighter and 5 inches shorter than the M-14. It has an automatic firing rate of 650-700 rounds per minute which slowed to 100-200 rounds a minute under continual fire. The effective firing range is about 460 meters and its maximum distance is 2350 meters. Early versions were made in part of black plastic by Mattel. Called Widow Maker, Black Rifle, and Mattel Toy Rifle.

M-163 Vulcan - A M113 armored personnel carrier with a Vulcan 20-mm Gatling gun. Nicknamed Vulcan.

M-17 protective mask - A gas mask.

M-18 claymore mine - The claymore mine.

M-18 smoke grenade - A smoke grenade.

M-18A1 - The bag for carrying the claymore mines.

M-19 Mortar - A 60-mm mortar that was muzzle loaded and fired from a tube held on a shoulder.

M-1911A1 - The standard military .45 cal semiautomatic pistol. Note the ammunition for this and the .45 cal machine gun was interchangeable.

M-1919A6 - The standard Browning .30 cal machine gun.

M-1944 AA gun - A long barreled antiaircraft gun.

M-1951 field cap - A cotton hat similar to a baseball cap worn until replaced in 1964, usually by officers with indoor assignments as the hat was hot outside.

M-1951 field jacket - A cold weather green jacket with four pockets, waist drawstring and button sleeves.

M-1955 flak jacket - The armored vest for Marines which was heavier than that issued to Army troops.

M-1956 combat field pack-See butt pack.

M-1961 combat field pack - See butt pack.

M-1964 field jacket - Similar to the 1951 field jacket but with a rain hood and Velcro at the sleeves.

M-1A1 - Thompson submachine gun.

M-2 Bouncing Betty - See Bouncing Betty mine.

M-2 Carbine - The M-1 improved to allow fully automatic firing.

M-2 HMG - The heavy .50 cal machine gun mounted on a Jeep or truck.

M-2 Mortar - The M-19, 60-mm mortar.

M-20 rocket launcher - The antitank rocket launched from a tube. Called Super Bazooka.

M-203 rifle - A M-16 rifle with a grenade launcher mounted under the rifle barrel. Called over-and-under.

M-21 - See M-14 sniper rifle.

M-24 cannon - The 20-mm cannon.

M-24 light tank - The light tank used by the French. Called Chaffee.

M-250 cargo carrier - An all terrain cargo carrier 8-tons. See M-553.

M-26 - Fragmentation grenade, also frag or Mike 26.

M-274 mule - A small flatbed field utility vehicle used by Army and Marines to haul cargo up to a half ton. The steering wheel rotated out to be used by a driver walking beside the vehicle. Called mule.

M-28 rifle grenade - An antitank grenade attached to the end of a rifle.

M-29 - The 81-mm mortar, American made.

M-29C - The American made amphibious cargo carrier. Also Weasel or Crab.

M-2A17 Flamethrower - A man-packed 45 lb. napalm dispensing flame thrower with a range of 20-45 meters. See Zippo.

M-3 Airborne Personnel Detector - XM-3.

M-3 TAP Suit - A Toxicological Agents Protective Suit.

M-30 - The 4.2 inch mortar.

M-33 - A fragmentation grenade.

M-34 - A white phosphorous grenade.

M-35 CBU - A incendiary cluster bomb that created a firestorm when detonated.

M-35 truck - A 2.5 ton truck. Called Duce and a Half, 6x6 and Six-By.

M-37 B1 - The ¾ ton truck.

M-38 mortar - The 120-mm mortar.

M-3A1 SMG - The .45 cal machine gun. Also called Grease Gun and Burp Gun.

M-4 Tank - The Sherman tank.

M-40 rifle - The Remington .308 cal, 7.62-mm high powered sniper rifle used by Marine sniper teams. Also Remington 700 and Varmint.

M-406 grenade - The standard high explosive grenade.

M-40A1 rifle - The 106-mm recoilless rifle that also could shoot beehive rounds like a shotgun.

M-41 - American made tank used by the South Vietnamese.

M-42 - A M-41 with antiaircraft guns. Duster.

M-43 mortar - Either the 120-mm or 160-mm mortar.

M-46 - Soviet made 130-mm gun.

M-48 - The Patton tank.

M-49 scope - A spotting scope.

M-5 bag - The large medical kit carried by Medics.

M-5 Grenade Launcher - A belt fed armament on the underside of a helicopter firing .40-mm grenades. Also Chunker or Thumper.

M-5 Medical Kit - See Unit One.

M-5 triggers - The antimotion triggers on booby traps allowing them to be safely moved and placed before arming the explosive by flipping the switch.

M-52 tractor - The 5-ton tractor used to pull a variety of trailers. See M-123 tractor.

M-53 SPA - The self propelled 155-mm Howitzer.

M-54 truck - The five-ton truck.

M-546 beehive round - A highly effective antipersonnel round containing 8,000 steel darts, each two inches in length and weighing 8 grams. A canister round.

M-548 cargo carrier - Operated as self-propelled ammo carrier for artillery batteries.

M-55 quad - A motorized gun mount with four .50 cal machine guns. Mounted on boat or truck for convoy protection or to a fixed base for camp protection.

M-55 SPA - The self propelled 8-inch Howitzer.

M-551 ARV - The Army turreted reconnaissance vehicle. Although classified as a reconnaissance vehicle, troops referred to it as a tank. See Sherman tank.

M-553 cargo carrier - Four wheel rough terrain vehicle This version was 10-tons. M-250 was 8-tons. Called GOER.

M-56 harness - See butt pack.

M-56 SPAT - The Army's 90-mm self propelled antitank gun.

M-561 cargo carrier - A small truck that had a pivot in the center of the bed to allow tight turns and rough terrain. Called Gamma Goat.

M-57 - hand detonator - The remote trigger for a claymore mine. Called clacker.

M-57 frag - A fragmentation grenade.

M-577 ACC - Armored command center or artillery firing center. A M-113 modified with added radio and artillery control gear. Also called Hightop or Commo Track.

M-578 VTR - The vehicle tracked retriever that had a crane on it. Called cherrypicker.

M-59 - A fragmentation grenade.

M-6 blasting caps - Detonators.

M-6 Quad MG - A machine gun.

M-60 AVLB (Armored Vehicle Launched Bridge) - A portable bridge, 60 feet in length carried on tanks able to span a 30 foot area and hold 60 tons. See Bailey bridge.

M-60 LMG - The standard light machine gun which was belt fed using 7.63-mm ammunition. Due to weight and firepower, these were usually mounted on trucks or helicopters. Called The Gun.

M-60 tank - A main battle tank, full-tracked, with a 105-mm gun.

M-61 gun pod - A 20-mm Vulcan cannon on a pod.

M-67 flamethrower - A Patton tank using a flame thrower in place of the front gun. Also Zippo tank.

M-67 Recoilless Rifle - A 90-mm antitank weapon held over a shoulder.

M-7 CS hand grenade - A tear gas emitting hand grenade.

M-72-LAW - A light weight antitank weapon firing a 66-mm HEAT rocket from a one-shot tube. See HEAT.

M-728 CEV - Army Combat Engineering Vehicle which was a modified tank with a bulldozer blade in front.

M-73 machine gun - The two gun version of the M-60 machine gun.

M-75 grenade launcher turret - The gun turret located under the nose of the Cobra or Huey helicopters to house the belt fed 40-mm grenade launcher. Nicknamed Hognose for the shape and location.

M-76 - cargo carrier - The amphibious tractor armed with a machine gun and able to carry 1.5 tons of gear or 10 Marines.

M-76 submachine gun - A Smith & Wesson 9-mm submachine gun for special clandestine operations.

M-79 buckshot round - A canister round.

M-79 flare - A flare used for illumination.

M-79 flechette round - A canister round.

M-79 grenade launcher - An American made single shot grenade launcher that looks like a single shot shotgun. It fired a 40-mm grenade at an effective distance of about 375 yards and a short range buckshot projectile. See Thumper.

M-8 armored car - A WWII era light armored car. Nickname Greyhound.

M-8 smoke grenade - A smoke grenade.

M-88 VTR - An Army medium armored recovery vehicle equipped with an A-frame boom and bulldozer blade.

M-8A1 Dozer Blade - A tank with a bulldozer blade in front.

M-day - (DOD, NATO, SEATO, CENTO, IADB) The term used to designate the day on which mobilization is to begin. See also D-day; K-day.

M-day force materiel requirement - (DOD) The quantity of an item required (on M-day minus one day) to equip and provide a materiel pipeline for authorized peacetime United States force levels, both active and reserve. See also mobilization reserves.

M-day materiel assets - (DOD) The total quantity of an item available in the military system worldwide on M-day to support the effective joint strategic objectives plan. It considers the current worldwide inventory (serviceable and reparable) of the item, adjustments in this inventory prior to M-day of the effective joint strategic objectives plan to provide for attrition and consumption, transfers out of or into the inventory and deliveries from funded and planned procurement to M-day of the effective joint strategic objectives plan. See also mobilization reserves.

M-day materiel requirement - (DOD) The quantity of an item required to be in the military system on M-day in order to equip, provide a materiel pipeline, and sustain the United States forces in the effective joint strategic objectives plan through the period prescribed for mobilization materiel planning purposes. It is the quantity by which the mobilization materiel requirement exceeds the mobilization materiel procurement capability and the mobilization materiel requirement adjustment. It includes the M-day force materiel requirement and the mobilization reserve materiel requirement. See also mobilization reserves.

M-day materiel status - (DOD) The status of M-day materiel assets, as compared to the M-day materiel requirement, is a means of assessing M-day materiel readiness. It is the difference between M-day materiel assets and the M-day materiel requirement. See also mobilization reserves.

M'aidez. - Help me, French. Pronounced "May Day".

M/Sgt - Master Sergeant.

M103A1 - A tank, full-tracked, with a 120-mm gun.

M103A1 - See tank, combat, full tracked, 170-mm gun.

M107 - The Soviet made 175-mm cannon used by the NVA.

M41 light tank - A light tank with a 76-mm gun. Also Walker Bulldog and Little Bulldog.

M42 - See Duster (antiaircraft weapon).

M48A2 tank - The large, combat, full-tracked, 90-mm gun and two .50 cal machine guns. Also Patton Tank.

M50 - A self-propelled, full-tracked, antitank weapon also used against bunkers had six 106-mm rifles. Light armor made it vulnerable to mines and loading it from the muzzle exposed the loader to enemy fire. Called Ontos or The Thing.

M51 HRV - The heavy recovery vehicle fitted with a crane and tow bar. Called Ox.

M60 - See tank, combat, full tracked, 105-mm gun.

MA - Mechanical ambush, this is the term for the American set booby trap.

MAAG - Military Assistance Advisory Group.

MAAV - Military Assistance Advisory Group, by which U.S. channeled funds to the French between 1950-1964.

MABS - Marine Air Base Squadron.

MAC - Military Airlift Command.

MACCORDS - The Civil Operations and Revolutionary Development Support Division of MACV.

Mace - (DOD, IADB) An improved version of the MGM-1C Matador, differing primarily in its improved guidance system, longer-range, low-level attack capability and higher-yield warhead. The MGM-13A is guided by a self-contained radar guidance system. The CGM - 13B is guided by an inertial guidance system. Designated as MGM-13.

mace - A VC booby trap consisting of a spiked rock or wood block on a rope that when released swung into the person tripping the wire.

Mach - 1. A speed indicator for supersonic aircraft, e.g. Mach One is the speed of sound, Mach Two is twice the speed of sound. 2. The definition of the speed of sound in the air is 661.5 knots at sea level, at 15 degrees C., the measurement is named for Ernst Mach. Pronounced mock.

Mach front - See Mach stem.

Mach no/yes - (DOD) In air intercept, means I have reached maximum speed and am not/ am closing my target.

Mach number - (DOD, NATO, SEATO, CENTO, IADB) The ratio of the velocity of a body to that of sound in the surrounding medium.

Mach stem - (DOD, NATO, CENTO) The shock front formed by the fusion of the incident and reflected shock fronts from an explosion. The term is generally used with reference to a blast wave, propagated in the air, reflected at the surface of the earth. In the ideal case the Mach stem is perpendicular to the reflecting surface and slightly convex (forward). The Mach stem is also called the Mach front.

Mach wave - See Mach stem.

machete - The long hacking tool for slashing away jungle foliage and vines.

machine gun - A rapid-firing, belt-fed gun. The .50cal M-2 could fire 500 rounds a minute and weighed about 80 pounds. The 7.62-mm M-60 could fire 100 rounds a minute and weighed about 20 pounds.

MACOV - Mechanized and Armor Combat Operations in Vietnam.

MACV (pronounced MAC-Vee) - Military Assistance Command, Vietnam. 1. The U.S. Army military advisers to the Vietnamese. 2. The overall command in Vietnam established in 1962 in Saigon.

MACVSOG - Military Assistance Command, Vietnam, Studies and Observation Group. Responsible for key intelligence and operations missions.

mad bomber - The Mortar Air Delivery System.

mad minute - Slang for a test firing or free fire session of automatic weapons.

mad monkeys - Staff personnel at the MACV.

MADS - The Mortar Air Delivery System.

MAF - Marine Amphibious Force.

MAG - 1. Marine Air Group. 2. Military Advisory Group.

mag - Magazine holding ammunition.

mag pouch - A pouch that held added magazines of ammunition.

Maggie's drawers - Red flag raised from target pit of firing range to indicate a complete miss of the target, a miss.

magnetic compass - (NATO) An instrument that uses a pivoted magnetic needle or other magnetic sensing element to align itself with the earth's magnetic lines of force to indicate direction. See also magnetic variation; grid magnetic angle; deviation.

magnetic declination - (DOD, NATO) The angle between the magnetic and geographical meridians at any place, expressed in degrees East or West to indicate the direction of magnetic North from true North. In nautical and aeronautical navigation the term magnetic variation is used instead of magnetic declination and the angle is termed variation of the compass or magnetic variation. Magnetic declination is not otherwise synonymous with magnetic variation which refers to regular or irregular change with time of the magnetic declination, dip or intensity. See also magnetic variation.

magnetic north - (DOD, NATO, CENTO, IADB) The direction indicated by the north-seeking pole of a freely suspended magnetic needle, influenced only by the earth's magnetic field.

magnetic tape - (DOD, IADB) A tape or ribbon of any material impregnated or coated with magnetic or other material on which information may be placed in the form of magnetically polarized spots.

magnetic variation - (DOD, NATO) The horizontal angle at a place between the true north and magnetic north measured in degrees and minutes east or west according to whether magnetic north lies east or west of true north. See also magnetic declination.

Magpie - A B-57 loaded with 750-pound bombs.

mail call - See incoming.

main airfield - (NATO, SEATO, CENTO, IADB) An airfield planned for permanent occupation in peacetime, at a location suitable for wartime utilization, and with operational facilities of a standard adequate to develop full use of its war combat potential. See also airfield; alternative airfield; departure airfield; redeployment airfield.

main armament - (DOD) The request of the observer or spotter to obtain fire from the largest guns installed on the fire support ship.

main attack - (DOD, NATO, SEATO, CENTO, IADB) The principal attack or effort into which the commander throws the full weight of the offensive power at his disposal. An attack directed against the chief objective of the campaign or battle.

main force - North Vietnamese soldiers, not Viet Cong guerrillas.

main line of resistance - (DOD, NATO, SEATO, CENTO, IADB) A line at the forward edge of the battle position, designated for the purpose of coordinating the fire of all units and supporting weapons, including air and naval gunfire. It defines the forward limits of a series of mutually supporting defensive areas, but does not include the areas occupied or used by covering or screening forces.

main man - Best friend.

main road - (DOD, IADB) A road capable of serving as the principal ground line of communication to an area or locality. Usually it is wide enough and suitable for two-way, all-weather traffic at high speeds.

main supply route - (DOD, NATO, CENTO) The route or routes designated within an area of operations upon which the bulk of traffic flows in support of military operations.

mainguard - (NFSN, CENTO, IADB) An element of an advanced guard. See also advanced guard.

mainliner - One who injects drugs.

maint - Maintenance.

maintenance (materiel) - (DOD, NATO, SEATO, CENTO, IADB) 1. All action taken to retain materiel in a serviceable condition or to restore it to serviceability. It includes inspection, testing, servicing, classification as to serviceability, repair, rebuilding, and reclamation. 2. All supply and repair action taken to keep a force in condition to carry out its mission 3. The routine recurring work required to keep a facility (plant, building, structure, ground facility, utility system, or other real property) in such condition that it may be continuously utilized, at its original or designed capacity and efficiency for its intended purpose.

maintenance area - (DOD, IADB) A general locality in which are grouped a number of maintenance activities for the purpose of retaining or restoring materiel to a serviceable condition.

maintenance engineering - (DOD, IADB) The application of techniques, engineering skills and effort, organized to insure that the design and development of weapon systems and equipment provide adequately for their effective and economical maintenance.

maintenance status - (DOD, IADB) 1. A non-operating condition, deliberately imposed, with adequate personnel to maintain and preserve installations, materiel, and facilities in such a condition that they may be readily restored to operable condition in a minimum time by the assignment of additional personnel and without extensive repair or overhaul. 2. That condition of materiel which is in fact, or is administratively classified as, unserviceable, pending completion of required servicing or repairs.

MAJ - Major (Army).

Maj - Major (Marine Corps, Air Force).

Maj Gen - Major General (Air Force).

MajGen - Major General (Marine Corps).

major disaster - See domestic emergencies.

major fleet - (DOD) A principal, permanent subdivision of the operating forces of the Navy with certain supporting shore activities. Presently there are two such fleets: the Pacific Fleet and the Atlantic Fleet. See also fleet.

major NATO commanders - (NATO) Major NATO commanders are: Supreme Allied Commander Atlantic, Supreme Allied Commander Europe, and Allied Commander-in - Chief Channel. See also commander(s).

major nuclear power - (DOD, NATO, CENTO, IADB) Any nation that possesses a nuclear striking force capable of posing a serious threat to every other nation.

major port - (DOD, NATO, CENTO, IADB) Any port with two or more berths and facilities and equipment capable of discharging 100,000 tons of cargo per month from oceangoing ships. Such ports will be designated as probable nuclear targets. See also port.

major water terminal - (DOD, NATO, CENTO, IADB) A water terminal with facilities for berthing numerous ships simultaneously at wharves and/or working anchorages, located within sheltered coastal waters adjacent to rail, highway, air and/or inland water transportation nets. It covers a relatively large area and its scope of operation is such that it is designated as a probable nuclear target. See also water terminal.

make a hole - Marine slang for get out of the way, coming through.

Make the scene with eighteen. - A phrase used on Armed Services Radio and Television as a reminder to use only 18 not the maximum of 20 rounds of ammunition in the M-16 rifle to avoid jamming.

Malay whip - A booby trap consisting of a log hung by two ropes that, when the trap was tripped, crashed into anyone on the trail.

malfunction junction - The Pentagon.

malingering - Goldbricking by pretending to be ill.

mama - The submarine from which troops were deployed.

mama-san - Slang for a older Vietnamese woman.

man Friday - A derogatory term for black soldiers appearing to suck up to white officers in hopes of getting lighter duty. From the character Friday in the novel Robinson Crusoe.

man movable - (DOD, NATO, CENTO) Items which can be towed, rolled, or skidded for short distances by an individual without mechanical assistance but which are of such size, weight, or configuration as to preclude being carried. Upper weight limit: approximately 425 pounds per individual.

man portable - (DOD) Items which are designed to be carried as a component part of individual, crew served or team equipment of the dismounted soldier in conjunction with his assigned duties. Upper weight limit: approximately 30 pounds.

man space - (DOD, IADB) The space and weight factor used to determine the combat capacity of vehicles, craft, and transport aircraft, based on the requirements of one man with his individual equipment. He is assumed to weigh between 222-250 pounds and to occupy 13.5 cubic feet of space. See also boat space.

man transportable - (DOD) Items which are usually transported on wheeled, tracked, or air vehicles, but have integral provisions to allow periodic handling by one or more individuals for limited distances (100-500 meters). Upper weight limit: approximately 65 pounds per individual.

Man, The Man - Black soldier slang for 1. White people. 2. Those in authority.

management - (DOD, IADB) A process of establishing and attaining objectives to carry out responsibilities. Management consists of those continuing actions or planning, organizing, directing, coordinating, controlling, and evaluating the use of men, money, materials, and facilities to accomplish missions and tasks. Management is inherent in command, but it does not include as extensive authority and responsibility as command.

management and control system (mobility) - (DOD) Those elements of organizations and/or activities which are part of, or are closely related to, the mobility system and which authorize requirements to be moved, to obtain and allocate lift resources, or to direct the operation of link-lift vehicles.

maneuver - (DOD, IADB) 1. A movement to place ships, troops, materiel, or fire in a better location with respect to the enemy. 2. A tactical exercise carried out at sea, in the air, on the ground, or on a map in imitation of war. 3. The operation of a ship, aircraft, or vehicle to cause it to perform desired movements. See also command post exercise; exercise; field exercise.

maneuverable reentry vehicle - (DOD) A reentry vehicle capable of performing preplanned flight maneuvers during the reentry phase. See also multiple reentry vehicle; multiple independently targetable reentry vehicle; reentry vehicle.

maneuvering area - (NATO) That part of an airfield used for takeoffs, landings and associated maneuvers. See also aircraft marshalling area.

manifest - (DOD, IADB) A document specifying in detail the passengers or items carried for a specific destination.

manipulative deception - (DOD) The alteration or simulation of friendly electromagnetic radiations to accomplish deception.

Manpack Personnel Detector-Chemical - The People Sniffer.

many (raid size) - (DOD) In air intercept usage, 8 or more aircraft. See also few (raid size).

map - (DOD, NESN, NFSN) A graphic representation, usually on a plane surface, and at an established scale, of natural and artificial features on the surface of a part or the whole of the earth or other planetary body. The features are positioned relative to a coordinate reference system. See also administrative map; battle map; chart index; chart series; chart sheet; controlled map; general map; intermediate scale map; large-scale map; line-route map; map chart; map index; map series; map sheet; medium-scale map; operation map; planimetric map; situation map; small-scale map; strategic map; tactical map; topographic map; traffic-circulation map; weather map.

map chart - (DOD, IADB) A representation of a land-sea area, using the characteristics of a map to represent the land area and the characteristics of a chart to represent the sea area, with such special characteristics as to make the map-chart most useful in military operations, particularly amphibious operations. See also map.

map convergence - (NATO) The angle at which one meridian is inclined to another on a map or chart. See also convergence.

map exercise - (DOD) An exercise in which a series of military situations is stated and solved on a map.

map index - (DOD, NESN, NFSN, CENTO, IADB) Graphic key primarily designed to give the relationship between sheets of a series, their coverage, availability, and further information on the series. See also map.

map reference - (NATO) A means of identifying a point on the earth's surface by relating it to information appearing on a map, generally the graticule or grid.

map reference code - (DOD, NATO, CENTO, IADB) A code used primarily for encoding grid coordinates and other information pertaining to maps. This code may be used for other purposes where the encryption of numerals is required.

map series - (DOD, NATO, CENTO, IADB) A collection of sheets having the same scale and cartographic specifications collectively identified by the producing agency.

map sheet - (DOD, NESN, CENTO, IADB) An individual map or chart, either complete in itself or part of a series.

march order - Artillery order to move to another location.

marching fire - 1. Infantry tactic of firing while walking. 2. Artillery tactic of firing at ever increasing heights so the impact areas walks away from the artillery's location. Also called walking fire.

MarDiv - Marine Division.

margin - (NATO) In cartography, the area of a map or chart lying outside the border.

marginal data - (NATO) All explanatory information given in the margin of a map or chart which clarifies, defines, illustrates and/or supplements the graphic portion of the sheet.

marginal information - See marginal data.

marginal weather - (DOD) Weather which is sufficiently adverse to a military operation so as to require the imposition of procedural limitations. See also adverse weather.

Marine Air Base Squadron - A non-tactical support area for an Air Squadron composed of motor pool, guard detail, etc.

Marine air command and control system - (DOD) A United States Marine Corps tactical air command and control system which provides the tactical air commander with the means to command, coordinate, and control all air operations within an assigned sector arid to coordinate air operations with other Services. It is composed of command and control agencies with communications-electronics equipment that incorporates a capability from manual through semiautomatic control.

Marine Air Control Squadron - (DOD, SEATO) The component of the Marine Air Control Group which provides and operates ground facilities for the detection and interception of hostile aircraft and for the navigational direction of friendly aircraft in the conduct of support missions.

Marine Air Group - The designation for the unit of aviation troops.

Marine Air Support Squadron - (DOD) The component of the Marine Air Control Group which provides and operates facilities for the control of support aircraft operating in direct support of ground forces.

Marine amphibious brigade - (DOD) A Marine air-ground task force built around a regimental landing team and a Marine aircraft group. The Marine amphibious brigade normally employs about one-third of the combat resources of one Marine division/wing team.

Marine amphibious corps - (DOD) A Marine air-ground task force built around two Marine divisions and two Marine aircraft wings. The Marine amphibious corps normally employs the full combat resources of two Marine division/wing teams.

Marine amphibious force - (DOD) A Marine air-ground task force built around a Marine division and a Marine aircraft wing. The Marine amphibious force normally employs the full combat resources of one Marine division/wing team.

Marine amphibious unit - (DOD) A Marine air-ground task force built around a battalion landing team and a provisional Marine aircraft group which is usually composed of an attack squadron and a helicopter squadron. The Marine amphibious unit normally employs about one-ninth of the combat resources of one Marine division/wing team.

Marine base - (DOD, SEATO) A base for support of Marine ground forces, consisting of activities or facilities for which the Marine Corps has operating responsibilities, together with interior lines of communication and the minimum surrounding area necessary for local security. (Normally, not greater than an area of 20 square miles.) See also base complex.

Marine Corps - The American service in the Vietnam war providing both ground and air operations.

Marine division/wing team - (DOD) A Marine Corps air-ground team consisting of one division and one aircraft wing, together with their normal reinforcements.

marine environment - (DOD) The oceans, seas, bays, estuaries, and other major water bodies including their surface interface and interaction with the atmosphere and with the land seaward of the mean high water mark.

Marine fishing - Using a grenade in a pond to kill fish for consumption.

Marine Logistics Flights - Flights to move men and/or supplies.

Marine stove - An improvised stove using an empty can and C-4 explosive which burns very hot.

Marineland - The region of I Corps. A play on the name of a marine park and aquarium.

maritime area - (NATO, SEATO, CENTO) A maritime theater of operations can be divided for the purposes of decentralization of command into maritime areas and subareas, e.g., Atlantic theater, which is divided into maritime area and subarea commands.

maritime control area - (DOD, IADB) An area generally similar to a defensive sea area in purpose except that it may be established any place on the high seas. Maritime control areas are normally established only in time of war. See also defensive sea area.

maritime operations - (NATO, SEATO, CENTO, IADB) Actions performed by forces on, under, or over the sea to gain or exploit control of the sea or to deny its use to the enemy.

maritime search and rescue region - (DOD) The waters subject to the jurisdiction of the United States; the territories and possessions of the United States (except Canal Zone and the inland area of Alaska) and designated areas of the high seas. See also search and rescue region.

mark - (DOD) 1. A call for fire on a specified location to orient the observer or spotter or to indicate targets. 2. A report made by the observer or spotter in firing illumination shells to indicate the instant of optimum light on the target. 3. An air control agency's term utilized to indicate the point of weapon release. It is usually preceded by the word, "STANDBY" as a preparatory command.

mark - Slang for a air speed indicator on the ground.

mark mark - (DOD) Command from ground controller for aircraft to release bombs; may indicate electronic ground controlled release or voice command to aircrew.

marker - (NATO, CENTO, IADB) A visual or electronic aid used to mark a designated point. See also beacon.

marker (land mine warfare) - See gap marker (land mine warfare); intermediate marker (land mine warfare); lane marker (land mine warfare); row marker (land mine warfare); strip marker (land mine warfare).

marker round - Artillery term for the first round fired when it is used as a reference point allowing the adjustment of subsequent rounds onto the target.

marker ship - (DOD, NATO, SEATO, CENTO, IADB) In an amphibious operation, a ship which takes accurate station on a designated control point. It may fly identifying flags by day and show lights to seaward by night. Note: SEATO term is "marker vessel".

marking panel - (DOD, NATO, CENTO) A sheet of material displayed for visual communications usually between friendly units. See also panel code.

marking panel - (SEATO, IADB) A sheet of material displayed by ground troops for visual signaling to friendly aircraft. See also panel code.

marking teams - (NATO, CENTO, IADB) Personnel landed in the landing area with the task of establishing navigational aids. See also pathfinder; pathfinder aircraft; pathfinders.

MARLOG - Marine Logistics Flights.

MAROP - Marine Operations.

MARS - Military Affiliate Radio Station, the communication link by which soldiers in Vietnam could call stateside by way of Signal Corps and ham radio operator linkages. See ham radio operators.

Mars generator - A gas operated generator used to flush hot air or chemicals into a tunnel used by the enemy.

Marsden matting - Perforated steel plates used for runway and other uses to provide a stable surface.

marshalling - (DOD, NATO, CENTO, IADB) 1. The process by which units participating in an amphibious or airborne operation group together or assemble when feasible or move to temporary camps in the vicinity of embarkation points, complete preparations for combat and prepare for loading. 2. The process of assembling, holding, and organizing supplies and/or equipment, especially vehicles of transportation, for onward movement. See also stage; staging area.

marshalling - (SEATO) 1. The process by which units participating in an amphibious or airborne operation move to temporary camps in the vicinity of embarkation points and airfields, complete preparations for combat, and prepare for loading. 2. The process of assembling, holding, and organizing supplies and/or equipment, especially vehicles of transportation, for onward movement.

Marston matting - See Marsden matting. Note called Marston from the town in North Carolina where it was first made. The more common name was Marsden matting.

Martin-Baker Fan Club - Aviation term for the select group who have ejected from airplanes. The ejection mechanism was made by Martin-Baker which maintains a listing of all ejections in which the life of the pilot (crew) was saved by their gear.

Marvin ARVIN - Slang for South Vietnamese troop.

MASH - Mobile Army Surgical Hospital.

Mason-Dixon Line - The DMZ. From the survey line in colonial America.

mass - (DOD, NATO, CENTO) 1. The military formation in which units are spaced at less than the normal distances and intervals. 2. The concentration of combat power.

mass (concentration) - (SEATO, IADB) 1. The concentration of combat power. 2. To concentrate or bring together, as to mass the fire of all batteries. 3. The military formation in which units are spaced at less than the normal distances and intervals.

mass cal - Hospital slang for mass casualties, usually a group of eight or more triggered this alert.

mass grave - A grave containing many persons, usually unidentified.

massaged - Killed.

massed fire - (DOD) 1. The fire of the batteries of two or more ships directed against a single target. 2. Fire from a number of weapons directed at a single point or small area. See also concentrated fire.

massing of fire - (DOD) 1. The fire of the battery of two or more ships directed against a single target. 2. Fire from a number of weapons, directed against a single target.

mast - Meeting with commanding officer. See requesting mast.

MAST - Mobile Army Surgical Team.

mast-head bombing - See minimum-altitude bombing and skip bombing.

master plot - (NATO, CENTO) A portion of a map or overlay on which are drawn the outlines of the areas covered by an air photographic sortie. Latitude and longitude, map and sortie information are shown.

Master Sergeant - The senior non-commissioned officer.

Master-at-Arms - Navy and Coast Guard title for the petty officer in charge of maintaining discipline on a ship, similar to Military Police.

MAT - Mobile Advisory Team of two officers, three enlisted men and one interpreter conducting training.

Mat - Vietnamese for "secret" stamped on documents.

MAT Team - Military Assistance and Training Team, a three or four man teams assigned to South Vietnamese units to train and assist in operations.

materials handling - (DOD, NATO, CENTO, IADB) The movement of materials (raw materials, scrap, semifinished, and finished) to, through, and from productive processes; in warehouses and storage; and in receiving and shipping areas.

materiel - (DOD, IADB) All items necessary for the equipment, maintenance, operation, and support of military activities without distinction as to their application for administrative or combat purposes; excluding ships or naval aircraft. See also equipment.

materiel cognizance - (DOD, IADB) Denotes responsibility for exercising supply management over items or categories of materiel.

materiel control - See inventory control.

materiel management - See inventory control.

materiel pipeline - (DOD, IADB) The quantity of an item required in the worldwide supply system to maintain an uninterrupted replacement flow.

materiel readiness - (DOD) The availability of materiel required by a military organization to support its wartime activities or contingencies, disaster relief (flood, earthquake, etc.), or other emergencies.

materiel requirements - (DOD, IADB) Those quantities of items of equipment and supplies necessary to equip, provide a materiel pipeline, and sustain a service, formation, organization, or unit in the fulfillment of its purposes or tasks during a specified period.

MATS - Military Air Transport Service.

Mattel toy rifle - The M-16 rifle when made by Mattel.

Mau Mau - 1. The group in Kenya that fomented rebellion in the 1950-60s. 2. Black power advocates. 3. As a verb meaning to agitate, riot, intimidate, in lower case mau mau.

Mauler - (DOD, IADB) A mobile, self-propelled mount guided missile designed for providing all-weather air defense of forward ground-combat elements against low-flying aircraft and short-range rockets/missiles. Designated as XMIM-46A.

maverick - Slang for lost or stolen vehicle.

maxi-ward - The Maxillofacial unit of a hospital for patients with facial wounds.

maximum effective range - (DOD, IADB) The maximum distance at which a weapon may be expected to deliver its destructive charge with the accuracy specified to inflict prescribed damage.

maximum effective range - (NATO, CENTO) The maximum distance at which a weapon may be expected to fire accurately to achieve the desired result.

maximum landing weight - (NATO, SEATO, CENTO, IADB) The maximum gross weight due to design or operational limitations at which an aircraft is permitted to land.

maximum ordinate - (DOD) The highest point along the trajectory of a projectile. The difference in altitude (vertical interval) between the origin and the summit.

maximum permissible concentration - See radioactivity concentration guide.

maximum permissible dose - (DOD, NATO, CENTO, IADB) That radiation dose which a military commander or other appropriate authority may prescribe as the limiting cumulative radiation dose to be received over a specific period of time by members of his command, consistent with current operational military considerations.

maximum power - An aviation term for using an afterburner.

maximum range - (DOD) The greatest distance a weapon can fire without consideration of dispersion.

maximum speed (transport vehicles) - (SEATO, IADB) The highest speed at which a vehicle can be driven for an extended period on a level, first-class highway without sustaining damage.

maximum sustained speed (transport vehicles) - (DOD, NATO, CENTO, IADB) The highest speed at which a vehicle, with its rated payload, can be driven for an extended period on a level, first-class highway without sustaining damage.

maximum take-off weight - (NATO, SEATO, CENTO, IADB) The maximum gross weight due to design or operational limitations at which an aircraft is permitted to take off.

maximum turn rate - The aviation measure of the degrees per second that a plane can turn in flight.

May day. - See mayday.

mayday - (DOD) Distress call, derived from the French M'aidez, help me.

MC - 1. Marine Corps. 2. Medical corps.

MC-1 - The Army T-10 parachute.

MCAS - Marine Corps Air Station.

MCCC - Marine Corps Command Center.

McGuire rig - A harness used to extract troops by helicopter when a landing area is not available.

MCI - Meal Combat Individual. A replacement in some units for the C-rations, later in the war.

McNamara's war - Slang for the Vietnam War.

MCPO - Master Chief Petty Officer, (Navy, Coast Guard).

MCPOCG - Master Chief Petty Officer of the Coast Guard (Special- senior person.) (Coast Guard).

MCPON - Master Chief Petty Officer of the Navy (Special- senior person) (Navy)

meaconing - (NATO, SEATO, CENTO, IADB) A system of receiving radio beacon signals and rebroadcasting them on the same frequency to confuse navigation. The meaconing stations cause inaccurate bearings to be obtained by aircraft or ground stations. See also beacon.

mean line of advance - (DOD) In naval usage, the direction expected to be made good over a sustained period.

mean point of impact - (DOD, NATO, CENTO, IADB) The point whose coordinates are the arithmetic means of the coordinates of the separate points of impact of a finite number of projectiles fired or released at the same aiming point under a given set of conditions.

mean sea level - (DOD, IADB) The average height of the surface of the sea for all stages of the tide, used as a reference for elevations.

mean sea level - (NATO, CENTO) The average sea level for a particular geographical location, obtained from numerous observations, at regular intervals, over a long period of time.

means of transport - See mode of transport.

measuring magnifier - (NATO, CENTO) A magnifying instrument incorporating a graticule for measuring small distances.

meat factory - Nurse's slang for the evacuation hospitals.

meat wagon - Slang for ambulance or APC used to remove wounded.

meatball - 1. The lighted circle that is an aid to landing a plane on a carrier by indicating if the plane is on the correct glidepath, high, low or to the side. 2. The optical landing glidescope system in general.

mechanical ambush - A booby trap set by U.S. troops, triggered as the enemy approached it.

mechanical mule - A small flat bed vehicle used for hauling heavy gear.

Med - Medical.

MED - Message Entry Device. Any of several data transmission devices.

Medal of Honor - The highest of the American military awards for battlefield bravery.

MEDCAP - Medical Civilian (or Civic) Assistance Program.

MedCAP - The medical clinic and assistance program to the civilian village population by the United States military. Also spelled MEDCAP.

MedEvac - Medical evacuation by helicopter. Also spelled MEDEVAC and medevac.

median lethal dose - (DOD, NATO, CENTO, IADB) 1. (nuclear) - The amount of radiation over the whole body which would be fatal to 50 percent of the animals or organisms in question in a given period of time. 2. (chemical) - The dose of toxic chemical agent which will kill 50 percent of exposed unprotected personnel. It is expressed in milligram minutes per cubic centimeter.

medic - Slang for any medical personnel in the field.

medical intelligence - (DOD) That category of intelligence which concerns itself with man as a living organism and those factors affecting his efficiency, capability, and well-being.

medical tag - A 4x7 inch paper tag with a string that tied it to the injured soldier's uniform. The tag was used by medics in the field to record treatment, medical status and identification to speed aid at the receiving medical facility.

medical treatment facility - (DOD, IADB) A facility established for the purpose of furnishing medical and/or dental care to eligible individuals.

Medical Unit Self-contained, Transportable - Field hospitals that were easily moved from one location to another but large enough to serve 30-90 patients. Abbreviated as MUST.

medium - (DOD) As used in air intercept, a height between two thousand and twenty-five thousand feet.

medium artillery - See howitzer, 155-mm.

medium atomic demolition munition - (DOD) A low yield, team portable, atomic demolition munition which can be detonated either by remote control or a timer device.

medium-altitude bombing - (DOD, IADB) Horizontal bombing with the height of release between 8,000 and 15,000 feet.

medium-angle loft bombing - (DOD, IADB) Type of loft bombing wherein weapon release occurs at an angle between 35 degrees and 75 degrees above the horizontal.

medium-lot storage - (DOD, IADB) Generally defined as a quantity of material which will require one to three pallet stacks, stored to maximum height. Thus, the term refers to relatively small lots as distinguished from definitely large or small lots. See also storage.

medium-range ballistic missile - (DOD) A ballistic missile with a range capability from about 600 to 1500 nautical miles.

medium-scale map - (DOD, IADB) A map having a scale larger than 1:600,000 and smaller than 1:75,000. See also map.

MEDTC - Military Equipment Delivery Team, Cambodia. Late in the war this group supplied gear and training on that gear to Cambodia.

meeting engagement - An unplanned meeting with enemy forces.

MEF - Marine Expeditionary Force.

megaton weapon - (DOD, NATO, CENTO, IADB) A nuclear weapon, the yield of which is measured in terms of millions of tons of trinitrotoluene explosive equivalents.

memory - See storage.

Menu - The code name for the secret series of bombing missions against Communist positions in Cambodia. Sub codes referenced the location of the bombing as follows: Breakfast (The Fish Hook area that is surrounded on three sides by Vietnam), Lunch (where Laos, Cambodia and Vietnam meet), Supper (a specific base), and Dessert (north of the Fish Hook).

Breakfast - Code for a bombing area in Cambodia. See Menu.

MER - Multiple Ejector Rack.

merchant intelligence - (DOD) In intelligence handling, communication instructions for reporting by merchant vessels of vital intelligence sightings. Also called MERINT.

merchant ship casualty report - (DOD, NATO, CENTO, IADB) A report by message, or other means, of a casualty to a merchant ship at sea or in port. Merchant ship casualty reports are sent by the escort force commander or other appropriate authority to the operational control authority in whose area the casualty occurred.

mere gook rule - Slang for the dehumanization of Asians thus justifying any action toward them.

merged - (DOD) In air intercept, a term meaning tracks have come together.

meritorious promotion - A promotion based on some exceptional circumstance, not the usual time or testing.

mermite - Insulated food containers which were a large chest, containing three smaller containers, usually one meat, one potato and one vegetable, warmed by boiling water and hot food being inserted at base before transport to the field by helicopter. Also Mermite.

mess hall - Dining room.

mess kit repair battalion - Mythical assignment for misfits and goof-offs.

message - (DOD, IADB) Any thought or idea expressed briefly in a plain or secret language, prepared in a form suitable for transmission by any means of communication.

message - (NATO, CENTO) Any thought or idea expressed briefly in a plain, coded, or secret language, prepared in a form suitable for transmission by any means of communications.

message center - (DOD) An element of a communications center, responsible for acceptance and processing of outgoing messages and for the receipt and delivery of incoming messages.

message center - (IADB) A communication agency charged with the responsibility for acceptance, preparation for transmission, receipt, and delivery of messages. See also communications/signal center.

message precedence - (IADB) Designations employed to indicate the relative order in which a message of one precedence designation is handled with respect to all other precedence designations. Precedence designations indicate: a. to the originator - the required speed of delivery to the addressee; b. to communications personnel - the relative order of handling and delivery; and c. to the addressee - the relative order in which he should note the message. See also flash message; immediate message; priority message; routine message; precedence.

met message - Meteorological message, a weather report.

meteorological data - (DOD, NATO, CENTO, IADB) Meteorological facts pertaining to the atmosphere, such as wind, temperature, air density, and other phenomena which affect military operations.

Metrical Division - Slang for the Americal Division, from the trademarked brand of low calorie drink.

metrology - (DOD) The science of measurement including the development of measurement standards and systems for absolute and relative measurements.

METTW - Elements used to evaluate a situation and formulate a plan and commands to implement that plan. Factors include: Mission, Enemy, Terrain, Tactics, Weather.

MF - 1. Mike Force. 2. Mother Fucker.

MFW - Multiple frag wounds.

MG - 1. Machine gun. 2. Military Government. 3. Major General (Army).

MGen - Major General. See MG.

MGF - Mobile Guerrilla Force.

MGH - Medium Green Helicopter.

MGM-13 - See Mace.

MGM-18 - See Lacrosse.

MGM-21A - See Entac.

MGM-29 - See Sergeant.

MGM-32 - See Entac.

MGM-5 - See Corporal.

MGM-51 - See Shillelagh.

MGR-1 - See Honest John.

MGR-3 - See Little John.

MGySgt - Master Gunnery Sergeant (Marine Corps).

MH - Medium Helicopter.

Mi - Mile.

MI - Military Intelligence.

MIA - Missing in Action.

MIA/BNR - Missing in Action/ Body Not Recovered.

Mickey Mouse ears - The huge earphones worn by a LSO on a carrier (and other on deck crew) that were noise blocking and essential for radio communication with pilots. The black color and rounded shape was reminiscent of the ears on the Disney cartoon character.

MicroSid - The smallest of the seismic detection devices. See MiniSid.

MICV - Mechanized Infantry Combat Vehicle.

mid rats - See midnight rations.

mid-range ballistic missile - (IADB) A ballistic missile with a range in the interval 500-3,000 nautical miles.

midcourse guidance - (DOD, IADB) The guidance applied to a missile between termination of the launching phase and the start of the terminal phase of flight. See also guidance.

middleman - (DOD) In air intercept, a term meaning very high frequency or ultrahigh frequency radio relay equipment.

midnight - (DOD) In air intercept, a code meaning change over from close to broadcast control.

midnight rations - The midnight meal on a carrier, usually from a snack bar or grill rather than a full mess. Featured were very greasy cheeseburgers that would slide off a plate in rough seas, called sliders.

midnight requisition - The unauthorized acquisition of supplies, theft.

MiG or MIG - The abbreviation for the Soviet made fighter jet, the Mikoyan i Gurevich.

MiG Screen - A aviation mission to block MiG access to ground troops.

MIG-15 - The subsonic aircraft used by the North Vietnamese up to 1964 as supplied by the Chinese.

MIG-17 - The subsonic aircraft used by the North Vietnamese as supplied by the Chinese.

MIG-19 - The supersonic aircraft used by the North Vietnamese Air Force post 1965.

MIG-21 - The supersonic aircraft used by the North Vietnamese Air Force post 1965.

MiGCAP - Combat Air Patrol specifically against MiG fighter jets.

Mighty Mike - 1. The portable air blower used by tunnel flushers to force gas into enemy tunnels. Also called Mighty Mite. 2. Marine slang for a Jeep.

Mighty Mite - See Mighty Mike.

Mike - The military phonetic alphabet designation for the letter "M".

Mike 26 - Fragmentation grenade.

Mike boat - See LCM-8 Landing craft.

Mike Force - Mobile Strike Force.

Mike Juliet - Marijuana.

mike minutes - Slang for when a patrol is moving out or another event is planned in the future such as moving out in three zero mikes (30 minutes).

Mike Papa - Military Police.

mike-mike - Slang for a millimeter.

mil - Angular mil. Angular milliradian. A measurement used on artillery gunsights. A mil is an angular measure that is 1/6400 of a circle in NATO countries or 1/18 of a degree.

MILCAP - The abbreviation for the Military Civil Assistance Program (South Vietnam).

militarily significant fallout - (DOD) Radioactive contamination capable of inflicting radiation doses to personnel which may result in a reduction of their combat effectiveness.

Military Affiliate Radio System - (DOD) A program conducted by the Departments of the Army, Navy, and Air Force in which amateur radio stations and operators participate and contribute to the mission of providing auxiliary and emergency communications on a local, national, or international basis as an adjunct to normal military communications.

Military Airlift Command - (DOD) The single manager operating agency for designated airlift service. Also referred to as MAC.

Military Airlift Command - The Air Force group responsible for air lifting troops, formerly called the Military Air Transport Service.

Military Assistance Advisory Group - (DOD, IADB) A joint Service group normally under the military command of a commander of a unified command and representing the Secretary of Defense which primarily administers the United States military assistance planning and programming in the host country.

Military Assistance Articles and Services List - (DOD) A Department of Defense publication listing source, availability, and price of items and services for use by the unified commands and Military Departments in preparing military assistance plans and programs.

Military Assistance Grant Aid Training - (DOD) That training provided under Military Assistance Program Grant Aid.

Military Assistance Program - (DOD, IADB) The United States program for providing military assistance under the Foreign Assistance Act of 1961, as amended, as distinct from Economic Aid and other programs authorized by the Act; includes the furnishing of defense articles and defense services through Grant Aid or Military Sales to eligible Allies, as specified by Congress.

Military Assistance Program Grant Aid - (DOD, IADB) Military assistance rendered under the authority of the Foreign Assistance Act of 1961, as amended, for which the United States receives no reimbursement.

Military Assistance Program Grant Aid Trainees - (DOD) Foreign nationals receiving training under the Grant Aid portion of Military Assistance Program training.

Military Assistance Program Supported Third Country Training - (DOD) Training provided not under United States supervision outside the continental United States in a country other than the country of program. Training may include United States assistance for costs of normal student travel and living allowance.

military assistance sales - (IADB) That portion of United States military assistance authorized by the Foreign Assistance Act of 1961. This assistance differs from Military Assistance Program Grant Aid in that it is purchased by the recipient country. See also foreign military sales.

military censorship - (DOD) All types of censorship conducted by personnel of the Armed Forces of the United States, to include armed forces censorship, civil censorship, prisoner of war censorship, and field press censorship. See also censorship.

military censorship - (IADB) All types of censorship conducted by personnel of the Armed Forces, to include armed forces censorship, civil censorship, prisoner of war censorship, and field press censorship. See also censorship.

military characteristics - (DOD, IADB) Those characteristics of equipment upon which depend its ability to perform desired military functions. Military characteristics include physical and operational characteristics but not technical characteristics.

military civic action - (DOD, I, SEATO, IADB) The use of preponderantly indigenous military forces on projects useful to the local population at all levels in such fields as education, training, public works, agriculture, transportation, communications, health, sanitation, and others contributing to economic and social development, which would also serve to improve the standing of the military forces with the population. (DOD, I) (United States forces may at times advise or engage in military civic actions in overseas areas.)

military currency - (DOD, NATO, CENTO, IADB) Currency prepared by a power and declared by its military commander to be legal tender for use by civilian and/or military personnel as prescribed in the areas occupied by its forces. It should be of distinctive design to distinguish it from the official currency of the countries concerned, but may be denominated in the monetary unit of either.

military currency - (SEATO) Currency prepared by a power and declared by its military commander to be legal tender for use by civilian and/or military personnel as prescribed in the areas occupied by its forces. Should be of distinctive design to distinguish it from the official currency of both the opposing powers, but may be denominated in the monetary unit of either.

Military Department - (DOD) One of the departments within the Department of Defense created by the National Security Act of 1947, as amended. See also Department of the Army; Department of the Navy; Department of the Air Force.

military education - (DOD, IADB) The systematic instruction of individuals in subjects which will enhance their knowledge of the science and art of war. See also military training.

military geographic documentation - (DOD, NATO, CENTO, IADB) Military geographic information which has been evaluated, processed, summarized, and published.

military geographic information - (DOD, NATO, CENTO, IADB) Comprises the information concerning physical aspects, resources, and artificial features which is necessary for planning and operations.

military geography - (DOD, IADB) The specialized field of geography dealing with natural and man-made physical features that may affect the planning and conduct of military operations.

military government - See civil affairs.

military government ordinance - (DOD, IADB) An enactment, on the authority of a military governor, promulgating laws or rules regulating the occupied territory under his control.

military governor - (DOD, NATO, CENTO, IADB) The military commander or other designated person who, in an occupied territory, exercises supreme authority over the civil population subject to the laws and usages of war and to any directive received from his government or his superior.

military grid - (NATO, SEATO, CENTO, IADB) Two sets of parallel lines intersecting at right angles and forming squares; the grid is superimposed on maps, charts, and other similar representations of the earth's surface in an accurate and consistent manner to permit identification of ground locations with respect to other locations and the computation of direction and distance to other points. See also grid; military grid reference system.

military grid reference system - (DOD, NATO, SEATO, CENTO, IADB) A system which uses a standard-scaled grid square, based on a point of origin on a map projection of the earth's surface in an accurate and consistent manner to permit either position referencing or the computation of direction and distance between grid positions. See also grid; military grid.

military intelligence - See intelligence.

military intervention - (DOD, IADB) The deliberate act of a nation or a group of nations to introduce its military forces into the course of an existing controversy.

military land transportation resources - (DOD) All military-owned transportation resources designated for common-user, over the ground, point-to-point use.

military load classification - (DOD, NATO, CENTO) The military load classification of a route, bridge or raft, is a class number which represents the safe load carrying capacity of the route, bridge or raft, and indicates the maximum vehicle class that can be accepted under normal conditions. See also classification of bridges and vehicles; route classification.

military necessity - (DOD, NATO, SEATO, CENTO, IADB) The principle whereby a belligerent has the right to apply any measures which are required to bring about the successful conclusion of a military operation and which are not forbidden by the laws of war.

military nuclear power - (DOD, NATO, CENTO) A nation which has nuclear weapons and the capability for their employment. See also nuclear power.

military occupation - (DOD, IADB) A condition in which territory is under the effective control of a foreign armed force. See also occupied territory; phases of military government.

Military Operations Specialty - The numerical designation of the occupation and specialty of any service personnel. See MOS.

military payment certificates - The currency issued to the military in Vietnam used in lieu of U.S. currency. See GI Play Money.

military platform - (DOD, NATO, CENTO) A side loading platform generally at least 300 meters/1000 feet long for military trains.

military police - The military personnel responsible for troop discipline, traffic control and guarding convoys, brigs and stockades. See Shore Patrol.

military posture - (DOD, IADB) The military disposition, strength, and condition of readiness as it affects capabilities.

military power - Aviation slang for operating a jet at full power without using the afterburner.

military requirement - (DOD, NATO, CENTO, IADB) An established need justifying the timely allocation of resources to achieve a capability to accomplish approved military objectives, missions, or tasks. See also objective force level.

Military Sealift Command - (DOD) The single manager operating agency for designated sealift service. Also referred to as MSC.

Military Service - (DOD) A branch of the Armed Forces of the United States, established by act of Congress, in which persons are appointed, enlisted, or inducted for military service and which operates and is administered within a military or executive department. The military Services are: the United States Army, the United States Navy, the United States Air Force, the United States Marine Corps, and the United States Coast Guard.

military standard requisitioning and issue procedure - (DOD) A uniform procedure established by the Department of Defense for use within the Department of Defense to govern requisition and issue of materiel within standardized priorities. Also referred to as MILSTRIP.

military standard transportation and movement procedures - (DOD) Uniform and standard transportation data, documentation, and control procedures applicable to all cargo movements in the Department of Defense transportation system. Also referred to as MILSTAMP.

military strategy - (DOD, IADB) The art and science of employing the armed forces of a nation to secure the objectives of national policy by the application of force, or the threat of force. See also strategy.

military traffic - (DOD) Department of Defense personnel, mail, and cargo to be, or being transported.

Military Traffic Management and Terminal Service - (DOD) The single manager operating agency for military traffic, land transportation, and common-user ocean terminals. Also referred to as MTMTS.

military training - (DOD, IADB) The instruction of personnel to enhance their capacity to perform specific military functions and tasks; the exercise of one or more military units conducted to enhance their combat readiness. See also military education.

milk run - Easy non-hazardous job.

million dollar wound - Non-crippling injury that required return to stateside.

Millitary Assistance Command Vietnam - MACV.

MILPHAP - Military Provincial Health Assistance Program.

milvan - (DOD) Military-owned demountable container, conforming to United States and international standards, operated in a centrally controlled fleet for movement of military cargo.

milvan chassis - (DOD) The compatible chassis to which the MILVAN is attached by coupling the lower four standard corner fittings of the container to compatible mounting blocks in the chassis, to permit road movement.

MIM-23 - See Hawk.

MIM-3 - See Nike Ajax.

MIM-14 - See Nike Hercules.

mine - See armed mine; antipersonnel mine (land mine warfare); antitank mine (land mine warfare); disarmed mine; drifting mine; inert mine (land mine warfare); mine (land mine warfare); oscillating type mine; phony mine (land mine warfare); practice mine (land mine warfare).

mine (land mine warfare) - (DOD, NATO, SEATO, CENTO, IADB) An explosive or other material, normally encased, designed to destroy or damage vehicles, boats, or aircraft, or designed to wound, kill, or otherwise incapacitate personnel. It may be detonated by the action of its victim, by the passage of time, or by controlled means.

See also anti-personnel mine (land mine warfare); anti-tank mine (land mine warfare); inert mine (land mine warfare); mine; phony mine (land mine warfare); practice mine (land mine warfare).

mine clearance (land mine warfare) - (DOD, NATO, SEATO, CENTO, IADB) The process of detecting and/or removing land mines by manual or mechanical means.

mine countermeasures - (DOD, IADB) Includes all methods for preventing or reducing damage or danger to ships, personnel, aircraft, and vehicles from mines.

mine defense - (DOD, NATO, CENTO, IADB) The defense of a position, area, etc., by land or underwater mines. A mine defense system includes the personnel and equipment needed to plant, operate, maintain, and protect the minefields that are laid.

mine hunting - (DOD, IADB) The branch of mine countermeasures based on determining the positions of individual mines and concentrating countermeasures on those positions, as opposed to techniques directed at a more extensive area suspected of containing mines. Mine hunting includes mine locating, clearance of located mine, and mine watching.

mine row (land mine warfare) - (DOD, NATO, SEATO, CENTO, IADB) A single row of mines or clusters. See also mine strip (land mine warfare).

mine strip (land mine warfare) - (DOD, NATO, SEATO, CENTO, IADB) Two parallel mine rows laid simultaneously six paces apart. See also mine row (land mine warfare).

mine warfare - (DOD, NATO, CENTO, IADB) The strategic and tactical use of mines and their countermeasures.

mine warfare forces (naval) - (DOD, IADB) Navy forces charged with the strategic and tactical use of naval mines and their counter-measures. Such forces are capable of offensive and defensive measures in connection with laying and clearing mines.

mine watching - (DOD, NATO, CENTO, IADB) The mine countermeasures procedure which detects, finds the position of, and/or identifies mines during the act of laying by the enemy.

minefield (land mine warfare) - (DOD, NATO, SEATO, CENTO, IADB) An area of ground containing mines laid with or without pattern. See also antiairborne minefield (land mine warfare); antiamphibious minefield (land mine warfare); antipersonnel minefield (land mine warfare); barrier minefield (land mine warfare); defensive minefield (land mine warfare); mixed minefield (land mine warfare); nuisance minefield (land mine warfare); phony minefield (land mine warfare); protective minefield (land mine warfare).

minefield gap (land mine warfare) - (DOD, NATO, CENTO, IADB) A portion of a minefield, in which no mines have been laid, of specified width to enable a friendly force to pass through the minefield in tactical formation. See also gap marker (land mine warfare).

minefield gap (land mine warfare) - (SEATO) A portion of a minefield, in which no mines have been laid, of specified width to enable a friendly force to pass through the minefield in tactical formation. It will seldom be less than 100 yards wide.

minefield lane (land mine warfare) - (DOD, NATO, IADB) A marked lane, unmined, or cleared of mines, leading through a minefield.

minefield marking - (DOD, NATO) Visible marking of all points required in laying a minefield and indicating the extent of such minefields.

minefield record - (DOD, NATO, CENTO, IADB) A complete written record of all pertinent information concerned on a minefield, submitted on a standard form by the other officer in charge of the laying operations.

minesweeping - (DOD, NATO, CENTO, IADB) The technique of searching for, or clearing mines using mechanical or explosion gear, which physically removes or destroys the mine, or produces in the area the influence fields necessary to actuate it.

minesweeping - (SEATO) The mine clearance procedure whereby a region of water is swept for mines either by covering or traversing it with mechanical or explosive gear which physically removes or destroys the mines, or by producing in the region the influence field necessary to actuate the mines.

mini-arc-light - A combined air and artillery strike.

Mini-Gun or Minigun - The electric operated Gatling gun that could shoot 6,000 rounds a minute, technically, a 7.62-mm weapon in prop planes and helicopters. See Puff the Magic Dragon.

minimize - (DOD, IADB) A condition wherein normal message and telephone traffic is drastically reduced in order that messages connected with an actual or simulated emergency shall not be delayed.

minimum attack altitude - (DOD) The lowest altitude determined by the tactical use of weapons, terrain consideration, and weapons effects which permits the safe conduct of an air attack and/or minimizes effective enemy counteraction.

minimum crossing altitude - (DOD) The lowest altitude at certain radio fixes at which an aircraft must cross when proceeding in the direction of a higher minimum en route instrument flight rules altitude.

minimum essential equipment - (DOD, IADB) That part of authorized allowances of Army equipment, clothing, and supplies needed to preserve the integrity of a unit during movement without regard to the performance of its combat or service mission.

Items common within this category will normally be carried by, or accompany troops to the port and will be placed aboard the same ships with the troops. As used in movement directives, minimum essential equipment refers to specific items of both organizational and individual clothing and equipment.

minimum normal burst altitude - (DOD) The altitude above terrain below which air defense nuclear warheads are not normally detonated.

minimum obstruction clearance altitude - (DOD) The specified altitude in effect between radio fixes on very high frequency omnirange airways, off-airway routes, or route segments which meets obstruction clearance requirements for the entire route segment and which assures acceptable navigational signal coverage only within 22 miles of a very high frequency omnirange.

minimum quality surveillance (petroleum) - (NATO, SEATO, CENTO, IADB) The minimum measures to be applied to determine and maintain the quality of bulk and packaged petroleum products in order that these products will be in a condition suitable for immediate use.

minimum range - (DOD) 1. Least range setting of a gun at which the projectile will clear an obstacle or friendly troops between the gun and the target. 2. Shortest distance to which a gun can fire from a given position.

minimum reception altitude - (DOD) The lowest altitude required to receive adequate signals to determine specific very high frequency omnirange/tactical air navigation fixes.

minimum safe altitude - (DOD) The altitude below which it is hazardous to fly, owing to presence of high ground or other hazards.

minimum safe altitude - (NATO, SEATO, CENTO, IADB) The altitude below which it is hazardous to fly, owing to presence of high ground or other obstacles. Note: The SEATO term is "minimum safety altitude".

minimum safe distance (nuclear) - (DOD, NATO, CENTO, IADB) The sum of the radius of safety and the buffer distance.

minimum warning time (nuclear) - (DOD, NATO, CENTO, IADB) The sum of system reaction time and personnel reaction time.

minimum-altitude bombing - (DOD, IADB) Horizontal or glide bombing with the height of release under 900 feet. It includes mast-head bombing which is sometimes erroneously referred to as "skip bombing". See also skip bombing.

minimums - The minimum of all conditions allowing flight.

MiniSid - A small seismic detection device. See MicroSid.

minor control - See photogrammetric control.

minor port - (DOD, NATO, CENTO, IADB) A port having facilities for the discharge of cargo from coasters or lighters only. See also port.

Minuteman - (DOD, IADB) A three-stage solid-propellant, second-generation intercontinental ballistic missile equipped with a nuclear war-head, designed for deployment in a hardened and dispersed configuration and in a mobile mode on railroad trains. It is a simple, smaller, lighter missile than earlier intercontinental ballistic missiles and is designed for highly automated remote operation. Designated as LGM-30.

misadventure - The death of a civilian by friendly fire, a MACV term.

misfire - (DOD, NATO, SEATO, CENTO, IADB) 1. Fail to fire or explode properly. 2. Failure of a primer or the propelling charge of a projectile to function, wholly or in part.

Missile A (division direct support missile) - (DOD) A simple low-cost, light-weight, air-transportable, mobile missile system providing sustained direct support for the battle group.

missile assembly-checkout facility - (DOD) A building, van, or other type structure located near the operational missile launching location designed for the final assembly and checkout of the missile system.

Missile B (division support missile) - (DOD) A light-weight missile system utilizing a self-propelled launcher, air-transportable and capable of sustained ground combat in support of divisions.

missile intercept zone - (DOD) That geographical division of the destruction area where surface-to-air missiles have primary responsibility for destruction of airborne objects. See also destruction area.

missile monitor - (DOD) A mobile, electronic, air defense fire distribution system for use at Army air defense group, battalion, and battery levels. It employs digital data to exchange information within the system and provides means for the Army air defense commander to monitor the actions of his units and take corrective action when necessary. It automatically exchanges information with adjacent missile monitor systems when connected with them by data links.

Missing in Action (MIA) - Any member of the armed services who is not accounted for at the end of a battle. The status of MIA remains until the remains are recovered or other proof of loss is made.

missing link - Second lieutenant.

missing man formation - Aviation term for a ceremonial aviation formation flown in memorial, such as over a funeral. The formation may range from a large parade formation that is clearly missing a plane as a static formation or be performed as an active maneuver in which a diamond formation approaches, the wingman peels off skyward, often trailing smoke, leaving the incomplete diamond formation to pass over the observers.

mission - (DOD, IADB) 1. The task, together with the purpose, which clearly indicates the action to be taken and the reason therefor. 2. In common usage, especially when applied to lower military units, a duty assigned to an individual or unit; to task. 3. The dispatching of one or more aircraft to accomplish one particular task.

mission - (NATO, SEATO, CENTO) 1. The task, together with its purpose, thereby clearly indicating the action to be taken and the reason therefor. 2. The dispatching of one or more aircraft to accomplish one particular task.

mission ready - The status of equipment ready for use. See NORS and NORS-G.

mission review report (photographic interpretation) - (DOD, NATO, CENTO) An intelligence report containing information on all targets covered by one photographic sortie.

mission type order - (DOD, IADB) 1. Order issued to a lower unit that includes the accomplishment of the total mission assigned to the higher headquarters. 2. Order to a unit to perform a mission without specifying how it is to be accomplished.

mission-essential materiel - (DOD) That materiel, which is authorized and available to combat, combat support, combat service support, and combat readiness training forces to accomplish their assigned mission.

mission-oriented items - (DOD) Items for which requirements computations are based upon the assessment of enemy capabilities expressed as a known or estimated quantity of total targets to be destroyed. See also combination mission/level of effort-oriented items; level of effort-oriented items.

Mitey Mite - See Mighty Mike.

mix-up, caution - (DOD) In air intercept, a term meaning mixture of friendly and hostile aircraft.

mixed - (DOD) A spotting, or an observation, by a spotter or an observer to indicate that the rounds fired resulted in an equal number of air and impact bursts.

mixed air - (DOD) A spotting, or an observation, by a spotter or an observer to indicate that the rounds fired resulted in both air and impact bursts with a majority of the bursts being airbursts.

mixed graze - (DOD) A spotting, or an observation, by a spotter or an observer to indicate that the rounds fired resulted in both air and impact bursts with a majority of the bursts being impact bursts.

mixed minefield (land mine warfare) - (DOD, NATO, SEATO, CENTO, IADB) A minefield containing both antitank and antipersonnel mines. See also minefield (land mine warfare).

Mixmaster - See O-1, an aircraft, derived from the trademarked name of a food mixer.

mobile air movements team - (NATO, CENTO) An air force team trained for operational deployment on air movement/traffic section duties.

Mobile Army Surgical Hospital - A small field hospital. Requires added transport support to be moved. Abbreviated as MASH.

mobile defense - (DOD, IADB) Defense of an area or position in which maneuver is used with organization of fire and utilization of terrain to seize the initiative from the enemy.

mobile support group (naval) - (DOD, NATO, CENTO, IADB) Provides logistic support to ships at an anchorage; in effect, a naval base afloat although certain of its supporting elements may be located ashore.

mobile training team - (DOD) A mobile training team consists of one or more United States personnel drawn from Service resources and sent on temporary duty to a foreign nation to give instruction. The mission of the team is to provide, by training instructor personnel, a military service of the foreign nation with a self-training capability in a particular skill.

mobility - (DOD, NATO, CENTO, IADB) A quality or capability of military forces which permits them to move from place to place while retaining the ability to fulfill their primary mission.

mobility system support resources - (DOD) Those resources that are required to: a. complement the airlift and sealift forces, and/or b. perform those work functions directly related to the origination, processing, or termination of a movement requirement.

mobilization - (DOD, NATO, SEATO, CENTO, IADB) 1. The act of preparing for war or other emergencies through assembling and organizing national resources. 2. The process by which the armed forces or part of them are brought to a state of readiness for war or other national emergency. This includes assembling and organizing personnel, supplies, and material for active military service.

mobilization base - (DOD, IADB) The total of all resources available, or which can be made available, to meet foreseeable wartime needs. Such resources include the manpower and material resources and services required for the support of essential military, civilian, and survival activities; as well as the elements affecting their state of readiness, such as (but not limited to) the following: manning levels, state of training, modernization of equipment, mobilization materiel reserves and facilities, continuity of government, civil defense plans and preparedness measures, psychological preparedness of the people, international agreements, planning with industry, dispersion, and stand-by legislation and controls.

mobilization exercise - (DOD, IADB) An exercise involving, either completely or in part, the implementation of mobilization plans.

mobilization materiel procurement capability - (DOD, IADB) The quantity of an item which can be acquired by orders placed on or after M-day from industry or from any other available source during the period prescribed for mobilization procurement planning purposes. See also mobilization reserves.

mobilization materiel requirement - (DOD) The quantity of an item required to support completely the United States forces in the effective joint strategic objectives plan through the period prescribed for mobilization materiel planning purposes. It includes the materiel required to equip and provide a materiel pipeline for the M-day forces (authorized peacetime United States forces, both active and reserve, on M-day minus one day), to support planned mobilization and to sustain in training, combat, or noncombat operations, as applicable, all United States forces in the effective joint strategic objectives plan. See also mobilization reserves.

mobilization materiel requirement adjustment - (DOD) The quantity of an item included in the mobilization materiel requirement, for the support of certain forces in the effective joint strategic objectives plan, which is also included in the peacetime force materiel requirement for the support of the same forces, in the event M-day does not occur as assumed. See also mobilization reserves.

mobilization reserve materiel objective - (DOD) That portion of the computed mobilization reserve materiel requirement which a Service or single manager recommends be stocked after considering the essentiality of the item to the overall mission, modernization, storage characteristics, and costs of storage and maintenance. This quantity may be the same as the computed mobilization reserve materiel requirement. See also mobilization reserves.

mobilization reserve materiel procurement objective - (DOD) The quantity of an item required to be procured in peacetime, in addition to the peacetime force materiel procurement objective, in order to support the effective joint strategic objectives plan. It is the quantity by which the mobilization reserve materiel objective exceeds the mobilization reserve stock. See also mobilization reserves.

mobilization reserve materiel requirement - (DOD) The quantity of an item, in addition to the M-day force materiel requirement required to be in the military supply system on M-day in order to support planned mobilization, to expand the materiel pipeline, and to sustain in training, combat, or noncombat operations, as applicable, all forces in the effective joint strategic objectives plan through the period prescribed for mobilization materiel planning purposes. It is the quantity by which the M-day materiel requirement exceeds the M-day force materiel requirement, or the quantity by which the mobilization materiel requirement exceeds the sum of the M-day force materiel requirement, the mobilization materiel procurement capability, and the mobilization materiel requirement adjustment. See also mobilization reserves.

mobilization reserve stock - (DOD) That portion of total materiel assets which is designated to meet the mobilization reserve materiel objective. See also mobilization reserves.

mobilization reserves - See general mobilization reserve materiel objective; general mobilization reserve stock; M-day force materiel requirement; M-day materiel assets; M-day materiel requirements; M-day materiel status; mobilization materiel procurement capability; mobilization materiel requirement; mobilization materiel requirement adjustment; mobilization reserve materiel objective; mobilization reserve materiel procurement objectives; mobilization reserve materiel requirement; mobilization reserve stock; peacetime force materiel assets; peacetime force materiel procurement objective; peacetime force materiel requirement; pre-positioned war reserve requirement; pre-positioned war reserve stock; total materiel assets; total materiel objective; total materiel procurement objective; total materiel requirement.

mock-up - (DOD, IADB) Model, built to scale, of a machine, apparatus, or weapon. It is used in studying the construction and in testing a new development, or in teaching personnel how to operate the actual machine, apparatus, or weapon. Mock-ups of ships, landing craft, and aircraft are used in training personnel to load, embark, and debark.

mode (identification friend or foe) - (DOD) The number or letter referring to the specific pulse spacing of the signals transmitted by an interrogator.

mode of transport - (DOD, NATO, CENTO, IADB) The various modes used for a movement. For each mode there are several means of transport. They are: a. inland surface transportation (rail, road and inland waterway); b. sea transport (coastal and ocean) ; c. air transportation; and d. pipelines.

Model 14 - See Randall knife.

Model 70 Winchester - The .30-06 sniper rifle used by Marines.

moderate damage - See nuclear damage (land warfare).

moderate risk (nuclear) - (DOD, NATO, CENTO, IADB) A degree of risk where anticipated effects are tolerable, or at worst, a minor nuisance. See also emergency risk (nuclear).

modification center - (DOD, IADB) An installation consisting of an airfield and of facilities for modifying standard production aircraft to meet certain requirements which were not anticipated at the time of manufacture.

MOH - Ministry of Health (South Vietnam).

Mohawk - See OV-1B, an aircraft.

Molotov Cocktail - Homemade explosive device, usually a bottle filled with gasoline and fused with a rag that is lighted and then thrown at a target.

Mom - Aviation slang for the carrier that is home to a pilot.

moment - (NATO, CENTO) In air transport, the weight of a load multiplied by its distance from a reference point in the aircraft.

Monday pills - Slang for the anti-malaria pills that were taken once a week, usually on a Monday.

monitoring - (DOD, NATO, CENTO, IADB) l. The act of detecting the presence of radiation and the measurement thereof with radiation measuring instruments. (NATO, CENTO, IADB) 2. The act of listening to, reviewing, and/or recording enemy, one's own, or other friendly forces' communications for the purpose of maintaining standards, improving communications, or for reference, as applicable. See also communications security monitoring.

monitoring - (SEATO) 1. The act of listening to, reviewing, and/or recording one's own or other friendly forces' communications for the purpose of maintaining standards, improving communications, or for reference. 2. The assessing with instruments for known or suspected radioactive hazards.

monkey strap - The tether between a helicopter frame and a door gunners. A safety strap.

Monopoly money - See military pay certificates.

monsoon - Rainy season with southwest wind and massive rainfall between April and October in Southern Asia.

Monster, The Monster - Slang for the PRC-77 radio.

Montagnard - The Vietnamese who lived in the rural hill areas, from the French for mountain dweller.

moonbeam - Marine slang for a flashlight.

Moonglow - A C-47 with flares.

moonshine - 1. Flares. 2. An aircraft that carries flares. 3. A call for assistance from a flare ship.

MOOT - Move out of town. A program to reduce the military presence in towns.

mopping-up - (DOD, NATO, SEATO, CENTO, IADB) The liquidation of remnants of enemy resistance in an area that has been surrounded or isolated, or through which other units have passed without eliminating all active resistance.

morgue - See zipper room.

morning report - The daily report of troop strength, transfers, removal by injury or death and transfers into a unit.

Moron Corps - The soldiers inducted at lower passing rates on the Armed Forces Qualification Test.

mortar - (DOD) Normally a muzzle-loading weapon with either a rifled or smooth bore. It usually has a shorter range than a howitzer, employs a higher angle of fire and has a tube length of 10 to 20 calibers. See also gun; howitzer.

mortar, 107-mm (4.2") (howtar) - (DOD) A Marine Corps modification mounting of a 4.2-inch mortar tube mounted on a 75-mm pack howitzer carriage.

Mortie - A mortar.

MOS - Abbreviation for the Military Occupation Specialty, this is the job title in the military. The specific job code added a number to the MOS to designate a specific job.

mosaic - (DOD, NATO, CENTO) An assembly of overlapping photographs which have been matched to form a continuous photographic representation of a portion of the earth's surface. See also controlled mosaic; uncontrolled mosaic.

mosquito boat - Slang for torpedo boat.

most ricki ticki - Right now, immediately, pidgin used in Okinawa.

mother - Abbreviation for mother fucker, a bastard or a rough assignment or area. Often pronounced "muther".

Mother - Aviation slang for the carrier that is home to a pilot.

mother bomb - The outer shell of a guava bomb.

mother-in-law - A bogie, from the mother-in-law being nuisance or pest.

Mother's Day Medal - See National Defense Service Medal.

Motor-T - Motor transport, the support staff who maintained motorized vehicles.

motorized unit - (DOD, NATO, SEATO, CENTO, IADB) A unit equipped with complete motor transportation that enables all of its personnel, weapons, and equipment to be moved at the same time without assistance from other sources.

mounting - (DOD, NATO, SEATO, CENTO, IADB) 1. All preparations made in areas designated for the purpose, in anticipation of an operation. It includes the assembly in the mounting area, preparation and maintenance within the mounting area, movement to loading points, and subsequent embarkation into ships, craft, or aircraft, if applicable. 2. A carriage or stand upon which a weapon is placed.

mounting area - (DOD, IADB) A general locality where assigned forces of an amphibious or airborne operation, with their equipment, are assembled, prepared, and loaded in shipping and/or aircraft preparatory to an assault. See also embarkation area.

mouse - The pointman on patrol.

mouse ears - See Mickey Mouse ears.

mouse trap - An ambush designed around some bait such as C-rations to draw the enemy into the open.

move out - The order to start walking a patrol.

movement control - (DOD, NATO, SEATO, CENTO, IADB) The planning, routing, scheduling, and control of personnel and supply movements over lines of communication; also an organization responsible for these functions.

movement control officer - (NATO, CENTO) An officer of the movement control organization responsible for the executive control of movement of military personnel and cargo by all means of transport.

movement credit - (NATO, CENTO) The allocation granted to one or more vehicles in order to move over a controlled route in a fixed time according to movement instructions.

movement directive - (DOD) The basic document published by the Department of the Army or the Department of the Air Force, or jointly, which authorizes a command to take action to move a designated unit from one location to another.

movement directive - (IADB) The basic document published by competent authority which authorizes a command to take action to move a designated unit from one location to another.

movement of shipping (in the early days of war) - See area evacuation; port evacuation; shipping movement policy.

movement order - (DOD, IADB) An order issued by a commander covering the details for a move of his command.

movement priority - (NATO, CENTO, IADB) The relative precedence given to each movement requirement.

movement report control center - (DOD, IADB) The controlling agency for the entire movement report system. It has available all information relative to the movements of naval ships and other ships under naval control.

movement report system - (DOD) A system established to collect and make available to certain commands vital information on the status, location, and movement of flag commands, commissioned fleet units, and ships under operational control of the Navy.

movement requirement - (DOD) A stated movement mode and time-phased need for the transport of units, personnel, and/or materiel from a specified origin to a specified destination.

movement restriction - (DOD, NATO, CENTO, IADB) A restriction temporarily placed on traffic into and/or out of areas to permit clearance of or prevention of congestion.

movement table - (DOD, NATO, SEATO, CENTO, IADB) A table giving detailed instructions or data for a move. When necessary, it will be qualified by the words road, rail, sea, air, etc., to signify the type of movement. Normally issued as an annex to a movement order or instruction.

moving havens - (DOD, IADB) Restricted areas established to provide a measure of security to submarines and surface ships in transit through areas in which the existing attack restrictions would be inadequate to prevent attack by friendly forces. See also moving submarine haven; moving surface ship haven.

moving submarine haven - (DOD, IADB) Established by Submarine Notices, surrounding submarines in transit, extending 50 miles ahead, 100 miles behind, and 15 miles on each side of the estimated position of the submarine along the stated track. See also moving havens.

moving surface ship haven - (DOD, IADB) Established by Surface Ship Notices and will normally be a circle with a specified radius centered on the estimated position of the ship or the guide of a group of ships. See also moving havens.

moving target indicator - (DOD, NATO) A radar presentation which shows only targets which are in motion. Signals from stationary targets are subtracted out of the return signal by the output of a suitable memory circuit.

MP - Military Police.

MPC - See Military Pay Certificates.

MQ-74 - Heat seeking targeting radar. Also snake eyes.

MR - Military Region.

Mr. No-Shoulders - A snake.

Mr. Zippo - Flamethrower.

MRE - Meals-Ready to Eat. Food that replaced C-rations. Slang term was Meals Rejected by Everyone.

MRF - Mobile Riverine Force.

MRP - Medical Rehabilitation Platoon. Marine slang was "the overweight platoon" to which recruits needing added physical fitness or weight management were assigned.

MS - Medical Services.

MSE - 1. Medical Services Corps. 2. Military Sealift Command (Navy).

MSG - Master Sergeant (Army).

MSgt - Master Sergeant (Marine Corps, Air Force).

MTB - Motor transport battalion.

MTT - Mobile Training Team.

Mud Marine - Slang for the Marine troops serving in an infantry capacity. See grunt.

mule - See M-274 mule. A small motorized platform for the 106-mm recoilless rifle and used for general hauling of heavy gear.

Multiple Ejector Rack - The rack that held and released ordinance from an aircraft.

multiple independently targetable reentry vehicle - (DOD) A delivery system which places one or more reentry vehicles over each of several separate targets. See also maneuverable reentry vehicle; multiple reentry vehicle; reentry vehicle.

multiple reentry vehicle - (DOD) The reentry vehicle of a delivery system which places more than one reentry vehicle over an individual target. See also maneuverable reentry vehicle; multiple independently targetable reentry vehicle; reentry vehicle.

multipurpose close support weapon - (DOD, IADB) A ground close support weapon capable of defilade delivery of a variety of warheads including nuclear.

mummy sack - Slang for a body bag,

music - (DOD) In air intercept, a term meaning electronic jamming.

MUST - Medical Unit Self-contained, Transportable. As it was inflated, it was nicknamed bubbles.

Mustang - Slang for an officer who rose from enlisted ranks or was given a battlefield promotion.

muster - A call for a quick assembly of troops.

muther - Slang for "mother" in the phrase mother fucker.

mutual aid - (NATO, CENTO, IADB) Arrangements made at government level between one nation and one or more other nations to assist each other. See also integrated logistic support; logistic assistance; reallocation of resources.

mutual support - (DOD, NATO, SEATO, CENTO, IADB) That support which units render each other against an enemy, because of their assigned tasks, their position relative to each other and to the enemy, and their inherent capabilities. See also cross-servicing; support.

MUV - Marine Unit Vietnam.

muzzle brake - (DOD) A device attached to the muzzle of a weapon which utilizes escaping gas to reduce recoil.

muzzle compensator - (DOD) A device attached to the muzzle of a weapon which utilizes escaping gas to control muzzle movement.

muzzle velocity - (DOD, IADB) The velocity of a projectile with respect to the muzzle at the instant the projectile leaves the weapon.

Mxd - Mixed artillery fire.

My _____ - When using the clock code to give a direction, it is assumed that the direction (3 o'clock) is from the speaker's position. For clarity, the speaker may further specify Enemy is at my three o'clock. See clock code.

My fun meter is pegged. - Unhappy, not having any fun.

My god! - See Choi oi.

My shit don't stink. - A phrase of supreme confidence.

mystery meat - A mess hall presentation appearing to be meat but having no clear identity.

N – NOVEMBER

N - Designated in the phonetic military alphabet as "November".

N-1 - See S-1.

N-2 - See S-2.

N-3 - See S-3.

N-4 - See S-4.

N-5 - See S-5.

NA - Not available.

NAB - 1. Naval Air Base. 2. Naval Advisory Board.

nadir - (NATO, CENTO) That point on the celestial sphere directly beneath the observer and directly opposite the zenith.

nadir point - See nadir.

NAF - Naval Air Facility.

nail - To kill.

nails - A flechette rocket.

Naked Fanny (Invert) - Air Force pilot's name for the Air force control center at Nakhon Phanom that assembled enemy air movement on a specialized computer (Invert).

Nam - Short for Vietnam.

nap-of-the-earth flying - To fly as close to the ground as possible, often at 3-6 feet for helicopters.

napalm - (DOD, IADB) A powder employed to thicken gasoline for use in flame throwers and incendiary bombs.

napalm - 1. Slang to drop or spray flaming napalm on the enemy. 2. Any jellied gasoline, specifically Napthhene-Palmitic.

napalm canisters - Empty canisters were used to drop supplies so the resupply mission would go undetected.

nape - See napalm.

narrow gate - Aviation term for setting radar homing and targeting selectors for a narrow range of targets.

NAS - National Academy of Science.

Nasty boat - Swedish made motorized patrol gunboats made by the Nasty company.

National Cemetery of the Pacific- The cemetery and registration point in Honolulu Hawaii for all missing and dead Armed Forces from Vietnam, Korea and WWII.

national censorship - (DOD) The examination and control under civil authority of communications entering, leaving, or transiting the borders of the United States, its territories, or its possessions. See also censorship.

national command - (NATO, SEATO, CENTO, IADB) A command that is organized by, and functions under the authority of, a specific nation. It mayor may not be placed under a (NATO) (SEATO) (CENTO) commander. See also command. (Note: IADB definition ends with the word "nation".)

national command authorities - (DOD) The President, the Secretary of Defense, the Joint Chiefs of Staff, or their authorized successors and alternates.

national commander - (NATO, CENTO) All national commanders, territorial or functional, who are normally not in the allied chain of command.

national component - (IADB) Any national forces of one or more Services under the command of a single national commander.

national component - (NATO, SEATO, CENTO) Any national forces of one or more Services under the command of a single national commander, assigned to any (NATO) (SEATO) (CENTO) commander.

National Defense Service Medal - Awarded to any U.S. service member serving in Vietnam between 1 January 1961 and 14 August 1974 regardless of the area of service or duration. Called the Mother's Day Medal as anyone who ever had a mother got one.

national emergency - (DOD) A condition declared by the President or the Congress by virtue of powers previously vested in them which authorize certain emergency actions to be undertaken in the national interest. Actions to be taken may include partial or total mobilization of national resources.

national force commanders - (NATO, SEATO, CENTO, IADB) Commanders of national forces assigned as separate elements of subordinate allied commands. See also commander(s).

national forces for the defense of the (NATO) (SEATO) (CENTO) area - (NATO, SEATO, CENTO) Non-allocated forces whose mission involves the defense of an area within the (NATO) (SEATO) (CENTO) area of responsibility. See also forces; NATO forces; SEATO forces.

national infrastructure - (DOD, NATO, SEATO, CENTO) Infrastructure provided and financed by a (NATO) (SEATO) (CENTO) member in its own territory solely for its own forces (including those forces assigned to or designated for (NATO) (SEATO) (CENTO)). See also infrastructure.

national intelligence - (DOD, IADB) Integrated departmental intelligence that covers the broad aspects of national policy and national security, is of concern to more than one department or agency, and transcends the exclusive competence of a single department or agency.

national intelligence estimate - (DOD) A strategic estimate of capabilities, vulnerabilities, and probable courses of action of foreign nations which is produced at the national level as a composite of the views of the intelligence community.

national intelligence surveys - (DOD) Basic intelligence studies produced on a coordinate interdepartmental basis and concerned with characteristics, basic resources, and relatively unchanging natural features of a foreign country or other area.

National Liberation Front - NLF, the communist front organization used to gain the affiliation of many noncommunist South Vietnamese with a platform of land reform, expulsion of foreigners, tax reform and other issues.

national military authority - (NATO, SEATO, CENTO, IADB) The governmental agency, such as Ministry of Defense or Service Ministry, empowered to make decisions on military matters on behalf of its country. This authority may be delegated to a military or civilian group or individual at any level appropriate for dealing with allied commanders or their subordinates.

national objectives - (DOD, IADB) Those fundamental aims, goals, or purposes of a nation, as opposed to the means for seeking these ends-toward which a policy is directed and efforts and resources of the nation are applied.

national policy - (DOD, IADB) A broad course of action or statements of guidance adopted by the government at the national level in pursuit of national objectives.

national strategy - (DOD, IADB) The art and science of developing and using the political, economic, and psychological powers of a nation, together with its armed forces, during peace and war, to secure national objectives. See also strategy.

national territorial commander - (NATO, SEATO, CENTO, IADB) A national commander who is responsible for the execution of purely national functions in a specific geographical area. He remains a national territorial commander regardless of any allied status which may be assigned to him. See also commander(s).

native sport - Slang for hunting the enemy.

NATO - North Atlantic Treaty Organization.

NATO forces - See forces allocated to NATO; national forces for the defense of the NATO area; other forces for NATO. See also force(s).

NATO intelligence subject code - (NATO) A numerical framework developed for indexing the subject matter of intelligence documents. In addition to the subject outline, it includes a system of alphabetical or numerical symbols for geographic areas which are used with the subject classification.

NATO unified product - (NATO) A standardized product which is used or is fully suitable for use by all NATO nations for a given end use. See also acceptable product; emergency substitute; standardized product.

natural disaster - See domestic emergencies.

nautical chart - See hydrographic chart.

nautical mile - (DOD, IADB) A measure of distance equal to one minute of arc on the earth's surface. (DOD) The United States has adopted the International Nautical Mile equal to 1,852 meters or 6,076.11549 feet.

Navaids - Navigational aids.

naval augmentation group - (NATO, SEATO, CENTO, IADB) A formed group of escort ships employed to augment the through escort of convoys when passing through areas known or suspected to be threatened by enemy forces.

naval base - (DOD, SEATO) A naval base primarily for support of the forces afloat, contiguous to a port or anchorage, consisting of activities or facilities for which the Navy has operating responsibilities, together with interior lines of communication and the minimum surrounding area necessary for local security. (Normally, not greater than an area of 40 square miles.) See also base complex.

naval beach group - (DOD, NATO, SEATO, CENTO, IADB) A permanently organized naval command, within an amphibious force, comprised of a commander, his staff, a beach-master unit, an amphibious construction battalion, and assault craft unit, designed to provide an administrative group from which required naval tactical components may be made available to the attack force commander and to the amphibious landing force commander to support the landing of one division (reinforced). See also shore party. Note: NATO, SEATO and CENTO definition uses the words "boat unit" instead of "assault craft unit".

naval beach unit - See naval beach group.

naval campaign - (DOD, NATO, CENTO, IADB) An operation or a connected series of operations conducted essentially by naval forces including all surface, subsurface, air, and amphibious troops, for the purpose of gaining, extending, or maintaining control of the sea.

naval construction force - (DOD) The combined construction units of the Navy, including primarily the mobile construction battalions and the amphibious construction battalions. These units are part of the operating forces and represent the Navy's capability for advanced base construction.

naval control of shipping officer - (DOD, NATO, CENTO, IADB) A naval officer appointed to form merchant convoys, control and coordinate the routing and movements of such convoys, independently sailed merchant ships and hospital ships in and out of a port or base, subject to the directions of the Operational Control Authority.

naval control of shipping organization - (DOD) The organization within the Navy which carries out the specific responsibilities of the Chief of Naval Operations to provide for the control and protection of movements of merchant ships in time of war.

naval district - (DOD) A geographically defined area in which one naval officer, designated commandant, is the direct representative of the Secretary of the Navy and the Chief of Naval Operations. The commandant has the responsibility for local naval defense and security and for the coordination of naval activities in the area.

naval flare - A signaling flare used for airplanes or helicopters to see.

Naval Flight Officer - A non-aviator who is trained in aviation support such as a Radio Intercept Officer or Bombardier/Navigator.

naval gunfire liaison team - (DOD, NATO, CENTO, IADB) Personnel and equipment required to coordinate and advise ground/landing forces on naval gunfire employment.

naval gunfire operation center - (DOD, NATO, CENTO, IADB) The agency established in a ship to control the execution of plans for the employment of naval gunfire, process requests for naval gunfire support, and to allot ships to forward observers. Ideally located in the same ship as the supporting arms coordination center.

naval gunfire spotting team - (DOD, IADB) The unit of a shore fire control party which designates targets, controls commencement, cessation, rate, and types of fire, and spots fire on the target. See also field artillery observer; spotter.

naval operation - (DOD, IADB) A naval action, or the performance of a naval mission, which may be strategic, tactical, logistic, or training; the process of carrying on or training for naval combat to gain the objectives of any battle or campaign.

naval or marine (air) base - (DOD, SEATO) An air base for support of naval or marine air units, consisting of landing strips, seaplane alighting areas, and all components of related facilities for which the Navy or Marine Corps has operating responsibilities, together with interior lines of communication and the minimum surrounding area necessary for local security. (Normally, not greater than an area of 20 square miles.) See also base complex.

naval port control office - (DOD, IADB) The authority established at a port or port complex to coordinate arrangements for logistic support and harbor services to ships under naval control and to otherwise support the naval control of shipping organization.

naval stores - (DOD, NATO, CENTO) Any articles or commodities used by a naval ship or station, such as equipment, consumable supplies, clothing, petroleum, oils, and lubricants, medical supplies, and ammunition. See also supplies.

naval support area - (DOD, NATO, SEATO, CENTO, IADB) A sea area assigned to naval ships detailed to support an amphibious operation. See also fire support area.

naval tactical data system - (DOD) Consists of a complex of data inputs, user consoles, converters, adapters, and radio terminals interconnected with high-speed general purpose computers and its stored programs. Combat data is collected, processed, and composed into a picture of the overall tactical situation which enables the force commander to make rapid, accurate evaluations and decisions.

NAVFORV - Naval Forces Vietnam.

navigation head - (DOD, NATO, SEATO, CENTO, IADB) A transshipment point on a waterway where loads are transferred between water carriers and land carriers. A navigation head is similar in function to a railhead or truckhead.

navigational grid - (NATO) A series of straight lines, superimposed over a conformal projection and indicating grid North, used as an aid to navigation. The interval of the grid lines generally of a multiple of 60 or 100 nautical miles. See also military grid.

Navy Achievement Medal - For leadership and professionalism by enlisted personnel.

Navy and Marine Corps Medal - Awarded for heroism in combat. It ranks just under the Distinguished Flying Cross.

Navy Cross - The second highest military award for bravery, along with the Air Force Cross and the Distinguished Service Cross.

navy hat - See Dixie Cup.

Navy SEAL - See SEAL.

NBC - Non-battle casualty.

NC - Nurse Corps.

NCAP - See night cap. Pronounced N cap.

NCM - Navy Court Martial.

NCMR - Navy Court of Military Review.

NCO - 1. Non-Commissioned Officer, usually a squad or platoon leader. 2. Derogatory: No chance outside to suggest no civilian employment would be available.

NCO Club - The club on a military base for noncommissioned officers.

NDP - Night Defensive Position.

near miss (aircraft) - (DOD, IADB) Any circumstance in flight where the degree of separation between two aircraft is considered by either pilot to have constituted a hazardous situation involving potential risk of collision.

near real time - (DOD) Delay caused by automated processing and display between the occurrence of an event and reception of the data at some other location. See also real time; reporting time interval.

neatlines - (NATO) The lines that bound the body of a map, usually parallels and meridians. Also called sheetlines.

NEC - Naval Enlisted Classified. The numerical code of all Navy and Coast Guard enlisted jobs.

necessary - Latrine.

neckerchief - The 24x36" bandana.

need to know - (DOD, SEATO, IADB) A criterion used in security procedures which requires the custodians of classified information to establish, prior to disclosure, that the intended recipient must have access to the information to perform his official duties.

negative - (DOD) As used in air intercept, means cancel, or no.

negative - (NATO, CENTO) In photography: 1. (black and white) An image on film, plate or paper in which the normal tones of the subject are reversed. 2. (color) An image on film, plate, or paper, in which colors appear as their complements.

negative objective - Radio code for search and rescue personnel that the pilot was found dead.

negative phase of the shock wave - (DOD) The period during which the pressure falls below ambient and then returns to the ambient value. See also positive phase of the shock wave; shock wave.

negative photo plane - (NATO, CENTO) The plane in which a film or plate lies at the moment of exposure.

negative suppression - An order not to return fire.

neglect - (DOD) In artillery and naval gunfire support, a report to the observer or spotter to indicate that the last round(s) was fired with incorrect data and that the round(s) will be fired again using correct data.

negligible risk (nuclear) - (DOD, NATO, CENTO, IADB) A degree of risk where personnel are reasonably safe, with the exceptions of dazzle or temporary loss of night vision. Note: NATO and CENTO term does not use the qualifier "(nuclear)".

Neptune - (DOD, IADB) A twin reciprocating engine, twin-jet, all weather, long-range, land-based antisubmarine aircraft. It is capable of carrying a varied assortment of search radar, nuclear depth charges, and homing torpedoes. It can be used for search, patrol, barrier, hunter-killer, and convoy escort operations. Designated as P-2.

NESN - An indication modifying a military definition that NATO approval has been granted for a term to be used in military use by the English speaking NATO nations (U.S., Canada, and United Kingdom).

Nestle's Quick - Slang for a NCO fresh out of school. From the trademarked chocolate powder to make instant chocolate milk.

net - Short from network, meaning radio frequency.

net (communications) - (DOD, NATO, SEATO, CENTO, IADB) An organization of stations capable of direct communications on a common channel or frequency.

net call sign - (DOD, NATO, SEATO, CENTO, IADB) A call sign which represents all stations within a net. See also call sign.

net weight - (DOD) Weight of a ground vehicle without fuel, engine oil, coolant, on vehicle materiel, cargo, or operating personnel.

net weight - (NATO, CENTO) Weight of a ground vehicle fully equipped and serviced for operation, including fuel, lubricants, coolant, vehicle tools and spares, but without crew, personal equipment, traction devices or payload. See also gross weight.

net weight (transport vehicles) - (SEATO, IADB) Weight of the vehicle fully equipped and serviced for operation, including fuel, lubricants, coolant, vehicle tools, and equipment, but without crew, personal equipment, traction devices, or payload. See also laden weight (transport vehicles); unladen weight (transport vehicles).

net, chain, cell system - (DOD) Patterns of clandestine organization, especially for operational purposes. Net is the broadest of the three; it usually involves: a. a succession of echelons; and b. such functional specialists as may be required to accomplish its mission. When it consists largely or entirely of non-staff employees, it may be called an agent net. <u>Chain</u> focuses attention upon the first of these elements; it is commonly defined as a series of agents and informants who receive instructions from and pass information to a principal agent by means of cutouts and couriers. <u>Cell system</u> emphasizes a variant of the first element of net; its distinctive feature is the grouping of personnel into small units that are relatively isolated and self-contained. In the interest of maximum security for the organization as a whole, each cell has contact with the rest of the organization only through an agent of the organization and a single member of the cell. Others in the cell do not know the agent, and nobody in the cell knows the identities or activities of members of other cells.

neutral state - (DOD, IADB) In international law, a state which pursues a policy of neutrality during war. See also neutrality.

neutrality - (DOD, IADB) In international law, the attitude of impartiality, during periods of war, adopted by third states toward belligerents and recognized by the belligerents, which creates rights and duties between the impartial states and the belligerents. In a United Nations enforcement action, the rules of neutrality apply to impartial members of the United Nations except so far as they are excluded by the obligation of such members under the United Nations Charter.

neutralization fire - (DOD, NATO, SEATO, CENTO, IADB) Fire which is delivered to hamper and interrupt movement, and/or the firing of weapons. See also fire.

neutralize - (DOD, IADB) As pertains to military operations, to render ineffective or unusable.

neutralize - Slang for kill.

neutralize track - (DOD) As used in air intercept, to render the target being tracked ineffective or unusable.

neutron induced activity - (DOD, NATO, CENTO, IADB) Radioactivity induced in the ground or an object as a result of direct irradiation by neutrons.

Never happen. - Slang for: 1. A very unlikely occurrence. 2. A hopeful statement that something will not happen.

new dos - New soldier in country and showing up in the late afternoon. Pronounced new-dues.

new man rule - The new man in an infantry unit is assigned to walk point. This both reduces exposure of seasoned troops as well as testing the new guy.

new meat - A new arrival.

new puppy - An ensign or second lieutenant.

newbie - Replacement personnel. Also spelled newby.

newfer - Replacement personnel.

Newport - A deep-water port built by the U.S. near Saigon.

Newyorkians - Puerto Ricans born in New York usually with minimal English skills.

next - Due to rotate out soon. See short.

Next of Kin - Nearest designated relative to be notified in the event of death or serious wound.

NFG - No fucking good.

NFO - Naval Flight Officer. An officer who is not a pilot, but in the aviation wing. Also called Non-Flying Object or No Future Occupation.

NFOD - No fear of death. Aviation term for the bravado pilots show.

NFSN - An indication modifying a military definition that NATO approval has been granted for a term to be used in military use by the French speaking NATO nations (France and Belgium).

NFWS - Navy Fighter Weapons School. The Topgun school.

NFZ - No Fire Zone.

NG - National Guard.

niact - Night action communication. A radio monitored 24 hours a day providing immediate night response.

Niagara - The operation of saturation bombing on preselected targets in Vietnam in support of the attack on Khe Sanh. The operation began on January 14, 1968 and ended March 31, 1968. During this intensive joint services operation involving Air Force, Navy and Marine fighter-bombers and bombers flew over 2,400 tactical fighter-bomber sorties and 2,700 bomber flights dropping over 110,000 tons.

Nice vapes. - Aviation compliment to a pilot putting out vapor trails from a high speed low altitude or high G force flight. A flashy fly by.

nickel - Slang for the number five.

nickel night - The practice of serving drinks for five cents on a set night of the week at bars on a base.

nicknames (exercise) - (NATO, SEATO, CENTO, IADB) Nicknames may be assigned formally or informally by any appropriate authority to an event, project, maneuver, exercise, test, or other activity for purposes other than to provide for the security of information. Nicknames will always consist of at least two separate words and should be short. Their most common use is for naming maneuvers and exercises.

nigger - Offensive term for Negro. Often slurred in a faux-Southern accent to be "nigra", offensive but not as blatantly so.

night angel - Slang for night flare dropping missions.

night belongs to Charlie - Phrase used to express the aversion of U.S. troops to night fighting.

night cap - (DOD) Night combat air patrol (written NCAP).

night effect - (DOD, NATO, CENTO) An effect mainly caused by variations in the state of polarization of reflected waves, which sometimes result in errors in direction finding bearings. The effect is most frequent at nightfall.

night fire - 1. The training class in flare and starlight scope use. 2. Night fire in the field.

night hawks - Night helicopter flights.

night kits - A gear package flown in to troops in the field including engineering stakes, barbed wire, bug juice, food, water, ammunition and mines.

night location - Spending the night in the field.

night owls - Code for the night operations to stop the enemy on the Ho Chi Minh Trail.

night patrol - Night field operations.

night vision - Special battery operated goggles increasing vision at night.

Nighthawk - The UH-1 Huey helicopter with spotlights on it.

Nike Ajax - (DOD, IADB) A mobile or fixed site, surface-to-air guided missile system designed to intercept and destroy manned bombers and air-breathing missiles. Designated as MIM-3.

Nike Hercules - (DOD, IADB) A mobile or fixed site, surface-to-air guided missile system, with nuclear warhead capability, designed to intercept and destroy manned bombers and air-breathing missiles at greater ranges and altitudes than the Nike Ajax. It also has a surface-to-surface capability. Designated as MIM-14.

Nike X - (DOD) An antimissile missile system for defense against ballistic missiles. The system includes a multifunction array radar which performs target acquisition, discrimination and tracking functions; a missile site radar which performs missile command and track, and target track and search functions; data processing equipment consisting of high speed digital computers; and Sprint missiles.

Nike Zeus - (IADB) A solid-propellant, guided, surface-to-air, antimissile missile, with nuclear warhead capability, for attacking intercontinental ballistic missiles. Designated as XLIM-49A.

nine - 1. Expressed in radio code and slang as niner. 2. The position to the left of the pilot in clock code.

Nine nine nine (999) - See Priority 999.

nine rule card - A card given to incoming troops with nine rules of conduct while in

Vietnam. In summary: 1. We are guests, 2. Join the people by learning their language and customs, 3. Treat women with respect, 4. Make friends, 5. Give Vietnamese the right of way, 6. Be alert for security issues, 7. Do not attract attention, 8. Avoid displays of wealth or status, 9. Be responsible for your actions and reflect honor on yourself and your country.

nine-to-five war - Slang for: 1. Business as usual. 2. No one gives a shit.

niner - Slang for the number nine.

ninety - Slang for the 90-mm long gun on a tank.

ninety day loss - Troops with less than 90 days left to serve were rotated to the rear and had little interest in their duties.

ninety day wonders - Graduates of the Officers Candidate School during the expedited training program.

ninety RCL, 90-mm RCL - See M-67 RCL.

ninety SPAT, 90-mm SPAT - See M-56 SPAT.

ninety-one Band-Aids - Slang for the MOS of an Army medic from 91-B, referencing the trademarked adhesive bandage.

ninety-one bedpans - Slang for the MOS of an Army medic from 91-B.

NIS - Naval investigative Service. Comparable to detectives in a civilian police force.

nit noi - No big deal, small shit, from the Vietnamese.

NJP - Non-judicial punishment.

NL - See night location.

NLF - National Liberation Front.

NLT - No later than.

NM - Nautical mile.

no chance outside - Derogatory term for NCO.

no fire/no fly - Slang for the area over which others should not fly or fire as troops were on the ground.

no fucking good - See Number ten.

No Future Occupation - See NFO.

no joy - (DOD) In air intercept, a code meaning, I have been unsuccessful, or I have no information.

no joy - 1. Aviation slang for failure to make a contact or kill. 2. General slang for any failure.

no sweat - Slang for an easy task, an achievable objective, an easy mission, no problem.

no visible results - Bomb damage assessment report classification.

no-clap medal - Good conduct medal.

No-Doze mission - Slang for a psychological operation using loudspeakers to play music and speeches for propaganda, often at night. From the No-Doze tablets to aid in staying awake.

no-fire line - (DOD) A line short of which artillery or ships may not fire except on request or approval of the supported commander, but beyond which they may fire at any time without danger to friendly troops.

no-fire line - (NATO, SEATO, CENTO, IADB) A line short of which artillery or ships do not fire except on request or approval of the supported commander, but beyond which they may fire at any time without danger to friendly troops.

no-go pills - See Polymagna.

no-load - Aviation slang on a carrier for a guy who has no future. An underachiever. From the test firing of the catapult before launching a plane that is done without the weight of a plane (load) on it.

no-no war in never-neverland - The secret war in Laos.

no-wind position - See air position.

node - (DOD) A location in a mobility system where a movement requirement is originated, processed for onward movement, or terminated.

NOFORN - A classification term meaning a document or message is not for foreign eyes.

Noggies - Australian slang for NVA/VC.

noise - 1. Radio static. 2. Gossip, idle chatter.

noise discipline - The amount of noise a soldier made in getting into position.

NOK - Next of Kin.

Nomex - Fire retardant in flight suits, trademarked brand.

nominal focal length - (DOD, NATO, CENTO) An approximate value of the focal length, rounded off to some standard figure, used for the classification of lenses, mirrors, or cameras.

nominal scale - See principal scale; scale.

nominal weapon - (DOD, NATO, CENTO, IADB) A nuclear weapon producing a yield of approximately 20 kilotons. See also kiloton weapon; subkiloton weapon.

non-commissioned officer - Ranks of E-5 to E-10. NCO.

Non-Flying Object - See NFO.

non-hacker - A poor soldier, one who is not hacking it, failing

non-qual - A Marine who fails to qualify at the rifle range.

non-vital cargo - (NATO, CENTO, IADB) A cargo of some value, loaded in peacetime, but which is not immediately required in its country of destination. See also cargoes.

nonair transportable - (DOD) That which is not transportable by air by virtue of dimension, weight and/or special characteristics or restrictions.

nonaligned state - (DOD, IADB) A state which pursues a policy of nonalignment.

nonalignment - (DOD, IADB) The political attitude of a state which does not associate, or identify itself with the political ideology or objective espoused by other states, groups of states, or international causes, or with the foreign policies stemming therefrom. It does not preclude involvement, but expresses the attitude of no precommitment to a particular state (or bloc) or policy before a situation arises.

nonappropriated funds - (DOD) Funds generated by Department of Defense military and civilian personnel and their dependents and used to augment funds appropriated by the Congress to provide a comprehensive, morale-building, welfare, religious, educational, and recreational program, designed to improve the well-being of military and civilian personnel and their dependents.

nonbattle casualty - (DOD, NATO, SEATO, CENTO, IADB) A person who is not a battle casualty, but who is lost to his organization by reason of disease or injury, including persons dying from disease or injury, or by reason of being missing where the absence does not appear to be voluntary or due to enemy action or to being interned. See also battle casualty; wounded.

noncom - NCO.

noncombatant - Military personnel not in combat by assignment, such as a cook.

noncontiguous facility - (DOD) A facility for which the Service indicated has operating responsibility, but which is not located on, or in the immediate vicinity of, a base complex of that Service. Its area includes only that actually occupied by the facility, plus the minimum surrounding area necessary for close-in security. See also base complex.

nondeferrable issue demand - (DOD) Issue demand related to specific periods of time which will not exist after the close of those periods, even though not satisfied during the period.

noneffective sortie - (DOD, IADB) Any aircraft dispatched which for any reason fails to carry out the purpose of the mission. Abortive sorties are included.

nonexpendable supplies and material - (DOD, IADB) Supplies which are not consumed in use and which retain their original identity during the period of use, such as weapons, machines, tools, and equipment.

nonexpendable supplies and material - (NATO, SEATO, CENTO) Items which are not consumed in use and which retain their original identity during the period of use, such as weapons, and which normally require further accounting.

nonfixed medical treatment facility - (DOD, IADB) A medical treatment facility designed to be moved from place to place, including medical treatment facilities afloat.

nonprogram aircraft - (DOD) All aircraft, other than active and reserve categories, in the total aircraft inventory, including X-models; aircraft for which there is no longer a requirement either in the active or reserve category; and aircraft in the process of being dropped from the total aircraft inventory. See also aircraft.

nonrecurring demand - (DOD) A request made on a one time basis for material. The material may be used to fill initial allowances, increases in stock levels or allowances, and for one time repair or rebuild requirements.

nonregistered publication - (DOD, NATO, SEATO, CENTO, IADB) A publication which bears no register number and for which periodic accounting is not required.

nonscheduled units - (DOD, NATO, CENTO, IADB) Units of the landing force held in readiness for landing during the initial unloading period, but not included in either scheduled or on-call waves. This category usually includes certain of the combat support units and most of the combat service support units with higher echelon (division and above) reserve units of the landing force. Their landing is directed when the need ashore can be predicted with a reasonable degree of accuracy.

Nordo - Slang for: 1. An aircraft without a radio communication capacity. 2. A person with less than acceptable skills.

normal impact effect - See cardinal point effect.

normal intelligence reports - (DOD, NATO, CENTO, IADB) A category of reports used in the dissemination of intelligence, which is conventionally used for the immediate dissemination of individual items of intelligence. See also intelligence reporting; specialist intelligence reports.

normal operations - (DOD) Generally and collectively the broad functions which the commander of a unified combatant command undertakes when he is assigned responsibility for a given geographic or functional area. Except as otherwise qualified in certain unified command plan paragraphs which relate to particular commands, "normal operations" of a unified command commander include: planning for and execution of operations in contingencies; limited war and general war; planning and conduct of cold war activities; planning for and administration of military assistance; and maintaining the relationships and exercising the directive or coordinating authority prescribed in JCS Pubs. 2, 3, and 4.

normal rules - The normal rules of engagement apply, that is the ability to return fire if fired on.

normal zone of fire - (IADB) The area within the zone of fire for which an artillery unit is normally responsible and within which its fire is normally directed. See also zone of fire.

NOROC - Armored panels in a helicopter.

NORS - Not operationally ready.

NORS-G - Not operationally ready - grounded.

northing - (NATO, CENTO, IADB) Northward (that is, from bottom to top) reading of grid values on a map.

Not worth a rat's ass - 1. Not worth the effort. 2. Motto of the U.S. tunnel rat team that sought out the enemy in tunnels whose motto was "Non Gratum Anus Rodentum".

notched - Getting or giving a minor wound.

notional ship - (DOD) A theoretical or average ship of anyone category used in transportation planning, e.g., a Liberty ship for dry cargo; a T-2 tanker for bulk petroleum, oils, and lubricants; a personnel transport of 2,400 troop spaces.

November - The military phonetic alphabet designation for the letter "N".

November Foxtrot Whisky - Phonetic alphabet for "no fucking way", an emphatic negative.

NS - Naval Station.

NSAM - National Security Action Memorandum.

NSC - National Security Council.

NSSM - National Security Study Memorandum Nuclear weapons, while not used in Vietnam, there was the capacity to do so.

Nth country - (DOD) A reference to additions to the group of powers possessing nuclear weapons-the next country of a series to acquire nuclear capabilities.

nub bush - A black female, from Nubian.

nuclear accident - See nuclear weapon(s) accident.

nuclear airburst - (DOD, NATO, SEATO, CENTO, IADB) The explosion of a nuclear weapon in the air, at a height greater than the maximum radius of the fireball. See also nuclear exoatmospheric burst; types of burst.

nuclear burst - See types of burst.

nuclear cloud - (DOD, NATO, CENTO, IADB) An all inclusive term for the volume of hot gases, smoke, dust, and other particulate matter from the nuclear bomb itself and from its environment, which is carried aloft in conjunction with the rise of the fireball produced by the detonation of the nuclear weapon.

nuclear column - (DOD, NATO, CENTO) A hollow cylinder of water and spray thrown up from an underwater burst of a nuclear weapon, through which the hot, high-pressure gases formed in the explosion are vented to the atmosphere. A somewhat similar column of dirt is formed in an underground explosion. See also camouflet; crater.

nuclear coordination - (DOD) A broad term encompassing all the actions involved with planning nuclear strikes including liaison between commanders for the purposes of satisfying support requirements or because of the extension of weapons effects into the territory of another.

nuclear damage (land warfare) - (DOD, NATO, CENTO, IADB) 1. light damage - Damage which does not prevent the immediate use of equipment or installations for which it was intended. Some repair by the user may be required to make full use of the equipment or installations. 2. moderate damage - Damage which prevents the use of equipment or installations until extensive repairs are made. 3. severe damage - Damage which prevents use of equipment or installations permanently.

nuclear damage assessment - (DOD, NATO, CENTO, IADB) The determination of the damage effect to the population forces, and resources resulting from actual nuclear attack. It is performed during the trans-attack and post-attack periods. It does not include the function of evaluating the operational significance of nuclear damage assessments.

nuclear defense - (DOD, NATO, CENTO, IADB) The methods, plans, and procedures involved in establishing and exercising defensive measures against the effects of an attack by nuclear weapons or radiological warfare agents. It encompasses both the training for, and the implementation of, these methods, plans, and procedures. See also radiological defense.

nuclear detonation detection and reporting system - (DOD, NATO, CENTO) A system deployed to provide surveillance coverage of critical friendly target areas and indicate place, height of burst, yield, and ground zero of nuclear detonations. See also bomb alarm system.

nuclear dud - (DOD) A nuclear weapon, which when launched at or emplaced on a target, fails to provide any explosion of that part of the weapon designed to produce the nuclear yield.

nuclear energy - (DOD) All forms of energy released in the course of a nuclear fission or nuclear transformation. See also atomic energy.

nuclear equipoise - (DOD) Not to be used. See nuclear stalemate.

nuclear exoatmospheric burst - (DOD) The explosion of a nuclear weapon above the sensible atmosphere (above 120 kilometers) where atmospheric interaction is minimal. See also nuclear airburst.

nuclear incident - (DOD) An unexpected event involving a nuclear weapon, facility, or component resulting in any of the following, but not constituting a nuclear weapon(s) accident: a. an increase in the possibility of explosion or radioactive contamination; b. errors committed in the assembly, testing, loading, or transportation of equipment, and/or the malfunctioning of equipment and materiel which could lead to an unintentional operation of all or part of the weapon arming and/or firing sequence, or which could lead to a substantial change in yield, or increased dud probability; and c. any act of God, unfavorable environment or condition resulting in damage to the weapon, facility, or component.

nuclear incident - (NATO, CENTO, IADB) An unexpected event involving a nuclear weapon, facility, or component but not constituting a nuclear weapon(s) accident.

nuclear logistic movement - (DOD) The transport of nuclear weapons in connection with supply or maintenance operations. Under certain specified conditions, combat aircraft may be used for such movements.

nuclear logistic movement - (NATO, CENTO, IADB) The transport of nuclear weapons or components of nuclear weapons in connection with supply or maintenance operations.

nuclear nations - (DOD, NATO, CENTO) Military nuclear powers and civil nuclear powers. See also nuclear power.

nuclear parity - (DOD, IADB) A condition at a given point in time when opposing forces possess nuclear offensive and defensive systems approximately equal in overall combat effectiveness.

nuclear power - (DOD, NATO, CENTO) Not to be used without appropriate modifier. See civil nuclear power; major nuclear power; military nuclear power. See also nuclear nations.

nuclear radiation - (DOD, NATO, CENTO) Particulate and electromagnetic radiation emitted from atomic nuclei in various nuclear processes. The important nuclear radiations, from the weapons standpoint, are alpha and beta particles, gamma rays, and neutrons. All nuclear radiations are ionizing radiations, but the reverse is not true; X-rays, for example, are included among ionizing radiations, but they are not nuclear radiations since they do not originate from atomic nuclei.

nuclear reactor - (DOD) A facility in which fissile material is used on a self-supporting chain reaction (nuclear fission) to produce heat and/or radiation for both practical application and research and development.

nuclear round - See complete round.

nuclear safety line - (DOD, NATO, IADB) A line selected, if possible, to follow well defined topographical features and used to delineate levels of protective measures, degrees of damage or risk to friendly troops, and/or to prescribe limits to which the effects of friendly weapons may be permitted to extend.

nuclear stalemate - (DOD, IADB) A concept which postulates a situation wherein the relative strength of opposing nuclear forces results in mutual deterrence against employment of nuclear forces.

nuclear strike warning - (DOD, IADB) A warning of impending friendly or suspected enemy nuclear attack.

nuclear support - (DOD) The use of nuclear weapons against hostile forces in support of friendly air, land, and naval operations. See also immediate nuclear support; preplanned nuclear support.

nuclear surface burst - (DOD, NATO, CENTO, IADB) An explosion of a nuclear weapon at the surface of land or water; or above the surface, at a height less than the maximum radius of the fireball. See also types of burst.

nuclear transmutation - (DOD) Artificially induced modification (nuclear reaction) of the constituents of certain nuclei, thus giving rise to different nuclides.

nuclear underground burst - (DOD, NATO, CENTO, IADB) The explosion of a nuclear weapon in which the center of the detonation lies at a point beneath the surface of the ground. See also types of burst.

nuclear underwater burst - (DOD, NATO, CENTO, IADB) The explosion of a nuclear weapon in which the center of the detonation lies at a point beneath the surface of the water. See also types of burst.

nuclear vulnerability assessment - (DOD, NATO, CENTO, IADB) The estimation of the probable effect on population, forces and resources from a hypothetical nuclear attack. It is performed predominantly in the pre-attack period; however, it may be extended to the trans-attack or post-attack periods.

nuclear warfare - (DOD, NATO, CENTO, IADB) Warfare involving the employment of nuclear weapons.

nuclear warning message - (DOD) A warning message which must be disseminated to all affected friendly forces any time a nuclear weapon is to be detonated if effects of the weapon will have impact upon those forces.

nuclear weapon - (DOD, NATO, CENTO, IADB) A device in which the explosion results from the energy released by reactions involving atomic nuclei, either fission or fusion, or both.

nuclear weapon degradation - (DOD) The degeneration of a nuclear warhead to such an extent that the anticipated nuclear yield is lessened.

nuclear weapon employment time - (DOD, NATO, CENTO, IADB) The time required for delivery of a nuclear weapon after the decision to fire has been made.

nuclear weapon exercise - (DOD, NATO, CENTO) An operation not directly related to immediate operational readiness. It includes removal of a weapon from its normal storage location, preparing for use, delivery to an employment unit, the movement in a ground training exercise to include loading aboard an aircraft or missile and return to storage. It may include any or all of the operations listed above, but does not include launching or flying operations. Typical exercises include aircraft generation exercises, ground readiness exercises, ground tactical exercises, and various categories of inspections designed to evaluate the capability of the unit to perform its prescribed mission. See also immediate operational readiness; nuclear weapon maneuver.

nuclear weapon maneuver - (DOD, NATO, CENTO) An operation not directly related to immediate operational readiness. It may consist of all those operations listed for a nuclear weapon exercise but is extended to include fly-away in combat aircraft not to include expenditure of the weapon. Typical maneuvers include nuclear operational readiness maneuvers and tactical air operations. See also immediate operational readiness; nuclear weapon exercise.

nuclear weapon(s) accident - (DOD, NATO, CENTO, IADB) Any unplanned occurrence involving loss or destruction of, or serious damage to, nuclear weapons or their components which results in an actual or potential hazard to life or property.

nuclear weapons state - See military nuclear power.

nuclear yields - (DOD, IADB) The energy released in the detonation of a nuclear weapon, measured in terms of the kilotons or megatons of trinitrotoluene required to produce the same energy release. Yields are categorized as: very low (less than 1 kiloton); low (1 kiloton to 10 kilotons); medium (over 10 kilotons to 50 kilotons); high (over 50 kilotons to 500 kilotons); or very high (over 500 kilotons). See also nominal weapon; subkiloton weapon.

nuclear yields - (NATO, CENTO) The energy released in the detonation of a nuclear weapon, measured in terms of kilotons or megatons of trinitrotoluene required to produce the same energy release.

nuclear, biological, chemical area of observation - (NATO, CENTO) A geographical area consisting of several nuclear, biological, chemical zones of observation, comparable to the area of responsibility of an Army or Army Group or an Allied Tactical Air Force.

nuclear, biological, chemical collection center - (NATO, CENTO) The agency responsible for the receipt, consolidation, and evaluation of reports of nuclear detonations, biological and chemical attacks, and resultant contamination within the nuclear, biological, chemical zone of observation and for the production and dissemination of appropriate reports and warnings. Agencies with similar functions, but with responsibilities for only part of the nuclear, biological, chemical zone of observation may be termed sub-collection centers.

nuclear, biological, chemical control center - (NATO, CENTO) The agency responsible for coordinating the efforts of all collection centers within the nuclear, biological, chemical area of observation. A control center may assume the function of the collection center for the area in which it is located.

nuclear, biological, chemical zone of observation - (NATO, CENTO) A geographical area which defines the responsibility for reporting and collecting information on enemy or unidentified nuclear detonations, biological or chemical attacks, and resultant contamination. Boundaries of nuclear, biological, chemical zones of observation, which may overlap, will be determined by the organization of the forces concerned.

nucleon - (DOD) The common name for a constituent particle of the atomic nucleus. It is applied to protons and neutrons, but it is intended to include any other particle that is found to exist in the nucleus.

nuclide - (DOD) All nuclear species, both stable (about 270) and unstable (about 500), of the chemical elements, as distinguished from the two or more nuclear species of a single chemical element which are called isotopes.

nudets - See nuclear detonation detection and reporting system.

nugget - Aviation slang for a pilot on his first carrier tour of duty.

nuisance minefield (land mine warfare) - (DOD, NATO, SEATO, CENTO, IADB) A minefield laid to delay and disorganize the enemy and to hinder his use of an area or route. See also minefield (land mine warfare).

numb nuts - A stupid or incompetent person.

numba one - The best (rarely pronounced as number one).

numba ten - The worst.

numba ten thousand - The very worst.

number of rounds - (DOD) A command or request used to indicate the number or projectiles per tube to be fired on a specified target.

number one - See numba one.

number ten - See numba ten.

number ten thousand - See numba ten thousand.

number tens, number 10s - GI slang for an illegal mixture of drugs, usually involving Speed and/or Quaaludes. Also Dimes.

numbered fleet - (DOD) A major tactical unit of the Navy immediately subordinate to a major fleet command and comprising various task forces, elements, groups, and units for the purpose of prosecuting specific naval operations. See also fleet.

numbered wave - See wave.

Numbers - The use of radio and the need for clarity in communication led to the use of words for numbers that could be confused for others as follows: 0 - ball, zippo, 00 - balls, 1 - one, 2 - two, duce, 3 - three, 4 - four, quad, 5 - nickel, fiver, 6 - six, 7 - seven, 8 - eight, 9 - niner, 10 - dime.

numby (pronounced nummy) - A stupid or incompetent person.

numerical scale - See representative fraction.

NVA - 1. The North Vietnamese Army. 2. A soldier in the North Vietnamese Army.

NVR - See no visible results.

nylon - Parachute.

nylon letdown - Aviation slang for the parachute drop after an ejection from a disabled airplane.

NZ - New Zealand.

O – OSCAR

O - 1. Designated in the phonetic military alphabet as "Oscar". 2. The designations, by pay grade, for Officers.

O-1 - Birddog. The Cesena made single engine high-wing spotter plane with the ability to go low and slow (which made an easy target).

O-1 - Second Lieutenant (Army, Marine Corps, Air Force), Ensign (Navy and Coast Guard).

O-10 - General (Army, Marine Corps) General Air Force Chief of Staff (Air Force), Admiral Chief of Naval Operations/Commandant of the Coast Guard (Navy, Coast Guard). See four star general.

O-11 - General of the Army (Special- during wartime only.) (Army), Fleet Admiral (Special- during wartime only.) (Navy), General of the Air Force (Special- during wartime only.) (Air Force). There is no rank of this level for the Coast Guard or Marine Corps.

O-2 - First Lieutenant (Army, Marine Corps, and Air Force), Lieutenant Junior Grade (Navy, Coast Guard).

O-2 - Super Skymaster, "Push me, Pull you", Mixmaster, the Cessna twin engine, Forward Air Control plane with excellent visibility. Used primarily by the Air Force.

O-3 - Captain (Army, Marine Corps, and Air Force), Lieutenant (Navy, Coast Guard).

O-4 - Major (Army, Marine Corps, and Air Force), Lieutenant Commander (Navy, Coast Guard).

O-5 - Lieutenant Colonel (Army, Marine Corps, and Air Force), Commander (Navy, Coast Guard).

O-6 - Colonel (Army, Marine Corps, and Air Force), Captain (Navy, Coast Guard).

O-7 - Brigadier General (Army, Marine Corps, and Air Force), Rear Admiral (Navy, Coast Guard). See one star general.

O-8 - Major General (Army, Marine Corps, Air Force), Rear Admiral (Navy, Coast Guard). See two star general.

O-9 - Lieutenant General (Army, Marine Corps, Air Force), Vice Admiral (Navy, Coast Guard). See three star general.

o-dark-thirty - Unspecified time in the very early morning while still dark. Also o'dark thirty.

o-o line - (DOD) A line for the coordination of field artillery observation, designated by the corps or force artillery commander and dividing primary responsibility for observation between the corps or force artillery and division artillery.

o'clock ____ - (DOD) In clock code section and at range indicated (heading of own aircraft being twelve o'clock). See also clock code position.

O' Club - Officer's Club. Also O Club.

O1E - Cessna light observation plane.

oak leaf cluster - Decoration to indicate more than one of the medal has been awarded. Called rat turds in the field.

OASD(PA) - Office of the Assistant Secretary of Defense, Public Affairs.

OASD(SA) - Office of the Assistant Secretary of Defense, Systems Analysis.

OB - Order of Battle.

objective - (DOD, NATO, SEATO, CENTO, IADB) The physical object of the action taken, e.g., a definite tactical feature, the seizure and/or holding of which is essential to the commander's plan.

objective area - (DOD, NATO, SEATO, CENTO, IADB) A defined geographical area within which is located an objective to be captured or reached by the military forces. This area is defined by competent authority for purposes of command and control.

objective force level - (DOD, IADB) The level of military forces that needs to be attained within a finite time frame and resource level to accomplish approved military objectives, missions, or tasks. See also military requirement.

obligated reservist - (DOD) An individual who has a statutory requirement imposed upon him by the Military Selective Service Act of 1967 or Section 651, Title 10 U.S.C. to serve on active duty in the armed forces or to serve while not on active duty in a reserve component for a period not to exceed that prescribed by the applicable statute.

oblique air photograph - (DOD, NATO, CENTO) An air photograph taken with the camera axis directed between the horizontal and vertical planes. Commonly referred to as an oblique: a. high oblique: One in which the apparent horizon appears; and b. low oblique: One in which the apparent horizon does not appear.

oblique air photograph strip - (DOD) Photographic strip composed of oblique air photographs.

obliquity - (DOD) The characteristic in wide-angle or oblique photography which portrays the terrain and objects at such an angle and range that details necessary for interpretation are seriously masked or are at a very small scale, rendering interpretation difficult or impossible.

observation post - (DOD, NATO, SEATO, IADB) A position from which military observations are made, or fire directed and adjusted, and which possesses appropriate communications; may be airborne. Note: SEATO definition ends with the word "communications". Note: most commonly a daylight visual observation as opposed to listening post which is night and sound based.

observed fire - (DOD, NATO, SEATO, CENTO, IADB) Fire for which the points of impact or burst can be seen by an observer. The fire can be controlled and adjusted on the basis of observation. See also fire.

observed fire procedure - (DOD, NATO, SEATO, CENTO, IADB) A standardized procedure for use in adjusting indirect fire on a target.

observer identification - (DOD) The first element of a call for fire. It is used to establish communication and to identify the observer or spotter.

observer-target line - (DOD) An imaginary straight line from the observer or spotter to the target. See also spotting line.

observer-target range - (DOD) The distance along an imaginary straight line from the observer or spotter to the target.

observers (exercise) - (IADB) Representatives who are invited to attend military exercises as observers.

observers (exercise) - (NATO, CENTO) Representatives from nations who are invited to attend as observers at exercises.

observers (exercise) - (SEATO) Representatives from SEATO nations who are invited to attend as observers at SEATO exercises.

obstruction - (NATO) A building or other obstacle rising up far enough above the surrounding surface to create a hazard to aircraft in flight.

occupation currency - See military currency.

occupation of position - (NATO, CENTO, IADB) Movement into and proper organization of an area to be used as a battle position.

occupied territory - (DOD, IADB) Territory under the authority and effective control of a belligerent armed force. The term is not applicable to territory being administered pursuant to peace terms, treaty, or other agreement, express or implied, with the civil authority of the territory. See also civil affairs agreement.

ocean convoy - (DOD, NATO, CENTO, IADB) A convoy whose voyage lies in general outside coastal waters. See also convoy.

ocean manifest - (DOD, NATO, CENTO, IADB) A detailed listing of the entire cargo loaded into anyone ship showing all pertinent data which will readily identify such cargo and where and how the cargo is stowed.

ocean station ship - (DOD, NATO, CENTO, IADB) A ship assigned to operate within a specified area to provide several services including search and rescue, meteorological information, navigational aid and communications facilities. Note: IADB definition ends with the word "communications".

oceanography - (DOD, NATO, CENTO) The study of the sea, embracing and integrating all knowledge pertaining to the sea and its physical boundaries, the chemistry and physics of sea water, and marine biology.

OCO - Office of Civil Operations in 1966 and the first part of 1967. Name changed to CORDS in 1967.

OCS - Officers Candidate School.

OCS Manual - Slang for a comic book.

OD - 1. Olive drab, the shade of green used in almost everything that is military issued. 2. Officer of the Day.

OE-1 - The Cessna observation plane.

OER - Officer Effeciency Report. The personnel and performance evaluation.

off - To kill.

office hours - Marine slang for an official inquiry or reprimand.

office pogue - Marine slang for a Marine on desk duty.

officer conducting the exercise - (NATO, SEATO, CENTO, IADB) The officer responsible for the conduct of an allocated part of the exercise both from the ORANGE and BLUE aspects. He will issue necessary supplementary instructions. In addition, he may be an exercise commander.

officer in tactical command (naval) - (DOD, NATO, CENTO, IADB) The senior officer present eligible to assume command or the officer to whom he has delegated tactical command.

officer material - Sardonic, not officer material, a goof off.

Officer of the Day - The on duty officer, a rotating administrative assignment. See OD.

officer scheduling the exercise - (NATO, SEATO, CENTO, IADB) The officer who originates the exercise and orders it to take place. He will issue basic instructions which will include the designation of exercise areas, the allocation of forces, and the necessary coordinating instructions. He will also designate the officers conducting the exercise.

official information - (DOD) Information which is owned by, produced by, or is subject to the control of the United States Government.

offset distance (nuclear) - (DOD, NATO, CENTO, IADB) The distance the desired ground zero or actual ground zero is offset from the center of an area target or from a point target.

offset point - (DOD) In air intercept, the offset point is a point in space relative to a target's flight path toward which an interceptor is vectored and from which the final or a preliminary turn to attack heading is made.

offshore patrol - (DOD, NATO, CENTO, IADB) A naval defense patrol operating in the outer areas of navigable coastal waters. It is a part of the naval local defense forces consisting of naval ships and aircraft and operates outside those areas assigned to the inshore patrol.

OH-13 - Bell helicopter. Also Sioux, Flying Bubble, Goldfish bowl

OH-23 - A three seat observation helicopter. Also Raven.

OH-58 - A light observation helicopter. Also Kiowa.

OH-6 - LOCH, Sperm, light observation helicopter made by Hughes with a crew of two and space for four combat equipped troops in the aft cargo area. These brought troops to battle areas, removed troops and could stay on station to call in artillery to the enemy that it had spotted.

OIC - Officer in Charge.

oil spot - A pacification program which selected a central spot for a base and the anti-Viet Cong activity was designed to spread from it like an oil spot.

oiler - (NATO, SEATO, CENTO, IADB) A naval or merchant tanker specially equipped and rigged for replenishing other ships at sea.

OJs - Marijuana cigarettes dipped in a liquid opium solution.

OJT - On the job training.

Old Breed - The First Marine Division.

old man - The commanding officer. Usually The Old Man.

Old Reliables - Ninth Infantry Division.

Oley - Radio code for wounded in action.

olive drab - The Army green color.

olive green - See olive drab.

OMH - Officer's Mess Hall.

on berth - (DOD) Said of a ship when it is properly moored to a quay, wharf, jetty, pier, or buoy or when it is at anchor and available for loading or discharging passengers and cargo.

on call - (DOD, NATO, CENTO, IADB) The term used to signify that a prearranged concentration, air strike, or final protective fire may be called for. See also call for fire; call mission.

on call target (nuclear) - (DOD) A planned nuclear target other than a scheduled nuclear target for which a need can be anticipated but which will be delivered upon request rather than at a specific time. Coordination and warning of friendly troops and aircraft are mandatory.

on call wave - See wave.

on line - The walking pattern in the jungle when a group could be fired on. This side-by-side approach allowed any soldier to shoot immediately without firing on another, as would occur if walking behind one another in a line.

on profile - Temporary medical restriction from some duty.

on scene commander - (DOD) The person designated to coordinate the rescue efforts at the rescue site.

on station - (DOD) 1. In air intercept usage, I have reached my assigned station. 2. In close air support and air interdiction, airborne aircraft in position to attack targets, or to perform the mission designated by control agency.

on station time - (DOD) The time an aircraft can remain on station. May be determined by endurance or orders.

on target - (DOD) In air intercept, my fire control director(s)/system(s) have acquired the indicated contact and is (are) tracking successfully.

on the carpet - In trouble.

on the deck - (DOD) At minimum altitude.

on the mouse - Aviation slang for the carrier flight deck radio system that had deck crew wearing huge earphone that looked like Mickey Mouse ears, that blocked flight noise and let them communicate with pilots and other crew.

on the rag - Pissed off, cranky, derogatory reference to menstruation.

one - Expressed in radio code or slang as penny.

one buck - Code for units that are stateside but ready to deploy to Vietnam on 48 hour notice.

one day's supply - (DOD, NATO, SEATO, CENTO, IADB) A unit or quantity of supplies adopted as a standard of measurement, used in estimating the average daily expenditure under stated conditions. It may also be expressed in terms of a factor, e.g., rounds of ammunition per weapon per day.

one hundred mile per hour tape - See hundred miles an hour tape.

one oh six - The 106-mm artillery.

one oh worst - The 101st Airborne Division.

One shot. One kill. - Marine sniper motto.

one-fifty-five Howitzer, 155-mm Howitzer - See M-114A1.

one-fifty-five SPA, 155-mm self propelled Howitzer - See M-109 155-mm SPA.

one-five-one, one-fifty-one - The M-151 Jeep.

one-forty rocket, 140-mm rocket - See BM14/21.

one-oh-five - The 105-mm artillery in general.

one-oh-five Howie, 105-Howie - See M-101A1 Howitzer.

one-oh-five recoilless, 105-mm recoilless - See M-40A1 RCL.

one-oh-five SPA, 105-mm SPA - See M-108 105-mm RCL.

one-oh-seven mortar, 107-mm mortar - See M-107/M38 mortar.

one-oh-seven recoilless, 107-mm recoilless - See PRC RCL.

one-oh-seven rocket, 107-mm rocket - See Type 63 rocket.

one-oh-six RCL, 106-mm RCL - See M-40A1 RCL.

one-seventy-five gun, 175-mm self-propelled gun - See M-107 175-mm gun.

one-seventy-fives, 175s - See M-107 175-mm gun.

one-sixty mortar, 160-mm mortar - See M43 160-mm mortar.

one-star general - Brigadier General.

one-thirty AA, 130-mm AAA - North Vietnamese antiaircraft gun.

one-thirty rocket, 130-mm rocket - Soviet-made long range cannon.

one-twenty millimeter mortar - Soviet made mortar.

one-twenty mortar, 120-mm mortar - See M38 mortar.

one-twenty-seven rocket, 127-mm rocket - See Zuni.

one-twenty-two - The 122-mm Communist rocket which had a range of 22 kilometers when using a booster.

one-twenty-two rocket, 122-mm rocket - See DKZ-B.

One, The One - The officer in charge of administration.

ONI - 1. Office of Navy Investigation. 2. Office of Naval Intelligence.

Ontos (rifle, self-propelled, full-tracked, multiple, 106-mm) - (DOD, IADB) A self-propelled, direct-fire, and antitank weapon. Armament consists of six 106-mm recoilless rifles, one 30 caliber machine gun, and four 50 caliber spotting rifles. Designated as M50.

OODA - Aviation term for the pilot's mental preparation for flight or battle, which is continually repeated: observation, orientation, decision, and action.

OP - See Observation Post.

OP2E - Twin engine propeller driven aircraft.

opcon - Operation control.

open improved storage space - (DOD, IADB) Open area which has been graded and hard surfaced or prepared with topping of some suitable material so as to permit effective material handling operations. See also storage.

open sheaf - (DOD) 1. The lateral distribution of the fire of two or more pieces so that adjoining points of impact or points of burst are separated by the maximum effective width of burst of the type shell used. 2. Term used in a "call for fire" to indicate that the observer desires a wider sheaf than the one being employed. See also parallel sheaf; sheaf; special sheaf.

open unimproved wet spaces - (DOD, IADB) That water area specifically allotted to and usable for storage of floating equipment. See also storage.

operating forces - (DOD, IADB) Those forces whose primary missions are to participate in combat and the integral supporting elements thereof. See also combat forces; combat service support elements; combat support elements.

operating level of supply - (DOD, IADB) The quantities of materiel required to sustain operations in the interval between requisitions or the arrival of successive shipments. These quantities should be based on the established replenishment period (monthly, quarterly, etc.). See also level of supply.

operation - (DOD, NATO, SEATO, CENTO, IADB) A military action or the carrying out of a strategic, tactical, service, training, or administrative military mission;

the process of carrying on combat, including movement, supply, attack, defense, and maneuvers needed to gain the objectives of any battle or campaign.

operation annexes - (DOD, IADB) Those amplifying instructions which are of such a nature, or are so voluminous or technical, as to make their inclusion in the body of the plan or order undesirable.

Operation Freeze - The policy of the Marine Corps to restrict a unit to quarters, do a roll call after a fragging incident, and continue the restriction until a suspect was identified.

Operation Frequent Wind - Code for the plan to evacuate the last Americans from Saigon.

Operation Homecoming - The operation resulting in the release and return of POWs after the Peace Accords were signed.

operation map - (DOD, IADB) A map showing the location and strength of friendly forces involved in an operation. It may indicate predicted movement and location of enemy forces. See also map.

operation order - (DOD, IADB) A directive issued by a commander to subordinate commanders for the purpose of effecting the coordinated execution of an operation.

operation order - (NATO, SEATO, CENTO) A directive, usually formal, issued by a commander to subordinate commanders for the purpose of effecting the coordinated execution of an operation. See also operation plan.

operation plan - (DOD, NATO, CENTO) 1. A plan for a single or series of connected operations to be carried out simultaneously or in succession. It is usually based upon stated assumptions and is the form of directive employed by higher authority to permit subordinate commanders to prepare supporting plans and orders. 2. The designation "plan" is usually used instead of "order" in preparing for operations well in advance. An operation plan may be put into effect at a prescribed time, or on signal, and then becomes the operation order. See also operation order.

operation plan - (SEATO, IADB) 1. A plan for operations extending over a considerable space and time and usually based on stated assumptions. It may cover a single operation or a series of connected operations to be carried out simultaneously or in succession. It is the form of directive employed by high echelons of command in order to permit subordinate commanders to prepare their supporting plans or orders. 2. The designation "plan" is often used instead of "order" in preparing for operations well in advance. An operation plan may be put into effect at a prescribed time, or on signal, and then becomes the operation order. See also operation order.

operational chain of command - (DOD, NATO, SEATO, CENTO, IADB) The chain of command established for a particular operation or series of continuing operations. See also administrative chain of command; chain of command.

operational characteristics - (DOD, IADB) Those military characteristics which pertain primarily to the functions to be performed by equipment, either alone or in conjunction with other equipment, e.g., for electronic equipment, operational characteristics include such items as frequency coverage, channeling, type of modulation, and character of emission.

operational characteristics - (NATO, CENTO) The specific military qualities of performance and capability required of an item of equipment to enable it to meet an agreed operational need.

operational command - (DOD, IADB) Those functions of command involving the composition of subordinate forces, the assignment of tasks, the designation of objectives and the authoritative direction necessary to accomplish the mission. Operational command should be exercised by the use of the assigned normal organizational units through their responsible commanders or through the commanders of subordinate forces established by the commander exercising operational command. It does not include such matters as administration, discipline, internal organization, and unit training except when a subordinate commander requests assistance. (DOD) (The term is synonymous with operational control and is uniquely applied to the operational control exercised by the commanders of unified and specified commands over assigned forces in accordance with the National Security Act of 1947, as amended and revised (10 United States Code 124).) See also administrative control; control.

operational command - (NATO, SEATO, CENTO) The authority granted to a commander to assign missions or tasks to subordinate commanders, to deploy units, to reassign forces, and to retain or delegate operational and/or tactical control as may be deemed necessary. It does not of itself include administrative command or logistical responsibility. (NATO, CENTO) May also be used to denote the forces assigned to a commander. See also command.

operational control - (NATO, SEATO, CENTO) The authority granted to a commander to direct forces assigned so that the commander may accomplish specific missions or tasks which are usually limited by function, time, or location; to deploy units concerned, and to retain or assign tactical control of those units. It does not include authority to assign separate employment of components of the units concerned. Neither does it, of itself, include administrative or logistic control. See also operational command.

operational control authority (naval) - (DOD, NATO, CENTO, IADB) The naval commander responsible for the control of movement and for protection of all allied merchant shipping within specified geographic limits.

operational environment - (DOD, IADB) As pertains to the military, it is a composite of the conditions, circumstances, and influences which affect the employment of military forces and which bear on the decisions of the commander.

operational evaluation - (DOD, IADB) The test and analysis of a specific end item or system, insofar as practicable under Service operating conditions, in order to determine if quantity production is warranted considering: a. the increase in military effectiveness to be gained; and b. its effectiveness as compared with currently available items or systems, consideration being given to: (1) personnel capabilities to maintain and operate the equipment; (2) size, weight, and location considerations; and (3) enemy capabilities in the field. See also technical evaluation.

operational intelligence - (DOD, IADB) Intelligence required for planning and executing all types of operations. See also intelligence.

operational intelligence - (SEATO) Intelligence required by operational commanders for planning and executing all types of operations.

operational interchangeability - (NATO, SEATO, CENTO, IADB) Ability to substitute one item for another of different composition or origin without loss in effectiveness, accuracy, and safety of performance.

operational missile - (DOD, NATO, SEATO, CENTO, IADB) A missile which has been accepted by the using Services for tactical and/or strategic use.

operational readiness - (DOD) The capability of a unit, ship, weapon system, or equipment to perform the missions or functions for which it is organized or designed. May be used in a general sense or to express a level or degree of readiness.

operational reserve - (DOD, NATO, SEATO, CENTO, IADB) An emergency reserve of men and/or material established for the support of a specific operation. See also reserve supplies.

operational testing - (DOD) A continuing process of evaluation which may be applied to either operational personnel or situations to determine their validity or reliability.

operationally ready - (DOD) 1. as applied to a unit, ship, or weapon system - Capable of performing the missions or functions for which organized or designed. Incorporates both equipment readiness and personnel readiness. 2. as applied to equipment - Available and in condition for serving the functions for which designed. 3. as applied to personnel-Available and qualified to perform assigned missions or functions.

operations center - See command center.

operations research - (DOD, IADB) The analytical study of military problems, undertaken to provide responsible commanders and staff agencies with a scientific basis for decision on action to improve military operations. Also known as operation research; operations analysis.

OPLAN - Operations plan.

Opns - Operations.

opportune lift - (DOD) That portion of lift capability available for use after planned requirements have been met.

opportunity target - See target of opportunity.

opportunity to excel - Aviation slang for a really bad task or assignment, which is nearly impossible to complete due to a lack of resources, time or mission. Also called an opportunity.

opposite numbers - (DOD) Officers (including foreign) having corresponding duty assignments within their respective military Services or establishments.

opposition - The enemy.

OpSum - Operation Summary.

optical axis - (NATO, CENTO) In a lens element, the straight line which passes through the centers of curvature of the lens surfaces. In an optical system, the line formed by the coinciding principal axes of the series of optical elements.

optical landing system - (DOD, IADB) A shipboard gyrostabilized or shore-based device which indicates to the pilot his displacement from a preselected glide path. See also ground-controlled approach.

optimum height - (DOD, NATO, CENTO) The height of an explosion which will produce the maximum effect against a given target.

optimum height of burst - (DOD) For nuclear weapons, the optimum height of burst for a particular target (or area) is that at which it is estimated a weapon of a specified energy yield will produce a certain desired effect over the maximum possible area. See also types of burst.

Option IV - Code for the secret plan for the evacuation of the Embassy and other key personnel from Saigon, ultimately implemented 29 April 1975.

orange forces - (IADB) Denotes those forces used in an enemy role during exercises. See also force(s).

orange forces - (NATO, SEATO, CENTO) Denotes those forces used in an enemy role during (NATO) (SEATO) (CENTO) exercises. See also force(s).

oranges (sour) - (DOD) In air intercept, a code meaning weather is unsuitable for aircraft mission.

oranges (sweet) - (DOD) In air intercept, a code meaning weather is suitable for aircraft mission.

orbit determination - (DOD) The process of describing the past, present, or predicted position of a satellite in terms of orbital parameters.

orbit point - (DOD, NATO, SEATO, CENTO, IADB) A geographically or electronically defined location over land or water, used in stationing airborne aircraft.

orbital injection - (DOD) The process of providing a space vehicle with sufficient velocity to establish an orbit.

orbiting - (DOD) In air intercept, means circling, or circle and search.

order - (DOD, NATO, SEATO, CENTO, IADB) A communication, written, oral, or by signal, which conveys instructions from a superior to a subordinate. (DOD, IADB) In a broad sense, the terms "order" and "command" are synonymous. However, an order implies discretion as to the details of execution whereas a command does not.

order and shipping time - (DOD, IADB) The time elapsing between the initiation of stock replenishment action for a specific activity and the receipt by that activity of the materiel resulting from such action. Order and shipping time is applicable only to materiel within the supply system, and it is composed of the distinct elements, order time and shipping time. See also level of supply.

order of battle - (DOD, NATO, SEATO, CENTO, IADB) The identification, strength, command structure, and disposition of the personnel, units, and equipment of any military force.

order of battle card (intelligence) - (NATO, CENTO, IADB) A single, or master, standardized card containing basic information on each enemy ground forces unit/formation providing all pertinent order of battle information.

order time - (DOD, IADB) 1. The time elapsing between the initiation of stock replenishment action and submittal of requisition or order. 2. The time elapsing between the submittal of requisition or order and shipment of materiel by the supplying activity. See also order and shipping time.

orderly room - The administrative office on base, which may include a recreation room for relaxation.

ordinary priority - (DOD) A category of immediate mission request which is lower than "urgent priority" but takes precedence over "search and attack priority," e.g., a target which is delaying a unit's advance but which is not causing casualties. See also immediate mission request; priority of immediate mission requests.

ordnance - (DOD) Explosives, chemicals, pyrotechnic and similar stores, e.g., bombs, guns and ammunition, flares, smoke, napalm.

Oreo - Slang for a black soldier who acted white, after the trademarked cookie that is a white cream filling between two black wafers.

organic - (DOD, IADB) Assigned to and forming an essential part of a military

organization (DOD) Organic parts of a unit are those listed in its table of organization for the Army, Air Force, and Marine Corps, and are assigned to the administrative organizations of the operating forces for the Navy.

organization of the ground - (DOD, NATO, SEATO, CENTO, IADB) The development of a defensive position by strengthening the natural defenses of the terrain and by assignment of the occupying troops to specific localities.

organizational equipment - (DOD, IADB) Referring to method of use, signifies that equipment, other than individual equipment, which is used in furtherance of the common mission of an organization or unit. See also equipment.

organizational maintenance - (DOD, IADB) That maintenance which is the responsibility of and performed by a using organization on its assigned equipment. Its phases normally consist of inspecting, servicing, lubricating, adjusting, and the replacing of parts, minor assemblies, and subassemblies.

organize - The assignment of personnel to activate a unit.

original destination (merchant shipping) - (NATO, CENTO, IADB) The original final destination of a convoy or of an individual ship (whether in convoy or independent). This is particularly applicable to the original destination of a voyage begun in peacetime. See also final destination; immediate destination; intermediate destination; terminal destination.

originating medical facility - (DOD, NATO, SEATO, CENTO, IADB) A medical facility that initially transfers a patient to another medical facility.

originator - (DOD, IADB) The command by whose authority a message is sent. The responsibility of the originator includes the responsibility for the functions of the drafter and releasing officer. See also drafter; releasing officer.

Orion - (DOD, IADB) A four-engine, turbo-prop, all-weather, long-range, land-based antisubmarine aircraft. It is capable of carrying a varied assortment of search radar, nuclear depth charges, and homing torpedoes. It can be used for search, patrol, hunter-killer, and convoy escort operations. Designated as P-3.

ORP - Objective Rally Point. The location designated for after-battle reunion to do a head count and determine the next action.

orthomorphic projection - (NATO, CENTO) One in which the scale, although varying throughout the map, is the same in all directions at any point, so that very small areas are represented by correct shape and bearings are correct.

Oscar - 1. The military phonetic alphabet designation for the letter "O". 2. Slang for Radio Telephone Operator.

oscillating type mine - (NATO, SEATO, CENTO, IADB) A moored mine hydrostatically controlled which maintains a pre-set depth below the surface of the water independently of the rise and fall of the tide. See also mine.

ossifer - Slang for officer.

other forces - (NATO, CENTO) Forces not assigned or earmarked for assignment to a (NATO) (CENTO) command which may, at some future date, cooperate with (NATO) (CENTO) forces or be placed under the operational command or operational control of a (NATO) (CENTO) commander in certain circumstances which should be specified.

other forces for SEATO - (SEATO) Forces, if any, not assigned or earmarked for a SEATO command but which might be available to a SEATO command in certain circumstances which should be specified. See also SEATO forces.

other theater - The secret war in Laos.

OTS - Officer Training School.

out - 1. No longer in Vietnam. 2. No longer in the service.

outbound traffic - (DOD) Traffic originating in continental United States destined for overseas or overseas traffic moving in a general direction away from continental United States.

outer fix - (DOD) A fix in the destination terminal area, other than the approach fix, to which aircraft are normally cleared by an air route traffic control center or a terminal area traffic control facility, and from which aircraft are cleared to the approach fix or final approach course.

outer transport area - (DOD, IADB) The area which is used for unloading operations during the initial phases of the assault and which is located inside the antisubmarine defense perimeter, but outside the effective range of enemy shore batteries. See also transport area.

outgoing/outgoing mail - Artillery fire directed toward the enemy.

outline map - (NATO) A map which represents just sufficient geographic information to permit the correlation of additional data placed upon it.

outline plan - (DOD, NATO, SEATO, CENTO, IADB) A preliminary plan which outlines the salient features or principles of a course of action prior to the initiation of detailed planning.

outside - Civilian life, usually "the outside".

outstanding - 1. Said mockingly of events or persons who are less than acceptable. 2. Marine slang for excellence, well done.

OUTUS - Outside the U.S.

OV-10 - Bronco, A twin turboprop made by North American as a counterinsurgency reconnaissance with armaments. It was faster and more armed than the O-2. Used by Air Force and Marines, designed for Marines.

OV-1B - Mohawk, the reconnaissance aircraft used exclusively by the Army for tactical battlefield support intelligence gathering. Made by Grumman, the twin turboprop aircraft was fitted with a variety of complex sensors including the "sniffers" which were troop detection devices, "SLAR" which was side looking airborne radar, infrared and other gear.

over - (DOD) A spotting, or an observation, used by a spotter or an observer to indicate that a burst(s) occurred beyond the target in relation to the spotting line.

over and under - The M-203 rifle with rifle barrel over a grenade launcher.

over the beach operations - See logistics over the shore operations.

over the fence - Crossing a border on a mission.

over the hill - 1. Marine slang for going AWOL. 2. Desertion.

over the hump - 1. Marine slang for passing the halfway point in an enlistment. 2. Generally a halfway mark on completion of any task.

over-the-shoulder bombing - (DOD, IADB) A special case of loft bombing where the bomb is released past the vertical in order that the bomb may be thrown back to the target. See also loft bombing; toss bombing.

overhead - Navy and Marine slang for the ceiling.

overhead clearance - (DOD, NATO, CENTO) The vertical distance between the route surface and any obstruction above it.

overhead grenade - A booby trap using a grenade above a man's head. A trip wire is attached to the pin in the grenade. When tripped, the pin is removed and the grenade explodes.

overlap - (DOD, NATO, CENTO) 1. In photography, the amount by which one photograph includes the same area covered by another, customarily expressed as a percentage. The overlap between successive air photographs on a flight line is called forward lap. The overlap between photographs in adjacent parallel flight lines is called side lap. 2. In cartography, that portion of a map or chart which overlaps the area covered by another of the same series.

overlap tell - (DOD) The transfer of information to an adjacent facility concerning tracks detected in the adjacent facilities' area of responsibility. See also track telling.

overlap zone - (DOD) A designated area on each side of a boundary between adjacent tactical air control systems wherein coordination and interaction between the systems is required.

overlay - (DOD, NATO, CENTO, IADB) A printing or drawing on a transparent or semi-transparent medium at the same scale as a map, chart, etc., to show details not appearing or requiring special emphasis on the original.

overlay - (SEATO) A transparent sheet bearing information designed to add or emphasize details when superimposed on a particular chart, map, drawing, tracing, or other representation.

overpressure - (DOD, NATO, CENTO, IADB) The pressure resulting from the blast wave of an explosion. It is referred to as "positive" when it exceeds atmospheric pressure and "negative" during the passage of the wave when resulting pressures are less than atmospheric pressure.

overprint - (DOD, NATO, CENTO, IADB) Information printed or stamped upon a map or chart, in addition to that originally printed, to show data of importance or special use.

override - 1. To issue added orders altering the initial order. 2. A tank commander's control panel allowing him to operate all controls and weapon systems which normally would be operated by his crew.

overrun control - (NATO, CENTO) Equipment enabling a camera to continue operating for a predetermined number of frames or seconds after normal cutoff.

overseas - (DOD) All locations, including Alaska and Hawaii, outside the continental United States.

overseas search and rescue region - (DOD) Overseas unified command areas (or portions thereof not included within the inland region or the maritime region). See also search and rescue region.

overshoot - 1. Aviation term in combat for flying past the aiming point of a target plane. 2. Aviation term in landing (carrier or airfield) for going past the point where wheels should touchdown. 3. Artillery term for rounds falling long. See long.

overt operation - (DOD) The collection of intelligence openly, without concealment.

overtake velocity - Aviation term for the speed required to catch up to another plane.

Ox - The M51 HRV.

P – PAPA

P - 1. Designated in the phonetic military alphabet as "Papa". 2. Piasters, Vietnamese currency that was replaced in 1978 by the dong.

P-2 - See Neptune.

P-3 - See Orion.

P-38 - 1. Small folding can opener used to remove the lid of a tin can that was packed in the C-ration box, about 38-mm in length. It was often worn on the dog tag chain which passed through a small hole in the opener. It was often used as an emergency screwdriver or small knife. Made by J.W. Speaker (stamped US Speaker), Washburn Corp. (stamped US Androck), and Mallin hardware (stamped US Mallin Shelby Ohio or US Shelby Co.). Nicknamed John Wayne. 2. Occasionally the P-38 was called by the name stamped on the side: Speaker, Shelby or Androck. 3. A prop plane of World War II vintage used as a spotter plane.

P-4 - Navy torpedo boat.

P-5 - Navy seaplane.

P-51 - A larger version of the P-38 lid remover, about 51-mm in length.

P-day - (DOD) That point in time at which the rate of production of an item available for military consumption equals the rate at which the item is required by the armed forces.

P2, P^2, P Square - Slang for an individual who is trying to drive you crazy.

PACAF - Pacific Air Force.

pace (ground forces:) - (NATO, IADB) The regulated speed of a column or element as set by the pace setter in order to maintain the average speed prescribed. (Note: IADB term does not use the qualifier "(ground forces)".)

pace man - The soldier who counted steps and reported to the patrol leader as each 100 meters was completed to provide location information, not to set the speed of travel.

pace setter - (DOD, NATO, CENTO) An individual, selected by the column commander, who travels in the lead vehicle or element to regulate the column speed and establish the pace necessary to meet the required movement order.

Pacific Stars and Stripes - The newspaper for troops.

Pacification - The tactic and objective of the American war effort in Vietnam by restoring the peace, development of democracy and reforming society through the U.S. efforts to provide protection and support to rural population to counter the Viet Cong influence.

pack - The radio pack.

packaged bulk petroleum - (IADB) Bulk petroleum which because of operational necessity is packaged and supplied (stored, transported, and issued) in 5-gallon cans or 55-gallon drums. See also petroleum.

packaged forces - (DOD) Force of varying size and composition preselected for specific missions in order to facilitate planning and training.

packaged petroleum - (IADB) Petroleum products (generally lubricants, greases, and specialty items) normally packaged by a manufacturer and procured, stored, transported, and issued in containers having a fill capacity of 55 gallons or less. See also petroleum.

packaged petroleum products - (DOD, NATO CENTO) Petroleum products (generally lubricants, oils, grease, and specialty items) normally packaged by a manufacturer and procured, stored, transported and issued in containers having a fill capacity of 55 United States gallons (45 imperial gallons) or less.

packboard - A flat board on a backpack harness to which irregularly shaped items could be secured for carrying.

PACOM - Pacific Command.

PACV - Patrol Air Cushioned Vehicle. See hovercraft.

padding - (DOD, IADB) Extraneous text added to a message for the purpose of concealing its beginning, ending, or length.

Paddles - Slang name for Landing Signal Officer on a carrier.

paddy foot - Trench foot.

paddy strength - Slang for combat strength.

padlocked - Aviation term for having a visual lock on an enemy aircraft. See locked.

PAE bag - Parachutist's Adjustable Equipment bag. The small pack carried on the front, as the parachute was on the back. Pronounced pay bag.

page 12 - See dash twelve.

painted - Aviation term for scanned on the cockpit radar.

pajamas - Nickname for traditional Vietnamese attire.

pallet - (DOD, NATO, CENTO) A flat base for combining stores or carrying a single item to form a unit load for handling, transportation and storage by materials handling equipment.

palletized unit load - (DOD, NATO, CENTO, IADB) Quantity of any item, packaged or unpackaged, which is arranged on a pallet in a specified manner and securely strapped or fastened thereto so that the whole is handled as a unit.

palm - Napalm. Also 'palm.

pan - (DOD) In air intercept, a code meaning the calling station has a very urgent message to transmit concerning the safety of a ship, aircraft, or other vehicle, or of some person on board or within sight.

Panama Control - The aviation control center in Da Nang.

pancake - (DOD) In air intercept, a code meaning land, or I wish to land (reason may be specified; e.g., "pancake ammo," "pancake fuel").

panel code - (DOD, NATO, CENTO) A prearranged code designed for visual communications usually between friendly units by making use of marking panels. See also marking panel.

panel code - (SEATO, IADB) A prearranged code designed for visual communications between ground units and friendly aircraft. See also marking panel.

panoramic air camera - (DOD, NATO) An air camera which, through a system of moving optics or mirrors, scans a wide area of the terrain, usually from horizon to horizon. The camera may be mounted vertically or obliquely within the aircraft, to scan across or along the line of flight.

panoramic ground camera - (DOD, NATO) A camera which photographs a wide expanse of terrain by rotating horizontally about the vertical axis through the center of the camera lens.

Papa - The military phonetic alphabet designation for the letter "P".

Papa Sierra - Platoon sergeant.

papa-san - Slang for older Vietnamese men.

paper pukes - Rear echelon personnel.

paper soldiers - Rear echelon personnel.

para drag drop - (NATO, CENTO) Ultra low level airdrop technique using the drag of an arrester parachute to extract and halt airdrop loads.

parachute - 1. Aviation term for the rescue device that fills with air and slows a fall of parachuting aviators, paratroopers, or goods being airdropped. 2. Infantry and artillery term for the parachutes on flares. See chute.

parachute deployment height - (DOD, NATO, CENTO) The height above the intended impact point at which the parachute or parachutes are fully deployed.

parachute flare - A small flare rocket on a parachute providing bright illumination.

parade deck - Parade ground.

parade formation - Aviation term for an aerial formation of multiple planes in which each plane is at 45 degrees off the leader's wing forming a V. Similar to cruise formation but with minimal distance between planes. This is the show-stopper flight formation at aviation shows in which there can be as little as a few feet between the wingtips as in the display flights of the Blue Angels.

paradrop - (NATO, CENTO) Delivery by parachute of personnel or cargo from an aircraft in flight. See also airdrop.

parajumper - Parachuting rescue specialists trained in medical, survival and survival who jumped from helicopters to rescue downed pilots.

parallactic angle - See angle of convergence.

parallax - (NATO, CENTO) In photography, the apparent displacement of the position of an object in relation to a reference point, due to a change in the point of observation.

parallax difference - (NATO, CENTO) The difference in displacement of the top of an object in relation to its base, as measured on the two images of the object on a stereo pair of photographs.

parallel sheaf - (DOD) A sheaf in which the planes of fire of all pieces are parallel. See also open sheaf; sheaf; special sheaf.

parallel staff - (DOD, NATO, SEATO, CENTO, IADB) A staff in which one officer from each nation, or Service, working in parallel, is appointed to each post. See also staff; integrated staff.

paramilitary forces - (DOD, I, IADB) Forces or groups which are distinct from the regular armed forces of any country, but resembling them in organization, equipment, training, or mission.

paramilitary operation - (SEATO, IADB) An operation undertaken by a paramilitary force.

paraphrase - (DOD, SEATO, IADB) To change the phraseology of a message without changing its meaning.

pararescue team - (DOD, IADB) Specially trained personnel qualified to penetrate to the site of an incident by land or parachute, render medical aid, accomplish survival methods, and rescue survivors.

Paris Accords - See Agreement on Ending the War and Restoring the Peace in Vietnam.

Paris Peace Accords - See Agreement on Ending the War and Restoring the Peace in Vietnam.

Parker 51 booby trap - Retreating Vietnamese often left booby trapped items they expected GIs to take for souvenirs. This fountain pen was often used.

parlimentaire - (DOD, IADB) An agent employed by a commander of belligerent forces in the field to go in person within the enemy lines for the purpose of communicating or negotiating openly and directly with the enemy commander.

parrot - (DOD) Identification Friend or Foe transponder equipment.

partial storage monitoring - (DOD, IADB) A periodic inspection of major assemblies or components for nuclear weapons, consisting mainly of external observation of humidity, temperatures, and visual damage or deterioration during storage. This type of inspection is also conducted prior to and upon completion of a movement.

partisan warfare - (DOD) Not to be used. See guerrilla warfare.

party packs - A pack of ten marijuana cigarettes.

pass - (DOD, IADB) A short tactical run or dive by an aircraft at a target; a single sweep through or within firing range of an enemy air formation.

pass - Aviation slang for: 1. An attempted carrier landing that did not work and required a fly-by. 2. In combat, the point where two fighters aiming for a head on collision pass by each other.

pass time (road) - (DOD, NATO, CENTO) The time that elapses between the moment when the leading vehicle of a column passes a given point and the moment when the last vehicle passes the same point.

passageway - Navy and Marine slang for a hallway.

passed over - Not promoted when a promotion is expected.

passenger mile - (DOD) One passenger transported one mile. For air and ocean transport, use nautical miles; for rail, highway, and inland waterway transport in the continental United States, use statute miles.

passing gas - 1. Aviation term for mid-air refueling. 2. Hospital slang for administering anesthesia.

passive air defense - (DOD, IADB) All measures, other than active air defense, taken to minimize the effect; of hostile air action. These include the use of cover, concealment, camouflage, deception, dispersion and protective construction. See also air defense.

passive air defense - (NATO, SEATO, CENTO) All measures, other than active defense, taken to minimize the effects of hostile air action. These include the use of cover, concealment, camouflage, dispersion, and protective construction. See also air defense.

passive communications satellite - See communications satellite.

passive defense - (DOD, NATO, CENTO, IADB) Measures taken to reduce the probability of and to minimize the effects of damage caused by hostile action without the intention of taking the initiative.

passive defense - (SEATO) Defense of a place without the employment of active weapons and without the expectation of taking the initiative.

passive homing guidance - (DOD, NESN, IADB) A system of homing guidance wherein the receiver in the missile utilizes radiation from the target. See also guidance.

password - (DOD, NATO, SEATO, CENTO, IADB) A secret word or distinctive sound used to reply to a challenge. See also challenge; countersign; reply.

patch - The area of a map assigned to one reconnaissance team.

patch guy - Pilot with significant experience, as demonstrated by multiple unit patches on flight suit/gear.

Pathet Lao - The Laotian communists led by the North Vietnamese Army.

pathfinder - (SEATO, IADB) An aircraft with a specially trained crew carrying dropping zone/landing zone marking teams, target markers, or navigational aids, which precedes the main force to the dropping zone/landing zone, or target.

pathfinder aircraft - (NATO, CENTO) An aircraft with a specially trained crew carrying drop zone/landing zone marking teams, target markers, or navigational aids, which precedes the main force to the drop zone/landing zone, or target.

pathfinder drop zone control - (DOD, IADB) The communication and operation center from which pathfinders exercise aircraft guidance.

pathfinder landing zone control - See pathfinder drop zone control.

pathfinder team - (NATO, CENTO) A team dropped or air landed at an objective to establish and operate navigational aids for the purpose of guiding aircraft to drop and landing zones.

pathfinders - (DOD, IADB) 1. Experienced aircraft crews who lead a formation to the drop zone, release point, or target. 2. Teams dropped or air landed at an objective to establish and operate navigational aids for the purpose of guiding aircraft to drop and landing zones. 3. A radar device used for navigating or homing to an objective when visibility precludes accurate visual navigation. 4. Teams, air delivered into enemy territory, for the purpose of determining the best approach and withdrawal lanes, landing zones, and sites for helicopter-borne forces.

patients - (DOD, NATO, SEATO, CENTO, IADB) All sick, injured, or wounded personnel receiving medical care or treatment.

patrol - (DOD, SEATO, IADB) A detachment of ground, sea, or air forces sent out by a larger unit for the purpose of gathering information or carrying out a destructive, harassing, mopping-up, or security mission. See also combat air patrol; combat/fighting patrol (ground); reconnaissance patrol (ground).

patrol - (NATO, CENTO) A detachment of ground, sea, or air forces sent out for the purpose of gathering information or carrying out a destructive, harassing, mopping-up, or security mission. See also combat air patrol; combat patrol; reconnaissance patrol (ground); standing patrol.

patrol (ground) - (NFSN, CENTO) A detachment sent out by a larger unit for the purpose of gathering information or carrying out, a harassing action, a destructive, mopping-up or security mission.

patrol boat - Used by U.S. Navy for river and coastal patrol.

patrol harness - Suspenders holding a pistol belt, two canteens, two ammo pouches, two grenades, a smoke grenade and a K-BAR knife.

pattern activity analysis - The analysis of enemy movement and tactics over a set period of time to anticipate future activity.

pattern bombing - (DOD, IADB) The systematic covering of a target area with bombs uniformly distributed according to a plan.

pattern laying (land mine warfare) - (DOD, NATO, SEATO, CENTO, IADB) The laying of mines in a fixed relationship to each other.

Patton tank - See M48A2 Tank.

pave fire - The Air Force's laser bomb system in which a lead plane "lit" a target with a laser, and held it on target while following plane(s) released "smart bombs" that went to the "lit" point.

Pave Knife - A F-4 jet with smart bombs.

pave nail - The LORAN navigation system

PAVN - People's Army of Vietnam (North). Also PAV. Later NVA.

pay advance - The payment of salary in advance to address an emergency or provide funds for leave expenses.

pay bag - See PAE bag.

payback - Slang for revenge, used in the phrase "payback is a motherfucker".

payload - (DOD, IADB) 1. The load (expressed in tons of cargo or equipment, gallons of liquid, or number of passengers) which the vehicle is designed to transport under specified conditions of operation, in addition to its unladen weight. 2. The warhead section in a military missile. 3. The satellite or research vehicle of a space probe or research missile.

payload - (NATO, CENTO) 1. The load (expressed in tons of cargo or equipment, gallons of liquid, or number of passengers) which the vehicle is designed to transport under specified conditions of operation, in addition to its unladen weight. 2. The warhead, its container, and activating devices in a military missile. 3. The satellite or research vehicle of a space probe or research missile. See also airlift; allowable cabin load (air); allowable cargo load (air); planned load (aircraft).

payload (aircraft) - (SEATO) The sum of the weight of passengers and cargo that an aircraft can carry.

payload (missile) - See payload, Part 2.

payload build-up (missile and space) - (DOD, IADB) The process by which the scientific instrumentation (sensors, detectors, etc.) and necessary mechanical and electronic sub-assemblies are assembled into a complete operational package capable of achieving the scientific objectives of the mission.

payload integration (missile and space) - (DOD, IADB) The compatible installation of a complete payload package into the spacecraft and space vehicle.

PBI - Poor bloody infantry.

PBR - River patrol boat, well armed.

PC - Personnel Carrier.

PCF - Patrol Boat Fast. Swift boat.

PCOD (Pussy Cut off Date) - The last date for sex which would guarantee the remediation of any venereal disease prior to the DEROS date, as infection would delay the exit from Vietnam. Normally set 6-8 weeks before DEROS.

PCS - Permanent Change of Station, orders to another assignment out of Vietnam.

PDS - Permanent Duty Station.

peacetime force materiel assets - (DOD) That portion of total materiel assets which is designated to meet the peacetime force materiel requirement. See also mobilization reserves.

peacetime force materiel procurement objective - (DOD) The quantity of an item required to be procured in peacetime to balance peacetime force materiel assets with the peacetime force materiel requirement. It is the quantity by which the peacetime force materiel requirement exceeds the peacetime force materiel assets. See also mobilization reserves.

peacetime force materiel requirement - (DOD) The quantity of an item required to equip, provide a materiel pipeline and sustain the authorized peacetime United States Forces, both active and reserve, and support the scheduled establishment through normal appropriation and procurement lead-time periods. See also mobilization reserves.

peak overpressure - (DOD, NATO, CENTO) The maximum value of overpressure at a given location which is generally experienced at the instant the shock (or blast) wave reaches that location. See also shock wave.

Peanut - Radio code for Killed in Action. Note earlier troops (60's) used Peanut for KIA, later troops (70's) referenced Peanut for WIA.

pecked line - (NATO) A symbol consisting of a line broken at regular intervals.

pecker checker - Slang for a Medic.

pecuniary liability - (DOD) A personal, joint, or corporate monetary obligation to make good any lost, damaged, or destroyed property resulting from fault or neglect. It may also result under conditions stipulated in a contract or bond.

pedicab - A three wheeled bicycle either pedaled or motor driven in which one or two passengers or packages are on a bench in front of the operator. See cyclo and rickshaw.

Pedro - Slang for the winch on Air Force helicopters used to extract downed flyers by using a harness or basket on a wire. Army would request "Pedro" assistance as needed.

pee halt - A bathroom break on a march.

pee pipe - See piss tube.

peepers - 1. Eyeglasses. 2. Night vision goggles.

peepsight - The small opening in a gun sight that you peep (look) through.

penalty box - Aviation term for the blackboard of shame on an aircraft carrier where a pilot's name is written if he screws up a landing by being so off the line to require a wave off.

pencil - A reporter initially, later any media (film crew or reporter).

pencil pusher - Those with administrative or desk jobs.

pencil whip - Marine slang for a written report that is an exaggeration or fiction.

penetration - (DOD, NATO, CENTO, IADB) A form of offensive maneuver which seeks to break through the enemy's defensive position, widen the gap created, and destroy the continuity of his positions. Note: NATO and CENTO term is "penetration (ground forces)".

penetration (air traffic control) - (DOD) That portion of a published high altitude instrument approach procedure which prescribes a descent path from the fix on which the procedure is based to a fix or altitude from which an approach to the airport is made.

penetration (intelligence) - (DOD) The recruitment of agents within, or the planting of agents or technical monitoring devices in, a target organization for the purpose of gaining access to its secrets or of influencing its activities.

penguin - Air Force ground crews due to wingless flightless status.

penny - Slang for the number one.

penny-nickel-nickel - Slang for the M109 155-mm howitzer.

penstock - (NATO) A valve or sluice on an open water channel.

Pentagon East - The Military Assistance Command, Vietnam at Tan Son Nhut air base a few miles outside Saigon. See MACV.

Pentagon Papers - The information on the war in Vietnam which was disclosed to the press and discredited much of the official information on the war. Officially known as The History of the U.S. Decision Making Process on Vietnam, the report was classified. It was released by Daniel Ellsberg to the New York Times which began publishing them on June 13, 1971. The effect of the publication domestically was to cast doubt on the credibility of the government.

people sniffer - An experimental device able to detect an elevated ammonia levels from sweat and urine as an indicator of enemy presence. The XM-2 was hand carried, and the XM-3 was lowered from a helicopter.

People's Army of Vietnam - The original name of the North Vietnamese Army. See PAVN and NVA.

People's Liberation Armed Forces or People's Liberation Forces - The Viet Cong.

perigee - (DOD, NATO, CENTO, IADB) The point at which a satellite orbit is the least distance from the center of the gravitational field of the controlling body or bodies.

perim - Perimeter.

perimeter defense - (DOD, IADB) A defense without an exposed flank, consisting of forces deployed along the perimeter of the defended area.

periodic intelligence summary - (DOD) A report of the intelligence situation in a tactical operation, normally produced at corps level or its equivalent, and higher, usually at intervals of twenty-four hours, or as directed by the commander. Also called PERINTSUM.

peripheral war - (DOD) Not to be used. See limited war.

perishable cargo - (DOD, IADB) Cargo requiring refrigeration, such as meat, fruit, and fresh vegetables, and medical department biologicals. See also cargo.

permafrost - (DOD, IADB) Permanently frozen subsoil.

permissive action link - (DOD) A device included in or attached to a nuclear weapon system to preclude arming and/or launching until the insertion of a prescribed discrete code or combination. It may include equipment and cabling external to the weapon or weapon system to activate components within the weapon or weapon system.

permit - Parachutist's insignia.

Pershing - (DOD, IADB) A mobile, solid-propellant, surface-to-surface guided missile, with a nuclear warhead capability, designed to support the field army by the attack of long-range ground targets. Designated as XMGM-31A.

personal locator beacon - (DOD, NATO, CENTO, IADB) A locator beacon capable of providing homing signals to help search and rescue operations. See also crash locator beacon.

personal property - (DOD) Property of any kind or any interest therein, except real property, records of the Federal Government, and naval vessels of the following categories: aircraft carriers, battleships, cruisers, destroyers, and submarines.

personnel - (DOD, IADB) Those individuals required in either a military or civilian capacity to accomplish the assigned mission.

personnel reaction time (nuclear) - (DOD, NATO, CENTO, IADB) The time required by personnel to take prescribed protective measures after receipt of a nuclear strike warning.

perspective grid - (NATO, CENTO) A network of lines drawn or superimposed on an oblique photograph representing the perspective of a grid on the ground or datum plane.

peta-prime - An petroleum product that was sprayed over dirt roads to hold dust down. In the tropical heat it melted easily.

Peter - Slang for phosphorous.

Peter pilot - The co-pilot in a helicopter.

petroleum - (DOD, NATO, CENTO) An oily, liquid solution of hydrocarbons which, when fractionally distilled, yields paraffin, kerosene, fuel oil, gasoline, etc. See also bulk petroleum products; packaged petroleum products; petroleum oils and lubricants.

petroleum intersectional service - (DOD, NATO, CENTO) An intersectional or interzonal service in a theater of operations that operates pipelines and related facilities for the supply of bulk petroleum products to theater Army elements and other forces as directed.

petroleum, oils and lubricants - (NATO, SEATO, CENTO, IADB) A broad term which includes all petroleum and associated products used by the armed forces.

Petty Officer - A noncommissioned officer in the Navy or Coast Guard.

PF - Popular Force, the South Vietnamese military like a National Guard.

PFC - Private First Class (Army, Marine Corps).

PFC - Slang for Proud Fucking Civilian, sarcastic reference to PFC rank.

PG - Patrol Gunboat.

PGM-11 - See Redstone.

PGM-17 - See Thor.

Phantom II - (DOD, IADB) A twin-engine, all-weather, supersonic, two-place jet fighter/ bomber designed for operating from aircraft carriers for interception and destruction of enemy aircraft, for troop support, and the delivery of relatively heavy loads of nuclear or non-nuclear weapons, in addition to carrying four Sparrow IUs or Sidewinders. This aircraft can be air refueled, or carry a tanker package for other aircraft. Designated as F-4.

phantom order - (DOD) A draft contract with an industrial establishment for wartime production of a specific product with provisions for necessary preplanning in time of peace and for immediate execution of the contract upon receipt of proper authority.

phase line - (DOD, IADB) The line utilized for control and coordination of military operations, usually a terrain feature extending across the zone of action. See also report line.

phases of military government - (DOD, IADB) 1. Assault - That period which commences with first contact with civilians ashore and extends to the establishment of military government control ashore by the landing force. 2. Consolidation - That period which commences with the establishment of military government control ashore by the landing force and extends to the establishment of control by occupation forces. 3. Occupation - That period which commences when an area has been occupied in fact, and the military commander within that area is in a position to enforce public safety and order. See also civil affairs; military occupation.

Phoenix Operation - The English term for the Phuong Hoang Program in which the South Vietnamese government sponsored a program from 1968 to 1971 which targeted the leaders, key members and followers of the Viet Cong infrastructure.

phonetic alphabet - (DOD, IADB) A list of standard words used to identify letters in a message transmitted by radio or telephone. The following are the authorized words, listed in order, for each letter in the alphabet: Alfa, Bravo, Charlie, Delta, Echo, Foxtrot, Golf, Hotel, India, Juliet, Kilo, Lima, Mike, November, Oscar, Papa, Quebec, Romeo, Sierra, Tango, Uniform, Victor, Whiskey, X-ray, Yankee, and Zulu.

phony mine (land mine warfare) - (DOD, NATO, SEATO, CENTO, IADB) An object used to simulate a mine in a phony minefield. It may be made of any available material. See also mine; mine (land mine warfare).

phony minefield (land mine warfare) - (DOD, NATO, SEATO, CENTO, IADB) An area of ground used to simulate a minefield with the object of deceiving the enemy. See also mine· field (land mine warfare).

phosphorus - The chemical that was in shells and grenades to disable as well as mark a location by intense light.

photo interpretation key - See imagery interpretation key.

photo nadir - (NATO, CENTO) The point at which a vertical line through the perspective center of the camera lens intersects the photo plane.

photoflash bomb - (DOD, NATO, CENTO, IADB) A bomb designed to produce a brief and intense illumination for medium altitude night photography.

photoflash cartridge - (DOD, NATO, CENTO, IADB) A pyrotechnic cartridge designed to produce a brief and intense illumination for low altitude night photography.

photogrammetric control - (DOD, NATO, CENTO) Control established by photogrammetric methods as distinguished from control established by ground methods. Sometimes called minor control.

photogrammetry - (DOD, NATO, CENTO) The science or art of obtaining reliable measurements from photographic images.

photographic coverage - (DOD) The extent to which an area is covered by photography from one mission or a series of missions or in a period of time. Coverage, in this sense, conveys the ideal of availability of photography and is not a synonym for the word photography.

photographic filter - (NATO, CENTO) A layer of glass, gelatine or other material used to modify the spectrum of the incidental light.

photographic intelligence - (DOD) The collected products of photographic interpretation, classified and evaluated for intelligence use.

photographic intelligence - (NATO, CENTO) The collected products of photographic interpretation, classified and evaluated for military use.

photographic interpretation - (NATO, CENTO) The extraction of information from photographs or other recorded images.

photographic panorama - (DOD) A continuous photograph or an assemblage of overlapping oblique or ground photographs which have been matched and joined together to form a continuous photographic representation of the area.

photographic reading - (NATO, CENTO) The simple recognition of natural or cultural features from photographs.

photographic scale - (DOD, NATO, CENTO) The ratio of a distance measured on a photograph or mosaic to the corresponding distance on the ground, classified as follows: very large scale: 1:6,000 and larger; large scale 1:6,000 to 1:12,000; medium scale 1:12,000 to 1:30,000; small scale 1:30,000 to 1:70,000; very small scale 1:70,000 and smaller.

photographic sortie - See imagery sortie.

photographic strip - (DOD) A series of successive overlapping photographs made from an aircraft flying a selected course or direction.

photographic strip - (NATO, CENTO) A series of successive overlapping photographs taken along a selected course or direction.

photomap - (DOD, NATO, CENTO) A reproduction of a photograph or photomosaic upon which the grid lines, marginal data, contours, place names, boundaries, and other data may be added.

Phuong Hoang Program - See Phoenix Operation.

physical characteristics - (DOD, IADB) Those military characteristics of equipment which are primarily physical in nature, such as weight, shape, volume, waterproofing, and sturdiness.

VIETNAM: THE WAR ZONE DICTIONARY IN THEIR OWN WORDS

physical security - (DOD, NATO, CENTO, IADB) That part of security concerned with physical measures designed to safeguard personnel, to prevent unauthorized access to equipment, facilities, material, and documents, and to safeguard them against espionage, sabotage, damage, and theft. See also communications security.

physical training - The exercise routine to get in combat fitness.

PI - Political influence. A notation of a personnel file noting the soldier was politically connected (e.g. father a congressman).

Piastre - Vietnamese currency.

PIC - Provincial Interrogation Center.

pick up brass - Recover spent brass shell casings from range or in field.

pick up zone - A predetermined area for troop pickup.

pick up zone - The area designated for the extraction of troops usually by helicopter, occasionally by truck.

pickle - Slang for bomb.

pickle switch - The bomber cockpit bomb release switch.

pickling - The bombing tactic of releasing bombs one at a time to expand the coverage area.

pictomap - (DOD) A topographic map in which the photographic imagery of a standard mosaic has been converted into interpretable colors and symbols by means of a pictomap process.

pictorial symbolization - (DOD, NATO, CENTO, IADB) The use of symbols which convey the visual character of the features they represent.

pie hole - Mouth, as in shut your pie hole, meaning be quiet.

piece - A rifle.

pig - The M-60 machine gun.

pigeon - (DOD) In air intercept, a code meaning the magnetic bearing and distance of base (or unit indicated) from you is _____ degrees _____ miles.

pile on - Tactic in which a small unit seeks and finds the enemy at which time massive support is given which "piles on" in the fight.

pillbox - (DOD, NATO, SEATO, CENTO, IADB) A small, low fortification that houses machine guns, antitank weapons, etc. A pillbox is usually made of concrete, steel, or filled sandbags.

pilot's trace - (DOD, NATO, CENTO) A rough overlay to a map made by the pilot of a photographic reconnaissance aircraft during or immediately after a sortie. It shows the location, direction, number, and order of photographic runs made, together with the camera(s) used on each run.

pineapple - Slang for hand grenade.

ping - Submarine and Navy slang for the noise a SONAR makes when it sees an object.

pinging on - Aviation term for paying close attention to what someone is saying or doing.

pink sheet - The pink paper sheet cover to secret documents.

pinkie - Aviation term for a twilight landing. While counted as a night landing, the twilight between sunset and real darkness that often has a pink hue, was a cheap way to get night landing credit.

pinpoint - (DOD, NATO, SEATO, CENTO, IADB) 1. A precisely identified point, especially on the ground, that locates a very small target, a reference point for rendezvous or for other purposes; the coordinates that define this point. 2. The ground position of aircraft determined by direct observation of the ground.

pinpoint photograph - (DOD) A single photograph or one or more stereopairs of a specific object or target.

pinpoint photograph - (NATO, CENTO) A single photograph or a stereo pair of a specific object or target.

PIO - 1. Public Information Office. 2. An individual assigned to the Public Information Office. 3. Pilot Induced Oscillation which is when the pilot guides the plane on a course that enhances the natural oscillation of the aircraft to roll (longitudinal), pitch (lateral) or yaw (vertical).

PIOCC - Provincial Intelligence and Operation Coordinating Center.

pip - The dot on a radar screen, also called a blip.

pipe - A pipe used for smoking marijuana or opium. See bong.

pipe cleaner - Prostitute.

pipeline - (DOD, NATO, SEATO, CENTO, IADB) In logistics, the channel of support or a specific portion thereof by means of which materiel or personnel flow from sources of procurement to their point of use.

PIRAZ - Positive identification and radar zone. The area around a Navy fleet in which aviation is controlled by the Navy, not land based control. See Red Crown.

piss and punk - Marine slang for bread and water punishment.

piss cutter - Marine slang for sharp creased folding cap that looks like an envelope. See cunt cap.

piss pot - GI helmet.

piss tube - A vertical tube buried half to two thirds in the ground. The exposed part was intended to be used as a urinal. These were made of cut up shell casings or of plastic pipe.

pissed - Angry.

pitch - (DOD) See tip.

pitch - In aviation, the lateral axis, e.g. nose up or down.

pitch liberty - Navy term for going ashore.

pith helmet - The fiber helmet worn by some in the North Vietnamese Army.

PJ - 1. Parajumper. 2. Photojournalist.

PKIA - Presumed killed in action.

PLA - People's Liberation Army.

PLAF - People's Liberation Armed Forces (Viet Cong). See PLF.

plan range - (NATO, CENTO) In air photographic reconnaissance, the horizontal distance from the point below the aircraft to an object on the ground.

planimetric map - (DOD, IADB) A map representing only the horizontal position of features. Sometimes called a line map. See also map.

planned load (aircraft) - (NATO, CENTO, IADB) A load that has been planned for a specific type of aircraft sortie. See also load (air).

planned resupply - (NATO, CENTO, IADB) The shipping of supplies in a regular flow as envisaged by existing preplanned schedules and organizations, which will usually include some form of planned procurement. See also elements of resupply.

planned target (nuclear) - (DOD) A nuclear target planned on an area or point in which a need is anticipated. A planned nuclear target may be scheduled or on call. Firing data for a planned nuclear target mayor may not be determined in advance. Coordination and warning of friendly troops and aircraft are mandatory.

planning factor (logistics) - (DOD, NATO, SEATO, CENTO, IADB) A properly selected multiplier, used in planning to estimate the amount and type of effort involved in a contemplated operation. Planning factors are often expressed as rates, ratios, or lengths of time.

planning staff - See central planning team.

planograph - (DOD, IADB) A scale drawing of a storage area showing the approved layout of the area, location of bulk, bin, rack, and box pallet areas, aisles, assembly areas, walls, doorways, directions of storage, office space, wash rooms, and other support and operational areas.

plant equipment - (DOD) Personal property of a capital nature, consisting of equipment, furniture, vehicles, machine tools, test equipment, and accessory and auxiliary items, but excluding special tooling and special test equipment, used or capable of use in the manufacture of supplies or for any administrative or general plant purpose.

plastic - Explosive that is malleable like clay. See C-4.

plastic range - (DOD, NATO, CENTO) The stress range in which a material will not fail when subjected to the action of a force, but will not recover completely, so that a permanent deformation results when the force is removed.

plastic spray packaging - See cocooning.

plastic zone - (DOD, NATO, CENTO) The region beyond the rupture zone associated with crater formation resulting from an explosion in which there is no visible rupture but in which the soil is permanently deformed and compressed to a high density. See also rupture zone.

plastique - French for C-4 plastic explosive.

plate - (NATO) 1. In cartography: a. a printing plate of zinc, aluminum or engraved copper; b. collective term for all "states" of an engraved map reproduced from the same engraved printing plate; c. all detail to appear on a map or chart which will be reproduced from a single printing plate (e.g. the "blue plate" or the "contour plate"). 2. In photography, a transparent medium, usually glass, coated with a photographic emulsion. See also diapositive; transparency.

platform drop - (NATO, CENTO) The airdrop of loaded platforms from rear loading aircraft with roller conveyors. See also airdrop; airdrop platform.

platoon - A unit of military organization led by a Lieutenant and composed of two to three squads.

Play Dough - Slang for bread in the C-rations from the clay-like trademarked modeling compound for children Play Doh.

PLF - 1. Parachute Landing Fall. 2. People's Liberation Forces. See PLAF.

plot - (DOD) 1. Map, chart, or graph representing data of any sort. 2. Represent on a diagram or chart the position or course of a target in terms of angles and distances from known positions; locate a position on a map or chart. 3. The visual display of a single geographical location of an airborne object at a particular instant of time. 4. A portion of a map or overlay on which are drawn the outlines of the areas covered by one or more photographs.

plot - (NATO, CENTO) In photographic interpretation, a portion of a map or overlay on which are drawn the outlines of the areas covered by one or more photographs. See also master plot.

plotting chart (navigation) - (NATO, CENTO, IADB) A chart designed for the graphical processes of navigation.

PO - Petty Officer, in general.

PO1 - Petty Officer 1st Class (Navy, Coast Guard).

PO2 - Petty Officer 2nd Class (Navy, Coast Guard).

PO3 - Petty Officer 3rd Class (Navy, Coast Guard).

pod formation - In aviation, a formation in which the positioning of the airplanes allows the overlapping coverage by the weapon pods on each ship.

pods - 1. Rubberized 500 gallon containers for liquids, usually water or fuel. 2. Aviation term for any aerodynamic attachment to an aircraft to hold sensors or arms.

pogey (also spelled pogue or poag) - Derogatory term for military personnel stationed in the rear in support duty away from the fighting. Source reputed to be from China Marines who were issued candy as part of rations. Candy was used as barter with prostitutes (which sounds like pogey). Candy morphed into pogey-bait and thence to candy used to bribe the useless guy in the rear.

pogey bait - Candy or other desirable non-issued item used in exchange for some administrative favor by administrative staff in the rear.

pogo - (DOD) In air intercept, a code meaning switch to communications channel number preceding "pogo". If unable to establish communications, switch to channel number following "pogo".

point - 1. The lead position. 2. The forward group or element in combat mission, 3. The individual who walked at the lead of a patrol (that followed him in a column).

point blank canister rounds - Artillery rounds shot directly at an enemy, parallel to the ground, not in an elevated angle of fire adjustment for distance.

point designation grid - (DOD, NATO, SEATO, CENTO, IADB) A system of lines, having no relation to the actual scale or orientation, drawn on a map, chart, or air photograph, dividing it into squares so that points can be more readily located.

point of no return - (DOD, NATO, SEATO, CENTO, IADB) A point along an aircraft track beyond which its endurance will not permit return to its own or some other associated base on its own fuel supply.

point target - (DOD) 1. A target of such small dimension that it requires the accurate placement of ordnance in order to neutralize or destroy it. 2. (nuclear) A target in which the ratio of radius of damage to target radius is equal to or greater than 5.

point target - (NATO, SEATO, CENTO, IADB) A target which requires the accurate placement of bombs or fire.

point target (nuclear) - See point target, Part 2.

point to point sealift - (DOD) The movement of troops and/or cargo in Military Sealift Command nucleus or commercial shipping between established ports, in administrative landings or logistics over the shore operations. See also administrative landing; administrative movement; logistics over the shore operations.

pointy end - Aviation term for the bow of the boat, used by carrier pilots to irritate Navy personnel.

POL - Petroleum products, such as oil, lubricants.

POL farm - A tank farm or supply depot for petroleum products.

polar coordinates - (DOD) The location of a point in a plane by the length of a radius vector, from a fixed origin in the plane, and the angle the radius vector makes with a fixed line in the plane. See also coordinates.

polar plot - (DOD) The method of locating a target or point on the map by means of polar coordinates.

Polaris - (DOD, IADB) An underwater/surface-launched, surface-to-surface, solid-propellant ballistic missile with inertial guidance and nuclear warhead. Designated as UGM-27. UGM-27A - 1,200 nautical mile range. UGM-27B - 1,500 nautical mile range. UGM-2:7C - 2,500 nautical mile range.

poles - Slang for pants, trousers.

police - To clean up the area.

police call - The order to clean up an area and allotted time to do so.

police up - Clean up an area.

political intelligence - (DOD) Intelligence concerning foreign and domestic policies of governments and the activities of political movements.

political warfare - (DOD, IADB) Aggressive use of political means to achieve national objectives.

politico-military gaming - (DOD) Simulation of situations involving the interaction of political, military, sociological, psychological, economic, scientific, and other appropriate factors.

Polymagna - Antidiarrheal pills.

poncho - Loose rain gear.

poncho liner - The nylon liner to the poncho that was used as a blanket.

Pond - Pacific Ocean.

Pony Express - 1. Courier flights in Vietnam. 2. Mail call from home, 3. POW secret communication code while confined.

Pony Soldiers - Slang for the First Cavalry Division.

pool - (DOD, IADB) 1. To maintain and control a supply of resources or personnel upon which other activities may draw. The primary purpose of a pool is to promote maximum efficiency of use of the pooled resources or personnel, e.g., a petroleum pool, a labor and equipment pool. 2. Any combination of resources which serve a common purpose.

poontang - Slang for sex.

poop - Marine slang for information, more than a rumor, less than official.

pop - To kill.

pop bleeders - Hospital slang for when a previously closed wound or incision begins to bleed again, usually heavily.

pop flare - A hand held flare launched for illumination.

pop smoke - To ignite a smoke flare or smoke grenade to signal location.

pop up - Aviation tactic of flying low to avoid detection and going to elevation only when needed to deploy weapons or bombs and then returning to low level flight.

pop-up target - To serve a tour of duty in Viet Nam, ironic reference to being a pop-up target on the firing range.

popeye - (DOD) In air intercept, a code meaning in clouds or area of reduced visibility.

poppers - Slang for Amyl Nitrate which was medically used for angina or illegally as a stimulant.

popping caps - Rapid shooting.

Popular Forces - The national army in South Vietnam usually assigned to a village area. See Regional Forces.

porcupine fence – Slang for the perimeter defense used by the North Vietnamese made of bamboo sticks, sharpened at the tip, embedded in the ground pointing out at a 30-90 degree angle to prevent or slow ground assaults. An abatis.

port - (DOD)) A place at which ships may discharge or receive their cargoes. It includes any port accessible to ships on the seacoast, navigable rivers or inland waterways. The term "ports" should not be used in conjunction with air facilities which are designated as aerial ports, airports, etc. See also destination port; major port; minor port; secondary port; water terminal.

port - The left side of a ship when facing forward.

port area - (NATO, SEATO, CENTO, IADB) The area coming within the authority of a given port committee or, in the absence of such a committee, another administrative agency with similar powers.

port capacity - (DOD, NATO, CENTO, IADB) The estimated capacity of a port or an anchorage to clear cargo in 24 hours usually expressed in tons. See also beach capacity; clearance capacity.

port complex - (DOD, NATO, SEATO, CENTO, IADB) A port complex comprises one or more port areas of varying importance whose activities are geographically linked either because these areas are dependent on a common inland transport system or because they constitute a common initial destination for convoys.

port evacuation - (NATO, CENTO, IADB) The removal of shipping from a port/water terminal except perhaps for a few ships dispersed within the immediate vicinity thereof. See also movement of shipping (in the early days of war).

Portable Truth Detectors - The imaginary device that identified friend or foe immediately. 2. A rifle barrel. See PTD.

pos - Position.

pos rep - Position report.

position - 1. Location. 2. Slang for the ready position in a pushup. 3. "The position" is assuming the position for a period of discipline, or while being lectured to for some infraction.

position defense - (NATO, CENTO, IADB) The type of defense in which the bulk of the defending force is disposed in selected tactical localities where the decisive battle is to be fought. Principal reliance is placed on the ability of the forces in the defended localities to maintain their positions and to control the terrain between them. The reserve is used to add depth, to block, or restore the battle position by counterattack.

positive - (NATO, CENTO) In photography, an image on film, plate or paper having approximately the same total rendition of light and shade as the original subject.

positive control - (DOD) The operation of air traffic in a radar/nonradar ground control environment in which positive identification, tracking, and direction of aircraft within an air space is conducted by an agency having the authority and responsibility therein.

positive identification and radar advisory zone - (DOD) A specified area established for identification and flight following of aircraft in the vicinity of a fleet-defended area.

positive phase of the shock wave - (DOD) The period during which the pressure rises very sharply to a value that is higher than ambient and then decreases rapidly to the ambient pressure. See also negative phase of the shock wave; shock wave.

possible - (DOD) A term used to qualify a statement made under conditions wherein some evidence exists to support the statement. This evidence is sufficient to warrant mention, but insufficient to warrant assumption as true.

post hostilities period - (DOD, IADB) That period subsequent to the date of ratification by political authorities of agreements to terminate hostilities.

Post Traumatic Stress Syndrome or Post Traumatic Stress Disorder - Recognized as a disorder in 1980 by the American Psychological Association the disorder is a delay in response to a trauma, such as battle experience typified by emotional numbness, re-experiencing the event, survivor guilt, difficulty in developing relationships, sleep disorders or depression. See delayed stress syndrome.

post-strike reconnaissance - (DOD) Missions undertaken for the purpose of gathering information used to measure results of a strike.

postattack period - (DOD) In nuclear warfare, that period which extends from the termination of the final attack until political authorities agree to terminate hostilities. See also post hostilities period; transattack period.

potato masher - Hand grenade made by Chinese communists. See Chi-comm.

pounce - (DOD) In air intercept, a code meaning I am in position to engage target.

POW - Prisoner of War.

powder train - Explosives expert, usually a SEAL.

powdered - Blown up, usually referring to an aircraft.

power band - A wristband made of braided shoelaces initially and other flat braided material later, indicating support for the Black Power movement. Most often worn by black soldiers but some white soldiers also wove and wore these.

power puke - Aviation term for the projectile vomiting that comes with severe airsickness.

practice mine (land mine warfare) - (DOD, NATO, SEATO, CENTO, IADB) A replica of a standard mine, having the same features and weight as the mine it represents. It is constructed to emit a puff of smoke or make a noise to simulate detonation. See also mine; mine (land mine warfare).

prang - To land a helicopter very hard.

PRC - Any infantry portable radio. Pronounced prick.

PRC-10 - A handheld battery operated radio, effective over short distances, like a big walkie talkie. Replaced by the PRC-25.

PRC-25 - The standard infantry radio, carried as a pack by the Radio Telephone Operator in the field (See Prick 25).

PRC-77 - A more complex and heavier version of the PRC-25 with a scrambler operating on a secure network. This radio had a scrambler device in it. See Secure net. See Monster.

PRD-74 - The radio used by mobile guerrilla forces beyond the range of the PRC-25.

pre-flight inspection - The inspection of an aircraft prior to takeoff to insure readiness.

pre-launch survivability - (DOD) The probability that a delivery and/or launch vehicle will survive an enemy attack under an established condition of warning.

pre-position - (DOD, NATO, CENTO, IADB) To place military units, equipment, or supplies at or near the point of planned use or at a designated location to reduce reaction time, and to insure timely support of a specific force during initial phases of an operation.

pre-positioned war reserve requirement - (DOD) That portion of the mobilization reserve materiel objective which strategic plans dictate be positioned prior to hostilities at or near the point of planned use or issue to the user, to insure timely support of a specific project or designated force during the initial phase of war, pending arrival of replenishment shipments. See also mobilization reserves.

pre-positioned war reserve stock - (DOD) The quantity of an item acquired and positioned against a pre-positioned war reserve requirement. See also mobilization reserves.

prearranged fire - (DOD, IADB) Fire that is formally planned and executed against targets or target areas of known location. Such fire is usually planned well in advance and is executed at a predetermined time or during a predetermined period of time. See also fire; on call; scheduled fire.

preassault operations - (DOD, NATO, CENTO, IADB) Operations conducted in the objective area prior to the assault. They include reconnaissance, minesweeping, bombardment, bombing, underwater demolition, and destruction of beach obstacles.

precautionary launch - (DOD) The launching of nuclear loaded aircraft under imminent nuclear attack so as to preclude friendly aircraft destruction and loss of weapons on the ground/carrier.

precedence - (DOD) 1. (communications) - A designation assigned to a message by the originator to indicate to communications personnel the relative order of handling and to the addressee the order in which the message is to be noted. 2. (reconnaissance) - A letter designation, assigned by a unit requesting several reconnaissance missions, to indicate the relative order of importance, within an established priority, of the mission requested. See also flash message; immediate message; priority message; routine message.

precedence - (NATO, SEATO, CENTO, IADB) A designation assigned to a message by the originator to indicate to communication personnel the relative order of handling and to the addressee the order in which the message is to be noted.

precision bombing - (DOD, IADB) Bombing directed at a specific point target.

precleared fire zone - Replacing the term free fire zone after political and public criticism of the suggestion that fire was excessive and unsupervised.

precursor - (DOD) An air pressure wave which moves ahead of the main blast wave for some distance as a result of a nuclear explosion of appropriate yield and low burst height over a heat absorbing (or dusty) surface. The pressure at the precursor front increases more gradually than in a true (or ideal) shock wave, so that the behavior in the precursor region is said to be nonideal.

predominant height - (NATO, CENTO) In air reconnaissance, the height of 51% or more of the structures within an area of similar surface material.

preemptive attack - (DOD, IADB) An attack initiated on the basis of incontrovertible evidence that an enemy attack is imminent.

preemptive war - (DOD) Not to be used. See preemptive attack.

preinitiation - (DOD) The initiation of the fission chain reaction in the active material of a nuclear weapon at any time earlier than that at which either the designed or the maximum compression or degree of assembly is attained.

preliminary demolition - (NATO, SEATO, CENTO, IADB) A target prepared for demolition preliminary to a withdrawal, the demolition of which can be executed as soon after preparation as convenient on the orders of the officer to whom the responsibility for such demolitions has been delegated.

preload loading - (DOD, NATO, SEATO, CENTO, IADB) The loading of selected items aboard ship at one port prior to the main loading of the ship at another. See also loading.

premature dud - See flare dud.

prep - 1. Preparation, in general. 2. Preparatory fire.

preparation fire - (DOD, NATO, SEATO, CENTO, IADB) Fire delivered on a target preparatory to an assault. See also fire.

preplanned air support - (DOD, NATO, SEATO, CENTO, IADB) Air support in accordance with a program planned in advance of operations. See also air support.

preplanned mission request - (DOD) A request for an air strike on a target which can be anticipated sufficiently in advance to permit detailed mission coordination and planning.

preplanned mission request (reconnaissance) - (DOD) A request for a mission on a target or in support of a maneuver which can be anticipated sufficiently in advance to allow detailed mission coordination and planning.

preplanned nuclear support - (DOD) Nuclear support planned in advance of operations. See also nuclear support; immediate nuclear support.

prescribed nuclear load - (DOD, NATO, CENTO) A specified quantity of nuclear weapons to be carried by a delivery unit. The establishment and replenishment of this load after each expenditure is a command decision and is dependent upon the tactical situation, the nuclear logistical situation, and the capability of the unit to transport and utilize the load. It may vary from day to day and among similar delivery units. See also special ammunition load.

prescribed nuclear stockage - (NATO, CENTO) A specified quantity of nuclear weapons, components of nuclear weapons, and warhead test equipment to be stocked in special ammunition supply points or other logistical installations. The establishment and replenishment of this stockage is a command decision and is dependent upon the tactical situation, the allocation, the capability of the logistical support unit to store and maintain the nuclear weapons, and the nuclear logistical situation. The prescribed stockage may vary from time to time and among similar logistical support units.

preset guidance - (DOD, IADB) A technique of missile control wherein a predetermined flight path is set into the control mechanism and cannot be adjusted after launching. See also guidance.

Presidential Unit Citation - An award to a unit for heroism, similar to that required for the award of a Distinguished Flying Cross, Navy Cross or Air Force Cross, as well as gallantry and teamwork in exceptionally difficult circumstances.

pressure altitude - (DOD, NATO, CENTO, IADB) An atmospheric pressure, expressed in terms of altitude which correspond to that pressure in the standard atmosphere. See also altitude.

pressure breathing - (DOD, NATO, CENTO, IADB) The technique of breathing which is required when oxygen is supplied direct to an individual at a pressure higher than the ambient barometric pressure.

pressure breathing - (SEATO) Technique in which oxygen is injected inside the respiratory ducts through a pressure higher than the ambient barometric pressure.

pressure front - See shock front.

pressure suit - (DOD, NATO, SEATO, CENTO, IADB) 1. (partial) - A skin-tight suit which does not completely enclose the body but which is capable of exerting pressure on the major portion of the body in order to counteract an increased intrapulmonary oxygen pressure. 2. (full) - A suit which completely encloses the body and in which a gas pressure, sufficiently above ambient pressure for maintenance of function, may be sustained. See also water suit.

pressurized cabin - (DOD, NATO, SEATO, CENTO, IADB) The occupied space of an aircraft in which the air pressure has been increased above that of the ambient atmosphere by compression of the ambient atmosphere into the space.

prestrike reconnaissance - (DOD) Missions undertaken for the purpose of obtaining complete information about known targets for use by the strike force.

preventive maintenance - (DOD, IADB) The care and servicing by personnel for the purpose of maintaining equipment and facilities in satisfactory operating condition by providing for systematic inspection, detection, and correction of incipient failures either before they occur or before they develop into major defects.

preventive war - (DOD, IADB) A war initiated in the belief that military conflict, while not imminent, is inevitable, and that to delay would involve greater risk.

prewithdrawal demolition target - (DOD) A target prepared for demolition preliminary to a withdrawal, the demolition of which can be executed as soon after preparation as convenient on the orders of the officer to whom the responsibility for such demolitions has been delegated.

PRG - Provisional Revolutionary Government.

prick - 1. Penis. 2. Slang for any of the field radios carried as backpacks in the field. See PRC.

Prick 10 - Slang for the PRC-10 radio.

Prick 25 - Slang for the PRC-25 radio.

Prick 74 - Slang for the PRC-274 radio.

Prick 77 - Slang for the PRC-77 radio.

pricksmith - An enlisted man in the medical corps.

Primaquine - An antimalarial drug.

primary censorship - (DOD, IADB) Armed forces censorship performed by personnel of a company, battery, squadron, ship, station, base, or similar unit on the personal communications of persons assigned, attached, or otherwise under the jurisdiction of a unit. See also censorship.

primary demolition belt - (DOD, IADB) A continuous series of obstacles across the whole front, selected by the division or higher commander. The preparation of such a belt is normally a priority engineer task. See also demolition belt.

primary interest - (DOD, IADB) Principal, although not exclusive, interest and responsibility for accomplishment of a given mission, including responsibility for reconciling the activities of other agencies that possess collateral interest in the program.

prime mover - (DOD, IADB) A vehicle, including heavy construction equipment, possessing military characteristics, designed primarily for towing heavy, wheeled weapons and frequently providing facilities for the transportation of the crew of, and ammunition for, the weapon.

principal operational interest - (DOD) When used in connection with an established facility operated by one Service for joint use by two or more Services, the term indicates a requirement for the greatest use of, or the greatest need for, the services of that facility. The term may be applied to a Service, but is more applicable to a command.

principal parallel - (NATO, CENTO) On an oblique photograph, a line parallel to the true horizon and passing through the principal point.

principal plane - (NATO, CENTO) A vertical plane which contains the principal point of an oblique photograph, the perspective center of the lens and the ground nadir.

principal point - (NATO, CENTO) The foot of the perpendicular to the photo plane through the perspective center. Generally determined by intersection of the lines joining opposite collimating or fiducial marks.

principal scale - (DOD, NATO) In cartography, the scale of a reduced or generating globe representing the sphere or spheroid, defined by the fractional relation of their respective radii. Also known as nominal scale. See scale.

principal vertical - (NATO, CENTO) On an oblique photograph, a line perpendicular to the true horizon and passing through the principal point.

print reference - (NATO, CENTO) A reference to an individual print in an air photographic sortie.

prior permission (air) - (DOD, NATO, CENTO, IADB) Permission granted by the appropriate national authority prior to the commencement of a flight or a series of flights landing in or flying over the territory of the nation concerned.

priority - (DOD, IADB) With reference to war plans and the tasks derived therfrom, an indication of relative importance rather than an exclusive and final designation of the order of accomplishment.

Priority 999 - Air Force Airlift's top priority for delivery of supplies. See nine nine nine (999) and Red Ball Express.

priority message - (DOD, IADB) A category of precedence reserved for messages which require expeditious action by the addressee(s) and/or furnish essential information for the conduct of operations in progress when routine precedence will not suffice. See also message precedence; precedence.

priority national intelligence objectives - (DOD) A guide for the coordination of intelligence collection and production in response to requirements relating to the formulation and execution of national security policy. They are compiled annually by the Washington Intelligence Community and flow directly from the intelligence mission as set forth by the National Security Council. They are specific enough to provide a basis for planning the allocation of collection and research resources but not so specific as to constitute in themselves research and collection requirements.

priority of immediate mission requests - See emergency priority; ordinary priority; search and attack priority; urgent priority.

priority of preplanned mission requests - (DOD) 1. Targets capable of preventing the execution of the plan of action. 2. Targets capable of immediate serious interference with the plan of action. 3. Targets capable of ultimate serious interference with the execution of the plan of action. 4. Targets capable of limited interference with the execution of the plan of action.

priority system for mission requests for tactical reconnaissance - (DOD) Priority I - Takes precedence over all other requests except previously assigned priorities. The results of these requests are of paramount importance to the immediate battle situation or objective. Priority II - The results of these requirements are in support of the general battle situation and will be accomplished as soon as possible after priorities I. These are requests to gain current battle information. Priority III - The results of these requests update the intelligence data base but do not affect the immediate battle situation. Priority IV - The results of these requests are of a routine nature. These requests will be fulfilled when the reconnaissance effort permits. See also precedence.

Prisoner of War - POW.

prisoner of war branch camp - (DOD, NATO, SEATO, CENTO) A subsidiary camp under the supervision and administration of the prisoner of war camp of which it is a branch.

prisoner of war cage - (DOD, NATO, SEATO, CENTO, IADB) A temporary construction, building, or enclosed area, to which prisoners of war are evacuated for interrogation and temporary detention pending further evacuation.

prisoner of war camp - (DOD, NATO, SEATO, CENTO, IADB) A camp of a semipermanent nature established in the communication zone, or zone of interior (home country) for the internment and complete administration of prisoners of war. It may be located on, or independent of, other military installations.

prisoner of war censorship - (DOD) The censorship of the communications to and from enemy prisoners of war and civilian internees held by the United States Armed Forces. See also censorship.

prisoner of war censorship - (IADB) The censorship of the communications to and from enemy prisoners of war and civilian internees. See also censorship.

prisoner of war collecting point - (DOD, NATO, SEATO, CENTO, IADB) A designated locality in a forward battle area where prisoners are assembled pending local examination for information of immediate tactical value and subsequent evacuation. Note: SEATO uses "front line area" instead of "forward battle area".

prisoner of war compound - (DOD, NATO, SEATO, CENTO, IADB) A subdivision of a prisoner of war enclosure.

prisoner of war enclosure - (DOD, NATO, SEATO, CENTO, IADB) A subdivision of a prisoner of war camp.

prisoner of war personnel record - (DOD, NATO, SEATO, CENTO, IADB) A form for recording photograph, fingerprints, and other pertinent personal data concerning the prisoner of war, including that required by the Geneva Convention.

prisoner of war processing station - (DOD, NATO, SEATO, CENTO, IADB) An installation established for the processing and temporary detention of prisoners of war pending assignment to camps.

prisoners of war - (DOD, IADB) Persons as defined in the Geneva Convention relative to the treatment of prisoners of war (12 August 1949, Part I, Article 4).

Private First Class - PFC.

probability of damage - (DOD, NATO, CENTO, IADB) The probability that damage will occur to a target expressed as a percentage or as a decimal.

probable - (DOD) A term used to qualify a statement made under conditions wherein the available evidence indicates that the statement is factual until there is further evidence in confirmation or denial.

probable error - See horizontal error.

probable error deflection - (DOD) Error in deflection which is exceeded as often as not.

probable error height of burst - (DOD) Error in height of burst which projectile/missile fuzes may be expected to exceed as often as not.

probable error range - (DOD) Error in range which is exceeded as often as not.

probably destroyed (aircraft) - (DOD, NATO, SEATO, CENTO, IADB) A damage assessment on an enemy aircraft seen to break off combat in circumstances which lead to the conclusion that it must be a loss although it is not actually seen to crash.

Probe Eye - An infrared sensing device able to detect the enemy in the dark.

processing - (NATO, CENTO) In photography, the operations necessary to produce negatives, diapositives or prints from exposed films, plates or paper.

proclamation - (DOD, IADB) A document published to the inhabitants of an area which sets forth the basis of authority and scope of activities of a commander in a given area and which defines the obligations, liabilities, duties, and rights of the population affected.

procurement - (DOD, IADB) The process of obtaining personnel, services, supplies, and equipment.

procurement lead time - (DOD, IADB) The interval in months between the initiation of procurement action and receipt into the supply system of the production model (excludes prototypes) purchased as the result of such actions, and is composed of two elements, production lead time and administrative lead time. See also initiation of procurement action; level of supply; receipt into the supply system.

production - (DOD, IADB) The conversion of raw materials into products and/or components thereof, through a series of manufacturing processes. It includes functions of production engineering, controlling, quality assurance, and the determination of resources requirements.

production base - (DOD, IADB) The total national industrial production capacity available for the manufacture of items to meet materiel requirements.

production lead time - (DOD, IADB) The time interval between the placement of a contract and receipt into the supply system of materiel purchased. Two entries are provided: a. (initial) - The time interval if the item is not under production as of the date of contract placement. b. (reorder) - The time interval if the item is under production as of the date of contract placement. See also procurement lead time.

production loss appraisal - (DOD, IADB) An estimate of damage inflicted on an industry in terms of quantities of finished products denied the enemy from the moment of attack, through the period of reconstruction, and to the point when full production is resumed.

professional co-pilot - A bad pilot.

proficiency training aircraft - (DOD) Aircraft required to maintain the proficiency of pilots and other aircrew members who are assigned to nonflying duties.

profile - A prohibition against specific types of duty due to an injury, noted in the personnel file.

proforma - (DOD, NATO, SEATO, CENTO, IADB) 1. A message, the nature of the successive elements of which is understood by prearrangement. 2. A standard form.

program aircraft - (DOD, IADB) The total of the active and reserve aircraft. See also aircraft.

program manager - See system manager.

progress payment - (DOD) Payment made as work progresses under a contract, upon the basis of costs incurred, of percentage of completion accomplished, or of a particular stage of completion. The term does not include payments for partial deliveries accepted by the Government under a contract, or partial payments on contract termination claims.

prohibited area - (DOD, NATO) A specified area within the land areas of a state or territorial waters adjacent thereto over which the flight of aircraft is prohibited. May also refer to land or sea areas to which access is prohibited. See also danger area; restricted area.

project - (DOD) A planned undertaking of something to be accomplished, produced, or constructed, having a finite beginning and a finite ending.

project manager - See system manager.

projectile - (NATO, SEATO, CENTO, IADB) An object projected by an applied exterior force and continuing in motion by virtue of its own inertia, as a bullet, bomb, shell, or grenade. Also applied to rockets and to guided missiles.

projection - (NATO) In cartography, any systematic arrangement of meridians and parallels portraying the curved surface of the sphere or spheroid upon a plane.

projection print - (DOD, NATO, CENTO) An enlarged or reduced photographic print made by projection of the image of a negative or a transparency onto a sensitized surface.

proliferation (nuclear weapons) - (DOD) The process by which one nation after another comes into possession of, or into the right to determine the use of nuclear weapons, each potentially able to launch a nuclear attack upon another nation.

pronto - (DOD) As quickly as possible.

propaganda - (DOD, I) Any form of communication in support of national objectives designed to influence the opinions, emotions, attitudes, or behavior of any group in order to benefit the sponsor, either directly or indirectly. See also black propaganda; grey propaganda; white propaganda.

propaganda - (NATO, SEATO, CENTO, IADB) Any information, ideas, doctrines, or special appeals disseminated to influence the opinions, emotions, attitudes, or behavior of any specified group in order to benefit the sponsor, either directly or indirectly. See also black propaganda; grey propaganda; white propaganda.

propellant - (DOD, NATO, SEATO, CENTO, IADB) That which provides the energy required for propelling a projectile. Specifically an explosive charge for propelling a bullet, shell, or the like; also a fuel, either solid or liquid, for propelling a rocket or missile.

propellant - (SEATO) That which provides the energy for propelling something; specifically an explosive powder charge for propelling a bullet, shell, or the like; also a fuel, either powder or liquid, for propelling a rocket or the like.

property - (DOD) 1. Anything that may be owned. 2. As used in the military establishment, this term is usually confined to tangible property, including real estate and materiel. 3. For special purposes and as used in certain statutes, this term may exclude such items as the public domain, certain lands, certain categories of naval vessels, and records of the Federal Government.

proportional navigation - (DOD) A method of homing navigation in which the missile turn rate is directly proportional to the turn rate in space of the line of sight.

protective clothing - (DOD, NATO, CENTO) Clothing especially designed, fabricated, treated to protect personnel against hazards caused by extreme changes in physical environment, dangerous working conditions, or enemy action.

protective minefield (land mine warfare) - (DOD, NATO, SEATO, CENTO, IADB) A minefield employed to assist a unit in its local, close-in protection. See also minefield (land mine warfare).

prototype - (DOD, SEATO, IADB) A model suitable for evaluation of design, performance, and production potential.

Provider - (DOD, IADB) An assault, twin-engine transport which can operate from short, unprepared landing strips to transport troops and equipment and evacuate wounded. Designated as C-123.

provisional unit - (NATO, SEATO, CENTO, IADB) An assemblage of personnel and equipment temporarily organized for a limited period of time for the accomplishment of a specific mission.

proword - A code word or number used to express a set message which is procedural in nature and not required to be secret. Example: break is used at the end of a message to end it.

proximity fuze - (DOD, NATO, SEATO, CENTO, IADB) A fuze designed to detonate a projectile, bomb, mine, or charge when activated by an external influence in the close vicinity of a target. The variable time fuze is one type of a proximity fuze. See also fuze.

PRP - People's Revolutionary Party.

PRS - The abbreviation for a hand held metal detector using a flat plate above the ground and headphones for the operator. Specific models have added descriptors such as AN/PRS-3.

PRU - Provincial Reconnaissance Unit.

prudent limit of endurance - (NATO, SEATO, CENTO, IADB) The time during which an aircraft can remain airborne and still retain a given safety margin of fuel.

PSC - Province senior advisor.

PSD - Public Safety Directorate, (CORDS).

PSDF - People's Self-Defense Force.

pseudomonas - A bacteria that was common in Vietnam and caused a variety of infections, noted for the blue-green pus that it generated.

pseudopursuit navigation - (DOD) A method of homing navigation in which the missile is directed toward the instantaneous target position in azimuth, while pursuit navigation in elevation is delayed until more favorable angle of attack on the target is achieved.

PSG - 1. Platoon Sergeant. 2. Pacification Studies Group (CORDS).

PSP - Perforated steel plate or perforated steel planking. See Marsden matting.

Psy Op - Psychological operations.

Psychedelic Cookie - The Ninth Division from the eight sided insignia.

psychological operations - (DOD, IADB) These operations include psychological warfare and, in addition, encompass those political, military, economic, and ideological actions planned and conducted to create in neutral or friendly foreign groups the emotions, attitudes, or behavior to support the achievement of national objectives.

psychological warfare - (DOD, IADB) The planned use of propaganda and other psychological actions having the primary purpose of influencing the opinions, emotions, attitudes, and behavior of hostile foreign groups in such a way as to support the achievement of national objectives. See also psychological warfare consolidation.

psychological warfare - (NATO, SEATO, CENTO) The planned use of propaganda and other measures, designed to influence the opinions, emotions, attitude, and behavior of enemy, neutral, or friendly groups in support of current policy and aims, or of a military plan.

psychological warfare consolidation - (DOD, IADB) Psychological warfare directed toward populations in friendly rear areas or in territory occupied by friendly military forces with the objective of facilitating military operations and promoting maximum cooperation among the civil populace. See also psychological warfare.

psyops - Psychological operations.

psywar - Psychological warfare.

PT - 1. Physical training. 2. Physical therapy.

PT Boat - Navy's torpedo boat.

PT-76 - Soviet made tank.

PTAT - Post Telegraph and Telephone System.

PTD - See Portable Truth Detectors.

ptomaine domain - Mess hall.

ptomaine palace - Mess hall.

PTT - 1. One of the three telephone systems in South Vietnam. Also ARVIN and tiger exchange. 2. A Saigon radio station.

pubic affairs - Slang for public affairs, or the office of disinformation.

public affairs - (DOD, IADB) Those public information and community relations activities directed toward the general public by the various elements of the Department of Defense.

public information - (DOD, IADB) Information of a military nature, the dissemination of which through public news media is not inconsistent with security, and the release of which is considered desirable by or non-objectionable to the responsible releasing agency.

PUC - Presidential Unit Citation.

pucker factor - The GI measurement of the level of fear by the tightness of the anal sphincter.

pucker-fucker - 1. Anal intercourse. 2. A homosexual.

Puff the Magic Dragon - 1. See C-47, the fixed wing aircraft with miniguns 2. the Cobra helicopter when equipped with a minigun capable of 6,000 rounds a minute giving the appearance of fire breathing, possibly from the song, Puff the Magic Dragon which was popular in that era 3. Smoking marijuana.

pugil stick - The padded stick used in basic training to simulate attack by a rifle with a fixed bayonet.

Puking Buzzards - The 101st Airborne Division, commonly called the Screaming Eagles.

pull device - The trip wire on a booby trap.

pull it out - To fix a bad situation, possibly from pull it out of the fire.

pull rank - To exert power, take advantage of position, usually to the disadvantage of another.

pull the pin - 1. To leave, as to run from area after a grenade pin is pulled. 2. End something.

pull up - 1. A sudden rise in the nose of a plane in level flight. 2. A recovery from a hard downward path.

pull-pitch - A warning by a helicopter pilot to crew that takeoff was imminent.

pull-up point - (DOD, NATO, CENTO, IADB) The point at which an aircraft must start to climb from a low level approach in order to gain sufficient height from which to execute the attack or retirement. See also air control team; contact point; forward air controller; turn-in point.

pulling lead - Aviation tactic of firing in front of an enemy aircraft so the trajectory and enemy plane collide. Pronounced leed.

pulse duration - (DOD) In radar, measurement of pulse transmission time in microseconds, that is, the time the radar's transmitter is energized during each cycle. Also called pulse length and pulse width.

pulse repetition frequency - (DOD) In radar, the number of pulses that occur each second. Not to be confused with transmission frequency which is determined by the rate at which cycles are repeated within the transmitted pulse.

pulsejet - (DOD, NATO, CENTO, IADB) A jet-propulsion engine, containing neither compressor nor turbine. Equipped with valves in the front which open and shut, it takes in air to create thrust in rapid periodic bursts rather than continuously.

punch - (DOD) In air intercept, a code meaning you should very soon be obtaining a contact on the aircraft that is being intercepted. (Only use with "air intercept" interceptions.)

punch out - Eject from an aircraft.

pungi sticks, pungi stakes - See punji sticks.

punji pit - The hole containing punji sticks that is covered or camouflaged.

punji sticks or punji stakes - Sharpened bamboo sticks hidden under brush or in a pit as a booby trap. The tips often had fecal material on them to induce infection in the puncture wound. These accounted for 2% of the combat wounds in Vietnam. Incorrectly spelled pungi.

purchase - (DOD, IADB) To procure property or services for a price; includes obtaining by barter. See also collaborative purchase; joint purchase; single department purchase.

purchase description - (DOD) A statement outlining the essential characteristics and functions of an item, service, or material required to meet the minimum needs of the Government. It is used when a specification is not available or when specific procurement specifications are not required by the individual Military Departments or the Department of Defense.

purchase description - (DOD) A statement outlining the essential characteristics and functions of an item, service, or material required to meet the minimum needs the Government. It is used when a specification is not available or when specific procurement specifications are not required by the individual Military Departments or the Department of Defense.

purchase description - (IADB) A statement outlining the essential characteristics and functions of an item, service, or material required to meet the minimum needs of the purchaser.

purchase notice agreements - (DOD) Agreements concerning the purchase of brand name items for resale purposes established by each military Service under the control of the Military Subsistence Supply Agency.

purchasing office - (DOD, IADB) Any installation or activity, or any division, office, branch, section, unit, or other organizational element of an installation or activity charged with the functions of procuring supplies or services.

purple - (DOD) In air intercept, a code meaning the unit indicated is suspected of carrying nuclear weapons. (i.e. "purple VB").

Purple Heart - The oldest of the military decorations dating to the Revolutionary War, awarded for being wounded or killed by an enemy or hostile force.

purple out zone - An emergency evacuation.

purple vision - Night vision, easily lost by exposure to white light, but not red.

push - Slang for radio frequency.

Push Me, Pull You - See O-2, an aircraft.

pushes - Medical slang for an unusually high number of incoming cases at once.

pushing the envelope - 1. Aviation for flying at or beyond the maximum tolerances. 2. Slang for pushing the rules or limits.

pussy cut off date - The last date for sex which would guarantee the remediation of any venereal disease prior to the DEROS date, as infection would delay the exit from Vietnam.

Puzzle Palace - 1. Slang for headquarters. 2. The Pentagon.

PV2 - Private 2 (Army).

PVT - Private (Army).

Pvt - Private (Marine Corps).

PX - Post Exchange. The military store for personal items on post. See BX.

PX Hero - A person who bought medals at the PX but did not earn them.

PX issue - The basic issue of clothes and gear.

PZ - Pick up zone.

Q – QUEBEC

Q - Designated in the phonetic military alphabet as "Quebec".

Q course - The qualification course for Special Forces.

Q-ship - See decoy ship.

Q-Star - See Quiet Star.

QH-50 - See Drone Antisubmarine Helicopter.

QM - Quartermaster.

QRC-160 - Quick reaction capability, a radar jamming device.

QT - Quick time.

QU-22 - Bonanza See U-8.

Quaaludes - A sedative, often abused.

quad - 1. Slang for the number four. 2. A quadraplegic individual.

Quad 50 - A four barrel configuration of .50 cal machine

Quad 60 - See XM-6 machine gun.

Quad U - See UUUU.

quadrant elevation - (DOD) The angle between the level base of the trajectory/horizontal and the axis of the bore when laid. It is the algebraic sum of the elevation, angle of site, and complementary angle of site.

quadriplegic - A person without use of four limbs. See quad and blinker.

Quail - (DOD) An air-launched decoy missile carried internally in the B-52 and used to degrade the effectiveness of enemy radar, interceptor aircraft, air defense missiles, etc. Designated as ADM-20.

Quartermaster - The NCO in charge of issuing property and supplies.

quartermaster property - Slang for a dead soldier as burial details were often in quartermaster area of responsibility.

quarters - Navy and Marine slang for residence area, living space.

Quebec - The military phonetic alphabet designation for the letter "Q".

queen of battle - The infantry, after the chess piece that is powerful and mobile.

Queen's Cobras - A Royal Thai infantry regiment.

quick fix - A temporary repair.

quick search procedure - (NATO, SEATO, CENTO, IADB) A method of search done as quickly as possible by searching the entire area on the outbound leg and by using twice as many aircraft as are normally used.

quick step - Slang for running in a crouched position from one bunker to the next.

quick time - A pace of 120 steps a minute with each step about 30 inches in length.

quicktrans - (DOD) Long term contract airlift service within continental United States for the movement of cargo in support of the logistic system for the military Services (primarily the Navy and Marine Corps) and Department of Defense agencies.

Quiet Star - A small observation plane made by Lockheed that was so quiet in operation so that it was almost not heard on the ground when flying at 1200 feet. The observer sat in front of the pilot. Less than a dozen were built. Also called the Q-Star.

quiz room - Interrogation room.

Quoc Ngu - The system for writing Vietnamese in Roman letters, originally devised by French missionary, now the common way to write the language.

Quonset hut - A building made of arched corrugated metal forming a half-pipe shape with a flat wall at either end.

R – ROMEO

R - 1. Designated in the phonetic military alphabet as "Romeo". 2. Designation of regimental duties.

R-1 - Designation for divisional administration.

R-2 - Designation for divisional intelligence.

R-3 - Designation for divisional operations. 2. Staff officer assignment at the divisional level as a tactical advisor.

R-4 - Designation for divisional supply.

r-max - Maximum range.

R. P. - Route Package.

R&R - Rest and Relaxation. Leave, usually out of Vietnam, once during the year, ranging from three to seven days, locations that were pre-designated. For those extending for a second tour of duty in Vietnam, a month of R&R was granted.

R4D - Navy and Marine version of the C-47 transport airplane.

RA - 1. Regular Army, the designation before the serial number of Americans who enlisted (See US). 2. Rear Admiral.

RA3 - See B-66.

RA5 - See A-5

RAAF - Royal Australian Air Force.

rabbit - 1. A white person. 2. See dog collar.

RABFAC - Small radar beacons used by Forward Air Controllers to direct artillery strikes.

rack - Marine term for bed or cot, as hit the rack to get some sleep. See bunk.

rack out - Get some sleep.

rack time - Getting rest or sleep.

rad - (DOD, NATO, CENTO, IADB) Unit of absorbed dose of radiation. It represents the absorption of 100 ergs of nuclear (or ionizing) radiation per gram of the absorbing material or tissue.

RAD - Research and Development (CORDS).

rad mon - Radiation monitoring of a person's exposure.

radar - (DOD, NATO, SEATO, CENTO, IADB) Radio detection and ranging equipment that determines the distance and usually the direction of objects by transmission and return of electromagnetic energy.

radar advisory - (DOD) The term used to indicate that the provision of advice and information is based on radar observation.

radar altimetry area - (DOD, NATO) A large and comparatively level terrain area with a defined elevation which can be used in determining the altitude of airborne equipment by the use of radar.

radar beacon - (DOD) A receiver-transmitter combination which sends out a coded signal when triggered by the proper type of pulse, enabling determination of range and bearing information by the interrogating station or aircraft.

radar burnthrough - The ability of radar to penetrate radar blocking efforts.

radar clutter - (NATO, CENTO) Unwanted signals, echoes, or images on the face of the display tube which interfere with observation of desired signals.

radar countermeasures - See electronic countermeasures.

radar coverage - (DOD, NATO, SEATO, CENTO, IADB) The limits within which objects can be detected by one or more radar stations.

radar deception - See electronic deception.

radar fire - (NATO, SEATO, CENTO, IADB) Gunfire aimed at a target which is tracked by radar. See also fire.

radar horizon - (NATO, CENTO) The line at which direct radar rays are tangential to the earth's surface.

radar imagery - (DOD) Imagery produced by recording radar waves reflected from a given target surface.

radar intelligence item - (NATO, CENTO) A feature which is radar significant but which cannot be identified exactly at the moment of its appearance as homogenous.

Radar Intercept Officer - The "second seat" in a fighter-bomber aircraft.

radar MQ-74 - Heat seeking targeting radar. Also snake eye.

radar netting - (DOD, NATO, CENTO) The linking of several radars to a single center to provide integrated target information.

radar netting station - (DOD, NATO, CENTO) A center which can receive data from radar tracking stations and exchange this data among other radar tracking stations, thus forming a radar netting system. See also radar netting unit; radar tracking station.

radar netting unit - (DOD) Optional electronic equipment which converts the operations central of certain air defense fire distribution systems to a radar netting station. See also radar netting station.

radar paint - Pilot's slang for the image on their radar scope.

radar picket - (DOD, NATO, CENTO, IADB) Any ship, aircraft, or vehicle, stationed at a distance from the force protected, for the purpose of increasing the radar detection range.

radar picket cap - (DOD) Radar picket combat air patrol.

radar picket escort ship - (DOD, IADB) These are escort ships modified to give increased combat information center, electronic countermeasures, and electronic search facilities. Designated as DER.

radar position - Aviation term for the three position missile selection switch on the control panel of the F-4

radar reconnaissance - (DOD) Reconnaissance by means of radar to obtain information on enemy activity and to determine the nature of terrain.

radar signal film - (DOD) The film on which is recorded all the reflected signals acquired by a coherent radar, and which must be viewed or processed through an optical correlator to permit interpretation.

radar signature - Aviation term for the distinctive radar pattern given by different airplanes when displayed on the radar screen.

radar silence - (DOD, NATO, CENTO, IADB) An imposed discipline prohibiting the transmission by radar of electromagnetic signals on some or all frequencies.

radar tracking station - (DOD) A radar facility which has the capability of tracking moving targets.

radarscope overlays - (NATO, CENTO) Transparent overlays for placing on the radarscope for comparison and identification of radar returns.

radarscope photography - (NATO, CENTO) A film record of the returns shown by a radar screen.

radiac - (DOD, NATO, SEATO, CENTO, IADB) A term devised to designate various types of radiological measuring instruments or equipment. (This term is derived from the words "radioactivity detection, indication, and computation", and is normally used as an adjective.)

radiac dosimeter - (DOD, NATO, CENTO, IADB) An instrument used to measure the ionizing radiation absorbed by that instrument.

radial - (DOD) A magnetic bearing extending from a very high frequency omnirange/tactical air navigation station.

radiant exposure - See thermal exposure.

radiation dose - (DOD, NATO, CENTO) The total amount of ionizing radiation absorbed by material or tissues, commonly expressed in rads. (DOD) The term radiation dose is often used in the sense of the exposure dose expressed in roentgens, which is a measure of the total amount of ionization that the quantity of radiation could produce in air. This should be distinguished from the absorbed dose, also given in rads, which represents the energy absorbed from the radiation per gram of specified body tissue. Further, the biological dose, in rems, is a measure of the biological effectiveness of the radiation exposure.

radiation dose - (IADB) The total amount of ionizing radiation absorbed by material or tissue.

radiation dose (dosage) - See radiation dose.

radiation dose rate - (DOD, NATO, CENTO, IADB) The radiation dose (dosage) absorbed per unit of time. (DOD) A radiation dose rate can be set at some particular unit of time (e.g., H+1hour) and would be called H+1 radiation dose rate.

radiation intensity - (DOD, NATO, CENTO, IADB) The radiation dose rate at a given time and place. It may be used coupled with a figure to denote the radiation intensity used at a given number of hours after a nuclear burst, e.g., RI3 is the radiation intensity 3 hours after the time of burst.

radiation scattering - (DOD, NATO, CENTO, IADB) The diversion of radiation (thermal, electromagnetic, or nuclear) from its original path as a result of interactions or collisions with atoms, molecules, or larger particles in the atmosphere or other media between the source of radiation (e.g., a nuclear explosion) and a point at some distance away. As a result of scattering, radiation (especially gamma rays and neutrons) will be received at such a point from many directions instead of only from the direction of the source.

radiation sickness - (NATO, CENTO) An illness resulting from excessive exposure to ionizing radiation. The earliest symptoms are nausea, vomiting, and diarrhea, which may be followed by loss of hair, hemorrhage, inflammation of the mouth and throat, and general loss of energy.

radiation situation map - (NATO, CENTO, IADB) A map showing the actual and/or predicted radiation situation in the area of interest.

radio - See PRC.

radio amplifier - A box that improved the quality and sound. See bitch box.

radio and wire integration - (DOD) The combining of wire circuits with radio facilities.

radio approach aids - (DOD, NATO, SEATO, CENTO, IADB) Equipment making use of radio to determine the position of an aircraft with considerable accuracy from the time it is in the vicinity of an airfield or carrier until it reaches a position from which landing can be carried out.

radio beacon - (NATO, SEATO, CENTO, IADB) A radio transmitter which emits a distinctive or characteristic signal used for the determination of bearings, courses, or location. See also beacon.

radio brevity code - The use of brief letters, numbers or codes to convey longer messages, not needed to be in code for secrecy. An informal and ever changing system of designations by which radio operators communicated location or status of personnel by using informal referents. For example, a map coordinate could be designated as "Buick" and radio orders given to go in relation to that coded position, not actual geographic names, which would be easily understood and draw fire.

radio call sign - Radio communications call signs designated the function of the speaker. Examples: 2 was the intelligence officer, 3 was the operations officer, 4 was the command NCO or Sergeant, 5 was the executive officer or second in command, 6 was the unit commander. Added alpha-numeric designations were made for units and operations, and frequently changed.

radio code - 1. Official terms used to denote military objectives, locations or strength. 2. Unofficial terms used by infantry radiomen for clarity over the static of the equipment and noise of battle. 3. The slang developed to disguise information such as Coors five for a five dead soldiers. 4. The extensive numeric list of unauthorized codes used by pilots to express displeasure or conduct non-military related chatter after complaints over the use of obscenity or private conversations. These varied from unit to unit or between services.

radio countermeasures - See electronic countermeasures.

radio deception - (DOD, IADB) The employment of radio to deceive the enemy. Radio deception includes sending false dispatches, using deceptive headings, employing enemy call signs, etc. See also electronic deception.

radio detection - (DOD, NATO, SEATO, CENTO, IADB) The detection of the presence of an object by radio location without precise determination of its position.

radio direction finding - (DOD, NATO, SEATO, CENTO, IADB) Radio location in which only the direction of a station is determined by means of its emissions.

radio direction finding data base - (DOD) The aggregate of information, acquired by both airborne and surface means, necessary to provide support to radio direction finding operations to produce fixes on target transmitters/emitters. The resultant bearings and fixes serve as a basis for tactical decisions concerning military operations, including exercises, planned or underway.

radio fix - (DOD, NATO, CENTO, IADB) l. The location of a friendly or enemy radio. transmitter, determined by finding the direction of the radio transmitter from two or more listening stations. 2. The location of a ship or aircraft by determining the direction of radio signals coming to the ship or aircraft from two or more sending stations, the locations of which are known.

radio guard - (DOD, IADB) A ship, aircraft, or radio station designated to listen for and record transmissions, and to handle traffic on a designated frequency for a certain unit or units.

radio navigation - (NATO, SEATO, CENTO, IADB) Radio location intended for the determination of position or direction or for obstruction warning in navigation.

radio range finding - (DOD, NATO, SEATO, CENTO, IADB) Radio location in which the distance of an object is determined by means of its radio emissions, whether independent, reflected, or retransmitted on the same or other wave length.

radio range station - (DOD, NATO, SEATO, CENTO, IADB) A radio navigation land station in the aeronautical radio navigation service providing radio equisignal zones. In certain instances a radio range station may be placed on board a ship.

radio recognition - (DOD, NATO, SEATO, CENTO, IADB) The determination by radio means of the friendly or enemy character, or the individuality, of another.

radio recognition and identification - See Identification Friend or Foe.

radio relay - The communications technique of extending the limited range of radio communications by using several short range radios in a chain so that a message sent from A to B is then sent by B to C and so on. The messages were designed to be very clear and short to avoid errors in retransmission.

radio silence - (NATO, SEATO, CENTO, IADB) A period during which all or certain radio equipment capable of radiation is kept inoperative. (In combined or United States joint or intra-Service communications the frequency bands and/or types of equipment affected will be specified.)

radio sonobuoy - See sonobuoy.

radio telegraphy - (NATO, SEATO, CENTO) The transmission of telegraphic codes by means of radio.

Radio Telephone Operator - The soldier carrying and managing the portable radio telephone packs in the field. Also RTO.

radio telephony - (NATO, SEATO, CENTO, IADB) The transmission of speech by means of modulated radio waves.

radioactivity - (DOD) The spontaneous emission of radiation, generally alpha or beta particles, often accompanied by gamma rays, from the nuclei of an unstable isotope.

radioactivity concentration guide - (DOD, NATO, CENTO) The amount of any specified radioisotope that is acceptable in air and water for continuous consumption.

radiological defense - (DOD, NATO, CENTO, IADB) Defensive measures taken against the radiation hazard resulting from the employment of nuclear and radiological weapons.

radiological monitoring - See monitoring and rad mon.

radiological operations - (DOD, NATO, CENTO, IADB) Employment of radioactive materials or radiation producing devices to cause casualties or restrict the use of terrain. Includes the intentional employment of fallout from nuclear weapons.

radiological survey - (DOD, NATO, CENTO, IADB) The directed effort to determine the distribution and dose rates of radiation in an area.

radiological survey flight altitude - (DOD, IADB) The altitude at which an aircraft is flown during an aerial radiological survey.

radius of action - (DOD, NATO, SEATO, CENTO, IADB) The maximum distance a ship, aircraft, or vehicle can travel away from its base along a given course with normal combat load and return without refueling, allowing for all safety and operating factors.

radius of damage - (DOD) The distance from ground zero at which there is a 0.50 probability of achieving the desired damage.

radius of integration - (DOD) The distance from ground zero which indicates the area within which the effects of both the nuclear detonation and conventional weapons are to be integrated.

radius of safety - (DOD, NATO, CENTO, IADB) The horizontal distance from ground zero beyond which the weapon effects on friendly troops are acceptable.

RADM - Rear Admiral (upper half) (Navy, Coast Guard).

RAG - River Assault Group, a South Vietnamese manned river patrol group.

rag boats - In riverine operations, the boats used by the South Vietnamese that carried about 25 men assigned to a River Assault Group.

rag stuffer - A parachute rigger who folded the parachute into the pack.

raid - (DOD, NATO, SEATO, CENTO, IADB) An operation, usually small scale, involving a swift penetration of hostile territory to secure information, confuse the enemy, or to destroy his installations. It ends with a planned withdrawal upon completion of the assigned mission.

Rail - First Lieutenant from the insignia which is a single silver bar.

rail capacity - (DOD, NATO, CENTO) The maximum number of trains which can be planned to move in both directions over a specified section of track in a 24-hour period.

railroad tracks - The insignia for captain. Captain's bars.

railway end-loading ramp - (DOD, NATO, CENTO) A sloping platform situated at the end of a track and rising to the level of the floor of the rail cars (wagons).

rainfall (nuclear) - (DOD) The water that is precipatated from the base surge clouds after an underwater burst of a nuclear weapon. This rain is radioactive and presents an important secondary effect of such a burst.

rainout - (DOD, NATO, CENTO, IADB) Radioactive material in the atmosphere brought down by precipitation.

rallier - A Viet Cong defector.

rally - A meeting time and place for a scattered reconnaissance team.

ram air turbine - The emergency system on aircraft that powers the electrical and hydraulic systems if the main power source fails by having the air flow operate an auxiliary generator.

RAMF - Rear area mother fucker. Someone with a desk job away from combat.

ramjet - (DOD, NATO, CENTO, IADB) A jet-propulsion engine containing neither compressor nor turbine which depends for its operation on the air compression accomplished by the forward motion of the engine. See also pulsejet.

ramp - 1. Aviation term for the runway apron. 2. Hospital term for the entry area to the hospital, as stairs would impede delivery of patients on litters in the field or gurneys in a fixed base hospital.

ramp alert - An aviation order placing all personnel and equipment on a 15 minute stand-by to takeoff status. Also hot pad alert and strip alert.

ramp strike - Aviation term for a crash caused by landing short on a runway or flight deck of a carrier.

ramp tramp - 1. Aviation term for the flight line supervisor. 2. Hospital term for a supervisor responsible for overall operations.

ramp up - Hospital slang for: 1. A warning to expect a surge in activity. 2. An increase in the intensity of work, whether from staff reduction, case complexity or increased admissions.

ramps - Aviation term for the adjustable air vents on supersonic aircraft which buffer the shock of going from subsonic to supersonic speed and regulate the air intake into the engines.

Ranch Hand - The C-123 tanker aircraft fitted with tanks to hold the defoliation liquid sprayed on the jungle.

Randall knife - A 7.5 inch fixed blade knife with a leather sheath and sharpening stone. Also Model 14.

random minelaying - See scattered laying (land mine warfare).

range - (DOD, NATO, CENTO, IADB) 1. The distance between any given point and an object or target. 2. Extent or distance limiting the operation or action of something, such as the range of an aircraft, ship, or gun. 3. The distance which can be covered over a hard surface by a ground vehicle, with its rated payload, using the fuel in its tank and in cans normally carried as part of the ground vehicle equipment. 4. Area equipped for practice in shooting at targets. In this meaning, also called target range.

range (transport vehicles) - (SEATO) The distance which can be covered by a vehicle with its rated payload over hard surfaces using the fuel in the tanks.

range card - Infantry term for an orientation card that showed position sectors and the direction of fire.

range marker - (NATO, CENTO) A single calibration blip fed on to the time base of a radial display. The rotation of the time base shows the single blips as a circle on the plan position indicator scope. It may be used to measure range.

range markers - (DOD, IADB) Two upright markers which may be lighted at night, placed so that when aligned, the direction indicated assists in piloting. They may be used in amphibious operations to aid in beaching landing ships or craft.

range resolution - (NATO, CENTO) The ability of the radar equipment to separate two reflecting objects on a similar bearing, but at different ranges from the antenna. The ability is determined primarily by the pulse length in use.

range spread - (DOD) The technique used to place the mean point of impact of two or more units 100 meters apart on the gun-target line.

Ranger roll - Wrapping clothing into a roll to hold above the head, out of water, when swimming or wading in deep water crossing streams or rivers.

Rangers - U.S. Army light infantry. See Sneaky Pete.

ranging - (DOD, NATO, CENTO, IADB) The process of establishing target distance. Types of ranging include echo, intermittent, manual, navigational, explosive echo, optical, radar, etc. See also spot.

rank - The military designation of an individual's position of authority in the military. Note, military rank designations are abbreviated in military records as all capital letters without periods.

RAP - Rear area pussy. Support troops not in combat.

Rapid Securing Device - A device on a carrier into which a helicopter lands to be secured on deck.

RAT - Ram Air Turbine.

rat fuck - A mission or activity doomed for failure.

rat patrol - Ambush patrols operating at night, usually four men in a Jeep with machine guns.

rat trap - Marine nickname for 2-3 man spider holes in which VC would hide in daylight.

rat turds - See oak leaf cluster.

rate of fire - (DOD, NATO, SEATO, CENTO, IADB) The number of rounds fired per weapon per minute.

rate of march - (DOD, NATO, CENTO, IADB) The average number of miles or kilometers to be travelled in a given period of time, including all ordered halts. It is expressed in miles or kilometers in the hour.

ratio print - (DOD) A print the scale of which has been changed from that of the negative by photographic enlargement or reduction.

ration card - The card given to soldiers allowing the purchase of a set amount of a product over a set time period, limiting access to some items such as liquor. However, given the black market, this control was easily bypassed.

ration dense - (DOD, IADB) Foods which, through processing, have been reduced in volume and quantity to a small compact package without appreciable loss of food value, quality, or acceptance, with a high yield in relation to space occupied, such as dehydrates and concentrates.

ration of shit - 1. A hard time. 2. Getting chewed out by a superior.

ration supplement pack - The added pack with rations containing bootlaces, candy, stationary, pipe tobacco pipe or cigarettes.

ration supply pack - See ration supplement pack.

ratline - (DOD) An organized effort for moving personnel and/or material by clandestine means across a denied area or border.

Raven - The OH-23 helicopter.

RB-26 - See B-26.

RB-47 - See Stratojet.

RB-57 - See Canberra.

RB-66 - See Destroyer.

RBF - Reconnaissance by fire.

RC-130 - See C-130.

RC-47 - See C-47.

RCA - Riot Control Agents such as tear gas.

RD - 1. Revolutionary Development. 2. Rural Development.

Rds - Rounds of ammunition.

RDML - Rear Admiral (lower half) (Navy, Coast Guard).

RE - Reports and Evaluation Division (CORDS).

RE Codes - The alpha-numeric code on the DD214 discharge form indicating the person's reenlistment status.

re-up - To re-enlist or extend a tour of duty.

react - The assistance one unit provided another unit under enemy fire.

reaction force - Relief reinforcements.

reaction time - (DOD, IADB) 1. The elapsed time between the initiation of an action and the required response. 2. The time required between the receipt of an order directing an operation and the arrival of the initial element of the force concerned in the designated area.

read - To understand or hear.

readiness condition - See operational readiness.

ready - (DOD) The term used to indicate that a weapon(s) is aimed, loaded, and prepared to fire.

ready box - The wood box where extra ammunition was stored.

ready cap - (DOD) Fighter aircraft in condition of "standby".

ready light - A light indication that some system is activated and ready to go, commonly on an instrument control panel or ordinance.

ready position (helicopter) - (NATO, CENTO, IADB) A designated place where a stick waits for the order to emplane in a helicopter.

real bush - An American/Caucasian female.

real estate - Territory gained or lost.

real property - (DOD) Lands, buildings, structures, utilities systems, improvements and appurtenances thereto. Includes equipment attached to and made part of buildings and structures (such as heating systems) but not movable equipment (such as plant equipment).

real time - (DOD) The absence of delay, except for the time required for the transmission by electromagnetic energy, between the occurrence of an event or the transmission of data, and the knowledge of the event, or reception of the data at some other location. See also near real time; reporting time interval.

real time - A computer that sorts and reports data almost instantly, rather than batch processing overnight or once a week.

reallocation of resources - (NATO, CENTO) The provision of logistic resources by the military forces of one nation from those deemed "made available" under the terms incorporated in appropriate (NATO) (CENTO) documents, to the military forces of another nation or nations as directed by the appropriate military authority. See also integrated logistic support; logistic assistance; mutual aid.

Rear Admiral - The rank is related historically to that of Commodore. The Navy and Coast Guard used Commodore as a rank and title at various times in its history, causing confusion as to actual pay grades and authority during the reductions after WWII. After the Vietnam War, the Navy and Coast Guard abandoned the Commodore rank and title, substituting two forms of Rear Admiral: Rear Admiral, lower half is abbreviated RDML at a pay grade of O-7 and Rear Admiral, upper half, is abbreviated RADM at pay grade O-8.

rear area - (DOD, IADB) The area in the rear of the combat and forward areas. See also Army service area; communications zone.

rear area pussy - Someone working in the rear area away from combat.

rear area security - (DOD, NATO, CENTO, IADB) The measures taken prior to, during, and/or after an enemy airborne attack, sabotage action, infiltration, guerrilla action, and/or initiation of psychological or propaganda warfare to minimize the effects thereof. See also area damage control; damage control; disaster control.

rear echelon (air transport) - (DOD, NATO, SEATO, CENTO, IADB) Elements of a force which are not required in the objective area.

rear guard - (DOD) Security detachment that protects the rear of a column from hostile forces. During a withdrawal, it delays the enemy by armed resistance, destroying bridges and blocking roads.

rear guard - (NATO, CENTO) The rearmost elements of an advancing or withdrawing force. It has the following functions: a. to protect the rear of a column from hostile forces; b. during the withdrawal, to delay the enemy; and c. during the advance, to keep supply routes open.

rearming - (DOD, IADB) 1. An operation that replenishes the prescribed stores of ammunition, bombs, and other armament items for an aircraft, naval ship, tank, or armored vehicle, including replacement of defective ordnance equipment, in order to make it ready for combat service. 2. Resetting the fuze on a bomb, or on an artillery, mortar, or rocket projectile, so that it will detonate at the desired time.

recce - Shortened version of reconnaissance. Pronounced like wreck-ee. Often misspelled as recky.

recce formation - Aviation term for an aerial formation of multiple planes in a combat spread in which each plane is at a 45-60 degree trail aft of the lead plane to cluster firepower. Pronounced like wreck-ee, from the word reconnaissance.

receipt into the supply system - (DOD, IADB) That point in time when the first item or first quantity of the item of the contract has been received at or is en route to point of first delivery after inspection and acceptance. See also procurement lead time.

reception - (DOD) 1. All ground arrangements connected with the delivery and disposition of air or sea drops. Includes selection and preparation of site, signals for warning and approach, facilitation of secure departure of agents, speedy collection of delivered articles, and their prompt removal to storage places having maximum security. When a group is involved, it may be called a reception committee. 2. Arrangements to welcome and provide secure quarters or transportation for defectors, escapees, evaders, or incoming agents.

reciprocal jurisdiction - (DOD) The exercise of court martial jurisdiction by one armed force over personnel of another armed force, pursuant to specific authorization by the President or by the Secretary of Defense.

recky - See reece.

reclama - (DOD, IADB) A request to duly constituted authority to reconsider its decision or its proposed action.

recognition - (NATO, CENTO, IADB) The determination by any means of the friendly or enemy character or of the individuality of another, or of objects such as aircraft, ships, or tanks, or of phenomena such as communications-electronics patterns.

recognition - (SEATO) The determination by any means of the friendly or enemy character or of the individuality of another.

recognition signal - (DOD, IADB) Any prearranged signal by which individuals or units may identify each other.

recoilless rifle (heavy) - (DOD, IADB) A weapon capable of being fired from either a ground mount or from a vehicle, and capable of destroying tanks.

recon - See reconnaissance.

recon gloves - Black leather gloves without a thumb or trigger finger, designed to be worn with a wool inner glove.

recon patrol - A patrol sent to get facts on the enemy status such as location, direction of movement, strength and any other information of assistance.

recon zone - The specific map grid of the area to be worked by a recon patrol.

reconnaissance - (DOD, NATO, CENTO, IADB) A mission undertaken to obtain, by visual observation or other detection methods, information about the activities and resources of an enemy or potential enemy; or to secure data concerning the meteorological, hydrographic, or geographic characteristics of a particular area.

reconnaissance by fire - (DOD, NATO, SEATO, CENTO, IADB) A method of reconnaissance in which fire is placed on a suspected enemy position to cause the enemy to disclose his presence by movement or return of fire.

reconnaissance by force - A tactic to discover the enemy not by stealth but by initiating an attack. Similar to search and destroy.

reconnaissance patrol - See patrol.

reconnaissance patrol (ground) - (NATO, SEATO, CENTO) A small patrol used to gain information of the enemy, preferably without his knowledge. See also combat air patrol; combat fighting patrol (ground); fighting patrol; patrol.

reconnaissance photography - (DOD) Photography taken primarily for purposes other than making maps, charts, or mosaics. It is used to obtain information on the results of bombing, or on enemy movements, concentrations, activities, and forces.

reconstitute - 1. To reactivate a unit that had been deactivated. 2. To rehydrate the freeze dried meals used later in the war.

reconstitution site - (DOD) A location selected by the surviving command authority as the site at which a damage or destroyed headquarters can be reformed from survivors of the attack and/or personnel from other sources, predesignated as replacements.

record as target - (DOD) The order used to denote that the target is to be recorded for future engagement or reference.

recovery airfield - (DOD, IADB) Any airfield, military or civil, at which aircraft might land post H-hour. It is not expected that combat missions would be conducted from a recovery airfield. See also airfield.

recovery and reconstitution - (DOD, IADB) Those actions taken by one nation prior to, during, and following an attack by an enemy nation to minimize the effects of the attack, rehabilitate the national economy, provide for the welfare of the populace, and maximize the combat potential of remaining forces and supporting activities.

rectification - (DOD, NATO, CENTO) In photogrammetry, the process of projecting a tilted or oblique photograph onto a horizontal reference plane.

recuperation - (DOD) Not to be used. See recovery and reconstitution.

recurring demand - (DOD, IADB) A request made periodically or anticipated to be repetitive by an authorized requisitioner for materiel for consumption or use or for stock replenishment.

recycle - To repeat some training.

red - 1. Generally a word indicating danger when describing an area or mission. See red LZ. 2. Communist.

red alert - Signal that enemy attack is immediate.

red ball - An enemy road or trail that can be used for high speed transportation.

Red Ball Express - See Priority 999.

Red Bird - Slang for the Cobra helicopter.

red bombs - Sleeping pills.

red book - The Uniform Code of Military Justice.

red broom handle - An enemy booby trap made by placing the explosive on a stake like a broom handle about 2-3 feet above ground so leg injury was significant when the trigger wire was tripped.

Red Cross - See American Red Cross.

Red Crown - Code for the U.S. Navy's radar control of aviation near an area defended by a fleet. See PIRAZ.

Red Diamond - Slang for the Fifth Infantry Division from the insignia.

red dog - Radio code for a squad size patrol.

red hat - A red tracer bullet.

red horse - The Air Force construction units able to do rapid airfield construction and repair.

red leg - Artilleryman, from the red stripe on their formal uniform trousers.

red LZ - A hot LZ, under fire.

red phone - The emergency telephone used only is the most extreme emergencies.

red smoke - A hot LZ, under fire.

red team - Armed helicopters.

redball - See red ball.

REDCOM - The Readiness Command composed of U.S. Army and Air Force units in the United States which were available for deployment.

redeployment - (DOD, IADB) The transfer of a unit, an individual, or supplies deployed in one area to another area, or to another location within the area, or to the zone of interior for the purpose of further employment.

redeployment airfield - (DOD, NATO, SEATO, CENTO, IADB) An airfield not occupied in its entirety in peacetime, but available immediately upon outbreak of war for use and occupation by units redeployed from their peacetime locations. It must have substantially the same standard of operational facilities as a main airfield. See also airfield; alternative airfield; departure airfield; main airfield.

redesignated site - (DOD) A surviving facility that may be redesignated as the command center to carryon the functions of an incapacitated alternate headquarters and/or facility.

redesignation - Renaming or renumbering a unit or ship.

Redeye - (DOD, IADB) A man-transportable guided missile, fired from the shoulder, designed to provide combat troops with the capability of destroying low-flying aircraft. Designated as XFIM-43A.

redeye - Slang, an overnight flight.

redistribution - (DOD, IADB) The act of effecting transfer in control, utilization, or location of material between units or activities within or among the military Services or between the military Services and other Federal agencies. (Note: IADB definition uses the words "governmental agencies" instead of "Federal agencies".)

reds - Sleeping pills, when being abused.

Redstone - (DOD, IADB) A mobile, liquid-propellant, surface-to-surface guided missile, with a nuclear warhead capability, designed to support the field army by attacking targets up to a range of 175 nautical miles. Designated as PGM-ll.

reduced charge - (DOD) The smaller of the two propelling charges available for naval guns.

reduction (photographic) - (DOD) The production of a negative, diapositive, or print at a scale smaller than the original.

reefer - (DOD, IADB) 1. A refrigerator. 2. A motor vehicle, railroad freight car, ship, aircraft, or other conveyance, so constructed and insulated as to protect commodities from either heat or cold.

reefer - 1. A marijuana cigarette. 2. Refrigerated truck when used as portable morgue.

reentry vehicle - (DOD, NATO, SEATO, CENTO, IADB) That part of a space vehicle designed to reenter the earth's atmosphere in the terminal portion of its trajectory. See also maneuverable reentry vehicle; multiple independently targetable reentry vehicle; multiple reentry vehicle.

reference box - See information box.

reference datum - (NATO, SEATO, CENTO, IADB) As used in the loading of aircraft, an imaginary vertical plane at or near the nose of the aircraft from which all horizontal distances are measured for balance purposes. Diagrams of each aircraft show this reference datum as balance station zero.

reference line - (DOD) A convenient and readily identifiable line used by the observer or spotter as the line to which spots will be related. One of three types of spotting lines. See also spotting line.

reference point - (DOD) A prominent, easily located point in the terrain.

reflected shock wave - (DOD) When a shock wave traveling in a medium strikes the interface between this medium and a denser medium, part of the energy of the shock wave induces a shock wave in the denser medium and the remainder of the energy results in the formation of a reflected shock wave which travels back through the less dense medium. See also shock wave.

reflex force - (DOD) (Pertaining to Air Force units.) That part of the alert force maintained overseas or at zone of interior forward bases by scheduled rotations.

refugee - (DOD, NATO, SEATO, CENTO, IADB) A civilian who by reason of real or imagined danger has left his home to seek safety elsewhere. See also displaced person; evacuee; expellee.

regiment - 1. Army term for armored cavalry. 2. Marine Corps term for three battalions.

regimental landing team - (DOD, IADB) A task organization for landing, comprised of an infantry regiment reinforced by those elements which are required for initiation of its combat function ashore.

regional boundaries - (SEATO, IADB) Lines which delineate geographical areas of the world for broad planning purposes.

Regional Forces - South Vietnamese army units operating at the district level. The local militia. See Popular Forces.

register - (NATO) In cartography, the fit of the components of a map, together or one with another, at each stage of production.

register glass - (NATO, CENTO) In photography, a glass plate at the focal plane, against which the film is pressed during exposure.

register marks - (NATO) In cartography, designated marks, such as small crosses, circles, or other patterns applied to original copy prior to reproduction to facilitate registration of plates and to indicate the relative positions of successive impressions.

registered matter - (NATO, SEATO, CENTO, IADB) Any classified matter registered, usually by number, and accounted for periodically.

registered publication - (NATO, SEATO, CENTO, IADB) A classified publication bearing a register number, as well as a long and short title, and for which periodic accounting is required.

registration - (DOD) The adjustment of fire to determine firing data corrections.

registration fire - (NATO, CENTO, IADB) Fire delivered to obtain accurate data for subsequent effective engagement of targets. See also fire.

registration point - (DOD) Terrain feature or other designated point on which fire is adjusted for the purpose of obtaining corrections to firing data.

regrade - (DOD, IADB) To determine that certain classified information requires, in the interests of national defense, a higher or a lower degree of protection against unauthorized disclosure than currently provided, coupled with a changing of the classification designation to reflect such higher or lower degree.

regroup airfield - (DOD, IADB) Any airfield, military or civil, at which post H-hour reassembling of aircraft is planned for the express purpose of rearming, recocking, and resumption of armed alert, overseas deployment, or conducting further combat missions. See also airfield.

Regt - Regiment.

regular - 1. Career or formal enlistment U.S. service personnel, not reserve service personnel. 2. North Vietnamese soldiers who were well trained and equipped.

regulated item - (DOD, NATO, SEATO, CENTO, IADB) Any item over which proper authority exercises close supervision of distribution to individual units or commands because the item is scarce, costly, or of a highly technical or hazardous nature. See also critical item; critical supplies and materials.

regulating station - (DOD, IADB) A command agency established to control all movements of personnel and supplies into or out of a given area.

regulatory signs - (NATO, SEATO, CENTO, IADB) Signs used by competent authority to regulate and control traffic. (Note: SEATO and IADB term is "regulatory signs (road transport)".)

Regulus - (DOD, IADB) A surface-to-surface, jet-powered guided missile. It is equipped with nuclear warhead, and launched from surfaced submarine, or cruiser. Designated as RGM-6/15.

rehab - 1. Rehabilitation. 2. Hospital slang for the rehabilitation unit of a hospital or the medical process of rehabilitation, usually out of Vietnam.

rehabilitation - (DOD, NATO, SEATO, CENTO, IADB) 1. The processing, usually in a relatively quiet area, of units or individuals recently withdrawn from combat or arduous duty, during which units recondition equipment and are rested, furnished special recreation facilities, filled up with replacements, issued replacement supplies and equipment, given training, and generally made ready for employment in future operations. 2. The action taken to prepare immobilized individuals, such as military prisoners and hospital patients, for their return to military duty or useful civilian employment. 3. The action performed in restoring an installation to authorized design standards.

reinforce - (SEATO, IADB) To strengthen by the addition of personnel or military equipment.

reinforcing - (DOD) A tactical mission in which one artillery unit augments the fires of another artillery unit.

relateral tell - (DOD) The relay of information between facilities through the use of a third facility. This type of telling is appropriate between automated facilities in a degraded communications environment. See also track telling.

relative aperture - (NATO, CENTO) The ratio of the equivalent focal length to the diameter of the entrance pupil of photographic lens expressed f:4.5, etc. Also called f-number; stop; aperture stop; or diaphragm stop.

relative biological effectiveness - (DOD, NATO, CENTO) The ratio of the number of rads of gamma (or X) radiation of a certain energy which will produce a specified biological effect to the number of rads of another radiation required to produce the same effect is the relative biological effectiveness of the latter radiation.

relative target altitude - (DOD) The difference between target altitude and interceptor altitude.

relay Huey - A communications helicopter that relayed radio messages to extend the distance that could be covered.

release altitude - (DOD, IADB) Altitude of an aircraft above the ground at the time of release of bombs, rockets, missiles, tow targets, etc.

release point - (NATO, CENTO) 1. In road movements, a well-defined point on a route at which the elements composing a column return under the authority of their respective commanders, each one of these elements continuing its movement towards its own appropriate destination. 2. In air transport, a point on the ground directly above which the first paratroop or cargo item is air dropped. See also computed air release point.

release point (road) - (DOD) A well defined point on a route at which the elements composing a column return under the authority of their respective commanders, each one of these elements continuing its movement towards its own appropriate destination.

releasing commander (nuclear weapons) - (DOD, NATO, SEATO, CENTO) A commander who has been delegated authority to approve the use of nuclear weapons within prescribed limits. See also commander(s); executing commander (nuclear weapons).

releasing officer - (DOD, IADB) A properly designated individual who may authorize the sending of a message for and in the name of the originator. See also originator.

reliability diagram - (NATO) In cartography, a diagram showing the dates and quality of the source material from which a map or chart has been compiled. See also information box.

reliability of source (intelligence) - See evaluation (intelligence).

relief - (NATO, IADB) Inequalities of elevation and the configuration of land features on the surface of the earth which may be represented on maps or charts by contours, hypsometric tints, shading or spot elevations.

relief in place - (DOD, NATO, CENTO) An operation in which, by direction of higher authority, all or part of a unit is replaced in an area by the incoming unit. The responsibilities of the replaced elements for the mission and the assigned zone of operations are transferred to the incoming unit. The incoming unit continues the operation as ordered.

relief in place - (SEATO, IADB) A combat operation in which, by direction of higher authority, all or part of a unit is replaced in a combat area by the incoming unit. The responsibilities of the replaced elements for the combat mission and the assigned zone of operations are transferred to the incoming unit. The incoming unit continues the operation as ordered. The replaced elements are withdrawn prior to the resumption of operations.

rem (roentgen equivalent mammal) - (DOD) One rem is the quantity of ionizing radiation of any type which, when absorbed by man or other mammal, produces a physiological effect equivalent to that produced by the absorption of 1 roentgen of X-ray or gamma radiation.

remaining forces - (DOD) The total surviving United States forces at any given stage of combat operations.

remains - The body of a deceased person.

REMF - Rear Echelon Motherfucker: 1. Derogatory term for a person in rear away from the fighting. 2. A person in the rear who is not lending support. Pronounced rim-f.

Remington 700 - The high powered sniper rifle used by Marine sniper teams.

Remington 870 - The shotgun.

Remington Raiders - Slang for the typists in administrative assignments. From Remington typewriters, not the arms manufacturer.

remote - An assignment in a rural or hostile area in which dependents can not accompany the service personnel.

rendezvous area - (DOD, IADB) In an amphibious operation, the area in which the landing craft and amphibious vehicles rendezvous to form waves after being loaded, and prior to movement to the line of departure.

reorder cycle - (DOD, IADB) The interval between successive reorder (procurement) actions.

reorder point - (DOD) 1. That point at which time a stock replenishment requisition would be submitted to maintain the predetermined or calculated stockage objective. 2. The sum of the safety level of supply plus the level for order and shipping time equals the reorder point. See also level of supply.

repair cycle aircraft - (DOD) Aircraft in the active inventory that are in or awaiting depot maintenance, including those in transit to or from depot maintenance.

repatriate - (DOD) A person who returns to his country or citizenship, having left his native country, either against his will or as one of a group who left for reason of politics, religion, or other pertinent reasons.

repeat - (DOD) An order or request to fire again the same number of rounds with the same method of fire.

repeat - Not to be used unless specifically calling for artillery fire. See say again.

replacement center - The military facility which processed incoming soldiers before assignment to their specific duty station.

replacement demand - (DOD, IADB) A demand representing replacement of items consumed or worn out.

replacement factor - (DOD, NATO, CENTO, IADB) The estimated percentage of equipment or repair parts in use that will require replacement during a given period due to wearing out beyond repair, enemy action, abandonment, pilferage, and other causes except catastrophes.

reply - (DOD, NATO, SEATO, CENTO, IADB) An answer to a challenge. See also challenge; countersign; password.

repo depot - The replacement or reassignment depot used for processing troops out of Vietnam.

report line - (NATO, SEATO, CENTO) The line utilized for control and coordination of military operations, usually a terrain feature extending across the zone of action. See also phase line.

reported unit - (DOD) A unit designation which has been mentioned in an agent report, captured document, or interrogation report, but available information is insufficient to include the unit in accepted order of battle holdings.

reporting post - (DOD, IADB) An element of the control and reporting system used to extend the radar coverage of the control and reporting center. It does not undertake the control of aircraft.

reporting time interval - (DOD) 1. In surveillance, the time interval between the detection of an event and the receipt of a report by the user. 2. In communications, the time for transmission of data or a report from the originating terminal to the end receiver. See also near real time.

Repose - The hospital ship. The other was the *Sanctuary*.

representative fraction - (DOD, NATO) The scale of a map, chart, or photograph expressed as a fraction or ratio. See also scale.

Republic of Vietnam - South Vietnam.

Republic of Vietnam Campaign Medal - The medal issued by the Republic of Vietnam to its armed forces and those of foreign governments for direct participation in operations from 1 January 1960 forward. The end period was not established for the medal as the Republic of Vietnam ceased to exist. See VSM for the medal issued by the U.S.

requesting mast - The right of any Marine to a meeting with the commanding officer, from colonial days in which Marines served on sailing ships and such meetings were "before the mast" in the captain's quarters.

required military force - (NATO, SEATO, CENTO, IADB) The armed forces necessary to carry out a military mission over a specified period of time.

required supply rate (ammunition) - (DOD, NATO, SEATO, CENTO, IADB) The amount of ammunition expressed in terms of rounds per weapon per day for ammunition items fired by weapons, and in terms of other units of measure per day for bulk allotment and other items, estimated to be required to sustain operations of any designated force without restriction for a specified period. (DOD, IADB) Tactical commanders use this rate to state their requirements for ammunition to support planned tactical operations at specified intervals. The required supply rate is submitted through command channels. It is consolidated at each echelon and is considered by each commander in subsequently determining the available supply rate within his command.

requirements - See military requirement.

requisition - (DOD, IADB) 1. An authoritative demand or request, especially for personnel, supplies, or services authorized but not made available without specific request; to make such a demand or request. 2. To demand or require services from an invaded or conquered nation.

requisitioning objective - (DOD, IADB) The maximum quantities of materiel to be maintained on hand and on order to sustain current operations. It will consist of the sum of stocks represented by the operating level, safety level, and the order and shipping time or procurement lead time, as appropriate. See also level of supply.

RESCAP - Rescue combat air patrol.

rescue combat air patrol - (DOD) Combat patrols which cover search and rescue operations. See also combat air patrol.

rescue coordination center - See search and rescue coordination center.

research - (DOD, IADB) All effort directed toward increased knowledge of natural phenomena and environment and toward the solution of problems in all fields of science. This includes basic and applied research.

reserve - (DOD) 1. Portion of a body of troops which is kept to the rear, or withheld from action at the beginning of an engagement, available for a decisive movement. 2. Members of the military Services who are not in active service but who are subject to call to active duty. 3. Portion of an appropriation or contract authorization held or set aside for future operations or contingencies and in respect to which administrative authorization to incur commitments or obligations has been withheld. See also general reserve; operational reserve; reserve supplies.

reserve aircraft - (DOD, IADB) Those aircraft which have been accumulated in excess of immediate needs for active aircraft and are retained in the inventory against possible future needs. See also aircraft.

reserve chute - The smaller of the two parachutes worn together, used if the main chute fails.

Reserve components - (DOD) Reserve components of the Armed Forces of the United States are: a. the Army National Guard of the United States; b. the Army Reserve; c. the Naval Reserve; d. the Marine Corps Reserve; e. the Air National Guard of the United States; f. the Air Force Reserve; and g. the Coast Guard Reserve. In each reserve component there are three reserve categories, namely: a Ready Reserve, a Standby Reserve, and a Retired Reserve. Each reservist shall be placed in one of these categories. (10 United States Code 261 and 267.)

Reserve Officer Training Corps - The system by which officers attended college while in training and were actively deployed upon graduation. See ROTC.

reserve supplies - (DOD, IADB) Supplies accumulated in excess of immediate needs for the purpose of insuring continuity of an adequate supply. Also called reserves. See also battle reserves; beach reserves; contingency retention stock; economic retention stock; individual reserves; initial reserves; unit reserves.

reserved demolition target - (DOD, NATO, SEATO, CENTO, IADB) A target for demolition, the destruction of which must be controlled at a specific level of command because it plays a vital part in the tactical or strategical plan, or because of the importance of the structure itself, or because the demolition may be executed in the face of the enemy. See also demolition target.

reserved route - (DOD, NATO, CENTO) A route the use of which is: a. allocated exclusively to a particular authority or formation; or b. intended to meet a particular requirement. See also route.

reserves - The system of each of the Armed Services and state National Guards of training individuals periodically to allow a call-up in the event of need. See weekend warrior.

residual contamination - (DOD, NATO, CENTO, IADB) Contamination which remains after steps have been taken to remove it. These steps may consist of nothing more than allowing the contamination to decay normally.

residual forces - (DOD) Unexpended portions of the remaining United States forces which have an immediate combat potential for continued military operations, and which have been deliberately withheld from utilization.

residual radiation - (DOD) Nuclear radiation caused by fallout, radioactive material dispersed artificially, or irradiation which results from a nuclear explosion and persists longer than one minute after burst. See also contamination; induced radiation; initial radiation.

residual radiation - (NATO, SEATO, CENTO, IADB) Nuclear radiation caused by fallout, radioactive material dispersed artificially, or irradiation as a result of a nuclear explosion. See also contamination; induced radiation.

resistance movement - (DOD) An organized effort by some portion of the civil population of a country to resist the legally established government or an occupying power and to disrupt civil order and stability.

resolution - (NATO, CENTO) The measure of the ability of a lens, a photographic material or a photographic system to distinguish detail under certain specific conditions. The measure of this ability is normally expressed in lines per millimeter or angular resolution.

responsibility - (DOD, IADB) 1. The obligation to carry forward an assigned task to a successful conclusion. With responsibility goes authority to direct and take the necessary action to insure success. 2. The obligation of an individual for the proper custody, care, and safekeeping of property or funds entrusted to his possession or under his supervision. See also accountability.

responsor - (DOD, IADB) An electronic device used to receive an electronic challenge and to display a reply thereto.

rest and recuperation - (DOD) The withdrawal of individuals from combat or duty in a combat area for short periods of rest and recuperation. This is commonly referred to as R&R. See also rehabilitation.

restitution - (NATO, CENTO) The process of determining the true planimetric position of objects whose images appear on photographs.

restitution factor - See correlation factor.

restraint factor - (NATO, CENTO) A factor normally expressed in multiples of the force of gravity which determines the required strength of lashings and tiedowns to secure a particular load.

restraint of loads - (DOD, NATO, CENTO) The process of binding, lashing, and wedging items into one unit onto or into its transporter in a manner that will insure immobility during transit.

restricted air cargo - (NATO, SEATO, CENTO, IADB) Cargo which is not highly dangerous under normal conditions, but which possesses certain qualities which require extra precautions in packing and handling.

restricted area - (DOD, IADB) 1. An area (land, sea, or air) in which there are special restrictive measures employed to prevent or minimize interference between friendly forces. 2. An area under military jurisdiction in which special security measures are employed to prevent unauthorized entry. See also air surface zones; controlled firing area; restricted areas (air).

restricted area - (NATO) An air space of defined dimensions above the land areas or territorial waters of the state within which the flight of aircraft is restricted in accordance with certain specified conditions. May also refer to land or sea areas to which access is restricted. See also danger area; prohibited area.

restricted areas (air) - (DOD, IADB) Designated areas established by appropriate authority over which flight of aircraft is restricted. They are shown on aeronautical charts and published in notices to airmen, and publications of aids to air navigation. See also restricted area.

restricted data - (DOD) All data (information) concerning: a. design, manufacture, or utilization of atomic weapons; b. the production of special nuclear material; or c. the use of special nuclear material in the production of energy, but shall not include data declassified or removed from the restricted data category pursuant to Section 142 of the Atomic Energy Act. (Section 11w, Atomic Energy Act of 1954, as amended.) See also formerly restricted data.

restricted zone - Aviation term for an area restricted from entry, flight or attack, often due to civilian populations or political rather than military issues.

restrictive fire plan - (DOD) A safety measure for friendly aircraft which establishes air-space that is reasonably safe from friendly surface delivered nonnuclear fires.

resume - (DOD) In air intercept usage, resume last patrol ordered.

resupply - (NATO, SEATO, CENTO, IADB) Resupply is the act of replenishing stocks in order to maintain required levels of supply.

resupply of Europe - (NATO) The shipping of supplies to Europe during the period from the outbreak of war until the end of such a requirement. These supplies to exclude any material already located upon land in Europe, but to include other supplies irrespective of their origin or location. See also elements of resupply.

retard - (DOD) A request from a spotter to indicate that he desires the illuminating projectile burst later in relation to the subsequent bursts of high explosive projectiles.

reticule - Aviation and Artillery term for the scale for measuring and aiming using lines (usually circles) around the center of an optical target on a radar or other electronic aiming device offering range and distance information.

retrofit action - (DOD) Action taken to modify inservice equipment.

retrograde cargo - Trash and unused materials removed from a battle to insure the enemy can not use or gain intelligence from the items.

retrograde maneuver - Retreat.

retrograde movement - (DOD, IADB) Any movement of a command to the rear, or away from the enemy. It may be forced by the enemy or may be made voluntarily. Such movements may be classified as withdrawal, retirement, or delaying action.

retrograde movement - Retreat (a word never to be used).

return load - (DOD, NATO, CENTO, IADB) Personnel and/or cargo to be transported by a returning carrier.

return to base - (DOD) Proceed to the point indicated by the displayed information. This point is being used to return the aircraft to a place at which the aircraft can land. Command heading, speed and altitude may be used, if desired.

reunification - One goal of the North Vietnamese.

reveille - 1. A wake up call. 2. The bugle tune played to alert a camp to awaken. 3. The bugle call.

reverse slope - (NATO, CENTO, IADB) Any slope which descends away from the enemy.

revetment - A protected area for the safe storage of equipment or helicopters such as a sandbagged reinforced hanger or warehouse.

revolving fund - (DOD) A fund established to finance a cycle of operations to which reimbursements and collections are returned for reuse in a manner such as will maintain the principal of the fund, e.g., working capital funds, industrial funds, and loan funds.

RF - Regional Forces.

RF-101 - The photoreconnaissance version of the Voodoo.

RF-4 - The photoreconnaissance version of the Phantom jet used by the Air Force and Marine aviation.

RF-8 - The photoreconnaissance version of the Crusader jet, used by the Navy and Marine aviation.

RF-PF RF/PF - Regional Forces - Popular Forces - Combined action by the Regional Forces (covering a district) and Popular Forces (covering local villages). See Regional Force. See Popular Force. Slang as ruff-puff.

RFZ - Restricted fire zone.

RGM-6/15 - See Regulus.

RHAW - Radar Homing and Warning system for aviation.

RHIP - Rank has its privileges. Pronounced as individual letters.

rhumb line - (NATO, IADB) A line on the surface of the earth cutting all meridians at the same angle.

ribbon - The small bar shaped colored ribbon worn as a military decoration on the chese of a uniform. Each ribbon is distinct in color(s) and design reflecting a specific award, accomplishment or area of service.

ricki ticki - Right now, immediately, pidgin used in Okinawa.

ricki-tick - See ricki-ticki.

rickshaw - A two wheeled carriage holding one or two passengers between the two large wheels while the operator pulled it from in front of the passengers. See pedicab.

ride bareback - To have sex without a condom. See bareback.

riding shotgun - The passenger in a vehicle providing security.

RIF - 1. Reconnaissance in Force, a heavily armed reconnaissance patrol. 2. Late in the war Reduction in Force, an administrative vehicle that retired career military personnel prior to the end of their obligation.

rifle - Infantryman.

rifle, self-propelled, full-tracked, multiple, l06-mm - See Ontos (rifle, self-propelled, full-tracked, multiple, l06-mm).

rig (verb) - (NATO, CENTO) To prepare a load for air drop.

rigger - 1. A person who packs parachutes. 2. A person who laid lines of explosive charges, particularly in the SEALS.

right (left) bank - That bank of a stream or river on the right (left) of the observer when he is facing in the direction of flow, or downstream. See left (right) bank.

right (or left) - A term used to establish the relative position of a body of troops. The person using the terms "left" or "right" is assumed to be facing in the direction of the enemy regardless of whether the troops are advancing toward or withdrawing from the enemy. See left (or right).

rik-tik - See ricki ticki.

RIM-2 - See Terrier.

RIM-24 - See Tartar.

RIM-50 - See Typhon.

RIM-55 - See Typhon.

RIM-8 - See Talos.

Ring Knocker Society - Slang for the added comradeship of those who graduated from the United states Military Academy at West Point. See West Point Protective Association.

RIO - Radio Intercept Officer.

riot control agent - (DOD, NATO, CENTO) A chemical that produces temporary irritating or disabling effects when in contact with the eyes or when inhaled.

ripple fire - Launching two or more missiles in a fast series.

risk - See degree of risk (nuclear).

RITA - Resister Inside the Army. An antiwar group of soldiers in Europe.

river mines - Mines placed in rivers.

river rats - U.S. Navy river and coastal patrol personnel.

river warfare - The overall plans for managing the enemy in a river and canal environment. See riverine operations.

riverine area - (DOD) An inland or coastal area comprising both land and water, characterized by limited land lines of communication, with extensive water surface and/or inland waterways that provide natural routes for surface transportation and communications.

Riverine Forces - U.S. forces operating in the river areas.

riverine operations - (DOD) Operations conducted by forces organized to cope with and exploit the unique characteristics of a riverine area, to locate and destroy hostile forces, and/or to achieve, or maintain control of the riverine area. Joint riverine operations combine land, naval, and air operations, as appropriate, and suited to the nature of the specific riverine area in which operations are to be conducted.

RL - Rocket launcher.

RLA - Royal Laotian Army.

RLAF - Royal Laotian Air Force.

RLG - Royal Laotian Government.

RLT - Regimental landing team.

RMK/BRJ - The initials of a huge construction consortium of several companies that built airports, hospitals and other large projects on government contract. Raymond International, Morrison-Knudson, Brown & Root, and the J.A. Jones Construction Company. It was one of the, if not the, largest government contractors of the war, building most of the infrastructure of the war effort.

RNO - Results not observed. An after bombing report if no destruction of the objective was observable.

ro-ro - Container shipments from roll on roll off.

roach coach - Mobile food kitchen.

road block - (NATO, SEATO, CENTO, IADB) A barrier or obstacle (usually covered by fire) used to block or limit the movement of hostile vehicles along a route.

road capacity - (DOD, IADB) The maximum traffic flow obtainable on a given roadway, using all available lanes, usually expressed in vehicles per hour or vehicles per day.

road clearance time - (DOD, NATO, CENTO) The total time a column requires to travel over and clear a section of the road.

road net - (DOD, IADB) The system of roads available within a particular locality or area.

road space - (DOD, NATO, SEATO, CENTO, IADB) The length of roadway allocated to and/or actually occupied by a column on a route, expressed in miles or kilometers.

road sweep - Checking the road for mines.

roadrunners - 1. South Vietnamese dressing like VC to infiltrate and secure information. 2. A convoy tactic by which roads were used frequently at a high speed for presence and to attempt to find the enemy randomly.

roamer - (NATO, CENTO) A series of grids constructed to common map scales and marked out on a sheet of transparent material. It is used to assist in determining map references.

ROC - Radio Operator Course.

rock and roll - Slang for firing a weapon on full automatic. Usually pronounced rock 'n' roll.

rockers - Lower stripes on noncommissioned officer's insignia resembling rails on rocking horse.

rocket - A cylindrical projectile, artillery. Rockets were deployed in Vietnam from ships, fixed wing airplanes and helicopters as well as by field forces.

rocket belt - The area from which the enemy could launch rockets, usually surrounding a fixed location like a city.

rocket city - Base under continual or frequent artillery fire.

rocket pocket - Any location from which a rocket could be launched. Used commonly in searching for the enemy rather than locating a U.S. rocket position.

rocket propulsion - (DOD, IADB) Reaction propulsion wherein both the fuel and the oxidizer, generating the hot gases expended through a nozzle, are carried as part of the rocket engine. Specifically, rocket propulsion differs from jet propulsion in that jet propulsion utilizes atmospheric air as an oxidizer whereas rocket propulsion utilizes nitric acid or a similar compound as an oxidizer. See also jet propulsion.

ROE - Rules of Engagement, the set of policies and directives that controlled when, where, and the degree of fighting.

roentgen - (NATO, CENTO) A unit of exposure dose of gamma (or X-) radiation.

Roger - Radio code for understood or agree. Often as Roger that, for emphasis.

ROK - Republic of Korea. Pronounced rock.

ROK Marines - Marines from Korea.

ROKAF - Republic of Korea Air Force.

roll - In aviation, the longitudinal axis of the plane (left or right). See tilt.

roll 'em - Showing the nightly movie on film reels through a projector in the rec room. One literally rolled the film reel. As in what time is the roll 'em.

roll back - (DOD) The process of progressive destruction and/or neutralization of the opposing defenses, starting at the periphery and working inward, to permit deeper penetration of succeeding defense positions.

roll out - Get out of bed, wake up and get going.

roll-in-point - (DOD) The point at which aircraft enter the final leg of the attack, e.g., dive, glide.

roll-up - (DOD, IADB) The process for orderly dismantling of facilities no longer required in support of operations and available for transfer to other areas.

roller conveyor - (NATO, CENTO) A materials handling aid containing rollers over which cargo is moved.

rolling scissors - Aviation defensive maneuver in which an airplane being chased pulls up fast (vertical) rolls over (barrel roll or rolling) and comes in behind the attacker. Also called vertical scissors.

Rolling Thunder - An operation 1965-69 which concentrated bombing on pre-planned targets in North Vietnam.

rollout - Aviation term for resuming normal flight after a maneuver or mission is completed.

roman candled - A parachute failure in which the fabric fouls and wraps around itself like the shaft of a roman candle.

Rome plow - A huge bulldozer used to clear or crush jungle areas. Specifically, the D7E bulldozer weighing 4600 pounds, capable of slicing through a 3 foot tree. Used for jungle clearing, the cab was enclosed and bulletproof. Made by the Rome company in Georgia. Also called "Hog Jaws".

Romeo - The military phonetic alphabet designation for the letter "R".

romp and stomp - Marine slang for marching and drill.

RON - Remain overnight in position which is in the field.

roof - The flight deck of a carrier.

rope - (DOD, NESN, CENTO, IADB) An element of chaff consisting of a long roll of metallic foil or wire which is designed for broad, low-frequency response. See also chaff.

rope-chaff - (DOD, NESN, CENTO, IADB) Chaff which contains one or more rope elements. See also chaff.

rotate - To return to military duty in the United States after a tour of duty in Vietnam. See Big R.

rotational hump - The fast rotation within a unit of more than a quarter of the unit within 30 days posing a training and organizational challenge.

ROTC - Reserve Officers Training Corps, the college program that combined military training and college education in American colleges. Also pronounced rot-cee.

rotor - The overhead blades of a helicopter.

rotor wash - The strong wind caused by the air being pushed into the ground from a helicopter's rotors at landing or takeoff.

Rototilling - Carpet bombing strategy named after motorized cultivator Rototiller that churns up the earth.

rough rider - The passenger in a vehicle providing security. See riding shotgun.

round - A bullet, artillery or mortar shell.

round eyes - 1. A Caucasian, Occidental. 2. An American female.

rounddown - The rear of a deck of an aircraft carrier which is rounded. Also spelled round-down.

rounds complete - (DOD) The term used to report that the number of rounds specified in fire for effect have been fired.

route - (DOD, NATO, CENTO) The prescribed course to be travelled from a specific point of origin to a specific destination. See also axial route; controlled route; despatch route; lateral route; reserved route; signed route; supervised route.

route classification - (DOD, NATO, CENTO) Classification assigned to a route using factors of minimum width, worst route type, least bridge, raft or culvert military load classification, and obstructions to traffic flow. See also classification of bridges and vehicles; military load classification.

route package - Any of six pre-planned bombing targets in Operation Rolling Thunder.

route transport operations (air transport) - (SEATO, IADB) Operations over an established air route.

routine medevac - 1. A removal of non-critical patients from an area within 12-24 hours when the injury was not life threatening. 2. The removal of dead soldiers.

routine message - (DOD, IADB) A category of precedence to be used for all types of messages which justify transmission by rapid means unless of sufficient urgency to require a higher precedence. See also precedence.

routines - Radio code for Killed in Action.

routing indicator - (DOD, IADB) A group of letters assigned to indicate: a. the geographic location of a station; b. a fixed headquarters of a command, activity, or unit at a geographic location; and c. the general location of a tape relay or tributary station to facilitate the routing of traffic over the tape relay networks.

row marker (land mine warfare) - (DOD, NATO, SEATO, CENTO, IADB) A marker, natural, artificial, or specially installed, located at the start and finish of a mine row where mines are laid by individual rows. See also marker (land mine warfare).

RP - Rendezvous Point.

RPC - River patrol craft.

RPD - A light machine gun used by North Vietnamese, the Ruchnoi Pulemet Degtyarev (See LMG).

RPD - Soviet made machine gun.

RPG - Rocket Propelled Grenade, used by the Viet Cong and the NVA.

RPG screen - A wall of chain link fencing placed around a parking area for vehicles to reduce the damage of RPG explosions to those vehicles.

RPV - Remotely piloted vehicle. A small unmanned surveillance aircraft flown by remote control.

Rqn - Requisition.

RR - 1. Radio relay to extend the range of a radio transmission. 2. Recoilless rifle.

RSD - Rapid securing device for helicopters landing on a carrier.

RSP - See ration supplement pack.

RT - Reconnaissance Team.

RTAF - Royal Thai Air Force.

RTB - Return to base.

RTO - Radio Telephone Operator.

rubber - A condom.

rubber bitch - The inflatable rubber air mattress which was heavy and unreliable in rough terrain.

rubber lady - See rubber bitch.

rubberneck flight - A non-combat flight for administrative functions, in particular flying news correspondents over battle areas or to set locations.

Ruby Queen - A brand of cigarettes.

RUC - Riverine utility craft.

ruck - See rucksack and ALICE.

ruck up - An order to get gear on and move out. See saddle up.

rucksack - The backpack issued by the Army to the infantry soldier.

rudder - 1. On airplanes, the movable air foil at the rear of a plane controlling the horizontal direction. 2. On ships, the underwater blade controlling the ship's direction.

rudder reversal - 1. An aviation term for a high speed roll and turn by using only the rudder control. This is used when an enemy plane is approaching from the front. The pilot uses only the rudder to turn, reduce speed, drop, and reverse direction so the enemy plane passes by him and he ends up with the enemy plane ahead of the him and vulnerable. 2. A defensive U-turn that becomes an offensive position, in aviation or in a debate.

ruff-puff - The combination of all South Vietnamese army functions, both the Regional (district wide), and Popular Forces (village) in South Vietnam.

Ruined his day. - Killed him.

rules of engagement - (DOD) Directives issued by competent military authority which delineate the circumstances and limitations under which United States forces will initiate and or continue combat engagement with other forces encountered.

rumor control - The pre-event discussion of the potential action.

run - (NATO, CENTO) That part of flight of one photographic reconnaissance aircraft during which photographs are taken.

run-up area - (NATO) A zone within the maneuvering area reserved for testing aircraft engines prior to take-off.

running a block - Slang for a soldier who drew enemy fire to expose their position and facilitate an ambush.

running fix - (NATO, SEATO, CENTO, IADB) The intersection of two or more position lines, not obtained simultaneously, adjusted to a common time.

running takeoff - A helicopter flight technique allowing an overloaded helicopter to get airborne. To accomplish this, when a straight hover/lift is not possible, a low hover is achieved and then forward movement allows a gradual increase in speed and altitude.

running trails - Surveillance of trails for enemy action, but not using the trail for a means of transit.

rupture zone - (DOD, NATO, CENTO) The region immediately adjacent to the crater boundary in which the stresses produced by the explosion have exceeded the ultimate strength of the medium. It is characterized by the appearance of numerous radial cracks of various sizes. See also plastic zone.

RUR-4 - See Weapon Alpha.

RUR-5A - See antisubmarine rocket.

RVN - Republic of Vietnam (South).

RVNAF - Republic of Vietnam (South) Air Force or Armed Forces.

S – SIERRA

S - 1. Designated in the military phonetic alphabet as "Sierra". 2. Designation of battalion duties.

S maneuver - Aviation tactic by swerving one way and then the other while flying level.

S-1 - Battalion administration.

S-2 - Battalion intelligence. Also see Tracker.

S-3 - Battalion operations.

S-4 - Battalion supply.

S-5 - Civil Affairs.

S-55 - See H-19.

S-56 - See CH-37.

S-58 - See CH-34.

S-60 - The M-60 antiaircraft gun.

S-61 - See SH-3.

S-ing - Aviation term for doing a series of S shaped turns.

S-turn - Aviation maneuver in which the plane continually shifts right to left while going forward at the same altitude. This confuses ground radar.

S&C - Secret and confidential.

S&D - Search and Destroy.

S&S - Supply and Service, the name of a support unit.

S&W 9-mm - See Hush Puppy.

SA - 1. Senior Advisor. 2. Small arms. 3. Small arms fire. 4. Aviation term for situational awareness. Keeping track of everything. 5. Seaman Apprentice (Navy and Coast Guard).

SAAFO - Special Assistant to the Ambassador for Field Operations.

sabot - (DOD, NATO, CENTO, IADB) Light-weight carrier in which a subcaliber projectile is centered to permit firing the projectile in the larger caliber weapon. The carrier fills the bore of the weapon from which the projectile is fired; it is normally discarded a short distance from the muzzle.

sabotage - (DOD) An act with an intent to injure, interfere with, or obstruct the national defense of a country by willfully injuring or destroying, or attempting to injure or destroy, any national defense or war material, premises, or utilities.

sabotage - (NESN, CENTO) An act with an intent to damage, interfere with, or obstruct by willfully damaging or destroying or attempting to damage or destroy material, premises, or utilities, in the interests of a foreign power or subversive political organization.

sabotage alert team - See security alert team.

Sabreliner - The twin engine jet transport. See T-39.

SAC - Strategic Air Command of the U.S. Air Force.

sack - 1. A bed. 2. To sleep. 3. To destroy the enemy.

sack out - Get some sleep.

SAD - Search and Destroy.

saddle - 1. The final attack position for a fighter pilot who is in position and ready to fire. Also in the saddle. 2. The dip in terrain between two mountain tops.

saddle up - Army order get going, from the old cavalry term.

SAF - Small arms fire.

safe area - (DOD) A designated area in hostile territory which offers the evader or escapee a reasonable chance of avoiding capture and of surviving until he can be evacuated.

safe burst height - (DOD, NATO, CENTO, IADB) The height of burst at or above which the level of fallout, or damage to ground installations, is at a predetermined level acceptable to the military commander. See also types of burst.

safe house - (DOD) An innocent-appearing house or premises established by an organization for the purpose of conducting clandestine or covert activity in relative security.

safety angle - See angle of safety.

safety distance (road) - (DOD, NATO, CENTO) The distance between vehicles traveling in column specified by the command in light of safety requirements.

safety height - See altitude; minimum safe altitude.

safety lanes - (DOD, NATO, CENTO, IADB) Specified sea lanes designated for use in transit by submarines and surface ships to prevent attack by friendly forces.

safety level of supply - (DOD, IADB) The quantity of materiel, in addition to the operating level of supply, required to be on hand to permit continuous operations in the event of minor interruption of normal replenishment or unpredictable fluctuations in demand. See also level of supply.

safety pin - The cotter pin restraining the spoon on a hand grenade that kept it safe until removed.

safety zone - (DOD, NATO, CENTO, IADB) An area (land, sea, or air) reserved for non-combat operations of friendly aircraft, surface ships, or ground forces.

safety zone - (SEATO) A restricted area (air, land, or sea) established to prevent or reduce interference between friendly forces engaged in noncombat operations.

safing - (DOD) As applied to weapons and ammunition, the changing from a state of readiness for initiation to a safe condition.

SAGE - An air defense system.

Saigon - The capitol city of South Vietnam.

Saigon commando - Soldier assigned to administrative duties in Saigon.

Saigon quickstep - Diarrhea.

Saigon tea - The watered down tea bought for bar girls as whiskey, at whiskey prices, while GIs drank booze.

VIETNAM: THE WAR ZONE DICTIONARY IN THEIR OWN WORDS

Saigon warrior - See Saigon commando.

Saint - (DOD) A satellite inspector system designed to demonstrate the feasibility of intercepting, inspecting, and reporting on the characteristics of satellites in orbit.

salt - Navy and Marine slang for a person with considerable experience. As in an old salt.

salted weapon - (DOD, NATO, CENTO) A nuclear weapon which has, in addition to its normal components, certain elements or isotopes which capture neutrons at the time of the explosion and produce radioactive products over and above the usual radioactive weapon debris. See also clean weapon.

salty - Marine term for 1. Stuck up person. 2. Person with an attitude, opinionated.

salty dog - Marine term for abandoned equipment.

salvage - (DOD, IADB) 1. Property that has some value in excess of its basic material content but which is in such condition that it has no reasonable prospect of use for any purpose as a unit and its repair or rehabilitation for use as a unit is clearly impractical. 2. The saving or rescuing of condemned, discarded, or abandoned property, and of materials contained therein for reuse, refabrication, or scrapping.

salvage group - (DOD, IADB) In an amphibious operation, a naval task organization designated and equipped to rescue personnel and to salvage equipment and materiel.

salvage procedure - (DOD, NATO, SEATO, CENTO, IADB) 1. The recovery, evacuation, and reclamation of damaged, discarded, condemned, or abandoned allied or enemy materiel, ships, craft, and floating equipment for reuse, repair, refabrication, or scrapping. 2. Naval salvage operations include harbor and channel clearance, diving, hazardous towing and rescue tug services, and the recovery of materiel, ships, craft, and floating equipment sunk offshore or elsewhere stranded.

salvo - (DOD) 1. In naval gunfire support, a method of fire in which a number of weapons are fired at the same target simultaneously. 2. In close air support/air interdiction operations, a method of delivery in which the release mechanisms are operated to release or fire all ordnance of a specific type simultaneously.

salvos - (DOD) In air intercept usage, means am about to open fire. Keep clear. (Magnetic bearing of the approximate line of fire from the firing unit or units may be indicated.) Type of fire may be indicated (e.g., salvos proximity - am about to open fire with variable time fused ammunition; salvos mushroom - am about to fire a special weapon.)

SAM - 1. Surface to air missile, in general. 2. Specifically, the North Vietnamese weapon, effective 30 miles horizontal and 11 miles vertical against U.S. aircraft. Surface to air missile, 35 foot long, called flying telephone poles.

SAM Song - Aviation slang for the instrument panel warning tone that a missile battery has been detected.

same mud-same blood - An expression of racial harmony, in particular in combat zones.

same old shit - Slang for everything is status quo and awful. See SOS.

same-same - GI term usually to Vietnamese listener that two items were identical.

sampan - A Vietnamese flat-bottomed boat usually rowed.

sanctuary - (DOD) A nation or area near or contiguous to the combat area which by tacit agreement between the warring powers is exempt from attack and therefore serves as a refuge for staging, logistic, or other activities of the combatant powers.

Sanctuary - The hospital ship. The other was the *Repose*.

sandbag - A fabric bag filled with sand or dirt and stacked to make protective walls.

sandbagging - Goldbricking.

sandpaper - Government issued toilet paper.

sandwich - Aviation maneuver for a two-plane element when they spot an enemy aircraft. They spread the distance between them, both turn and bring the enemy aircraft between them.

Sandy - See A-1 Skyraider, an aircraft.

sanitize - (DOD) Revise a report or other document in such a fashion as to prevent identification of sources, or of the actual persons and places with which it is concerned, or of the means by which it was acquired. Usually involves deletion or substitution of names and other key details.

sanitize - Slang for assassinate.

SAP - See special attention personnel.

sapper - 1. A Viet Cong insurgent armed with explosives, usually grenades. 2. One who penetrated the base perimeter and tossed grenades or satchel charges. 3. A small leather or canvas blackjack with a lead weight at one end used to disable an opponent. Also called a sap or zapper.

sapper team - An enemy component of two or three soldiers armed with explosives with the goal of entering a base and blowing up personnel and equipment.

SAR - Search and Rescue.

SARC - Surveillance and Reconnaissance Center. A central data analysis location.

SARCAP - Search and Rescue Combat Air Patrol.

Sarg - Sergeant.

SARTAF - Search and Rescue Task Force.

satchel charge - An explosive device with a handle for carrying it, more powerful than a grenade.

satellite and missile surveillance - (DOD) The systematic observation of aerospace for the purpose of detecting, tracking, and characterizing objects, events, and phenomena associated with satellites and inflight missiles, friendly and enemy. See also surveillance.

SATS - Short Airfield for Tactical Support. An airstrip that can be build in 24-48 hours and be able to support fighter aircraft on a round the clock basis. This land based portable runway made of pierced aluminum with an arresting cable and catapult like an aircraft carrier.

saucer cap - The Army service cap with a flat top and small brim similar to what police officers wear.

saunter - (DOD) In air intercept, a term meaning fly at best endurance.

say again - Used to request a repetition of something on the radio. Repeat is never used as that is the order to repeat the last artillery firing.

scale - (NATO) The ratio between the distance on a map, chart, or photograph and the corresponding distance on the ground measured in the same units. See also bar scale; conversion scale; graphic scale; linear scale; nominal scale; numerical scale; photographic scale; principal scale; representative fraction.

scale (photographic) - See photographic scale.

scaling law - (DOD, NATO, CENTO) The mathematical relationship which permits the effects of a nuclear explosion of given energy yield to be determined as a function of distance from the explosion (or from ground zero), provided the corresponding effect is known as a function of distance for a reference explosion, e.g., of 1-kiloton energy yield.

scan - (DOD) In air intercept, a term meaning search sector indicated and report any contacts.

scan - (NATO) In electromagnetic or accoustic search, one complete rotation of the antenna. It may determine a time base.

scan (elint) - (DOD) The motion of an electronic beam through space searching for a target. Scanning is produced by the motion of the antenna or by lobe switching.

scan period - (DOD) The time period of basic scan types (except conical and lobe switching) or the period of the lowest repetitive cycle of complex scan combinations. The basic unit of measurement is degrees/mils per second or second per cycle.

scan type - (DOD) The path made in space by a point on the radar beam; for example: circular, helical, conical, spiral, or sector.

Scared Horse - The 11th Armored Cavalry Regiment from its horse insignia.

scattered laying (land mine warfare) - (DOD, NATO, SEATO, CENTO, IADB)

The laying of mines without regard to pattern.

scene of action commander - (DOD, NATO, CENTO) In antisubmarine warfare, the commander at the scene of contact. He is usually in a ship, or may be in a fixed wing aircraft, helicopter or submarine.

Sch - Schedule.

schedule of fire - (DOD) Groups of fires or series of fires fired in a definite sequence according to a definite program. The time of starting the schedule may be ON CALL. For identification purposes schedules may be referred to by a code name or other designation.

scheduled fire - (DOD, IADB) A type of pre-arranged fire executed at a predetermined time.

scheduled maintenance - (DOD, IADB) Periodic prescribed inspection and/or servicing of equipment accomplished on a calendar, mileage, or hours of operation basis. See also organizational maintenance.

scheduled service (air transport) - (DOD, NATO, SEATO, CENTO, IADB) A routine air transport service operated in accordance with a timetable.

scheduled target (nuclear) - (DOD) A planned target on which a nuclear weapon is to be delivered at a specific time during the operation of the supported force. The time is specified in terms of minutes before or after a designated time or in terms of the accomplishment of a predetermined movement or task. Coordination and warning of friendly troops and aircraft are mandatory.

scheduled wave - See wave.

scheme of maneuver - (DOD) The tactical plan to be executed by a force in order to seize assigned objectives.

science fiction - Slang for Special Forces.

scientific and technical intelligence - (DOD, IADB) The product resulting from the collection, evaluation, analysis, and interpretation of foreign scientific and technical information which covers: a. foreign developments in basic and applied research and in applied engineering techniques; and b. scientific and technical characteristics, capabilities, and limitations of all foreign military systems, weapons, weapon systems, and material, the research and development related thereto, and the production methods employed for their manufacture.

scientific intelligence - (DOD, IADB) Not to be used. See scientific and technical intelligence.

scissors - Aviation tactic for attack or defense in fighter air combat, to attack one cuts the angle between them and the enemy, to defend the pilot goes in the opposite of the attacker, the mutual maneuvering resembles the action of scissors.

scoch - Pronounced sco-sh. See scochi.

scochi - Slang for a small amount of anything from the Japanese.

Scoop - Information, often from a rumor.

Scooter - See A-4, an aircraft.

scope - 1. The radar display screen. 2. Nickname for the Radar Intercept Officer (See RIO).

scope tow - Using the periscope of a submerged submarine as the attachment point for an inflatable raft such as the IBS doughnut to tow it.

Scopehead - Radarman.

Scorpion - (DOD, IADB) An all-weather interceptor with twin turbojet engines. Its armament consists of air-to-air rockets with nuclear or non-nuclear warheads. Designated as F-89.

Scoshie Tiger - See F-5, an aircraft, slang name from the Japanese for small, scoshie.

scout track - An armored cavalry assault vehicle used by a recon team.

scouts out - A call to get assembled and move out for the cavalry.

SCPO - Senior Chief Petty Officer (Navy and Coast Guard).

scramble - (DOD) Takeoff as quickly as possible (usually followed by course and altitude instructions).

scrambled eggs - The gold braid and embellishment on the visor of the hat of senior officers.

scrambler - An electronic device that altered radio or other electronic transmissions so they could not be understood by anyone other than the intended recipient.

screamers - Artillery shells modified in the field to create a screaming sound to demoralize the enemy. The modification was made by soldiers in the field by inserting metal such as a razor blade between the fuse and shell. Also called whistler.

Screaming Chickens - See Screaming Eagles.

Screaming Eagles - The 101st Airborne Division.

screen (Navy) - (DOD) An arrangement of ships, submarines and/or aircraft for the protection of a unit or main body against attack by submarines, aircraft or missiles.

scribing - (NATO) In cartography, a method of preparing a map or chart by cutting the lines into a prepared coating.

script - See MPC.

scrounge - To acquire, usually though marginally legal means. See midnight requisition.

SCUBA - Self-contained underwater breathing apparatus.

scut work - Hospital slang for any routine menial work, usually something nasty like bandage and tissue disposal.

scuttlebutt - 1. Rumors. 2. Marine slang for water fountain on a ship, where gossip is exchanged.

scuz rag - Rags or a braided mop used for cleaning floors.

SDC - Self-defense Corps. The local militia in South Vietnam.

SEA - Southeast Asia.

sea bag - Navy slang for a large cylindrical cloth storage bag, similar to a duffle bag but having a snap hook closure at the top.

Sea Bat - (DOD, IADB) An antisubmarine warfare helicopter equipped with active/passive sonar, acoustic homing torpedoes, and instrument/night flight capability. Designated as SH-34G.

sea control operations - (DOD) The employment of naval forces, supported by land and air forces, as appropriate, to achieve military objectives in vital sea areas. Such operations include destruction of enemy naval forces, suppression of enemy sea commerce, protection of vital sea lanes, and establishment of local military superiority in areas of naval operations.

Sea Dragon - The operation by the Navy from 1966 to 1968 to interdict supplies by sea to coincide with Operation Rolling Thunder to interdict supply movement by land.

sea echelon - (DOD, NATO, CENTO, IADB) A portion of the assault shipping which withdraws from or "remains out of the transport area during an amphibious landing and operates in designated areas to seaward in an on-call or unscheduled status.

sea frontier - (DOD, IADB) The naval command of a coastal frontier, including the coastal zone in addition to the land area of the coastal frontier and the adjacent sea areas.

sea going bellhop - Navy slang for Marines.

Sea Gull - A pilot who does not like to fly.

Sea Horse - CH-34 helicopter.

Sea King - The search and rescue helicopter.

Sea Knight - See Ch-46, a helicopter.

sea lawyer - Marine slang for a self-appointed expert.

Sea Sprite - A utility helicopter.

Sea Stallion - A heavy lifting helicopter. See CH-53

sea story - Marine slang for an exaggeration.

sea superiority - (DOD) That degree of dominance in the sea battle of one force over another which permits the conduct of operations by the former and its related land, sea, and air forces at a given time and place without prohibitive interference by the opposing force.

sea supremacy - (DOD) That degree of sea superiority wherein the opposing force is incapable of effective interference.

sea surveillance - (DOD, NATO, CENTO, IADB) The systematic observation of surface and subsurface sea areas by available and practicable means primarily for the purpose of locating, identifying and determining the movements of ships, submarines, and other vehicles, friendly and enemy, proceeding on or under the surface of the world's seas and oceans. See also surveillance.

sea surveillance system - (DOD, NATO, CENTO, IADB) A system for collecting, reporting, correlating, and presenting information supporting and derived from the task of sea surveillance.

sea-air-land team - (DOD) A group of officers and men specially trained and equipped for conducting unconventional and paramilitary operations and to train personnel of allied nations in such operations including surveillance and reconnaissance in and from restricted waters, rivers, and coastal areas. Commonly referred to as SEAL team.

sea-launched ballistic missile - (DOD, IADB) A missile launched from a submarine or surface ship.

SEABEE - The section of the U.S. Navy that is responsible for construction and engineering of military facilities, roads, airstrips, housing and schools in some areas of Vietnam. See also See-Bee and CB.

SEAL - The U.S. Navy commando troops trained to operate on sea, in air, and on land. See Black Berets.

SEAL Forces - Acronym for Sea Air and Land, U.S. Navy commandos.

SEAL Trident - The insignia of the SEAL Forces. See Budweiser.

sealed cabin - (DOD, NATO, SEATO, CENTO, IADB) The occupied space of an aircraft characterized by walls which do not allow any gaseous exchange between the ambient atmosphere and the inside atmosphere and containing its own ways of regenerating the inside atmosphere.

SEALORDS - Acronym for South East Asia Lake Ocean Delta Strategy, a combined effort by the U.S. Navy and the South Vietnamese forces to cut supply lines from Cambodia.

search - (DOD, IADB) 1. An operation to locate an enemy force known or believed to be at sea. 2. A systematic reconnaissance of a defined area, so that all parts of the area have passed within visibility. 3. To distribute gunfire over an area in depth by successive changes in gun elevation.

search and attack priority - (DOD) The lowest category of immediate mission request involving suspected targets related to the enemy tactical or logistical capabilities, e.g., those which are not inhibiting a unit's advance but by their fleeting nature and tactical importance should be located and destroyed. See also immediate mission request; priority of immediate mission requests.

search and avoid - Derogatory summary of South Vietnamese Army operations.

search and clear - To sweep through an area and kill or scatter the enemy.

search and delight mission - Slang for R&R.

search and destroy - The tactic of the American and South Vietnamese troops to identify an enemy location and destroy it and the enemy troops.

search and rescue - (DOD, NATO, CENTO, IADB) The use of aircraft, surface craft, submarines, specialized rescue teams and equipment to search for and rescue personnel in distress on land or at sea. See also component search and rescue controller; joint rescue coordination center. See SAR.

search and rescue - (SEATO) The use of aircraft, surface craft, submarines and other special equipment employed in search and/or rescue of personnel.

Search and Rescue Combat Air Patrol - Abbreviated as SARCAP

search and rescue coordination center - (DOD, IADB) A primary search and rescue facility suitably staffed by supervisory personnel and equipped for coordinating and controlling search and rescue operations. It may be operated jointly or unilaterally.

search and rescue coordinator - (DOD, IADB) The designated search and rescue representative of the area commander with overall responsibility and authority for operation of the joint rescue coordination center, and for joint search and rescue operations within the geographical area assigned.

search and rescue mission coordinator - (DOD, IADB) A search and rescue controller selected by the search and rescue coordinator to direct a specific mission.

search and rescue region - See inland search and rescue region; maritime search and rescue region; overseas search and rescue region.

search and sweep - See search and clear.

search attack unit - (DOD) The designation given to one or more ships separately organized or detached from a formation as a tactical unit to search for and destroy submarines.

search mission (air) - (DOD, NATO, SEATO, CENTO, IADB) An air reconnaissance by one or more aircraft dispatched to locate an object or objects known or suspected to be in a specific area.

searching fire - (DOD, NATO, CENTO, IADB) Fire distributed in depth by successive changes in the elevation of the gun. See also fire.

SEAsia - Southeast Asia.

Seasprite - A ship-based helicopter. See SH-2. Also Sea Sprite.

SEATO - Southeast Atlantic Treaty Organization.

SEATO forces - See forces allocated to SEATO; national forces for the defense of the SEATO area; other forces for SEATO.

seavan - (DOD) Commercial or Government-owned (or leased) shipping containers which are moved via ocean transportation without bogey wheels attached, i.e., lifted on and off the ship.

second balloon - A Second Lieutenant.

second hat - Assistant Drill Instructor.

Second Lieutenant - Abbreviated as: 2LT (Army), 2ndLt (Marine Corps), 2d Lt (Air Force).

second seat - 1. Co-pilot. 2. Radar Intercept Officer.

second strike - (DOD, IADB) The first counter-blow of a war. (Generally associated with nuclear operations.)

second strike capability - (NATO, CENTO) The ability to survive a first strike with sufficient resources to deliver an effective counterblow. (Generally associated with nuclear weapons).

secondary armament - (DOD) In ships with multiple-size guns installed, that battery consisting of guns next largest to those of the main battery.

secondary censorship - (DOD) Armed forces censorship performed on the personal communications of officers, civilian employees, and accompanying civilians of the Armed Forces of the United States, and on those personal communications of enlisted personnel of the armed forces not subject to armed forces primary censorship or those requiring reexamination. See also censorship.

secondary port - (DOD, NATO, CENTO, IADB) A port with one or more berths, normally at quays, which can accommodate ocean-going ships for discharge. See also port.

secondary rescue facilities - (DOD, IADB) Local airbase-ready aircraft, crash boats, and other air, surface, subsurface, and ground elements suitable for rescue missions, including government and privately operated units and facilities.

secondary road - (DOD, IADB) A road supplementing a main road, usually wide enough and suitable for two-way all-weather traffic at moderate or slow speeds.

secondary water terminal - (DOD, NATO, CENTO, IADB) A coastal area with no facility for placing deep draft ships alongside a wharf. Secondary water terminals are established on beaches that desirably are adjacent to rail lines and/or a good coastal highway. At secondary water terminals, shipping is unloaded at anchorages located from one to five miles offshore, and the cargo and personnel unloaded are landed in the terminal area by ship-to-shore lighters. The scope of operation is so limited that it is not designated as a probable primary nuclear target. See also water terminal.

secret - See defense classification.

SecState - Secretary of State.

section - (DOD) 1. As applied to ships or naval aircraft, a tactical subdivision of a division. It is normally one-half of a division in the case of ships, and two aircraft in the case of aircraft. 2. A subdivision of an office, installation, territory, works, or organization; especially a major subdivision of a staff. 3. A tactical unit of the Army and Marine Corps. A section is smaller than a platoon and larger than a squad. In some organizations the section, rather than the squad, is the basic tactical unit. 4. An area in a warehouse extending from one wall to the next; usually the largest subdivision of one floor.

section - (IADB) 1. A subdivision of an office, installation, territory, works, or organization; especially a major subdivision of a staff. 2. An area in a warehouse extending from one wall to the next; usually the largest subdivision of one floor.

section - Aviation term in the Air Force for a two-plane formation with the wingman's plane to the side and slightly behind the lead plane. See two ship element formation.

Section 212 - The Army Regulation governing psychiatric discharge.

Section Eight - 1. The obsolete term from WWII for a discharge from the service for being mentally unfit to serve. 2. Referring to a person who is acting odd/crazy.

section formation - The basic air tactical formation of two planes, one as the lead and the other as the wingman.

sector - (DOD, NATO, SEATO, CENTO, IADB) 1. A defense area designated by boundaries within which a unit operates, and for which it is responsible. 2. One of the sub-divisions of a coastal frontier. See also area of influence; zone of action.

sector controller - (NATO, SEATO, CENTO, IADB) An officer appointed to act on behalf of a sector commander in a sector operations center. He is responsible for the operational control of all active air defenses in the sector area in coordination with those of adjacent sectors. In these tasks he is subject to overall direction by the group or command controller.

sector of fire - (DOD, NATO, CENTO, IADB) An area which is required to be covered by fire by an individual, weapon or a unit.

sector scan - (NATO) Scan in which the antenna oscillates through a selected angle.

secure - Navy and Marine slang for: 1. Tie down. 2. Put something in its proper place. 3. Lock it up. 4. Stop doing something.

secure (operations) - (DOD, NATO, SEATO, CENTO, IADB) To gain possession of a position or terrain feature, with or without force, and to make such disposition as will prevent, as far as possible, its destruction or loss by enemy action.

secure net - The coded radio transmissions through the PRC-77 radio.

security - (DOD, IADB) 1. Measures taken by a command to protect itself from espionage, observation, sabotage, annoyance, or surprise. 2. A condition which results from the establishment and maintenance of protective measures which insure a state of inviolability from hostile acts or influences. 3. With respect to classified matter, it is the condition which prevents unauthorized persons from having access to official information which is safeguarded in the interests of national defense. 4. Protection of supplies or supply establishments against enemy attack, fire, theft, and sabotage.

security - (NATO, CENTO) A condition which results from the establishment of measures which protects designated information, personnel, systems, components and equipment against hostile persons, acts, or influences. See also physical security.

security alert team - (DOD, IADB) Two or more security force members who form the initial reinforcing element responding to security alarms, emergencies, or irregularities.

security certification - (DOD, NATO) A certification issued by competent national authority to indicate that a person has been investigated and is eligible for access to classified matter to the extent stated in the certification. (Note: DOD definition does not use the word "national".)

security classification - (NATO, SEATO, CENTO, IADB) A category or grade assigned to defense information or materiel to indicate the degree of danger to (NATO) (SEATO) (CENTO) national security that would result from its unauthorized disclosure and the standard of protection required to guard against unauthorized disclosure. See also defense classification.

security clearance - (DOD, NATO, CENTO, IADB) An administrative determination by competent national authority that an individual is eligible, from a security standpoint, for access to classified information. (Note: DOD definition does not use the word "national".)

security countermeasures - (NATO, SEATO, CENTO, IADB) Measures designed to impair the effectiveness of an unfriendly or hostile attack upon security.

SEE-BEES - See SEABEES, Construction Battalion.

seen the elephant - To have been under enemy fire. A full sentence is noted from the Mexican War is "I have heard the owl and seen the elephant."

seismic intrusion device - Any of several electronic devices designed to signal any enemy movement.

SEL - Suspected enemy location.

selected reserve forces - (DOD) Those units and individuals within the Ready Reserve designated by their respective Services and approved by the Joint Chiefs of Staff as so essential to initial wartime missions as to require priority over other reserves.

selective identification feature - (DOD) A capability which, when added to the basic Identification Friend or Foe system, provides the means to transmit, receive, and display selected coded replies.

selective identification feature - (NATO, CENTO) Airborne pulse-type transponder which provides automatic selective identification of aircraft in which it is installed - to friend-or-foe identification installations, whether ground, shipboard, or airborne.

selective loading - (DOD, NATO, SEATO, CENTO, IADB) The arrangement and stowage of equipment and supplies aboard ship in a manner designed to facilitate issues to units. See also loading.

selective ordinance - Slang for napalm.

Selective Service - The federal agency responsible for registering and reviewing men 18-26 years old, verifying medical suitability for service or applying any of the several reasons for deferral or exemption from service. See draft.

selenodesy - (DOD, IADB) That branch of applied mathematics which determines, by observation and measurement, the exact positions of points and the figures and areas of large portions of the moon's surface, or the shape and size of the moon.

selenodetic - (DOD, IADB) Of or pertaining to, or determined by selenodesy.

self-destroying fuze - (DOD, NATO, SEATO, CENTO, IADB) A fuze designed to burst a projectile before the end of its flight. See also fuze.

self-help - Any acquisition or construction done by the user or recipient that shortcut the normal channels.

semiactive homing guidance - (DOD, NESN, IADB) A system of homing guidance wherein the receiver in the missile utilizes radiations from the target which has been illuminated by an outside source. See also guidance.

semicontrolled mosaic - (NATO, CENTO) A mosaic which is composed of photographs of approximately the same scale laid so that major ground features match their geographical coordinates. See also mosaic.

semifixed ammunition - (DOD, NATO, SEATO, CENTO, IADB) Ammunition in which the cartridge case is not permanently attached to the projectile. See also ammunition.

Seminole - See U-8 The Beechcraft twin Bonanza.

Semper Fi - The slang version of the Marine Corps motto. See Semper Fidelis.

Semper Fidelis - Latin for always faithful, the Marine Corps motto, indicating commitment both to country and each other.

senior officer present afloat - (DOD) The senior line officer of the Navy, on active service, eligible for command at sea, who is present and in command of any unit of the operating forces afloat in the locality or within an area prescribed by competent authority. He is responsible for the administration of matters which collectively affect naval units of the operating forces afloat in the locality prescribed.

senior squid - Senior naval hospital corpsman.

sensitive - (DOD) Requiring special protection from disclosure which could cause embarrassment, compromise, or threat to the security of the sponsoring power. May be applied to an agency, installation, person, position, document, material, or activity.

sensor - (DOD, NATO, IADB) A technical means to extend man's natural senses; an equipment which detects and indicates terrain configuration, the presence of military targets, and other natural and man-made objects and activities by means of energy emitted or reflected by such targets or objects. The energy may be nuclear, electromagnetic, including the visible and invisible portions of the spectrum, chemical, biological, thermal, or mechanical, including sound, blast, and earth vibration.

SEP - Separate.

separate-loading ammunition - (DOD, NATO, SEATO, CENTO, IADB) Ammunition in which the projectile and charge are loaded into a gun separately. See also ammunition.

separation - 1. Aviation term for the distance between aircraft flying in formation. 2. Aviation term for the distance between a pilot and enemy aircraft. 3. Discharge from the service.

separation maneuver - Aviation term for increased speed to attack or defend in combat.

SERE - Survival, evasion, resistance, and escape.

Sergeant - (DOD, IADB) A mobile, inertially guided, solid-propellant, surface-to-surface missile, with nuclear warhead capability, designed to attack targets up to a range of 75 nautical miles. Designated as MGM-29.

serial - (DOD, NATO, SEA TO, CENTO, IADB) An element or a group of elements within a series which is given a numerical or alphabetical designation for convenience in planning, scheduling, and control.

serial - Slang for a line of Huey helicopters on mission. Seven were needed to move a platoon, twenty-two were required to move a full infantry company.

serial assignment table - (DOD, IADB) A table which is used in amphibious operations and shows the serial number, the title of the unit, the approximate number of personnel; the material, vehicles, or equipment in the serial; the number and type of landing craft and/or amphibious vehicles required to boat the serial; and the ship on which the serial is embarked.

serial number - 1. A unique identification number for large equipment, weapons and personnel. 2. The specific alpha-numeric number assigned to all Armed Forces personnel. The alpha designation reflects the person's enlistment status as follows: US was drafted, RA enlisted, ER was a reservist, O was for officers.

seriously ill - (DOD, NATO, CENTO, IADB) A patient is seriously ill when his illness is of such severity that there is cause for immediate concern but there is no imminent danger to life. See also very seriously ill.

seriously wounded - (DOD, IADB) A stretcher case. See also wounded.

SERTS - Screaming Eagle Replacement Training School.

serum albumin - A blood expander carried by medics and administered intravenously to wounded soldiers with significant blood loss.

service ammunition - (DOD, IADB) Ammunition intended for combat, rather than for training purposes.

service force - (DOD, IADB) A naval task organization which performs missions for the logistic support of operations.

service group - (DOD, IADB) A major naval administrative and/or tactical organization, consisting of the commander and his staff, designed to exercise operational control and administrative command of assigned squadrons and units in executing their tasks of providing logistic support of fleet operations.

Service Medal - See Vietnam Service Medal.

service ribbon - A ribbon worn on the uniform representing a service medal.

service squadron - (DOD, IADB) An administrative and/or tactical subdivision of a naval service force or service group, consisting of the commander and his staff, organized to exercise operational control and administrative command of assigned units in providing logistic support of fleet units as directed.

service star - A small metal star placed on a ribbon to indicate multiple awards of that ribbon. A bronze star is for each additional award. A silver star is for five additional awards.

service stripe - A sleeve stripe for enlisted personnel indicating three years of service in the army or four years of service in the Navy, Marine Corps and Coast Guard. See hash mark or zebra.

service test - (DOD, IADB) A test of an item, system of materiel, or technique conducted under simulated or actual operational conditions to determine whether the specified military requirements or characteristics are satisfied. See also tests.

service troops - (DOD, IADB) Those units designed to render supply, maintenance, transportation, evacuation, and hospitalization, and other services required by air and ground combat units to carry out effectively their mission in combat. See also combat service support elements; troops.

servicing - See common servicing; cross-servicing; joint servicing. See also inter-Service support.

set - A party.

seven and seven - 1. Seven days of R&R followed by seven days of leave. 2. A drink of 7-Up and Seven Crown whiskey.

seven eighty two gear - The standard Marine infantry issue of combat gear. The equipment list included: pack, haversack, blankets, poncho, poncho liner, shelter half (including tent pole, pegs and lines) extra boots, socks and underwear, first aid kit, K-Bar knife, E-tool, two canteens, shaving kit, mess kit, extra uniform. This augments the uniform and weapon issuance. When combined with ammunition and weapons including grenades and mines, the weight could be 65-70 pounds of gear.

seven point - See seven point sixty-two.

seven point sixty-two, 7.62-mm minigun pod - See XM-18 minigun.

Seventeenth Parallel, 17th Parallel - The demarcation between North and South Vietnam.

Seventh Fleet - The Navy in operations in Vietnam.

seventy-five recoilless, 75-mm recoilless - See PRC RCL.

seventy-nine launcher, 79 - The M-79 grenade launcher.

severe damage - See nuclear damage (land warfare).

sewer trout - Mess hall fish.

SF - Special Forces.

SFC - Sergeant First Class (Army).

SGM - Sergeant Major (Army).

SGN - Saigon.

SGT - Sergeant (Army).

Sgt - Sergeant (Marine Corps).

Sgt. Rock - 1. A comic book character who was an heroic WWII veteran and twice a good as life. 2. Anybody who was acting heroic.

SgtMaj - Sergeant Major (Marine Corps).

SgtMajMarCor - Sergeant Major of the Marine Corps (Special- during wartime only.) (Marine Corps).

SH-3 - The Sea King Sikorsky helicopter.

SH-34G - See Sea Bat.

shack up - To live off base, with a girlfriend, both being prohibited.

shackle - Encrypting to allow radio communication of sensitive information.

Shadow - The C-119 aircraft with a searchlight.

shadow factor - (NATO, CENTO) A multiplication factor derived from the sun's declination, the latitude of the target and the time of photography, used in determining the heights of objects from shadow length. It is also known as tan alt.

Shake 'n Bake - A Sergeant who attended NCO school and earned rank after a very short training period, possibly named from the trademarked seasoned breading product that produced a faster oven baked chicken.

shakedown - The search for contraband (drugs, weapons, etc.) conducted on troops rotating home. See amnesty box.

shallow fording - (DOD, NATO, CENTO, IADB) The ability of a self-propelled gun or ground vehicle equipped with built-in waterproofing, with its wheels or tracks in contact with the ground, to negotiate a water obstacle without the use of a special waterproofing kit. See also deep fording; flotation.

shallow fording - (SEATO) The ability of a vehicle or gun equipped with built-in waterproofing with its suspension in contact with the ground, to negotiate a water obstacle without the use of special waterproofing kit.

sham - A fake injury.

shaped charge - An explosive charge which was designed to direct its energy and force in one direction.

shavetail - A new lieutenant. Dating back to civil war in which new unbroken mules had their tails shaved so handlers could quickly distinguish trained and trusted animals from the new ones.

Shawnee - A personnel carrying helicopter.

sheaf - (DOD) Planned planes of fire which produce a desired pattern of bursts with rounds fired by two or more weapons. See also open sheaf; parallel sheaf; special sheaf.

sheetlines - See neatlines.

Shelby - One of the makers of the P-38 can opener.

shell (specify) - (DOD) A command or request indicating the type of projectile to be used.

shelling report - (DOD, NATO, CENTO, IADB) Any report of enemy shelling containing information on caliber, direction, time, density, and area shelled.

shelter half - Marine term for the individual part of a two-man tent used in the field.

Sheridan - See M551 ARV.

Sherman tank - See M4 Tank.

Sherwood Forest - Any large land burning operation.

shielding - (DOD, NATO, CENTO, IADB) 1. Material of suitable thickness and physical characteristics used to protect personnel from radiation during the manufacture, handling, and transportation of fissionable and radioactive materials. 2. Obstructions which tend to protect personnel or materials from the effects of a nuclear explosion.

shift (radar) - (NATO, CENTO) The ability to move the origin of a radial display away from the center of the cathode ray tube.

shifting fire - (DOD) Fire delivered at constant range at varying deflections: used to cover the width of a target which is too great to be covered by an open sheaf.

Shillelagh - (DOD, IADB) A weapon system including gun launcher and fire control system mounted on the main battle tank and assault reconnaissance vehicle for employment against enemy armor, troops, and field fortifications. Designated as MGM-51.

Shining Brass - The code name for the operation by which U.S. Special Forces entered Laos between 1965 and 1968, the same operation was renamed in 1968 as Prairie Fire, and again in 1971 as Phu Dung (Foo Young).

ship - Short for airship, or Army helicopter

ship combat readiness - See combat readiness.

ship haven - See moving havens.

ship will adjust - (DOD) In naval gunfire support, a method of control in which the ship can see the target and, with the concurrence of the spotter, will adjust.

ship-to-shore movement - (DOD, NATO, SEATO, CENTO, IADB) That portion of the assault phase of an amphibious operation which includes the deployment of the landing force from the assault shipping to designated landing areas.

shipping - (DOD, NATO, CENTO, IADB) A term applied collectively to those ships which are used to transport personnel or cargo, or both; often modified to denote type, use, or force to which assigned.

shipping control - (DOD, NATO, SEATO, CENTO, IADB) All matters pertaining to convoy organization, routing, reporting, and diversion of shipping of all allied nations and neutrals under charter thereto. It does not include cognizance over the general employment and allocation of shipping, harbor movements, loading, and unloading, etc., which are functions of other agencies. It does not include cognizance or control over the assignment, employment, operations, or tactical procedures of the patrol or escort forces which are related but separate functions of the naval commanders.

shipping designator - (DOD, IADB) A code word assigned to a particular overseas base, port, or area, for specific use as an address on shipments to the overseas location concerned. The code word is usually four letters and may be followed by a number to indicate a particular addressee.

shipping movement policy - (NATO, CENTO) The (NATO) (CENTO) policy for the conduct of all merchant shipping in the early days of war. See also movement of shipping (in the early days of war).

shipping time - (DOD, IADB) The time elapsing between the shipment of materiel by the supplying activity and receipt of materiel by the requiring activity. See also order and shipping time.

shit burning - The sanitation technique in which oil drums were used for latrines and later kerosene ignited in the drum.

shit can - Marine slang for: 1. To dispose of, quit. 2. Garbage can.

shit city - Vietnam.

shit faced - Drunk.

shit on a shingle - Creamed beef on toast. See SOS.

shit paper - Toilet paper.

shit sandwich - A tough battle or firefight.

shit-kicker - 1. Western novel. 2. Cowboy boots.

shitbird - Marine slang for goldbricker or troublemaker. Also shit bird.

Shithook - The Sky hook, CH-47 helicopter.

shitter - Latrine.

shock front - (DOD, NATO, CENTO, IADB) The boundary between the pressure disturbance created by an explosion (in air, water, or earth) and the ambient atmosphere, water, or earth.

shock wave - (DOD, NATO, CENTO, IADB) The continuously propagated pressure pulse formed by the blast from an explosion in air by the air blast, underwater by the water blast, and underground by the earth blast. See also reflected shock wave.

shoe tag - A four-part paper tag fastened to a paratrooper's boot with identification and loading and parachuting order, copies to loadmaster, jumpmaster, soldier and headquarters.

shoebox mine - An explosive set inside a shoeshine boy's shoebox and detonated remotely. Often shoeshine boys were unaware of the planted charge which was detonated when a GI got a shoe shine.

shoot an azimuth - 1. Aviation for taking a bearing reading. 2. The technical term for using a compass.

shoot and scoot - Artillery technique in which the firing unit moves after firing to avoid return fire.

shooter - Aviation slang for the catapult operator on a carrier.

Shooting star - A single engine jet fighter. See F-80.

shoran - (DOD, IADB) A precise short-range electronic navigation system which uses the time of travel of pulse-type transmission from two or more fixed stations to measure slant-range distance from the stations. Also, in conjunction with suitable computer, used in precision bombing. (This term is derived from the words "short-range navigation".)

shore fire control party - (DOD, IADB) A specially trained unit for control of naval gunfire in support of troops ashore, consisting of a spotting team to adjust fire and a naval gunfire liaison team to perform liaison functions for the supported battalion commander.

shore bombardment lines - (NATO, CENTO, IADB) Ground lines established to delimit bombardment by friendly surface ships.

shore party - (DOD, NATO, SEATO, CENTO, IADB) A task organization of the landing force, formed for the purpose of facilitating the landing and movement off the beaches of troops, equipment, and supplies; for the evacuation from the beaches of casualties and prisoners of war; and for facilitating the beaching, retraction, and salvaging of landing ships and craft. It comprises elements of both the naval and landing forces. See also beachmaster unit; beach party; naval beach group. (Note: SEATO term has qualifier" (beach group)".)

shore patrol - Navy personnel assigned to duty as military police.

shore-to-shore movement - (DOD, IADB) The assault movement of personnel and materiel directly from a shore staging area to the objective, involving no further transfers between types of craft or ships incident to the assault movement.

short - (DOD) A spotting, or an observation, used by an observer to indicate that a burst(s) occurred short of the target in relation to the spotting line.

short - See short timer.

Short Airfield for Tactical Support - A land based portable runway made of pierced aluminum with an arresting cable and catapult like an aircraft carrier. See SATS.

short arm inspection - A medical inspection of genitals for signs of venereal disease.

short distance navigational aid - (NATO, SEATO, CENTO, IADB) An equipment or system which provides navigational assistance to a range not exceeding 200 statute miles/ 320 kilometers.

short final - A helicopter on its final approach to landing.

short haul convoy - (NATO, CENTO) A convoy whose voyage lies in general in coastal waters and whose ports/water terminals of departure and arrival lie in different countries. See also convoy.

Short Little Ugly Fella - See A-4, also SLUF.

short round - (DOD) 1. The unintentional or inadvertent delivery of ordnance on friendly troops, installations, or civilians by a friendly weapon system. 2. A defective cartridge in which the projectile has been seated too deeply.

short round - Slang for any artillery round falling short of the target, without regard to what it hit.

short stick - 1. The designation of a person with less than sixty days of service left in Vietnam, as in he has a short stick. See short timer's stick. 2. Getting a bad deal or assignment. From drawing the short stick or straw.

short supply - (DOD, IADB) An item is in short supply when the total of stock on hand and anticipated receipts during a given period is less than the total estimated demand during that period.

short takeoff and landing - (DOD, NATO, CENTO, IADB) The ability of an aircraft to clear a 50-foot obstacle within 1500 feet of commencing takeoff, or in landing, to stop within 1500 feet after passing over a 50-foot obstacle.

short time - 1. A brief sexual encounter. 2. The end of a love affair.

short timer - A person approaching end of his tour of duty.

short timer's attitude - Apathy or resistance to work. See Give a fuck.

short timer's stick - A stick with notches cut into it in the last sixty days of service in Vietnam. Some military personnel took a stick from the field at about the point in which they had two months to serve in Vietnam before returning stateside. Each day they would cut or whittle away at the stick so that as they had less time until departure the stick shortened.

short title - (DOD, NATO, SEATO, CENTO, IADB) A short, identifying combination of letters, and/or numbers assigned to a document or device for purposes of brevity and/or security.

short-range ballistic missile - (DOD, IADB) A ballistic missile with a range capability up to about 600 nautical miles.

shot - (DOD) A report that indicates a gun or guns have been fired.

shotgun - 1. A weapon similar to a rifle that fired multiple small projectiles, shot. 2. The armed guard in the passenger seat of a vehicle. 3. The doorgunner in a helicopter.

shotgun bong - The use of a shotgun barrel as a bong for smoking marijuana.

shotgun envelope - A routing envelope with holes in the side so contents are visible.

shrapnel - The fragments of a bomb casing or other material such as gravel expelled at detonation of a bomb or mine.

Shrike - The AGM-45 air to ground missile.

Shrink - Psychiatrist.

shuttered fuze - (NATO, CENTO) A fuze in which inadvertent initiation of the detonator will not initiate either the booster or the burst charge. See also fuze.

shuttle bombing - (DOD, IADB) Bombing of objectives, utilizing two bases. By this method, a bomber formation bombs its target, flies on to its second base, reloads, and returns to its home base, again bombing a target if required.

Shylocker - The unit loan shark who would loan money to other soldiers at high rates of interest. From the character Shylock in Shakespeare's play The Merchant of Venice.

SI - Seriously ill.

sick - (DOD) In air intercept, a code meaning equipment indicated is operating at reduced efficiency.

sick bay - An area for routine medical care.

sick bay commando - A soldier, often a recruit, who goes on sick call to avoid work.

sick call - 1. The daily time to report for non-critical medical attention. 2. The daily report of ambulatory soldiers reporting for treatment.

side lap - See overlap.

side oblique air photograph - (DOD) An oblique photograph taken with the camera axis at right angles to the longitudinal axis of the aircraft.

side-looking airborne radar - (DOD, NATO, CENTO) An airborne radar, viewing at right angles to the axis of the vehicle, which produces a presentation of terrain or moving targets. (DOD) Commonly referred to as SLAR.

Sidewinder - (DOD, IADB) A solid-propellant, air-to-air rocket with nonnuclear warhead, and infrared, heat-seeking homer. Designated as AIM-9.

SIDS - Seismic Intrusion Device.

Sierra - The military phonetic alphabet designation for the letter "S".

Sierra Hotel - SH. Aviation slang over the radio for being shit hot, high praise for a maneuver perfectly done or some other exceptional piece of flying.

SIF - Selective Identification Feature, the radio device to indicate the identity of aircraft on radar (See IFF).

sighting - (DOD, IADB) Actual visual contact. Does not include other contacts, which must be reported by type, e.g., radar and sonar contacts. See also contact report.

SIGINT - Signal Intelligence unit of U.S. National Security Agency responsible for code breaking and intelligence related to national security under the executive office of the government.

signal - (DOD, NATO, SEATO, CENTO, IADB) 1. As applied to electronics, any transmitted electrical impulse. 2. Operationally, a type of message, the text of which consists of one or more letters, words, characters, signal flags, visual displays or special sounds, with prearranged meanings and which is conveyed or transmitted by visual, acoustical, or electrical means.

signal area - (NATO) An area on an airfield used for the display of ground signals.

signal center - (DOD) A combination of signal communication facilities operated by the Army in the field and consisting of a communications center, telephone switching central and appropriate means of signal communications. See also communications center.

signal hill - Any hill on which radio antennas were placed to increase reception distances.

signal intelligence - (DOD, IADB) A generic term which includes both communication intelligence and electronic intelligence. Also called SIGINT. See also intelligence.

signal letters - (DOD) The international visual and radio call sign of a ship. See also international call sign.

signal operation instructions - (DOD, IADB) A series of orders issued for technical control and coordination of the signal communication activities of a command. (DOD) In Marine Corps usage, these instructions are designated communication operation instructions.

signal security - (DOD, IADB) A generic term which includes both communications security and electronic security. See also security.

signal-to-noise ratio - (DOD) The ratio of the amplitude of the desired signal to the amplitude of noise signals at a given point in time.

signals support - (NATO, SEATO, CENTO, IADB) The provision of personnel and equipment from other forces for the establishment of a special or supplementary communications system.

signature (target) - (DOD, NATO, CENTO, IADB) The characteristic pattern of the target displayed by detection and identification equipment.

signed route - (DOD, NATO, CENTO) A route along which a unit has placed directional signs bearing its unit identification symbol. The signs are for the unit's use only and must comply with movement regulations.

significant tracks - (DOD, NATO, CENTO) Tracks of aircraft or missiles which behave in an unusual manner which warrants attention and could pose a threat to a defended area. (Note: NATO and CENTO term has the qualifier "air defense".)

silk - A parachute, named for the original fabric used in the canopy.

silk shack - The place where parachutes are packed.

Silver Star - The third highest decoration for heroism in combat.

simultaneous engagement - (DOD) The concurrent engagement of hostile targets by combination of interceptor aircraft and surface-to-air missiles.

sin loi - Spelled as pronounced, Vietnamese for "I am sorry". Properly spelled xin loi.

single department purchase - (DOD, IADB) A method of purchase whereby one department buys particular commodities for another department or departments. See also purchase.

single digit fright - A nervous state of a soldier with less than 10 days to serve in a combat zone who is subject to being ordered continue there rather than being rotated out.

single digit midget - A soldier with fewer than ten days to serve in the combat zone.

single manager - (DOD) A Military Department or Agency designated by the Secretary of Defense to be responsible for management of specified commodities or common service activities on a Department of Defense-wide basis.

Sioux - See CH-13

sit map - A situation map.

sit-rep - A situation report.

sit-rep Alpha Sierra - Radiocode for situation report all secure.

situation map - (DOD, NATO, SEATO, CENTO, IADB) A map showing the tactical or the administrative situation at a particular time. See also map.

situation report - (DOD, NATO, SEATO, CENTO, IADB) A report giving the situation in the area of a reporting unit or formation.

SIW - Self Inflicted Wound.

six - 1. The radio code or call for the unit commander. 2. Aviation term for the position in the clock code for a location directly behind the pilot. 3. To eliminate something (deep six it).

Six Actual - The unit commander, not the next in line or a substitute.

six by - A large flat bed truck, often having wooden sides and a canvas top over the bed of the truck.

six by six - The M-35 truck.

six pack - A six passenger open bed truck.

six six and a kick - The maximum punishment after a general court martial. Six months loss of pay, six months confinement at hard labor and a dishonorable discharge.

six to six - Two commanders talking on the radio, 6 to 6.

sixteen - Slang for a M-16 rifle.

sixty - See M-60, an American mortar.

sixty mike-mike - See M-60, an American mortar.

sixty mortar, 60-mm mortar - See M-19 60-mm mortar.

sixty one - A Communist mortar.

sixty tubes, 60-mm tubes - See M-19 60-mm mortar.

sixty-one mortar, 61-mm mortar - See Type 31 mortar.

sixty-six file - Officer's personnel file.

skate - An easy task.

skid lid - Helmet.

skin paint - (DOD) A radar indication caused by the reflected radar signal from an object.

skin tracking - (DOD) The tracking of an object by means of a skin paint.

skip bombing - (DOD, IADB) A method of aerial bombing in which the bomb is released from such a low altitude that it slides or glances along the surface of the water or ground and strikes the target at or above water level or ground level. See also minimum-altitude bombing.

skip it - (DOD) In air intercept, means do not attack, cease attack, cease interception.

Skipper - 1. Slang for the rank of Captain, in any service, not just Navy. 2. Affectionate term for commanding officer.

skirmish - A minor engagement with the enemy.

skirmish line - Marine Corps infantry formation in which every other man in a line facing the enemy was a few paces back.

skivvies - 1. Underwear, rarely worn in the field. 2. Hookers.

skivvy house - Whorehouse.

Skoshi cab (also scochi, skosh) - A small Japanese taxi, derivative scoch means anything small, as in "just a skosh of water with my scotch, please".

SKS - A Soviet 7.62-mm semi automatic carbine, the Somonov.

skunk - Radar and aviation term for an unidentified object refelected on the radar screen.

sky - To leave.

sky out - To leave suddenly.

sky pilot - Chaplain.

sky up - To leave.

Skycrane - The CH-54 helicopter, a huge dual rotor helicopter. Also Sky Crane.

Skyhawk - (DOD, IADB) A single-engine, turbojet attack aircraft designed to operate from aircraft carriers, and capable of delivering nuclear and/or nonnuclear weapons, providing troop support, or conducting reconnaissance missions. It can act as a tanker, and can itself be air refueled. It possesses a limited all-weather attack capability, and can operate from short, unprepared fields. Designated as A-4.

Skyhawk - Note: Made by Douglas, in several models A-4 C/E/F. Also called Tinkertoy, or Heinemann's Hot Rod after the designer, Ed Heinemann. Also Sky Hawk.

Skyknight - See F-3D, an aircraft. Later designated F-10.

Skymaster - A WWII era transport airplane. Also Sky Master.

Skyraider - (DOD, IADB) A single reciprocating-engine, general-purpose attack aircraft designed to operate from aircraft carriers built by Douglas. It is capable of relatively long-range, low-level nuclear and nonnuclear weapons delivery, mine-laying, reconnaissance, torpedo delivery, and troop support. Designated as A-1.

Skyraider - Note: The attack-bomber was made for the Navy and Air Force and used for RESCAP and FAC missions. The strengths of the plane were its heavy armament, ability to go low and slow to look for downed pilots and crew in rescue situations and the loiter on target to coordinate mission timing. Its weakness is its slowness that made it vulnerable to attack. Also Sky Raider. Commonly called Spad, or Sandy. Other Nicknames: Able Dog, Hobo, Firefly; Zorro, The Big Gun, Old Faithful, Old Miscellaneous, Fat Face (AD-5 version), Guppy (AD-5W version), Q-Bird (AD-1Q/AD-5Q versions), Flying Dumptruck (A-1E), Crazy Water Buffalo (South Vietnamese nickname).

Skyray - (DOD, IADB) A single-engine, single-pilot, supersonic, limited all-weather jet fighter designed for operating from aircraft carriers for interception and destruction of enemy aircraft. Armament includes the Side-winder. Built by Douglas. Used until 1964. Designated as F-6.

skyspot - The coordinates and altitude from which bombs were released per computer controlled or generated data.

Skytrain - The Douglas built DC-3, armed with miniguns and used for flare drops and night close support. Designated C-47. Known as Puff the Magic Dragon.

Skywagon - Cessna 180 Single engine prop small plane.

Skywarrior - (DOD, IADB) A twin-engine, turbojet, tactical all-weather attack aircraft designed to operate from aircraft carriers, and capable of delivering nuclear or non-nuclear weapons, and conducting reconnaissance, or minelaying missions. Its range can be extended by in-flight refueling. It has a crew of four. Designated as A-3. (Air Force version is the B-66.)

Skywarrior - Note: Built by Douglas. Used in the early days of the war as a strategic bomber, later it was used as an in air refueling tanker and for reconnaissance.

slack - 1. The patrol position directly behind the point. 2. Leeway as in the phrase cut me some slack.

slackman - The man directly behind the lead or point man in a patrol, responsible for protecting the pointman.

slagging rag - A slow opening parachute.

SLAM - Search, locate, annihilate, and monitor.

slant - Derogatory term for Vietnamese.

slant range - (DOD, NATO, SEATO, CENTO, IADB) The line of sight distance between two points not at the same elevation.

SLAR - Side Looking Radar, used to detect camouflaged targets.

slated items - (DOD) Bulk petroleum and packaged bulk petroleum items which are requisitioned for oversea use by means of a consolidated requirement document, prepared and submitted through joint petroleum office channels. Packaged petroleum items are requisitioned in accordance with normal requisitioning procedures. See also petroleum.

slice - (DOD, IADB) An average logistic planning factor used to obtain estimates of requirements for personnel and materiel. A personnel slice, e.g., generally consists of the total strength of the stated basis combatant element, plus its proportionate share of all supporting and higher headquarters personnel.

slice - Aviation term for a full speed drop with more than 90 degrees of banking.

Slick - 1. See UH-1, a Huey helicopter. 2. A Mark-80 low drag bomb, named for its fast drop and sleek configuration (See fats).

slick sleeves - A recruit or Private with no service stripes.

slider - Navy and carrier aviation term for a hamburger fried in so much grease and covered with cheese that it is guaranteed to slide off a plate when the ship rocks in heavy seas.

sliding into new arms - Putting on a fresh shirt.

sliding into new legs - Putting on fresh trousers.

slightly wounded - (DOD, IADB) A casualty that is a sitting or a walking case. See also wounded.

slop chute - 1. A beer hall for enlisted men on base. 2. A diner or marginal restaurant.

slope - Derogatory term for Asians.

Slow CAP - The slower of the combat air patrol aircraft.

SLUF - Short Little Ugly Fella, See A-7, an aircraft.

slung load - A load of cargo in a sling under a helicopter.

slushies - Australian slang for Vietnamese civilian workers on a base.

SMA - Sergeant Major of the Army (Special- during wartime only.) (Army).

smack - Heroin.

smacker - Heroin user.

small arms - (DOD, IADB) All arms, including automatic weapons, up to and including .60 caliber and shotguns.

small arms ammunition - (DOD, IADB) Ammunition for small arms, i.e., all ammunition up to and including .60 caliber, and all gauges of shotgun shells.

small circle - (NATO, CENTO, IADB) A circle on the surface of the earth, the plane of which does not pass through the earth's center.

small-lot storage - (DOD, IADB) Generally considered to be a quantity of less than one pallet stack, stacked to maximum storage height. Thus, the term refers to a lot consisting of from one container to two or more pallet loads, but is not of sufficient quantity to form a complete pallet column. See also storage.

small-scale map - (DOD, IADB) A map having a scale smaller than 1:600,000. See also map.

smart bomb - A bomb guided by a laser light at the target site or other electronic systems.

smear - To napalm.

Smell-O-Meter - The experimental people sniffer.

Smelling apple pie. - About to go stateside.

SMG - Submachine gun.

Smiling Jack - 1. A shark. 2. Called out as a shark warning.

Smith Corona commandos - Rear area clerks and typists, from a brand of typewriter.

Smitty Harris tap code - See tap code.

smoke - 1. To kill as in to smoke the enemy. 2. To inhale marijuana smoke.

Smoke 'em if you got 'em. - The announcement of a break in action or a work detail, just enough time to smoke a cigarette.

smoke grenade - The M-18.

smoke screen - (DOD, NATO, CENTO, IADB) Cloud of smoke used to mask either friendly or enemy installations or maneuvers.

smoke stack - Smoke from the enemy rifle disclosing his position.

Smokey Bear - Drill Sergeant, from the hat shape worn by both.

smoking hole - The site of aircraft crash.

smoking lamp - Navy and Marine slang for authorization to smoke. Permitted when the smoking lamp is lit, not when the smoking lamp is out.

SMSgt - Senior Master Sergeant (Air Force).

smudge pots - Canisters that burned oil to make smoke (smudge). Normally used as a frost inhibitor in citrus groves, however, in Vietnam they were set up around bases as the oily smoke served to confuse radar and provided a visual interference as well.

SN - Seaman (Navy and Coast Guard).

SNAFU - Situation Normal-All Fucked Up.

snake - 1. Taking a short sleep, a nap. 2. Penis.

Snake - A Cobra helicopter.

snake eater - Green Beret.

snake eye - The heat seeking MQ-74 radar component of a bomb.

Snakeye - A bomb designed for low elevation and slow drop delivery. Designed much like the slick except for retracted tail fins that were triggered by an arming wire after dropped. The fins slowed the descent.

snap report - (DOD) Not to be used. See Joint Tactical Air Reconnaissance/Surveillance Mission Report.

snap report - (SEATO, IADB) A preliminary report of observations by air crews rendered by intelligence personnel immediately following interrogation and dispatched prior to compilation of a detailed mission report.

snap roll - Aviation maneuver that spins a plane on its longitudinal axis quickly.

snap up - Aviation term for a fast climb, usually to get a better aim.

snatch - 1. A rescue mission. 2. A kidnap mission, 3. Female crotch.

SNB - The Twin Beech aircraft, called C-45 by the Air Force, used by all three services and Air America. Pronounced sneeb. See Bugmasher.

Sneaky Pete - See Rangers.

snooping and pooping - Marine slang for reconnoitering.

snoopy - A poncho liner.

snot locker - Nose.

snow - (DOD) In air intercept, a term meaning sweep jamming.

snuffy - 1. A young Marine. 2. Marine slang for any Marine. 3. A menial task.

snuggle up - Aviation term for an order to close a formation and reduce the space between planes.

soap rounds - Ammunition in which the lead projectile was replaced with soap and the gunpowder reduced so it could be used in close quarters to shoot rats and not harm people.

sofar - (DOD) The technique of fixing an explosion at sea by time difference of arrival of sound energy at several separate geographical locations. (The term is derived from the words "sound fixing and ranging".)

soft bomb - A fragmentation bomb.

soft missile base - (NATO, CENTO, IADB) A launching base that is not protected against a nuclear explosion.

soft ordinance - Napalm.

soft target - Personnel or unarmored vehicles subject to damage from small arms fire.

SOI - Signal Operating Instructions. The radio handbook of instructions and a directory of unit call signs and frequencies.

soil shear strength - (DOD, NATO) The maximum resistance of a soil to shearing stresses.

SOL - Shit out of luck. Pronounced as three letters, not a word.

solatium - A grievance payment made for emotional injury.

Soldiers Medal - The fifth highest medal for non-combat action that involved personal risk.

sole survivor rule - The Army policy of not sending the last surviving son of a family into combat.

sonar - (DOD, NATO, CENTO, IADB) A sonic device used primarily for the detection and location of underwater objects. (This term is derived from the words "sound navigation and ranging".)

sonic - (DOD, NATO, CENTO, IADB) Of or pertaining to sound or the speed of sound. See also speed of sound.

sonobuoy - (DOD, NATO, CENTO, IADB) A sonar device used to detect submerged submarines which when activated relays information by radio. It may be active directional or nondirectional, or it may be passive directional or nondirectional.

SOP - Standard operating procedure. See also standing operating procedure.

Sorry 'bout that. - A generally sarcastic comment.

sortie - (DOD, IADB) 1. A sudden attack made from a defensive position. In this meaning, it is sometimes called a sally. 2. An operational flight by one aircraft. 3. To depart from a port or anchorage, with an implication of departure for operations or maneuver. See also mission.

sortie (air) - (NATO, SEATO, CENTO) An operational flight by one aircraft.

sortie number - (DOD, NATO, CENTO) A reference used to identify the images taken by all the sensors during one air reconnaissance sortie.

sortie plot - (DOD) An overlay representing the area on a map covered by imagery taken during one sortie.

sortie reference - See sortie number.

SOS - 1. Same old shit. 2. Shit on a shingle, creamed beef on toast.

soul brother - A black soldier.

soul city - The section of Saigon that catered to black soldiers.

sound off - 1. To count cadence while marching. 2. Speak up in an assertive voice. 3. Complaining.

source - (DOD) 1. A person, thing, or activity from which intelligence, information is obtained. 2. In clandestine activities, a person (agent), normally a foreign national, in the employ of an intelligence activity for intelligence purposes. 3. In interrogation activities, any person who furnishes intelligence information" either with or without the knowledge that the information is being used for intelligence purposes. In this context, a controlled source is in the employment or under the control of the intelligence activity and knows that his information is to be used for intelligence purposes. An uncontrolled source is a voluntary contributor of information and mayor may not know that the information is to be used for intelligence purposes.

South Vietnamese time - The regular time in South Vietnam used by civilians which was one hour ahead of the U.S. military and that used in North Vietnam. See gulf time, golf time.

souvenir - A gift, Vietnamese spin on the French word.

Souvenir me. - A request for a gift or begging.

SP - 1. Shore patrol. 2. Self-propelled.

VIETNAM: THE WAR ZONE DICTIONARY IN THEIR OWN WORDS

SP pack - A cellophane wrapped packet in C-rations containing cigarettes, occasionally pipe tobacco and toiletries.

space A - 1. The space available on aircraft for added passengers. 2. Flying space A in an aircraft. 3. Getting a free ride.

space assignment - (DOD) An assignment to the individual Departments/Services by the appropriate transportation operating agency of movement capability which completely or partially satisfies the stated requirements of the Departments/Services for the operating month and which has been accepted by them without the necessity for referral to the Joint Transportation Board for allocation.

space cadet - A show off, usually a young pilot.

space defense - (DOD, IADB) All measures designed to reduce or nullify the effectiveness of hostile acts by vehicles (including missiles) while in space.

Spacetrack - (DOD) A global system of radar, optical and radiometric sensors linked to a computation and analysis center in the North American Air Defense Command combat operations center complex. The Spacetrack mission is detection, tracking, and cataloging of all man-made objects in orbit of the earth. It is the Air Force portion of the North American Air Defense Command Space Detection and Tracking System. See also Spadats; Spasur.

Spad - See A-1, an aircraft.

Spadats - (DOD, IADB) A space detection and tracking system capable of detecting and tracking space vehicles from the earth, and reporting the orbital characteristics of these vehicles to a central control facility. See also Spacetrack; Spasur.

span of detonation (atomic demolition munition employment) - (DOD) That total period of time, resulting from a timer error, between the earliest and the latest possible detonation time. 1. early time: The earliest possible time that an atomic demolition munition can detonate; 2. fire time: That time the atomic demolition munition will detonate should the timers function precisely without error; 3. late time: The latest possible time that an atomic demolition munition can detonate.

spank - Aviation term for what you do to the enemy in a dogfight when you win.

Sparks - Nickname for a Radio Telephone Operator.

Sparky - Nickname for a Radio Telephone Operator.

Sparrow - (DOD, IADB) An air-to-air solid-propellant rocket with nonnuclear warhead and electronic-controlled homing. Designated as AIM-7.

spasm war - (DOD) Not to be used. See general war.

Spasur - (DOD) An operational space surveillance system with the mission to detect and determine the orbital elements of all man-made objects in orbit of the earth. The mission is accomplished by means of a continuous fan of continuous wave energy beamed vertically across the continental United States and an associated computational facility. It is the Navy portion of the North American Air Defense Command/Continental Air Defense Command Space Detection and Tracking System. See also Spacetrack; Spadats.

SPC - Specialist (Army).

Speaker - One of the makers of the P-38 can opener.

special (or project) equipment - (DOD, IADB) Equipment not authorized in standard equipment publications but determined as essential in connection with a contemplated operation, function, or mission. See also equipment.

special agent - (DOD) A person, either United States military or civilian, who is a specialist in military security or the collection of intelligence or counterintelligence information.

special ammunition supply point - (DOD, IADB) A mobile supply point where special ammunition is stored and issued to delivery units.

special assignment airlift requirements - (DOD) Airlift requirements, including directed/coordinated exercises, which require special consideration due to the number of passengers involved, weight or size of cargo, urgency or movement, sensitivity, or other valid factors which preclude the use of channel airlift.

special atomic demolition munition - (DOD, IADB) A very low yield, man-portable, atomic demolition munition which is detonated by a timer device.

special attention personnel - See special person list, watch list, SAP.

special cargo - (DOD, IADB) Cargo which requires special handling or protection, such as pyrotechnics, detonators, watches, and precision instruments. See also cargo.

special feces - Special Forces.

special flight - (DOD, NATO, SEATO, CENTO, IADB) An air transport flight, other than a scheduled service, set up to move a specific load.

Special Forces - (SEATO) Military personnel with cross training in basic and specialized military skills, organized into small multiple-purpose detachments with the mission to train, organize, supply, direct, and control indigenous forces in guerrilla warfare and counterinsurgency operations, and to conduct unconventional warfare operations.

Special Forces - See United States Army Special Forces Green Berets.

Special Forces popcorn - Amphetamines.

special job cover map - (NATO, CENTO) A small scale map used to record progress on photographic reconnaissance tasks covering very large areas. As each portion of the task is completed, the area covered is outlined on the map.

special operations - (DOD, IADB) Secondary or supporting operations which may be adjuncts to various other operations and for which no one Service is assigned primary responsibility.

Special Services - 1. The recreational services offered by the military for off-duty time such as libraries, lounges. 2. The unit providing the services.

special sheaf - (DOD) Any sheaf other than parallel, converged, or open. See also open sheaf; parallel sheaf; sheaf.

special staff - (DOD, IADB) All staff officers having duties at a headquarters and not included in the general (coordinating) staff group or in the personal staff group. The special staff includes certain technical specialists and heads of services, e.g., quartermaster officer, antiaircraft officer, transportation officer, etc. See also staff.

special weapons - (DOD, IADB) A term sometimes used to indicate weapons grouped for special procedures, for security, or other reasons. Specific terminology, e.g., nuclear weapons, guided missiles, is preferable.

special-equipment vehicle - (DOD, IADB) A vehicle consisting of a general-purpose chassis with special-purpose body and/or mounted equipment designed to meet a specialized requirement. See also vehicle.

special-purpose vehicle - (DOD, IADB) A vehicle incorporating a special chassis and designed to meet a specialized requirement. See also vehicle.

specialist intelligence reports - (DOD, NATO, CENTO, IADB) A category of specialized, technical reports used in the dissemination of intelligence. See also intelligence reporting.

specific intelligence collection requirement - (DOD) An identified gap in intelligence holdings that may be satisfied only by collection action, and which has been validated by the appropriate requirements control authority. Commonly referred to as SICR.

specific search - (DOD) Reconnaissance of a limited number of points for specific information.

specified command - (DOD) A command which has a broad continuing mission and which is established and so designated by the President through the Secretary of Defense with the advice and assistance of the Joint Chiefs of Staff. It normally is composed of forces from but one Service.

Spectre - The AC-130 with weapons.

spectrum of war - (DOD, IADB) A term which encompasses the full range of conflict: cold, limited, and general war.

speed - Slang for amphetamine.

speed of advance - (DOD) In naval usage, the speed expected to be made good over the distance along a route. See also mean line of advance.

speed of sound - (DOD, NATO, CENTO, IADB) The speed at which sound travels in a given medium under specified conditions. The speed of sound at sea level in the Inter - national Standard Atmosphere is 1108 ft. per second, 658 knots, 1215 km/hour. See also hypersonic; sonic; subsonic; supersonic; transonic.

speedbrakes - Aviation term for the flaps on the wings that slow the plane in flight and on landing.

speedjeans - See G-suit.

Sperm - See OH-6, an aircraft whose shape resembled a sperm.

spider hole - Slang for a very small enemy dugout or fox hole used for hiding during daylight.

spider trap - See spider hole.

SPIES-rig - Suspended Personnel Insertion and Extraction System. A harness and line system for placing and removing troops from specific locations that are hard to access or particularly risky. Like the STABS or McGuire rig.

spigot - See sprag.

spike buoy - An electronic sensor mounted on a metal stake that is manually placed in the ground.

spike pit - A booby trap, usually on a path, consisting of a pit with a camouflaged opening and spiked bamboo at the bottom.

spiked gun - A gun or artillery piece rendered useless to the enemy when it must be left behind.

spin stabilization - (DOD, IADB) Directional stability of a projectile obtained by the action of gyroscopic forces which result from spinning of the body about its axis of symmetry.

spit and polish - Detailed, orderly, attention to detail.

spit shine - The glistening mirrored finish on leather shoes.

spitting - (DOD) In air intercept, a code meaning I am about to lay, or am laying, sonobuoys. I may be out of radio contact for a few minutes. If transmitted from the submarine it indicates that the submarine has launched a sonobuoy.

splash - (DOD) Word transmitted to an observer or spotter five seconds before the estimated time of the impact of a salvo or round.

splash - Aviation carrier slang for: 1. Landing in water. 2. A time estimate of when fuel will be expended and a plane will splash down. See state.

splashed - (DOD) In air intercept, a code meaning enemy aircraft shot down (followed by number and type).

splib - A term for black soldiers, from south Philadelphia lower income black, also spelled spliv. See WASP.

splib cookies - Chocolate wafer sandwich cookies filled with white creme. See chuck cookies.

splinters round - Australian slang for a beehive round.

split cameras - (DOD, NATO, IADB) An assembly of two cameras disposed at a fixed overlapping angle relative to each other. See also fan cameras.

split pair - See split vertical photography.

split plane maneuvering - Aviation term for the coordinated action and positioning of two different types of planes at different altitudes.

split S - Aviation term for a method a reversing the plane's direction (horizontal) and increasing or decreasing altitude (vertical) in one continuous action.

split vertical photography - (DOD, NATO, CENTO) Photographs taken simultaneously by two cameras mounted at an angle from the vertical, one tilted to the left and one to the right, to obtain a small sidelap.

spliv - See splib.

SPN - Separation Number Program. An entry on the DD-214 discharge form that indicated the reason for the separation in addition to the type of separation (honorable, etc.). Pronounced spin.

spoiling attack - (DOD, IADB) A tactical maneuver employed to seriously impair a hostile attack while the enemy is in the process of forming or assembling for an attack. Usually employed by armored units in defense by an attack on enemy assembly positions in front of a main line of resistance or battle position.

spoking (radar) - (NATO, CENTO) Periodic flashes of the rotating time base on a radial display. Sometimes caused by mutual interference.

Sponson box - The tool box on the fender or side of an armored vehicle.

sponsor - (DOD) Military member or civilian employee with dependents.

sponsor (exercise) - (NATO, SEATO, CENTO, IADB) The commander who conceives a particular exercise and orders that it be planned and executed either by his staff or by a subordinate headquarters.

spoofer - (DOD) In air intercept, means a contact employing electronic or tactical deception measures.

spook - 1. To kill. 2. To frighten. 3. Slang for a spy. 4. Derogatory for a black soldier.

spook drop - The night parachute drop of a clandestine team usually very few.

Spooky - A prop aircraft with a minigun mounted in the door. 2. A helicopter with a minigun mounted in the door (See Minigun, Puff the Magic Dragon).

spooled up - Aviation term for excited.

spoon - 1. Slang for cook. 2. The curved lever on the side of a grenade held in place with a cotter pin. When the pin is in place it is "safe".

spot - (DOD, IADB) 1. To determine, by observation, deviations of ordnance from the target for the purpose of supplying necessary information for adjustment of fire. 2. To place in a proper location. See also adjustment of fire.

spot - (NATO, SEATO, CENTO) 1. To determine by observation, deviations of gunfire from the target for the purpose of supplying necessary information for the adjustment of fire. 2. To place in a proper location. See also adjustment of fire.

spot elevation - (DOD, NATO, CENTO, IADB) A point on a map or chart whose elevation is noted.

spot jamming - (DOD, NATO, CENTO, IADB) The jamming of a specific channel or frequency. See also barrage jamming; electronic jamming; jamming.

spot net - (DOD, IADB) Radio communication net used by a spotter in calling fire.

spot report - (DOD) A concise narrative report of essential information covering events or conditions that may have an immediate and significant effect on current planning and operations which is afforded the most expeditious means of transmission consistent with requisite security. (Note: In reconnaissance and surveillance usage, "spot report" is not to be used. See Joint Tactical Air Reconnaissance/Surveillance Mission Report.)

spot size - (NATO, CENTO) The size of the electron spot on the face of the cathode ray tube.

spotter - (DOD, IADB) An observer stationed for the purpose of observing and reporting results of naval gunfire to the firing agency. He also may be employed in designating targets. See also field artillery observer; naval gunfire spotting team.

spotter plane - The small plane that flew over a combat area, located both enemy and friendly troops and dropped colored smoke flares to indicate the position and enemy/friendly status. These smoke indicators then were used by others for support decisions on aviation or artillery.

spotter round - Artillery term for the first round fired, which is then used to adjust aim to get on the target.

spotting - (DOD) A process of determining by visual or electronic observation, deviations of artillery or naval gunfire from the target in relation to a spotting line for the purpose of supplying necessary information for the adjustment or analysis of fire.

spotting line - (DOD) Either the gun-target line, the observer-target line, or a reference line used by the observer or spotter in making spot corrections. See also gun-target line; observer-target line; reference line.

sprag - (NATO, CENTO) A projection preventing the movement of platforms or pallets in the side guidance rails in an aircraft cabin.

spray - Infantry term for firing intensely, usually on full automatic.

spray dome - (DOD, NATO, CENTO) The mound of water spray thrown up into the air when the shock wave from an underwater detonation of a nuclear (or atomic) weapon reaches the surface. See also dome.

spread formation - Aviation term for the tactical formation in which the aircraft are widely spread, often several hundred feet apart, as opposed to close formation flying.

spreading fire - (DOD) A notification by the spotter or the naval gunfire ship, depending on who is controlling the fire, to indicate that fire is about to be distributed over an area.

Sprint - (DOD) A guided, surface-to-air, high acceleration, antimissile missile with nuclear warhead capability employed in the Nike X System.

SPT - Support.

SPTrps - Special Troops.

spud locker - 1. Navy and Marine slang for pantry. 2. Aviation term for the part of a carrier flight deck not suited for landing as it is well down the fantail, historically above the pantry.

Sqdn - Squadron.

squad - The military unit commanded by a Sergeant.

squadron - (DOD, IADB) 1. An organization consisting of two or more divisions of ships, or two or more divisions (Navy) or flights of aircraft. It is normally, but not necessarily, composed of ships or aircraft of the same type. 2. The basic administrative aviation unit of the Army, Navy, Marine Corps, and Air Force.

square - A cigarette.

square away - Get organized, put stuff away.

squared away - Ready for action, prepared, organized.

squash bomber - The F-105 jet.

squash rot - Medical slang for any brain disease.

squawk - (DOD) A radio code meaning switch Identification Friend or Foe master control to "normal" (Mode and Code as directed) position.

squawk flash - (DOD) A radio code meaning actuate Identification Friend or Foe I/P switch.

squawk low - (DOD) A radio code meaning switch Identification Friend or Foe master control to "low" position.

squawk may day - (DOD) A radio code meaning switch Identification Friend or Foe master control to "emergency" position.

squawk mike - (DOD) A radio code meaning actuate Identification Friend or Foe MIC switch and key transmitter as directed.

squawk standby - (DOD) A radio code meaning switch Identification Friend or Foe master control to "standby" position.

squawking (_____) - (DOD) A radio code meaning showing Identification Friend or Foe in Mode (_____) indicated.

squelch - The radio microphone had a button to press to talk. This created a squelch, or radio silence, cutting off incoming and making outgoing transmission possible. Pressing the squelch button caused a noticeable sound change for the recipient while the sender did not need to talk. The squelch button was used for transmitting enemy location information silently as follows: one squelch for enemy close, two for all clear.

squib - (DOD, IADB) A small pyrotechnic device which may be used to fire the igniter in a rocket or for some similar purpose. Not to be confused with a detonator which explodes.

squid - 1. Naval hospital corpsman. 2. Marine slang for any Navy personnel.

SR - Seaman Recruit (Navy and Coast Guard).

SR-71 - An aircraft made by Lockheed as a fast, high altitude reconnaissance plane, also called Blackbird, or Habu.

SR-71 - The Blackhawk jet.

SrA - Senior Airman (Air Force).

SRAO - Supplemental Recreational Activities Overseas. The Red Cross.

SRB - Service Record Book. Marine Corps service record.

SRO - Senior Ranking Officer.

SRV - Socialist Republic of Vietnam.

SS - See submarine.

SSBN - See fleet ballistic missile submarine.

SSG - 1. Staff Sergeant (Army) 2. See guided missile submarine.

SSGN - See guided missile submarine.

SSgt - Staff Sergeant (Marine Corps, Air Force).

SSN - See submarine.

SSS - Selective Service System. The national draft in the U.S. for men 18 and older.

SSZ - Specified strike zone, the later designation for the free fire zone.

STAB - SEAL Team Assault Boat.

stable base film - (DOD, NATO, CENTO) A particular type of film having high stability in regard to shrinkage and stretching.

STABO rig - A harness worn by troops to allow extraction by helicopter and as a base for carrying gear. The under-leg straps were usually not used in the field, but were unfolded and fastened before extraction. From stabilized body.

stack arms - The order to stack three or more rifles in a standing pyramid, which keeps them clean and ready to use.

stack pencils - 1. A pointless assignment. 2. Killing time.

stack trooper - Army slang for a model soldier.

staff - See combined staff; general staff; integrated staff; joint staff; parallel staff; special staff.

Staff Sergeant - The second lowest NCO rank.

staff supervision - (DOD, IADB) The process of advising other staff officers and individuals subordinate to the commander of the commander's plans and policies, interpreting those plans and policies, assisting such subordinates in carrying them out, determining the extent to which they are being followed, and advising the commander thereof.

stage - (DOD, NATO, CENTO, IADB) 1. To process, in a specified area, troops which are in transit from one locality to another. See also marshalling; staging area. 2. An element of the missile or propulsion system that generally separates from the missile at burnout or cutoff. Stages are numbered chronologically in order of burning. 3. (NATO, CENTO) The part of an air route from one air staging unit to the next.

staged crews - (DOD, IADB) Aircrews specifically positioned at intermediate airfields to take over aircraft operating on air routes, thus relieving complementary crews of flying fatigue and speeding up the flow rate of the aircraft concerned.

staged crews - (NATO, CENTO) Aircrews prepositioned at specific points along an air route to allow the continuous operation of the aircraft.

staging area - (DOD, NATO, SEATO, CENTO, IADB) 1. (amphibious or airborne) - A general locality between the mounting area and the objective of an amphibious or airborne expedition, through which the expedition or parts thereof pass after mounting, for refueling, regrouping of ships, and/or exercise, inspection, and redistribution of troops. 2. (other movements) - A general locality, containing accommodations for troops, established for the concentration of troop units and transient personnel between movements over the lines of communication. See also marshalling; stage.

staging base - (DOD, IADB) 1. An advanced naval base for the anchoring, fueling, and refitting of transports and cargo ships, and for replenishing mobile service squadrons. 2. A landing and takeoff area with minimum servicing, supply, and shelter provided for the temporary occupancy of military aircraft during the course of movement from one location to another.

stand by - Prepare to do something.

stand down - 1. The return of an infantry unit from the field to the base camp, usually followed by a three day rest period. 2. Later in the war to mean a unit being withdrawn from service in Vietnam and transferred stateside. 3. Suspend action, stop the operation.

stand in the door - Parachutist term for the position just before jumping from a plane.

stand tall - Come to attention.

stand to - Directive to man stations at full strength.

Standard - The AGM 75A surface to air missile which was converted to air to ground use.

standard advanced base units - (DOD, IADB) Personnel and materiel organized to function as advanced base units, including the functional components which are employed in the establishment of naval advanced bases. Such advanced base units may establish repair bases, supply bases, supply depots, airfields, air bases, or other naval shore establishments at overseas locations; e.g., Acorns, Cubs, Gropacs, and Lions. (Note: IADB definition stops with the words "naval shore establishments".)

standard load - (NATO, CENTO) A load which has been preplanned as to dimensions, weight, and balance, and designated by a number or some classification.

standard parallel - (DOD, NATO, CENTO, IADB) A parallel on a map or chart along which the scale is as stated for that map or chart.

standard pattern (land mine warfare) - (DOD, NATO, SEATO, CENTO, IADB) The agreed pattern to which mines are normally laid.

standardization - (DOD) The process by which the Department of Defense achieves the closest practicable cooperation among the Services and Defense agencies for the most efficient use of research, development, and production resources, and agrees to adopt on the broadest possible basis the use of: a. common or compatible operational, administrative, and logistic procedures; b. common or compatible technical procedures and criteria; c. common, compatible, or interchangeable supplies, components, weapons, or equipment; and d. common or compatible tactical doctrine with corresponding organizational compatibility.

standardization - (IADB) The process by which the participating countries achieve the closest practicable cooperation and agree to adopt on the broadest possible basis the use of: a. common or compatible operational, administrative, and logistic procedures; b. common or compatible technical procedures and criteria; c. common, compatible, or interchangeable supplies, components, weapons, or equipment; and d. common or compatible tactical doctrine with corresponding organizational compatibility.

standardization - (NATO, SEATO, CENTO) The process by which member nations achieve the closest practicable cooperation among forces, the most efficient use of research, development, and production resources, and agree to adopt on the broadest possible basis, the use of: a. common or compatible operational, administrative, and logistic procedures; b. common or compatible technical procedures and criteria; c. common, compatible, or interchangeable supplies, components, weapons, or equipment; and d. common or compatible tactical doctrine with corresponding organizational compatibility.

standardization agreement (CENTO) - (CENTO) The record of an agreement among several or all of the member nations to adopt like or similar military equipment, ammunition, supplies and stores; and operational, logistic and administrative procedures. National acceptance of a CENTO allied publication may be recorded as a Standardization Agreement (STANAG).

standardization agreement (NATO) - (NATO) The record of an agreement among several or all of the member nations to adopt like or similar military equipment, ammunition, supplies, and stores; and operational, logistic, and administrative procedures. National acceptance of a NATO allied publication issued by the Military Agency for Standardization may be recorded as a Standardization Agreement (STANAG).

standardization agreement (SEATO) - (SEATO) The record of an agreement among several or all of the member nations to adopt like or similar military equipment, ammunition, supplies, and stores; and operational, logistic, and administrative procedures. National acceptance of a SEATO allied publication issued by the Military Planning Office may be recorded as a Standardization Agreement (SEASTAG).

standardized product - (NATO, CENTO, IADB) A product that conforms to specifications resulting from the same technical requirements.

standby - 1. The order to wait in position for added orders. 2. The status of waiting in position.

standing operating procedure - (DOD, NATO, SEATO, CENTO, IADB) A set of instructions covering those features of operations which lend themselves to a definite or standardized procedure without loss of effectiveness. The procedure is applicable unless prescribed otherwise in a particular case. Thus, the flexibility necessary in special situations is retained.

standing order - (DOD, NATO, CENTO, IADB) Promulgated orders which remain in force until amended or cancelled.

standing order - (SEATO) An order of relative permanence.

standing patrol - (NATO, CENTO, IADB) A patrol which will be of a strength decided by the commander allotting the task. Its task may be reece, listening, fighting, or a combination of these. It differs from a recce, fighting, or listening patrol in that, having taken up its allotted position, it is not free to maneuver in the performance of its task without permission. See also patrol.

star shell - Artillery term for a shell that provided illumination above a combat area.

starboard - The right side of a ship when facing forward.

starch - Slang for plastic explosive.

starchies - A starched utility uniform.

Starfighter - (DOD, IADB) A supersonic, single-engine, turbojet-powered, tactical and air superiority fighter. The tactical version employs cannons or nuclear weapons for attack against surface targets, and is capable of providing close support for ground forces. The interceptor version employs Sidewinders and/or cannons. Designated as F-104.

Starlifter - (DOD, IADB) A large cargo transport made by Lockheed, powered by four turbo-fan engines, capable of intercontinental range with heavy payloads and airdrops. Designated as C-141.

starlight scope - Night scope.

Stars and Bars - The Confederate flag, used as a symbol of white supremacy.

Stars and Stripes - The free U.S. military published newspaper provided to military personnel stationed outside the U.S.

start line-See line of departure, Part 1.

start point - (NATO, CENTO) A well defined point on a route at which a movement of vehicles begins to be under the control of the commander of this movement. It is at this point that the column is formed by the successive passing, at an appointed time, of each of the elements composing the column. In addition to the principal start point of a column there may be secondary start points for its different elements.

stat - Medical order for immediate action, usually verbal due to the urgency.

state - Aviation term which is a request from a carrier to a pilot to state your flight time status. Say your state. The reply is in hours and minutes to splash (landing in the sea). Such as Three plus ten to splash meaning three hours ten minutes of fuel left.

State - The United States State Department.

state and regional defense airlift - (DOD) The program for use during an emergency of civil aircraft other than air carrier aircraft.

state chicken - (DOD) In air intercept, a code meaning I am at a fuel state requiring recovery, tanker service, or diversion to an airfield.

state lamb - (DOD) In air intercept, a code meaning I do not have enough fuel for an intercept plus reserve required for carrier recovery.

state of readiness-armed (demolition) - (DOD, NATO, SEATO, CENTO, IADB) Demolition is ready for immediate firing.

state of readiness-safe (demolition) - (DOD, NATO, SEATO, CENTO, IADB) A demolition target upon or within which the demolition agent has been placed and secured. The firing or initiating circuits have been installed, but not connected to the demolition agent. Detonators or initiators have not been connected or installed.

state tiger - (DOD) In air intercept, a code meaning I have sufficient fuel to complete my mission as assigned.

stateless person - (DOD, NATO, SEATO, CENTO, IADB) A person who is without citizenship.

stateside - In the United States.

static line (air transport) - (DOD, NATO, SEATO, CENTO, IADB) A line attached to a parachute pack and to a strop or anchor cable in an aircraft so that when the load is dropped the parachute is deployed automatically.

static line cable - See anchor cable (air transport).

station - (DOD, IADB) 1. A general term meaning any military or naval activity at a fixed land location. 2. A particular kind of activity to which other activities or individuals may come for a specific service, often of a technical nature, e.g., aid station. 3. An assigned or prescribed position in a naval formation or cruising disposition; or an assigned area in an approach, contact, or battle disposition. 4. Any place of duty or post or position in the field to which an individual, or group of individuals, or a unit may be assigned. (DOD) 5. One or more transmitters or receivers or a combination of transmitters and receivers, including the accessory equipment necessary at one location, for carrying on radio communication service. Each station will be classified by the service in which it operates permanently or temporarily.

station authentication - (DOD, IADB) A security measure designed to establish the authenticity of a transmitting or receiving station.

station time (air transport) - (DOD, NATO, CENTO, IADB) Time at which crews, passengers, and cargo are to be on board and ready for the flight.

Stations of the Cross - Marine slang for the many processing points that must be passed to get required clearances to go on leave or reassignment such as medical, operational, quartermaster, armory, and the unit's orderly room. From the religious depiction of the many reflections by Christ while carrying the cross on the way to the crucifixion.

staybehind - (DOD) Agent or agent organization established in a given country to be activated in the event of hostile overrun or other circumstances under which normal access would be denied.

steady - (DOD) In air intercept, a code meaning am on prescribed heading, or straighten out immediately on present heading or heading indicated.

steam and cream - Slang for: 1. The steam rooms that also had prostitutes. 2. Getting the full range of services of such an establishment.

steel pot - The GI helmet.

Steel Tiger - 1. The air strikes used in Laos on the Ho Chi Minh Trail. 2. Air strikes against enemy transport trucks strategy.

Steer _____ - (DOD) In air intercept, close air support and air interdiction, means set magnetic heading indicated to reach me (or _____).

steering dot - Aviation term for the dot on a radar screen indicating a lock on a target.

stellar guidance - (DOD, IADB) A system wherein a guided missile may follow a predetermined course with reference primarily to the relative position of the missile and certain preselected celestial bodies. See also guidance.

stereogram - (NATO, CENTO) A stereoscopic set of photographs or drawings correctly oriented and mounted for stereoscopic viewing.

stereographic coverage - (DOD) Photographic coverage with overlapping air photographs to provide a three-dimensional presentation of the picture; sixty percent overlap is considered normal, and fifty-three percent is generally regarded as the minimum.

stereoscope - (NATO, CENTO) A binocular optical instrument for helping an observer to view photographs or diagrams in order to obtain a three dimentional impression.

stereoscopic cover - (NATO, CENTO) Photographs taken with sufficient overlap to permit complete stereoscopic examination.

stereoscopic model - (NATO, CENTO) The mental impression of an area or object seen as being in three dimensions when viewed stereoscopically on photographs.

stereoscopic pair - (NATO, CENTO) Two photographs with sufficient overlap of detail to make possible stereoscopic examination of an object or an area common to both.

stereoscopic vision - (NATO, CENTO) The ability to perceive three-dimensional images.

stereoscopy - (NATO, CENTO) The science which deals with three-dimensional effects and the methods by which they are produced.

sterile - 1. Clandestine term for unmarked and untraceable weapon. 2. A uniform without insignias.

sterilize - (DOD) To remove from material to be used in covert and clandestine operations, marks or devices which can identify it as emanating from the sponsoring nations or organization.

sterilizer (mine) - (DOD, IADB) A device incorporated in a mine to detonate or make the mine inactive after a certain preset period of time.

stern - The rear of a ship or aircraft.

stern attack - (DOD) In air intercept, an attack by an interceptor aircraft which terminates with a heading crossing angle of 45 degrees or less. See also heading crossing angle.

Sterno - A trademarked name of a jellied hydrochemical compound that when lighted is used for heating or cooking food.

stewburner - A cook.

stick (air transport) - (DOD, NATO, SEATO, CENTO, IADB) A number of paratroopers who jump from one aperture or door of an aircraft during one run over a drop zone.

stick commander (air transport) - (DOD, NATO, SEATO, CENTO, IADB) A designated individual who controls parachutists from the time they enter the aircraft until their exit. See also jumpmaster.

sticks - Trousers.

stiffs - Dead bodies.

Stinger - The AC-119 gunship.

stingray - Marine recon patrols using guerrilla tactics.

stitched - Killed.

stock control - (DOD, NATO, CENTO, IADB) Process of maintaining data on the quantity, location, and condition of supplies and equipment due in, on-hand, and due-out, to determine quantities of materiel and equipment available and/or required for issue and to facilitate distribution and management of materiel. See also inventory control.

stock coordination - (DOD, IADB) A supply management function exercised usually at department level which controls the assignment of material cognizance for items or categories of material to inventory managers.

stock level - See level of supply.

stock record account - (DOD) A basic record showing by item the receipt and issuance of property, the balances on hand and such other identifying or stock control data as may be required by proper authority.

stockage objective - (DOD, IADB) The maximum quantities of materiel to be maintained on hand to sustain current operations. It will consist of the sum of stocks represented by the operating level and the safety level. See also level of supply.

stockpile to target sequence - (DOD) 1. The order of events involved in removing a nuclear weapon from storage, and assembling, testing, transporting, and delivering it on the target. 2. A document which defines the logistical and employment concepts and related physical environments involved in the delivery of a nuclear weapon from the stock-pile to the target. It may also define the logistical flow involved in moving nuclear weapons to and from the stockpile for quality assurance testing, modification and retrofit, and the recycling of limited life components.

stockpile to target sequence - (NATO, CENTO) The order and permutations of events involved in removing a nuclear weapon from storage, and assembling, testing, transporting, and delivering it on the target.

STOL - Short takeoff and landing aircraft.

stop squawk - (DOD) A radio code meaning turn Identification Friend or Foe master control to "off".

stoppage - A gun jam.

stopper - A fortified line of fire used to stop forward movement of the enemy.

storage - (DOD) 1. Pertaining to a device in which data can be stored and from which it can be obtained at a later time. The means of storing data may be chemical, electrical, or mechanical. 2. A device consisting of electronic, electrostatic, electrical, hardware or other elements into which data may be entered, and from which data may be obtained as desired. 3. The erasable storage in any given computer. Synonymous with memory. See also ammunition and toxic material open space; bulk storage; igloo space; large-lot storage; medium-lot storage; open improved storage space; open unimproved wet space; small-lot storage.

stores - See naval stores; supplies.

stowage diagram - (DOD, NATO, SEATO, CENTO, IADB) A scaled drawing included in the loading plan of a ship for each deck or platform showing the exact location of all cargo. The diagram also contains pertinent items of the following data for each cargo space and deck stowage area: overall dimensions, location of obstructions, dimensions of the overhead hatch opening, dimensions of bow door or stern gate opening, minimum clearances to the overhead, bale cubic capacity, square feet of deck area and the capacity of booms. See also stowage plan.

stowage factor - (DOD) The number which expresses the space, in cubic feet, occupied by a long ton of any commodity as prepared for shipment, including all crating or packaging.

stowage plan - (DOD, IADB) A completed stowage diagram showing what materiel has been loaded and its stowage location in each hold, between-deck compartment, or other space in a ship, including deck space. Each port of discharge is indicated by colors or other appropriate means. Deck and between-deck cargo normally is shown in perspective, while cargo stowed in the lower hold is shown in profile, except that vehicles usually are shown in perspective regardless of stowage. See also stowage diagram.

STP - Slang for an experimental drug (Dom) used to treat mental illness. When abused it was a hallucinogenic. STP were initials for serenity, tranquility, and peace.

strafe - Aviation term for the rapid and repeated firing of the plane's guns at ground targets.

strafing - (DOD) The delivery of automatic weapons fire by aircraft on ground targets.

straight leg - Slang for infantryman.

straightjacket mission - A mission with very strict operational boundaries.

strak (also strac) - Slang for the person who went absolutely by the official military rules and regulations. See The Book.

stranger (bearing, distance, altitude) - (DOD) In air intercept, means an unidentified aircraft, bearing, distance, and altitude as indicated relative to you.

strangle - (DOD) A code meaning switch off equipment indicated.

strangle parrot - (DOD) A radio code meaning switch off Identification Friend or Foe equipment.

straphanger - 1. Useless person. 2. One who just went along for the ride. 3. Not a unit member.

strapping - (DOD, IADB) 1. An operation by which supply containers, such as cartons or boxes, are reinforced by bands, metal straps, or wire placed at specified intervals around them, drawn taut, and then sealed or clamped by a machine. 2. Measurement of storage tanks and calculation of volume to provide tables for conversion of depth of product in linear units of measurement to volume of contents.

strategic advantage - (DOD, IADB) The over-all relative power relationship of opponents which enables one nation or group of nations effectively to control the course of a military/ political situation.

Strategic Air Command - The U.S. Air Force section that operated the heavy bombers

(B-52, etc.) and were responsible for the land based nuclear missiles.

strategic air transport - (DOD, SEATO) The movement of personnel and materiel by air in accordance with a strategic plan.

strategic air transport operations - (NATO, CENTO) The carriage of passengers and cargo between theaters by means of: 1. Scheduled services. 2. Special flights. 3. Air logistic support. 4. Aeromedical evacuations.

strategic air warfare - (DOD, IADB) Air combat and supporting operations designed to effect, through the systematic application of force to a selected series of vital targets, the progressive destruction and disintegration of the enemy's war-making capacity to a point where he no longer retains the ability or the will to wage war. Vital targets may include key manufacturing systems, sources of raw material, critical material, stockpiles, power systems, transportation systems, communication facilities, concentrations of uncommitted elements of enemy armed forces, key agricultural areas, and other such target systems.

strategic air warfare - (NATO, SEATO, CENTO) Air operations designed to effect the progressive destruction and disintegration of the enemy's war-making capacity.

Strategic Army Forces-See United States Strategic Army Forces.

strategic concentration - (DOD, NATO, SEATO, CENTO, IADB) The assembly of designated forces in areas from which it is intended that operations of the assembled force shall begin so that they are best disposed to initiate the plan of campaign.

strategic concept - (DOD, NATO, SEATO, CENTO, IADB) The course of action accepted as the result of the estimate of the strategic situation. It is a statement of what is to be done expressed in broad terms sufficiently flexible to permit its use in framing the basic undertakings which stem from it. See also basic undertakings.

strategic intelligence - (DOD, NATO, CENTO, IADB) Intelligence which is required for the formation of policy and military plans at national and international levels.

strategic map - (DOD, IADB) A map of medium scale, or smaller, used for planning of operations, including the movement, concentration, and supply of troops. See also map.

strategic material (critical) - (DOD, IADB) A material required for, essential uses in a war emergency, the procurement of which in adequate quantity, quality, or time, is sufficiently uncertain, for any reason, to require prior provision of the supply thereof.

strategic mission - (DOD, IADB) A mission directed against one or more of a selected series of enemy targets with the purpose of progressive destruction and disintegration of the enemy's war-making capacity and his will to make war. Targets include key manufacturing systems, sources of raw material, critical material stockpiles, power systems, transportation systems, communication facilities, and other such target systems. As opposed to tactical operations, strategic operations are designed to have a long-range, rather than immediate, effect on the enemy and his military forces.

strategic plan - (DOD, IADB) A plan for the overall conduct of a war.

strategic reserve - (DOD, IADB) That quantity of material which is placed in a particular geographic location due to strategic considerations or in anticipation of major interruptions in the supply distribution system. It is over and above the stockage objective. See also level of supply.

strategic transport aircraft - (DOD, NATO, CENTO) Aircraft designed primarily for the carriage of personnel and/or cargo over long distances.

strategic transport aircraft - (SEATO) Aircraft designed primarily for the carriage of personnel and/or cargo between theaters.

strategic vulnerability - (DOD, IADB) The susceptibility of vital elements of national power to being seriously decreased or adversely changed by the application of actions within the capability of another nation to impose. Strategic vulnerability may pertain to political, geographic, economic, scientific, sociological, or military factors.

strategic warning - (DOD, IADB) A notification that enemy-initiated hostilities may be imminent. This notification may be received from minutes to hours, to days, or longer, prior to the initiation of hostilities. See also strategic warning lead time; strategic warning post-decision time; strategic warning pre-decision time; tactical warning.

strategic warning lead time - (DOD) That time between the receipt of strategic warning and the beginning of hostilities. This time may include two action periods: strategic warning pre-decision time and strategic warning post-decision time. See also commanders estimate of the situation; strategic concept; strategic warning.

strategic warning post-decision time - (DOD) That time which begins after the decision, made at the highest levels of government(s) in response to strategic warning, is ordered executed and ends with the start of hostilities or termination of the threat. It is that part of strategic warning lead time available for executing pre-hostility actions to strengthen the national strategic posture; however, some preparatory actions may be initiated in the pre-decision period. See also strategic warning; strategic warning lead time.

strategic warning pre-decision time - (DOD) That time which begins upon receipt of strategic warning and ends when a decision is ordered executed. It is that part of strategic warning lead time available to the highest levels of government (s) to determine that strategic course of action to be executed. See also strategic warning; strategic warning lead time.

strategy - (DOD, IADB) The art and science of developing and using political, economic, psychological, and military forces as necessary during peace and war, to afford the maximum support to policies, in order to increase the probabilities and favorable consequences of victory and to lessen the chances of defeat. See also military strategy; national strategy.

Stratofortress - (DOD, IADB) An all-weather, intercontinental, strategic heavy bomber powered by eight turbojet engines. It is capable of delivering nuclear and nonnuclear bombs, air-to-surface missiles and decoys. Its range is extended by in-flight refueling. Made by Boeing having a crew of six with the largest ordinance delivery capacity of the bombers used in Vietnam. Designated as B-52.

Stratofreighter - (DOD, IADB) A strategic aerial tanker-freighter powered by four reciprocating engines. It is equipped for in-flight refueling of bombers and fighters. Designated as KC-97.

Stratojet - (DOD) An all-weather strategic medium bomber. It is powered by six turbojet engines. It has intercontinental range through in-flight refueling. The Stratojet is capable of delivering nuclear and nonnuclear bombs. RB-47 is the reconnaissance version of the B-47. Designated as B-47.

Stratolifter - The military version of the Boeing 707 passenger airliner.

stratosphere - (DOD, NATO, CENTO) The layer of the atmosphere above the troposphere in which the change of temperature with height is relatively small. See also atmosphere.

Stratotanker - (DOD, IADB) A multipurpose aerial tanker-transport powered by four turbojet engines. It is equipped for high-speed, high-altitude refueling of bombers and fighters. Designated as KC-135.

Stream (_____) - (DOD) Dispensing of chaff (solid/random interval/bursts).

stream takeoff - (DOD, NATO, CENTO, IADB) Aircraft taking off in trail/column formation.

streamer - 1. Parachutists slang for a parachute that fails to open all the way, but streams above him. 2. An useless person.

Strela - Soviet made missile.

strength - See economic potential; unit strength.

strength group - (DOD) A surface action group (unit) (element) composed of the heaviest combatant ships available with their aircraft and assigned screen.

strength of enemy forces - (IADB) The description of an enemy unit or force in terms of men, weapons, and equipment. See also effective strength of enemy forces; initial strength of enemy forces.

stretch out - (DOD, IADB) A reduction in the delivery rate specified for a program without a reduction in the total quantity to be delivered.

stretcher - See litter.

stretcher patient - See litter patient.

strike - (DOD, NATO, CENTO, IADB) 1. An attack which is intended to inflict damage on, seize or destroy an objective.

strike - Slang, to barhop.

strike force - (DOD, IADB) A force composed of appropriate units necessary to conduct strikes, attack or assault operations. See also task force.

strike photography - (DOD, NATO) Air photographs taken during an air strike.

striker - 1. Special Forces strike unit member. 2. Navy slang for an enlisted man seeking advancement.

strings - 1. The ropes dangling from helicopters to which solders tie themselves for extraction. 2. A series of sensors in the field to detect enemy movement.

strip alert - See ramp alert.

strip marker (land mine warfare) - (DOD, NATO, SEATO, CENTO, IADB) A marker, natural, artificial, or specially installed, located at the start and finish of a mine strip. See also marker (land mine warfare).

strip plot - (NATO, CENTO) A portion of a map or overlay on which a number of photographs taken along a flight line is delineated without defining the outlines of individual prints.

strobe - A handheld flashing light to assist in night landings of helicopters in the field.

stroke book - A porn magazine.

strong point - (DOD, NATO, SEATO, CENTO, IADB) A key point in a defensive position, usually strongly fortified and heavily armed with automatic weapons, around which other positions are grouped for its protection.

strop - (DOD, NATO, CENTO, IADB) In air transport, a length of webbing connecting the static line to the anchor cable.

strop (air transport) - (SEATO) The length of webbing connecting the static line to the anchor cable.

stuffer - Parachutist's term for parachute rigger, one who folds and packs the parachute.

sub collection centers - See nuclear, biological, chemical collection center.

subdued rank and insignia - The muted colors on rank and insignia patches to allow peer recognition but make the colors less visible to the enemy.

subgravity - (DOD, NATO, SEATO, CENTO, IADB) A condition in which the resultant ambient acceleration is between 0 and one G.

subkiloton weapon - (DOD, NATO, CENTO, IADB) A nuclear weapon producing a yield below one kiloton. See also kiloton weapon; nominal weapon.

sublimited war - Not to be used. No substitute recommended.

submarine sanctuaries - (DOD, IADB) Restricted areas which are established for the conduct of non-combat submarine or antisubmarine exercises. They may be either stationary or moving and are normally designated only in rear areas. See also moving havens.

submarine - (DOD, IADB) A warship designed for under-the-surface operations with primary mission of locating and destroying ships, including other submarines. It is capable of various other naval missions. SSNs are nuclear powered. Designated as SS and SSN. See also fleet ballistic missile submarine.

submarine base - (NATO, SEATO, CENTO, IADB) A base providing logistic support for submarines.

submarine havens - (NATO, SEATO, CENTO, IADB) Specified sea areas for submarine noncombat operations including: a. submarine sanctuaries announced by the area, fleet, or equivalent commander; b. areas reserved for submarine operations and training in non-combat zones; and c. moving areas, established by "Submarine Notices", surrounding submarines in transit, extending 50 nautical miles ahead, 100 nautical miles behind, and 15 nautical miles on each side of the estimated position of the submarine along the stated track. See also moving havens. (Note: SEATO definition Part c does not include "nautical.")

submarine launched missile - See sea-launched ballistic missile.

submarine patrol areas - (DOD, NATO, CENTO, IADB) A stretch of water determined in all directions by specific geographic limits assigned to a submarine's action.

submarine patrol zones - (DOD, NATO, SEATO, CENTO, IADB) Restricted sea areas established for the purpose of permitting submarine operations, unrestricted by the operations or possible attack of friendly forces.

submarine rocket - (DOD, IADB) Submerged, submarine-launched, surface-to-surface rocket with nuclear depth charge or homing torpedo payload, primarily antisubmarine. Popular name is Subroc. Designated as UUM-44A.

submarine safety lanes - See safety lanes.

submarine striking forces - (DOD, IADB) Submarines having guided or ballistic missile launching and/or guidance capabilities formed to launch offensive nuclear strikes.

Subroc - See submarine rocket.

subsidiary demolition belt - (DOD, IADB) A supplement to the primary belt to give depth in front or behind, or to protect the flanks. See also demolition belt.

subsonic - (DOD, NATO, CENTO, IADB) Of or pertaining to speeds less than the speed of sound. See also speed of sound.

substitute transport-type vehicle - (DOD, IADB) A wheeled vehicle designed to perform, within certain limitations, the same military function as military transport vehicles, but not requiring all the special characteristics thereof. They are developed from civilian designs by addition of certain features, or from military designs by deletion of certain features. See also vehicle.

subversion - (DOD, I, SEATO, IADB) Action designed to undermine the military, economic, psychological, morale, or political strength of a regime. See also unconventional warfare.

subversion - (NATO, CENTO) Action designed to undermine: a. the military, economic, psychological, morale, or political strength of a nation; and b. the loyalty of the subjects.

subversive political action - (DOD, SEATO, IADB) A planned series of activities designed to accomplish political objectives by influencing, dominating, or displacing individuals or groups who are so placed as to affect the decisions and actions of another government.

subversive activity - (DOD) Anyone lending aid, comfort, and moral support to individuals, groups, or organizations which advocate the overthrow of incumbent governments by force and violence is subversive and is engaged in subversive activity. All willful acts which are intended to be detrimental to the best interests of the government and which do not fall into the categories of treason, sedition, sabotage, or espionage will be placed in the category of subversive activity.

suck up - A subordinate trying to get favors from a superior. A kiss ass.

sucking chest wound - A wound in which the lung collapses and death will follow if the hole is not plugged immediately. The use of cellophane from cigarette packs was commonly used as an immediate field patch to restore lung function until medical assistance was available.

sugar reports - 1. Letters from stateside, usually from a girlfriend. 2. Reports made more positive then factual.

summary areas - (NATO, SEATO, CENTO, IADB) Defined areas of sea. For each of these areas, a separate estimated position summary (covering own shipping and forces) and enemy information summary messages are made daily by officers conducting the exercise. These messages are for the information of warships and sea-going commands at sea in the particular area, and certain specified shore authorities.

summit - (DOD) The highest altitude above mean sea level that a projectile reaches in its flight from the gun to the target; the algebraic sum of the maximum ordinate and the altitude of the gun.

SUPCOM - Supreme Command.

super bazooka - The M-20 rocket launcher.

super grunt - Slang for Marine recon patrol members.

Super Sabre - (DOD, IADB) A supersonic, single-engine, turbojet-powered, tactical and air superiority fighter capable of delivering either nuclear or nonnuclear bombs, rockets, and Bullpup missiles against surface targets, or cannons and Sidewinder missiles against airborne targets. It is capable of providing close support for ground forces; and it can be refueled in flight. Designated as F-100.

Super Skymaster - See O-2, an aircraft.

Superfortress - (DOD) A tactical aerial tanker powered by four reciprocating engines and two turbojet engines. It is capable of simultaneous aerial refueling of three fighter-type aircraft by the probe and drogue method. Designated as KB-50.

supersonic - (DOD, NATO, CENTO, IADB) Of or pertaining to speed in excess of the speed of sound - See also speed of sound.

supervised route - (DOD, NATO, CENTO) A roadway over which control is exercised by a traffic control authority by means of traffic control posts, traffic patrols or both. See also route.

Supper - Code for a bombing area in Cambodia. See Menu.

supplement - (NATO, SEATO, CENTO, IADB) A supplement is a separate publication, related to a basic publication and prepared for purposes of promulgating additional information or summaries, and may include extracts from the basic publication. (SEATO, IADB) A supplement may have a different classification from that of the basic publication, and may not be registered regardless of whether or not the basic publication is registered.

Supplemental Recreational Activities Overseas (SRAO) - The official title of the Red Cross operation.

supplies - (DOD) All items necessary for the equipment, maintenance, and operation of a military command, including food, clothing, equipment, arms, ammunition, fuel, materials, and machinery of all kinds. See also stores. For planning and administrative purposes supplies are divided as noted below. The subclassification materiel designators (A through T) may be used in combination with the designated subclassifications to further define a portion of a class of supply for planning purposes, e.g., use of Class V AL to designate ammunition, air missile. Additional codes may be utilized by the Services to satisfy a specific requirement. This additional permissive coding is not to be utilized in lieu of that designated for the major classification and subclassification. a. <u>Class I</u>-Subsistence including gratuitous health and welfare items. Subclassifications for Class I are: A-Air (inflight rations); R-Refrigerated subsistence;

S-Nonrefrigerated subsistence (less combat rations); C-Combat rations (including gratuitous health and welfare items). b. <u>Class II</u>-Clothing, individual equipment, tentage, organizational tool sets and tool kits, hand tools, administrative, and housekeeping supplies and equipment. Subclassifications for Class II are: B-Ground support materiel (includes power generators and construction, barrier, bridging, fire fighting, petroleum, and mapping equipment); E-General supplies; F-Clothing and textiles; M-Weapons; and T-Industrial supplies (includes bearings, block and tackle, cable, chain, wire rope, screws, bolts, studs, steel rods, plates and bars). c. <u>Class III</u>-Petroleum, oils, and lubricants: Petroleum fuels, lubricants, hydraulic and insulating oils, preservatives, liquid and compressed gases, bulk chemical products, coolants, deicing and antifreeze compounds, together with components and additives of such products, and coal. Subclassifications for Class III are: A-Air; and W-Ground (surface). d. <u>Class IV</u>-Construction: Construction materials to include installed equipment, and all fortification/barrier materials. (No subclassifications.). e. <u>Class V</u>-Ammunition: Ammunition of all types (including chemical, biological, radiological, and special weapons), bombs, explosives, mines, fuzes, detonators, pyrotechnics, missiles, rockets, propellants, and other associated items. Subclassifications for Class V are: A -Air; and W-Ground. f. <u>Class VI</u>-Personal Demand Items (Nonmilitary Sales Items). (No subclassifications.). g. <u>Class VII</u>-Major End Items: A final combination of end products which is ready for its intended use; e.g., launchers, tanks, mobile machine shops, vehicles. Subclassifications for Class VII are: A -Air; B-Ground support materiel (includes power generators and construction, barrier, bridging, fire fighting, petroleum, and mapping equipment); D-Administrative vehicles (commercial vehicles utilized in administrative motor pools); G-Electronics; K-Tactical vehicles; L-Missiles; M-Weapons; and N-Special weapons. h. <u>Class VIII</u>-Medical Materiel Including Medical Peculiar Repair Parts. (No subclassifications.). i. <u>Class IX</u>-Repair Parts and components to include kits, assemblies, and subassemblies, reparable and nonreparable, required for maintenance support of all equipment. Subclassifications for Class IX are the same as Class VII with addition of T-Industrial supplies (includes bearings, block and tackle, cable, chain, wire rope, screws, bolts, studs, steel rods, plates and bars). j. <u>Class X</u>-Materiel to Support Nonmilitary Programs; e.g., Agricultural and Economic Development, Not included in Classes I-IX. (No subclassifications.)

supply - (DOD, IADB) The procurement, distribution, maintenance while in storage, and salvage of supplies, including the determination of kind and quantity of supplies. a. (producer phase)-That phase of military supply which extends from determination of procurement schedules to acceptance of finished supplies by the military Services. b. (consumer phase)-That phase of military supply which extends from receipt of finished supplies by the military Services through issue for use or consumption.

supply by air - See airdrop; air movement.

supply control - (DOD, IADB) The process by which an item of supply is controlled within the supply system, including requisitioning, receipt, storage, stock control, shipment, disposition, identification, and accounting.

supply management - See inventory control.

supply point - (DOD, NATO, SEATO, CENTO, IADB) Any point where supplies are issued in detail.

support - (DOD, IADB) 1. The action of a force which aids, protects, complements, or sustains another force in accordance with a directive requiring such action. 2. A unit which helps another unit in battle. Aviation, artillery, or naval gunfire may be used as a support for infantry. 3. A part of any unit held back at the beginning of an attack as a reserve. 4. An element of a command that assists, protects, or supplies other forces in combat. See also interdepartmental/agency support; international logistical support, inter-Service support.

support - (NATO, SEATO, CENTO) The action of a force or portion thereof, which aids, protects, complements, or sustains any other force.

supporting aircraft - (DOD, IADB) All active aircraft other than unit aircraft. See also aircraft.

supporting arms - (DOD, IADB) Air, sea, and land weapons of all types employed to support ground units.

supporting arms coordination center - (DOD, IADB) A single location on board an amphibious command ship in which all communication facilities incident to the coordination of fire support of the artillery, air, and naval gunfire are centralized. This is the naval counterpart to the fire support coordination center utilized by the landing force. See also fire support coordination center.

supporting artillery - (DOD, IADB) Artillery which executes fire missions in support of a specific unit, usually infantry, but remains under the command of the next higher artillery commander.

supporting fire - (DOD, NATO, SEATO, CENTO, IADB) Fire delivered by supporting units to assist or protect a unit in combat. See also close supporting fire; deep supporting fire; direct supporting fire; fire.

Supreme Six, Supreme-6 - Slang for God, God's call sign.

surface burst - See nuclear surface burst.

surface code - See panel code.

surface striking forces (naval) - (DOD, IADB) Forces which are organized primarily to do battle with enemy forces or to conduct shore bombardment. Units comprising such a force are generally incorporated in and operate as part of another force, but with provisions for their formation into a surface striking force should such action appear likely and/or desirable.

surface zero - See ground zero.

surface-to-air missile - (DOD, IADB) A surface-launched missile designed to operate against a target above the surface.

surface-to-air missile envelope - (DOD) That air space within the kill capabilities of a specific surface-to-air missile system.

surface-to-air missile installation - (DOD) A surface-to-air missile site with the surface-to-air missile system hardware installed.

surface-to-air missile site - (DOD) A plot of ground prepared in such a manner that it will readily accept the hardware used in a surface-to-air missile system.

surface-to-surface missile - (DOD, IADB) A surface-launched missile designed to operate against a target on the surface.

surplus property - (DOD) Any excess property not required for the needs and for the discharge of the responsibilities of all federal agencies, including the Department of Defense, as determined by the General Services Administration.

surplus property - (IADB) Any excess property not required for the needs and for the discharge of the responsibilities of all governmental agencies.

Surv - Surveillance aircraft.

surveillance - (DOD, NATO, CENTO, IADB) The systematic observation of aerospace, surface, or subsurface areas, places, persons, or things by visual, aural, electronic, photographic, or other means. See also air surveillance; satellite and missile surveillance; sea surveillance.

surveillance approach - (DOD) An instrument approach conducted in accordance with directions issued by a controller referring to the surveillance radar display.

survey - Navy and Marine slang for dispose of by logging out of stock and usage.

survey control point - (DOD) A survey station used to coordinate survey control.

survey information center - (DOD) A place where survey data are collected, correlated, and made available to subordinate units.

survey photography - See air cartographic photography.

Survival Assistance Officer - The officer reporting a death of a soldier to the next of kin, accompanying his body, and assisting the next of kin in funeral arrangements.

survival straws - A water purification system built into a straw.

susceptibility - (DOD) The degree to which a device, equipment or weapons system is open to effective attack due to one or more inherent weaknesses.

suspension strop - (DOD, NATO, CENTO, IADB) A length of webbing or wire rope between the helicopter and cargo sling.

Suzy - Slang for the girlfriend left stateside.

SV - 1. South Vietnam. 2. Security vehicle.

SVC - Service.

swab - Navy and Marine slang for a mop or mopping.

swab jockey - Marine slang for Navy personnel.

swabbie - Slang for Navy personnel. Also spelled swabee.

SWAG - Scientific wild ass guess.

Swamp Rats - First Battalion, 18th Infantry.

Swatow - A North Vietnamese gunboat.

sweat hog - An overweight soldier.

Sweaty Betty - Slang for an American female easily available for sex.

sweep - (DOD) To employ technical means to uncover planted microphones or other surveillance devices. See also technical survey.

sweep - 1. Infantry term for troops search a village. 2. Aviation term for fighter jets looking for and taking on enemy planes as targets present themself.

sweet - Aviation term for everything working properly.

Swift Boats - U.S. Navy patrol boats on coast and rivers.

swifties - Slang for crew of Swift Boats

swinging dick - Any male soldier.

swinging man trap - See Malay whip.

switchblade - Infantry and recon term for attacking the enemy with his own weapons.

synthesis - (DOD, IADB) In intelligence usage, the examining and combining of processed information with other information and intelligence for final interpretation.

syrette - A one-use syringe of morphine carried in the field. The needle is attached to a collapsible tube which is squeezed to inject the morphine.

system manager(s) - (DOD) A general term of reference to those organizations directed by individual managers, exercising authority over the planning, direction, and control of tasks and associated functions essential for support of designated weapons or equipment systems. The authority vested in this organization may include. such functions as research, development, procurement, production, materiel distribution, and logistic support, when so assigned. When intended to relate to a specific system manager, this term will be preceded by the appropriate designation (e.g., Chinook System Manager, Sonar System Manager, F-4 System Manager). This term will normally be used in lieu of system support manager, weapon system manager, program manager, and project manager when such organizations perform these functions.

system support manager - See system manager.

T – TANGO

T - Designated in the phonetic military alphabet as "Tango".

T and E tripod - The large tripod used to support the .50 cal machine gun that allowed adjustment in all directions for fine targeting.

T and T - See T&T.

T-10 parachute - The nylon main parachute worn on a harness on the back. See MC-1.

T-10 reserve parachute - The smaller nylon reserve parachute worn over the chest.

T-21 - The Czech made rifle used by the North Vietnamese.

T-28 - A World War II vintage trainer prop aircraft that was converted to be a bomber by the Vietnamese Air Force (South). See Trojan.

T-33 - See F-80.

T-34 - A Soviet made tank.

T-39 - See Sabreliner.

T-54 - A Soviet made tank of WWII vintage that is medium sized.

T-56 - The standard issue rifle for the North Vietnamese Army and the Viet Cong, produced in China as a copy of the AK-47.

T-6 - The D7E tractor.

T-85 - A Soviet made tank.

T-block - A plastic plug that, when inserted into the breech of a rifle, prevented an accidental discharge.

T-LAR - "That looks about right". An estimate. Also spelled TLAR. Pronounced Tee lar.

T/Sgt - Technical Sergeant.

T&T - Hospital slang for a wound that is through and through, meaning the projectile entered and exited the body. Pronounced TNT. Also spelled T and T.

TA 50 - A standard issue of combat clothes and gear.

TA-1 - Field telephone. Unlike a battery powered medium to long range radio (PRK) these were self-powered by a hand cranked generator and had a short range. Their use was for immediate and close range communication, often until lines could be laid or better radios brought to the area. It was about the size of a fishing tackle box, with a lid and handset looking like a residential telephone.

TA-4 - A two-seater version of the A-4 Phantom jet used for Forward Air Control.

TAADS - The Army Authorization Documents System. Also AADS.

Tabasco - 1. The trademarked hot sauce relished in the C-ration packs. 2. Slang for napalm when in lower case as tabasco.

table of organization - See establishment.

table of organization and equipment - See establishment.

TAC - 1. True Air Speed. 2. Tactical Air Command.

Tac Air - 1.Tactical Air Support, Air Force term. 2. Fighter bombers.

tac wire - Tactical wire. The use of coils of barbed wire to interrupt the forward movement of the enemy.

tac-log group - (DOD, IADB) Representatives designated by troop commanders to assist Navy control officers aboard control ships in the ship-to-shore movement of troops, equipment, and supplies.

TACA - Tactical Air Control Airborne, the operation of designating targets, directing other planes to the target and assessing damage, often the leader of the flight.

TACAN - A U.S. navigation system.

TACC - Tactical Air Control Center, the command center for all air activity for a set sector.

tacit arms control agreement - (DOD, IADB) An arms control course of action in which two or more nations participate without any formal agreement having been made.

tactical aeromedical evacuation - (DOD, NATO, SEATO, CENTO, IADB) That phase of evacuation which provides airlift for patients from the combat zone to points outside the combat zone, and between points within the communications zone.

tactical air command - (DOD) 1. An Air Force organization designed to conduct offensive and defensive air operations in conjunction with land or sea forces. 2. A designation of one of the subordinate commands of the Air Force.

tactical air command center - (DOD) The principal United States Marine Corps air operation installation from which aircraft and air warning functions of tactical air operations are directed. It is the senior agency of the Marine Corps Air Command and Control System from which the Marine Corps tactical air commander can direct and control tactical air operations and coordinate such air operations with other Services.

tactical air commander - See tactical air force.

tactical air commander (ashore) - (DOD) The officer (aviator) responsible to the landing force commander for control and coordination of air operations within the landing force commander's area of responsibility when control of these operations is passed ashore.

tactical air control center - (DOD, NATO, SEATO, CENTO, IADB) The principal air operations installation (land or ship-based) from which all aircraft and air warning functions of tactical air operations are controlled.

tactical air control group - (DOD, IADB) 1. (land-based)- A flexible administrative and tactical component of a tactical air organization which provides aircraft control and warning functions ashore for offensive and defensive missions within the tactical air zone of responsibility. 2. (ship-based)- An administrative and tactical component of an amphibious force which provides aircraft control and warning facilities afloat for offensive and defensive missions within the tactical air command area of responsibility.

tactical air control party - (DOD) A subordinate operational component of a tactical air control system designed to provide air liaison to land forces and for the control of aircraft. See also air control team.

tactical air control party - (IADB) A subordinate operational component of the landing force tactical air control system designed to provide air liaison functions and for the control of aircraft from a forward observation post. The tactical air control party operates at division, regimental, and battalion levels. See also air control team.

tactical air control party support team - (DOD) An Army team organized to provide armored combat and/or special purpose vehicles and crews to certain tactical air control parties.

tactical air control squadron - (DOD, IADB) 1. (land-based)- A flexible administrative component of a tactical air control group, known as TACRON, which provides the control mechanism for a land-based tactical air control center, a tactical air direction center, or tactical air control parties. 2. (ship-based)- An administrative and tactical component of the tactical air control group, known as TACRON, which provides the control mechanism for the ship-based tactical air direction center or the ship-based tactical air control center.

tactical air control system - (DOD) The organization and equipment necessary to plan, direct, and control tactical air operations and to coordinate air operations with other Services. It is composed of control agencies and communications-electronics facilities which provide the means for centralized control and decentralized execution of missions.

tactical air controller - (DOD) The officer in charge of all operations of the tactical air control center (afloat). He is responsible to the tactical air officer for the control of all aircraft and air warning facilities within his area of responsibility. See also air controller.

tactical air controller - (NATO, SEATO, CENTO, IADB) The officer in charge of all operations of the tactical air control center. He is responsible to the tactical air commander for the control of all aircraft and air warning facilities within his area of responsibility. See also air controller.

tactical air coordinator (airborne) - (DOD, IADB) An officer who coordinates, from an aircraft, the action of combat aircraft engaged in close support of ground or sea forces.

tactical air direction center - (DOD) An air operations installation under the overall control of the tactical air control center (afloat)/tactical air command center, from which aircraft and air warning service functions of tactical air operations in an area of responsibility are directed. See also tactical air director.

tactical air direction center - (IADB) An air operations installation under the overall control of the tactical air control center, from which aircraft and aircraft warning service functions of tactical air operations in an area of responsibility are directed. See also tactical air director.

tactical air director - (DOD, IADB) The officer in charge of all operations of the tactical air direction center. He is responsible to the tactical air controller for the direction of all aircraft and air warning facilities assigned to his area of responsibility. When operating independently of a tactical air control center (afloat), the tactical air director assumes the functions of the tactical air controller. See also tactical air direction center.

tactical air force - (DOD, NATO, SEATO, CENTO, IADB) An air force charged with carrying out tactical air operations in coordination with ground or naval forces.

tactical air observer - (DOD) An officer trained as an air observer whose function is to observe from airborne aircraft and report on movement and disposition of friendly and enemy forces, on terrain, weather, and hydrography and to execute other missions as directed.

tactical air officer (afloat) - (DOD) The officer (aviator) under the amphibious task force commander who coordinates planning of all phases of air participation of the amphibious operation and air operations of supporting forces en route to and in the objective area. Until control is passed ashore, he exercises control over all operations of the tactical air control center (afloat) and is charged with: a. control of all aircraft in the objective area assigned for tactical air operations, including offensive and defensive air; b. control of all other aircraft entering or passing through the objective area; and c. control of all air warning facilities in the objective area.

tactical air operation - (DOD, NATO, SEATO, CENTO, IADB) An air operation involving the employment of air power in coordination with ground or naval forces to: a. gain and maintain air superiority; b. prevent movement of enemy forces into and within the objective area and to seek out and destroy these forces and their supporting installations; and c. join with ground or naval forces in operations within the objective area, in order to assist directly in attainment of their immediate objective.

tactical air operations center - (DOD) A subordinate operational component of the Marine Air Command and Control System designed for direction and control of all en route air traffic and air defense operations, to include manned interceptors and surface-to-air weapons, in an assigned sector. It is under the operational control of the Tactical Air Command Center.

tactical air reconnaissance - (DOD) The use of air vehicles to obtain information concerning terrain, weather, and the disposition, composition, movement, installations, lines of communications, electronic and communication emissions of enemy forces. Also included are artillery and naval gunfire adjustment, and systematic and random observation of ground battle area, targets, and/or sectors of airspace.

tactical air support - (DOD, NATO, SEATO, CENTO, IADB) Air operations carried out in coordination with surface forces which directly assist the land or naval battle. See also air support.

tactical air support element - (DOD) An element of a United States Army division, corps, or field army tactical operations center consisting of G-2 and G-3 air personnel who coordinate and integrate tactical air support with current tactical ground operations.

tactical air transport - (SEATO, IADB) The use of air transport in direct support of: a. airborne assaults; b. carriage of air transported forces; c. tactical air supply; d. evacuation of casualties from forward airfields; and e. clandestine operations.

tactical air transport operations - (DOD, NATO, CENTO) The carriage of passengers and cargo within a theater by means of: l. Airborne operations: a. parachute assault; b. helicopter borne assault; and c. air landing. 2. Air logistic support. 3. Special missions. 4. Aeromedical evacuation missions.

tactical area of responsibility - (DOD) A defined area of land for which responsibility is specifically assigned to the commander of the area as a measure for control of assigned forces and coordination of support. Commonly referred to as TAOR.

tactical bomb lines - (IADB) Lines (land) prescribed by a troop commander beyond which he considers that properly coordinated bombing would not endanger his own forces. See also bomb lines.

tactical call sign - (DOD, NATO, SEATO, CENTO, IADB) A call sign which identifies a tactical command or tactical communication facility. See also call sign.

tactical command ship - (DOD, IADB) A warship, converted from a light cruiser, and designed to serve as a command ship for a fleet/force commander. It is equipped with extensive communication equipment. Designated as CC.

tactical control - (NATO, SEATO, CENTO, IADB) The detailed and, usually, local direction and control of movements or maneuvers necessary to accomplish missions or tasks assigned.

tactical diversion (naval) - (SEATO, IADB) A modification for operational reasons to the route, or the rate of progress along the route, including waiting periods in a holding anchorage, of a ship or convoy without alteration of its ultimate destination.

tactical emergency - Code for a critical field unit in danger of being overrun. This assessment and order can only be made by General staff who then may redeploy other troops.

tactical information processing and interpretation system - (DOD) A tactical, mobile, land-based, automated information-handling system designed to store and retrieve intelligence information and to process and interpret imagery or nonimagery data. Also called TIPI.

tactical intelligence - (DOD) Intelligence which is required for the planning and conduct of tactical operations. Essentially, tactical intelligence and strategic intelligence differ only in scope, point of view, and level of employment.

tactical loading - See combat loading; unit loading.

tactical locality - (DOD, NATO, SEATO, CENTO, IADB) An area of terrain which, because of its location or features, possesses a tactical significance in the particular circumstances existing at a particular time.

tactical map - (DOD, IADB) A large-scale map used for tactical and administrative purposes. See also map.

tactical nuclear weapon employment - (DOD) The use of nuclear weapons by land, sea, or air forces against opposing forces, supporting installations or facilities, in support of operations which contribute to the accomplishment of a military mission of limited scope, or in support of the military commander's scheme of maneuver, usually limited to the area of military operations.

tactical operations center - (DOD) A physical groupment of those elements of an Army general and special staff concerned with the current tactical operations and the tactical support thereof.

tactical reserve - (DOD, NATO, SEATO, CENTO, IADB) A part of battalion, regiment, or similar force, held initially under the control of the commander as a maneuvering force to influence future action.

tactical transport aircraft - (DOD, NATO, CENTO) Aircraft designed primarily for the carriage of personnel and/or cargo over short or medium distances.

tactical troops - (DOD, IADB) Combat troops, together with any service troops required for their direct support, who are organized under one commander to operate as a unit and engage the enemy in combat. See also troops.

tactical unit - (DOD, IADB) An organization of troops, aircraft, or ships which is intended to serve as a single unit in combat. It may include service units required for its direct support.

tactical vehicle - (DOD, IADB) A vehicle having military characteristics designed primarily for use by forces in the field in direct connection with, or support of, combat or tactical operations, or the training of troops for such operations. See also vehicle.

tactical warning - (DOD, IADB) 1. A notification that the enemy has initiated hostilities. Such warning may be received any time from the launching of the attack until it reaches its target. See also strategic warning. (DOD) 2. In satellite and missile surveillance, a notification to operational command centers that a specific threat event(s) is occurring. The component elements that describe threat events are: <u>Country of origin</u>-country or countries initiating hostilities. <u>Event type and size</u>-identification of the type of event and determination of the size or number of weapons. <u>Country under attack</u>-determined by observing trajectory of an object and predicting its impact point. <u>Event time</u>-time the hostile event occurred.

tactics - (DOD, IADB) 1. The employment of units in combat. 2. The ordered arrangement and maneuver of units in relation to each other and/or to the enemy in order to utilize their full potentialities.

TAD - Temporary active duty or temporary additional duty.

tadpole - The OH-6 helicopter. See Sperm.

tag - The paper tag tied to a wounded soldier by a medic with medical status and treatment information and identification data.

tag and bag - Removing a dead body by attaching an identification tag the soldier and bagging the body for removal from the field.

tail - The last man in a patrol, infantry or aviation.

tail end Charlie - The last man in a patrol formation.

tail rotor chain bracelets - The drive chain of a tail rotor worn by helicopter crews as a bracelet.

taildragger - 1. The small prop airplanes. 2. Any plane with a three-wheel landing structure in which two landing wheels forward of center and a smaller one was under the tail. 3. A lazy person.

take down - Destroy.

take fire - Be shot at.

take out - Kill.

talk quick - Radio slang for a secure communications system.

tally ho - (DOD) Target visually sighted (presumably the target I have been ordered to intercept). This should be followed by initial contact report as soon as possible. The sighting should be amplified if possible (e.g., "tally-ho pounce," or "tally-ho heads up").

Talos - (DOD, IADB) A shipborne, surface-to-air missile with solid-propellent rocket/ram-jet engine. It is equipped with nuclear or non-nuclear warhead, and command, beam-rider homing guidance. Designated as RIM-8.

tan alt - See shadow factor.

tanglefoot - Slang for a barbed wire laid in a mesh pattern at ankle height to impede passage.

Tango - The military phonetic alphabet designation for the letter "T".

Tango Charlie - Request for a time check.

Tango India Charlie - See troops in combat (enemy contact).

Tango November - For the offensive slang token nigger.

Tango Uniform - Slang for tits up, meaning dead, inoperative, impossible to survive the situation, from the ranching description of a cow with its tits up in a ditch-impossible to extract and save.

tank farm - The fuel storage depot.

tank, 76-mm gun - (DOD, IADB) A tracked vehicle providing light armor protection against small arms fire and shell fragments. Primary role of this vehicle is armored reconnaissance. Designated as M41.

tank, combat, full-tracked, 90-mm gun - (DOD, IADB) A fully armed combat vehicle providing mobile fire power and crew protection for offensive combat, armed with one 90-mm gun, one 50-caliber machine gun, and one 30-caliber machine gun. Designated as M48A2.

tank, combat, full-tracked, l05-mm gun - (DOD, IADB) A heavy, fully armored combat vehicle providing mobile fire power and crew protection for offensive combat, armed with one l05-mm gun, one 50 caliber machine gun, and one 30-caliber machine gun. Designated as M60.

tank, combat, full-tracked, 120-mm gun - (DOD, IADB) A heavy, fully armored combat vehicle armed with one 120-mm gun, one 30-caliber machine gun, and one 50-caliber machine gun. Designated as Ml03A1.

tank, main battle - (DOD, IADB) A tracked vehicle providing heavy armor protection and serving as the principal assault weapon of armored and infantry troops. The new main battle tank will mount the Shillelagh.

tanker - Soldier in tank unit.

tanker bar - A tool used on tracked vehicles like tanks.

tanker boots - Combat boots with double wrap leather straps over the laces, worn by tank personnel. Also called wrap boots.

tanker grenade - An improvised explosive for defense when the enemy is too close for the use of the tank's guns. Usually made of barbed wire wrapped around two pounds of C-4 or TNT.

tans - The summer khaki uniform.

TAOI - Tactical area of influence. An area in which the presence of the enemy may impact planning or operations.

TAOR - Tactical area of responsibility.

tap - To kill.

tap codes - A system used by American POWs in confinement to communicate. Similar to Morse code, the POWs would tap walls or pipes to convey messages. The code was developed using 25 letters in a 5x5 grid, so the tap would indicate row and letter position on that row. The omitted letter was K, letting C act as both C and K.

tape and turn - The infantryman's strategy of taping two banana clips of ammunition together, in a reverse orientation, so that when the ammunition in one clip is expended, you simply remove it, turn the taped unit, and insert the second clip, saving the time needed to find a second clip.

tapioca mill - A whorehouse.

taps - The bugle call played at the end of ceremonies and the end of the day for lights out.

tar baby - A hashish addict.

TARCAP - Target Combat Air Patrol. Fighters flying defense for bombers.

TARFU - Things are really fucked up.

target - (DOD) 1. A geographical area, complex, or installation planned for capture or destruction by military forces. 2. In intelligence usage, a country, area, installation, agency, or person against which intelligence operations are directed. 3. An area designated and numbered for future firing. 4. In gunfire support usage, an impact burst which hits the target.

target acquisition - (DOD, NATO, CENTO, IADB) The detection, identification, and location of a target in sufficient detail to permit the effective employment of weapons. See also target analysis.

target analysis - (DOD, NATO, CENTO, IADB) An examination of potential targets to determine military importance, priority of attack, and weapons required to obtain a desired level of damage or casualties.

target approach point - (DOD, NATO, SEATO, CENTO, IADB) In air transport operations, a navigational checkpoint over which the final turn into the drop zone/landing zone is made. See also initial point.

target area survey base - (DOD, NATO, CENTO) A base line used for the locating of targets or other points by the intersection of observations from two stations located at opposite ends on the line.

target array - (DOD) A graphic representation of enemy forces, personnel, and facilities in a specific situation, accompanied by a target analysis.

target bearing - (DOD, IADB) 1. (true)- The true compass bearing of a target from a firing ship. 2. (relative)- The bearing of a target measured in the horizontal from the bow of one's own ship clockwise from 0 degrees to 360 degrees, or from the nose of one's own aircraft in hours of the clock.

target cap - (DOD) Target combat air patrol.

target classification - (DOD) A grouping of targets in accordance with their threat to the amphibious task force and its component elements, targets not to be fired upon prior to D-day and targets not to be destroyed except on direct orders.

target combat air patrol - (DOD) A patrol of fighters maintained over an enemy target area to destroy enemy aircraft and to cover friendly shipping in the vicinity of the target area in amphibious operations. See also combat air patrol.

target complex - (DOD, NATO, SEATO, CENTO, IADB) A geographically integrated series of target concentrations. See also target.

target concentration - (DOD, IADB) A grouping of geographically proximate targets. See also target; target complex.

target data inventory - (DOD) A basic targeting program which provides standardized target data in support of the requirements of the Joint Chiefs of Staff, military departments, and unified and specified commands for target planning' coordination and weapons application.

target date - (NATO, SEATO, CENTO, IADB) The date on which it is desired that an action be accomplished or initiated.

target director post - (DOD, IADB) A special control element of the tactical air control system. It performs no air warning service but is used to position friendly aircraft over predetermined target coordinates, or other geographical locations, under all weather conditions.

target discrimination - (DOD, NATO, CENTO) The ability of a surveillance or guidance system to identify or engage anyone target when multiple targets are present.

target dossiers - (DOD, NATO, SEATO, CENTO, IADB) Files of assembled target intelligence about a specific geographic area.

target folders - (DOD, NATO, SEATO, CENTO, IADB) The folders containing target intelligence and related materials prepared for planning and executing action against a specific target.

target grid - (NATO, CENTO, IADB) Device for converting the observer's target locations and corrections with respect to the observer target line to target locations and corrections with respect to the gun target line.

target illustration print - (NATO, CENTO) A single contact print or enlarged portion of a selected area from a single print, providing the best available illustration of a specific installation or pin-point target.

target information sheet - (NATO, CENTO, IADB) Brief description of the target, completing the "descriptive target data". It should include technical and physical characteristics, details on exact location, disposition, importance, and possible obstacles for an aircraft flying at low altitudes.

target intelligence - (DOD, NATO, SEATO, CENTO, IADB) Intelligence which portrays and locates the components of a target or target complex and indicates its vulnerability and relative importance.

target list - (DOD) The listing of targets maintained and promulgated by the senior echelon of command; it contains those targets which are to be engaged by supporting arms, as distinguished from a "list of targets" which may be maintained by any echelon as confirmed, suspect, or possible targets for informational and planning purposes.

target materials - (DOD, IADB) Graphic, textual, tabular, or other presentations of target intelligence, primarily designed to support operations against designated targets by one or more weapon systems. Target materials are suitable for training, planning, executing, and evaluating such operations.

target number (artillery) - (NATO, CENTO, IADB) The reference number given to the target by the fire control unit.

target of opportunity - (DOD, IADB) 1. A target visible to a surface or air sensor or observer, which is within range of available weapons and against which fire has not been scheduled or requested. (DOD) 2. (nuclear) A nuclear target observed or detected after an operation begins that has not been previously considered, analyzed or planned for a nuclear strike. Generally fleeting in nature, it should be attacked as soon as possible within the time limitations imposed for coordination and warning of friendly troops and aircraft.

target of opportunity - (NATO, CENTO) A target which appears during combat and which can be reached by ground fire, naval fire, or aircraft fire, and against which fire has not been scheduled.

target pattern - (DOD) The flight path of aircraft during the attack phase. Also called attack pattern.

target priority - (DOD) A grouping of targets with the indicated sequence of attack.

target range - See range.

target response (nuclear) - (DOD, NATO, CENTO, IADB) The effect on men, material, and equipment of blast, heat, light, and nuclear radiation resulting from the explosion of a nuclear weapon.

target status board - (NATO, SEATO, CENTO, IADB) A wall chart maintained by the air intelligence division of the joint operations center. It includes target lists, locations, priority and status of action taken. It may also include recommended armament and fuzing for destruction.

target system - (DOD, NATO, CENTO, IADB) 1. All the targets situated in a particular geographic area and functionally related. (DOD) 2. A group of targets which are so related that their destruction will produce some particular effect desired by the attacker. See also target complex.

target system component - (DOD, IADB) A set of targets belonging to one or more groups of industries and basic utilities required to produce component parts of an end product such as periscopes, or one type of a series of interrelated commodities, such as aviation gasoline.

Tarhe - The CH-54 helicopter. Named for the Wyandot Indian chief whose name translated as crane.

tarmac - The paved hard surface for landing strips.

Tartar - (DOD, IADB) A shipborne, surface-to-air missile with solid-propellant rocket engine and nonnuclear warhead. Designated as RIM-24.

Tarzan - The infantry slang for the person volunteering to walk point. From the jungle hero of literature and comic books.

TAS - True Air Speed.

task component - (DOD, IADB) A subdivision of a fleet, task force, task group, or task unit, organized by the respective commander or by higher authority for the accomplishment of specific tasks.

task element - (DOD, SEATO, IADB) A component of a naval task unit organized by the commander of a task unit or higher authority.

task fleet - (DOD, IADB) A mobile command consisting of ships and aircraft necessary for the accomplishment of a specific major task or tasks which may be of a continuing nature.

task force - (DOD, NATO, SEATO, CENTO, IADB) 1. A temporary grouping of units under one commander, formed for the purpose of carrying out a specific operation or mission. 2. A semipermanent organization of units under one commander for the purpose of carrying out a continuing specific task. 3. A component of a fleet organized by the commander of a task fleet or higher authority for the accomplishment of a specific task or tasks. See also force(s).

Task Force 77 - Code for the Navy's Seventh Fleet.

task group - (DOD, SEATO, IADB) A component of a naval task force organized by the commander of a task force or higher authority.

task organization - (DOD, SEATO) 1. In the Navy, an organization which assigns to responsible commanders the means with which to accomplish their assigned tasks in any planned action. 2. An organization table pertaining to a specific naval directive.

task unit - (DOD, IADB) A component of a naval task group organized by the commander of a task group or higher authority.

taxi dancer - A bar girl who dances with GIs for money.

taxi girl - A hooker who hung around a base gate.

taxiway - (NATO, SEATO, CENTO, IADB) A specially prepared or designated path on a land airfield for the use of taxiing aircraft.

tbo - Time before overhaul. The projected hours of flight or time of operation of land or water craft before maintenance.

TBS - 1. The Basic School. The Marine Corps school in Quantico Virginia. 2. Talk between ships (either naval or aircraft).

TC - 1. Tactical commander. 2. Tank Commander.

TCB - Tropical chocolate bars, which did not melt in the heat.

TDY - Temporary duty.

team - A small, often temporary, group of soldiers for a set mission.

team uniform - 1. Radio code for the radio frequency assigned to a specific team. These were changed frequently. 2. Changing the radio frequency and announcing it to keep all in the company on the same frequency.

tear gas - See CS gas.

tech rep - 1. A technical representative from a provider of a weapon or other gear to train or review its use. 2. A CIA employee posing as a tech rep to introduce a new weapon of gear to be field tested and evaluated.

technical assistance - (DOD) The providing of advice, assistance, and training pertaining to the installation, operation, and maintenance of equipment.

technical characteristics - (DOD, IADB) Those characteristics of equipment which pertain primarily to the engineering principles involved in producing equipment possessing desired military characteristics, e.g., for electronic equipment, technical characteristics include such items as circuitry, and types and arrangement of components.

technical escort - (DOD) Individuals technically qualified and properly equipped to accompany designated material requiring a high degree of safety and/or security during shipment.

technical evaluation - (DOD, IADB) The study and investigations by a developing agency to determine the technical suitability of material, equipment, or a system, for use in the military Services. See also operational evaluation.

technical information - (DOD, IADB) Information, including scientific information, which relates to research, development, engineering, test, evaluation, production, operation, use, and maintenance of munitions and other military supplies and equipment.

technical intelligence - (DOD, IADB) Not to be used. See scientific and technical intelligence.

technical intelligence - (NATO, SEATO, CENTO) Intelligence concerning foreign technological developments, performance and operational capabilities of foreign materiel, which now or may eventually have a practical application for military purposes. It is the end product resulting from the processing and collation of technical information.

technical specifications - (NATO, CENTO, IADB) A detailed description of technical requirements stated in terms suitable to form the basis for the actual design development and production processes of an item having the qualities specified in the operational characteristics. See also NATO basic military requirement; operational characteristics.

technical supply operations - (DOD, IADB) Operations performed by supply units or technical supply elements of supply and maintenance units in acquiring, accounting for, storing, and issuing Class II and IV items needed by supported units and maintenance activities.

technical survey - (DOD) A complete electronic and physical inspection to ascertain that offices, conference rooms, war rooms, and other similar locations where classified information is discussed are free of monitoring systems. See also sweep.

tee-tee - Very small. Sometimes spelled ti-ti.

telecommunication - (DOD, NATO, SEATO, CENTO, IADB) Any transmission, emission, or reception of signs, signals, writing, images, and sounds or information of any nature by wire, radio, visual, or other electromagnetic systems. (Note: SEATO definition uses the word "intelligence" instead of "information.")

teleconference - (DOD, NATO, SEATO, CENTO, IADB) A conference between persons remote from one another but linked by a telecommunications system.

teleran system - (DOD, IADB) A navigational system which: a. employs ground-based search radar equipment along an airway to locate aircraft flying near that airway; b. transmits, by television means, information pertaining to these aircraft and other information to the pilots of properly equipped aircraft; and c. provides information to the pilots appropriate for use in the landing approach.

television imagery - (DOD) Imagery acquired by a television camera and recorded or transmitted electronically.

temperature gradient - (DOD) At sea, a temperature gradient is the change of temperature with depth; a positive gradient is a temperature increase with an increase in depth, and a negative gradient is a temperature decrease with an increase in depth.

temporary cemetery - (DOD, NATO, SEATO, CENTO, IADB) A cemetery for the purpose of: a. the initial burial of the remains if the circumstances permit, or b. the reburial of remains exhumed from an emergency burial.

ten - Expressed in radio code or slang as dime.

ten forty-nine - Form 1049, the Army request for transfer form.

ten gallon can of rotor wash - The imaginary supply that rookies were sent to supply to request as a prank. See rotor wash for the proper use.

ten thousand dollar paper - The GI life insurance paid $10,000 on death.

Ten-Pin Theory - The political theory of the French from 1946 to 1954 that the loss of their colony in Vietnam would result in the immediate loss of other colonies, like a bowling ball hitting pins.

tent peg - Stupid or worthless soldier.

TER - Triple Ejector Rack. The bomb rack often attached to the underside of the wing of an aircraft (See MER).

terminal clearance capacity - (DOD) The amount of cargo or personnel that can be moved through and out of a terminal on a daily basis.

terminal control area - (DOD, NATO, CENTO, IADB) A control area or a portion thereof normally situated at the confluence of air traffic service routes in the vicinity of one or more major airfields. See also airway; controlled airspace; control area; control zone (air).

terminal destination (merchant shipping) - (NATO, CENTO, IADB) The last port/water terminal or anchorage of an independent or convoy to which routing instructions have been issued. It is not necessarily the final destination. See also final destination; immediate destination; intermediate destination; original destination.

terminal guidance - (DOD, IADB) 1. The guidance applied to a guided missile between mid-course guidance and arrival in the vicinity of the target. 2. Electronic, mechanical, visual, or other assistance given an aircraft pilot to facilitate arrival at, operation within or over, landing upon, or departure from an air landing or airdrop facility. See also guidance; homing phase; terminal phase.

terminal operations - (DOD) The reception, processing, and staging of passengers, the receipt, transit storage and marshalling of cargo, the loading and unloading of ships or aircraft, and the manifesting and forwarding of cargo and passengers to destination.

terminal phase - (DOD, IADB) The period of flight of a missile between the end of midcourse guidance and impact. See also terminal guidance.

terminal port - (NATO, SEATO, CENTO, IADB) The final port of an independent or convoy to which routing instructions have been issued. It is not necessarily the destination.

terminal velocity - (DOD, NATO, CENTO, IADB) 1. Hypothetical maximum speed a body could attain along a specified flight path under given conditions of weight and thrust if diving through an unlimited distance in air of specified uniform density. 2. Remaining speed of a projectile at the point in its downward path where it is level with the muzzle of the weapon.

terminate with extreme prejudice - The CIA term for a person targeted for assassination.

Terne - (DOD, IADB) A Norwegian-designed, antisubmarine, ahead-thrown rocket comparable to Weapon Alpha. It is designed for installation in ships of 500 to 1,000 tons.

terrain exercise - (DOD, IADB) An exercise in which a stated military situation is solved on the ground, the troops being imaginary and the solution usually being in writing.

terrain intelligence - (DOD, SEATO, IADB) Processed information on the military significance of natural and man-made characteristics of an area.

terrain study - (DOD, IADB) An analysis and interpretation of natural and man-made features of an area, their effects on military operations, and the effect of weather

VIETNAM: THE WAR ZONE DICTIONARY IN THEIR OWN WORDS

and climate on these features.

terrestrial environment - (DOD) The earth's land area, including its manmade and natural surface and sub-surface features, and its interfaces and interactions with the atmosphere and the oceans.

terrestrial reference guidance - (DOD, IADB) The technique of providing intelligence to a missile from certain characteristics of the surface over which the missile is flown, thereby achieving flight along a predetermined path. See also guidance.

Terrier - (DOD, IADB) A surface-to-air missile with solid-fuel rocket motor. It is equipped with radar beam rider or homing guidance and nuclear or nonnuclear warhead. Designated as RIM-2.

Terrier land weapon system - (DOD, IADB) A surface-to-air missile system, utilizing the Terrier RIM-2B and Terrier RIM-2C missile with ground-launching and guidance equipment, developed specifically for amphibious operations. (DOD) This equipment is a lighter and land-mobile version of the Navy system.

TESTICLES - The LRRP team motto standing for the qualities they had as a team: Teamwork, Enthusiasm, Stamina, Tenacity, Initiative, Courage, Loyalty, Excellence and Sense of Humor.

tests - See service test; troop test.

Tet - 1. The lunar new year holiday in Vietnam. 2. The NVA attack in 1968 called the Tet Offensive.

Tetracycline - A commonly used antibiotic particularly for treating VD.

Texaco - Aviation slang for a flying tanker that did mid-air refueling. From the brand of gasoline.

TF - Task Force.

TFR - Terrain Following Radar. Aviation radar in some planes to use in low level flying to spot and warn of obstacles on the ground ahead.

tfrd - Transferred.

TFX - See F-111, an aircraft.

TH-55A - The Army training helicopter at Fort Rucker, Alabama.

thank you - Cam on.

the gun - The M-60 machine gun.

the telegram - Notification to next of kin that their relative was wounded. See the visit.

the visit - Notification to next of kin that their relative was killed. See the telegram.

theater - (DOD) The geographical area outside continental United States for which a commander of a unified or specified command has been assigned military responsibility.

theater of operations - See area of operations.

theater of war - See area of war.

There it is! - An expression of a truth finally coming to light, as in I told you so.

thermal energy - The energy emitted from the fireball as thermal radiation. The total amount of thermal energy received per unit area at a specified distance from a nuclear explosion is generally expressed in terms of calories per square centimeter.

thermal exposure - (DOD, NATO, CENTO, IADB) The total normal component of thermal radiation striking a given surface throughout the course of a detonation; expressed in the units: calories per square centimeter.

thermal imagery (infrared) - (NATO, CENTO) Imagery produced by measuring and recording electronically the thermal radiation of objects.

thermal pulse - (DOD, IADB) The radiant power versus time pulse from a nuclear weapon detonation.

thermal radiation - (DOD, NATO, CENTO, IADB) 1. The heat and light produced by a nuclear explosion. (DOD) 2. Electromagnetic radiations emitted from a heat or light source as a consequence of its temperature; it consists essentially of ultraviolet, visible, and infrared radiations.

thermal X-rays - (DOD, NATO, CENTO) The electromagnetic radiation, mainly in the soft (low-energy) X-ray region, emitted by the extremely hot weapon debris by virtue of its extremely high temperature.

Thermit - A brand of thermite. See thermite.

thermite - A mix of powered aluminum and metal oxide which produces a high heat, used in incendiary bombs and in welding.

thermite grenade - An incendiary grenade that could melt metal or start fires.

thermonuclear - (DOD, NATO, CENTO) An adjective referring to the process (or processes) in which very high temperatures are used to bring about the fusion of light nuclei, with the accompanying liberation of energy.

thermonuclear weapon - (DOD, NATO, CENTO, IADB) A weapon in which very high temperatures are used to bring about the fusion of light nuclei such as those of hydrogen isotopes (e.g., deuterium and tritium) with the accompanying release of energy. The high temperatures required are obtained by means of fission.

Thing - The Thing was the Marine slang for the Ontos antitank vehicle.

thingamabob - The name for any piece of gear or component in lieu of knowing or using the technical term (such as gizmo hoo-ha, or doodad).

things on springs - An inspection of gear in a barracks in which gear is on a bunk.

third area conflict - (DOD) Not to be used. See cold war; general war; guerrilla warfare; limited war.

third hat - The assistant drill instructor in charge of discipline.

third herd - Slang for any unit with "third" in its name.

thirty caliber, .30 cal - Ammunition or a gun using ammunition rated as .30 caliber.

thirty eight, thirty-eight S&W, .38 S&W - A .38 cal Smith & Wesson pistol.

thirty Mike Mike, 30 Mike Mike - A 30-mm cannon. See XM-140

Thirty-Three - A Vietnamese beer, 33.

thirty-year man - A career Army person, a lifer.

Thor - (DOD) A liquid-propellant, one-stage, rocket-powered intermediate range ballistic missile equipped with nuclear warhead. It is also equipped with an all inertial guidance system.

thousand meter stare - A glazed expression, looking past the horizon, checking-out, a symptom of fatigue or post traumatic stress.

thousand pounders - Big bombs with explosive power of a thousand pounds of TNT. Slang for swimming pool makers.

thousand yard stare - See thousand meter stare.

three - 1. Expressed in radio code and slang as trey. 2. As a clock code position, the target is to the right of the observer, see clock code position. 3. In Army call signs, the operations officer.

three down and locked - Aviation term for having landing gear in position for landing. The reply to the tower of pre-landing status.

three finger fuck off - Pointless activity.

three hairs - A Vietnamese female with little pubic hair.

three heart rule - A general policy that after three wounds (Purple Hearts) you could rotate out of combat at least and usually go stateside.

three heart ticket - The Army policy of removing a soldier from combat on his request after being wounded in three separate events.

Three hearts and you're out. - The expression summarizing the Army policy of removing a soldier from combat on his request after being wounded in three separate events.

three nine line - Aviation combat term for: 1. The imaginary line between your three clock position (right side) and nine clock position (left side). 2. The goal of keeping your enemy aircraft ahead of this line, e.g. in front of you.

three point - Parachutists bad landing on ass, boots and head.

three point C and B - Parachutists really bad landing as a crash and burn in addition to landing on ass, boots and head.

three quarter, ¾ ton, - A three quarter ton truck.

three up and down - A master sergeant for the insignia with three stripes on top and three on the bottom. Also three up and three down.

three up and two down - A sergeant first class from the insignia.

three whisker mine - Slang for the M-16 mine that had three antenna like projections.

three-quarter - A three quarter ton truck.

three-star general - Lieutenant General.

Three, The Three - The officer assigned to operations.

throttle back - Aviation slang for slow down, take it easy.

throttle jockey - A jet pilot, usually of fighter jets.

throwing hands - A fistfight.

Thud - See F-105, an aircraft.

thumper - 1. The M-5 grenade. 2. M-74 grenade launcher.

Thunderchief - (DOD, IADB) A supersonic, single-engine, turbojet-powered tactical fighter capable of delivering nuclear weapons as well as non-nuclear bombs and rockets. It is also capable of close support for ground forces. Its range can be extended by in-flight refueling. It is equipped with the Sidewinder missile. The aircraft is capable of all-weather attack. Designated as F-I05.

ti ti - See tee tee.

TIC - Target Information Center. The data reviewing operation that selected targets from intelligence reports.

ticket - 1. The tag completed by medics detailing a soldier's wounds and medical status. See tag. 2. The duty assignment that is required for promotion. See ticket punching.

ticket home - An injury sufficient to be sent stateside.

ticket punching - Slang decisions made to further a career rather than for the good of the operation. Based on the criteria for promotion of serving in combat as well as other training and operational experience, combat was one punch on the list on the ticket.

tie down - See lashing.

tie down point - (NATO, CENTO) An attachment point provided on or within a vehicle for securing cargo.

tie-down diagram - (DOD, NATO, CENTO) A drawing indicating the prescribed method of securing a particular item of cargo within a specific type of vehicle.

tie-down point pattern - (DOD, NATO, CENTO) The pattern of tie down points within a vehicle.

tied on - (DOD) The aircraft indicated is in formation with me.

Tiger - (DOD, IADB) A single-engine, single-seat, supersonic jet fighter designed for operating from aircraft carriers for the interception and destruction of enemy aircraft, and the support of troops ashore. Armament consists of Sidewinders, cannons, and rocket packs. Designated as F-11.

tiger - Slang for patrol and ambush elements.

Tiger beer - Slang for Biere La Rue brewed in Saigon that had a tiger on the label.

tiger cage - The small cage in which American prisoners of war were held. It was so small that it did not allow one to sit or lie down, also called cramper.

tiger country - Australian slang for enemy territory.

tiger exchange - One of the three telephone systems in South Vietnam. Also ARVIN and PTT.

tiger ladies - Vietnamese women working in construction for U.S. contractors.

Tiger Paw beer - A Vietnamese beer nicknamed tiger piss.

tiger piss - 1. Local beer. 2. Tiger Paw beer.

tiger stripes - See tiger suit.

tiger suit - A tiger striped pattern of jungle camouflage.

Tiger Track - An experimental vehicle with articulated tracks. The XM-571. Also Tiger Tracks.

tiger trap - A large hole dug in a road and disguised into which tanks and other vehicles would fall.

tight - Close to someone as in a good friend.

Tilly - Aviation slang nickname for the crane on the flight deck of a carrier that removes disabled planes.

tilt - (NATO, CENTO) In air photography, the camera rotation about the longitudinal axis of the aircraft. Also known as roll. See also tilt angle.

tilt angle - (NATO, CENTO) The angle between the axis of an air camera and the vertical relative to the longitudinal axis of the aircraft. The angle at the perspective center between the photograph perpendicular and the plumb line. See also angle of depression.

time and material contract - (DOD, IADB) A contract providing for the procurement of supplies or services on the basis of: a. direct labor hours at specified fixed hourly rates (which rates include direct and indirect labor, overhead, and profit); and b. material at cost.

time fuze - (DOD, NATO, SEATO, CENTO, IADB) A fuze which contains a graduated time element to regulate the time interval after which the fuze will function. See also fuze.

time in the barrel - 1. A shitty job. 2. Duty at Con Thien.

time of attack - (DOD, IADB) The hour at which the attack is to be launched. If a line of departure is prescribed, it is the hour at which the line is to be crossed by the leading elements of the attack.

time of delivery - (DOD, IADB) The time at which the addressee or responsible relay agency receipts for a message.

time of flight - (DOD) The time in seconds from the instant a weapon is fired, launched, or released from the delivery vehicle or weapons system to the instant it strikes or detonates.

time of origin - (DOD, IADB) The time at which a message is released for transmission.

time of receipt - (DOD, IADB) The time at which a receiving station completes reception of a message.

time on target - (DOD, NATO, CENTO, IADB) 1. The method of firing on a target in which various artillery units and naval gunfire support ships so time their fire as to assure all projectiles reaching the target simultaneously. 2. Time at which aircraft are scheduled to attack/photograph the target. (DOD) 3. The actual time at which aircraft attack/photograph the target. 4. The time at which a nuclear detonation is planned at a specified desired ground zero.

time on target (air) - See time on target, Parts 2 and 3.

time on target (artillery) - See time on target, Part 1.

time over target (nuclear) - See time on target, Part 4.

time over target conflict - (DOD) A situation wherein two or more delivery vehicles are scheduled such that their proximity violates the established separation criteria for yield, time, distance or all three.

time pencil - A time delayed detonator shaped like a fat pencil that allowed the duration of the delay to be set.

time to go - (DOD) During an air intercept, the time to fly to the offset point from any given interceptor position; after passing the offset point, the time to fly to the intercept point.

TIN - Transaction Identification Number.

Tin City - Guam.

tin foil - Anti-radar chaff.

tin foil airstrip - A landing strip made of aluminum matting.

tin pot - Helmet.

Tinactin - A cream for athlete's foot.

Tinkertoy - See A-4, an aircraft, nicknamed from the trademarked name of the children's toy.

tip - (NATO, CENTO) In air photography, the camera rotation about the transverse axis of the aircraft. Also known as pitch.

tip the scale - The overall tactic of gaining the advantage over the enemy in any confrontation so that the enemy is placed on the defensive.

tips - (DOD) External fuel tanks.

TIRS - Terrorist Incident Reporting System.

Titan - (DOD, IADB) A liquid-propellant, two-stage, rocket-powered intercontinental ballistic missile equipped with a nuclear warhead. Designated as HGM-25, it is guided by radio-inertial guidance and the LGM-25C, an improved version of the HGM-25, is guided by all-inertial guidance and equipped with a higher-yield warhead. The system is for deployment in a hardened and dispersed configuration.

title block - See information box.

titling strip - (NATO, CENTO) The information added to negatives and/or positives, in accordance with regulations to identify and provide reference information.

tits machine - Aviation slang for a classic perfect airplane, no current crafts need apply, this is old school.

titty - The female breast.

titty club - Bars providing nude entertainment.

titty deep - See foxhole.

TK-2 GFS kit - The gun system on a helicopter to fire at the enemy on the ground.

TM and B School - A special infantry school on tunnels, mines and booby traps.

TM-41 Anti-tank mine - A Soviet made anti-tank mine.

TNT - 1. The explosive, specifically Trinitrotoluene. 2. See T&T.

TNT equivalent - (DOD, NATO, CENTO, IADB) A measure of the energy release from the detonation of a nuclear weapon, or from the explosion of a given quantity of fissionable or fusionable material, in terms of the amount of trinitrotoluene which would release the same amount of energy when exploded.

TO - Table of Organization. The organizational chart showing relationships of elements and the personnel of each by number and rank.

toadsticker - A bayonet.

TOC - Tactical Operations Center.

toe popper - The M-14 small land mine.

TOE, TO&E - Table of Organization and Equipment.

TOG Rule - The saying to justify any personal injury or property damage to the Vietnamese as being less than human, from the phrase, They're only Gooks.

Toi com biet. - I do not understand.

Toi mat - "Top secret" stamped on Vietnamese documents.

toke - To smoke dope.

token nigger - The offensive term for the one black soldier in a unit.

tolerance dose - (DOD, IADB) The amount of radiation which may be received by an individual within a specified period with negligible results.

Tom - A black soldier making a career of the military. From Uncle Tom, a subservient black person.

Tomcat - See F-14.

tone - (NATO, CENTO) Each distinguishable shade variation from black to white on photographs.

tool - Penis.

tooth to tail ratio - The ratio of soldiers in combat (tooth) to soldiers in rear echelon support (tail), expressed as the number of personnel needed to support one combat soldier. That ranged from: 1:5 to 1:8 during different times.

Top - A first sergeant.

Top Gun - See TOPGUN.

TOPGUN - The U.S. Navy Fighter Weapons School at the Naval Air Station Miramar, California, near San Diego, that trained fighter pilots. Also Topgun.

Top Kick - A first sergeant.

top off - 1. Fill a tank completely with gas. 2. Aviation slang for mid-air refueling.

top secret - See defense classification.

topical chocolate bars - Chocolate bars that did not melt in the tropical heat.

topographic base - See chart base.

topographic map - (DOD, IADB) A map which presents the vertical position of features in measurable form as well as their horizontal positions. See also map.

topside - Navy and Marine slang for above deck, upstairs.

torch - 1. To burn a village. 2. British and Commonwealth NATO troop slang for a large flashlight.

torching - 1. Pilot slang for the flames of an external fire when a fuel tank or line is hit or ruptures. 2. Infantry slang for burning a village.

torpedo boat - A high speed surface boat that could launch torpedoes as well as being armed with machine guns.

torpedo defense net - (DOD, NATO, CENTO, IADB) A net employed to close an inner harbor to torpedoes fired from seaward or to protect an individual ship at anchor or underway.

toss bombing - (DOD, IADB) A method of bombing where an aircraft flies on a line towards the target, pulls up in a vertical plane, releasing the bomb at an angle that will compensate for the effect of gravity drop on the bomb. Similar to loft bombing; unrestricted as to altitude. See also loft bombing; over-the-shoulder bombing.

TOT - Time on target.

total materiel assets - (DOD) The total quantity of an item available in the military system world wide and all funded procurement of the item with adjustments to provide for transfers out of or into the inventory through the appropriation and procurement lead-time periods. It includes peacetime force material assets and mobilization reserve stock. See also mobilization reserves.

total materiel objective - (DOD) The sum of the peacetime force materiel requirement and the mobilization reserve materiel objective. See also mobilization reserves.

total materiel procurement objective - (DOD) The quantity of an item required to be procured in peacetime in order to balance total materiel assets with the total materiel objective when the objective exceeds assets. It is also the sum of the peacetime force materiel procurement objective and the mobilization reserve materiel procurement objective. See also mobilization reserves.

total materiel requirement - (DOD) The sum of the peacetime force materiel requirement and the mobilization reserve materiel requirement. See also mobilization reserves.

total nuclear war - (DOD) Not to be used. See general war.

total war - (DOD) Not to be used. See general war.

totem pole - Slang for the chain of command. Getting promoted is climbing the totem pole.

tourniquet - 1. The medical technique of applying a tight band or belt to the arm or leg to stop massive bleeding from that limb. 2. The NVA/VC technique of applying tourniquets to each arm and leg before entering into a suicide mission to extend the period of time they could fire.

TOW - Tube-launched, Optically-tracked, Wire-guided Missile. A missile that trails a wire as an antenna allowing it to be guided in its flight by an operator on the ground.

tower rat - A soldier serving guard duty in a tower.

tower week - The middle week of paratrooper school, in which parachute jumps from a tower are a key element of training.

toxic attack - (SEATO) An attack directed at man, animals, or crops, using injurious agents of radiological, biological, or chemical origin.

toxic chemical, biological, or radiological attack - (DOD, NATO, CENTO, IADB) An attack directed at man, animals, or crops, using injurious agents of radiological, biological, or chemical origin.

TP - Troops.

TPQ - Ground controlled radar bombing that directs a plane to a release point in the air.

TPQ flights - Bombing runs in which the release of bombs is directed by ground radar.

TPQ-10 - The portable radar system.

tr - Transportation.

TR-20 - A two-way radio used by civilian authorities.

tracer - A bullet or other projectile that leaves a visible trail of smoke and/or light as it is fired. The tracer ammunition was placed to fire at about every ten or twelve rounds. U.S. tracers were red phosphorous while NVA/VC used green phosphorus.

trach - See tracheotomy.

trach tube - 1. The medical device used to hold open the tracheotomy incision. 2. The barrel of a ball point pen used in field emergencies. 3. Slang for a ball point pen.

tracheotomy - The emergency medical procedure to treat a collapsed windpipe and restore breathing. Field first aid training was given to troops to cut into the windpipe just above the collarbone and insert something to hold the incision open until medical assistance was available. Often the tube of a ball point pen was used. Similarly, if a knife was not immediately available, the P-38 can opener was used. Many carried a P-38 on their dog tag chain for just such occasions.

track - (DOD, IADB) 1. A series of related contacts displayed on a plotting board. 2. To display or record the successive positions of a moving object. 3. To lock onto a point of radiation and obtain guidance therefrom. 4. To keep a gun properly aimed, or to point continuously a target locating instrument at a moving target. 5. The actual path of an aircraft above, or a ship on, the surface of the earth. The course is the path which is planned; the track is the path which is actually taken. 6. One of the two endless belts on which a full-track or half-track vehicle runs. 7. A metal part forming a path for a moving object, e.g., the track around the inside of a vehicle for moving a mounted machine gun.

track - (NATO, CENTO) 1. To display or record the successive positions of a moving object; also to lock on to a point of radiation and obtain guidance therefrom. 2. To keep a gun properly aimed, or to point continuously a target-locating instrument at a moving target. 3. The projection on the surface of the earth of the path of an aircraft or ship the direction of which path at any point is usually expressed in degrees from North (true, magnetic or grid). 4. One of two endless belts on which a full-track or half-track vehicle runs. 5. A metal part forming a path for a moving object.

track - (SEATO) 1. To display or record the successive positions of a moving object; also to lock onto a point of radiation and obtain guidance therefrom. 2. To keep a gun properly aimed or to point continuously a target locating instrument at a moving target. 3. The actual path of an aircraft above, or a ship on, the surface of the earth. The course is the path which is planned; the track is the path actually taken. 4. One of the two endless belts on which a full-track or half-track vehicle runs. 5. A metal part forming a path for moving object, e.g., the track around the inside of a vehicle for moving a mounted machine gun. 6. An unimproved rough route suitable for sustained use by animal-drawn transport and normally not motorable.

track - 1. Slang for an armored personnel carrier (APC) or any vehicle on metal track treads.

track correlation - (DOD) Correlating track information for identification purposes using all available data.

track crossing angle - (DOD) In air intercept, the angular difference between interceptor track and target track at the time of intercept.

track telling - (DOD) The process of communicating air surveillance and tactical data in formation between command and control systems and facilities within the systems. Telling may be classified into the following areas: back tell; cross tell; forward tell; lateral tell; overlap ten; and relateral tell. See also back tell; cross tell; forward tell; lateral tell; overlap tell; relateral tell.

Tracker - (DOD, IADB) A twin-reciprocating-engine, antisubmarine aircraft capable of operating from carriers, and designed primarily for the detection, location, and destruction of submarines. Designated as S-2.

tracker team - A small team of a scout dog, handler, and other specially trained soldiers who found the enemy or recovered lost or injured soldiers through visual and tracking methods. Most combat tracker teams used five men and one dog, often a black labrador retriever.

tracking - (DOD) In air intercept, means by my evaluation, target is steering true course indicated.

tracks - 1. Slang for an armored personnel carrier. 2. The trail of marks on skin from repeated injections of heroin, often on the forearm.

tractor - 1. The motor and cab part of a tractor-trailer vehicle like a moving van. 2.

A low speed high torque vehicle for hauling or pushing like a tractor with a blade clearing land.

tractor group - (DOD, IADB) A group of landing ships in an amphibious operation which carries the amphibious vehicles of the landing force.

trade school - West Point.

Trader - The small utility transport plane for personnel, parts and mail. The C-1.

traffic circulation map - (DOD, IADB) A map showing traffic routes and the measures for traffic regulation. It indicates the roads for use of certain classes of traffic, the location of traffic control stations, and the directions in which traffic may move. Also called a circulation map. See also map.

traffic control police (road transport) - (NATO, SEATO, CENTO, IADB) Any persons ordered by a military commander and/or by national authorities to facilitate the movement of traffic and to prevent and/or report any breach of road traffic regulations.

traffic density - (DOD, NATO, CENTO, IADB) The average number of vehicles that occupy one mile or one kilometer of road space, expressed in vehicles per mile or per kilometer.

traffic flow - (DOD, NATO, CENTO) The total number of vehicles passing a given point in a given time. Traffic flow is expressed as vehicles per hour.

traffic flow security - (DOD, IADB) The protection resulting from features, inherent in some cryptoequipment, which conceal the presence of valid messages on a communications circuit, normally achieved by causing the circuit to appear busy at all times.

traffic information (radar) - (DOD) Information issued to alert an aircraft to any radar targets observed on the radar display which may be in such proximity to its position or intended route of flight to warrant its attention.

traffic pattern - (DOD) The traffic flow that is prescribed for aircraft landing at, taxiing on, and taking off from an airport. The usual components of a traffic pattern are upwind leg, crosswind leg, downwind leg, base leg, and final approach.

trafficability - (DOD, NATO, CENTO, IADB) Capability of terrain to bear traffic. It refers to the extent to which the terrain will permit continued movement of any and/or all types of traffic.

trail - (DOD) Track (or shadow). (The words "landward" or "seaward" may be used to indicate from which side of enemy unit to shadow.)

trail blazing - See cutting trail.

trail formation - Aviation term for two or more planes following the lead plane at the same altitude and directly behind the lead plane. Also called ladder formation or column formation. See lead trail formation for only two planes.

trail marker - See cairn.

trailer - (DOD) Aircraft which are following and keeping under surveillance a designated airborne contact.

train - (DOD, IADB) 1. A service force or group of service elements which provides logistic support, e.g., an organization of naval auxiliary ships or merchant ships attached to a fleet for this purpose; similarly, the vehicles and operating personnel which furnish supply, evacuation, and maintenance services to a land unit. (DOD) 2. Bombs dropped in short intervals or sequence.

train headway - (NATO, CENTO) The interval of time between two trains boarded by the same unit at the same point.

train path - (NATO, CENTO) The opportunity offered to a train to move along a given route. This opportunity is reflected in timings. The whole of the train paths on any given route constitutes a time table.

train wreck - 1. Medical slang for a patient with multiple major wounds and injuries. 2. A messed up situation. Also spelled trainwreck.

training aids - (DOD, IADB) Any item which is developed and/or procured with the primary intent that it shall assist in training and the process of learning.

trajectory - See ballistic trajectory.

transattack period - (DOD) 1. In nuclear warfare, the period from the initiation of the attack to its termination. 2. As applied to the Single Integrated Operational Plan, the period which extends from execution (or enemy attack, whichever is sooner) to termination of the Single Integrated Operational Plan. See also postattack period.

transfer area - (DOD, IADB) In an amphibious operation, the water area in which the transfer of troops and supplies from landing craft to amphibious vehicles is effected.

transfer loader - (DOD, NATO, CENTO, IADB) A wheeled or tracked vehicle with a platform capable of vertical and horizontal adjustment used in the loading and unloading of aircraft, ships, or other vehicles.

transient - (DOD, IADB) 1. Personnel, ships, or craft stopping temporarily at a post, station, or port to which they are not assigned or attached, and having destination elsewhere. (NATO, SEATO, CENTO) 2. An individual awaiting orders, transport, etc., at a post or station to which he is not attached or assigned.

transient area - See staging area.

transient forces - (DOD, IADB) Forces which pass or stage through, or base temporarily within, the area of responsibility of another command but are not under its operational control.

transition altitude - (DOD, NATO, CENTO, IADB) The altitude at or below which the vertical position of an aircraft is controlled by reference to true altitude.

transition level - (DOD, NATO) The lowest flight level available for use above the transition altitude. See also altitude; transition altitude.

transmission factor (nuclear) - (DOD, NESN, CENTO, IADB) The ratio of the dose inside the shielding material to the outside (ambient) dose. Transmission factor is used to calculate the dose received through the shielding material. See also half thickness; shielding.

transmission security - See communications security.

transonic - (DOD, NATO, CENTO, IADB) Of or pertaining to the speed of a body in a surrounding fluid when the relative speed of the fluid is subsonic in some places and supersonic in others. This is encountered when passing from subsonic to supersonic speeds and vice versa. See also speed of sound.

transparency - (DOD, NATO) An image fixed on a clear base by means of a photographic, printing, chemical or other process, especially adaptable for viewing by transmitted light. See also diapositive.

transponder - (DOD, NATO, SEATO, CENTO, IADB) A transmitter-receiver capable of accepting the electronic challenge of an interrogator and automatically transmitting an appropriate reply.

transponder india - (DOD) International civil aviation organization/secondary surveillance radar.

transponder sierra - (DOD) Identification Friend or Foe mark X (selective identification feature).

transponder tango - (DOD) Identification Friend or Foe mark X basic.

transport area - (DOD, IADB) A sea area in the proximity of the landing beaches of an amphibious assault for transport unloading operations. See also helicopter transport area; inner transport area; outer transport area.

transport capacity - (NATO, CENTO, IADB) The capacity of a vehicle is defined by the number of persons, the tonnage (or volume) of equipment which can be carried by this vehicle under given conditions.

transport control center (air transport) - (DOD, NATO, SEATO, CENTO, IADB) The operations center through which the air transport force commander exercises control over the air transport system.

transport group (amphibious) - (DOD, NATO, CENTO, IADB) A subdivision of an amphibious task force, composed primarily of transports.

transport network - (DOD, NATO, CENTO, IADB) The complete system of the routes pertaining to all means of transport available in a particular area. It is made up of the network particular to each means of transport.

transport stream - (DOD, NATO, CENTO, IADB) Transport vehicles proceeding in trail formation.

transport vehicle - (DOD, IADB) A motor vehicle designed and used without modification to the chassis, to provide general transport service in the movement of personnel and cargo. See also vehicle.

transportation emergency - (DOD) A situation created by a shortage of normal transportation capability and of a magnitude sufficient to frustrate military movement requirements, and which requires extraordinary action by the President or other designated authority to insure continued movement of essential Department of Defense traffic.

transportation operating agencies - (DOD) 1. (military) - These agencies are the Military Traffic Management and Terminal Service, under the Department of the Army, the Military Sealift Command, under the Department of the Navy, and the Military Airlift Command, under the Department of the Air Force. 2. (civil) - Those Federal agencies having responsibilities under national emergency conditions for the operational direction of one or more forms of transportation; they are also referred to as Federal Modal Agencies or Federal Transport Agencies.

transportation priorities - (DOD) Indicators assigned to eligible traffic which establish its movement precedence. Appropriate priority systems apply to the movement of traffic by sea and air. In times of emergency, priorities may be applicable to continental United States movements by land, water, or air.

trap - 1. Aviation term for the arresting gear on a carrier to halt a plane's forward progress while landing or a helicopter landing in a rapid securing device. See RSD. 2. A booby trap, usually one with a pit in it.

trash - Slang for the chest ribbons worn by officers. Also fruit salad.

trash bagger - Parachutist's term for a parachute rigger.

trash hauler - 1. Aviation term for a general transport aircraft. 2. The pilot of a general transport aircraft.

traumatic amputation - Loss of a body part in a non-surgical means such as explosion.

travel bureau - Graves Registration.

traverse - (DOD, NATO, CENTO, IADB) 1. To turn a weapon to the right or left on its mount. 2. In surveying, a series of straight lines running from point to point, the distances and angles being accurately measured.

tread head - Tank operator.

treason - (DOD) Violation of the allegiance owed to one's sovereign or state; betrayal of one's country.

tree crusher - A three-wheeled tree demolition machine.

tree eater - Special Forces.

tree line - A line of trees either naturally occurring or planted as a windbreak or property line. See hedgerow

trench burial - (DOD, NATO, SEATO, CENTO, IADB) A method of burial resorted to when casualties are heavy whereby a trench is prepared and the individual remains are laid in it side by side, thus obviating the necessity of digging and filling in individual graves. See also burial.

trench foot - Immersion foot. A painful condition of feet and legs caused by prolonged exposure to water and dampness.

trend - (DOD) The straying of the fall of shot, such as might be caused by incorrect speed settings of the fire support ship.

tri-camera photography - (NATO, CENTO) Photography obtained by simultaneous exposure of three cameras systematically disposed in the air vehicle at fixed overlapping angles relative to each other in order to cover a wide field. See also fan camera photography.

triage - Medical term for the initial classification and sorting of field wounded and incoming hospital patients for their priority for treatment. Three classifications were used (although the terms seemed to vary slightly): a. walking wounded (Those whose injuries were attended to as soon as emergencies were addressed, also called routine), b. immediate (Those needing emergency intervention to life threatening injuries, also called priority), and c. expecteds (Those whose injuries were beyond medical correction and who were removed to die discretely, also called emergency).

Triangle - The Iron Triangle near Saigon.

trick - A specific work shift.

trick chief - The NCO in charge of a shift.

trig list - (DOD) A list published by certain Army units which includes essential information of accurately located survey points.

trigger time - Time in combat.

trim size - (NATO) The size of a map or chart sheet when the excess paper outside the margin has been trimmed off after printing.

trimetrogon photography - (DOD) Not to be used. See fan camera photography.

trip flare - A flare set to ignite by a trip wire, often used as an early warning around a camp's perimeter.

trip wire - 1. A hidden or nylon line used as a detonator when moved. 2. A booby trap. 3. A soldier with a knack for finding trouble.

triple A - Antiaircraft artillery.

triple canopy - The three layers of dense jungle foliage. See double canopy.

Triple Nickel - The 555th Tactical Squadron.

triple point - (DOD) The intersection of the incident, reflected and fused (or Mach) shock fronts accompanying an air burst. The height of the triple point above the surface, i.e., the height of the Mach stem, increases with increasing distance from a given explosion.

tripping - One under the influence of a hallucinogen, such as LSD.

trippy - Slang for: 1. Being under the influence of a hallucinogen. 2. Things just being weird or out of control.

Trojan - 1. The T-28 aircraft. 2. The trademarked condom.

troll - Aviation term for flying a random pattern looking for the enemy, as in trolling for fish.

troop basis - (DOD, IADB) An approved list of those military units and individuals (including civilians) required for the performance of a particular mission by numbers, organization and equipment, and, in the case of larger commands, by deployment.

troop safety (nuclear) - (DOD) An element which defines a distance from the proposed burst location beyond which personnel meeting the criteria described under degree of risk will be safe to the degree prescribed.

troop space cargo - (DOD, IADB) Cargo such as sea or barracks bags, bedding rolls or hammocks, locker trunks, and office equipment, which is normally stowed in an accessible place. This cargo will also include normal hand-carried combat equipment and weapons to be carried ashore by the assault troops. See also cargo.

troop test - (DOD, IADB) A test conducted in the field for the purpose of evaluating operational or organizational concepts, doctrine, tactics, and techniques, or to gain further information on materiel. See also tests.

trooper - An infantryman.

troops - (DOD, IADB) A collective term for uniformed military personnel (usually not applicable to naval personnel afloat). See also airborne troops; combat service support elements; combat support troops; combat troops; service troops; tactical troops.

troops in combat (enemy contact) - See engaged. Also Tango India Charlie.

Tropic Lightening - The U.S. 25th Infantry Division from the lightening on the insignia.

tropical immersion foot - See immersion foot.

tropical storm - (DOD, IADB) A tropical cyclone in which the surface wind speed is at least 34, but not more than 63 knots.

tropopause - (DOD, NATO, CENTO) The transition zone between the stratosphere and the troposphere. The tropopause normally occurs at an altitude of about 25,000 to 45,000 feet in polar and temperate zones, and at 55,000 feet in the tropics. See also atmosphere.

troposphere - (DOD, NATO, CENTO) The lower layers of atmosphere, in which the change of temperature with height is relatively large. It is the region where clouds form, convection is active, and mixing is continuous and more or less complete. See also atmosphere.

tropospheric scatter - (DOD) The propagation of radio waves by scattering as a result of irregularities or discontinuities in the physical properties of the troposphere.

tropospheric scatter - (NATO, CENTO) An over-the-horizon ground-to-ground radio system which utilizes the reflective properties of the troposphere to provide a multi-channel communications system.

trops - Tropical khaki uniform.

truck war - Infantry and aviation term for missions specifically designed to disrupt trucking of troops or supplies.

true airspeed - The calibrated speed corrected for density and altitude factors. See airspeed

true altitude - (DOD, NESN, CENTO, IADB) The height of an aircraft as measured from mean sea level.

true convergence - (DOD, NATO) The angle at which one meridian is inclined to another on the surface of the earth. See also convergence.

true horizon - (NATO, CENTO) The boundary of a horizontal plane passing through a point of vision, or in photogrammetry, the perspective center of a lens system.

true north - (DOD, NATO) The direction from an observer's position to the geographic North pole. The North direction of any geographic meridian.

trunk air route - (NATO, SEATO, CENTO, IADB) An established air route along which strategic moves of military forces can take place.

TS - Top Secret.

TSgt - Technical Sergeant (Air Force).

TSN - The Ton Son Nhut Air Base.

TT-33 - A pistol used by the North Vietnamese.

tube artillery - An artillery firing device such as a gun barrel or tube, not rocket driven.

tube sock - A sock without a set heel, like a tube. Often used to contain cans of extra rations or other items to carry in the field.

tube steak - 1. A hot dog. 2. Penis.

tuck under - Aviation term for the flight dynamic of some high speed jets to nose down when approaching the speed of sound.

tunnel - A unique feature of the war in Vietnam was the extensive use of tunnels by the Viet Cong. Some were in the field as secret military installations or small hideouts while others were large enough to house factories and hospitals.

tunnel flusher - A high powered air blower used to push smoke or gas into enemy tunnels.

tunnel pistol - The .44 cal Magnum pistol.

tunnel rats - U.S. soldiers specializing in locating, searching, and clearing tunnels used by the Viet Cong.

Tunnels Mines and Booby Traps School - A special training class in Vietnam

TUOC - Tactical Unit Operations Center.

turbojet - (DOD, IADB) A jet engine whose air is supplied by a turbine-driven compressor, the turbine being activated by exhaust gases.

turd SID - The Seismic Intrusion Device shaped like dog droppings. The experimental design was changed to look like wood chips once they figured out there were no dogs in the areas of intended use.

turds - See oak leaf cluster.

turkey jerk - 1. A massage parlor. 2. A hand job in a massage parlor.

turn radius - Aviation term for the radius of a circle made by a specific aircraft when making a full circle turn, including air speed, altitude and other data which would alter the distance.

turn to - Marine slang for start working, begin.

turn-in point - (DOD, NATO, CENTO, IADB) The point at which an aircraft starts to turn from the approach direction to the line of attack. See also air control team; contact point; pull-up point.

turnaround - (DOD, NATO, SEATO, CENTO, IADB) The length of time between arriving at a point and departing from that point. It is used in this sense for the turnaround of shipping in ports, and for aircraft refueling and rearming. See also turnaround cycle.

turnaround cycle - (DOD, NATO, SEATO, CENTO, IADB) Used in conjunction with vehicles, ships, and aircraft and comprises the following: loading time at home; time to and from destination; unloading and loading time at destination; unloading time at home; planned maintenance time and, where applicable, time awaiting facilities. See also turnaround.

turnback - A Student in Officer's candidate School who needs to repeat classes or drop out.

turning point (land mine warfare) - (DOD, NATO) A point of the centerline of a mine strip or row where strips or rows change direction.

turret - The top of a tank holding the tank commander and often the guns for the tank.

turtles - Replacements, based on their slow arrival.

TWA - Teeney-Weenie-Airlines. Slang for helicopter transportation, a play on the large airline TWA, Trans World Airlines.

twat - Vagina.

tweak - Fine tune something.

Tweetybirds - The A-37 airplane. Dragonfly.

Twelfth General Order - Don't get caught. General Orders were standing orders, this is a sarcastic play on that basic rule set.

twelve o'clock - The position directly ahead of the reporter. Often reported as my twelve o'clock or my twelve. See clock code positions.

Twenty Mike-Mike - The 20-mm gatling gun on fighter airplanes.

Twenty Third Psalm, 23rd Psalm - The variant of the Lord's Prayer often written on helmet covers as one of the following: Yea, though I walk through the Valley of the Shadow of Death, I shall fear no evil for I am the baddest (or meanest) mother fucker (or son of a bitch) in the Valley.

twenty two hundred - Ten p.m., the time of curfew in safe towns.

twenty-five, 25-mm AA - Soviet made antiaircraft gun.

twink - 1. A second lieutenant. 2. A new recruit.

twinkle - The starlight scope for night vision, from the nursery rhyme that starts Twinkle twinkle little star.

TWIX - Military telegram.

two - 1. The radio call sign of the unit's Intelligence Officer. 2. Expressed in radio code or slang as duce.

two by two, 2X2 - The gauze pad in medical kits that is fastened with tape over a wound.

two digit fidget - Getting jumpy as the end of tour approaches. Avoiding any hazardous activity in the last 90 days in Vietnam.

two digit midget - A short timer.

two heart ticket - The informal rule that two combat wounds let you transfer out of combat. See Purple Heart.

two hots and a Charlie - A ration of two hot meals and one C-ration.

Two Shades of Soul - Slang for the 173d Airborne Brigade, in part because it was a harmonious racially integrated group.

two ship element - See two ship formation.

two ship formation - Aviation term for a two-plane formation with the wingman's plane to the side and slightly behind the lead plane. Called section in the Air Force.

two shop, the two shop - The intelligence section.

two-man rule - (DOD) A system designed to prohibit access by an individual to nuclear weapons and certain designated components by requiring the presence at all times of at least two authorized persons each capable of detecting incorrect or unauthorized procedures with respect to the task to be performed. Also referred to as the two-man concept or two-man policy.

two-oh-one file, **201 file** - The designation of the personnel file in the Army. See jacket.

two-seventy-five rocket, 2.75-inch rocket - See XM-159C rocket.

two-seventy-fives, 2.75-inch flechettes - See Nails

two-star general - Major General.

two-twelve - Section 212 of the Army Regulations dealing with cause for discharge for psychiatric reasons, including drug addiction.

two-up - (NATO, CENTO, IADB) A formation with two elements disposed abreast; the remaining element(s) in rear.

Two, The Two - The officer assigned to intelligence.

Type 24 MMG - A Soviet made Maxim machine gun.

Type 31 - A Soviet made light mortar.

Type 50 SMG - A Soviet made submachine gun.

Type 51 pistol - A Soviet made pistol.

Type 53 - A Soviet made mortar.

Type 54 - A Soviet made heavy machine gun.

Type 56 SKS - A Soviet made rifle. See lifer's dream.

Type 59 grenade - A grenade.

Type 59 pistol - A pistol.

Type 62 - A Soviet made light tank.

Type 63 - A rocket.

Type 68 - A Chinese copy of the Soviet made SKS rifle used by the North Vietnamese.

Type 69 - A rocket propelled grenade.

type command - (DOD, IADB) An administrative subdivision of a fleet or force into ships or units of the same type, as differentiated from a tactical subdivision. Any type command may have a flagship, tender, and aircraft assigned to it.

type load - See standard load.

types of burst - See airburst; fallout safe height of burst; height of burst; high air-burst; high altitude burst; low airburst; nuclear airburst; nuclear surface burst; nuclear underground burst; nuclear under-water burst; optimum height of burst; safe burst height.

Typhon - (DOD, IADB) A surface-to-air missile of advanced design for installation on carriers, cruisers, frigates, and destroyers, and for use against high performance aircraft and short-range tactical missiles. It will be equipped with either a nuclear or non-nuclear warhead. Designated as RIM-50/ RIM-55.

U – UNIFORM

U - Designated in the phonetic military alphabet as "Uniform". 2. The aviation designation of utility aircraft.

U-10 - The single engine STOL prop aircraft.

U-17 - See Skywagon.

U-2 - The Air Force's high altitude reconnaissance and surveillance airplane.

U-21 - See Ute.

U-6 - See Beaver.

U-8 - See Seminole.

U-shaped ambush - An ambush in which two leading prongs are used.

U.S. - 1. Abbreviation for United States. 2. Leading alpha designation on serial number of a draftee.

UA - Unauthorized absence.

UAM - Underwater to air missile.

UCMJ - Uniform Code of Military Justice. 1. Military law. 2. The book containing the military law.

UD - Undesirable Discharge.

UDT - Underwater demolition teams.

UFC-10 - Aviation designation of the emergency radio beeper

UGM-27 - See Polaris.

UGS - Unattended ground sensor. The seismic, audio and magnetic sensors which were monitored to indicate troop movement.

UH-1A - The technical designation for the helicopter known as the Huey, Slick, Iroquois, and Huey Gunship. This was the multipurpose helicopter made by Bell to transport troops, run medevacs, and when equipped with miniguns and rocket pods to be a gunship.

UH-1B - An upgrade of the UH-1A including greater range and firepower.

UH-1C - An upgrade of the UH-1B. Also called Huey or Cobra gunship.

UH-1D - An upgrade of the UH-1B with greater capacity and firepower.

UH-1E - The UH-1B as configured for use by the Marines and usually for observation.

UH-1F - An upgrade of the UH-1A called the Green Hornet.

UH-1H - An upgrade of the UH-1D.

UH-1L - The UH-1B as configured for use by the Navy.

UH-1N - The twin engine version of the UH-1D.

UH-2 - See Seasprite.

UH-34D - Sea Horse medium transport helicopter.

ultimate weapon - 1. Infantryman. 2. Portable Truth Detector.

Ultra Hot - The F-105 jet.

ultraviolet imagery - (DOD) That imagery produced as a result of sensing ultraviolet radiations reflected from a given target surface.

UMZ - Ultra Militarized Zone. Sarcastic slang for the DMZ

UN - The United Nations.

unaccompanied - A tour of duty to a location that does not allow dependents to accompany the member of the Armed Forces.

unass - To stand up from a seated position, get up.

unbloused - Pant legs not tucked into boot tops. See bloused.

uncharged demolition target - (DOD, NATO, SEATO, CENTO, IADB) A demolition target which has been prepared to receive the demolition agent, the necessary quantities of which have been calculated, packaged, and stored in a safe place. Installation instructions have been prepared. See also demolition target.

unclassified matter - (DOD, NATO, SEATO, CENTO, IADB) Official matter which does not require the application of security safeguards, but the disclosure of which may be subject to control for other reasons. See also classified matter.

Uncle - The United States.

Uncle Sam - The United States.

Uncle Sucker - The United States.

Uncle Sugar - The United States.

uncontrolled mosaic - (DOD, NATO, CENTO) A mosaic composed of uncorrected photographs, the details of which have been matched from print to print without ground control or other orientation. Accurate measurement and direction cannot be accomplished. See also controlled mosaic; mosaic.

unconventional warfare - (DOD, IADB) Includes the three interrelated fields of guerrilla warfare, evasion and escape, and subversion. Unconventional warfare operations are conducted within enemy or enemy-controlled territory by predominantly indigenous personnel, usually supported and directed in varying degrees by an external source.

unconventional warfare - (NFSN, CENTO) General term used to describe operations conducted for military, political, or economical purposes within an area occupied by the enemy and making use of the local inhabitants and resources.

unconventional warfare forces - (DOD) United States forces having an existing unconventional warfare capability consisting of Army Special Forces and such Navy, Air Force, and Marine units as are assigned for these operations.

understowed cargo - See flatted cargo.

underwater demolition - (DOD, NATO, SEATO, CENTO, IADB) The destruction or neutralization of underwater obstacles; this is normally accomplished by underwater demolition teams.

underwater demolition team - (DOD) A group of officers and men specially trained and equipped for making hydrographic reconnaissance of approaches to prospective landing beaches; for effecting demolition of obstacles, clearing mines in certain areas; locating, improving, and marking of useable channels; channel and harbor clearance; acquisition of pertinent data during preassault operations, including military information; and visual observation of the hinterland to gain information useful to the landing force; and for performing miscellaneous underwater and surface tasks within their capabilities.

underway replenishment forces - (NATO, SEATO, CENTO, IADB) A task force of fleet auxiliaries (consisting of oilers, ammunition ships, stores issue ships, etc.) adequately protected by escorts furnished by the responsible operational commander. The function of this force is to provide underway logistic support for naval forces. An underway replenishment force may be organized in underway replenishment groups, units and elements in accordance with the standard doctrine for task organization. See also force(s).

underway replenishment group - (DOD, IADB) A task group configured to provide logistic replenishment of ships underway by transfer-at-sea methods.

unfriendlies - The enemy.

uni-Service command - (DOD) A command comprised of forces of a single Service.

Unified Action Armed Forces - (DOD) A publication setting forth the principles, doctrines, and functions governing the activities and performance of the Armed Forces of the United States when two or more Services or elements thereof are acting together.

unified command - (DOD) A command with a broad continuing mission under a single commander and composed of significant assigned components of two or more Services, and which is established and so designated by the President, through the Secretary of Defense with the advice and assistance of the Joint Chiefs of Staff, or, when so authorized by the Joint Chiefs of Staff, by a commander of an existing unified command established by the President.

Uniform - 1. The military phonetic alphabet designation for the letter "U". 2. The specified set of clothing for the season and assignment governed by regulation and orders of the day. 3. The UHF radio and its frequencies.

Uniform Code of Military Justice - The authority for military law.

unilateral arms control measure - (DOD, IADB) An arms control course of action taken by a nation without any compensating concession being required of other nations.

unit - (DOD, NATO, SEATO, CENTO, IADB) 1. Any military element whose structure is prescribed by competent authority, such as a table of organization and equipment; specifically, part of an organization. 2. An organizational title of a subdivision of a group in a task force. 3. A standard of basic quantity into which an item of supply is divided, issued, or used. In this meaning, also called unit of issue.

unit aircraft - (DOD, IADB) Those aircraft provided an aircraft unit for the performance of a flying mission. See also aircraft.

unit combat readiness - See combat readiness.

unit emplaning officer - (NATO, CENTO) In air transport, a representative of the transported unit responsible for organizing the movement of that unit.

unit loading - (DOD, NATO, CENTO, IADB) The loading of troop units with their equipment and supplies in the same ships, aircraft, or land vehicles. See also loading.

unit loading - (SEATO) The loading of troop units with their equipment and supplies in the same vessels. See also loading.

unit of issue - (DOD, IADB) In its special storage meaning, refers to the quantity of an item; as each number, dozen, gallon, pair, pound, ream, set, yard. Usually termed unit of issue to distinguish from "unit price". See also unit.

unit one - Medical kit. Infantry had a small one on each man. Medics had a larger kit.

unit personnel and tonnage table - (DOD, IADB) A table included in the loading plan of a combat-loaded ship as a recapitulation of totals of personnel and cargo by type, listing cubic measurements and weight.

unit reserves - (DOD, IADB) Prescribed quantities of supplies carried by a unit as a reserve to cover emergencies. See also reserve supplies.

unit strength - (NESN, NFSN) As applied to a friendly or enemy unit, relates to the number of personnel, amount of supplies, armament equipment and vehicles and the total logistic capabilities. See also strength.

United Service Organization - A civilian charitable organization providing military personnel with morale and recreational events and locations. In particular, known for tours of celebrities into the rear of war zones for open air variety shows.

United States Air Force Academy - The Air Force academy in Colorado Springs, Colorado.

United States Armed Forces - (DOD) Used to denote collectively only the regular components of the Army, Navy, Air Force, Marine Corps, and Coast Guard. See also Armed Forces of the United States.

United States Army Nurse Corps - The nurses in the U.S. Army, all of whom volunteered for service and additionally for duty in the war zone.

United States Army Special Forces - (DOD) Military personnel with cross training in basic and specialized military skills, organized into small, multiple-purpose detachments with the mission to train, organize, supply, direct, and control indigenous forces in guerrilla warfare and counterinsurgency operations, and to conduct unconventional warfare operations.

United States Civilian Internee Information Center - (DOD) The national center of information in the United States for enemy and United States civilian internees.

United States controlled shipping - (DOD) That shipping under United States flag plus those selected ships under foreign flag which are considered to be under "effective United States control," i.e., which can reasonably be expected to be made available to the United States in time of national emergency.

United States country team - (DOD) The senior, in-country, United States coordinating and supervising body, headed by the Chief of the United States diplomatic mission, usually an ambassador, and composed of the senior member of each represented United States department or agency.

United States Information Service - The U.S. agency responsible for radio broadcasts of news and information about and relevant to the United States in foreign countries. See USIS.

United States Military Academy - The Army's military academy at West Point, New York. Also called West Point.

United States Military Service Funded Foreign Training - (DOD) Training which is provided to foreign nationals in United States military Service schools and installations under authority other than the Foreign Assistance Act of 1961.

United States Naval Academy - The Navy's academy at Annapolis, Maryland. Also called Annapolis.

United States Prisoner of War Information Center - (DOD) The national center of information in the United States for enemy and United States prisoners of war.

United States Strategic Army Forces - (DOD) That part of the Army, normally located in the continental United States, which is trained, equipped, and maintained for employment at national level in accordance with current plans.

universal polar stereographic grid - (DOD) A military grid prescribed for joint use in operations in limited areas and used for operations requiring precise position reporting. It covers areas between the 80 degree parallels and the poles.

unknown - (DOD) A code meaning information not available (not used to mean an unidentified target).

unkwn - Unknown or unavailable.

unladen weight (transport vehicles) - (SEATO, IADB) Net weight of the vehicle plus the driver, the driver's personal equipment and the traction devices when they are normally part of the vehicle equipment. See laden weight (transport vehicles); net weight (transport vehicles). (Note: SEATO term does not include "(transport vehicles)".)

unlimited war - (DOD) Not to be used. See general war.

unload - Aviation term for: 1. A steep dive to gain maximum speed before leveling and bombing or strafing. See loading/unloading. 2. To dump all ordinance as fast as possible. Also unload ordinance.

unobserved fire - (NATO, CENTO, IADB) Fire for which the points of impact or burst are not observed.

unpremeditated expansion of a war - (DOD) Not to be used. See escalation.

unpremeditated war - (DOD) Not to be used. See accidental attack.

unsurveyed area - (NATO) Areas on a map or chart where both relief and planimetric data are unavailable. These areas are usually labelled "unsurveyed". Or an area on a map or chart which shows little or no charted data because accurate information is limited or not available.

unwarned exposed - (DOD, NATO, CENTO, IADB) The vulnerability of friendly forces to nuclear weapon effects. In this condition, personnel are assumed to be standing in the open at burst time, but have dropped to a prone position by the time the blast wave arrives. They are expected to have areas of bare skin exposed to direct thermal radiation, and some personnel may suffer dazzle. See also warned exposed; warned protected.

up - (DOD) 1. A correction used by an observer or a spotter in time fire to indicate that an increase in height of burst is desired. 2. A term used in a call for fire to indicate that the target is higher in altitude than the point which has been used as a reference point for the target location.

up - Operational, working.

up and locked - Aviation slang for someone who is oblivious to his surroundings and posing a danger to others. Brain on hold. From an attempt to land a plane with the landing gear up and locked.

up north - In North Vietnam.

up to speed - Aviation slang for someone who has the latest information, is fully trained and ready to go.

uppers - 1. Amphetamines. 2. Any stimulant, usually illegally obtained.

urgent dustoff - A request for medical evacuation by helicopter when loss of life or limb is imminent. The highest priority of evacuation.

urgent priority - (DOD) A category of immediate mission request which is lower than emergency priority but takes precedence over ordinary priority, e.g., enemy artillery or mortar fire which is falling on friendly troops and causing casualties or enemy troops or mechanized units moving up in such force as to threaten a break-through. See also immediate mission request; priority of immediate mission request.

US - The prefix before the serial number of Army draftees before 1969, when social security numbers were used. See also RA.

USA - United States of America.

USAF - United States Air Force.

VIETNAM: THE WAR ZONE DICTIONARY IN THEIR OWN WORDS

USAID - United States Agency for International development, an aid program.

USARV - 1. United States Army, Republic of Vietnam. 2. The command that addressed the operation of all U.S. troops in Vietnam, based at Long Binh.

USAVN - U.S. Army Viet Nam organized July 1965.

USCG - United States Coast Guard.

USCMA - United States Court of Military Appeals.

use up - To kill.

USIA - United States Information Agency. The successor organization to the United States Information Service.

using agency - (SEATO) In relation to code-words, the agency, including member governments, to which a codeword is allocated for use and which assigns to the word a special meaning.

USMACV - United States Military Assistance Command, Vietnam.

USMC - United States Marine Corps.

USN - United States Navy.

USNS - United States Naval Ship.

USO - See United Service Organization.

USOM - United States Operations Mission. Economic support via Saigon offices.

USS - United States Ship.

USSF - United States Special Forces.

Ute - The U-21 helicopter.

utilities - Marine term for fatigue uniform, the olive drab green field uniform.

UTM Universal Transmercador - The map making and labeling system used by the military in Vietnam. Under this system, a series of metric coordinates rather than longitude and latitude are used to locate a place. This permits location of a site within 100 meters. The designations are in a six digit series following the designation YD. See YD.

UUM-44A - See submarine rocket.

UUUU - Abbreviation for the phrase used to summarize the mission in South Vietnam "The unwilling led by the unqualified doing the unnecessary for the ungrateful." Or the phrase "We the unwilling led by the unqualified to kill the unfortunate and die for the ungrateful." See Quad U.

UW - Unconventional Warfare.

V – VICTOR

V - Designated in the military phonetic alphabet as "Victor".

V device - The metal "V" attached to a ribbon of a medal that may be awarded either for valor or meritorious service to indicate valor.

V formation - See the aviation term parade formation.

V-100 - An armored car with a machine gun mounted on it, often used by Military Police.

V-A - The Selective Service System draft classification for males no longer eligible for the draft by reason of age, 26 if no deferment, 36 if deferred with extended liability. Pronounced five A.

V-ring - Slang for dead, from a target centered in the v-ring of a rifle sight.

VA - 1. Vice Admiral. 2. Veterans Administration. See green machine.

VADM - Vice Admiral (Navy and Coast Guard).

Valpak - See B-4 bag. A suitcase.

valuable cargo - (NATO, CENTO, IADB) A commodity which may be of value during a later stage of the war. This will comprise such things as basic raw materials and manufactured goods. See also cargoes. (Note: IADB term is "valuable supply cargo".)

value engineering - (DOD) An organized effort directed at analyzing the function of Department of Defense systems, equipment, facilities, procedures and supplies for the purpose of achieving the required function at the lowest total cost of effective ownership, consistent with requirements for performance, reliability, quality, and maintainability.

vampire - A night sniper.

vanguard - (IADB) An element of the advanced guard. See also advanced guard.

vapor trail - See condensation trail.

variability - (DOD, NATO, CENTO, IADB) The manner in which the probability of damage to a specific target decreases with the distance from ground zero; or, in damage assessment, a mathematical factor introduced to average the effects of orientation, minor shielding and uncertainty of target response to the effects considered.

variable time fuze - (DOD, NATO, SEATO, CENTO, IADB) A fuze designed to detonate a projectile, bomb, mine, or charge when activated by external influence other than contact in the close vicinity of a target. See also fuze.

variant - (DOD, IADB) 1. One of two or more cipher or code symbols which have the same plain text equivalent. 2. One of several plain text meanings that are represented by a single code group; also called alternative.

variation (navigation) - (SEATO, IADB) The horizontal angle at a place between the true north and magnetic north measured in degrees and minutes east or west according to whether magnetic north lies east or west of true north. See also declination.

Varmint - The M-40 rifle. The Remington high powered sniper rifle used by Marine sniper teams.

vat-B - See weather.

VATLS - The Visual Airborne Target Locator System. An Army system using a high powered telescope for spotting enemy locations.

VC - Viet Cong - The North Vietnamese guerilla forces. 2. An individual who was a member of the Viet Cong.

VCC - Viet Cong Captured.

VCI - Viet Cong Infrastructure. The political organization within the VC.

VCS - Viet Cong Suspect.

VD - Venereal disease. Particularly noteworthy as troops would not be released for return stateside until medically cleared.

Vector _____ - (DOD) A heading issued to an aircraft to provide navigational guidance by radar.

vector - (DOD) In air intercept, close air support and air interdiction usage, alter heading to magnetic heading indicated. Heading ordered must be in three digits; e.g., "vector" zero six zero (for homing, use "steer").

vector control - Pest control, particularly those carrying disease such as rats and mosquitos.

vectored attacks - (DOD, NATO, CENTO, IADB) Attacks in which a weapon carrier (air, surface, or subsurface) not holding contact on the target, is vectored to the weapon delivery point by a unit (air, surface, or sub-surface) which holds contact on the target.

vegetable - Hospital slang for a patient without cognition. Severe brain damage.

vegetable patch - Hospital slang for the ward for head trauma cases.

vehicle - (DOD, NATO, CENTO, IADB) A self-propelled, boosted, or towed conveyance for transporting a burden on land, sea, or through air or space. See also amphibious vehicle; combat vehicle (fighting); commercial-type vehicle; special-equipment vehicle; special purpose vehicle; substitute transport-type vehicle; tactical vehicle; transport vehicle.

vehicle cargo - (DOD) Wheeled or tracked equipment, including weapons, which require certain deck space, head room, and other definite clearance. See also cargo.

vehicle commander (ground) - (DOD, NATO, CENTO) The leader of a vehicle crew appointed for each mission. He is responsible for crew discipline and the execution of the mission.

vehicle summary and priority table - (DOD, IADB) A table listing all vehicles by priority of debarkation from a combat-loaded ship. It includes the nomenclature, dimensions, square feet, cubic feet, weight, and stowage location of each vehicle, the cargo loaded in each vehicle, and the name of the unit to which the vehicle belongs.

verification - (DOD, IADB) In arms control, any action, including inspection, detection, and identification, taken to ascertain compliance with agreed measures.

verify - (DOD, NATO, SEATO, CENTO, IADB) 1. To insure that the meaning and phraseology of the transmitted message conveys the exact intention of the originator. (DOD) 2. A request from an observer, a spotter, or a fire control agency to reexamine firing data and report the results of the reexamination.

vertical air photograph - (DOD, NATO, CENTO) An air photograph taken with the optical axis of the camera perpendicular to the earth's surface.

vertical and/or short takeoff and landing - (DOD, IADB) Vertical and/or short takeoff and landing capability for aircraft.

vertical butt stroke - A move in rifle/bayonet fighting in which the rifle is held perpendicular to the ground and then rotated so the butt (shoulder piece) of the rifle hits under the enemy's chin.

vertical envelopment - (DOD, IADB) A tactical maneuver in which troops, either air dropped or air landed, attack the rear and flanks of a force, in effect, cutting off or encircling the force.

vertical interval - (DOD) Difference in altitude between two specified points or locations, e.g., the battery or firing ship and the target; observer location and the target; location of previously fired target and new target; observer and a height of burst; battery or firing ship and a height of burst, etc.

vertical loading - (DOD, NATO, SEATO, CENTO, IADB) A type of loading whereby items of like character are vertically tiered throughout the holds of a ship, so that selected items are available at any stage of the unloading. See also loading.

vertical probable error - (DOD) The product of the range probable error and the slope of fall.

vertical replenishment - A resupply by helicopter.

vertical scissors - Aviation defensive maneuver in which an airplane being chased pulls up fast (vertical) rolls over (barrel roll or rolling) and comes in behind the attacker.

Also called rolling scissors.

vertical separation - (DOD, NATO, SEATO, CENTO, IADB) A specified vertical distance measured in terms of space between aircraft in flight at different altitude or flight levels.

vertical strip - (DOD) A single flightline of overlapping photos. Photography of this type is normally taken of long, narrow targets such as beaches or roads.

vertical takeoff and landing - (DOD, NATO, CENTO, IADB) The capability of an aircraft to take off and land vertically and to transfer to or from forward motion at heights required to clear surrounding obstacles.

VERTREP - Vertical Replenishment. Helicopter resupply.

very high - (DOD) A height above fifty thousand feet.

very low - (DOD) A height below five hundred feet.

very seriously ill - (DOD, NATO, CENTO, IADB) A patient is very seriously ill when his illness is of such severity that life is imminently endangered.

vet - Veteran.

veteran - One who has served in the military.

vets - Vietnamese for pests such as mites and chiggers.

VFR - Visual flight rules. Aviation rules when visibility is not restricted. See IFR.

VHF - Very High Frequency radio and its frequencies.

vic - Vicinity.

Victor - The military phonetic alphabet designation for the letter "V".

Victor Charlie - The phonetic designation for the letters, "VC", the Viet Cong.

VID - Visual identification. Aviation term for the visual confirmation of an aircraft's identity when radar is not clear.

Viet Cong - 1. The fighting force of the communist. 2. The communist Vietnamese in the south.

Viet Cong Hunting Club - Out on patrol.

Viet Minh - A contraction from Vietnam Doc Lap Dong Minh (League for Vietnamese Independence), the term was devised in the communist party meeting of 1941 and later was used to describe both the communists and nationals in Vietnam who fought the French from 1946 to 1954.

Viet Nam - The spelling used in the 1960's and 70's, as in North Viet Nam, South Viet Nam, or Viet Nam.

Viet shits - Diarrhea.

Viet speak - The mixture of Vietnamese, English, French, and other Asian languages mixed together in random portions to be understood.

Vietnam - 1. The generally adopted spelling of either North or South Vietnam in the late 1970's, although inconsistent between news media and military. 2. The spelling of the united country, formally the Socialist Republic of Vietnam.

Vietnam Campaign Medal - See Republic of Vietnam Campaign Medal.

Vietnam flu - Venereal disease. Gonorrhea.

Vietnam People's Army - North Vietnam soldiers.

Vietnam Service Medal - The military award by the United States to members of its Armed Forces serving in Vietnam, Laos, Cambodia, and Thailand or in close support thereof during the war from 15 November 1961 to 28 March 1973 or during the evacuation of Saigon 29 April to 30 April 1975. It replaces the Armed Forces Expeditionary Medal issued for service prior to 1965. The ribbon consists of three vertical red stripes on a field of yellow bordered by two vertical green bars. Also VSM. Not to be confused with the Republic of Vietnam Campaign Medal.

Vietnamese car wash - A business set up outside a base that did provide a wash for dirty vehicles and added services such as a barber shop and whorehouse.

Vietnamization - 1. The designation of President Nixon's program to phase out U.S. troops in Vietnam and turn the war over to Vietnamese troops. 2. The act of troop withdrawal.

Viggie - Slang for the Vigilante plane.

Vigilante - (DOD, IADB) 1. A supersonic, twin-engine turbojet, tactical, all-weather attack aircraft designed to operate from aircraft carriers, and capable of delivering nuclear or nonnuclear weapons. It possesses electronic countermeasures equipment, long-range radar and automatic pilot guidance features. It has a crew of pilot and bombardier. It has in-flight refueling capabilities. Designated as A-5. 2. A self-propelled air defense weapon employing an improved rapid-fire 37-mm gun.

vignetting - (NATO) In cartography, a technique of graduated shading to emphasize the outline of a feature.

village - A group of dwellings larger than a hamlet but smaller than a town.

village deer - Dog meat.

ville - A town or village, from the French word.

Visibility _____ - (DOD) In air intercept usage, visibility (in miles) is _____.

visibility range - (DOD, NATO, CENTO) The horizontal distance (in kilometers or miles) at which a large dark object can just be seen against the horizon sky in daylight.

visual call sign - (DOD, NATO, SEATO, CENTO, IADB) A call sign provided primarily for visual signaling. See also call sign.

visual report - (DOD) Not to be used. See in-flight report

vital area - (DOD) A designated area or installation to be defended by air defense units.

vital ground - See key terrain.

vivax - One of the two types of malaria. See falciparum.

VNA - Vietnamese Army (South).

VNAF - Vietnamese Air Force (South).

VNMC - Vietnamese Marine Corps (South).

VNN - Vietnamese Navy (South).

VNSF - Vietnamese Special Forces. (South).

voice call sign - (DOD, NATO, SEATO, CENTO, IADB) A call sign provided primarily for voice communication. See also call sign.

Voice of Vietnam - The North Vietnamese radio broadcast in English to Southeast Asia.

void - 1. Marine Corps term for relieving someone of duty or a special assignment such as a Drill Instructor. 2. Slang for someone with an empty head, a dummy.

void tank - Navy term for a large equipment hold.

Voodoo - (DOD, IADB) A supersonic, twin-engine, turbojet-powered aircraft utilized in three versions: a. the F-101A is a single-place tactical fighter capable of delivering either nuclear or nonnuclear weapons, and of providing close support for ground forces; b. the F-101B is a two-place, tandem cockpit, all-weather fighter interceptor capable of destroying hostile aircraft with Genie air-to-air rockets or Falcon missiles; and c. the RF-101 is a single-place, tactical, photographic reconnaissance aircraft for support of both ground and air forces. Designated as F-101.

VPA - Vietnam People's Army (North).

VSI - Hospital slang for very seriously ill.

VSM - See Vietnam Service Medal.

VT - Vertically timed. Artillery term for rounds timed to explode at a set distance above the ground.

Vulcan - A 20-mm Gatling gun mounted in fighter aircraft.

vulnerability - (DOD) 1. The susceptibility of a nation or military force to any action by any means through which its war potential or combat effectiveness may be reduced or its will to fight diminished. 2. The characteristics of a system which causes it to suffer a definite degradation (incapability to perform the designated mission) as a result of having been subjected to a certain level of effects in an unnatural (manmade) hostile environment.

vulnerability program - (DOD) A program to determine the degree of, and to remedy insofar as possible, any existing susceptibility of nuclear weapon systems to enemy countermeasures, accidental fire, and accidental shock.

vulnerability study - (DOD) An analysis of the capabilities and limitations of a force in a specific situation to determine vulnerabilities capable of exploitation by an opposing force.

vulture's row - Aviation term for the side of a carrier where mechanics loitered on the flight deck waiting to pick apart the injured planes and repair them.

VVA - Vietnam Veterans of America.

VVAW - Vietnam Veterans Against the War.

VWP - Vietnamese Worker's Party, the Communist Party of North Vietnam.

W – WHISKEY

W - 1. Designated by the word "Whiskey" in the phonetic military alphabet. 2. The designations, by pay grade, for Warrant Officers.

W-1 - Warrant Officer (Army and Marine Corps). No Navy, Coast Guard or Air Force rank at this pay grade.

W-2 - Chief Warrant Officer 2 (Army, Marine Corp, Navy, Coast Guard). No Air Force rank at this pay grade.

W-3 - Chief Warrant Officer 3 (Army, Marine Corp, Navy, Coast Guard). No Air Force rank at this pay grade.

W-4 - Chief Warrant Officer 4 (Army, Marine Corp, Navy, Coast Guard). No Air Force rank at this pay grade.

W-5 - Chief Warrant Officer 5 (Army, Marine Corp, Navy). No Coast Guard or Air Force rank at this pay grade.

WAAPM-CBU - Wide area anti-personnel munition. A cluster bomb.

WAC - A member of the Woman's Army Corps.

wading crossing - See deep fording; shallow fording.

WAG - "Wild assed guess", speculation, made up facts.

wagon train defense - Infantry slang for the defensive strategy of placing soldiers in a circle around an encampment for protection, similar to "circling the wagons" of a wagon train when attacked.

wagon wheel - Marine Corps slang for the circle of marching recruits after physical training as a cool-down mode.

wagon wheel defense - 1. Infantry term for a defensive strategy for a small number of troops on patrol in which all lie down with feet at the hub of a wheel and each looking out, resembling the spokes on a wagon wheel. 2. Aviation term for two or more planes to fly in a wide circle while moving forward each with the ability to protect the rear of another plane.

wait a minute bush/vine - Any thorny tree, bush or vine that could hang up clothing, inflict cuts and impede progress.

waiting position (fast coastal forces) - (NATO, CENTO, IADB) Any geographical position in which fast patrol boats can be kept ready for operations at immediate notice.

wake-up - 1. The last day of duty in Vietnam. 2. Part of the exit countdown by those about to leave Vietnam, by adding a day to the phrase, so four and a wake up means only four days until shipping out to stateside.

walk in the sun - Troop movement without risk of combat.

walk to the wire - The area with electronic intrusion sensors outside a base that would alert the base if someone walked toward the base perimeter.

Walker bulldog - The M41 tank.

Walking Dead - The First Battalion Ninth Marine Regiment for the high casualties.

walking fire - 1. The infantry strategy of firing while walking. 2. Artillery tactic of firing at ever increasing heights so the impact areas walks away from the artillery's location. Also called marching fire.

walking patient - (DOD, NATO, CENTO, IADB) A patient not requiring a litter while in transit.

walking patient - (SEATO) A patient requiring only sitting accommodation while in transit.

walking point - 1. The front soldier in a patrol. 2. Anyone taking leadership on a dangerous mission.

walking rounds - A gunner's strategy to fire short of a target and use the tracers to correct the targeting and walk the rounds forward into the target.

walking tracers - See walking rounds.

walking wounded - 1. Hospital slang for the least critical classification in entry triage. 2. An ambulatory injured person. 3. Slang for those with mental health issues or psychological damage who are not in a hospital setting.

Wall - The Wall is the common term for the Vietnam Veterans Memorial in Washington, D.C. While its dedication in 1982 is beyond the time frame of this collection, it is an important part of this time as it recognizes all veterans for their service and honors over 50,000 men and the eight women who gave their lives in that war.

Wallaby Airlines - The Australian Air Force.

Walleye - Slang for the AGM-62 air to ground missile, delivered by a plane, it was guided to its target by a television screen.

Walter Wonderful - Walter Reed Army Hospital in Washington, D.C.

waltz - Infantry slang for hand to hand combat.

war air service program - (DOD) The program designed to provide for the maintenance of essential civil air routes and services, and to provide for the distribution and redistribution of air carrier aircraft among civil air transport carriers after withdrawal of aircraft allocated to the Civil Reserve Air Fleet.

war belt - Marine Corps slang for the web waist belt that held ammo pouches and canteens.

war game - (DOD, NATO, CENTO, IADB) A simulation, by whatever means, of a military operation involving two or more opposing forces, using rules, data, and procedures designed to depict an actual or assumed real life situation.

war gas - (SEATO, IADB) Any chemical agent (liquid, solid, or vapor) used in war, which produces poisonous or irritant effects on the human body. See also chemical agent.

war of attrition - The theory of war in which you win by exhausting the resources of your enemy, both personnel and supply.

War Powers Act - The Act passed by Congress in November 1973 requiring the President to consult with Congress before military forces are committed. Presidential power extends to a 60 day commitment of forces and an added 30 if certified in writing to congress that the safety of the forces requires the continued stay. The 90-day limit can be exceeded only by act of Congress.

war reserve (nuclear) - (DOD) Nuclear weapons material stockpiled in the custody of the Atomic Energy Commission or transferred to the custody of the Department of Defense and intended for employment in the event of war.

war reserves - (DOD, NATO, SEATO, CENTO, IADB) War reserves are stocks of material amassed in peacetime to meet the increase in military requirements consequent upon an outbreak of war. War reserves are intended to provide the interim support essential to sustain operations until resupply can be effected. See also reserve supplies.

warehouse chart - See planograph.

warhead - (DOD, NATO, CENTO, IADB) That part of a missile, projectile, torpedo, rocket, or other munition which contains either the nuclear or thermonuclear system, high-explosive system, chemical or biological agents or inert materials intended to inflict damage.

warhead mating - (DOD) The act of attaching a warhead section to the rocket, or missile body, torpedo, airframe, motor or guidance section.

warhead section - (DOD, NATO, CENTO, IADB) A completely assembled warhead including appropriate skin sections and related components.

warm body - Any soldier.

warned exposed - (DOD, NATO, CENTO, IADB) The vulnerability of friendly forces to nuclear weapon effects. In this condition, personnel are assumed to be prone with all skin covered and with thermal protection at least that provided by a two-layer summer uniform. See also unwarned exposed; warned protected.

warned protected - (DOD, NATO, CENTO, IADB) The vulnerability of friendly forces to nuclear weapon effects. In this condition, personnel are assumed to have some protection against heat, blast, and radiation such as that afforded in closed armored vehicles or crouched in fox holes with improvised overhead shielding. See also unwarned exposed; warned exposed.

warning area - See danger area.

warning net - (DOD, IADB) A communication system established for the purpose of disseminating warning information of enemy movement or action to all interested commands.

warning order - (DOD, NATO, SEATO, CENTO, IADB) A preliminary notice of an order or action which is to follow. It is designed to give subordinates time to make necessary plans and preparations.

warning red - See air defense warning conditions.

Warning Star - The EC-121 with radar.

warning white - See air defense warning conditions.

warning yellow - See air defense warning conditions.

Warrant Officer - A rank between NCO and Officer.

wash out - Aviation term for failing flight school.

WASP - A Caucasian with some background of privilege, from white Anglo Saxon Protestant.

waste - To kill.

wasted - 1. Killed. 2. Loaded on drugs or alcohol.

watch - 1. To stand guard, in general. 2. Navy term for a shift of a set percent of all available personnel, usually about half and those not on watch are on-call in the event of emergencies.

watch list - The unofficial and unacknowledged list of the sons of influential people. Soldiers on this list got special attention and less dangerous assignments. See special attention personnel.

water bottle break - Pilot slang for taking a break to hydrate. Heat and exertion on a flight would dehydrate aviators by 3-5 pounds.

water buffalo - 1. The large tanker on wheels that holds drinking water for troops, or non-potable water for construction uses. 2. The animal in Vietnam used for plowing and cart-pulling.

water cannon - A high pressure water pumping and nozzle mechanism that could be used offensively by Navy personnel to erode embankments, foxholes and other earthen fortifications along riverbanks to expose the enemy.

water point - A Vietnamese establishment near a base that offered a washing service for trucks and other vehicles, and other services such as a barber shop and whorehouse.

water purification tablets - Iodine tablets used to kill disease causing organisms in water that was replenished from streams while on patrol. The taste was masked by using unsweetened Kool-Aid.

water suit - (DOD, NATO, SEATO, CENTO, IADB) A G-suit in which water is used in the interlining thereby automatically approximating the required hydrostatic pressure gradient under G forces. See also pressure suit.

water taxi - A small powered boat that is covered (or enclosed) used for passenger travel from one area to another over water.

water terminal - See alternate water terminal; major water terminal; secondary water terminal. See also port.

water-walker - One who is impervious, who does the impossible, Christ-like.

wave - (DOD, NATO, CENTO, IADB) A formation of forces, landing ships, craft, amphibious vehicles or aircraft, required to beach or land about the same time. Can be classified as to type, function, or order as shown: a. assault wave; b. boat wave; c. helicopter wave; d. numbered wave; e. on-call wave; and f. scheduled wave.

waveoff - Aviation term for the order given by a Landing Signal Officer (by flag or radio) not to land on a carrier.

wax - To kill.

waypoint - (DOD) In air operations, a point or a series of points in space to which an aircraft may be vectored.

Weapon Alpha - (DOD, IADB) A 12.75" rocket-propelled depth charge with a range of about 1,000 yards. Designated as RUR-4.

weapon debris (nuclear) - (DOD, NATO, CENTO) The residue of a nuclear weapon after it has exploded; that is, the materials used for the casing, and other components of the weapon, plus unexpended plutonium or uranium, together with fission products.

weapon system - (DOD, NATO, CENTO, IADB) A weapon and those components required for its operation. (The term is not precise unless specific parameters are established.)

weapon system manager - See system manager.

weapon systems officer - The aviator assigned to manage the radar, munitions and firing in a F-4. Also called WSO, or guy in back (as opposed to the pilot who was in the front seat).

weapon-target line - (DOD, IADB) An imaginary straight line from a weapon to a target.

weapons assignment - (DOD) The process by which weapons are assigned to individual air weapons controllers for use in accomplishing an assigned mission.

weapons lost/weapons found - The report on the loss of allied weapons and gain of enemy weapons. Also weapons lost/weapons captured.

weapons of mass destruction - (DOD, IADB) In arms control usage, weapons that are capable of a high order of destruction and/or of being used in such a manner as to destroy large numbers of people. Can be nuclear, chemical, biological, and radiological weapons, but excludes the means of transporting or propelling the weapon where such means is a separable and divisible part of the weapon.

weapons recommendation sheet - (DOD, NATO, SEATO, CENTO, IADB) A sheet or chart which defines the intention of the attack, and recommends the nature of weapons, and resulting damage expected, tonnage, fuzing, spacing, desired mean points of impact, and intervals of reattack.

weapons state of readiness - (DOD) The degree of readiness of air defense weapons which can become airborne or be launched to carry out an assigned task. The states of readiness are expressed in numbers of weapons and numbers of minutes. Weapons states of readiness are defined as follows: a. 2 minutes - Weapons can be launched within two minutes, b. 5 minutes - Weapons can be launched within five minutes, c. 15 minutes - Weapons can be launched within fifteen minutes, d. 30 minutes - Weapons can be launched within thirty minutes, e. 1 hour - Weapons can be launched within one hour, f. 3 hours - Weapons can be launched within three hours, or g. released - Weapons are released from defense commitment for a specified period of time.

weapons system - Aviation term for the combination of the aircraft, electronic avionics, ordinance, and crew.

Weasel - The M-29C - The American made amphibious cargo carrier.

weather ("vat B") - (DOD) Short form weather report, giving: a. V - Visibility in miles. b. A - Amount of clouds, in eights. c. T - Height of cloud top, in thousands of feet. d. B -Height of cloud base, in thousands of feet. (The reply is a series of four numbers preceded by the word "weather". An unknown item is reported as "unknown".)

weather central - (DOD, IADB) An organization which collects, collates, evaluates, and disseminates meteorological information in such manner that it becomes a principal source of such information for a given area.

weather forecast - (DOD, IADB) A prediction of weather conditions at a point, along a route, or within an area for a specified period of time.

weather map - (DOD, IADB) A map showing the weather conditions prevailing, or predicted to prevail, over a considerable area. Usually, the map is based upon weather observations taken at the same time at a number of stations. See also map.

weather minimum - (DOD) The worst weather conditions under which aviation operations may be conducted under either visual or instrument flight rules. Usually prescribed by directives and standing operating procedures in terms of minimum ceiling, visibility or specific hazards to flight.

weave - Aviation term for having two elements of a formation cross back and forth in front of each other at the same altitude while moving forward to increase surveillance and security.

web gear - 1. A canvas belt with shoulder straps used by the infantry to carry ammunition and other gear. 2. The canvas belt without shoulder straps used by others.

web seats - Temporary or removable seating in a cargo aircraft.

weed - Slang for marijuana.

weekend warrior - Reservists.

weenie - 1. A wimp. 2. Anyone stationed in the rear away from harm.

weenie mobile - See Wienermobile.

weight and balance sheet - (DOD, NATO, CENTO, IADB) A sheet which records the distribution of weight in an aircraft and shows the center of gravity of an aircraft at takeoff and landing.

well - (DOD) As used in air intercept, means equipment indicated is operating efficiently.

VIETNAM: THE WAR ZONE DICTIONARY IN THEIR OWN WORDS

well connected - See drag.

West Point - See United States Military Academy.

West Point Protective Association - 1. The imaginary fraternity of Army officers who graduated from West Point. 2. The inference that West Point grads more than looked out for each other. See ring knockers.

wet job - An assassination.

wet read - reading photographs of reconnaissance while still wet with developing and fixing solutions.

WETSU - Abbreviation for "we eat this shit up".

wetting down - An informal, often drunken, party paid for by a newly promoted person, putting at least the difference in the old and new salaries into a bar tab. Naval in origin, the wetting was to wet the new stripe or insignia to age it to match the old stripes. Toasts and roast-like short speeches are common.

WHA - Wounded by Hostile Action.

Whale - See F3D, an aircraft.

WHAM - Winning the hearts and minds of the Vietnamese people, the goal of the counter-insurgency movement.

what luck - (DOD) As used in air intercept, means what are/were the results of assigned mission?

what state - (DOD) As used in air intercept, means report amount of fuel, ammunition, and oxygen remaining.

what's up - (DOD) As used in air intercept, means is anything the matter?

wheel - 1. Aviation term for a maneuver in which two planes circle while moving forward on the same altitude to provide mutual defense. 2. SEAL term for the officer in charge of that unit.

wheel base - (NATO, CENTO, IADB) The distance between the centers of two consecutive wheels. In the case of vehicles with more than two axles or equivalent systems, the successive wheel bases are all given in the order front to rear of the vehicle.

wheel jockey - Truck driver.

wheel load capacity - (DOD) The capacity of airfield runways, taxiways, parking areas, or roadways to bear the pressures exerted by aircraft or vehicles in a gross weight static configuration.

which transponder - (DOD) A code meaning report type of transponder fitted- Identification Friend or Foe, Air Traffic Control Radar Beacon System, or Secondary Surveillance Radar.

Whifferdale - See Whifferdill.

Whifferdill - An aviation maneuver that sharply changes both the vertical and horizontal axis at the same time to reverse direction and prepare for the next maneuver. It can be offensive or defensive in its use. Simply put it is a steep climb (or dive) and a sharp turn Also wingover or Whifferdale.

whirlybird - Any helicopter.

Whiskey - 1. The military phonetic alphabet designation for the letter "W". 2. The radio code for a soldier who is KIA.

Whiskey Charlie - Who cares?

Whiskey Delta - Weak dick. A pilot that can not fly well.

Whiskey Papa - White phosphorous.

whistler - See screamer.

white bird - A light observation helicopter (See LOH).

White Christmas - Code for the playing of the song "I'm Dreaming of a White Christmas" on the radio as the signal to evacuate the embassy in Saigon.

white envelope - 1. The white envelope dropped on VC positions offering amnesty and safe conduct if they left the VC and worked for the South. 2. The program in which the amnesty was offered to VC.

white lie ward - Hospital slang for the hopeless ward, particularly at the Da Nang hospital.

white mice - South Vietnamese military police, from the white helmets they wore.

white on rice - 1. The American perspective on something. 2. Being right.

white phosphorus - The chemical in an artillery shell or flare that burned hot and bright giving off intense illumnation and smoke.

White Power - The white supremacist movement, in opposition to the Black Power movement.

white propaganda - (DOD, I, NATO, SEATO, CENTO, IADB) Propaganda disseminated and acknowledged by the sponsor or by an accredited agency thereof. See also propaganda.

white psych - The CIA term for favorable propaganda which strengthens a regime.

white radio - Radio broadcasts openly attributed to the side making them.

white sidewalls - A military haircut close on sides to resemble white wall tires.

white team - Observation helicopters.

whiteout - (DOD, NATO, CENTO) Loss or orientation with respect to the horizon caused by sun reflecting on snow and overcast sky.

WIA - Wounded in action.

wicker heads - Derogatory for Vietnamese, from wearing straw hats.

Wickums - Armored self-propelled rail cars used by the South Vietnamese.

widow maker - 1. A mechanical ambush, a booby trap, (See MA). 2. The M-16 rifle, for its unreliability in early models.

width of sheaf - (DOD, IADB) Lateral interval between center of flank bursts or impacts. The comparable naval gunfire term is deflection pattern.

Wienermobile - The Chinook helicopter for the resemblance to the Oscar Mayer Wienermobile.

WIEU - Weekly Intelligence Estimate Update.

wilco - Radio code for will comply.

wild geese - Mercenaries.

Wild Weasel - Slang for aircraft equipped with electronic devices to defend against the enemy use of the surface to air missiles. The usual aircraft was the F-105. The usual gear was the Electronic Counter Measure (ECM) that picked up the missile radar and jammed it. Other actions included evasive flying or dropping foil strips to jam the radar.

will not fire - (DOD) A term sent to the spotter or other requesting agency to indicate that the target will not be engaged by the fire support ship.

willie fuds - The flying radar planes that had no ordinance just radar.

willie peter - Abbreviation for white phosphorous used in an artillery rounds.

willie peter bag - A waterproof bag to keep things dry.

willie peter grenade - A grenade containing white phosphorous that gives off high light and burns or melts everything it touches.

Willie the Whale - The large slow EF-10 Korean made airplanes used early in the war.

Wilson cloud - See condensation cloud.

WIMP - Weak, incompetent, malingering pussy.

Winchester - 1. Radio code for being out of ammunition. 2. The classic western carbine.

wind shear - (DOD, IADB) A change in space of wind direction and magnitude.

window - (NATO, SEATO, CENTO, IADB) Strips of frequency-cut metal foil, wire, or bars usually dropped from aircraft or expelled from shells or rockets as a radar countermeasure. See also chaff.

wing - (DOD) 1. An Air Force unit composed normally of one primary mission group and the necessary supporting organizations, i.e., organizations designed to render supply, maintenance, hospitalization, and other services required by the primary mission groups. Primary mission groups may be functional, such as combat, training, transport, or service. 2. A fleet air wing is the basic organizational and administrative unit for naval land and tender-based aviation. Such wings are mobile units to which are assigned aircraft squadrons and tenders for administrative control. 3. A balanced Marine Corps task organization of aircraft groups/squadrons together with appropriate command, air control, administrative, service, and maintenance units. A standard Marine Corps aircraft wing contains the aviation elements normally required for the air support of a Marine division. 4. A flank unit; that part of a military force to the right or left of the main body.

wing over - See Whifferdill.

wing wiper - Aviation slang for aviation personnel in the Marine Corps in support positions, not pilots.

wingman - 1. The plane that protects the lead plane in a formation, just off and to the rear of the lead plane's wing. 2. A friend that can be relied on to protect you.

wire - 1. Perimeter trip wires for a booby trap. 2. Perimeter.

wire hangers - Troops at the rear with ability to hang up clothing.

withdrawal action - (DOD, NATO, SEATO, CENTO, IADB) A maneuver whereby a force disengages from an enemy force in accordance with the will of the commander.

withhold (nuclear) - (DOD) The limiting of authority to employ nuclear weapons by denying their use within specified geographical areas of certain countries.

Wizard - Psychiatrist.

WO - Warrant Officer (Marine Corps).

WO1 - Warrant Officer (Army).

Woman Marines - Females in the United States Marine Corps. See BAM.

Woman's Army Corps - The separate branch of the United States Army for women. It was later integrated into the Army in 1978. See WAC.

wood line - See hedgerow.

wooden bomb - (DOD) A concept which pictures a weapon as being completely reliable and having an infinite shelf life while at the same time requiring no special handling, storage or surveillance.

wooden round - See wooden bomb.

woofing - Meaningless chatter.

word - The word is the confirmed official information, the straight scoop.

word one - Unable to reply or get in "word one".

working anchorage - (NATO, CENTO, IADB) An anchorage where ships lie to discharge cargoes overside to coasters or lighters. See also emergency anchorage.

working capital fund - (DOD) A revolving fund established to finance inventories of supplies and other stores, or to provide working capital for industrial-type activities.

working hard - Getting it done.

world - Anyplace other than Vietnam, especially the United States. Also The World.

world geographic reference system - See georef.

world news - A letter from home.

world of hurt - A bad situation. See deep shit.

wounded - See critically wounded; seriously wounded; slightly wounded. See also battle casualty.

wounded in action - (DOD, NATO, SEATO, CENTO, IADB) A battle casualty other than "killed in action" who has incurred an injury due to an external agent or cause. The term encompasses all kinds of wounds and other injuries incurred in action, whether there is a piercing of the body, as in a penetrating or perforated wound, or none, as in the contused wound; all fractures, burns, blast concussions, all effects of biological and chemical warfare agents, the effects of exposure to ionizing radiation, or any other destructive weapon or agent.

WP - White phosphorus.

WPB - Patrol craft of Coast Guard, an 80 foot cutter.

wrap boots - See tanker's boots.

wrong - (DOD) A proword meaning your last transmission was incorrect, the correct version is _____ .

WSO - The weapons systems officer.

WX - Aviator's abbreviation for weather.

X – X-RAY

X - 1. Designated in the phonetic military alphabet as "X-Ray". 2. Liquid oxygen, used to supply oxygen to pilots as it is more compact to store than is gaseous oxygen in an tank. 3. The alpha designation for experimental equipment.

X-15A - (DOD) A manned, rocket-powered, hypersonic research vehicle capable of operating at extremely high altitudes. The vehicle is air-launched from a B-52 Stratofortress and piloted to a landing.

x-axis - (DOD, IADB) A horizontal axis in a system of rectangular coordinates; that line on which distances to the right or left (east or west) of the reference line are marked, especially on a map, chart, or graph.

X-Ray - 1. The military phonetic alphabet designation for the letter "X". 2. Radio call sign for a reconnaissance patrol.

x-scale - (NATO, CENTO) On an oblique photograph, the scale along a line parallel to the true horizon.

xe tho - The north Vietnamese bicycle pack frame that allowed several hundred pounds of supplies to be carried on a bicycle.

xenon lights - High intensity search lights.

XFIM-43A - See Redeye.

Xin loi. - Vietnamese for I'm sorry. Often said sarcastically by troops in a sorry 'bout that tone. Pronounced, and often spelled, as sin loi.

XM - Designation for experimental model.

XM-12 - A gun pod on the Vulcan.

XM-129 - A grenade launcher.

XM-13 - A gun pod with a grenade launcher.

XM-14 - A gun pod with an enclosed machine gun.

XM-140 - A cannon that used a huge amount of ammunition.

XM-148 - A rifle put into service as the M-203.

XM-158 - A folding fin rocket launched for helicopters.

XM-159 - A folding fin rocket.

XM-16 - The XM-6 machine gun when paired with a mount for a rocket pod.

XM-174 - A grenade launcher.

XM-18 - A minigun used on Cobra gunships.

XM-2 - The "people sniffer" carried by troops used to detect ammonia associated with sweat and urine.

XM-21 - A twin minigun system on Huey gunships.

XM-22 - An air-to-ground missile system.

XM-23 - A dual machine gun mount for helicopters.

XM-24 - A machine gun mount located in the cargo bay.

XM-25 - A gun pod for the high speed 20-mm cannon.

XM-258 - A shotgun flechette round.

XM-27 - A gravel mine.

XM-27E1 - A minigun mounted on the side of Loach helicopters.

XM-28 Mask - A protective mask.

XM-28 Turret - A gun turret for a helicopter.

XM-3 - The "people sniffer" carried by helicopters used to detect ammonia associated with sweat and urine.

XM-30 - A cannon.

XM-31 - A cannon pod.

XM-32 MG - A dual mounted pair of machine guns on the sides of a helicopter.

XM-33 - A system of forward facing machine guns for the CH-47 helicopter.

XM-45E1 - A armored cargo carrier.

XM-5 - A grenade launcher.

XM-52 - A smoke screen device fitted into the exhaust system of a helicopter. The benefit was a fog of heavy oil smoke to disguise ground movement; however, the slow speed needed to lay the fog left the helicopter as an easy target.

XM-571 - An experimental vehicle with articulated tracks. See Tiger Track.

XM-59 - A system by which a .50 cal machine gun was mounted to one side and a dual .60 cal machine gun to the other.

XM-6 - A machine gun with four guns synchronized to fire together.

XM-8 - A gun mount on a helicopter.

XM-93 - A minigun system that could be operated by a gunner, or locked in place and fired by the pilot.

XM-94 - A grenade launcher in the door of a helicopter that could be fired by the gunner or locked in place and fired by the pilot.

XM134 - A six-barrel minigun. Also XM-134.

XM3 - A rocket launcher. Also XM-3.

XM70-115-mm - See boosted rocket field artillery weapon.

XMGM-31A - See Pershing.

XMIM-46A - See Mauler.

XO - Executive Officer.

Xu - A unit of currency in North Vietnam, like a penny made of aluminum (100 xu=1 dong).

Y – YANKEE

Y - Designated the phonetic military alphabet as "Yankee".

y-axis - (DOD, IADB) A vertical axis in a system of rectangular coordinates; that line on which distances above or below (north or south) the reference line are marked, especially on a map, chart or graph.

y-scale - (NATO, CENTO) On an oblique photograph, the scale along the line of the principal vertical, or any other line, inherent or plotted which, on the ground, is parallel to the principal vertical.

Yabuta - A motorized junk in the South Vietnamese navy.

Yankee - The military phonetic alphabet designation for the letter "Y". 2. An American.

Yards - Slang for the Montagnard soldiers.

yaw - 1. Aviation term for an airplane's movement on its vertical axis so the nose goes side to side (left or right). 2. Naval term for a ship drifting off course briefly.

YD - The cartographic map designation for a grid of 100,000 meters square from the Universal Transmercator (UTM) (See UTM).

yellow on rice - Slang for the Vietnamese point of view, being wrong. See white on rice.

yellow sheet - Aviation term for the form completed by a pilot after a flight that reports a mechanical or electronic problem with the aircraft.

YFND - A Navy barge used for storage.

YFR - A small ship used as a lighter and resupply craft.

yield - See nuclear yields.

YO-3A - A small observation plane. See Quiet Star.

Yo-Yo - Aviation maneuver in which the plane either climbs to slow or dives to accelerate while turning, either to defend against an attacker or find a better position for attack. The maneuver is named for Yo-Yo Noritake, the Chinese pilot inventing it in WWII, not for the toy spinning disk on a string. See High Yo-Yo and low Yo-Yo

You souvenir me. - A request by a Vietnamese for a gift. A begging phrase. Also Souvenir me.

Your _____ - When using the clock code to give a direction, it is assumed that the direction (3 o'clock) is from the speaker's position. For clarity, the speaker may further specify Enemy is at YOUR three o'clock. See clock code.

Your dick falls off and then you step on it. - A phrase used to describe a very embarrassing moment. Also phrased as, Then I stepped on my dick.

Your home away from home. - The slogan of the USO.

YR-71 - A Navy repair barge.

YRBM - A Navy floating river patrol base.

YTB - A large Navy tugboat.

YTL - A small Navy tugboat.

Z – ZULU

Z - Designated in the phonetic military alphabet as "Zulu".

Z marker beacon - (NATO, SEATO, CENTO, IADB) Equipment identical with the fan marker except that it is installed as part of a four-course radio range at the intersection of the four range legs, and radiates vertically to indicate to aircraft when they pass directly over the range station. It is usually not keyed for identification. Also known as cone of silence marker. See also beacon.

z-scale - (NATO, CENTO) On an oblique photograph, the scale used in calculating the height of an object. Also the name given to this method of height determination.

Z-time - Zulu time. Greenwich mean time. See golf time.

zap - To kill.

zapper - See sapper.

zebra - 1. Enlisted personnel with several service stripes, 2. A noncommissioned officer, due to insignia stripes.

zero - Expressed in radio code and slang as ball.

zero dark thirty - Any early morning time before light. Also o-dark-thirty.

zero delay - An automatic opening parachute used on ejection, e.g. no delay between ejection and deployment.

zero in - To correct sights on a rifle to insure accuracy at a preset range.

zero point - (DOD) The location of the center of a burst of a nuclear weapon at the instant of detonation. The zero point may be in the air, or on or beneath the surface of land or water, dependent upon the type of burst, and it is thus to be distinguished from ground zero.

zero zero - Expressed in radio code and slang as balls. For example a helicopter numbered 009 would be referred to as balls niner.

zero-length launching - (DOD, NATO, CENTO, IADB) A technique in which the first motion of the missile or aircraft removes it from the launcher.

zero-zero - 1. An aviation term for no visibility, fogged in, coming from zero ceiling (visibility up) and zero visibility (forward). 2. Slang clueless, ignorant.

ZI - Zone of the Interior (the United States).

zip - 1. Nothing, nada, zero. 2. Derogatory term for the Vietnamese.

zipper heads - A derogatory term for the Vietnamese.

zipper room - Morgue.

zippers - (DOD) Target dawn and dusk combat air patrol.

Zippo - 1. The trademarked brand of wind-proof flip-top personal cigarette or cigar lighter, usually chrome. 2. Slang for flamethrower, 3. Slang for the number zero, 4. assignments whose numeric code ended in a zero.

Zippo boats - Boats with flamethrowers.

Zippo mission - A mission involving the lighting homes aflame in villages. Also Zippo job.

Zippo tank - The M67 flamethrower tank.

Zippo track - The M-132 armored personnel carrier with a flamethrower.

zit - A derogatory term for the Vietnamese.

zone - See air defense identification zone; air surface zones; combat zone; communications zone; control zone; dead zone; demilitarized zone; drop zone; landing zone; rupture zone; safety zone; submarine patrol zones. See also area.

zone fire - (DOD, IADB) Artillery or mortar fires that are delivered in a constant direction at several quadrant elevations. See also fire.

zone I (nuclear) - (DOD) A circular area, determined by using minimum safe distance as the radius and the desired ground zero as the center, from which all armed forces are evacuated. If evacuation is not possible or if a commander elects a higher degree of risk, maximum protective measures will be required.

zone II (nuclear) - (DOD) A circular area (less zone I), determined by using minimum safe distance II as the radius and the desired ground zero as the center, in which all personnel require maximum protection. Maximum protection denotes that armed forces personnel are in "buttoned up" tanks or crouched in foxholes with improvised overhead shielding.

zone III (nuclear) - (DOD) A circular area (less zones I and II), determined by using minimum safe distance III as the radius and the desired ground zero as the center, in which all personnel require minimum protection. Minimum protection denotes that armed forces personnel are prone on open ground with all skin areas covered and with an overall thermal protection at least equal to that provided by a two-layer uniform.

zone of action - (DOD, NATO, SEATO, CENTO, IADB) A tactical subdivision of a larger area, the responsibility for which is assigned to a tactical unit; generally applied to offensive action. See also sector.

zone of fire - (DOD) An area within which a designated ground unit or fire support ship delivers, or is prepared to deliver, fire support. Fire may or may not be observed. See also contingent zone of fire.

zone of fire - (IADB) An area within which a particular unit delivers, or is prepared to deliver, fire. See also contingent zone of fire; normal zone of fire; zone of responsibility.

zone of responsibility - (IADB) A predetermined area of enemy terrain which supporting ships are responsible for covering by fire on known targets or targets of opportunity and by observation. See also zone of fire.

zoom - Aviation maneuver in which a maximum high speed level flight is then converted into a steep climb.

zoombag - A flight suit, particularly for jet pilots.

zoomie - 1. Slang for a pilot. 2. Graduates of the Air Force Academy.

zot - Zero, a loser.

ZPU - A small caliber belt-fed 14.5-mm weapon that was used against American aircraft. Pronounced zip-u.

Zs - Sleep.

Zulu - 1. The military phonetic alphabet designation for the letter "Z". 2. Radio code for a casualty report, 3. Referencing Greenwich mean time

zulu time - ((DOD, NATO, CENTO) Greenwich mean time.

Zuni - (DOD, IADB) An air-to-surface unguided rocket with solid propellant. Can be armed with various types of heads, including flares, fragmentation, and armor piercing.